1,000,000 Books

are available to read at

---◆---

www.ForgottenBooks.com

---◆---

Read online
Download PDF
Purchase in print

ISBN 978-1-332-40464-3
PIBN 10422585

1 MONTH OF
FREE
READING

at
www.ForgottenBooks.com

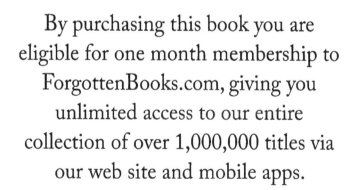

By purchasing this book you are eligible for one month membership to ForgottenBooks.com, giving you unlimited access to our entire collection of over 1,000,000 titles via our web site and mobile apps.

To claim your free month visit:

www.forgottenbooks.com/free422585

English
Français
Deutsche
Italiano
Español
Português

www.forgottenbooks.com

Mythology Photography **Fiction**
Fishing Christianity **Art** Cooking
Essays Buddhism Freemasonry
Medicine **Biology** Music **Ancient**
Egypt Evolution Carpentry Physics
Dance Geology **Mathematics** Fitness
Shakespeare **Folklore** Yoga Marketing
Confidence Immortality Biographies
Poetry **Psychology** Witchcraft
Electronics Chemistry History **Law**
Accounting **Philosophy** Anthropology
Alchemy Drama Quantum Mechanics
Atheism Sexual Health **Ancient History**
Entrepreneurship Languages Sport
Paleontology Needlework Islam
Metaphysics Investment Archaeology
Parenting Statistics Criminology
Motivational

POLITICAL ECONOMY

BY CHARLES GIDE

PROFESSOR OF SOCIAL ECONOMICS IN THE
FACULTY OF LAW IN THE UNIVERSITY OF
PARIS

AUTHORIZED TRANSLATION FROM THE THIRD
EDITION (1913) OF THE "COURS D'ÉCONOMIE
POLITIQUE"

D. C. HEATH & CO., PUBLISHERS
BOSTON   NEW YORK   CHICAGO

TRANSLATOR'S PREFACE

THIS third edition of Professor Gide's *Cours d'Économie politique* has been carefully revised by its author in order not only to bring the figures up to date, but, so far as is possible within the limits of one volume, to keep abreast of the latest changes in facts and ideas. It will be found, therefore, that new chapters have been added and several of the old ones entirely rewritten.

As the book was written primarily to help French students in preparing for their examinations in the Law Faculty of Paris, the method employed by the author has been not so much to exhaust a few subjects, as to cover the whole ground of Political Economy, dealing with each question in a concise but critical way.

The translator has done his best to follow the thought of the author. Nothing distinctively French has been eliminated, and it may be that examples in the text will be found to apply at times to French rather than to American conditions. But it has been thought good for the student of Political Economy to see the fundamental and familiar questions of his science pose themselves in slightly different forms under the influence of another race and another tradition. So he is reminded of the human element which is at once the main difficulty and the main interest of Political Economy.

The American edition varies in certain minor details from the English edition. The notes inserted in order to adapt the translation to meet more satisfactorily the needs of students in this country are signed AM. ED. The American publishers are indebted to Dr. C. W. A. Veditz, translator of an earlier edition of Gide's work, and to Dr. H. C. Metcalf, Professor of Political Science in Tufts College, for valuable assistance in preparing this edition.

CONTENTS

INTRODUCTORY

PART II: THE ORGANISATION OF PRODUCTION

CHAPTER I : HOW PRODUCTION IS REGULATED

CHAPTER II : THE DIVISION OF LABOUR

CHAPTER III : THE CONCENTRATION OF PRODUCTION

CHAPTER IV : ASSOCIATION FOR PRODUCTION

BOOK II : CIRCULATION

BOOK III: DISTRIBUTION

PART I: THE DIFFERENT MODES OF DISTRIBUTION

CHAPTER I: THE PRESENT MODE OF DISTRIBUTION

CHAPTER II: THE SOCIALIST MODES OF DISTRIBUTION

PART II: THE DIFFERENT CLASSES OF SHARERS

INTRODUCTION

CHAPTER I: LANDLORDS

PAGE

CHAPTER II : THE CAPITALIST *RENTIER*

CHAPTER III : WAGE-EARNERS

CHAPTER IV : THE *ENTREPRENEUR*

CHAPTER V: THE DESTITUTE

CHAPTER VI: THE STATE

BOOK IV : CONSUMPTION

INTRODUCTORY

CHAPTER I: ECONOMIC SCIENCE

I: THE OBJECT OF POLITICAL ECONOMY

THE celestial bodies, the globe, the elements within it, the animals and vegetables that cover its surface, these, and the relations existing between them, are all objects of distinct sciences called the *Physical and Natural Sciences.*

There are, however, other objects in this vast world no less worthy of our study, namely, ourselves—mankind. Men live in society, they cannot live otherwise; relations thus arise among them, and these form the subject-matter of a different group of sciences, called the *Social Sciences.*[1] For every distinct relationship between men—moral, juridical, economic, political, religious or linguistic (language being the vehicle of all the others)—there is a distinct science, known respectively as *Ethics, Law, Political Economy, Politics,* the science of *Religions* and that of *Languages.*[2]

True, the boundary lines between the social sciences, all of which deal ultimately with the same object—namely, man as a social being—cannot be so sharply drawn as those between such sciences as geology, botany, and zoology, which deal with entirely dissimilar objects. The classification of the social sciences will always be more or less artificial, resorted to rather for the sake of facilitating study, and to help out the small reach of our understanding, than because of any natural division between them.

Thus, Auguste Comte considered irrational any separation of the sciences which deal with human societies. He admitted but one single science embracing all the aspects of these societies, to which

---

[1] Formerly they were called the Moral and Political Sciences, and the section of the *Institut de France* which relates to them still bears that name.

[2] There is also *History,* which studies the order of facts, and the science of *Statistics,* which collects and classifies all facts capable of being expressed in figures. It must be remarked, however, that these two sciences, unlike those mentioned above, do not have as their object a special category of social facts, but apply to all, even to facts other than those of the social sciences. There is a history not only of Political Economy but of Religion, of Morals, even of the formation of living species and of stars. So also there are judicial, moral, political, and demographical statistics as well as economic and financial statistics.

he gave the name, now classic, of *Sociology* [1]; and he deprecated, in particular, every attempt to make Political Economy a distinct science. He has not been followed, because, for the purposes of study, it was impossible to refuse to the social sciences the right to be considered separately. As regards the three sciences which touch each other most closely—Ethics, Law, and Political Economy—their boundary lines will always be more or less fluctuating, certain institutions, such as property, the transmission of goods, the wage-system, coming under the jurisdiction of all three at once ; a happy interpenetration, moreover, and one very profitable to these sister-sciences. We have only to notice that the same object may be examined from different points of view, and to know how to recognise the different standpoints of the moralist, the jurisconsult, and the economist. Now, this is not very difficult. *To do one's duty, to exercise one's rights, to provide for one's wants*, are three fairly distinct ends of human activity. And it is this last one which is the object of Economic Science.

We may say, then, without being too exacting as regards a definition which, in spite of a hundred or so treatises, is still to be found, that, of all the relations which exist between human beings living in society, Political Economy deals with those alone which tend to the satisfaction of their material wants, with all that concerns their well-being.[2] It stands to the social body somewhat as physiology does to the human body.

The tendency to-day is to divide this science into two branches of study.

On the one hand, *Political Economy pure* (sometimes called

---

[1] Sociology is much studied at the present time, but no exact definition of its subject-matter has yet been given ; nor has it been clearly determined whether it is merely a synthesis of all the social sciences or whether it has distinct characteristics of its own. See the numerous discussions on this subject in the *Annales de l'Institut international de Sociologie.*

[2] It used often to be said, and is still to-day, that Political Economy is the "science of wealth." But this definition has the objection of turning the attention from the real object of economic science—man and his wants—to outside objects, which are but the means by which man satisfies his wants. What is known as an economic, or social, law, even when its object is apparently "things," applies in reality to man. To say that corn is going up in price means that men, for some reason or other, want more of it. And this is not a mere matter of words. This subversion of the true point of view has brought on some economists the reproach of reasoning as if man were made for wealth, not wealth for man. There is, moreover, a further objection to defining Political Economy by wealth, namely, that the word wealth itself, as we shall see later, is not easy to define.

So far so good, but then try all men from this generally progressive out look to try to do away in soc. dg. except as "cycles"

Economics) studies the spontaneous relations that arise between men living together, as it might study the relations that arise between any bodies whatsoever, "those necessary relations which derive from the nature of things," as Montesquieu said. It does not set out to judge them, either from the moral or from the practical point of view, but simply to *explain what is*. In so far, it tries to follow the methods of a natural, or even of a mathematical, science.

On the other hand, *Social Economy* studies rather the voluntary relations that men create among themselves—associations, written laws, institutions of all kinds—with a view to improving them. Its object is to find out the best means of doing this. It partakes, therefore, more of the character of the moral sciences, as seeking *what ought to be*, and of the arts, as seeking *what must be done*. This is why it is sometimes called, outside of France, *Social Politics*.[1]

This separation is necessary for specialists, but, by dissociating theory and practice, it greatly detracts from the interest of the subject. We shall not, therefore, adopt it in our present treatise, but shall deal with Social as well as Political Economy.

The economic phenomena first to attract attention were those connected with *production*. The Physiocrats and Adam Smith studied hardly any others. Ricardo and the second generation of economists applied themselves more particularly to analysing the phenomena of *distribution*. And these are still the two main divisions of Political Economy—or rather, the two aspects under which the same phenomena present themselves ; for, after all, it is practically the same phenomena that we find again on either side. Obviously the connection between the two questions, " How is wealth produced ? " and " To whom does it belong ? " is a close one.[2] This is, however, no reason for not studying them separately.

In production itself, it was not long before a distinction was drawn between the phenomena of production properly speaking and those of *circulation*—*i.e.* between the ways of creating wealth and those of transporting or of exchanging it. The latter, indeed, are of enormous importance and have a physiognomy entirely their own.

---

[1] Social Economy must not be confused with *applied* Political Economy. The latter points out the best practical ways of increasing the wealth of a country, such as banks, railways, monetary or commercial systems, etc. Social Economy aims above all at making men happier by providing them, not only with more comfort, but with more security, independence, leisure ; it has, consequently, the working classes more specially in view.

[2] "To whom *does* it belong ? " is a legal question. "To whom *ought it to belong* ? " is a question lying in the borderland between economics and ethics —AM. ED.

Still, this division is in answer rather to didactic convenience than to any logical necessity, since, as we shall see, exchange is, at bottom, but a mode of production.[1]

There is another category of facts, which, since the time of J. B. Say, has often constituted a separate section, that, namely, which relates to the *consumption* of wealth. At first sight it would seem as if this category ought to be the most important ; for consumption—in other words, the satisfaction of wants—is evidently the end and final cause of all economic activity. Yet many economists refuse to give consumption a separate place, and this branch of Political Economy is nearly always sacrificed, if not altogether omitted, in treatises, lectures and examinations. We hold, on the contrary, that a distinct place must be kept for it, a place which will become larger as we become more alive to the growing importance of the part played by the consumer in the economic order.

II : WHETHER THERE ARE NATURAL LAWS IN POLITICAL ECONOMY

WHEN we apply the word " science " to any branch of human knowledge, we are giving it no mere empty title ; we mean to state that the facts with which it deals *are connected by certain constant relations which have been discovered and which are called laws.*

In some spheres the sequence of facts is so obvious that even minds least accustomed to scientific speculation cannot help noticing it.

We have only to raise our eyes to the heavens to realise the regularity with which the stars march nightly across the skies, the moon accomplishes her monthly phases, the sun makes his annual journey through the constellations. In the remotest days of history, shepherds watching their flocks and sailors steering their barques had already

---

[1] An interesting discussion of these classifications will be found in Mr. Pierson's scholarly work, *Principles of Economics*, besides a kindly criticism of the classification adopted in our book. Mr. Pierson commends us for beginning with the study of value, but thinks that the part devoted to consumption is useless. He holds that distribution ought to be studied before production, as the latter cannot be understood without the former. This is true, but the reverse might also be said. Nowadays, the classic division into four parts—production, circulation, distribution and consumption—is considered out of date, partly because, having served for a century, it is felt that it is quite time to revise it, and also because facts, better studied than they used to be, show a multiplicity and interdependence demanding fuller explanation. Most writers outside of France have abandoned it. Still, no simpler or more convenient division has yet been found.

recognised the periodic nature of these movements, and had laid the foundations of a true science, the oldest of all, astronomy.

The phenomena manifested in the constitution of organic and inorganic bodies are not so simple, and the order of their co-existence or succession is not so easy to grasp.

Thus long centuries were necessary before human reason, lost in the labyrinth of things, succeeded in disentangling the guiding thread, in recognising order and law in these facts, too, and in creating the physical, chemical and biological sciences.

Little by little, the idea of a constant order in phenomena penetrated all spheres, even those which seemed, at first sight, as if they must be for ever closed to it. The very winds and waves, which poets had made the emblem of inconstancy and caprice, were made to own the sway of this universal order. Mankind became aware of the great laws which govern the currents of the atmosphere and of the sea, and meteorology—the physics of the globe—in turn was founded. Nothing, even to the results of the bet or the combinations of the dice, but has been brought under the calculation of probabilities. Chance itself henceforward has its laws.

The day was at last to come when this great idea of a Natural Order of things, after invading step by step like a conquering power all the regions of human knowledge, was to penetrate the sphere of social facts. It is to the Physiocrats, as we shall see, that the honour is due of having first recognised and proclaimed the existence of this " natural government " of things.

Still, there are many who shrink from accepting this assimilation of the social, with the physical, sciences. To their minds, there is an insurmountable barrier between them : for the latter are of the realm of Necessity, while the former are of the realm of Liberty.

The proof, they say, is, that in sciences of the physical order the scientist, given a certain fact, is always able to *foresee* with certainty the fact which will succeed or accompany it. The astronomer will announce an eclipse a thousand years off, and almost to a second ; the chemist, each time he combines two substances in a crucible, knows just what body will result and what its properties will be ; the geologist will enumerate the various layers of earth that will be met with in piercing a tunnel or in sinking a shaft. But the economist, the historian, the statesman, what can they foresee in regard to social and political facts ? At most they can but hazard a few conjectures, only too often contradicted by events. Foresight here may sometimes be the intuition of genius, but it has nothing of the nature of science about it.

This common objection, however, comes of a twofold error as to the meaning of the expressions *natural law* and *free-will*.

The mistake in the case of *natural law* lies in picturing it as a power commanding obedience and bearing a sword, like the figure of Law in allegorical pictures. Now, natural law expresses nothing more than certain relations which arise *spontaneously* between things or men, relations which can only be spoken of as necessary *if certain previous conditions have been fulfilled*. Atoms of oxygen and of hydrogen are not forced to form water, but *if* an atom of the former element and two of the latter are brought into contact under certain conditions of temperature, pressure, etc., water will result. In the same way, men are not forced to sell or buy, but *if* a man disposed to sell meets a man disposed to buy, and *if* their claims are not irreconcilable, they will necessarily strike a bargain at a price which may be determined—and this will none the less be a free contract.

As for *free-will*, the mistake lies in looking upon it as a sort of capriciousness, the power of " taking one's own way." But a moment's reflection will convince us that to act without any appreciable reason is precisely what characterises the state of dementia. The rational man, on the contrary, obeys in his conduct certain motives—in a word, *he does not make up his mind without cause*. Now, every social or economic law is merely a forecast of the conduct of men, and its scientific value is measured by the number of cases in which it comes true.[1]

No doubt these forecasts are often contradicted by events.[2] But this happens also in the natural sciences. Every thinking man is convinced that wind and rain, hail and storm, are not the result of chance : he does not doubt that they are governed by

[1] " An *economic law* is a statement that a certain course of action may be expected under certain conditions from the members of an industrial group " (Marshall, *Principles of Economics*, vol. i, p. 87 (1890). Moreover, in the last few years, belief in necessity—that is to say, in such an interlinking of all phenomena that things cannot be other than they are, and that a strong enough intelligence could put all these relations into formulæ—has lost much ground in science, and a belief in a certain *contingency*, as it is called, *i.e.* in the existence of more ways than one open to evolution, none of which can be foreseen because all are equally possible, appears no longer incompatible with true science. (See Boutroux, *De la contingence des lois de la nature*, and Bergson, *L'évolution créatrice*.)

[2] One argument given against the existence of natural laws in social matters is the fact that many things do not turn out as *foreseen*. This simply proves our ignorance. Just think how many times things do not turn out as we have *willed*. Does not this prove that there are causes at work in this world stronger than the will of man ?

natural laws. Yet forecasts in this sphere are no more exact than in that of economics. The coming of a commercial crisis may be foretold longer in advance than that of a cyclone, and railway transit from Lyons to Marseilles is certainly less irregular than is the flow of water in the Rhone whose banks it follows, although the one is kept going by men and the other by the sky. If our predictions in Political Economy are always uncertain and shortsighted, the reason is to be sought not in the fantasies of free-will, but simply in our ignorance of the true causes. If men ever become infinitely wise, probably foresight in economic matters will be exercised with as much certainty as in the case of the celestial bodies.

True, it would be absurd to pretend to foretell the acts and doings of an individual; but that is of no interest to the economist. He is not a fortune-teller. What matters to him is the *conduct of men, considered as a whole. Averages* are all that is necessary to establish our theoretical laws and our practical institutions.[1]

Observe, too, that those practical persons who deny most energetically the possibility of foresight in economic matters, do not fail to use it in the ordinary course of their lives and in the daily conduct of their affairs. Every man who speculates—and who is there who does not ?—is using, so far as he is able, scientific foresight. The financier who invests in railway shares foresees a continuous and progressive increase of traffic along a certain line, and, by the very fact of paying a high price for his shares, professes, whether he means to or not, his firm confidence in the regularity of an economic law. Yet it is quite certain that each individual and each parcel travelling along the line is doing so only because some one has *willed* it.

III: HOW ECONOMIC SCIENCE WAS CONSTITUTED

It was in the year 1615, in a French book called *Le Traicté de l'Œconomie politique*, by Antoine de Montchrétien, that Political Economy first received the name by which it is known to-day.

The word *economy* was already in use, and one of Xenophon's books even bears this title : but the ancients meant by it domestic economy (*oikos*, house ; *nomos*, rule, law). The adjective *political*, in use from the time of Montchrétien, indicates that the economy in question is no longer that of the household, but that of the city, the nation ; and this new name coincided with a historical

---

[1] Statistics have shown, over and over again, the almost infallible regularity with which the most important facts of human life, such as marriages, occur equally with the most insignificant, such as the posting of a letter unaddressed.

revolution, the rise of the great modern States. We might have adopted an expression sometimes used, and said *Social Economy*, instead of Political Economy. The etymological meaning in either case is the same (the adjective " political " is, however, better suited to the word " economy," as coming also from the Greek). But the word " social," as we have pointed out, is used for a somewhat different branch of study (see page 3).

Some of the questions which to-day are called economic, have attracted the attention of man from the earliest times : questions of money, commerce, and the ways by which individuals and the State may grow wealthier. The Fathers of the Church had condemned luxury, inequality of wealth, and loans at interest. The ancients, among them Aristotle, had accurately analysed the nature of money, the separation of trades, and the forms of acquiring property. But they had not seen the connection between these different questions nor thought of making them the object of one single science. Such problems belonged rather to the province of the philosopher than to that of the man of science. They were dealt with in a practical manner, in the form of good advice given either to sovereigns or to individuals.

The discovery of America gave the first stimulus to the formation of a true economic theory, in the course of the sixteenth and particularly the seventeenth centuries. What had formerly been mere counsels became now a system of co-ordinate and reasoned precepts. Countries like France, Italy and Great Britain watched, with anxious eyes, Spain drawing treasures from her mines in the New World, and wondered how they, too, could procure gold and silver. A book by an Italian, Antonio Serra, published in 1613, bore the significant title, *A Brief Discourse on the Possible Means of causing Gold and Silver to abound in Kingdoms where there are no Mines.* They thought to find the way by selling manufactured goods to foreign countries, and to this end they tried hard to develop foreign trade and home manufacturing by a complicated and artificial system of regulations. This was what has been called the Mercantile System.[1]

In the middle of the eighteenth century we find a lively reaction against all " system " taking place in France. The dream now was of a return to " nature," and any arrangement that appeared artificial was repudiated. The whole literature of the eighteenth century was impregnated with this idea, and political science, with Rousseau and Montesquieu, took its inspiration therefrom.

[1] See *infra,* the chapter on *Commercial Policy.*

L'Esprit des Lois opened with the immortal words, " Laws are the necessary relations which derive *from the nature of things,*" and in his preface to the same work Montesquieu declared : " I have not drawn my principles from my prejudices but from the nature of things."

It was only then that economic science was really evolved. A physician of Louis XV, named Quesnay, published, in 1758, *Le Tableau économique,*[1] and had quite a group of eminent men as his disciples. They called themselves *Economists,* and were later referred to as the *Physiocrats.*[2]

The school of the Physiocrats brought into the science two new ideas diametrically opposed to the mercantile system.

(1) That of the existence of a " natural and essential order of human societies " (such is the actual title of a book by one of the Physiocrats, Mercier de la Rivière). We have only to recognise the truth of this principle in order to realise the necessity of conforming to it. It is of no use, then, to devise laws, regulations, or systems : all we have to do is to leave things alone, *laisser faire.*

(2) That of the pre-eminence of agriculture over commerce and industry. For the Physiocrats, the earth, that is to say Nature, is the sole source of wealth ; she alone gives a net product ; all classes of society save the agricultural classes are sterile.

The first of these principles was destined to serve not only as the ground-work of a regular policy which was to last half a century and to accomplish great things under the name of the liberal policy,[3] but as a definitive basis to the whole edifice of economic science. Facts, indeed, can serve as basis for a science only in so far as we recognise relations of cause and effect between them—" a natural and essential order."

The second, on the contrary, although a happy reaction against the mistakes of the mercantile system, was itself, as we shall see

---

[1] There had previously appeared an *Essai sur la nature du commerce,* by Cantillon (published in 1755, but already written in 1725). This book has just been brought to light again by the English economists, and has been referred to by one of them as the first methodical treatise of Political Economy. But this work, which was not very well known, influenced the development of the science only through the Physiocratic school, which borrowed largely from it.

[2] The word " Physiocracy " is made up of two Greek words meaning literally " government of nature."

[3] An illustrious economist of the same period, Turgot, without sharing the error of the Physiocratic school, was the first to apply this policy when intendant of Limoges, and afterwards as minister of Louis XVI. He decreed in the first place *liberty of exchange,* abolishing internal customs and duties on grain, and then went on to decree *liberty of labour* by abolishing the guilds.

later, infected with an error which was rapidly to undermine the authority of this school.

The appearance of Adam Smith's *Inquiry into the Nature and Causes of the Wealth of Nations*, in 1776, marked a turning-point in the history of Political Economy. It secured to the British school an uncontested pre-eminence for nearly a century, and brought to its author the somewhat exaggerated title of " Father of Political Economy."

Adam Smith rejected the second principle of the Physiocrats, and gave industry its legitimate place in the production of wealth, but he splendidly confirmed and developed the first—*i.e.* the belief in natural economic laws and in the principle of *laisser faire*, at least as a rule of practical conduct.

He was, moreover, far ahead of the Physiocrats in observing facts and drawing lessons from history ; and he so widened the field of economic science that its boundaries have remained practically the same to this day.

Shortly after Adam Smith there appeared simultaneously in England two economists whose theories, extolled by some and execrated by others, were to impress their mark for the space of a century on economic science : Malthus, whose celebrated " law " in regard to the increase of population (1798), though apparently confined to a special sphere, was to have considerable influence on the whole science of economics ; Ricardo (1817), no less celebrated for his law on *land rent* and his abuse of the abstract and purely deductive method. In France, at the same time, Jean Baptiste Say was publishing his *Traité d'Économie politique* (1803). This work, remarkable mainly for its clearness of style, the admirable arrangement of its plan and the classification of its ideas, did not contribute so fruitfully to the formation of the science as did the works of the masters just mentioned. Nevertheless, translated into all the languages of Europe, it was the first really popular treatise on Political Economy, and has served more or less as a model for the innumerable classical manuals which have since appeared.

It was in this last book, more particularly, that Political Economy was set forth in the light of a natural science, that is to say, as purely descriptive. Adam Smith had defined it as proposing " to enrich both the people and the sovereign," thus giving it a practical aim. J. B. Say, improving on this definition, wrote : " I should prefer to say that the object of Political Economy is to make known the means by which wealth *is* formed, *is* distributed, and *is* consumed," meaning thereby that, in the economic order, everything proceeds of itself, spontaneously, automatically.[1]

From this time Political Economy may be considered as having reached its final classical form. But it was not long before it became divided into a large number of schools, the distinctive features of which we shall briefly indicate.[2]

CHAPTER II : THE VARIOUS ECONOMIC SCHOOLS

I: SCHOOLS AS DISTINGUISHED BY THEIR METHODS

" METHOD " is the name given in scientific language to the road which must be followed in order to arrive at the truth.

The *deductive* method starts from certain general data accepted as indisputable, and, by a process of logical reasoning, deduces from them an indefinite series of propositions. Geometry may be given as typical of the sciences which use the deductive method. We may also cite, as an example familiar to law students, the science of Law itself, particularly Roman Law, where the jurisconsult, starting from a few principles laid down by the Twelve Tables, or in the *Jus Gentium*, builds up the marvellous monument of reason, the Pandects. This is also called 'the *abstract* method, because it endeavours to simplify phenomena by reducing them to the one element that is to be studied, eliminating all the rest.

The *inductive* method starts from the observation of particular facts, and rises therefrom to general propositions; for example, from the *fact* that all bodies fall, to the *law* of gravitation.

It is a point of keen controversy which of these two methods is best adapted to Economic Science.

There is no doubt that it was by the deductive method that Political Economy was originally constituted. It was on a small number of principles considered as axiomatic, or suggested by very general observations—such as the increase of population, the law

---

[1] The title of his book speaks for itself : *Traité d'Économie politique—ou simple exposition de la manière dont se forment, se distribuent et se consomment les richesses.*

[2] To complete these brief indications, as also those of the next chapter, see *Histoire des Doctrines Économiques depuis les Physiocrates jusqu'à nos jours*, written in collaboration with M. Rist.

of diminishing returns—that the economists of the Classical school erected the columns and framework of their fine monument.[1] Indeed, for the whole structure of Political Economy they would have been content with the single principle that man always seeks to obtain a maximum of satisfaction with a minimum of effort. They sought to simplify the object of their study by considering man as a being moved solely by self-interest, the " homo œconomicus," identical in every country and every age, and by abstracting every other disturbing motive.

But half a century ago the efficacy of this method began to be contested.

The new school recommended the *inductive* method, that which Bacon introduced some centuries ago into the physical and natural sciences with such splendid results. In the economic domain this is known to-day as the *realistic* method, particularly in Germany, where it is almost exclusively followed. This school gave up looking for general laws governing an abstract man, and sought only historical laws, governing men of a particular society and a particular time.[2] It confined itself to the patient observation and accumulation of social facts, as revealed to us, at the present day by statistics and information obtained from travellers, in the past by history. It is also called the Historical school,[3] because it maintains that history, by showing us how economic and social institutions have

---

[1] One of the most absolute of theorists in this connection was Nassau Senior, professor at Oxford (1830-1840). He brought the whole of Political Economy down to four axioms, not one of which is accepted to-day as it stands.

[2] It was, however, looking for something entirely different from that which the Classical Economists were seeking —AM. ED.

[3] It was in Germany that this method was first applied to Economic Science, as it had been applied to Law by Savigny. It may be said to date from the publication of Roscher's *Grundriss zu Vorlesungen über die Staatswirthschaft nach geschichtlicher Methode* (1843). Its principal representatives at the present time in Germany are Professors Bücher, Brentano, Lexis, Schmoller, and Wagner (the latter more particularly a State Socialist). Among French writers, we may mention our colleague, M. Cauwès (*Cours d'Économie politique*, 1883, 1st ed.).

The application of the historical method to the social sciences was brilliantly inaugurated in France about the same date by the publication of Le Play's book, *Les Ouvriers Européens* (1885), and has been faithfully carried on ever since by the *le Play* school, so called after its founder, chiefly through " monographs on working-men's families." But the historical method is used so differently by the French school that it would be a great mistake to confuse it with the German school. Le Play, starting from the principle that there is nothing to invent in social matters, looks mainly to the past for lessons and examples, and is very conservative as regards a programme of action. The German school looks to the past only for the germ or roots of what has become the present, and is very progressive and even radical in its programme for the future.

'been formed, alone can throw light on the true nature of social facts.

The result is that the universality and permanence which the Classical school attributed to economic phenomena, and which it erected into natural laws, have vanished.[1]

This method is, no doubt, safer than the other, since it refrains from all bold generalisation. But we may doubt whether it is as fruitful. For it would be an illusion to think that the use of the purely inductive method will ever be of such service in the social, as it has been in the physical and natural sciences ; and this for two reasons :

First, facts are much more difficult to observe in the social sciences. Paradoxical as it may seem, just because they touch us more closely, because we are not mere spectators but actors as well, we are unable to see them clearly. Secondly, they are infinitely more diverse. Whoever has seen a single grasshopper has seen all ; but whoever has seen a single miner has seen nothing. In reality, the observation of economic and social facts is a task infinitely beyond the power of the individual, and can only be the collective work of thousands of human beings putting their observations together, or of States using for this purpose the powerful means of investigation at their disposal. It has meant a complete new science, that of *Statistics*. For example, surely the simplest fact that the social sciences can study is the number of persons who compose a given society. Yet, it is obvious that an isolated observer is quite powerless to determine this number. Public bodies alone are capable of undertaking the task. Even so, the official census is far from guaranteeing perfect accuracy, particularly if it be a question of ascertaining the numbers under special categories, say the number of landowners or of millionaires.

Again, the mere observation of facts could never have given such wonderful results in the natural sciences, had it not been for the help of a particular method of observation, carried on under certain artificial conditions, called *experiment*. Now, in the social sciences direct experiment is impossible. The chemist, the physicist, even the biologist (though in his case it is becoming more difficult), can always place the phenomena they want to study in certain artificially determined conditions, which they can vary at will. To study the respiration of an animal, they may place it under the bell-jar of a pneumatic apparatus and regulate the air-pressure.

[1] Along with the historical and realistic methods, we must place one which, under the name of *historical materialism*, has been advocated by the so-called Scientific, or rather, Marxian, socialism (see *infra*, p. 24).

But the economist, even were he also a legislator or an all-powerful despot, has not this power.[1]

In the matter of experiment, if such, indeed, it may be called, he has to be content with comparing the results of different legislations or systems. In France, for example, he will compare the working of the State railways with that of the great companies ; or again, he will study the effects of old-age pensions in Belgium and in Germany. But his conclusions will always be uncertain and controversial, since conditions from one place to another are never quite similar.

He is obliged to study the facts as they appear to him, without the power of isolating them from the other facts with which they are interwoven. He can isolate them only in imagination, by *supposing* that this or that phenomenon occurs *alone :* hence his constant reference, often unjustly ridiculed, to the ways and doings of a Crusoe. But it is clear that, through it, this would-be experimental method falls back into the very abstraction it seeks to avoid.

The Historical school then, in thus disparaging the processes and methods of the Deductive school, shows itself somewhat pretentious, if not a little ungrateful. After all, it still works within the categories laid down by the older school. It has not re-made the science ; it has simply—though this is no small thing—brought a new spirit into it. On its own side, it lays itself open to criticism. By fixing its attention on the observation of facts, and on the changes that take place in different nations and at different epochs, it tends too much to become merely erudite, and to lose sight of the general conditions which everywhere determine economic phenomena. It runs the risk of remaining purely descriptive. To accumulate millions of facts is useless ; there can be no science until relations are discovered between them. If we had to give up the attempt to discover permanent relations and general laws beneath the changing manifestations of phenomena, we should have to give up all idea of making a science of Political Economy. Now, however dangerous to science rash hypotheses may be, they

---

[1] Nevertheless, reference is constantly being made in Political Economy to *experiments.* It is said that this or that nation has tried the experiment of Protection, or of the regulation of labour, and has come out successfully or the reverse. But experiments of this sort are not by any means the same as *experimentation* in the scientific sense. And the proof is that, for all the centuries during which different nations have been making the experiment of Protection or of Free Trade, the problem is hardly any nearer solution than at the beginning. Mr. Pierson very justly remarks that most mistakes, or at least what are considered so to-day, passed formerly for the result of experiment.

are infinitely less so than such an avowal of impotence. However just may be the ridicule directed at the abstract man, the "homo œconomicus" of the Classical school, we are bound to admit that the human race does possess certain general characteristics. And history itself is the best proof of this, since it shows us that, whenever human societies are placed under similar conditions, they reproduce similar types : viz., feudalism in Europe in the twelfth century and in Japan up till the nineteenth century ; the successive forms of property and marriage ; the simultaneous use of precious metals for money ; similarity of funeral rites, and even of fairy tales, such as that of Tom Thumb, which the "folk-lorists" find to-day with little variation all over the world.

The use of the abstract method—the "let us suppose," so familiar to the Ricardian and so obnoxious to the Historical school—cannot therefore be rejected altogether. The labyrinth of economic fact is much too intricate for us ever to find our way, or to unravel those fundamental relations which are the material of every science, by the help of observation alone. We have to appeal not only to abstraction, but to imagination, *i.e.* to hypothesis, in order to bring light into this darkness and order into this chaos.

The true method proceeds by three stages :

(1) *By observing facts*, without any preconceived idea, particularly those facts which appear at first sight the most insignificant.

(2) *By imagining* a general explanation, which will enable us to connect groups of facts in the relation of cause to effect : in other words, by formulating a *hypothesis*.

(3) *By verifying* the soundness of this hypothesis, ascertaining either by experiment in the strict sense, or, if not, by observation of a special nature, whether it fits the facts.

This is, moreover, the method employed even in the physical and natural sciences. All the great laws which form the basis of modern science—beginning with Newton's law of gravitation—are but *verified* hypotheses. We may go further, and say that the great theories which have served as basis for the scientific discoveries of our time—for example, that of the existence of ether in the physical sciences, and the doctrine of evolution in the natural sciences—are only hypotheses *not yet verified*.[1]

---

[1] See Claude Bernard's *Introduction à l'étude de la médecine expérimentale* and H. Poincaré's *Rôle de l'hypothèse*. As Jevons pointed out in his *Principles of Science*, the method employed by the sciences to reach the truth is like that used unconsciously by those who try to find the answers to puzzles on the last pages of illustrated papers. To guess the meaning of these puzzles they

The mistake of the Classical school, then, lay not in making too much use of the abstract method, but simply in taking too often an abstraction or a hypothesis for the reality : as, for example, after assuming its " homo œconomicus," moved solely by personal interest, which it had a perfect right to do, to believe in his real existence or to see nothing besides him in the economic world.

And this school is by no means dead. It lives again at the present day in two new schools.

First, the *Mathematical* school, which looks on the relations that arise between men, under every given circumstance, as relations of equilibrium, similar to those studied in applied mathematics, and, like them, susceptible of being expressed in algebraic equations. To this end, the problem must be reduced to a number of given conditions, the rest being abstracted exactly as is done in applied mathematics.[1]

Secondly, the *Psychological school*, also called the Austrian school, from the nationality of its most eminent exponents,[2] which devotes itself exclusively to the theory of value, making it the centre of economic science. And, as value, according to this school, is only the expression of man's desires, economic science is naturally reduced to a study of man's desires, and of the causes which affect their intensity—that is to say, to a very subtle psychological analysis. For is not the old Classical principle of maximum satisfaction with minimum effort, which it has rejuvenated under the name of the *hedonistic* principle (from a Greek word meaning pleasure, enjoyment), altogether psychological ?

These two schools, then, as we see, carry the deductive method to its extreme consequences. But we must give them the credit of not falling, like the old Deductive school, into the trap of their own speculations. They set forth their hedonistic principle and their

---

imagine some meaning or other, and then ascertain whether it really fits the figures or pictures ; if it does not, it is a hypothesis to be rejected. They then go on to imagine others until they have better luck or lose courage altogether. The seeker will never find anything in the facts unless he has already in his mind some mental forecast of the truth.

[1] The Mathematical school, inaugurated without success by Cournot in France (*Recherches sur les principes mathématiques de la théorie des richesses*, 1838) many years ago, has recently been brought into credit by Jevons, Marshall and Edgeworth in England, Walras (a Frenchman) in Switzerland, Pantaleoni and Vilfredo Pareto in Italy, Gossen and Launhardt in Germany, Irving Fisher in the United States.

[2] Professors Karl Menger, Böhm-Bawerk, and Wieser. The subtle theories of this school have been well summed up in a little book by Professor W. Smart, *Introduction to the Theory of Value* (2nd edition, 1910).

abstractions as no more than *hypotheses* necessary to establish the science pure.[1]

On the other hand, if the abstract method of Ricardo has come to life again in the Mathematical and Psychological schools, we may also say that the naturalistic method of J. B. Say has come to life again in the *Organic school.* This last makes Political Economy an annex of natural history and biology, by assimilating human societies to living beings, and all their institutions to analogous organs, thus transposing physiological laws into the realm of social laws.[2] The railway system corresponds to the arterial and venous system, telegraph wires to the nervous system, the rich are the " adipose tissue," and the Stock Exchange is the " heart."

But this last school, which had a momentary success, has lost much ground. A number of sociologists to-day object to such assimilation. Herbert Spencer himself, who, most brilliantly of all, had worked out this analogy in his *Principles of Sociology,* protested

[1] " Political Economy pure," says M. Walras in his *Éléments d'Économie politique pure,* " is essentially the theory of the determination of prices, under a hypothetical system of absolute free competition." M. Pantaleoni even makes the hitherto unheard-of admission (*Principii di Economia pura*) : " The question whether the hedonistic or psychological hypothesis from which all economic truths are deduced coincides *or not* with the motives that actually determine man's actions, does not affect in any way the accuracy of the truths deduced from it."

[2] See Schaeffle's great work, *Bau und Leben des Socialen Körpers* ; R. Worm's *Organisme et Société.* This school points out in particular :

That every organic body is composed of innumerable cells, each with its own life and individuality, so that every living being is in reality nothing more than an *association* of thousands of millions of infinitely small individualities, which, as Claude Bernard says, unite and are yet distinct like men holding one another by the hand.

That every organic being is subject to the law of the *physiological division of labour.* In the lowest organisms, all functions are undifferentiated, and the organs are merged in a formless and homogeneous mass ; but as organisation becomes more perfect the different functions of nutrition, reproduction, loco-motion, etc., become differentiated, each disposing of a special organ Thus the more divided the physiological labour, the more perfect the organism.

That every living being is the seat of a perpetual movement of *exchange* and *circulation,* an exchange of services and even of materials ; for it is obvious that, if a function of the organism is to become specialised in one single organ, the other organs must fulfil the other functions essential to life and communicate the benefits to it.

That even *credit* is as indispensable to the functioning of living beings as it is to that of the social organism. " If an organ in the individual body or in the body politic is suddenly called into great action, that it may continue responding to the increased demand, there must be an extra influx of the materials used in its actions ; it must have credit in advance of function discharged " (H. Spencer, *Principles of Sociology,* part ii, chap. ix).

later against any attempt to assimilate living organisms and human societies.[1]

II : SCHOOLS AS DISTINGUISHED BY THEIR SOLUTIONS

IT is not merely in regard to method that economists differ in opinion. On such questions as their programme of action, their *social policy*, as the Germans call it, that is to say, the *solutions* to be proposed, they are divided into almost as many schools as are philosophers. This is undeniably a sign of weakness. And it is little enough consolation to say that Political Economy has been in existence hardly more than a century, and that this defect will pass with age. Other sciences, scarcely more than a generation old, have managed to constitute a body of principles solid enough to secure the almost unanimous adherence of those who are interested in them. We need not lose all hope of ultimately finding a similar unanimity among economists as regards the methods of observing facts, and of explaining the relations between them ; but, unfortunately, as regards the ends to be kept in view, the ideals to strive for, and the right methods of realising them, such a hope is hardly possible. Differences such as these cannot cease until the moral, political and social unity of the human race is realised.

In the economic movement of the present time, we may distinguish five schools, or tendencies, with very marked characteristics.

(A) THE LIBERAL SCHOOL

THE first of these schools, sometimes called the *Classical* school, because all the founders of Political Economy—the Physiocrats, Adam Smith, Ricardo, J. B. Say, J. S. Mill [2]—belong to it ; sometimes the *Individualist* school, because it sees in the individual at

---

[1] And an eminent Sociologist, M. Tarde, has broken still more resolutely with this tendency, declaring that the " science of sociology " will not begin to develop until it has finally cut the umbilical cord that binds it to its mother, biology. But even this is too great a concession, for we do not in the least believe that biology is " the mother " of sociology.

[2] To quote further, among deceased writers only : Dunoyer (*Liberté du Travail*, 1845), Bastiat (*Harmonies*, 1848), Courcelle-Seneuil and Léon Say, in France ; MacCulloch, Senior and Cairnes, in England ; Ferrara in Italy ; Carey and Walker in the United States. The English Liberal school is sometimes called the Manchester school, as it was in Manchester that its Free Trade principle carried the day. It is in France that this school has retained, up till now, the largest number of followers—nearly all the economists of the *Institut* and of the *Société d'Économie politique*, etc. The late M. de Molinari, ex-editor of the *Journal des Économistes*, was its head, and his successor, M. Yves Guyot, its truest representative.

once the motive force and the end of economic activity ; and sometimes called ironically by its adversaries the *Orthodox* school, because
of the somewhat dogmatic character of its assertions and the disdain
it has somewhat too frequently shown to so-called heretics, has
declared over and over again that it will accept no other name than
that of the *Liberal school*. It is better, therefore, to keep to this
last name exclusively ; for besides being quite characteristic of it,
the word "liberal" fits in well with its time-honoured formula,
laisser faire, laisser passer. But is it really a school ? Its partisans
deny this somewhat loftily, claiming to represent the science itself.
They give themselves the simple name of Economists, a name which
even their opponents for the most part allow them. It is true that
the origins of this school go back to those of economic science itself.
Its doctrine is very simple, and may be summed up in three points :

(*1*) Human societies are governed by natural laws which we
cannot change even if we would, since they are not of our own
making. *Even if we could, we should have no interest in changing them*,
because they are good, or at least the best possible.[1] The task of
the economist is limited to discovering the play of these natural
laws, and the duty of individuals and of governments is to try to
regulate their conduct by them.

(*2*) These laws are in no way opposed to man's liberty or to
individual effort, the first and sole motive in social evolution. They
are, on the contrary, merely the *expression of the relations which
arise spontaneously* between men living in society when left to
themselves and free to act according to their interests. Where this
is the case, a *harmony* arises between these apparently antagonistic
individual interests, a *harmony* which is in the essence of the
natural order, and far superior to any artificial combination that
could be imagined.

(*3*) The rôle of the legislator, then, if he would secure social
order and progress, is limited to developing, as far as possible, these
individual initiatives, to removing all that might impede them, and
to preventing them simply from prejudicing one another. Consequently the *intervention of authority should be reduced to the
minimum* indispensable to the security of each and all—in a word,
to *laisser faire*.[2]

---

[1] " The laws which govern capital, wages, the distribution of wealth are as
good as they are inevitable. They gradually raise the level of mankind "
(Leroy-Beaulieu, *Précis d'Économie politique*).

[2] " We assert that it is enough to observe them (these natural laws), levelling
the natural obstacles that impede their action and, above all, refraining from

Such a conception is certainly not lacking either in simplicity or grandeur. Whatever may be the fate in store for it, it at least possesses the merit of having helped to constitute economic science ; and if other doctrines are one day to take its place, it will none the less remain the foundation on which they will have built.

But it has been justly reproached with a strong tendency to optimism, that is to say, a tendency to palliate injustices and to present evils as a condition of progress : poverty, for example, as a necessary sanction of the law which imposes labour and foresight on mankind.[1] This tendency is most marked in the French school,[2] and has drawn upon it the epithet of " hard," an epithet which is quite out of place as we are speaking of a scientific conception, but which must be taken as meaning that this school has become hateful to those who are suffering and who are looking for some alleviation of their woes. What matter, it might answer, if such be the truth ! But this is the very point. Its doctrine seems to be inspired less by a truly scientific spirit than by a predetermination to justify the existing order of things. The following criticisms may be urged against it :

(1) First, the idea that the existing economic order is the *natural* order in the sense that it is the spontaneous result of natural laws and of liberty, and that it is, therefore, if not all that it should be, at least *all that it can be*, does not seem well founded. History shows that this order is only too often the result either of war and brutal conquest (the appropriation of the soil of England and Ireland by a small number of landlords, for instance, has its

putting artificial obstacles in their way, for the condition of mankind to be as good as is consistent with the advancement of his knowledge and his industry. Our gospel may therefore be summed up in these four words : ' laisser faire, laisser passer ' " (De Molinari, *The Natural Laws of Political Economy*). The same idea has been expressed in the somewhat sophistical words, " Political Economy is no more the art of organising societies than astronomy is the art of turning the planets." The whole of Bastiat's celebrated *Harmonies Économiques* is nothing but a development of this idea.

[1] " It is good that there should be lower places in society for families who behave badly. Poverty is this much-dreaded hell " (Dunoyer, *Liberté du Travail*).

[2] It reached its height in Bastiat's *Harmonies économiques*, and in Dunoyer's *La Liberté*, but it is also to be found in the writings of contemporary economists. See M. Paul Leroy-Beaulieu's book on the distribution of wealth, which bears the significant sub-title " or the tendency to a lesser inequality of conditions."

This optimism is much less marked in the English school, which, in some respects, shows itself distinctly *pessimistic*, particularly in the theories of Ricardo, Malthus, and even of J. S. Mill, regarding the laws of population, of rent, of wages, as fixed by the minimum of subsistence, of diminishing returns, of the stationary State, etc., which we shall discuss further on.

origin in conquest, usurpation, or confiscation) or of legislation dictated by certain classes of society for their own profit (succession laws, fiscal laws, etc.). If, therefore, the world were to be made over again, under conditions of absolute liberty, there is nothing to prove that it would at all resemble the world of to-day.

(2) Secondly, even if the prevailing order were the natural order, we should still have no reason to conclude that the economic facts and institutions, such as property and the wage-system, which exist to-day must be of a permanent and immutable nature. Any such conclusion would be a pure sophism. If, as contemporary science tends to believe, the natural law *par excellence* is that of evolution, then we must admit that natural laws, *far from excluding the idea of change, always presuppose it.* If, for example, we claim that, just as the wage-system (*salariat*) succeeded serfdom and slavery, so it, in its turn, must disappear, and give place to co-operation or some other unnamed state, our line of argument may be criticised, but it cannot be accused of being in contradiction with natural laws, since, by these same natural laws, the flower follows the seed and the fruit follows the flower on one and the same plant.

(3) Admitting that the economic order is subject to natural laws, we have still less right to conclude that these laws are necessarily good, or at least the best possible. There is no apparent reason why Nature should have the happiness of mankind as her end. Moreover, to hold that man is condemned always to abstention is to have too low an opinion of human activity, which is, indeed, exerted daily, and in the most effective manner, in modifying facts of the physical order in accordance with our wants. And this reasoned action of man on natural phenomena is in no wise incompatible with the idea of natural law : it is, on the contrary, closely bound up with it.[1]

No doubt there are facts which, by their immensity or their remoteness, are beyond the reach of human action : phenomena of the astronomical, geological, or even meteorological order. All that we can do in this case is to submit to them in silence. Our faculty of foresight is not able to save us from the shock of a comet or from an earthquake. But how many other spheres there are in which our knowledge is almost supreme ! Most of the more important compounds of inorganic chemistry have been created by the scientist in his laboratory. When we see the cattle-breeder and the horticulturist

---

[1] As M. Espinas pertinently says (*Sociétés animales*): " If human activity were incompatible with the order of phenomena, the act of boiling an egg would have to be considered a miracle."

ceaselessly modifying animal and vegetable forms and creating new races, it would seem as if living nature allowed herself to be moulded as docilely as inert matter. Even atmospheric phenomena do not altogether escape the action of human industry, which, by the judicious clearing and planting of forests, makes bold to modify the *régime* of the winds and waters, and to repeat, as it were, the miracle of the prophet Elijah, by bringing down from heaven the rain and the dew.

A fortiori, may our activity affect economic facts, for the very reason that they are the acts of man, and we have thus direct hold over them.[1] Here, no doubt, as in the sphere of the physical sciences, our action is confined within certain limits which science seeks to determine, and which all men, whether acting individually through private enterprise, or collectively through legislation, should endeavour to respect. Bacon's well-known adage, *naturæ non imperatur nisi parendo* (we can only govern nature by obeying her), is to the point here. Alchemy tried hard to turn lead into gold ; chemistry has given up this vain attempt, since it has realised that these are two simple, or at least two irreducible, bodies ; but it has not given up trying to turn coal into diamonds, since it has found that they are but one body in two different states. The Utopian tortures nature uselessly for that which she cannot give ; the scientist asks her only for what he knows is possible. But the sphere of this " possible " is infinitely vaster than the Classical school imagined.

(B) THE SOCIALIST SCHOOLS

THE Socialist doctrine is as old as the Classical doctrine : we may even say that, chronologically, it came first ; for there were socialists long before economists were heard of. Still, it was not until economics had become scientific in character that socialism, in sheer antagonism to it, took distinct form. As the tenets of these schools are mainly critical and are very divergent, they are much more difficult to formulate than those of the preceding school. We may, however, sum them up as follows : [2]

---

[1] Even the representatives of the Determinist school, who deny free-will (and this cannot surely be the case of the school which calls itself "Liberal "), allow man the power of modifying the order of things in which he lives. They simply make the reservation that every modifying act of man is itself necessarily predetermined ; but this is a question of pure metaphysics which we need not consider here. (See, besides, what we have said on this subject, p. 6, note 1.)

[2] Leaving aside the long line of precursors which may be traced back to Plato, socialism has had for its chief representatives during the last century : in France, Saint-Simon (*Système Industriel*, 1821), Fourier (*Association domestique agricole*, 1822), Proudhon (*Qu'est-ce que la propriété?* 1840) ; in England,

(*1*) All the Socialist schools see the essential cause of social disorder in the concentration of wealth in the hands of a small number of parasites, who thus have the power to exploit the masses and to make the many work for the profit of the few : *paucis humanum genus vivit.*

They therefore look for a new order of things, in which the private ownership of capital and its obverse side, the wage-system, will be, if not altogether abolished, at least more and more limited. And according as these schools are more or less exacting on this essential point, they may be classed thus : the *communists*, who want the abolition of private property in everything ; the *collectivists*, who demand the abolition of private property only in goods necessary for production ; the *agrarian socialists*, who are content with the abolition of private property simply in immovable goods, lands and houses.

For the rest, the features of the future society are very hazy.[1] The older socialists (Sir Thomas More, Saint-Simon, Fourier), disdainfully called Utopians, whose doctrines to-day are quite unjustly discredited, built their whole structure in one piece on some *a priori* principle of justice ; they proposed *systems*. The collectivists, who take the proud title of *scientific socialists*, refuse to propose systems, and confine themselves to showing how the future society will create itself and is already doing so under our eyes. The most original and interesting part of their thesis is that wherein they show this future society already contained in embryo, as it were, within those of our modern societies that are ready to give birth to it.

(*2*) These Socialist schools by no means claim, as the Classical economists accuse them of doing, that the social order can be changed from top to bottom by a revolution or a decree. They also believe in evolution ; but they hold that revolution, meaning thereby the sudden bursting forth of a latent and slowly ripening process, is one of the normal modes of evolution, and not of social evolution only, but of biological and geological evolution also. Earthquakes are one of the factors which determined the present form of our globe,

Owen (whose principal work, *New Views of Society*, was published in 1812) ; in Germany, Karl Marx (*Kapital*, vol. i, 1867, and three posthumous volumes), Lassalle (*Bastiat und Schulze Delitzsch*, 1864). France gave the strongest impulse to socialism up to the middle of the nineteenth century, since when it is the Germans who have given it its characteristic physiognomy.

[1] See, however, various anticipatory descriptions of this future society from the Collectivist point of view in Schaeffle's *Quintessence of Socialism* and in *Le régime socialiste*, by George Renard.

and the chicken has to break its shell before it can come out of the egg   Every birth, indeed, is a kind of revolution.

We may even say that the Socialist schools are more determinist than the Liberal school in this, that they assert the all-powerfulness of the environment over the individual.   This was the doctrine of Owen and Fourier, and in the Marxian school it became confirmed under the name of *historical materialism.*   By it is meant that facts of the economic order, particularly those relating to productive and industrial technique, *determine all social facts,* even the highest and apparently most remote facts of the political, moral, religious, and æsthetic orders.   Marx wrote : " In changing their mode of production, men change all their social relations.   The hand-mill will give you society with the suzerain ;   the steam-mill, society with the industrial capitalist."   And the socialists make bold to explain by purely economic causes the advent of Christianity, the Reformation, or the Renaissance, the struggle of the Guelphs and Ghibellines, or of the Whigs and Tories, and anything else besides.[1]

Still, this determinism has not the fatalistic character attributed to it.   For, even if social evolution is determined by the substitution of the steam-mill for the hand-mill, it must not be forgotten that both are products of human industry, and that consequently the collective action of mankind is itself the first factor of this evolution which bears it along and outstrips it.

(*3*) The Socialist schools are generally inclined to widen, as far as possible, the scope of collective powers, whether represented by the State, the communes, or working-men's associations, since their aim really is to transform into a public service all that is to-day in the hands of private enterprise.

It is, however, simply as a transitional measure, in order to transform individual into collective enterprises, that socialists advocate the extension of the functions of the State.   Once this is accomplished they will abolish the State altogether. For, far from being in favour of it, they profess the greatest contempt for it as it is to-day ; the " bourgeois State," as they call it—that is to say, the State as

---

[1] See, in particular, Loria's eloquent book, *Economic Bases of Social Organisation.* This doctrine of *historical materialism* obviously contains some truth, inasmuch as in order to do anything at all man must first eat, and economic facts in this sense precede all others   But it is one thing to say that a certain understructure is the necessary basis of all civilisation, and quite another to say that it determines this civilisation.   It is simply the ground from which flora of all descriptions may spring.   Besides, the Marxian socialists themselves no longer accept this doctrine in an absolute sense, and its value now lies mainly in its protest against the *ideological* method.

politician and employer with the same interests as individuals. In their plans for social reorganisation socialists avoid even the use of the word State, employing rather the word Society. In the socialist scheme, the State is to drop its political character altogether and become simply economic; eventually it will be no more than the committee of management of a kind of immense co-operative society, embracing the whole country. This is where the distinction comes in between Socialism pure or Labour-Socialism (" Democratic " Socialism, as it is called in Germany), and the State Socialism which we shall discuss presently.

(*4*) Lastly, the outstanding characteristic of present-day socialism is that it is exclusively *working class*, that is to say, it admits no other interests than those of the working class and considers the interests of the other classes of society as necessarily antagonistic to those of the workers.[1] The middle classes, or capitalists, have played their part, which was the forming of the present society, but, having become parasites, they must now be eliminated. Hence the emphasis laid on *class conflict*, which is the essential principle of the socialist programme. This characteristic, it must be observed, did not exist in the older socialism, nor even in that of 1848; nor is it to be found in the present form of socialism which goes by the name of *Anarchism*.[2] The working-class or proletariat nature of socialism has become confirmed only since the advent of Marxian Socialism,

---

[1] Fourier wanted a world in which every one was happy, " even the rich."

[2] Among the various Socialist schools, the *Anarchist* school stands out with such marked features that a special category should be reserved for it. The word "*Socialistic*," indeed, hardly applies to it, since its characteristics, on the contrary, are an ultra-individualism and a horror of all regulation and all constraint. It appears rather as an extreme development of the Liberal school, for it stands, like the latter, for perfect freedom (it calls itself quite readily "socialisme *libertaire* "). But, while the Liberal school is content to reduce the rôle of the legislator to a minimum, the Anarchist school does away with law altogether. It shares the optimism of the former school and exalts, like it, the harmony of natural instincts when left to themselves. But where it differs greatly from the Liberal school and allies itself to Socialism is in its belief that private property is incompatible with the full independence of the individual, or, at least, that it can give independence to some only by taking it from others. As M. Wilfred Monod, a Christian Socialist, has cleverly put it, " Is not what is called *private* property what *de-prives* others ? " The Anarchist theory is generally supposed to have originated in Russia; one reason being that it has mostly been taught by two Russians, Bakunin (who died in 1876) and Kropotkine; and another, that it is generally confused with Nihilism, although this doctrine, which is mainly political, has no connection with it. In reality, however, the Anarchist doctrines have spread in hardly any but the Latin countries—France, Spain and Italy.

and it is most clearly stated at the present day in *Syndicalism,* which, as the name indicates, has taken for its organ the syndicate, since the syndicate, by definition, can be composed only of workers. For the same reason the Revolution is prophesied to-day in the specifically working-class form of the General Strike.

It is impossible in this chapter to weigh the grievances of the Socialist school against the existing order of society ; we shall come upon them constantly in the course of this book. We may say here, however, that the rapid growth of socialism in every land is easily explained by the elements of truth which it contains, and that, in so far as it is a *critical* doctrine, it has had rather a salutary influence than otherwise on the minds and tendencies of our time.

But as a *positive* doctrine, *i.e.* as a plan for reorganising the economic conditions under which we live, it has failed. All the systems which it formerly proposed, after having recruited a few enthusiastic disciples, have either been abandoned or linger simply as vague hopes. As for Collectivism, or the so-called Scientific Socialism, it has refused to formulate a plan of organisation, and has even had to disavow the plans prematurely sketched out by some of its bolder spirits. We shall return to the discussion of Collectivism, however, in Book III.

(C) STATE SOCIALISM—THE RÔLE OF THE STATE

THIS doctrine is by no means to be confounded with the preceding one. It comes forward, on the contrary, as an antidote to such socialism, and is, as a rule, looked on with as much favour by governments, and sometimes by despots, as the former is by revolutionaries. It is one, in its origins, with the Historical school. The latter school first split off from the Classical school on a question of method only, but was not long in differentiating itself in its tendencies and its programme also. It began by rejecting altogether the characteristic principle of the Liberal school, *laisser faire.* It gave science a *practical aim,* and considered the old distinction between art and science as out of date, at least where the social sciences are concerned. It thus came back to the conception of the first economists. It holds, indeed, that we cannot think of modifying economic institutions in any other direction than that indicated by history; but that, along that particular line, we can and must do so; science, therefore, contains art, just as the past contains the future. What *is,* what *will be,* what *must be,* are inseparable. For example, while the Classical school considers the private ownership of land and the wage-system as final institutions, due to necessary and general causes, the Historical school looks on them simply as historical categories, due to diverse causes, which have taken on very varying forms in different countries and at different times.[1]

For the very reason that this school attaches so little importance to the idea of natural law (see p. 12), it attaches great importance to that of *positive laws*, emanating from the legislator, and sees in them one of the most powerful factors of social evolution.[2] It is, therefore, inclined to extend considerably the scope of State action, and does not share in any way in the antipathies or the distrust of the Liberal school in this respect.

State Socialism has, of late, had a great influence both on the minds of men and on legislation. The great legislative movement known as *Labour Legislation*, which began in the last quarter of the nineteenth century, the treaties concluded among States for the international regulation of labour, the moral and often pecuniary support lent by the State to a host of social institutions, are in large measure due to it. It has certainly rendered great service to economic science by widening the narrow, factitious point of view, which had quite satisfied the Classical school, with its intentional simplicity and irritating optimism. It has stirred economic science out of its systematic aloofness, and has tried to find some other answer to the old question of human poverty, " What is to be done ? " than the mere barren *laissez faire*.

It has been of use, too, in showing how the extreme mistrust of the State manifested by the Liberal school, which scarcely leaves the State any other rôle than that of preparing its own gradual abdication, has neither a scientific nor a historical justification. The rôle of the State has been an important one, and in spite of certain appearances it is becoming more so.

[1] Further, if we are to believe the Historical school, the hedonistic principle itself is by no means an innate instinct, universal, existing from all time.   In primitive societies (and even nowadays in societies in which men have kept their primitive habits) the principle of man's life is not to get the greatest gain.   It is only in his relations with foreigners, *i.e.* with enemies—for the two words were synonymous to the ancients—that he has acquired it ; and it was in proportion as trade with the outside world grew, swallowing up and dominating private relationships, that the churlish rule of the market (the frontier march), where exchange was made at the sword's point, became the law of economic relations (see Brentano, *Une leçon sur l'Économie classique, Revue d'Économie politique,* 1889).

[2] " The laws with which political economy is concerned are not laws of nature ; they are decreed by the legislator.   The former escape the action of man's will ; the latter issue from it " (De Laveleye, *Éléments d'Économie politique,* p. 17).

In the first place, the State has always made the laws, and it is the laws which give rise to rights. And what an influence, even from a purely economic point of view, have Law and Right had on social relations, through property, heredity, contracts, sales, loans, hires! True, it is said, the State does not create laws or rights, but simply gives a sort of formal consecration, as it were, to what custom has already created. It is for this reason, said the Physiocrats, that the word *legislator* is used, not *legisfactor*. Without disregarding the element of truth contained in this, or falling into the opposite extreme, like Hegel, whose conception of the State as the conscience of the nation has had so much influence on the growth of State Socialism in Germany, it is easy to show how inadequate is this conception. When we see the State to-day prohibiting by law the use of absinthe, pornographical publications, gambling, do we really think that it is only following and consecrating custom ? Is it not rather fighting custom ?

Such as it is, and badly organised as it may have been, we must not forget that the State, to go no further than the economic sphere, has done great and fine things in history which private initiative had been powerless to effect—the abolition of slavery, of serfdom, of guilds, the regulation of labour, the protection of children, the laying of roads, the sanitation of cities. No doubt these reforms were instigated in the first instance by individuals. Can we ever forget the part played by Wilberforce and Mrs. Beecher-Stowe in the abolition of negro slavery, or that of Lord Shaftesbury in the delivering of children from factory labour ? It is evident that the State must be set in motion by individuals, and that it can act only by means of individuals—the State is always some one, whether hero or mere official—nevertheless, it is by the power of the State that the good intentions of these individuals come to be realised.[1]

There are only two serious objections to State Socialism.

The first, an objection of principle, is that the State, even when carrying out reforms good in themselves, can, as a rule, only do so by law, *i.e.* by constraint. But we must point out that in every association, even voluntary, individuals have to submit to the will of the majority, *i.e.* to constraint. The State, again, does not always act by coercion. Very often it works by way of *example*, as

[1] See in this connection Dupont White, *l'Individu et l'État* (1865) ; Hamilton, *Le développement des fonctions de l'État dans leurs rapports avec le droit constitutionnel* (*Revue d'Économie politique*, 1891) ; Cauwès, *Cours d'Économie politique*, vol. i, Book I, 3rd edit.

employer in its yards and workshops ; or by way of *help*, as when it creates roads, ports, canals, telegraph lines, or subsidises industries, such as railways, or institutions due to private initiative—*e.g.* benefit societies, loan societies, unemployment and superannuation funds, etc., or when it directly organises institutions in order to hand them over to those for whom they have been created, such as professional schools, savings banks, insurance, etc.

The second, a practical objection, is that the State has often shown the most deplorable incapacity for dealing with economic matters, and often, too, has allowed itself to become a party instrument rather than the organ of the common good.[1] This is only too true, but these defects are due not so much to the nature of the State as to its organisation. We see no essential reason why the State, which, after all, is but an association, should necessarily be inferior to any other of the large companies which are taking over more and more the direction of economic affairs. It must not be forgotten that, even in the countries most advanced from the democratic point of view (particularly in these, we might say), the State has been organised *solely in view of its political, not of its economic, functions*, the latter being even subordinated to the former. We have only to point to the influence of electoral interests when the building of a railway is at stake. The rudimentary division of labour in a government, the instability of its power, the arbitrary way in which public offices are distributed, the rough-and-ready organisation of universal suffrage, which often does not even represent the will of the majority, may render the State at present unfit to deal with economic questions. But we may be permitted to hope that, so soon as it is constituted with due regard to its new duties, it will be able to exercise a more economic and effective action than has hitherto been the case.

These general remarks are enough for our present purpose ; we shall come across the question of State intervention and the criticism which it calls forth, in each of the four main divisions of this book :

In *production*, the State as industrial *entrepreneur*, or as subsidising and controlling certain private enterprises ;

In *circulation*, the State as regulating banks and international trade, and minting money ;

In *distribution*, the State interfering in the distribution of fortunes by its laws on property, inheritance, loans at interest, leases,

[1] See Herbert Spencer's celebrated pamphlet, *Man versus the State*.

wages, and taking its own share by a tax on the income of each citizen ;

Even in *consumption*, certain forms of which the State prohibits or controls.

(D) CHRISTIAN SOCIAL REFORM

THIS school shows two tendencies, which start from the same point but follow quite opposite directions. They correspond to the two great branches of the Christian religion to which the countries most advanced, economically, belong.[1]

(*1*) The Catholic school, like the Classical school, firmly believes in the existence of natural laws, which it calls *laws of Providence*, that govern social as well as physical facts.

Only, it believes that the working of these laws of Providence may be profoundly disturbed by a wrong use of man's liberty, and that this is precisely what has taken place. Through the fault of man, through Adam's sin, the world is not what it ought to be, what God would have had it be. Unlike the Liberal school, this school is not at all optimistic. It does not consider the social order as good, nor even as naturally tending to become better. Above all, it has no confidence in the *laisser faire* policy for restoring harmony and securing progress, since, on the contrary, it sees in this proud faith in freedom (which it calls *liberalism*) the true cause of social disorganisation.

The vehemence of the criticisms which the Catholic school directs against the present order of things, against capitalism, profit, and interest—which it still stigmatises, as it did in the Middle Ages, by the name of usury (*usura vorax*)—against corporations, free trade, and all forms of internationalism, in particular against competition, has earned for it, on the part of the Liberal Economists, the name of *Catholic Socialism*. This name it strenuously disclaims ; and, in spite of certain points of view common to both, it differs *toto orbe* from the Socialist school. In the first place, it aims in no way at abolishing the fundamental institutions of the present social order—property, succession, the wage-earning system—but rather at consecrating them by imbuing them with the Christian spirit. In the second place, it has no belief in evolution, or in the indefinite progress of the human race and looks less to the future for its ideal than to a revival of the spirit which animated the institutions of the past, and procured for man a relatively happy life : to a return

[1] For fuller details, see *Catholic Socialism*, by Nitti, translated into English, 1895.

to country life, for instance, and to the professional guilds of employers and workmen.

In general, this school is not hostile to the intervention of the State, which is, after the Church, " the minister of God . . . for good." [1] It goes the length of formally claiming intervention, in order to secure to the working classes the seventh day of rest, the regulation of labour, and even a just wage. Still, a small section of the Catholic school is as much opposed to State intervention as is the Liberal school itself, and this question has given rise to lively quarrels among its members.[2]

It is to this Liberal branch (in the economic sense of the word) of the Catholic school that the school of Le Play, to which we have already referred *à propos* of method, is attached. But his school is still one with the Catholic school : *first,* in the predominance which it gives to moral and religious feeling in the economic order ; *secondly,* in its distrust of evolution and natural progress, and its lively hostility to the " false dogmas " of the French Revolution ; *thirdly,* in the very great importance which it attaches to the organisation and stability of the family (the *stock*), the preservation of patrimony, and the freedom of bequest.[3] As its aim is above all to restore order and social peace, it hopes to attain this by a threefold authority : that of the *father* in the family, that of the *employer* in the workshop, that of the *Church* in society ; but this is on condition of reciprocal duties on the part of these " social authorities."

The strongest objection that can be urged against this school, putting aside all controversy bearing on politics and religion, was formulated long ago by J. S. Mill, when he said, " all privileged and powerful classes as such, have used their power in the interest of their own selfishness." [4] There is good reason to fear that the authority of the directing classes, if ever the task of solving the social question were entrusted to them alone, would but confirm the sad fact pointed out by Mill.

---

[1] St. Paul, *Epistle to the Romans,* chap. xiii, verse 4.

[2] For the interventionist Catholic school, see Father Antoine's *Cours,* and for the anti-socialist and anti-interventionist school, M. Rambaud's *Traité d'Économie politique.*

[3] Le Play's school is itself divided into two branches : one which has remained faithful to Le Play's teachings as regards social policy and the solution of social questions, and which has *La Réforme Sociale* for its organ in France ; the other, a dissenting school, which has devoted itself more particularly to method and to the classification of social facts. Its leaders were Demolins and the Abbé de Tourville, and its organ *La Science sociale.*

[4] *Principles of Political Economy,* edited by W. J. Ashley, p. 754.

(2) The Protestant school takes no more kindly to the actual economic order. It, too, denounces competition and the pursuit of gain. It accepts property, but mainly as a social *function*. It believes that the world must be radically transformed in order to approximate to the " Kingdom of God," the coming of which all the faithful must expect and already be preparing *on this earth.*

Nevertheless, in its programme it does not present the same unity as the Catholic school. It assumes different aspects in different countries.

In England, the " Christian Socialists," as they were called (Kingsley, Maurice, etc.), took a large part in the co-operative movement of the middle of the nineteenth century, and co-operative association still appears to English and American Christian Socialists as the form best suited to a Christian society in so far as, by eliminating competition and profit, and by putting into practice mutual help, it is superior as an ideal to trade associations which, in their view, are more of a nature to encourage corporative egoism. Is not every Protestant church, in fact, a co-operative association ? In the Anglican Church, however, there is an important movement for the nationalising of landed property : " The earth is the Lord's and the fullness thereof."

In Germany, the Protestant school made its first appearance with Pastor Stoecker under a somewhat anti-Semitic aspect and went hardly further than State Socialism. To-day it is rapidly turning towards Social Democracy, *i.e.* towards Collectivism. The same is true of Switzerland.[1]

(E) THE " SOLIDARITY " SCHOOL

SUMMARY though our review of the various schools is, we cannot pass over in silence one which is of recent date, but whose influence is rapidly increasing—the school which has taken for its motto the word " Solidarity."

Solidarity, or the mutual dependence of men, so clearly visible in the division of labour, in exchange, and, as regards succeeding generations, in heredity, had already been pointed out as a fact by Leroux, Bastiat, and Auguste Comte. But they looked on it as a natural law which had no need of human assistance, and was far

[1] In France, although the number of Protestants is small, there are no less than three Christian-Social associations, the oldest of which, founded in 1887, stops at co-operation, while the second and the third (quite a small school) go as far as communism. See the review, *Le Christianisme Social*, edited by M. Gounelle.

from being always a blessing. For solidarity in evil (*e.g.* the transmission of diseases by contagion or heredity) is more obvious than solidarity in good. It appeared to them, moreover, contrary to justice, according to which each man is responsible only for his own acts.

The Solidarity school, on the other hand, would transform solidarity from a bare fact into a rule of conduct, a moral duty, nay, more, an obligation sanctioned by law. What reason does it give for doing so ? Simply that, as each one of our acts has its incidence. for good or for ill, on our fellows and *vice versa*, our responsibility and our risks are enormously increased. If there are miserable beings in existence, we must help them : first, because we are probably to some extent the *authors* of their misery, by the way in which we have directed our businesses, our investments, our purchases. or by the example which we have set,—and being thus responsible, it is our *duty* to help them ; secondly, because we know that we, or our children, may one day be the *victims* of their suffering ; their disease will poison us, their depravity will demoralise us ; it is, therefore, our *interest*, rightly understood, to help them.

Human society, then, must be transformed into a kind of large association of mutual aid, in which natural solidarity, adjusted by the goodwill of each, or, lacking this, by legal restraint, will become justice ; in which each man will bear his share in the burden of the others, and will receive his share of their gains. And to those who fear thereby to lessen individuality, self-dependence, self-help, the reply must be, that individuality is strengthened and developed no less in helping others than in helping oneself.[1]

The Solidarity school is distinct from the Socialist school in that it upholds what are called the bases of the present social order—property, succession, freedom of bequest—and the inequalities to which they give rise ; but it lessens these inequalities by binding the weak to the strong in a thousand bonds of voluntary association. It also sanctions the intervention of the State in all cases where, by regulating labour, insanitary dwellings, the adulteration of food, etc., the law can prevent the degradation of the masses ; or where, by methods of compulsory insurance and providence, it tends to inculcate a spirit of solidarity in the various classes. It must not be forgotten that the State itself is but the most ancient and imposing form of solidarity among men. No doubt, solidarity acquires its full moral significance only when it is *willed*, but the

---

[1] Vinet, the Protestant critic, has put it admirably : " To give oneself, one must possess oneself."

solidarity imposed by law may be indispensable in preparing the ground from which free co-operation is later to blossom.[1]

This doctrine has had the rare privilege of rallying round it adherents from all points of the compass :—followers of the old French idealist socialism of Fourier and of Leroux ; disciples of Auguste Comte ; mystics and æsthetes inspired by Carlyle, Ruskin, or Tolstoy ; churchgoers no less than those who come from biological laboratories.[2] But this good fortune is perhaps due to the fact that its programme is as yet somewhat hazy. It is for this reason that it has made but few recruits among the ranks of professional economists.

[1] M. Léon Bourgeois has sought to give a juridical form to this somewhat vague conception of solidarity. Every man, he says, *is born with a debt to society*, in virtue of a tacit contract (which he calls a *quasi-contract*). This tacit contract is the result of the collective advantages—fruit of the labour of all—in which he shares. He must therefore begin by paying this debt, by contributing, for example, to the insurance; relief and education of his fellow men, and by other modes of contribution yet to be determined. Not until this preliminary condition has been fulfilled should economic freedom and private property be given full play. (See *La Solidarité*, by Léon Bourgeois, and also the volume, *Essai d'une Philosophie de la Solidarité*, a series of lectures given by the Solidarists in 1902, at the *École des Hautes Études Sociales*.) The objection to this ingenious theory is that there cannot be debtors without creditors. And it is not easy to see to whom in society the name of creditor or debtor should be applied. And this is a point of importance ! At first sight it might seem as if the rich were the debtors and the poor the creditors (the latter are generally referred to as the " disinherited "). But this is by no means certain. For it is quite possible that the rich man may, in reality, have given much more to society than he has received—a great inventor, for instance—and that the poor man, on the other hand, may be incapable or an invalid, and have given nothing in exchange for what he has received. Are children, for example, under this theory, creditors or debtors ?

[2] Above all, this doctrine has had the good fortune to provide a large political party, the so-called Radical party (of which M. Léon Bourgeois is one of the leaders), with the social and economic programme which it needed in order to remain distinct from Individualist-Liberalism and Collectivist-Socialism. It has enabled this party to uphold the principle of private property, while recognising the rights of the proletariat, and to adopt as its aim the abolition of the wage-system, while refusing to accept the class conflict as a means to it.

CHAPTER III: WANTS AND VALUE

I: THE WANTS OF MAN

MAN's wants are the motive force of all economic activity, and consequently the starting-point of the entire science of Economics. The whole of Political Economy might, therefore, be brought under this chapter.

Every living being, in order to exist, develop, and attain its ends, feels the need of borrowing elements from the outside world ; and when these elements are lacking, it first suffers and then dies. From the plant (and even from the crystal) up to man, this necessity grows as individuality grows. Every want, then, in a living being gives birth to a *desire*, and consequently to an *effort* to obtain certain outside objects,[1] since the possession of them brings him a satisfaction.

Man's wants have various characteristics, each of which is of great importance, for on each depends some great economic law.

(*1*) They are *unlimited in number*. It is this fact which dis-

---

[1] The words *want* and *desire*, though often used indiscriminately (as we ourselves shall use them), must not be confused. Want has a physiological origin : it consists in a feeling on the part of an organism that something is lacking, and in a vague groping after what is missed. But the organism is, as yet, ignorant of the exact object that will satisfy it. It is not until instinct, invention, or chance has revealed the object that it is *desired*, and that, secondarily, the means of obtaining it are desired. Desire is rather psychological. Thus, the want to eat exists naturally, but the desire for bread or for *pâté de foie gras* could only arise after corn had been discovered or some progress made in the culinary art. All men, again, feel a physiological want of stimulating and narcotic drugs, owing to causes as yet but little understood; but this want remains unexpressed so long as tobacco, opium and morphine, etc., have not been discovered. Only then are these objects desired, and, for their sake, the pipe and the Pravaz syringe. There is also a want in man for independence ; but it is not until the ownership of a piece of land appears to him the best means of securing this that land begins passionately to be desired. It is with this idea that M. Tarde made the proposition which, at first sight, appears paradoxical—" the first cause of all economic desire is invention " (*Logique sociale*, chap. viii).

We see, then, that desire is created by want and dies out as soon as want is satisfied ; but, as wants are permanent, desire as a rule, is not long in reappearing, and after it has been satisfied in the same way several times a habit is created, that is to say, a specialised want, *e.g.* not merely the want to smoke or to drink, but to smoke a pipe or to drink absinthe. These secondary wants, which spring from habit, are sometimes called " artificial," to distinguish them from primary wants, but we must not forget the proverb, " habit is second nature." Although, in the first instance, it springs from desire, a secondary want becomes also, in the long run, physiological.

tinguishes man from the animals and is the mainspring of civilisation in the literal sense of the word. For to civilise a people—look, for instance, at colonisation—is no more than to rouse new wants within it.

It is with the wants of mankind as with those of a child. At his birth he needs nothing but warmth and some milk; little by little, he requires more varied food, more complex garments, toys. Each year that passes brings some new want, some new desire. In primitive societies man feels almost nothing but the primary wants, the physiological ones of which we have just spoken. But the more he sees, the more he learns, the more is his curiosity wakened, and the more quickly do his desires grow and multiply. To-day we have a thousand wants—of comfort, of hygiene, of cleanliness, of education, of travel, of correspondence—unknown to our forefathers. And it is certain that our grandchildren will have still more. If we could get into communication with a higher being than man, on some other planet, we should certainly find in him an infinity of wants of which we, in this world, can have no idea.[1]

This infinite multiplication of wants, then, has created modern civilisation and all that is called progress. This is not to say that men are the happier for it. It has often been pointed out that the multiplication of desires and of the objects of desire—in other words, of wealth—has no necessary connection with the increase of happiness.[2] It is even open to us to ask whether nature here, as in the multiplication of species, is not making a dupe of man; for no sooner is one want satisfied than another takes its place, and man is thus spurred on to pursue an end that is ever vanishing before him. As a striking example of this, we may point to the state of mind

[1] We have no standard by which to draw up a scale of wants. Their relative importance might perhaps be fairly well measured by the order of their *appearance* in historic or prehistoric times, if Sociology provided us with precise enough records. It is evident that want of *food* was the first. That of *defence* against animals or other men must have followed closely on it. This explains the very ancient and dread import of the want of *arms*, which probably took as great, or even greater a place in the life and work of the men of the Stone Age than it holds in the budgets of civilised countries of the twentieth century. But it is a curious and unexpected fact that the want of *adornment* preceded that of clothing. This want is first among those which separate man from the animals. As Théophile Gautier remarks, " No dog ever had the idea of putting on earrings, and the stupid Papuans who eat clay and earthworms deck themselves out with shells and coloured berries." On the other hand, the want of *rapid communication* between men did not arise till much later, but it has developed extraordinarily of late years.

[2] See, for example, an interesting chapter on this subject in Durkheim's *La Division du Travail* (Book II, chap. i).

of the man of to-day, in which envy and exasperation become more frequent as well-being increases. Should we not rather hope that this multiplication of wants will one day cease, or, at least, slow down ? Would it not be better for us to turn our energies rather toward reducing our wants than to increasing our wealth ?

Such, indeed, was the opinion of the wise men of antiquity, and, later, of those inspired by the Christian doctrine. Others again, particularly since the eighteenth century, maintain, on the contrary, that frugality always brings with it slackness and routine.[1]

But this is a question pertaining to Ethics, not to Political Economy. We agree, however, that it is a desirable thing that economic wants, *i.e.* those which aim solely at wealth, should be reduced in number and intensity, and should occupy a smaller place in the life of individuals than is at present the case. But on one condition only ! *That they give place to other wants of a nobler kind* (see *infra*, p. 39). For, if we were simply to suppress them without putting others in their place, we should be thrusting social life back toward the animal level. Woe to the races too easily satisfied, whose desires do not reach beyond the narrow circle of a near horizon, and who ask but a handful of ripe fruit to live on, and a wall to shade them from the sun when they sleep ! They will not be long in disappearing from an earth which they have not known how to turn to account.

Moreover, even purely economic wants are not altogether lacking in moral value. Each new want is an additional *bond* between men, since we cannot, as a rule, satisfy it without the help of our fellows ; in this way the feeling of solidarity becomes stronger. The man who has no wants, the anchorite, is sufficient to himself : this is just what he should not be. As for the working classes, we should be glad, and not concerned, that new wants and desires torment them unceasingly ; were it not for this, they would have remained in perpetual bondage.

(2) Wants are *limited in capacity*. This is one of the most important propositions of Political Economy, since on it, as we shall see, the new theory of value is based. A want is limited in capacity in the sense that a fixed quantity of any one object is enough to satisfy it. Man needs only a certain amount of bread to still his hunger, and a certain quantity of water to quench his thirst. Further, a

---

[1] In a celebrated book of the eighteenth century, *The Fable of the Bees*, by Mandeville, the author declares that history proves that there never has been a frugal nation in the world that was not at the same time poor ; his meaning being, not frugal because poor, which goes without saying, but poor because frugal. Nevertheless, it is the frugal nations that have conquered the world. See also Voltaire, *Défense du Mondain*, and, *infra*, the chapter on *Luxury*.

want becomes gradually less intense in proportion as it approaches the point of satiety, *i.e.* the point where it is extinguished and gives place to disgust or even suffering.[1] There is no worse torment than the want of water ; but one of the cruellest tortures of the Middle Ages, the " water torture," consisted in forcing water into the victim's stomach.

The more natural a want is, *i.e.* the more *physiological*, the more clearly marked is its limit. It is easy to say how many ounces of bread and how many pints of water are necessary and sufficient for a man. On the other hand, the more artificial a want is, *i.e.* the more *social*, the more elastic does the limit of satisfaction become. It would be no easy matter to say how many horses would satisfy a sportsman, how many yards of lace a society woman, or how many rubies an Indian rajah ; harder than all, to say how many gold and silver coins would be enough to bring a civilised man to the point of crying " Stop ! " Yet we may say that, even in these categories of wealth, there is a limit ; that satiety is inevitable even in them, and that each new object added to those already possessed causes a rapid decrease in the pleasure felt.

It is in the case of money that satiety is most rare, and seems least likely ever to be reached. Why ? For the simple reason that money is the sole form of wealth that answers, not to one definite want, but to all possible wants ; thus it never ceases to be desired until all desires have been satisfied, a condition which pushes back the limit of satisfaction almost indefinitely. Still, it is evident that an extra five-franc piece does not give a millionaire anything like the pleasure which it gives to some poor wretch. Buffon, a great man though not an economist, had already pointed it out : " the crown piece of the poor man which is to pay for an object of prime necessity, and the crown piece that completes the sack of a rich financier, are two units of the same order in the eyes of a mathematician ; but morally, one is worth a louis, the other less than a hard."[2]

[1] Compare the series, well known to mathematicians, which gradually descends to zero, and then begins to ascend again, but with a negative value. The different degrees of want are the positive terms of the series ; the different degrees of disgust are the negative terms ; zero is satiety.

[2] This is precisely one of the arguments on which the present policy of the progressive income-tax is based. And just as there is a limit *at the top*, so there is a limit *at the bottom*. I mean that each want demands a minimum quantity of satisfaction, below which there is none. To be shod or gloved I must have two boots or two gloves ; one alone would be of no use. To enjoy an automobile I must have the income necessary for using it. If not I can do nothing with it.

(3) Wants *compete with one another*, that is to say, in most cases a want can expand only at the expense of other wants, which it either pushes out or absorbs. Very often, too, they are *interchangeable*, so that they may be easily substituted for one another, like the parts of guns or bicycles. Just as, according to the proverb, " one nail drives out another," so one want drives out another. And here we have the basis of a very important economic law called the Law of Substitution.[1] It has been found, in different countries, that the increased use of the bicycle and the motor car has considerably injured not only the sale of saddle-horses and carriages, but, what is still more unexpected, the manufacture of pianos !

The law of substitution is of capital importance, in that it acts as a sort of safety-valve for the consumer ; when the satisfaction of a want becomes too costly by the ordinary means, he substitutes, for instance, a bicycle for a horse, a newspaper for a book, a café-concert for a theatre, etc. This law allows him to escape the exactions of the producer invested with a monopoly, when the law of competition among producers, which is enough, as a rule, to protect the consumer, is no longer operative. The consumer has only to fall back on some other object, which perhaps does not answer his want quite so well, but which will do nevertheless. It is by the law of substitution that the omnipotence of Trusts is limited. In the case of wants of the physiological order, the field of possible substitution is somewhat small ; but in the case of luxuries, it is unlimited. A man may quite well substitute the theatre for hunting, or a woman a motor car for a pearl necklace.

Hygiene and morals are making use of this law in their endeavour to replace the lower and more animal wants by wants of a higher order. In the fight against alcoholism, for instance, temperance societies have found no plan more successful than the opening of temperance refreshment rooms, where the consumer is gradually accustomed to drink tea or coffee. Observe that a material want may be replaced by an intellectual or a moral one, *e.g.* the public-house may give place to the lecture-room, or a workman may go without " refreshment " in order to put aside a sum for insurance, strikes, or propaganda.

(4) Wants are *complementary, i.e.* they generally go together and can hardly be satisfied separately. Of what use is a single glove or shoe, a carriage without a horse, or a motor car without

---

[1] See in M. Paul Leroy-Beaulieu's *Traité d'Économie politique* numerous instances of the law of the substitution of wants.

petrol. To withstand the cold, a man must not only have an overcoat, he must have dined well. The want of food, in a civilised man at any rate, implies the want of a large number of objects—a table, a chair, table-linen, plates, glasses, knives and forks, etc. Sometimes, even, to obtain the maximum of satisfaction—as at a banquet— the want of food is associated with æsthetic pleasures—flowers, lights, crystals, dresses, music, etc.[1]

(5) Wants, even when artificial, once satisfied tend to recur regularly, to become fixed and to pass into *habits*; to become, as has been well expressed, "second nature." This law, too, is of great importance, especially in determining wages. It is not easy to lower the ordinary level of existence, the *standard of life*. There was a time when the working man wore neither linen nor boots ; when he had neither coffee nor tobacco, and ate no meat nor wheaten bread. To-day, the want of these things has become so inveterate, so firmly established, that a working man who could no longer satisfy it, and who found himself suddenly reduced to the condition of his fellows at the time of St. Louis, or Henry IV, would certainly perish.

Lastly, if we remember that a habit transmitted during a long succession of generations tends to become perpetuated by *heredity*, and that the senses become more subtle and more exacting, we shall understand how despotic a power a want may eventually acquire which at first seemed quite futile and insignificant.

II : UTILITY

WHAT most nearly concerns us in the outside world, so far, at any rate, as our support and well-being are concerned, is the property which a certain number of objects possess of satisfying some one or other of our wants. This property is called *utility* (from the Latin, *uti*, to use.)

---

[1] M. Tarde remarks, with his usual happiness of expression, "The well-being at which economic activity aims is a choir, not a solo, of wants harmoniously satisfied " (*Psychologie économique*, vol. i, p. 95).

This law of complementary wants had been stated and analysed by Fourier. He called it *la Composite*, and made of it a special passion, "the most beautiful of the twelve passions, the one which enhances the value of all the others. . . . It is born only of the association of the pleasures of the senses and of the soul." What Fourier called the passions, and analysed minutely, but with a puerile psychology, were simply wants at an acute stage.

We must not mistake goods called *complementary* because they are connected in consumption, with goods called complementary because they are connected in production, such as coal and gas, corn and straw, and all by-products in general. (See *infra*, *Integration of Industry*.)

Unfortunately, this word is a source of some confusion, since it has already a meaning in everyday language which does not at all correspond with its economic significance. The word *useful* is, as a rule, opposed either to the word *harmful* or to the word *superfluous*. It implies a certain moral judgment. It is applied only to objects which satisfy wants considered good. We are unwilling to speak of the *utility* of lace or of absinthe. In its economic sense, on the contrary, the word utility signifies nothing more than the property of satisfying some need or desire, and this utility is measured solely by the intensity of this need or desire.

To avoid continual misunderstanding, it would be better to substitute some other word. The older economists used the expression *value in use*. M. Vilfredo Pareto proposed that of " *ophelimity*," [1] a Greek word expressing the relation of fitness between an object and a desire. But this term has not been accepted. We ourselves, in the first edition of this book (1883), suggested the word *desirability*, which has the twofold advantage of assuming nothing in regard to the morality or reasonableness of the desire. But it also has been rejected.[2]

Let us, however, under whatever name we choose, analyse this fundamental property of objects.

Not all the things which surround us, animal, vegetable, or mineral, by any means possess it. Only a very small number—hardly more than two hundred species out of some hundreds of thousands in the animal kingdom—are really utilities.

For an object to be useful, two conditions are necessary :

(*1*) We must have discovered *a certain relation between the physical properties of the object and one of our wants*.[3] If bread is useful, it is because, on the one hand, we need food, and on the other, corn contains just the elements eminently suited for our nourishment. If the diamond is eagerly sought for, it is because it is the nature of man, as well as of certain animals, to take pleasure in things that sparkle, and the diamond, by reason of its superior refractive power, possesses just this property of flashing incomparable fires.

Notice, that of the two terms of this relationship, it is man, not the object, which is by far the more important (see p. 2, note 2). We might perhaps think, on the contrary, that the satis-

---

[1] *Cours d'Économie politique*, 1896.

[2] M. Landry, in his *Manuel d'Économique*, criticises the word as expressing "rather what we *ought* to desire than what we *actually do* desire." Perhaps so. *Appetibility* is the word which, etymologically and psychologically, would better express the meaning.

[3] See above, p. 35, note 1.

faction we expect from things is due to certain properties in them ; that the utility of gold is of the same nature as its weight, or its brightness, or its chemical resistance ; that utility is attached to objects like a physical quality. This is not so. It comes into existence only when desire wakens, and vanishes so soon as desire dies out. It follows desire from object to object, as the shadow follows the butterfly, and rests only where desire rests. It is *subjective*, not *objective*. If only for this reason the word *desirability* would be much clearer than the word utility ; for, of the two terms of the relation, man and the object, it puts man in the foreground, whereas the word utility puts him in the background.

The correspondence of an object with our wants is not always due to Nature. It may be imposed by custom, fashion, beliefs. For centuries more or less authentic relics have been looked upon as priceless wealth by reason of the virtues attributed to them, and mineral waters and pharmaceutical products have been sought after whose curative powers are extremely doubtful. Old-fashioned dresses, books no longer read, pictures no more admired, money that no longer passes, remedies that no longer cure—what a list we might make of forms of wealth whose utility is as fleeting and fugitive as the want which creates it ! And yet, if a collector were to set his desire—perhaps the most intense of all—on these dead forms of wealth, he would give them a new lease of life, and they would immediately assume a far higher value than ever they had in their former existence.

According to scientists, alcohol and the drinks derived from it, possess none of the virtues attributed to them ; they neither warm nor fortify. But what of that ! It is, alas, enough that thousands of men, in all countries, believe that they have these utilities for them to become a form of wealth—and wealth that runs to millions, from which even States themselves draw part of their revenue.

(2) But it is not sufficient for us to know that an object possesses the property of satisfying our wants : we must be able actually to apply it to the satisfaction of these wants. An object must not only be recognised as useful : it must be *capable of being used*. And this is not always possible. There are forests rotting where they stand, for lack of the power to exploit them. There are rivers, even in France, which contain gold that cannot be extracted economically. We know that there are enormous forces latent in the rise and fall of the tides, in streams, in molecular attraction ; but of all this we can make nothing, at any rate in the present state of our knowledge.

Probably there is not a single body in the world which might not be of use to man and increase his wealth. But, so long as it is unknown, it is as useless as are the fertile lands or precious metals that an astronomer might discover in Venus or Mars.

Does this property of satisfying our wants, of giving us pleasure, belong only to *things* (*res*, as the Roman jurisconsults called them) ? Assuredly we find it in acts too, in the deeds and behaviour of our fellow men. There is no question that many among them bring us great joy and are even *useful* in the economic sense of the word, satisfying our wants without the instrumentality of any material wealth. The doctor gives us health, the professor knowledge, the judge justice, the policeman security, the literary man or the artist give the loftiest and purest pleasures, and our servant does our errands. There is nothing more useful to man than man. These satisfactions are undoubtedly of an equal, or even of a higher order than those which things bring us, and we show the value we set on them by the high price we are willing to pay for them. In this case, it is true, we more readily employ the word *service* than utility.. But what of that ? Are we not continually saying of some object or other—a bicycle, a pocket ink-bottle, etc.—that it has "done us good service," just as we say to our friends, in words that are no less scientifically exact, " at your service " ?

What name are we to give to those objects and acts which possess this precious quality of satisfying our wants, of being useful or desirable ? We have to make the extraordinary admission that there is no adequate word to describe what is the very object of economic science. Jurisconsults use the Latin word *bona*, *goods* (French, *biens*) and it is perhaps the best word. Still, it implies, like the word utility, a certain moral appreciation. We should perhaps hesitate a little to apply the word " goods " to a burglar's outfit. Economists employ the word wealth, but this has the serious drawback of being already used in ordinary language in the sense of *fortune* as opposed to *poverty*. It is not easy to realise that the flowers in the field, pure water, fresh air, even a piece of bread, may be called wealth. Yet all these things possess in a high degree the property of making us live and enjoy life. ˙

The word wealth, moreover, implies another idea besides that of *enjoyment*, namely, that of *power*. This is indeed its etymological sense (compare the German *reich* = *empire* and *rich*). And this second idea is quite as important as the first. Enjoyment cannot be carried beyond a certain limit. If the pursuit of wealth, then, brought enjoyment only, it, too, would stop short at that limit.

But it is this other side of wealth, this desire for power over men and things, that pushes human effort beyond all assignable limit, and gives rise to the American millionaires, who are so aptly called the Oil, Steel, and Cotton Kings.

Wealth-*enjoyment* may be said to express itself in income, wealth-*power* in capital. And, as we shall see further on, present-day socialism may be said to aim at abolishing wealth as an instrument of power used by man over his fellows. while allowing it to remain as a means of enjoyment. It is doubtful, however, whether it will ever succeed in dissociating these two functions of wealth ; and were it to do so, it is the less noble of the two which it would leave in existence.

There is another drawback to the word wealth. It is difficult to apply it to the acts of men or to anything other than material objects. A doctor's consultation, a prima donna's song, the cut of a hairdresser, can hardly be said to be forms of wealth. And yet, as we have just seen, there is as much *utility* in all these acts as in any material object whatsoever.[1]

What, then, are we to do ? There is no other course .but to resign ourselves to using the words " goods " or " wealth," mentally translating them as " anything of the nature to satisfy an economic desire."

III : WHAT IS VALUE ?

ALL desirable things are not desired in the same degree. We establish an order of preference among them ; we classify them. It is here that the idea of *value* appears.

It is generally taught that value is inseparable from exchange, and cannot be conceived of apart from it. With this, however, we do not agree. Even Crusoe on his island had a scale of comparisons, for we find him saving first from the wreck the objects *he desired most*. And if ever a communist society were to be realised, we should

---

[1] The question whether wealth is necessarily material has long been a matter of discussion among economists. There is no need here to sum up the *pros* and *cons* of the discussion. They may be found in M. Bloch's *Progrès des Sciences économiques*, vol. i, and in an article by M. Turgeon, in the *Revue d'Économie politique*, 1892. Suffice it to say that most economists to-day are inclined to include, under the name wealth, immaterial as well as material products. It was the French school, under J. B. Say, which first took up this attitude ; and the conception of Political Economy as a psychological science, by placing the idea of wealth not in things but in us. finally consecrated it. (See p. 2, note 2.)

find exchange disappear, but not the idea of value. Having said so much, however, we admit that, in our societies, it is nearly always exchange which determines the comparison between two or more forms of wealth ; it is exchange which brings value out from its unconscious slumber, and makes it declare itself in the figure written on each object of commerce. We shall return, then, to Value in the chapter on Exchange, but this general introduction would be quite incomplete if we were to omit all mention of the idea of value. For this idea dominates not merely the exchange and circulation of wealth, but distribution, production, consumption, in fact, the whole of Political Economy.

Let us try, then, to obtain a clear conception of the idea of value, the most important, but also, alas, the most obscure in the whole of economic science.

The idea of value is more complex than that of utility. It is distinguished from the latter in particular by two characteristics :

(1) Value implies the idea of classification, of a relation between two or more things ; 'or rather, since things are here but the accessories, of a classification between wants or desires. It is concerned not simply with desirability, but with the *degree of desirability*.

It is this that distinguishes it from utility, which can exist alone, like the want to which it answers. When I say that a particular thing, say a gun or a horse, is *useful*, I make a perfectly clear and definite statement ; but if I say that a gun or a horse is worth——this statement is incomplete, and even unintelligible ; for what is it worth ? To be understood, I shall have to say that it is worth so much money ; or, if we are among savages, so many pieces of cotton-stuff, or so many elephants' tusks, *i.e.* I shall have to compare it with some other form of wealth.

Value is, therefore, a *relative* notion, of the same order as size or weight. If there were but one single body in the whole world, we should not be able to say whether it were large or small ; nor, in the same way, whether it had great or little value.[1]

---

[1] From this relative nature of value, it follows that we can never speak of a rise or fall of *all* values at once. Such a statement would have no meaning. If value is nothing but a classification, a hierarchy established among different forms of wealth, how can we imagine them all rising or falling at the same time ? Before any can rise in the scale some must necessarily give place to them and *come down*. Might not this statement have some sense if we meant by it simply that all men's desires may increase or diminish at the same time ? If, for instance, civilised societies are really moving toward the stationary state that Mill foresaw, in which men's minds will cease to be filled with the single anxiety

It is true that we constantly say of some object or other that it has " great value," without adding more ; but the term of comparison is none the less present, though implied. We mean, for example, that the diamond is of great value in relation to the unit of money, in which case we are comparing it with this other value called a coin ; or that it holds a high rank in the totality of wealth, in which case we are comparing it with all other forms of wealth collectively. So, too, when we say that platinum is heavy, without expressing any comparison, we mean that it represents a great many kilogrammes, *i.e.* we are relating it to the unit of weight (a litre of water); or that, of all known bodies, it is among the heaviest.

(2) Value implies *scarcity*, that is to say—for this word needs explaining no less than does utility—an insufficient quantity in relation to the quantity demanded.[1] This is obviously a *sine qua non*. For if there is more of a commodity than is wanted it cannot claim to have any value at all, *e.g.* drinking water in most countries, virgin soil in countries as yet unoccupied, and, only too often, alas, manual labour in our cities. 'Why ? For the simple reason we gave when analysing wants (p. 37)—that every want and every desire disappears so soon as it is *satiated*, and turns into actual repulsion against the object formerly coveted. But surely, it will be said, water remains useful even when one's thirst has been quenched. Yes, it is useful in the sense that it always contains, physically, the properties which quench our thirst ; but, economically, it is no longer desirable either for me or for anyone else, since every one has enough and to spare.[2]

The more nearly the quantity of anything approaches the point where want is satisfied, the lower does its value tend to fall; the further away it goes from this point, the higher does its value tend to rise.

to pursue wealth, might we not truly say that then all things will have less value ? No ! Not so long as the relation existing between them, the *degree* of desirability, remained the same. If, for instance, it were found one day that the force of gravity had decreased, this would not mean that objects *weighed* less : gold would still be nineteen times heavier than water.

[1] Scarcity taken by itself, *i.e.* when not brought into relation with demand or with want, has no influence whatever on value. Cherries are no less rare at the end of the season than at the beginning ; but, as they are only wanted when they are a novelty, scarcity at the end of the season gives them no value. Suppose I were to write a tragedy, my manuscript would be the only copy in the world : this would be the maximum of scarcity, but would confer no value on it.

[2] This, it may be added, is only true of drinking-water. Water that is to serve for purposes of irrigation, for pleasure grounds, or for motive power has a distinct and even a great value, for the reason that there is not enough of it to satisfy all who want to turn it to account in these particular ways.

Hence the curious consequence—we might almost say economic paradox—that by increasing the quantity of a commodity we often diminish the sum of values it represents, and *vice versa* by reducing the quantity we increase the sum of values. This law was known and practised by the spice merchants of the Dutch East Indies, who destroyed a part of their harvest when they judged it too plentiful, and it is to-day the underlying principle of manufacturers' associations or "pools," which restrict the production of coal or alcohol under penalty of a fine.

Suppose that by the touch of a fairy's wand, or simply by the continuous progress of science and industry, all objects were to become as abundant as running water or as the sand on the seashore, and that men, to satisfy their desires, had but to draw on them at will. Is it not evident that all these objects would lose their value through the simple fact of their superabundance ; that, for an individual, they would have no more and no less value than water or grains of sand ?

Thus we come to the conclusion that, in the land of Cockaigne, social wealth would be at its maximum, and yet no man would be rich, since all would be equal before the non-value of things, just as to-day king and beggar are equal before the light of the sun.[1]

IV : WHAT MAKES VALUE ?

WE have just said that value implies a classification, a comparison, or preference. Now why do we prefer one thing to another ? Why

---

[1] This is the question which J. B. Say considered the most thorny in Political Economy, and which he put in these terms : " As wealth is composed of the value of things possessed, how can it be that a nation is wealthier in proportion as the things in it are lower in price ? " (*Cours d'Économie politique*, part iii, chap. v). And Proudhon, in his *Contradictions économiques*, defied " every serious economist " to answer it. The supposed difficulty lies in this that, in the first part of the sentence, Say, in defining wealth as a " sum of values," uses the word wealth in its *individual* sense, viz., value in exchange. The wealth of an individual is composed of the totality of the goods he possesses valued in money, so that the more of these things there are in existence, the less they are worth. In the second part of his sentence, " the nation is richer in proportion as the things in it are lower in price," he uses the word wealth in the *social* sense, that of abundance.

When in years of plentiful harvest France is overflowing with corn and wine, it is said to be a " good year." But it is by no means so for the proprietors, who sell their corn and wine at a low price. Mme. de Sévigné, who did not trouble about Political Economy, fully realised it when she wrote from her chateau at Grignan (October 1673) : " Everything here is bursting with corn and I have not a ' sol.' I cry famine over a heap of corn."

do we say that one thing is worth more than another ? Why, for example, is one kilogramme of gold worth about 10,000 kilogrammes of bread ? This is the question which has been the torment of economists for over a century. Each generation fondly imagines that it has given a categorical answer,[1] but the next is still unsatisfied, and tries to dig more deeply into the problem.

We might well ask if it is not insoluble, like so many other problems that man has set himself and has had to renounce. If, as the proverb says, " there is no accounting for taste," must we not likewise say that the causes of human tastes and desires defy all analysis ? According to Ricardo, each man has a standard of his own by which he estimates the value of his enjoyments, and this standard is as variable as human nature.

But to give up the attempt to draw a few general principles from these individual preferences would be to give up the idea of Political Economy as a science. And economists have not only tried to determine the causes of value, but have done their best to reduce them to one single cause. Only they have not been able to agree on this cause. Utility ? scarcity ? difficulty of acquisition ? cost of production ? cost of reproduction ? Each of these has found its partisans, but nearly all have been abandoned.

The *Utility* theory, using the word utility in its ordinary sense as the property of answering to man's most urgent necessities, was not able to stand against this obvious objection : why does the diamond rank highest and water lowest in the scale of values ? For water is surely the one thing of all others that corresponds to man's most frequent and urgent want, ἄριστον μὲν ὕδωρ, said the poet Pindar ?

But this theory was supplemented as a rule by the addition of the element of Scarcity ; and some economists (Senior and the elder Walras) even considered scarcity a sufficient explanation in itself, utility being naturally implied in the word scarcity, as a scarcity that is useless would be meaningless. Although this closely approximates to the theory of final utility, which is generally adopted to-day, it is misleading since it puts in the first place that which is really secondary. It is only for the collector that the chief and sometimes sole merit of things lies in their scarcity. Scarcity, in itself,

---

[1] J. S. Mill declared, in 1848 : " Happily, there is nothing in the laws of value which remains for the present or any future writer to clear up ; the theory of the subject is complete " (*Principles of Political Economy*, 1909, Book III, chap. i).

is not an attraction ; it is merely the obstacle which gives an impetus to desire.[1]

There are but two explanations to-day which dispute the ground, and the first has almost entirely lost its standing. They are the *labour* theory and the *final utility* theory.

(A) THE LABOUR THEORY

THE labour theory of value has held a prominent place in the history of economic doctrine. Taught for the first time, though in somewhat uncertain fashion, by Adam Smith, strongly asserted by Ricardo, it has rallied round it economists of the most opposite schools, from optimists like Bastiat to socialists like Karl Marx.[2]

This theory, be it understood, does not deny that utility— *i.e.* the property of satisfying some human want or desire, is the primordial condition of all value. We must have taken leave of our senses to imagine that a thing that is of no earthly use could have any value, however much labour had gone to its making.

---

[1] *Difficulty of acquisition* is a better expression than scarcity, as it groups in two words many of the elements which may influence value. But it passes over in silence the most essential one—desire. Nothing could be more difficult than to draw up a pebble from the bottom of the Atlantic ; but this gives it no value.

The *cost of reproduction,* a theory dear to the heart of the American economist, Carey, and to the Italian, Ferrara, differs from the preceding one only in that it looks at the trouble that will be necessary to replace the object, not at that spent in acquiring it.

As for the *law of supply and demand,* if it is able to explain (and that with reservations which we shall discuss later) the *variations* of value, it is unable to explain the origin or the cause of value. To say that a thing has more value or less, according as more or less of it is demanded or offered, is like saying that a pendulum swings more to one side or the other according as it is pushed more to right or to left. But this does not explain the cause (force of gravity) which brings it back to the vertical position.

For the explanation of *cost of production,* see *infra,* p. 53, note 1.

[2] " It is natural," says Adam Smith, " that what is usually the produce of two days' or two hours' labour should be worth double of what is usually the produce of one day's or one hour's labour " (*Wealth of Nations*, Book I, chap. vi).

Ricardo refers to labour " as being the foundation of all value, and the relative quantity of labour as almost exclusively determining the relative value of commodities " (*Principles of Political Economy*, chap. i, sect. ii).

Karl Marx declares that " that which determines the magnitude of the value of any article is the amount of labour socially necessary . . . for its production " (*Kapital*, chap. i).

In spite of their apparent identity, the explanations of value given by these three eminent economists are, at bottom, quite different. But we cannot enter into these distinctions here (See *History of Economic Doctrines*, by Gide and Rist, English translation).

But, according to this school, if utility is the condition of value it is certainly not the cause of value. The basis of value is man's labour, and everything is worth more or less according as it has cost more or less to make.

At first sight this theory is very attractive.

In the first place, it appears more scientific than the others. It gives as the foundation of value a precise, objective, quantitative notion, something that can be measured. To say that this watch is worth twice as much as that because it represents twice as much labour, is to say something that satisfies our reason. The explanation seems valid, and, in any case, may be verified. But to say that it is worth double because its utility is twice as great, is to say something that barely enlightens us.

In the second place, it satisfies more fully our sense of justice by making a moral element—labour—the basis of value. It is from this side more particularly that it has attracted so many generous minds. If we could succeed in proving that the value of everything that has been appropriated, beginning with land, is proportional to the labour it has cost, it would not, of course, follow that the wealth appropriated by each man would be equivalent to the product of *his labour;* for he might quite well have appropriated a value created by some one else's labour. But at any rate the problem of crediting each man with a value equal to the product of his labour would be much simplified, and it would become easier to establish the social organisation solidly on a principle of justice.[1]

It must be remarked, however, that this " moral " motive is not altogether convincing ; for labour itself, if useless, cannot pretend to moral value. Even admitting, what is not always the case, that labour implies at least good intentions, we must not forget the saying, " The road to Hell is paved with good intentions."

But from the economic point of view the explanation is still less satisfactory, for the following reasons :

(*1*) If the value of a thing originated in, or consisted in, the labour

---

[1] Notice, however, that this explanation has been used for two contrary ends, as much in defence of private property as against it. The optimist school asserts that the values appropriated by each individual are, as a rule—save in the case of disturbances, exploitation, thefts, from which the most civilised countries are not exempt—*the fruit of the labour of the proprietor or his forbears. Cf.* Bastiat, Fontenay, Paul Leroy-Beaulieu. This, in particular, is the defence given for landed property, although the proof is, in this case, more troublesome.

The Socialist school, on the other hand, asserts that the values appropriated are, in general, the *fruit of the labour of others.*

devoted to its production, that value ought to remain unchange-able, since, as Bastiat says, " *past* labour is not susceptible of more or less." Now every one knows, on the contrary, that the value of an object is continually varying, precisely because it depends on demand or desire. It is quite evident, then, that these variations are altogether independent of the labour of production. Besides, *a priori*, it is absurd to think that the value of a thing can thus depend on a fact irrevocably past. The question of value would be ended there and then ; there could be no going back on it. " What's done is done," as Lady Macbeth said.

To this it may perhaps be replied that the labour to be taken as measure of value is not past, but present labour—*i.e.* not the labour actually devoted to producing the object in question, but the labour which would be necessary, under existing social conditions, to reproduce the same object—the *labour of reproduction.*[1] But, in that

---

[1] Karl Marx gave practically this answer when he declared that the matter at issue was not the individual labour given to the production of an object, but the *social labour*, as measured by the number of hours required *on an average* for its production. Bastiat, trying to solve the same difficulty, declared that it was not the labour of the person who had produced the article that was to be considered, but simply the *labour saved* to the man who would become possessed of it. And as, to save anyone labour, was, according to Bastiat, to render him a service, the author of the *Harmonies* thus arrived at a definition of value as *the relation between two exchanged efforts*, and declared that the cause and measure of value was *service rendered*.

It is a very fine and distinctly modern idea to see in social relationship an exchange of services ; but, as an explanation of value, it resolves itself into a simple tautology. To the question " Why has a diamond more value than a pebble ? " the answer is, " Because in giving me a diamond you are doing me a greater service than in giving me a pebble." A truism, indeed, which none will contest. But I have only to answer that, if the service done me by giving me a diamond is greater than the service done me by giving me a mere pebble, it is simply because the diamond has more value than the pebble. We are turning in a circle. It is not, after all, the service done by the person who gives me an article which determines its value ; it is, on the contrary, the value of the article given which determines and measures the service rendered (see our criticism of this theory in the *Revue d'Économie politique*, June 14, 1887, and its defence by M. Cauwès, vol. i, p. 308).

Note, moreover, that, in amending the original theory in this way, we are at the same time depriving it of the merit which it, at any rate, had of satisfying the idea of justice. We have admitted, indeed, that there would be a certain harmony if it could be proved that the value of an article possessed is proportional to the trouble which its possessor has taken to produce it ; but we deny that this harmony exists if, as on Bastiat's theory, value is simply proportional to the trouble saved, which consequently *has not been taken*, or, as on Karl Marx's theory, to the average of labour, and is consequently *independent of individual effort.*

case, we are no longer speaking of labour as a constituent element of value, but of labour as a measure of value—quite a different matter.

(2) If labour were the cause of value, then for equal labours there should always be equal values, and for unequal labours unequal values. Now, every moment we see objects—say, a loin or a tail of the same animal—which have cost the same labour, selling at very different prices, simply because their value is determined by quality, in other words, by their respective utility ; and inversely, objects which have cost very different amounts of labour selling at the same price—*e.g.* a bushel of wheat grown on land which produces fifteen to the acre, and a bushel of wheat of the same quality grown on land which produces fifty. It is on this very phenomenon that the law, so celebrated in Political Economy by the name of *rent,* is founded. As we shall see, it always implies a surplus in the selling price of an object over its cost of production—*i.e.* over its cost in labour. Now, rent exists more or less everywhere.[1]

(3) If labour were the cause of value, where there was no labour there could be no value. Now, there are innumerable things which have value of their own without any labour, simply because they are useful and much sought after : mineral or petroleum springs, guano deposited by sea-birds, the stretches of sandy beach at Camargues, which only the open winds have ploughed and which sell at a high price for vineyards, ground in Paris round the Champs Elysées ; or, again, which acquire a new value without labour— *e.g.* wine kept in a cellar.

(4) Lastly, the theory that value is created by labour strongly suggests the idea that value is a *product* of labour. Now this is a false idea. We may say of utility that it is a product of labour, for it is labour which, by a change of place or of form or of motion, adapts an object or an act to our wants. But we cannot say the same of value. For value is not a product. As we shall see, value does not lie in things at all ; it comes from outside. We must think of value as an illumination thrown on objects from the searchlight of our own desires. As the ray turns this way or that, it causes the objects of the outer world to start forth from the darkness, only to disappear again into the night so soon as it has passed over them. They have had a value ; they have one no longer.

---

[1] Ricardo did not deny the existence of rent, seeing that it was he himself who discovered it in the case of land (see p. 508, *The Law of Rent*) ; but the explanation which he gives of it only confirms the incontestable fact, that two objects of the same quality, that is to say, of the same utility, necessarily have the same value, however unequal may be the amounts of labour which they cost.

But, while criticising the above theory and refusing to admit that value is, in the words of Karl Marx, *human labour crystallised*, we would not go so far as to say that there is no relation between labour and value. Labour acts indirectly on value by acting on quantity, by creating abundance or scarcity of an object. This, however, brings us to the second theory of value, that of final utility.[1]

(B) FINAL UTILITY

THIS second theory is, in a way, the converse of the previous one. Whereas the first attaches itself to the idea of the *effort* made, this last attaches itself to the idea of the *satisfaction* obtained.

The theory of final utility, though directly descended from the old utility theory, is much superior to it in the distinction which it has drawn between the utility of a thing considered as a whole, *in genere*, and the utility of each *unit* of it. It has shown that the only utility that matters to us is that of the unit.

When we make the old objection that water is very useful and yet has no value, what do we mean ? Are we referring to all the fresh water that exists on the surface of the globe ? In this case it would be absolutely false to maintain that it has no value. It would have an incalculable value if it belonged to an individual or to a State, if it could be sold. Are we speaking of the quantity of water contained in a jug or in a bucket ? Probably, for this is the only quantity that can really concern us. Still, we cannot say whether the water in the bucket is useful or not. That depends.

Let us suppose, for example, that the quantity of water that I have at my disposal daily is distributed into a number of buckets. The first bucket is to serve for quenching my thirst ; it will have a maximum utility. The second is to serve for cooking purposes ; its utility will be less, but still great. The third I shall use for washing myself ; its utility will be less still. The fourth is to be given to my horse to drink, the fifth is to water my dahlias, the sixth to wash my kitchen floor, and the seventh is of no use to me at all. I shall not

---

[1] The labour theory tends at the present day to renew itself under the name of the *cost of production* theory. If, by cost of production, we mean the *sum of the prices paid for the different productive services*, wage, interest, rent, etc., this simply amounts to explaining the value of the product by the value of the elements which constitute it ; to explaining the sale price by the cost price. And this gives us no information as to the causes or origin of value, since it is only explaining one value by another. If, by cost of production, we mean the quantity *of labour and the quantity of time* used in producing a thing (and this is what Ricardo meant by it), then this practically amounts to the explanation criticised in the text, with this difference, that it includes, in the trouble or effort necessary for production, not only labour but capital.

even trouble to draw it from the well. And if some evil genius were to amuse himself by bringing me a tenth, twentieth, or hundredth bucket, till I was nearly deluged, not only would these last not be useful but they would be a positive nuisance. These buckets, therefore, cannot be called either useful or the reverse, as they offer a whole gamut of *decreasing utility*, from infinity to zero and even below.

Let us stop mentally at bucket number six, the last that has any utility at all, but which has still enough utility to be worth drawing from the well. We are able to assert, strange though it may seem, that not one of the other buckets can have a higher value than is measured *by the utility of this last*. Why ? Because, come what may, it is by the obtaining or losing of this last unit that we measure our enjoyment or privation. Suppose that bucket number one, my drinking water, is upset. Shall I make a great outcry, declaring that I am condemned to die of thirst ? Clearly I shall not go without a drink on that account ! All I need do is to sacrifice another bucket in its place, and obviously the bucket that is of least use to me—that is to say, the last one drawn. This is why the last determines the value of all the others. And as, in our country at any rate, the last bucket has but a trifling value (it would be otherwise probably in an African village) we have the reason why water has so little value. It is because its *final utility* is in reality extremely small.[1]

---

[1] *Final utility* must, therefore, be carefully distinguished from *total utility*. The latter consists in the sum of the utilities, added together, of all the buckets of water, and is, therefore, always much greater than the utility of the last alone. This is why the total utility of water is immense, although the utility of *a single bucket of water* may be small.

The adjective *final* is not altogether satisfactory. It has been criticised as implying the idea of a descending series, a method of numbering to be adopted for the purpose of demonstration, but not corresponding to reality. Some economists prefer the term *marginal utility*. It might be better still to say *liminal utility*.

In his fine work, too much neglected to-day, on *Le commerce et le Gouvernement* (1776), the philosopher Condillac had anticipated this explanation of value and had, in this direction, far outstripped his contemporaries, the Physiocrats : " The value of things increases by scarcity and diminishes by abundance. It may even by abundance diminish to a point where it disappears. A thing that is superabundant will be without value whenever it cannot be turned to account, *since it will then be absolutely useless*." Then follows the example of water drawn from a river or in the desert (part i, chap. i).

Franklin had said, still more simply, in *Poor Richard's Almanac*, that it is when the well is dry that we know the value of water.

But it was not till the middle of the nineteenth century that this theory of final utility appears to have been formulated for the first time by Dupuit (1844) and by a German, Gossen (1854). The works of both had remained totally unknown until Jevons in England (1871-1873), Walras in Switzerland, Karl Menger in

Let us now put out of our minds all idea of the *order* of the buckets, as the numbering of them was resorted to only to help out our proof, and is no longer of any use. For it is evident now that all the buckets are identical and interchangeable, and that consequently they have all the same value. This value is precisely that which corresponds to the last want satisfied or frustrated.

To sum up this demonstration :

Value is determined by subjective utility.

This utility is not the same for each unit possessed ; and it gradually decreases, since the intensity of a want diminishes as the number of units possessed increases.

It is the utility of the last unit possessed (the least useful, since it corresponds to the last want satisfied) which determines and limits the utility of all the others.

We are bound to admire this theory as a very delicate and true psychological analysis of man's wants and their varying intensity. Still, it only revives an older doctrine, that of Senior and the elder Walras, which placed the cause of value in scarcity—scarcity of a desirable object, of course, as scarcity otherwise would not create value (see *supra*, p. 46). Final utility is, in fact, only the scientific name for *scarce* utility. The merit of this theory lies in the fact that it has reconciled the two older explanations, utility and scarcity, by showing that they are inseparable, and that utility, in the economic sense of the word, varies with quantity ; that it is, as the mathematicians say, a " function " of the quantity.

Final utility not only implies scarcity, it implies also difficulty of acquisition. For scarcity, or limitation of quantity, is hardly ever the primary fact. In our economic state scarcity is merely a relative fact. There is not a single product of Nature, still less of human industry, the quantity of which is so strictly limited that it cannot be increased by taking the trouble. If diamonds are rare, it is not because Nature has issued, as it were, a limited number of specimens and has then broken the mould ; it is because it requires a great

Austria, and Clark and Patten in the United States, created this theory anew. The fact that, without knowing each other, these authors arrived simultaneously at practically the same conclusions is, on the face of it, a presumption in favour of its truth. This theory has found its principal representatives in Austria— not only Karl Menger but Böhm-Bawerk and Wieser. It is rarely taught in France, even in books. See, however, M. Colson's *Cours d'Économie politique*, and M. Landry's recently published *Manuel d'Économique*.

An excellent summary of this subtle theory is to be found in a small book by Professor Smart, of Glasgow University, *An Introduction to the Theory of Value* (2nd edition, 1910), unfortunately not translated into French.

deal of trouble or luck to find them, and the quantity in existence can only be increased with difficulty. If chronometers are scarce, it is not because there are only a certain limited number in the world. It is because the manufacture of a good chronometer takes time and special skill, and the quantity of them is thus limited by the time and labour available. It would even be rash to assert that the number of Raphael's pictures is absolutely limited ; for it is not at all impossible that others, hitherto unknown, may one day or other be found in some barn or ancient church.

Even explaining value by final utility, then, we cannot leave out of account the greater or lesser facility for multiplying wealth. So true is this that the mere possibility—say, the discovery of how to crystallise carbon into diamonds—before any practical application had been made of it, may be quite enough to bring down their value.[1]

These, then, are the two main theories of value. Is it absolutely necessary to choose between them ? No. Each represents one side of the truth. The human mind, possessed with the desire for unity, seeks in everything one single cause. But why may not value have two poles, two faces—utility and labour, pleasure and pain ? If, as we have just said, we are to discard the somewhat rough-and-ready idea that labour alone creates value, we must nevertheless admit that the effort necessary to produce an object does influence our desires.

If we ask ourselves why we attach a certain value to an object, we feel, on a little reflection, that we may give two different and, in some ways, opposite answers. We may become attached to things either because of the *pleasure* we get from the possession of them, or because of the *trouble* it has cost us to obtain them. Is not maternal love, the most intense of all affections, itself made up of these two elements ?

The solitary producer, Crusoe, values his corn not merely in proportion to his hunger, but in proportion to the effort which he has made to grow it, and which he will have to make over again, if the hail happens to beat it down before harvest time.

And this reasoning applies still more forcibly to a state of society in which almost all a man's goods come to him through exchange— in which no one can obtain an object unless he gives another in return. As buyer and consumer a man thinks mainly of the pleasure

---

[1] We would add that this theory, which seems quite clear so long as we are speaking of individual value—*value in use*, as the older economists called it— becomes much more involved when we come to explain *value in exchange*, and, as we shall see, only succeeds in explaining it by a *tour de force* of abstraction.

which the objects he wants to obtain will bring him ; as seller and producer he thinks above all of the sacrifice which the object he is giving up has cost him, and of the trouble which he will eventually have to replace it. Thus, simultaneously, or in turn, these two feelings are at work in his thoughts, and value comes and goes between them like a shuttlecock between two battledores.[1]

V : HOW VALUE IS MEASURED

SINCE value is degree of desirability, if we are to measure the value of an object, we ought to be able to measure the intensity of the desire which it excites in us. Is this possible ? Yes, if we are content to compare—and this is all that matters to us—two desires from the point of view of their intensity. Just as, in measuring the weight of a body, we compare the force of the earth's attraction for it with the force of the earth's attraction for some other body, so we can measure the value of an object by comparing the force which attracts us to it with that which attracts us to some other object. True, we have not scales in which to weigh our desires, but we have a means of determining them, no less accurate, namely. exchange. In every exchange each party is called on to make a certain sacrifice in order to satisfy his desire. He must give up a certain quantity of the wealth he possesses in order to obtain the wealth he covets. Now, it is clear that the extent of the sacrifice to which he consents is a very good measure of the intensity of his desire. If the Basuto gives ten oxen for a wife, have we not reason to assert that, for him, the woman is ten times as desirable as an ox ?

The keener the appreciation we have of an object in our possession, the greater must be the quantity of any other wealth offered to us to waken in us an equally intense desire for it, and to turn the scale in its favour. We are right, therefore, in saying that the value in exchange of an object is measured by the quantity of other things for which it can be exchanged, or, more shortly, by its purchasing power.[2]

If, then, I may obtain eight, ten, or twelve sheep in exchange for

---

[1] Compare Marshall, who declares that value is determined both by final utility and by cost of production, and is maintained in equilibrium between these two opposing forces like the keystone of an arch.

This is also the opinion of Vilfredo Pareto, who says : "Value is born of the contrast between tastes and obstacles."

[2] But we must beware of saying, as is too often done, that purchasing power is *what constitutes* value. It is our desire alone that confers value. Purchasing power is but an *effect* of value, just as the power of attraction of an electro-magnet is but an effect of the current passing through it.

C

an ox, I shall say that the value of an ox is eight, ten, or twelve times as great as that of a sheep; or inversely, that the value of a sheep is eight, ten, or twelve times less than that of an ox, which may be put thus: *the values of any two commodities are always in inverse proportion to the quantities exchanged.* The more we must give of any commodity in exchange, the less it is worth, and the less we need give, the more it is worth.

As in weighing: when the balance is in equilibrium, the weights of the objects may be said to be in inverse proportion to the quantities weighed. If ten sheep must be put in one scale to balance a single ox, it is because the weight of a sheep is only one-tenth that of an ox.

But to get a clear idea of size, weight, value, or any quantitative notion whatever, it is not enough to compare and measure objects by twos: we must have a *common measure* for all. Thus, in measuring lengths, either some part of the human body (foot, thumb) is taken as standard of comparison, or a definite fraction of the earth's circumference, the metre. In measuring weights, under the metric system a definite weight of distilled water has been taken as standard of comparison.

The function of a common measure is to compare *two things situated in different places*, which consequently cannot be compared directly, or to compare *one thing at different moments*, and to find out whether it has varied, and in what proportion. The inch allows us to compare the height of the Laplander with that of the Patagonian, and the amount of the difference between them. And if the inch is still in use some thousands of years hence, it will enable the man of that day to compare his stature with that of the man of to-day, and to ascertain whether it has decreased.

To measure value, then, it is not enough to compare one value with another, as is done in barter; we must take the value of some one specific thing as term of comparison. But what thing?

Every different nation and different epoch has used a different measure. Homer said that Diomede's armour was worth one hundred oxen. A few years ago, a Japanese would have said that it was worth so many hundredweights of rice; an African negro, so many yards of cotton stuff; a Canadian trapper, so many fox or otter skins.

Yet it is a remarkable fact that civilised peoples have been practically of one mind in choosing the value of precious metals, gold, silver and copper, particularly the first two, as standard or measure of values. All of them make use of a small ingot of gold or silver, which they call a pound sterling, a franc, a mark, a dollar, a rouble, etc. To measure the value of any object whatever, they compare it with the value of this small weight of gold or silver which serves as monetary unit ; that is to say, they try to find out how many of these little ingots must be given up in order to obtain the article in question ; and if, for example, ten must be given up, they say that the article is worth ten francs, or pounds, etc. This is its *price*.

The price of a thing is, then, the expression of the relation which exists between its value and the value of a certain weight of gold or silver, or, more strictly, *its value expressed in money*. And as, in every civilised country, money is the sole measure of values used, the word price has become synonymous with the word value.[1]

Why have the precious metals been chosen as the common measure of values ? Because they have two properties peculiar to them which allow of their fulfilling this function, if not perfectly, at least better than any other known object.

These two properties are : *facility of transport*, since they contain great value in small bulk ; and *durability*, or the property of being chemically unalterable. Thanks to the first of these two properties, the value of the precious metals is, of all values, that which varies least from place to place : thanks to the second, it is that which varies least from year to year. And this twofold invariability in space and in time is the essential condition of every good measure. Still, we shall see further on that, when we take long periods of time, or even one generation, this invariability is illusory (see *Historical Sketch of Money*).

Might we have found a better measure ? Others have been proposed, and first among them *wheat*.

Such a choice is at first sight surprising. For, if we consider the value of this article in different places or at different times, we see that there are few things which show more marked variations. We may see a hectolitre of wheat [2] selling at the same moment for twenty francs in France, fifteen francs in London, and for as little even as three or four francs in some regions of Siberia. And wheat may vary greatly from one year to another, according as the harvest is good or bad.

The answer to this is that, though the value of wheat is incomparably more variable than that of the precious metals over space, or even over short periods of time, it is, on the contrary, much more stable over long periods. Wheat answers to a physiological want that is permanent, and scarcely varies. No other commodity offers to the same degree this twofold character—of being almost indispensable up to the limit of the quantity necessary to feed a man, and of being

[1] See p. 221, section on *Exchange Value or Price*.
[2] Hectolitre = about 2¾ bushels.—*Translator*.

altogether useless beyond that limit ; for no one cares to eat more than his fill. In spite, therefore, of the sudden and severe oscillations which the caprices of the weather cause in the production of wheat, the law of demand and supply tends always to bring back production to the level marked by physiological want, and all the more forcibly if its equilibrium happens to have been momentarily disturbed.

It is true, then, that, as regards variations in value, wheat shows exactly the opposite virtues and defects to those which characterise the precious metals. But this is not enough to entitle it to play the part of money : at best it is good only for the function of a complementary or corrective measure. And it has, in fact, often been employed by statisticians as a good means for checking estimates of the cost of living at different epochs in history.

It has been suggested, again, that the *wages* of the lowest class of working man, the manual labourer, who just makes a bare living, should be taken as the common measure of value. This proposal starts from the idea that the absolute necessities of a man's life must be a constant quantity. But we have only to refer to what we said on Wants (p. 85) and to what we say, further on, of Wages (p. 590), to realise that such an assumption is quite contrary to facts.

The best measure would seem to be the trouble taken, the effort expended, in the production of an article. For we may claim, with good reason, that men will take more trouble to produce a thing in proportion as their desire for it is stronger; in other words, in proportion as they see more value in it. Just as, in exchange, we measure the value of an article by the sacrifice of another article which some person is willing to make to obtain it—by the quantity of money given by the buyer, for instance—may we not likewise measure its value by the sacrifice of time and trouble, by the number of blows of hammer or pickaxe, that men are ready to give to produce it ? It was with this meaning that Adam Smith said : " Labour was the first price, the original purchase-money that was paid for all things." [1]

Unfortunately, it is hopeless to look for a measure of value in

[1] We must not confuse this theory with that which makes labour the cause of value, and think that we are contradicting ourselves by accepting it after having rejected the latter. Here we are looking on labour, not as the *cause*, but as the *effect* or manifestation of value, or rather, of the desire which constitutes value. Now, if we admit that labour is an effect of value, it is surely a most scientific process to measure a cause by its effect. It is in this way that heat is measured by the expansion of mercury in the thermometer.

Theoretically this measure of value would be even better than the preceding ones, since all of those confine themselves to measuring one value *by another value,* comparing them together so that only a relative result can be reached. I measure the value of wheat by that of gold ; but if in a hundred years I find that

trouble or effort, since they themselves would need to be measured, and we have no dynamometer which could do this.

For want of anything better, then, we have had to be content with gold and silver as measures of values. We may, however, try to rectify the errors to which they give rise.

VI : HOW THE STANDARD OF VALUE IS CORRECTED— INDEX NUMBERS

Is there any way of *finding out* and *correcting* the apparent variations due to the variation in the standard of value ? These are two distinct questions.

Obviously the only method of *finding out* the variations in the value of money is by comparing that value with the values of other products. It would be useless to try to discover them in the coin itself, since, by definition, the little ingot of 20 francs is always worth 20 francs.

Suppose, however, we take a carefully drawn-up list of the prices of all commodities without exception, at a given moment, and suppose that ten years later a new list is drawn up showing, on comparison with the old one, that all prices *without exception* have gone up 100 per cent.—*i.e.* have doubled. We are able to assert, on this hypothesis, that the value of money has, in reality, fallen 50 per cent.—*i.e.* one half. Since all things which used to cost one shilling now cost two, two shillings are no longer worth more than one, and money has, in consequence, lost half its value.[1]

What justifies us in drawing such a conclusion ?

This, namely, that such a phenomenon as *a general and uniform rise in prices* admits of only two explanations. Either facts are as they appear—*i.e.* all commodities have undergone a general and identical rise in value—or the one single thing, money, has fallen, no the same weight of gold is worth twice as much wheat I cannot know which of the two values has varied (see *infra, Money*). On the contrary, the trouble that I am willing to take to satisfy my desire allows me to get at the very root of value, to measure the degree of desirability, and thus to compare any value with itself. It allows us to say, *e.g.* whether the desire for wheat is less intense to-day than a hundred years ago (of which, indeed, there is no doubt).

There is the same difference between money and labour, taken as measures of value, as there is between the scales and the pendulum in measures of weight. The scales only allow us to compare the respective weights of two bodies, while the pendulum measures the cause of heaviness, *i.e.* the earth's attraction. It shows us, *e.g.* what the scales cannot do, by how much this attraction decreases as we go up a mountain.

[1] A most illuminating discussion of Index Numbers and related subjects is furnished by Professor Irving Fisher, of Yale University, in his book on *The Purchasing Power of Money* (Macmillan, 1911).—Am. Ed.

other change having taken place meanwhile in the value of the other commodities. Which of these two explanations are we to accept? Common sense does not allow of a moment's hesitation. The second is as simple and clear as the first is unlikely, owing to the extraordinary combination of circumstances which it assumes. For how are we to imagine a cause capable of acting simultaneously and equally on the value of objects which are as different as possible in utility, quantity, and mode of production—a cause that can force up at the same time and in equal proportions the value of silk and coal, corn and diamonds, laces and wines, land and manual labour, and all the other objects which have no connection with one another? To prefer this second explanation, would be as senseless as to prefer Ptolemy's explanation of the movements of the astral bodies, according to which the whole heavens move round from east to west, to that of Copernicus, according to which our own globe simply moves from west to east. Now, even without any direct proof, there can be no hesitation between these two explanations. For how can we imagine that astral bodies so different in nature as the sun, moon, planets, stars, nebulæ, and set at such enormous distances from one another, will march like soldiers at a review, keeping their ranks and distances? The line of argument is the same in the case of a uniform upward movement of prices. It can only be explained rationally as a kind of optical illusion, an *apparent* upward movement caused by a real downward movement of money.[1]

The facts do not, of course, present themselves in the simple way we have imagined. We shall never find an absolutely general and uniform rise of prices. As the value of each thing has its own peculiar causes of variation, we shall find that the prices of some goods have risen in very different proportions, while some have remained stationary and others have even fallen. Still, supposing, by means of careful calculations, we can strike a general average—say, a rise of 10 per cent.—this average can only be explained, for the very reasons we have just given, by an equal fall in the value of money.[2]

With the object of finding this general average, economists have

---

[1] See Cournot, *Doctrines économiques.*

[2] Let us borrow another comparison from the domain of astronomy. It has been proved that the so-called fixed stars are in reality moving, and moving in quite diverging directions. Yet some persons have thought that they could perceive a general movement of these towards a definite point in the heavens. And we have no other way of explaining this general movement than by considering it as an optical illusion produced by the fact that our solar system is moving toward the opposite pole, which is marked by the constellation of Hercules; a movement which some astronomers have tried to measure.

drawn up tables known as Index Numbers. It is impossible to include all commodities in such tables ; the principal ones only are chosen. The choice of these is a somewhat delicate matter, as it may influence the results. If our object be to estimate the influence of these variations on the cost of living rather than to determine ·the variations of the standard of money, we should choose the articles of largest consumption, and should multiply their price by a co-efficient proportional to their importance in our budget of expenditure. Having chosen, say, fifty or one hundred articles, we should then take as starting-point their price at some fixed epoch. Which price should we take : wholesale or retail ? This will depend upon the use we intend to make of the table. The prices once ascertained are added together and written opposite the year chosen. The same is done for all the years that follow, and on comparing the totals we see at a glance whether the aggregate of prices has increased or diminished. To facilitate calculations and the reading of the tables, the total for the year selected as standard of comparison is expressed as 100, the totals for all the other years being given in proportional figures.

Thus, to take the best-known Index Number,[1] that of the English statistician Sauerbeck, we have the following figures (giving only maxima and minima) :

1818–1827	.	.	.	.	.	.	111
1848–1857	.	.	.	.	.	.	89
1858–1867	.	.	.	.	.	.	100 { the year chosen as standard
1890–1899	.	.	.	.	.	.	66
1900–1909	.	.	.	.	.	.	73 .

We see at once from these figures that prices fell, or, inversely, the buying power of money rose, during the whole of the last century, but that, since the beginning of the twentieth century, the movement has been in the opposite direction, and the rise has been greatly accentuated the last few years.

It is also possible to put the same tables graphically by representing each price by a vertical line (an ordinate) of proportional length, the upper ends of these being joined by a curve.

These tables cannot give very reliable results, since there is obviously a good deal that is arbitrary in the way in which they are

[1] In France there is the Index Number of the *Bureau de Statistique*, and another drawn up by M. de Foville ; in the United States, that of the Bureau of Labour and that of the Aldrich Senate Report. The first was that of Newmarch, which appeared, in 1859, in the *Journal of the Statistical Society*, of which he was editor : it comprised only nineteen articles.

drawn up. Still, when we compare the Index Numbers drawn up in different countries under slightly different methods, we find that on the whole they agree fairly well.

Supposing that the variations of the monetary standard can be exactly measured, is it possible, in practice, to correct them so as to maintain an artificial invariability of the standard as is done in the case of astronomical instruments.? Such corrections would be very useful in preventing the disturbances and prejudices caused at present by these variations in economic relations, particularly in long-term loans or leases, in the salaries of officials, in the redemption of government stock, &c.

It is possible. Tables of these variations, for instance, might be published at fixed intervals, *which would serve as official standard by which to correct the errors that result in practice from the use of coin as a measure of values.* This would allow debtors, for example, who had borrowed £100 to acquit themselves by paying back only £90— or, *vice versa,* would force them to repay £110, according as the value of money had gone up or down.[1]

The correction might also be rendered automatic by making the weight of money vary in inverse ratio to its depreciation. Thus if the franc were found to be worth no more than half a franc, it would be struck from an ingot weighing double, so that it would retain its ancient value, and the creditor, official, or fund-holder, paid with these new francs, would lose nothing.

Under such a monetary system there would be no longer a *visible* rise or fall in prices, for goods would always be exchanged for the same sum of money, for the same number of francs. Under the present system the value of money changes because its weight does not change. Under the new system the value of money would be invariable because its weight would be variable, but the public would hardly notice the change in its weight any more than it notices the change in its value to-day.

Only, to carry out this system, it would be necessary periodically, at short intervals, to withdraw all the money from circulation and remelt it. This would be inconvenient for the public and costly for the State.

Still, it might be possible, while leaving the price of money intact, to give it a legal value varying with the variations shown by the Index Numbers. This system would be a midway course between the two preceding ones. (See *infra, Variations in Price.*)

[1] An analogous table, called a Table of Reference. had been proposed by Lowe as far back as 1822, and another by Scrope in 1833.

BOOK I: PRODUCTION

PART I: THE FACTORS OF PRODUCTION

By virtue of a tradition that goes back to the first economists, three agents have always been distinguished in production : Land, Labour, and Capital. This threefold division is convenient for purposes of classification, and there is no need, so far as we can see, to depart from it, at any rate in an elementary book like the present.

But some mistaken notions concerning it must first be cleared away. Classical Political Economy has always shown a deplorable tendency to put these three factors of production on an equal footing. Now, the parts they play are very unequal.

Of the three, Labour is the only one which can claim the title of *agent* of production, in the strict sense of the word. Man alone plays an active part ; he alone takes the initiative in every act of production.

Land, or rather Nature—for we mean, by land, not merely the soil under cultivation but our whole material environment, solid, liquid, and gaseous—plays an absolutely passive part : all that it does is to yield to the solicitations of man, more often than not after long resistance. None the less, Nature is an indispensable condition whenever we would produce material wealth. She may even, with good right, be called the primary factor of production. For she does not merely accompany the action of labour ; she exists before there is any labour. Human activity cannot exercise itself on nothing. It does not work by *fiat*. It must find its indispensable materials outside of itself, and it is nature which furnishes these.

The third factor, Capital, plays, like Nature, a purely passive part, and has no claim to the title of agent ; but, unlike Nature, Capital cannot be termed a primary factor of production. It is only a factor of a subordinate order, derived logically and chronologically from the other two. Capital, as we shall presently see more clearly, is a product both of Labour and of Nature, set apart for purposes of production. The best name for it would be that of *instrument*, using the word in its widest sense.

We may point out that each of the three factors of production appeared in its own time on the economic stage. In the primitive societies of hunters, fishers, and shepherds, Nature alone furnished nearly all that was necessary. When we come to antiquity, we find Labour joining with nature, first in agriculture, later in industry.

Lastly, in our modern societies Capital has appeared, and has so dominated. the other two that the social system of the present day is commonly referred to as the *capitalist system.*

It is evident that, like all classifications, this is in some respects arbitrary. Often, in reality, the three factors cannot be separated. Land that has been cleared, drained, and cultivated, becomes a product of labour, consequently capital. Man's organs—for instance, the throat of the singer, the fingers of the skilled operator—are obviously natural agents ; and man himself becomes capital when, by means of education, brain and body have become a storehouse of acquired knowledge.[1]

CHAPTER I: NATURE

By the word Nature must be understood, not a definite factor of production—for such a word would imply but a vague entity—but the sum of pre-existent elements furnished by the world in which we live.[2]

In order that man may be able to produce, nature must furnish him with a *suitable environment,* with *raw material* that he can turn to account, and very often, too, with *motive forces* to assist his labour. We might also add, with *time,* since time, as well as space, is a condition of our existence.

I: THE ENVIRONMENT

It seems, at first sight, as if man can make no change in the environment in which Nature has placed him. But what marks the superiority of one organism over another, is just the facility with which it can adapt its environment to itself, instead of adapting itself to its environment. And this is borne out in a marked degree in the case of man. He cannot, it is true, create mines where there

---

[1] It is therefore nonsense to ask whether labour can produce *alone* without nature. We may be tempted to answer Yes when we think of the production of immaterial wealth, of services. But we should be forgetting that, even in this case, labour is never *alone.* It implies first a living body, then an environment, an atmosphere, sound, light, etc. Man cannot even speak into nothingness.

[2] The word *land* was formerly used instead of nature. The terms are equivalent if, by land, we mean not merely the soil fit for cultivation, but the whole earth and its atmosphere. Obviously, the superficial crust of our planet is the only portion of the universe which can serve as the field of our economic activity. But, as savage tribes have been known to use iron fallen from aerolites, and as all motive force (winds, watercourses, and the heat stored in coal) is derived from the heat of the sun. the word nature is, scientifically, the more exact.

are none ; but he is able, by his improvements, to manufacture soil
fit for cultivation, and to turn into arable land what was before
but barren marsh or gulfs like the Zuyder Zee. He cannot change
the great lines which nature has drawn, but he is able to modify
them on the slightest encouragement. He can, for example, complete a network of internal navigation ; overcome mountain barriers
by means of roads, and inlets of the sea by tunnels ; or he may
sever Africa from the Old World and South America from the New,
and thus make two islands out of what were peninsulas. He cannot,
of course, change the climate, but by afforestation on a large scale,
by appropriate husbandry, and by other means of which we have
not as yet the secret, human industry may one day be able to modify
considerably the course of wind and weather.

The environment consists :

(1) Of the *atmosphere*, which contains the oxygen indispensable
to life and which satisfies man's most urgent and continuous need.
To be deprived of it for one or two minutes only is enough to cause
death. But, as the composition of the atmosphere is the same
at every point of the earth's surface, and as there is everywhere
an overwhelming abundance of it, this precious commodity is of no
economic interest. Still, according as it is temperate, moist, or
sunny, by means of the rainfall and the flow of the watercourses—
in a word, through all that is included under the word *climate* —the
atmosphere has a decisive influence on the cultivation of the soil
and on all the arts of civilisation. If a piece of barren ground
at Nice or at St. Moritz fetches a high price per square yard,
it is for a right not to the soil, but to the fresh air and sunshine
which cannot be found elsewhere.[1]

[1] The branch of Le Play's school which, following M. Demolins, broke away
from his doctrine, looks on this matter of geographical environment as the
basis of the whole of social science. It distinguishes three categories of soil
which give rise to three types of primitive societies : The *steppes*, which produce
pastoral peoples ; the *seashores*, which produce *fisherfolk ;* and the *forest*, which
produces *hunting peoples.* These are the fundamental types of simple societies,
that is to say, of societies which live solely on the spontaneous products of the
soil. Nay, more, this school even traces back to them, as by direct descent, all
complex, or, in other words, civilised societies. And it ingeniously points to the
primitive state of the soil as the origin and sole cause of all the actual forms of
property, family, government, etc. (see *La Science Sociale*, wherein this system
has been expounded many a time, and M. Brunhes' books on Geography). But
this " geographical determinism," although suggestive in some ways, is very
much exaggerated. Karl Marx's school seems to be nearer the truth in pointing
out that the influence of the physical environment decreases in proportion as
that of the economic environment increases, since man becomes less dependent
on nature in proportion as he creates for himself an artificial environment. It

Tropical countries may have seen the blossoming of brilliant civilisations : they have never seen the rise of laborious and industrially productive races. There nature seems to discourage production as much by her bounty as by her violence. In those happy climes where bread grows like fruit, where clothing and housing are hardly necessary, man comes to rely upon nature, and spares himself all effort. On the other hand, the physical forces in those regions are so violent, so irresistible in their different manifestations—torrential rains, floods, earthquakes, cyclones—that man, dismayed, does not dream of subduing them and of turning them to his own ends. Enough for him if he can but defend himself against them. In our temperate countries, on the contrary, nature is so niggardly that she obliges man to depend largely on his own efforts ; but she is sufficiently calmed down to allow herself to be domesticated by human industry. Here she encourages productive activity both by what she withholds and by what she gives.

(2) Of *territory*, under which come the geographical situation, maritime or inland ; the orological features, which determine the courses of the rivers and of the great ways of communication ; the richness of the soil and of the subsoil. Who can measure the influence which the insular situations of England or of Japan [1] have had on their industrial and commercial development ? And if we would seek the reason why the African continent, familiar to the ancients, the seat of the oldest known civilisation, that of Egypt, has remained until quite lately beyond the pale of economic activity, while the two Americas, discovered barely four centuries ago, are crossed in all directions by trade currents, we must look for it in the difference between their river systems. The rivers of the New World flow into the sea through immense estuaries, and are so interlaced that one can pass from the tributaries of the Plata River to those of the Amazon, and thence to those of the Orinoco, or

is rather on man's physical constitution that the physical environment exercises its mysterious but certain influence. The Americans of the United States are gradually evolving towards a type not unlike the native Indians, and the Australians towards that of the native race of Australia.

[1] For maritime ports and navigable highways, see *infra;* the chapter *Transport.*

If any proof were wanted of the importance of the rôle that the "silver streak" has played in the destinies of England, it would be found in the curious uneasiness which took possession of this nation, in spite of its commercial and Free Trade spirit, at the mere prospect of being connected with the Continent by a submarine tunnel ; and in the categorical refusal of the British Government, notwithstanding the *entente cordiale,* to countenance the project, though it could easily have been carried out, and had already been started.

from the basin of the Mississippi to the Great Lakes, almost without leaving the waterway. The African rivers, on the other hand, though no less vast, oppose to all explorers, in their lower reaches, a barrier of insurmountable cataracts or of pestilential marshes, save only the Nile; and what an incomparable rôle it has played as the father of civilisations and of wealth!

The chemical constitution of the soil has no less influence, for it is this which makes agricultural wealth. If China is able to feed her teeming millions, it is to her " yellow land " that she owes it; and Russia is equally indebted to her rich " black land "— rich is the exact word, for, according to geologists, her soils contain over £600,000,000 sterling of nitrogen and phosphoric acid.

And yet, in its natural state, such wealth of soil is of no great use to man. In fact, it is rather an obstacle than otherwise, owing to the exuberant vegetation, which the pioneer finds it his first labour to clear, a labour often done with a wastefulness that he has later to deplore. Nowadays man is regretting the forests he has levelled, and is doing his best to preserve those that remain in various parts of Africa and South America.[1]

Until last century the subsoil had hardly any influence on the evolution of societies; to-day its effect is preponderant, and has contributed in no small degree to the change that has taken place in the relative positions of nations, politically as well as economically. Iron and coal do not merely drive industry; they build ships and forge cannon. If we compare the total world-production of the principal product of the subsoil, namely coal, with that of the principal product of the soil, namely wheat, we see that the production of coal to-day exceeds £600,000,000 sterling,[2] while that of wheat scarcely

---

[1] Regarding the ownership of forests, see p. 462, *The Right of Property in regard to its Object and its Subject.*

[2] Pricing the ton at 12s. 6d., a figure much below its actual value. According to the figures given by the Board of Trade, the production of coal, slightly over 1 billion tons, was distributed in 1911 as follows. We give the figures for 1891 for the sake of comparison:

	1891 Million tons	1011 Million tons.
United States	150 .	. 443
England	185 .	. 272
Germany	74 .	. 158
France	25 .	. 38
Belgium	20 .	. 23
Seventeen other countries	134 .	. 116
	588	1050

To the production of coal must be added that of petroleum, which seems likely

exceeds £640,000,000 sterling.[1] Thus the harvests from the subsoil will soon surpass in value those of the soil.

In regard to subsoil, France does not rank either among the most richly dowered or the most poverty-stricken countries. She has some good coal deposits, but these are not well situated, being neither near the sea, as in England, nor near some large navigable way, as in Germany, and one of her best was taken away when Lorraine was severed from her. She produces nevertheless nearly forty million tons, but as she consumes sixty millions she has a deficit of twenty million tons, and this deficit will steadily increase. As regards iron, however, she stands among the first countries of Europe, thanks to a process by which phosphoric ores, hitherto useless, are being utilised.[2]

The question of territory includes also the question of room— an indispensable condition of all production. Man must have a certain amount of room on the earth, if only for the sole of his foot ; he must have a little more if he is to lie down, more still if he is to build a house, and a great deal more if he is to sow corn or keep cattle.

Now, so soon as the population of a country becomes fairly dense, this question of room becomes menacing. When human beings, following their social instincts, crowd together in one of those great ant-heaps, London, New York, Paris, Berlin, the space necessary for lodging them soon runs short. We find land acquiring a greater value than the buildings on it, be they marble palaces. And the social consequences of this are disastrous, as we shall see when we come to the question of house rents. It would be absurd, of course, to fear

to be substituted for coal with advantage, especially in the navy. It exceeds to-day 43 million metric tons (28 millions of which are for the United States and 10 millions for Russia). The coal-mines of the United States employed 725,000 persons in 1910.—AM. ED.

[1] Taking wheat as 8s. 4d. the cwt. The total production of wheat in the world is estimated at 1600 million cwts., 160 or 180 millions of which are produced in France alone, which stands third in rank after the United States and Russia in absolute figures, but by far and away the first if we take the figure in relation to population and territory. The value of the wheat crop in the United States in 1910 was $625,000,000.—AM. ED.

[2] The total world-production of iron amounts to 145 million tons, the largest producers being :

		Million tons
United States	. . . .	58
Germany	. . . .	28
France	. . . .	16
England	. . . .	15·5
Sweden	. . . .	5·5

But, as regards the actual wealth of the seams, France stands first in Europe.

that a day may come when there will be no more dwelling space for man on this earth; but it would not be absurd to wonder if there will always be space enough to grow his food. For it requires a fair amount of ground to feed a man. True, the progress in civilisation and in agriculture is ever tending to reduce the quantity. Among hunting tribes, for instance, it takes several square leagues to feed an individual; among pastoral peoples, a square mile or so; among agricultural peoples, a few acres are enough, and still less is required as cultivation becomes intensive.[1] China, thanks to her intensive cultivation, which almost resembles market gardening, is able to make two and a half acres support several men. Still, however far back we may push it, the fatal limit is always there, to keep the human race uneasy as to its future fate.

It is evident that the earth, being limited in size, cannot support more than a certain number of inhabitants. This fact is the basis of the famous Malthusian laws, which we shall discuss later. Nature, said Malthus, by famine, disease, and war, checks the excess of population and brings the latter down to a figure proportionate to the size and fertility of countries.

The discovery of the New World and the opening up of Central Africa and of Australasia have ensured us enough room for many a generation. But, with the human race increasing at an average rate of fifteen millions a year, these reserves of the future will soon be used up. And there is no hope now of discovering new ones. Before the end of the next half-century the last piece of vacant land will be occupied, the last stake driven in, and the human race will have to be content with its domain of thirty milliard acres, without any prospect of increasing it by new conquests. Its only consolation will be Regnard's verse written, with a pride that was hardly justified by circumstances, on a rock in Lapland:

" *Hic stetimus tandem nobis ubi defuit orbis.*"

II : RAW MATERIAL

THE *inorganic materials* of which the earth's crust consists, to the small depth to which we have been able to penetrate, and the *organic substances* which originate from the living things (vegetable

---

[1] The density of population is as follows: Among the Greenland Eskimos and the natives of the Amazon forest (hunting tribes), from 2 to 3 inhabitants per *thousand* square kilometres; among the Kirghiz and Turcomans of Central Asia (pastoral people), from 1 to 2 inhabitants per square kilometre; in European Russia (agricultural country), 24 inhabitants per square kilometre; in England and Belgium (industrial countries), 240 and 260 inhabitants per square kilometre; in France there are only 74 inhabitants per square kilometre.

and animal) on its surface, provide industry with the raw material it requires, and form the primary element of all wealth. Some of these materials nature has scattered lavishly around ; of others she has shown herself very miserly.

Even those which exist in large quantities may be rare in some particular region. Fresh water is a form of wealth that is generally looked on as unlimited. Yet there is no great town that has a large enough water-supply, nor where costly and sometimes colossal works have not been necessary to obtain it. There are countries where irrigation is of such vital importance that one might almost, in their connection, speak of "hydraulic politics."[1] And this scarcity of water has given rise to very curious forms of ownership, different, as a rule, from those in land. Sometimes, as in Egypt and Algeria, water is the property of the State, which distributes it gratis, but by the mere fact of doing so wields over it a sovereign power. Sometimes, as in the celebrated *huertas* of Valentia or in the Algerian oases, it belongs to more or less co-operative communities.

When the material which man requires is transportable, human industry can counteract the disadvantages of unequal distribution by removing it from one place to another. It is for this reason that transport, as we shall see, is a veritable act of production. But matter, owing to its weight and inertia, is sometimes very difficult to move, and the effort and cost necessary to overcome this resistance increase with the distance to be covered. The transport industry cannot, therefore, altogether neutralise the natural inequalities of countries. Coal, simply because of its small economic density (*i.e.* its small value compared with its weight), cannot be carried great distances save by sea or canal. Where there is only a land route or railway it cannot be utilised beyond a certain limited radius.

[1] See M. Brunhes' interesting book on *l'Irrigation dans la Péninsule Ibérique et dans l'Afrique du Nord*, and Fromentin's picture of the " water distributor " at Laghouat, in *Un Été au Sahara :* " He is an old man with a grey beard, a sort of Saturn, armed with a pickaxe for a scythe and holding an hour-glass in his hand. A string, divided off by knots, attached to the hour-glass, is used to mark the number of times he has turned his clock. . . . When he has come to the end of his string, the gardens of the canton have had enough to drink and the moment has come to change the course of the water. The old man rises, destroys the dam with a blow of his axe, and begins to rebuild the other one with earth, pebbles, and straw."

There are *four* aspects, not *one*, to the water problem : (1) There is the question of *drinking-water* for towns, a problem which is becoming almost insoluble and certainly more and more costly for the large towns ; (2) of *irrigation water* for purposes of cultivation ; (3) of *water for motive power* in industry, the so-called " white " and " green " coal ; (4) of *water as a highway or means of transport* (for the last two, see Book II, chap. ii, section v, *Canals and Navigable Ways.*

Lastly, as regards natural materials that are extremely rare, the moulds of which have, so to speak, been broken, man is sometimes able to discover the processes of nature, and to re-create them artificially, e.g. he may manufacture diamonds by crystallising coal. He may also find a substitute for the object he wants in some substance of analogous properties. This he often succeeds in doing, and he would always succeed were his knowledge greater. For, in the infinite variety of organic and inorganic bodies, many possess like characteristics, and may, to some extent, be substituted for one another: e.g. silk made from cellulose for that of the silk-worm; vegetaline made from cocoanut for butter; the seed of the corozo tree of Columbia for ivory; acetylene for coal-gas. This replacing of one thing by another is, moreover, only an instance of the " Law of Substitution," of which we have already spoken (p. 39).

III : MOTIVE FORCES

THE work of production consists, as we have seen, simply in the displacing of matter. The resistance offered by the inertia of matter is often very great, and man's muscular power is, after all, slight. From early times, then, but particularly since the abolition of slavery and of the gratuitous use of human force, man has tried to make good his deficiency in this respect by the aid of certain motive forces with which Nature supplies him.

It is by means of machines that man makes use of these natural forces. The machine is a tool with this difference, that, instead of being moved by the hand of man, this tool is worked by a natural force.[1]

It should be remarked that the more powerful these natural forces, the more time and trouble does it cost mankind to turn them

---

[1] True, in ordinary language, instruments, whenever they are complex, are termed machines, even when they are worked directly by man; as, for instance, the sewing machine, the typewriting machine—we even call the bicycle a machine. But this way of speaking is not scientific.

Tools or instruments can also greatly increase a man's force. A child, by means of a hydraulic press, can exert a pressure theoretically unlimited; and Archimedes boasted, and rightly, that with a lever and a fulcrum he could lift the world. It has, however, been calculated that, even supposing he found this fulcrum, and worked continuously for some millions of years, he would hardly succeed in lifting it more than a hair's-breadth. For it is a law of mechanics that in using instruments a man *loses in time what he gains in force.* Now, time, as we have seen, is a very precious element, and one of which we must be very sparing. The advantages which we obtain by using instruments are, therefore, in practice somewhat limited, whereas a machine worked by motive force gives a gain of both time and power.

to his own ends. And this is only natural, for *resistance increases in direct ratio to power.*

This is why man has been able to utilise only four or five natural forces in production : the muscular force of *animals,* the motive force of *wind* and of *water,* the expansive force of *gases* (in particular steam and explosive gas), and, quite lately, *electrical energy,* which is, as a rule, simply a transformation of the last two. But there are any number of other forces known and unknown. The waves raised by the wind on the surface of the sea, the tide that breaks twice a day on thousands of miles of coast-line, are truly inexhaustible reservoirs of power. And the forces we see are nothing to those the existence of which we are only able to guess— to mention but the energy latent in the molecular combinations which radium has revealed to us. According to M. Gustave Le Bon, if the intra-atomic energy contained in a gramme of matter, *e.g.* in a one centime piece, could be set free, it would be strong enough to drive a goods train more than four times round the globe.

The domestication of certain animals, the horse, ox, chamois, elephant, reindeer, etc., provided man with his first natural force for transport, traction, and ploughing.[1] This was already a valuable conquest, for the animal is proportionally stronger than man. The strength of a horse is estimated at seven times that of a man, while his upkeep costs less. But these animals are limited in number, and become fewer as the population of a country increases, since a great deal of space is required for their food. Thus they represent but a relatively small motive force. France, however, in spite of her railways and automobiles, still employs at the present day over three million horses and two million plough oxen. The United States Department of Agriculture in 1910 estimated the number of horses in that country at twenty-three millions.

The motive power of winds and rivers was always used for transport, but up till quite lately it had hardly ever been used in industry, save for turning wind and water mills. The watermill, which dates from the earliest centuries of the Christian era, marks the invention of the first machine, properly speaking, in the sense of an instrument worked by a natural force.[2]

But of these two natural forces, one, wind, is as a rule too

[1] The number of these living motors is not necessarily bound to decrease through the competition of inanimate motors. Railways did not reduce the number of horses. Automobiles, however, have reduced them in Paris from 134,000 in 1900 to 75,000 in 1910.

[2] It has been celebrated in the much-quoted verses of a poet in the Greek anthology—Antiparos.

feeble, or at least too intermittent;[1] the other, though more powerful and more easily captured, has the serious drawback of being localised at certain places.[2] It was not till Newcomen (1705) and James Watt (1769) used heat to increase the pressure of steam in a cylinder that the marvellous instrument of modern industry, the steam engine, was created.[3] And what gives steam its inestimable advantage is the very fact that it is *artificial*, that it has been created not by Nature but by man. For this reason man can employ it, *when, where,* and *as* he will. It is mobile, portable, and continuous, and there is no limit, theoretically at any rate, to the pressure at which it can be produced.[4]

Now, however, water is coming to the front as a motive force, since a way has been discovered, not only of *transporting* it long distances, but of dividing it into such infinitely small quantities

[1] In Denmark, however, it is becoming more and more utilised in the production of electrical energy.

[2] The motive-power of the Niagara Falls is estimated at three and a half million h.p.—much more than is necessary to drive all the factories in France. Only a small portion of this power is being utilised, but the privilege to use almost a third of it has already been granted, to the great consternation of lovers of the picturesque.

[3] I say "marvellous" in respect of the services it renders. In reality, the steam engine is a very defective instrument. It utilises only a very small quantity, one-tenth at most, of the heat produced by coal combustion. There is an enormous loss between the furnace and the boiler, and considerable loss again between the boiler and the engine proper. Hence the remark of M. Le Bon: " I hope that well within the next twenty years the last specimen of this clumsy machine will have taken its place in the museums side by side with the stone axes of our primitive ancestors."

[4] Water heated at a temperature of 516°, by no means a high temperature, would be enough to produce a pressure of 1,700,000 atmospheres : more than enough to lift the Himalayas. The only difficulty would be to find a vessel of sufficient resisting power to hold it.

Motive-power in France is distributed as follows:

Railways	7,000,000
Ships (not including the navy)	1,200,000
Industry	3,550,000
Automobiles	400,000
	12,150,000

France is far from occupying the first rank, however. America employs about 15 million h.p. and Germany 8,831,000 in industry alone.

The aggregate motive-power employed in the *manufactures* of the United States was 5,954,655 in 1890 ; 10,409,625 in 1900 ; and 14,641,544 in 1905. Of this total steam furnished 76·9 per cent in 1890, and 73·9 per cent. in 1905 ; gas and gasoline furnished one-tenth of 1 per cent. in 1890, and 2 per cent. in 1905 ; water-wheels furnished 21·1 per cent. in 1890, and 11·3 in 1905 ; electric motors furnished three-tenths of 1 per cent. in 1890, and 7·9 in 1905.

that its force is able to radiate freely round the point where nature has apparently chained it. Thus the Rhone which, since it first began to flow, has spent itself uselessly in wearing pebbles, now flows through the lofty chambers of the Croix-Rousse to work the looms of the silk-weavers of Lyons. Motive power in the form of gas and water is already distributed in our houses, and we have only to turn a tap or press a button to obtain it.[1]

But water works by speed, not by mass. Of what use, for instance, as motive power, are the thousands of millions of cubic metres that sleep in a lake, or in a quiet river like the Seine ? We have, therefore, to utilise it mainly at its maximum incline, *i.e.* at waterfalls, and to go for our power as near as possible to the sources of rivers and to the glaciers that feed them. Hence, M. Bergès, an engineer of Grenoble, as far back as 1868 called this new force " *white coal* " (*houille blanche*), a name by which it has ever since been known. By this he did not mean, as is usually thought, running water in general, but the glacier as a reservoir of stored forces.

By a happy coincidence which, in other times, would have passed for an act of Providence, and which must be due to some unknown cause, the countries that are poorest in black coal have been most richly endowed by nature with white coal. In Europe, for instance, Switzerland, Northern Italy, and Scandinavia, which have not an atom of black coal, own magnificent resources of white coal ; while countries so rich in mines as England, Belgium, and Germany have few rivers or waterfalls available for motive power. In America, again, Canada and Brazil, which appear to have hardly any coal mines at all, have enormous resources in their waterfalls.[2] France· has been fairly well endowed in both respects, since, without being destitute of black coal (see *supra*, p. 70), she possesses quite a large quantity of hydraulic power, estimated at 8 to 10 million horse-power. This, if she knew how to utilise it, would not only relieve her of the annual tribute which she has to pay abroad for the twenty million tons of coal she is forced to import, but would even allow her to export some power.[3]

---

[1] As regards the question whether hydro-electric machines might not save small industry, see *infra Home Work*.

[2] The motive force of watercourses in Brazil is estimated at the fabulous figure of 800 million horse-power.

[3] For six millions of hydraulic horse-power, working no more than ten hours a day, would represent a combustion of exactly twenty million tons of coal, and it would cost no more to keep them going night and day. As yet, however, less than 1,000,000 hydraulic horse-power is being utilised in France, half of which is employed in the old-fashioned turning of flour and saw mills, and the

Unfortunately, the fact that speculators are already buying up these forces puts a serious obstacle to their being utilised in this way.[1]

Both of these fuels are, however, limited. Black coal, a treasure buried, as it were, in palæontological times, on which we are drawing like spendthrifts, is consumed with use, and will soon be at an end. White coal, though it is not consumed with use—for here we are drawing on income, not capital—does not increase as rapidly as we need it; and the present shrinkage of the glaciers and the conjectured lessening of the rainfall may even be threatening us with a decrease of hydraulic motive force. We may, therefore, ask with some anxiety, what will become of industry if one day, for lack of black or white fuel, it must extinguish its fires and stop its dynamos?

Some indeed already dream of seeking heat from the source of all power, the sun itself. But even if they were to succeed, such borrowed power would have one great drawback, that it would be even less at man's disposal, *when, where,* and *as* he wanted it, than the other natural forces. For the sun is not always and everywhere shining. If one day it were to become the power that drives our factories, this would be a heavier blow for England than the competition of white coal! The fogs of the North Sea would become her shroud, and it would be to the midst of the Sahara that human industry would go to build its capitals.

IV: THE LAW OF DIMINISHING OR NON-PROPORTIONAL RETURNS

As land, raw material, and even natural forces are limited, it follows, as a matter of course, that production, of which they are the necessary factors, is also limited.

rest for the lighting of towns, for tramways, railways, the manufacture of paper from wood, and of various chemical products, in particular of aluminium, the price of which, thanks to the "white coal," has fallen from seventy francs to one franc fifty centimes per kilogramme. In Norway, hydraulic horse-power is used for manufacturing chemical manures (nitrates).

The cost of installing hydraulic power (dams, pipes, turbines, and electric machines) varies according to the situation. But once done, the cost of upkeep per horse-power is almost nil, whereas, in the case of coal, on the other hand, it is relatively high each horse-power consuming one kilogramme of coal per hour. Black coal is still, however, the main source of power used. In France, there are over 11,000,000 h.p. of steam-power as against 800,000 h.p. of water-power.

[1] As regards the difficult question of the right of property over the motive force of water, see *infra,* p. 462. *The Right of Property in regard to its Object.*

It is in extractive industry that the limit of production is most apparent. When a mine is exhausted operations are brought to a standstill. Indeed, this generally happens some time before the mine is empty, since extraction ceases to pay, although it may become remunerative again when metallurgy has made further progress.

Hunting, which played so great a part in primitive societies, has disappeared from among productive industries in civilised countries, for the good reason that it has ceased to be remunerative in spite of all the regulations made to protect it. Even in the deserts of Africa and the solitudes of the Poles, the spoil of elephants,[1] ostriches, beavers, otters, and whales is beginning to run short. Sea-fishing, owing to the immense reservoir from which this natural wealth is drawn, is still a great industry, giving a livelihood to 150,000 persons in France and producing about one hundred and fifty million francs.[2] But the exhaustion of the fisheries along the French coasts is a subject of lamentation among the seafaring population, who are forced to equip stronger boats and follow the fish to the deep sea. The extermination of birds for hats, food, or from sheer stupidity, results in the swarming of insects and all the vermin which devour harvests. The disappearance of forests, and consequently of wood for carpentry, is already an accomplished fact in more than one European country, particularly in England. France, which at the time of the Gauls was one immense forest, and which, even by the Middle Ages, the labours of the western monks had but partially cleared, has now only about one-sixth of its surface under forest (nine and a half million hectares out of fifty-three millions).[3] The proportion varies in different countries. In England it is less than 5 per cent., but in Germany it is about one-fourth of the whole territory, in Austria-Hungary and Russia one-third, and in Sweden almost one-half. It might have been expected that the increasing substitution of iron for wood in the building of houses and of ships would have prolonged the life of the forests. Unfortunately, other industries have arisen which consume even more timber. At the present moment the paper industry, chiefly for newspapers, is the greatest forest consumer. There are daily papers in the United States each of which devours a whole forest per annum.

[1] 800,000 kilogrammes of elephants' tusks are imported annually into France, which, taking an average tusk at 20 kilogrammes, would represent 40,000 elephants. But this figure must be doubled at least, some say quadrupled, to cover waste and the number of small elephants uselessly slaughtered or abandoned.

[2] The fisheries of the United States gave products in 1908 valued at over $54,000,000, and furnished employment for 143,881 persons.—AM. ED.

[3] [It will be remembered that a hectare is about two and a half acres.—C. A.]

The chestnut forests of Corsica are being at this moment completely destroyed for the manufacture of gallic acid.[1]

True, in the case of living organisms, industry, by reversing its processes, may to some extent ward off the fate that threatens them. Hunting may give place to breeding,[2] fishing to pisciculture,[3] the clearing of the forest to planting ; [4] that is to say, we may pass from the category of purely extractive industry to that of cultivative industry like agriculture.   But here also we are met by a twofold limitation.

(1) In the first place, agricultural production is limited by the supply of mineral elements, indispensable to the life of plants. All land, even the most fertile, contains only a certain amount of nitrogen, potash, and phosphoric acid, and every harvest absorbs these little by little.   It is true that the art of agriculture succeeds not only in restoring to the earth the elements taken from it, but in enriching it also by the addition of new elements.   But it must be remembered that the sources from which the farmer obtains these wealth-giving substances are themselves limited.   Natural manure returns to the earth only a part of what the animals have consumed ;

[1] A conference for the " conservation of national resources," composed of Governors and special experts of the different States of the United States, was held in 1908.   It was opened by President Roosevelt with a speech of which the following is a summary :

The natural resources of the country, which are the ultimate basis of the power and the continuance of the nation, are being rapidly exhausted.   Already we see a limit approaching to the land that is not yet under cultivation.   The United States began with an unrivalled heritage of forests ; already half of the building timber has disappeared.   The United States began with larger coal-fields than those of any other nation and with iron-ore which was deemed inexhaustible.   Many competent persons now declare that the coal and iron are coming to an end.   The enormous accumulations of mineral oil and gas have to a great extent disappeared.   The natural water-ways still remain ; but, owing to carelessness and other causes, they have so deteriorated that there is less navigation on them than there was fifty years ago.   Lastly, the United States found, at the start, lands of unrivalled fertility, but have so impoverished these that their power of production is decreasing instead of increasing.

[2] This is already being done with some success in the case of certain animal species threatened with extinction : the ostrich in Central Africa, the blue fox in the islands of Alaska, crocodiles in Florida.

[3] Pisciculture is apparently carried on successfully in China.   In France a beginning has been made by stocking some watercourses with small fish, but these attempts are being frustrated by inveterate and unpunished poaching. In sea-fishery, pisciculture is more difficult (except in the case of oysters, which are raised in beds), but an attempt might at least be made to prevent the destruction of young fish by enforcing the regulations regarding the size of the nets the zones or close seasons for the fishing of certain species, etc.

[4] See infra, The Ownership of Forests.

while chemical manures, such as phosphates, nitrates, guano, etc., are of mineral origin, and their supply may be quickly exhausted.

(2) Agricultural production is further limited by the conditions of *space* and *time* indispensable for animal or vegetable life ; and these conditions are much more rigid and less easy to modify than in industrial production. The farmer is reduced to playing an almost passive part. He must wait patiently while nature does her work by laws which he still but imperfectly understands and the conditions of which he is unable to change. Months must pass before the grain which sleeps in the furrow turns to corn in the ear, and long years elapse before the acorn becomes an oak. Every plant, again, needs a minimum amount of room in which to spread its roots and breathe. The manufacturer, on the contrary, subjects matter in his factories to processes which, as a rule, are simple, the physical and chemical laws of which are much less mysterious than are the laws of life. Proof of this is that he has mastered them and makes them work to his orders with mechanical precision. He is not hemmed in by the inexorable cycle of the seasons; summer and winter, day and night he can fire his furnaces and drive his looms.[1]

Doubtless there is not a single piece of land from which the farmer could not, in the last resort, obtain a larger return. But, after a certain stage in agricultural industry, he can do this only at the cost of increasing labour, and there comes a moment when the effort

[1] Since the limitation which agricultural industry meets with is due to the fact that it is dealing with living things, we might ask why it does not try to overcome this obstacle by boldly dispensing with the aid of those mysterious forces and by turning its efforts to the manufacture of wholly artificial food-stuffs, in the same way as a manufacturer makes chemical products ? For we know that all the tissues of living things, whether animal or vegetable, are formed solely of carbon, oxygen, hydrogen, nitrogen, and a very small amount of a few mineral salts, all of which are elements that exist in superabundance in the earth's crust and in the atmosphere. Theoretically, therefore, the problem does not seem insoluble, and chemists look upon it as on the eve of solution. Certain it is that if one of them were ever to solve it, he would accomplish much more than was ever dreamed of by the alchemists. He would overturn the most fundamental laws of Political Economy. For if food could ever be entirely manufactured, *agriculture would become useless*. Man would ask nothing more of the earth than the space he needs for the soles of his feet, and a single acre of land would be able to feed as dense a population as now crowds into our large cities. So far, however, the law *omne vivum ex vivo* has not been superseded. Chemical synthesis has, it is true, succeeded in creating bodies which hitherto have been produced only by living beings—for example, urea—but it has not been able to create foodstuffs, in spite of Berthelot's prophecies.

necessary to get this return is quite out of proportion to the return itself.

Take, for example, a hectare of land which produces fifteen hecto-litres of wheat—about the average yield in France. Suppose that these fifteen hectolitres of wheat represent one hundred days of labour or three hundred francs of cost. The *law of diminishing returns* states that, to make this land yield thirty hectolitres of wheat, *more than* two hundred days˙ labour and *more than* six hundred francs will have to be spent ; that is to say, in order to get twice the result it may be necessary to put out three, four, or even ten times as much labour and expense !

The experience of every day bears out this law. Ask any intelligent farmer if his land cannot produce more than it is doing. He will answer : " Certainly ; the wheat crop would be larger if I chose to lay on more manure, to plough deeper, to clear the soil of the smallest weed, to double-dig, to dibble each grain by hand, and again, if I were to protect the harvest against insects, birds, and parasitical weeds." And if you ask him why he does not do all these things, he will answer : " Simply because it would not pay ; the˙increase in the harvest would cost more than it would be worth." There is a point of equilibrium, therefore, in the productiveness of land, a limit beyond which the farmer will not go. Not that he cannot go beyond it if he will, but that he has *no interest in doing so*.

If it were otherwise, if the return from a given piece of land could be indefinitely increased simply by increasing proportionally the labour and capital applied, landowners would certainly not fail to do so. Instead of spreading their capital and labour over a large domain, they would concentrate it on the smallest possible piece of ground ; for the latter would be much easier to work. But, in this case, the face of the earth would not be as it is to-day. The very fact that this is not done, that lands less fertile and less well situated are continually being brought under cultivation, is proof enough that, in practice at any rate, we cannot expect more than a certain return from any one piece of land (see Book III., *Land Rent*).[1]

Now, the law of diminishing returns does not apply only to the agricultural and extractive industries. It is a general law of pro-duction, and may be put as follows : beyond a certain point, every increase in the return requires a more than proportional expenditure

---

[1] Agricultural statistics for France show a somewhat slow and very irregular, though none the less constant, increase in the return per hectare. The following

of energy. Thus, to double the speed of a ship or a dirigible balloon, the power of the engine may perhaps have to be increased more than a hundredfold.[1]

V: THE ILLUSIONS TO WHICH MACHINERY HAS GIVEN RISE

NATURAL forces, imprisoned by machinery, work such wonders that we have become almost too used to them. Not only do they enable us to do our former tasks with an almost bewildering *speed*, *facility*, and *precision*, but they have allowed us to accomplish new ones of which we did not dream. To take but two examples— journalism and railways—which have profoundly modified the political, intellectual and moral, as well as the economic conditions of modern life : each of these is the creation of the steam engine.[2]

are the figures for wheat in ten-yearly averages (the last period given being twelve years) ; the third column gives the increase for each period in percentages for greater clearness :

1820–1829	.	.	.	.	.	.	11·80	..	100·00
1830–1839	.	.	.	.	.	.	12·36	..	104·75
1840–1849	.	.	.	.	.	.	13·66	..	115·76
1850–1859	.	.	.	.	.	.	13·95	..	118·22
1860–1869	.	.	.	.	.	.	14·36	..	121·69
1870–1879	.	.	.	.	.	.	14·46	..	122·44
1880–1889	.	.	.	.	.	.	15·44	..	130·85
1890–1899	.	.	.	.	.	.	16·19	..	137·20
1900–1911	.	.	.	.	.	.	17·67	..	149·75

We see that the return per hectare for the whole century (or at least for 91 years) rose from 12 hectolitres to 17⅔ hectolitres, an increase of nearly one-half. But if we divide this period into two, we find that, from 1820–1879, the return rose from 11·80 to 14·46, less than 22·5 per cent. in 59 years ; while from 1880–1911 we find that it rose from 14·46 to 17·67, an increase of 22·2 per cent. in 32 years, or a little more in half the time. This encouraging result is due mainly to the use of chemical manures, which has become very general during the last 20 years, especially since the creation of agricultural syndicates.

For the United States, the average yield of wheat per acre, if we express the product for 1896–1905 as 100, is indicated by the following figures : 1866–1875, 88·1 ; 1876–1885, 91·1 ; 1886–1895, 94·1 ; 1896–1905, 100 ; 1906, 114·8 ; 1907, 103·7 ; 1908, 103·7 ; 1909, 117.—AM ED.

[1] Theoretically, it is calculated that the power should increase as the cube of the speed. Thus, in the case of an airship, to double the speed we must multiply the power by 8 (2 × 2 × 2). But, in actual fact, the force required is much greater still. Take a ship of 20,000 h.p. going at the rate of 20 knots. To gain a knot, *i.e.* 5 per cent., the power of the machine must be increased by about 8000 h.p., and to bring the speed up to 25 knots the power would have to be raised to 60,000 or 70,000 h.p., *i.e.* tripled.

[2] A copy of a newspaper like *The Times* or some large American daily amounts, including advertisements, to about half the size of a volume like the

After the marvels of the present day, what may we not expect of the future ? Already we can see man almost freed from the necessity of toiling for his daily bread, working only three or four hours a day—a socialist has even put it at one hour twenty minutes —and yet producing more than enough to keep the whole human race in plenty.

Is there not, in France, at this moment twelve million horse-power producing a force of more than 120 million men ? [1] Now since there are, at most, not more than ten million men of an age to furnish productive labour, if we were to divide this 120 millions by the ten millions the productive power of each man would be multiplied by twelve ; or, rather, to put it more picturesquely, every French worker would henceforth have a dozen slaves in his service. This should put him almost in the position of the Roman patrician. For it would allow him to add the pleasures of idleness to those of wealth. Thanks, therefore, to this new form of slavery which might rep'ace the ancient servitude, there is no reason why the man of to-morrow should not live the noble life of the ancients, and, like the Greeks in the Agora or the Romans in the Forum, consecrate to politics, art and gymnastics, or to high thinking, the hours taken from material labour. The only difference would be that what was once the privilege of the few would then be the lot of all.

To dissipate such illusions we must first ask what it is we are expecting from machinery. An increase of wealth, or a reduction of labour—in other words, more leisure ? Or both ?

(*1*) If it is an increase of wealth that we are looking for, it must be pointed out that, of the 12,000,000 horse-power working in France, i iore than three-fourths is used for transport purposes only, in the form of locomotives or steamships. Now, the latter have certainly caused a considerable revolution by pushing back the limits which

present. Suppose that 100,000 copies are printed. This is equivalent 'to 50,000 volumes of the same size as this. How many copyist: would it take to produce by hand these 50,000 volumes in ten hours, *i.e.* in the same time as it takes to print the newspaper ? Say that each copyist wrote ten pages an hour, 400,000 copyists at least would be needed.

[1] One h.p., calculated at 75 kilogrammetres, represents a little more than the power of an ordinary horse, and as the power of the latter is estimated at seven times that of a man, it may be said that the force of 1 h.p. represents about ten times that of a man. But, as the work of the horse-power may be continuous, *e.g.* on steamships, while that of a man or a horse cannot last more than eight or ten hours a day, we may say that the labour furnished by 1 h.p. in a steam-engine represents twenty to twenty-five times that of a man. The giant machines of modern steamships produce as much as 80,000 h.p. This is equivalent to 1,500,000 rowers.

distance imposes upon the free movement of individuals, upon the exchange of products and upon the communication of ideas, thus accentuating the solidarity of the human race. In this they have performed a moral service the value of which cannot be exaggerated. But they cannot exactly be said to increase the number of products. They do so for the time being by *bringing them from distant places* ; but this is clearly only a provisional state of affairs, due to the fact that these places are still thinly populated and do not as yet need to keep all their produce for their own consumption.[1]

The goods the increase of which would most benefit mankind are agricultural products ; for the first condition of material well-being is to be fed, and, if possible, well fed. But this is precisely the domain in which up till now machinery has done least. In France, less than 200,000 h.p., that is to say, less than 2 per cent. of the total, is employed in agriculture.

Even in the agricultural industry the effect of most machines is to accelerate labour, not to increase the quantity of articles produced. The threshing machine, the sugar-crushing machine, even the Chicago machines which transform pork into sausages, do not add one atom to the sum of our wealth, to our stock of corn, of sugar, of meat.

There is another industry of capital importance as regards the well-being of man, that of house-building. Now, to this kind of production machinery, save under exceptional conditions, is hardly ever applied.[2]

It is, therefore, in a more limited field than we thought—in fact, that of manufacture only—that the use of the natural forces has yielded all that might have been expected in quantity and cheapness. In this particular sphere we may say that it has gone even beyond the mark, since it has resulted in superabundance, and has, as we shall see, forced manufacturers to come to agreements among themselves to restrict production.[3]

(2) Are we looking for a reduction of labour? Fifty years ago

[1] We may say, however, that, since the recent discovery of how to combine atmospheric nitrogen with other elements by means of electricity, machines, by producing powerful chemical fertilisers, cause an increase in the earth's yield.

[2] Machinery has been used for constructing iron frameworks, for lifting materials, and here and there for cutting and polishing the stones ; even, in a few out-of-the-way cases, for removing houses bodily.

[3] The English mills produce enough yards of cotton stuff to go 120 times round the earth (five billion yards). There would be nothing to hinder them from making a covering of cotton for the whole globe, if only they could be sure of selling it !

J. S. Mill wrote the melancholy words: "It is questionable if all the mechanical inventions yet made have lightened the day's toil of any human being." It is certainly true that, since they were written, the length of the working day has been much reduced in every country. But this was not due to machinery. It was, on the contrary, the prolonging of the working hours caused by machinery which finally brought about the intervention of the legislature. Moreover, the shortening of the working day has been counterbalanced by the more intense nature of the labour—a labour more nervous than muscular, it is true, but none the less wearing to the physique of the workman.[1]

As for the increase of leisure to be expected from the use of machinery, does it not rather face us in the form of an increase of unemployment ? This last scourge seems to be the most serious of all the consequences of the use of machinery ; and it is this which is at the root of the long and bitter animosity of the working classes towards machinery. It deserves a separate chapter of its own.

VI : WHETHER MACHINERY IS DETRIMENTAL TO THE WORKING CLASS

IF one horse-power does the work of ten men, every new horse-power should enable one man to do the work of ten, and nine men are thus apparently thrown out of employment. And, as each of the nine men will do his best to keep his place, they will underbid one another and bring down wages. It is because, rightly or wrongly, this consequence appeared inevitable to the workers, that they often destroyed the machines, and sometimes sought to kill the inventor. Even to-day the introduction of new machinery sometimes provokes strikes.

Are the workers altogether mistaken in their idea ? The classical economists, bent on proving that there cannot be a contradiction, in our economic organisation, between the interest of society and the interest of individuals, turned all their efforts toward showing that machinery, on the contrary, brings more employment and more well-being to the working classes. The three classical arguments are :[2]

(1) *Cheapness.* Every mechanical invention, they say, results in

---

[1] There are spinning frames with from 1000 to 1400 spindles turning at the rate of 180 revolutions a second. The worker who watches them has charge of two, and, in the United States, of four or five of these frames.—AM. ED.

[2] For the position of the Liberal school on this famous question, see Levasseur, *Precis d'Economie politique*, and as the most recent book, Daniel Bellet, *La machine et la main-d'œuvre humaine* (1912).

a lowering of the cost of production and consequently in a reduction of prices. Thus, even supposing that his wages are reduced, the worker will benefit, as a consumer, by the fall in prices from which he suffers as a producer.

The answer to this is, that the worker obtains no compensation if the article in question is not one which he consumes. The mechanical manufacture of certain laces may have brought down their price, but, as the poor woman who makes them is not in the habit of wearing them, this is no compensation for her.

Even supposing the article is one which the worker is in the habit of consuming, the quantity he consumes is probably minute, and his compensation therefore negligible. The stocking-knitter, who has lost her wages owing to the invention of the knitting machine, will not be easily consoled by the prospect of henceforth buying cheap stockings.

If the compensation of which they speak is to be real, *mechanical progress must take place in all branches of production at once* so that the subsequent fall in prices may be general and simultaneous. In this case, it might truthfully be said that the halving of his wage would matter little to the worker, since all his expenses would be halved too. Unfortunately, we have just shown that mechanical inventions are being carried into only a few branches of production, and affect but little the main items of the poor man's budget, namely, food and lodging.

(2) *Increase of production.* Every mechanical invention, they continue, by the very fact that it brings down prices, is bound to stimulate production. Thus it brings back in the long run the workers which it had for the time being displaced. Instead of taking work from them, it creates work for them. Examples in support of this contention are endless. Compare, for instance, the number of printers to-day, since the great increase in the output of books which has followed the invention of printing, with the handful of copyists in the Middle Ages.[1]

In answer to this it may be said, first, that, though increase in

---

[1] Another more precise example. In England, in 1835, the number of workers employed in the cotton spinning-mills was 220,000 ; to-day it is over 700,000. Yet it is in this industry that machinery has done such wonders.

Caroll D. Wright, in his *Industrial Evolution of the United States,* gives some striking examples of economy in labour through machinery.

Machinery has, besides, created a number of entirely new industries, among these the construction of machinery itself, thus opening new outlets to labour. The recently started automobile and cycle industry employs 100,000 workers in France.—Am. Ed.

output is a frequent consequence of a fall in prices, it does not always take place, as in the following cases : (a) Whenever the want which an article satisfies is a limited one. The example of coffins has become classical, but there are many other articles, such as wheat, salt, umbrellas, spectacles, musical instruments, a fall in the price of which would only very slightly raise consumption. It may sometimes, as in the case of certain articles of luxury, lessen it. Indeed, we may say that articles, the consumption of which increases in direct proportion to a fall in prices, are very rare. If boots were to fall to half their price, should we really wear out twice as many ?[1] (b) Whenever an industry is bound up with other industries. This is a frequent case. The production of bottles and barrels is limited by that of liquors. No matter how their price may fall, if there is no more wine to put in them no more will be sold than before. In the same way the production of watch springs is limited by that of watches; the production of rivets by that of rails and boilers ; that of rails and boilers, again, by other causes independent of prices, such as the development of transport, mining output, etc.

Further, even supposing that consumption were to increase proportionally, or more than proportionally, to the fall in prices, it will take time, in some cases even generations, for this evolution to take place. Time must be allowed for the former prices to come down, the more so as manufacturers, in their own interests, will resist the fall, and the public, accustomed to the old prices, will not hasten it. Competition will in the end win, but rival industries are not built up in a day. More time, again, must be allowed before the fall in price can bring the article within reach of those strata of society which do not easily change their likings and their needs. And, during all this time, what is the worker to do who is obliged to live from day to day ? For his grandchildren perhaps there will be compensation, but not for him.

(3) *Employment for the unemployed.* All employment of machinery which economises hand-labour must, they say, of necessity, be a gain to some one ; either to *the producer in the form of increased profit*, if he continues to sell his articles at the old prices, or to *the consumer in the form of lessened expenditure*, if, as is more likely, the price of the article is reduced to the level of the new cost of production. The money that does not go into the pockets of the dismissed workers is not therefore lost. We find it again in the

---

[1] In the United States in 1845 there were 46,000 bootmakers, representing at that time about 2·4 per cent. of the population. In 1900 there were 162,000, *i.e.* 2·1 per cent. of the population. Their number had therefore relatively decreased.

pockets of the manufacturers or of the consumers.   Now what does
the manufacturer do with his new savings ?   He must spend them
or invest them ; there is no other alternative.   In ei.her case, therefore, the money is bound to go to encourage industry by purchasing
new articles or to develop production by furnishing new capital.

Ultimately, then, every mechanical invention " sets free " not
only a certain quantity of labour, but a certain quantity of capital ;
and as these two elements have a great affinity, and cannot do
without each other, they will in the end meet and combine.

This, in particular, is Bastiat's line of argument.   In the abstract
it is true ; but we are bound to ask, " Where and when will this
combination take place ?   Will it be six years hence, and at the
other end of the world ? "   Perhaps the economies made by the
consumer will go to construct a canal at Panama, or a railway in
China.   Capital once freed has no difficulty in finding employment ·
it has wings and can fly whither it will.   The worker is not so mobile :
he is not fit for every kind of work, nor can he easily go to the
other end of the world in search of it.   In the long run he will turn
to a new trade ; but, in doing so, he will probably lose some of his
acquired skill, and in consequence his wage will be reduced.   In
any case the crisis will be long and painful, and, as it recurs at each
new invention, unemployment becomes a chronic condition.

This, then, is the problem.   But it must be pointed out that it
is not due specifically to machinery.   All *economic progress*, whether
it takes the form of mechanical inventions or of new methods of
organising labour, *cannot but result in rendering a certain amount of
labour useless*.   And, given the organisation of our modern societies,
founded as they are on the division of labour, in which each of us
makes a living by some definite kind of work, it is impossible that
this progress, of whatever sort it be, should not render some one's
labour superfluous.   It is the inevitable anomaly.   For this reason
the workers are hostile not only to machinery, but to every improvement which tends to increase production in the industry by which
they live.   One of the rules of the Trade Unions is the limiting of
the output of labour, with the object, not merely of harassing the
employer, but of reducing unemployment.

We may urge that this working-class policy is inspired by class
egoism, that it is contrary to the general interest, which requires
abundance and cheapness, and that it will be broken inevitably by
economic evolution.   The most enlightened workers themselves
admit it.   They deny that they are hostile to machinery from any

spirit of backwardness. Machinery, they grant, would be a benefit to them, as to all, if it belonged to the community. In such a case its sole effect would be to reduce the hours of labour for every one without depriving anyone of his living. But, under the actual economic system, the appropriation of machinery by the capitalists involves the expropriation of the wage-earners.

What they demand, in the meantime, is, that, as a result of a new invention, the wage-earner should not suffer dismissal, or a reduction of wage, but, on the contrary, should share in the advantages realised, by a reduction of hours, or an increase of wage.[1]

For the future, we have reason to hope that the painful shocks caused by mechanical inventions will become slighter. It is evident that the appearance of a new machine in an industry already working with machinery cannot cause a revolution approaching that which was occasioned by the introduction of the first mechanical loom in the weaving industry. We may even be allowed to prophesy that the great mechanical revolution which marked the nineteenth century is coming to a close. History, in fact, shows us, in the economic evolution of humanity, periods of sudden change followed by long periods of a more or less stationary nature. It is, therefore, quite likely that the great economic revolution of the present day will be followed by a long period of rest, or at least of very slow progress, somewhat similar to the long and peaceful periods which preceded it.[2] In all probability the invention of the steam-engine has already given all the results that it is able to give. It may be said that other more perfect machines will 'be invented. Perhaps; but even so, is it likely that the substitution of these unnamed machines for the steam-engine will produce a revolution in any way to be compared with that which resulted from the substitution of the steam-engine for handicraft?

The system of railways is almost complete over the whole of Europe, and will be so over the whole world within the next half-century. This, too, is a transformation which will not need to be repeated. Can we imagine that the carrying of passengers or goods by balloon or aeroplane will have the same economic consequences

---

[1] In printing establishments where linotypes are used, the French typographers' Trade Union demanded 12 francs a day not only for those who were working the machines, but for their comrades who were working by hand.

[2] J. S. Mill, in an eloquent and much-quoted passage, prophesies that the continuous fall in the price of products will bring about a "stationery state," in which we shall see "the stream of human industry finally spread itself out into an apparently stagnant sea" (*Principles of Political Economy*, Book IV, chap. viii, p. 746; edit. W. J. Ashley).

as the substitution of the railway for vehicular traffic ? Lastly, within the next few generations the human race will be settled on all that remains of the earth's surface ; there will be no more unoccupied lands, and the disturbing effect produced by the competition of new countries on our old markets will cease.

VII : EMIGRATION AND COLONISATION

WITH the various facts which we have been discussing—the limitation of land and natural resources, the law of diminishing returns, the slowing-down of social evolution as a prelude, perhaps, to a stationary state—we must connect two kindred facts of primary importance in the history not only of mankind, but of the animal, and even of the vegetable, world, *Emigration* and *Colonisation*.

To what are these displacements of population due ? The emigrations of the past were not, as we might think, caused by over-population or lack of space. It was often from the least-populated countries that the strongest currents of emigration started.[1] The forests and steppes which the barbarians left behind them were still deserts. But, however sparse a population may be, it will be too large if it lacks natural resources or means of turning these to

[1] From the figures given below for the five years 1906-1910, we see that there is no relation between density of population and emigration. If Italy, with a dense population, has a large figure for emigration, we see that Germany, on the other hand, with an equally large population, has quite an insignificant one. Conversely, Portugal, Ireland, Spain, and Norway, with a density of population much below that of France, have an emigration figure forty to a hundred times greater.

	Density per square kilometre.		Emigration per 100,000 Inhabitants.
Belgium	252	..	238
England	240	..	623
Italy	121	..	1155
Germany	120	..	42
France	74	..	15
Scotland	60	..	1258
Portugal	59	..	695
Ireland	52	..	1142
Spain	38	..	676
Norway	7	..	942

See the *Annuaire Statistique* for 1911, pp. 154 and 163. Emigration from England and Portugal increased enormously in 1911-1912, having doubled in England and trebled in Portugal. Thirty years ago emigration from Germany was ten times greater than to-day, her rise in prosperity having momentarily checked it. It is beginning again strongly.

account. The Norwegians have difficulty in finding enough arable land between their fjords and their glaciers. The Irish and the Italians are certainly not destitute of land, but they are without access to it, absorbed as it is by the large estates. The problem is one not of space, but of resources. Thus to-day it is lack of wages which is determining in great part the currents of emigration and is sending the working men of Western Europe to the two Americas.

We might perhaps think that colonisation is only a consequence of emigration. This is not so.

Emigration and colonisation are two phenomena which generally go together, but are nevertheless distinct. Emigration is a demographical phenomenon : it is often found without colonisation, as, for instance, when it takes place into a country already constituted and independent. This is the case not only in the inter-European emigrations, which bring into France numbers of Italians and Belgians, but more particularly in the great current of emigration which for a century has been peopling the republics of the two Americas.

Colonisation is a political fact : it is the taking possession of territories unoccupied or occupied by so-called uncivilised peoples, though this distinction is sometimes very arbitrary. It may exist without emigration if the occupation is effected by soldiers and officials who pass through the colony without settling there. This is what happens, unfortunately, in many of the French colonies. Climatic conditions may sometimes absolutely prevent immigration.

The work of emigration has scarcely begun ; that of colonisation is reaching its end, as hardly any more vacant land remains on this planet. It is for this reason that countries, particularly those which have come late to the division, are disputing so tenaciously mere deserts and marshes. As Cecil Rhodes said : " Wherever there is room there is hope." Who knows what wealth some new invention or new need may cause to spring from the soil or the subsoil ? We take when we can : we find out later.[1]

---

[1] Some countries have been able by colonisation to increase their territory ten or a hundredfold. The following figures give the area of a few countries in relation to the area of their colonial possessions :

	Area of the home country.		Area of the colonies.	Relation.
British Isles	315,000 square kilometres		30,000,000	1 to 95
Belgium	30,000	,, ,,	2,500,000	1 ,, 83
Holland	33,000	,, ,,	2,000,000	1 ,, 60
Portugal	89,000	,, ,,	2,000,000	1 ,, 22
France	536,000	,, ,,	9,500,000	1 ,, 18
Germany	540,000	,, ,,	2,800,000	1 ,, 5

(See *Principes de Colonisation*, by M. Arthur Girault.)

In vain do the economists of the liberal school, hostile as a rule to colonisation,[1] point out to their governments that they are undertaking a thankless task ; that it would be better for them to avoid the heavy cost of these conquests ; that they would profit no less by the wealth of these new countries if they peacefully sent thither their emigrants and their capital. Brazil and the Argentine Republic are much better colonies for the Italians and Germans than those which cost them so dear on the African coast. This reasoning has so far convinced no government. Before such arguments can be conclusive, we must suppose that the other countries, which will certainly not miss the chance of being first occupants, will allow the whole world to benefit by their colonial enterprise. This, however, they will not do. Without absolutely refusing admission to foreign immigrants and their capital, they will keep the best concessions in land, mines, railways, etc., for their own countrymen, and will be sure to reserve the markets by protective duties.

Even the policy of the open colony, which Great Britain has pursued with such splendid liberalism, procures many advantages to the home country. Thanks to this policy, Britain has been able to extend her colonial empire in all directions without incurring too great a hostility on the part of other nations, who know that it is to their advantage also ; and she finds in her colonies splendidly paid posts for the younger sons of her families. The political connection between the mother country and the conquered country, though it may be the cause of prolonged bitterness and hatred, nevertheless creates moral and economic ties which become continually closer, and which may outlive the eventual rupture of the political bond. By means of her schools, the mother country ends sooner or later by imposing her language on the natives—at least those of the better classes. Now, community of language creates an intellectual and sometimes a commercial clientèle.

Colonies differ greatly in character, but they may be reduced to two main types :[2]

(1) *Colonies of settlement*, the object of which is to receive the overflow population from the mother country, the swarm from the hive. The climatic conditions in such colonies must not differ too much from those of the home country, or the immigrants can neither

---

[1] With the exception, however, of M. Leroy-Beaulieu, who has constituted himself the champion of colonisation during the last thirty years (see his well-known book, *La Colonisation chez les peuples modernes*).

[2] For the administration of colonies, which is outside the scope of our book, see Girault, *op. cit.*

live there, nor, what is more difficult, perpetuate their race. But such coincidence is rare. England is almost the only country that has been able to lay hold of regions where the white man finds a familiar soil and a friendly sky—excepting perhaps Russia, if, as we really should, we count Siberia and Central Asia as colonies. France, too, has a fine though somewhat narrow belt of land opposite her coasts, on the north of Africa. But, for the other countries, colonies of settlement are now hardly possible. Still, it is not inconceivable that the progress at present being made in hygiene may one day enable the white man to become acclimatised to regions that are to-day considered uninhabitable.

(2) *Colonies of exploitation*, the object of which is not land on which to settle, but natural wealth. This is the type of colony which has brought untold riches to civilised societies in the shape of gold, silver, diamonds, ivory, spices, sugar, coffee, chocolate, cotton, quinine, india-rubber, and precious woods, all of which were, in the first instance, and still are, colonial products. Whereas settlement colonies are *agricultural*, those of exploitation are *commercial*, the natural wealth of the country, which is destined solely for export, being exploited and even monopolised by trading companies. These companies have played a great part in colonisation. We have only to call to mind the famous East India Company. Even to-day, whenever immense and almost unexplored territories. such as those of the Congo, are to be exploited, governments, as a rule, prefer to hand over the working of them to private companies, and to invest these with part of their sovereignty.[1]

The history of colonisation in both of the above forms is, it must be admitted, a cruel one. Colonies of settlement have nearly everywhere expropriated the native population and sometimes exterminated it.[2] Colonies of exploitation, as a rule, have been more

---

[1] This is not the case with the French companies of the Congo, which are invested with privileges of an economic order only. But as, over immense tracts, the natives may buy and sell only through the companies, the agents of these exercise a *de facto* sovereignty.

[2] It is an interesting fact that Spanish colonisation, the most horrible of all, apparently, in the greed and ferocity of its " conquistadores," has nevertheless left behind a large part of the native population in the Spanish-American colonies, while English colonisation, more humane in its methods, has ended in the complete disappearance of the native population of North America and Australia. The fact is, that economic competition between a strong race and a weak one is much more deadly than are individual acts of cruelty. The glory of French colonisation is that, in spite of isolated atrocities, the native population has increased in nearly all the colonies. In Algeria it is increasing even more rapidly than is that of the colonists themselves.

sparing of the lives of the natives, since native labour could not be replaced, but they have subjected the natives to a *régime* which cannot be better described than by the name itself, " exploitation." The scandals of the Belgian, and even of the French, colonial companies on the Congo, have been surpassed by the atrocities of the companies which collect rubber in Peru.

The justification for colonisation by conquest is, that the pressure of existence on the human race is too great to allow of land not turned to account by its owners lying uncultivated for an indefinite time. Expropriation is thus upheld on grounds of public utility, or rather of the utility of mankind. And we should consider this a sufficient reason if expropriation were accompanied by the same guarantees as are observed in the case of individuals, and if it left the natives at least as well off as they were before. These guarantees would be more effective if sanctioned by international agreements, such as the Berlin Act for the Congo. For freedom of trade is, of itself, some protection against commercial exploitation.[1]

CHAPTER II : LABOUR

1: THE PART PLAYED BY LABOUR IN PRODUCTION

To realise its ends, and principally to obtain the necessities of life, every living thing is obliged to do a certain amount of work. The very seed must make an effort before it can raise the crust of hardened earth that covers it and breathe the air and light. The oyster, fixed in its bed, opens and shuts its shell to draw in the nourishing elements from the water round it. The spider spins its web ; the fox and the wolf go hunting. Nor does man escape this common law ; he, too, can only satisfy his wants by continuous effort. This effort, unconscious in the plant and instinctive in the animal, becomes in man a deliberate act, and goes by the name of *Labour*.

But are there not some forms of wealth which man can obtain without labour, which Nature freely bestows on him ? This is a nice point.

In the first place, it must be observed that, of all the forms of wealth which come under the heading of *products*, there is not one that does not involve a certain amount of labour. This is implied

---

[1] For commerce with colonies see *infra*, the chapter on *Commercial Policy*.

in the very etymology of the word, product—*productum, drawn from somewhere*. And what should have drawn it from somewhere, if not the hand of man ? Before we can satisfy our desire for fruit, even the fruit which Nature has spontaneously given us—pines, bananas, dates, or the shellfish, which in Italy are called sea-fruit (*frutti di mare*)—we must first take the trouble to gather it. Now, the gathering is certainly labour, and a form of labour which may become very irksome.

We seldom, indeed, realise what a great part labour plays even in the making of products which are often inaccurately termed " natural." We are inclined to think, for example, that everything that grows in the earth—corn, vegetables, fruit—is a free gift of the earth, *alma parens rerum*. In reality, most of the plants used for man's food have been, if not created, at least so modified by the cultivation and labour of hundreds of generations, that, to this day, botanists have not been able to discover their original types.¯ Wheat, maize, lentils, beans, are nowhere to be found in their natural state. And the plants which we do find growing wild are singularly different from their cultivated brethren. The difference between our bunches of grapes and the acid berries of the wild vine ; between the juicy vegetables and fruits of our gardens and the leathery roots and bitter, sometimes poisonous, berries of the wild varieties, is so great that we may well look on our fruit and vegetables as artificial and as a veritable creation of human industry.[1] And the proof of this is that, if the unremitting labour of cultivation be relaxed for a few years, these products immediately degenerate, that is to say, they return to their natural state and lose all the virtues which human industry has given them.

Even in the case of forms of wealth which cannot be called " products," because *they exist before any act of production*—the soil, in the first instance, and all the materials, organic and inorganic, with which it supplies us : the bubbling spring of water or petroleum, the primeval forest, the natural prairie, the stone quarry, the coal or metal mine, the waterfall which turns the mill wheel or the turbine, the guano bed deposited by sea-birds, the teeming fishery—we must bear in mind :

(*1*) That these natural forms of wealth exist as wealth, *i.e.* as things of use and value, only in so far as human intelligence has been able, first, *to discover their existence*, and, secondly, to *recognise the properties in them which render them fit to satisfy some one or other*

---

[1] The gods, said Xenophon, sell us all good things for the price of our labour.

of our wants. Take, *e.g.* a piece of land, say wheat-growing land in America. If it is wealth, it is so only because some pioneer, following in the footsteps of Christopher Columbus, has revealed the existence of this particular spot. Now, discovery, whether of a New World or of a mushroom, always presupposes a certain amount of labour.

(2) That this natural wealth cannot be *utilised, i.e.* cannot minister to the satisfaction of man's wants, until it has undergone a certain amount of labour. Virgin soil, for example, must be cleared ; the spring of mineral water must be captured and bottled ; mushrooms and shellfish must be gathered and cooked.

II : HOW LABOUR PRODUCES

THREE different aspects of labour must be distinguished.

(1) *Manual Labour.* This is indispensable in the production of material wealth. The raw material of all wealth must always be transformed, or, at any rate, extracted. Now, this is primarily the handiwork of man.

The marvels which the hand of man can do belong almost to the sphere of the miraculous. Yet man has by no means " fairy fingers." His handiwork is nothing more than muscular energy directed by intelligence ; its result is not different from that of any other motive force, viz., *a displacement.*[1]

The displacement may consist either *in changing the place of the object itself,* or in *changing the arrangement of its component parts.* In the latter case, we say that the object has undergone a transformation. But all transformation is, after all, only a displacement. The exquisite forms which clay assumes under the hand of the potter or the sculptor, the rich and intricate designs which the thread follows in the hands of the lace maker, are but the effects produced by the displacing of molecules of clay or threads of tissue. All that man by his labour can do is to stir, separate, join, transpose, superimpose, arrange—mere movements. Take bread, for instance. It will be seen that all the processes in its production—ploughing, sowing, reaping, winnowing, sifting, kneading, putting into the oven—are nothing but displacements of matter. The true changes which take place in the constitution of bodies, the changes which modify their

---

[1] This had been already pointed out, in 1771, by the Italian economist, Verri. It must, however, be said that if man has less muscular energy than the animals, he has, as a rule, more dexterity. This he owes above all, as the name indicates (dexterity, from *dextera* = right hand), to that marvellous organ, the hand.

physical and chemical properties, are not of man's handiwork. All that man does is to arrange the materials in the right order; to put the seed into the earth, the vintage into the vat, the ore into the furnace. The rest is Nature's work. Hers is the mysterious evolution which brings forth the plant from the germ; the fermentation which produces alcohol from a sugary juice; the chemical combination which makes steel from coal and iron.

When we realise how weak is this motive force of man, how limited its action, we are the more amazed that it has been strong enough to transform the whole world.

(2) The labour of *Invention*. This is purely intellectual, but it is no less indispensable to production than manual labour. For there is not one of the things utilised by man, not a single one of his productive acts, that has not had to be invented. It is owing to the labour of invention that mankind's heritage is daily increasing. At one moment we have industry making shining aluminium, light and strong, from the clay which lies as mud on our streets; the next, it is converting foul coal residue into perfumes or into dyes more splendid than Tyrian purple. True, the number of things which we know how to use is still small compared with the immense number of things of which we, as yet, make nothing. Of the 140,000 known species in the vegetable kingdom, cultivation makes use of less than 300, while, of the hundreds of thousands of species in the animal kingdom, there are hardly 200 which we have been able to turn to account.[1] And in the inorganic world the proportion is not much larger. But the list of our riches is daily becoming longer, and we have every reason to think that, if our knowledge were perfect, there would not be a single blade of grass or a single grain of sand in the whole world, for which we should not have discovered some use.

It is not only the different forms of wealth which have to be discovered. The ways of transforming them and of utilising them—manual labour, that is to say, in all its forms, each movement of the weaver's fingers or of the blacksmith's arms—has had to be invented by some first artisan. And this labour of invention never comes quite to a standstill. It enters into the humblest work and prevents it from becoming crystallised into mere routine. Invention, in the economic sense of the word, is not the flash from the mind of a man of genius; it is simply the adaptation of a new means to an end [2]

---

[1] De Candolle, *Origines des plantes cultivées*, p. 366.

[2] M. Tarde (*Logique Sociale*), however, sees in invention much more than a simple category of labour. For him it is the first cause of all wealth, because it is the first cause of all want and desire, of which wealth is but the object. And

D'

It must be borne in mind that, once an invention has been made, it may be used for any number of acts of production, or rather, of reproduction. This is precisely what makes it so difficult for the legislator to regulate and protect the rights of property of the inventor.

(*3*) The labour of *Supervision*. All productive enterprises, carried on in a collective form, require supervision. Now supervision, in itself, constitutes a very effective form of labour, and its importance is increasing with the tendency of modern industry to take the form of large-scale production.

III: ON THE EVOLUTION OF IDEAS CONCERNING THE PRODUCTIVENESS OF LABOUR

IT is curious to follow the evolution of economic doctrine in regard to the word "productive." Confined at first to a single category of labour, the use of the word was gradually extended till it is now applied indiscriminately to all.

(*1*) The Physiocrats reserved it for agricultural labour only (and also for the industries of hunting, fishing, mining), refusing the title of productive to any other form of labour, even to that of manufacturing. The reason they gave was, not that the agricultural industries alone furnish the material of all wealth, other industries simply making use of this material, but that they are the only industries in which nature works along with man and creates a net product.

(2) The definition of the Physiocrats was beyond all question too narrow. Material, as delivered to us by the agricultural and extractive industries, is, as a rule, quite unfit for consumption. It has to go through many modifications, and these modifications are precisely the concern of manufacture. Manufacture is, therefore, the indispensable complement of the other two industries. Without it the process of production would be as incomplete as a play without the last act. Of what use is the ore at the pit-head, if it is not to pass through the forge or the foundry? Of what use is wheat, if it is not to pass through the hands of the miller and the baker? Were it not for the work of the spinner, flax would be of no more use than the nettle. What right, then, have we to refuse the name of

---

he protests against any confusing of invention (intuition, joy) with labour (effort, pain). In his view there is the same difference between the two as between the pleasures of conception and the pains of child-birth. Still, remembering Buffon's remark that " genius is long patience," we may be inclined to think that invention, too, is only one of the aspects of labour.

productive to labour, without which this wealth would be useless
—would not even be wealth ?

As for the idea that the extractive and agricultural industries
create wealth, while the manufacturing industry only *transforms* it,
this is an entire mistake. The agriculturist creates nothing. He,
too, does but transform the simple elements borrowed from the soil
and the atmosphere. He makes his wheat with water, potash, silica,
phosphates, and nitrates, exactly as the soap manufacturer makes
soap with soda and fats.

And from the time of Adam Smith down, there has been no
hesitation in extending the word productive to manufactures.

(3) There has been greater hesitation in the case of the transport
industry, for the reason that transport does not apparently modify
the object in any way. Is not a parcel the same when it arrives
at its destination as when it was despatched ? This, it was said,
was a characteristic difference between the transport, and the manufacturing, industries.

But this distinction is not very philosophical. Every displacement of bodies is essentially a modification of them. It is, indeed,
as we have just seen, the only modification which we are able to
impose on matter. If, then, we hold that displacement is a
modification not essential enough to be called productive, we must
likewise refuse to apply that term to the extractive industries.
For what difference is there between the labour of the miner who
brings the ore or the coal from the bottom of the pit to the surface,
and that of the carrier who transports it from the pit-head to the
works ? Unless, indeed, we would argue that displacement is only
productive when it takes place vertically, and ceases to be so as soon
as it is in a horizontal direction. It is hardly necessary to point
out further, that, just as the manufacturing industry is the indispensable complement of the agricultural and extractive industries, so
transport is the indispensable complement of these three industries.
What would be the use of stripping cinchona trees in the Brazilian
forests, of taking guano from the Peruvian islands, of hunting
ivory in South Africa, if there were no sailors and carriers to transport
these products to the places where they are to be employed ? Of
what good is it to own the finest harvest in the world, if it cannot
be transported for want of roads ?

(4) There has been still longer hesitation in applying the word
productive to commercial industry.

It may, in fact, be noted that a commercial operation, reduced to
the bare juridical act, that of buying in order to sell (such is the legal

definition of an act of commerce), does not imply any creation of wealth. This was the doctrine of the Physiocrats, and even of Dunoyer. Commerce, they said, may bring a great deal of money to the man who undertakes it, but it adds nothing to the general wealth.

On the other hand, it must be observed that the industry of commerce can hardly be separated from that of transport. There was no separation, as we shall see, till a fairly recent date, and even to-day the merchants are the real directors of the world's traffic. The carrying trade does but execute their behests. They under-take, moreover, to *preserve* goods in the form of stock and also to *modify* them to some extent. The draper cuts his cloth for his customers, the grocer roasts his coffee. Lastly, even reduced to a pure and simple exchange, the mere fact of transferring the ownership of a thing from the hands of the man who cannot use it, to those of the man who can and will, must be considered productive. For to *render useful a thing which is useless,* is the whole secret of production (*cf. infra, Exchange*).

(5) But it is on the question of labour which consists only in services, as in the liberal professions, that the discussion has been most acute. It may perhaps seem strange to apply the word " productive " to the labour of a judge who pronounces a sentence, or to that of a surgeon who amputates a leg. Where are their products ? Where is the wealth they have created ?

It is enough to point out, however :

(*a*) That, if they do not create material wealth, they none the less create utilities in the form of services rendered. And it is utility, not the actual substance to which it may be attached, that is the object of production.

(*b*) That, in the social organism, thanks to the law of the division of labour which we shall study further on, there is such solidarity between all the various forms of man's labour that it is not possible to separate them. And immaterial services are an indispensable condition of the production of all material wealth. Take, for example, the production of bread. We should have no hesitation in putting under the heading of productive labour the work of the ploughman, the sower, the reaper, the carrier, the miller, and the baker, beginning with Triptolemus, or whoever he was who invented the plough, and all his successors who discovered the different varieties of cereals, or who found out the rotation of crops or the methods of intensive culture. But we cannot stop short at strictly manual labour. It is clear that the work of the farmer, or of the landowner, is of great use in the production of wheat, even though he may not put a hand to the plough; just as the labour of the shepherd is useful in the production of wool, though he does not do the shearing himself. Nor can we neglect the engineer who drew up the plan for irrigation, the architect who built the houses and barns.

Must we stop short here? We may, no doubt; and it is just here that many economists draw the dividing line between labour which should be called productive because it adds a new utility to an object, and labour which, though useful, ought not to be called productive, because it consists only in services rendered (cf. supra, p. 43, the distinction between *wealth* and *service*). But have not the labours of the rural constable who scares away marauders, of the Public Prosecutor who arraigns them, of the judge who condemns them, contributed to the production of wheat, as well as the labour of the soldier who has protected the harvests against a still worse ravager—the armies of an enemy?

And what are we to say of the labour of those who have made the farmer and his men what they are, of the schoolmaster who gave them the rudiments of agriculture or the means of acquiring them, of the doctor who kept them in good health? Is it a matter of indifference, even in the production of wheat, whether the workers are educated and healthy; whether they live in a state of order and security and enjoy the benefits of good government and good laws? Have we even a right to set apart, as entirely unconnected with the production of corn, such remote labours as those of writers, poets, and artists? May not a real taste for agricultural labour be developed in society by novelists who draw scenes of country life, or by poets who celebrate the charms of work in the open fields, and who teach us to say with the author of the *Georgics*:

> O fortunatos nimium sua si bona norint
> Agricolas !

Where, then, are we to draw the line? We see the circle of productive labour widening out till it reaches the extreme limit of society, just as concentric circles on the face of the waters spread out from their centre till they are lost in the distance. No doubt, it may be said, the forms of labour we have just been considering have not all contributed in the same way to the production of corn; some have acted directly, others indirectly. But it is a fact that *not one of these labours,* from that of the ploughman to that of the President of the Republic, *can be suppressed without detriment to the production of wheat.*

There is no ground even for establishing an order of precedence among them as regards their economic utility. Judging by the importance of the economic wants they satisfy, we might be tempted to give the first place to the labour of invention and discovery ; the second to that of agriculture ; the third to that of manufacture ; the fourth to that of transport, and the last to the labours of commerce and public functions. But if the country is badly governed or has no means of transport, all its agricultural wealth will be of no use to it. Still, we should fall into no less serious an error if we were to think that, because every trade or profession may be considered productive, it is a small matter whether one expands more or less than another. The truth is that, while every profession is useful within the limits of the wants which it satisfies, it becomes harmful beyond these limits, because it becomes parasitical. What is required is a right *proportion between the producing capacity of each profession or group and the importance of the need it has to satisfy.* Unfortunately, such equilibrium is far from being realised in our civilised societies.[1] Thus we see some countries spending thousands of millions in developing their means of transport, without taking the trouble to find out whether they will have anything to transport. So, too, as agriculture becomes more and more deserted, we find the number of persons engaged in small trade, or in Government offices, daily increasing. And it is not without reason that we complain

---

[1] The *Census of Industries and Professions*, published, in 1910, by the French Board of Trade, gives the following figures for France :

	1886.		1906.
Agriculture, forests . . .	52·2 per cent.	..	44·8 per cent.
Industry and transport . .	33·6 ,,	..	36·5 ,,
Commerce	7·0 ,,	..	10·5 ,,
Liberal professions . . .	7·2 ,,	..	8·2 ,,

From this table it appears that, in the short period of twenty years, the proportion of men employed in the first two groups, which are the only directly productive ones, has gone down from 85 8 per cent. to 81 3 per cent., *i.e.* over 5 per cent. (the fact that the decrease is not greater is partly due to the neutralising effect of the development of railways), while the proportion of men employed in the last two groups—unproductive according to the old use of the word—has risen from 14·2 per cent. to 18·7 per cent., *i.e.* nearly one-third.

The figures for the United States in 1870 and 1900 are as follows :

	1870.		1900.
Agriculture, fisheries, mining .	49 per cent.	..	38 per cent.
Manufactures	20 ,,	..	22 ,,
Commerce and transportation .	10 ,,	..	16 ,,
Liberal professions . . .	3 ,,	..	4 ,,
Personal service . . .	18 ,,	..	20 ,,

AM. ED.

of the growing number of intermediaries and functionaries, and of the exorbitant share which they take from the product of the labour of all. We shall see, further on, that the co-operative societies for consumption aim precisely at removing the evil which results from this multiplication of traders.

IV : PAIN AS AN ELEMENT OF LABOUR

THERE is no denying the fact that mankind does not work by natural impulse, but only under the pressure of external circumstances. Children work for prizes, or from a spirit of emulation, or from fear of punishment ; men, from want, desire of gain, ambition, and professional honour. Most men work hard only to hasten the moment when they need no longer work. We must conclude, then, that all productive labour involves a certain amount of pain. This is a law of capital importance in Political Economy. If labour did not involve pain, economic phenomena would be quite other than they are. For example, neither slavery nor machinery would have existed, since the sole object of these was to do away with a certain amount of labour.

Why is labour painful ? Although every one feels it so, it is not easy to give a reason for it. Labour is, after all, but a form of human activity. And activity in itself is not painful. To act is to live. It is complete inactivity, on the contrary, which is a torment, and a torment so great that, if it is too prolonged, as in solitary confinement, it kills the prisoner or sends him mad.

Is it that labour always involves a certain *effort*, and that man is by nature a lazy animal ? This is not a sufficient explanation. Many exercises are looked on as pleasures : mountain climbing, canoeing, bicycling, motoring, flying, sport of all kinds, including dancing, require much more intense efforts than those of labour, and yet many men devote themselves passionately to these exercises.

In a game, however, effort is voluntary and free ; it seeks and finds its satisfaction in itself ; it is its own end. In labour, on the contrary, the effort is imposed by the necessity of attaining a certain end, viz., the satisfaction of a want. The effort in this case is simply the preliminary condition of an enjoyment to come. It is what is called a task. That is why it is painful. I can see but one difference between the boatman who rows for amusement and a waterman who rows for labour, between an Alpine climber and the guide who accompanies him, between a girl who spends her night at a ball and a dancer who appears in a ballet : it is that the former row, climb, and dance with the sole aim of rowing, climbing, and dancing, while the latter do so to earn their living. But this is quite enough to cause the same activities to be looked on as pleasure in the one case and pain in the other. Candide found it pleasant to " cultivate his garden." He would not have found it pleasant if he had had to grow vegetables for the market. The tourist, who follows a road simply for the sake of a walk, finds it inviting, but the rural postman, who takes it morning and evening for a particular purpose, always finds it long and tiring. Now, labour is simply a road along which almost all mankind must go in order to live.. Man works to earn his living ; he does not work for pleasure.

A good proof that the painfulness of labour comes from the fact that it is imposed on man, is that it varies in direct ratio to constraint and in inverse ratio to freedom. It was at its maximum in the case of the Roman slave attached to the grindstone, or the galley slave tied to his bench. It is still great in the case of the wage-earner who has to earn his daily bread. It is at its minimum in that of the peasant who lovingly ploughs his own field, of the director of trusts who organises the battle of millions as a general marshals his army, of the artist who expresses an idea on canvas or in marble. From this it is but a step to the conclusion that labour could be deprived entirely of its painful character under a social *régime* in which the pressure of hunger and misery should no longer be felt. And this step has been taken by most socialists. Fourier gave " attractive labour " as the pivot of the society of the future which he proposed to organise, declaring that, if labour is painful, it is due solely to the defective organisation of our modern societies. In his " Phalanstery " he prided himself on transforming labour into pleasure by free choice of callings, variety of occupations, shortness of tasks, *esprit de corps*, emulation, and a thousand other combinations, some ingenious, others fantastic : in a word, by turning the labours of the ploughman, smith, carpenter, shoemaker, etc., into so many kinds of sport.[1] If Louis XVI, he said, took pleasure in making locks, why should not all men end by working for pleasure ? And we are bound to admit that labour will certainly become less and less painful as men become richer and more independent ; for it will gradually lose its character of a task imposed by necessity, and will take on that of a free activity. Still, even if the law of labour ceases to be an economic necessity, it will remain as a moral law, a duty of social solidarity. And it

[1] See Fourier, *Œuvres choisies*, small edition, Guillaumin. Almost all socialists and anarchists of to-day take the same position.

would be a contradiction to imagine that labour will ever become play.[1]

In any case, as things are, every man who works is subject to the action of two forces : on the one hand, the *desire of obtaining some enjoyment ;* on the other, the *desire of avoiding the pain which the labour of obtaining this causes him.* He will continue, or desist from, his labour according to which of these two motives weighs down the balance.

As Jevons remarked, prolonged labour grows more and more painful, while the satisfaction expected from it diminishes as the most pressing wants begin to be satisfied.[2] So that of the two desires, that which impels a man to labour, and that which impels him to stop, it is evident that the second will sooner or later be victorious. Take a labourer drawing buckets of water from a well. His fatigue increases with every bucket he has to draw. The utility of each bucket, on the other hand, decreases ; for, if the first is indispensable for his food, the second is wanted merely for watering his cattle, the third for washing purposes, the fourth for watering his garden, the fifth for cleaning his courtyard, etc. At what number, then, will he stop ? This will depend to some extent on his power of resistance to fatigue, but more particularly on the scale of his wants. The Eskimo, who sees no other utility in water than that of quenching his thirst, will stop at the first or second bucket. But the Dutchman, who feels the need of washing the very roof of his house, will perhaps have to draw fifty before he has enough.

If, to the stimulus of present and actual wants, be added the stimulus of wants to come—if, for example, in a country where water is scarce, the labourer bethinks him of filling a cistern against days of drought—producing activity may be greatly increased. But this faculty of balancing an immediate pain against a far-off satisfaction, a faculty whose real name is *forethought,* belongs

---

[1] Some sociologists nevertheless claim that labour began as play, *i.e.* that, in order to secure discipline and regularity in labour, man's movements were made to follow those of the dance and physical games (see Büchner, *Arbeit und Rhythmus*). But there has always been this essential difference between labour and play, that the end of labour is production, while the end of play is pleasure. Labour, therefore, on its own definition could only become play by ceasing to be productive of wealth. This does not mean that play may not bring an incidental gain to the player. The gambler who plays at Monaco may become rich or may ruin himself, but he produces nothing.

[2] See M. Imbert's curious studies in his *Vies ouvrières* on the measuring of pain in manual labour.

only to the well-to-do classes of civilised races.   The savage and the
pauper are equally improvident.

V : TIME AS AN ELEMENT OF LABOUR—
THE LENGTH OF THE WORKING LIFE

IF time, as we have said, may be considered a factor of production [1]
iu nature's work—for time is needed for fruit to ripen and wine
to ferment—it may be said to hold a predominant place in the work ˙
of man.   Between the moment when a piece of work is begun
and the moment when its results may be expected, a certain amount
of time always elapses.   This length of time is, as a rule, longer in
proportion as the operation is productive.   In hand-to-mouth
labour, such as hunting, fishing, the gathering of wild fruits, a few
hours are enough ; but, when we come to agricultural labour, industrial enterprises, or those engineering works that are the honour of
our time, viz., mines, artesian wells, railways, tunnels, canals, the
time needed to complete them is enormous and proportionate to
the greatness of the results.   About forty years, for instance, will
have elapsed between the day when the first blow of an axe sounded
on the Isthmus of Panama and the day on which the first ship
passes through it.

But, if time may be said to be a factor of production in the casc
of nature's work, it appears, on the contrary, in the case of man's
work as an obstacle of the same nature as pain or effort.   We
cannot, indeed, say in the case of man as we can in that of nature,
that time costs nothing.   Time costs man a great deal, as we
find implied in the English proverb, " Time is money," and in the
more picturesque French one, " Time is the stuff of which life is
made."   Now, this " stuff " is measured out to man with no generous
hand, and labour is treated still more grudgingly.   For man is far
from being able to devote his whole life to labour.   Leaving out
of account the incalculable time wasted by laziness or in useless
occupations, there remain the facts :

(*1*) That man *cannot work every hour of the day*.   Time must be
taken off for sleep and meals ; and experience has shown that

---

[1] As also of destruction, of course.   But the action of time as a destroying
agent, *tempus edax rerum,* is much more striking than its action as an agent of
production.   In reality, time does not *act* in either case ; it is one of the conditions
of the action of forces which work in the direction both of production and of
consumption.   A lapse of time is as indispensable in the formation of a grain of
corn, or in the building of a cruiser, as in the formation of rust.

nothing is to be gained in productiveness by trying to prolong the working day. Formerly it was fourteen or fifteen hours ; the pressure of law and of trade unions has reduced it, in almost every country, to ten or eleven hours ; and in Australia it is no more than eight hours, or only one-third of the day.

(2) That man *cannot work all the days of the year*. There is no country but has a certain number of holidays. England and America rigorously observe the Sunday, while the English take the Saturday afternoon as well. In Russia, the number of Saints' days is incredible. Days of illness, too, must be allowed for. It is rare for even the most industrious worker to reach an average of 300 days' work in the year. The official figure given for France is 295.

(3) That *man cannot work all the years of his life*. The years of childhood and old age must be deducted. The useful life, that during which a man can earn his living, begins, in the case of a working man, at the age of fourteen or fifteen, and rarely extends beyond fifty-five, thus giving a length of forty years.[1] In the liberal professions, the active life continues beyond the age of fifty-five, but then, on the other hand, it begins much later. In fact, the productive period of a life of eighty years is hardly more than one-half, and the number of hours effectively devoted to labour hardly more than one-sixth.

A country is most favourably situated, demographically, when the greater part of its population belongs to the useful period of life. The ideal condition, from the purely economic point of view, would be that in which there were no children and no old men, since these two categories are unproductive. Such a situation is, of course, impossible. Still, new countries peopled for the most part by immigration approximate to it ; for immigrants, when they arrive, have already reached manhood, and their children are as a rule grown up. Sometimes, indeed, immigrants are not allowed to land after they have reached a certain age. This is distinctly one of the factors of the economic prosperity of new countries.[2]

---

[1] More than one quarter of the male population (262 per 1000 in France) die before reaching the age of eighteen. This is an enormous waste for society, as they have been brought up at a dead loss. Most of them, however, die in their early years, and this somewhat brings down the cost

[2] A country is also well off if the *average life is long*. Still, the *active life* is not necessarily connected with the average life. For imagine two countries, one in which everybody dies at thirty, and another in which half the population dies at birth, while the other half lives to sixty ; the average life would be the

Countries such as France, where the birth-rate is very low, are situated, demographically, somewhat like new countries. For, as births are less numerous, the proportion of adults in the population is evidently greater. The proportion of old men is, of course, also large, which somewhat reduces the economic advantage.[1]

The need of time in every productive operation, and of a longer period of time the more productive the operation is to be, is, as we shall see, one of the main causes of the importance of capital and of the privileged position of those who possess it. For the worker, while awaiting the fruits of his labour, must needs live on advances, and it is the capitalist alone who is in a position to furnish them. Naturally the capitalist will not do this for nothing.

VI : APPRENTICESHIP AND PROFESSIONAL EDUCATION

ALL manual labour consists of a series of combined movements, invented by the cleverest workers in the course of ages, and transmitted from one generation to another, partly by word of mouth or by written instruction, but mainly by sight, imitation, and practice. This teaching is called, from the point of view of the one who receives it, *apprenticeship*.[2]

Apprenticeship, particularly in the Middle Ages when it seems

same in both, and yet the second country would be much better off as regards the useful life, since there it would be forty years instead of ten.

[1] The distribution of ages in the three following countries per 1000 inhabitants is :

	Under 20 years.	20 to 60 years.	Over 60 years.
England	452	473	75
Germany	449	471	80
France .	357	525	118

France counts, therefore, 54 per 1000 more adults of from 20 to 60 years than Germany, which, out of a population of 39 millions, means 2,106,000 more persons at the useful stage of life. This compensates in some small measure for her inferiority of population for military service and industry.

[2] It is generally taught that the three grades, *apprenticeship, journeymanship,* and *mastership* succeeded each other, and that each worker had to pass through all three in the course of his professional life. This is not quite exact. The apprentice could become a master without passing through the journeyman stage, if there was a vacant place for him. When, however, the place of master became scarce and hard to obtain, journeymanship became a sort of necessary stage. Did apprenticeship still remain obligatory when, finally, the day came on which journeymen could no longer aspire to become masters ? There is some doubt on this point. In any case, it is the journeyman who is the father of the modern workman.

to have reached its highest perfection, was as important a period of life, as long and relatively as costly, for the sons of the working classes, as is the student period for the sons of the middle classes of to-day. It, too, had its final diploma, viz., its masterpiece. It was an individual training which took the form of a contract between the master and the apprentice, a contract involving obligations and severe penalties on both sides. The master had to train the apprentice thoroughly to his trade; the apprentice had to give implicit obedience. And this contract might last for years, according to the trade. In this way there was created the admirable class of artisans—a name synonymous with artist—that marked the Middle Ages. There was no fear that the apprentice, once trained, would compete with his former master; for, according to the regulations of the corporation, he could set up for himself only if a master's place were vacant. Very often he succeeded his own master, especially if, as sometimes happened, he had married his master's daughter.

To-day the situation is entirely changed. The complaint now is of the lack of apprenticeship and, consequently, of good workmen. This is one of the questions about which a great deal has been written of late years. The causes of the change are not hard to find. The following are the principal ones:

(1) In large industry, apprenticeship has become, in the first place, almost *useless*, because, with the introduction of machinery and the division of labour, each worker is called on to do, for his whole life-work, only one specialised task. What is the use in learning to make a whole shoe, if the worker is never to do anything but guide the machine for sewing the soles or for fastening the uppers? In the second place, it has become almost *impossible*, because the head of a large factory has other things to do than to act as instructor or teacher to a troop of apprentices.[1]

(2) In small industry, where such training would still be possible, e.g. in that of the shoemaker who works to order, the employer does not care to give it; for he has no longer any authority or means of control over his apprentice, and he is not anxious to create a

---

[1] We may also point out another reason in France, namely, that in factories employing children under eighteen years, or women of any age, along with men, French law prescribes a working day of ten hours, whereas in factories in which only men are employed, the legal length of the day is twelve hours. The result is that many employers, in order to avail themselves of the long day, systematically refuse to employ young persons, and consequently to make apprentices. As the ten hours' day is, however, tending to become more general, the undesirable effects of this discrimination are becoming less felt.—AM. ED

competitor whom nothing can hinder from opening a shop over the way. This is a risk to which managers of large dressmaking establishments are frequently exposed on the part of their fore-women. Apprenticeship is not compatible with free competition.

(3) But, if employers care little about apprenticeship, parents care still less. What matters most to them is, not that their children should learn a trade, but that they should earn wages as soon as possible. Now, a serious apprenticeship is incompatible with the payment of a wage to the apprentice. It is the apprentice, on the contrary, who should pay the master, as in the Middle Ages. There is, besides, the fact that the children themselves are ambitious to earn a man's wage in order to be independent of their parents. The employer, then, falling in with the desire of the parents and of the children—which coincides with his own interest—does not take apprentices, or if he takes them nominally, makes semi-workers of them (*petites mains*, as they are called in France), paying them half-wages, and taking as much as possible out of them.[1]

This is quite enough to explain why there are hardly any apprentices left. It has not been proved, moreover, that, from the purely economic point of view, industry suffers much from it; for the knowledge and special skill of the individual worker may be replaced, to some extent, by the knowledge and skill of the engineer who directs the whole. Still, the disappearance of apprenticeship is seriously felt in the highly skilled engineering industries, which, in France especially, it is important to safeguard. It is a matter of regret, too, from the educational point of view. For not only would apprenticeship react against the mechanical evolution which tends to confine the workman to a monotonous and specialised task; it would also be a means of giving him some heart in his work, for which he cannot possibly care save in so far as he understands it and sees its place in the whole.

Various measures have therefore been proposed for reviving apprenticeship,[2] such as the drawing up of a genuine contract,

---

[1] Still, it sometimes happens that employers find it to their advantage to engage these so-called apprentices, since they pay them half-wages and make use of them in the place of real workmen: hence the incessant struggle on the part of the trade unions for the limitation of the number of apprentices—a struggle fully justified. since these apprentices, when they become workmen, are no longer able to find employment.

[2] In France there is only one old law, that of 1851, on apprenticeship, which declares that " the master is to teach his apprentice progressively and completely the art, trade, or profession which is the object of the contract "; but it suggests no method of attaining this end.

the clauses and execution of which would be controlled by local boards of trade (*Conseils de Prud'hommes*) or by the trade unions, which imperatively claim this mission. But it would be difficult to induce employers, even with the compensations suggested for those who should take apprentices (*e.g.* reduction in taxation), to accept such control over their apprentices on the part of the trade unions, particularly if this control were to take the form of visits to the factory. In any case, no suggestion is offered as to how to overcome the resistance of the persons chiefly concerned—the parents and children themselves—unless we are to go the length of making the contract of apprenticeship compulsory, like the entrance examinations to public offices.

Owing to these difficulties, a solution has been sought in another direction, viz., in *technical education* given outside of the workshop in special schools. This system has the great advantage of giving the young workman general knowledge which should fit him for several trades at once, thus allowing him later to change more easily from one trade to another, and to suffer less from unemployment. These technical schools have, as a fact, shown admirable results in various countries, especially in Germany. But they, also, are not without their difficulties.

(*1*) In the first place, to benefit by this course of teaching, the young workman must have some free time. One of two ways will secure this : (*a*) An interval may be reserved for it between the time when he leaves the primary school (at the age of thirteen years in France) and his entrance to the workshop. In this case, however, the law will have to raise the age at which children are admitted into factories to fifteen or sixteen years, as otherwise the parents will prefer to send them to the factory rather than to the school. (*b*) A certain number of hours may be reserved out of his time in the factory in order to attend classes. For it can no longer be a question of schools, properly speaking, but of classes at hours which will be least inconvenient for him. And it will not be enough to give him the opportunity of attending these classes ; some means will have to be found of making his attendance compulsory. This is the system adopted in Germany and proposed in France.[1] In Germany,

---

[1] The *Conseil Supérieur du Travail*, in 1906, expressed the wish that young workmen, from the age of thirteen to sixteen, should be obliged to attend classes during a certain number of hours taken from their work, not, however, to exceed eight hours a week.

In Germany, legislation has a twofold aim :

(*a*) To oblige young workmen, whether apprentices or not, to attend the

the onus of ensuring attendance at the classes falls, and rightly, on the employer, not on the parents.

(2) In the second place, experience seems to show that technical teaching may complete, but cannot replace, apprenticeship. The old saying that " one can learn to forge only by being a smith " holds good. It is difficult to choose the right teachers. Those who are teachers by profession are not acquainted with the practical side. Workmen, on the other hand, do not know how to teach out of the shop. The students at such schools have no knowledge of what to do when they begin work. They are soon dismissed by the employer, or, humiliated, withdraw of their own accord. Many, on leaving the technical school, do not even go to a workshop. As they have lost touch with their fellow workmen and with the working class, and have become, so to speak, demi-intellectuals, they seek an outlet in the liberal professions or in public offices, or expect at least an overseer's post. Trade unionists look on these schools with no friendly eye, declaring that they turn out " blacklegs," men inspired with the employers' spirit, who tend to rise above their class.

(3) In the third place, the cost of technical training must be taken into account. In the technical schools at Paris, each student costs from 430 to 1250 francs, an average of more than 800 francs. We can see how this would mount up if we were to give such teaching to, say, 1,000,000 children of the working classes. And if we count that two-thirds of these children will not become workers, and consequently will not turn to account the outlay spent on them, we can see what an enormous waste it would be.[1]

technical schools, where there is an extraordinary variety of classes appropriate to each trade—classes for waiters, chimney-sweeps, etc.

(b) To encourage the use of the contract of apprenticeship. It stimulates employers by making the right to train apprentices a kind of honour to the man on whom it is conferred.

In England, young workers from the age of twelve to fourteen only do *half time, i.e.* one half-day or one day in two.

[1] Technical instruction in France is given in two quite distinct classes of schools, the one controlled by the Minister of Public Instruction, the other by the Minister of Commerce.

The former, called *Écoles primaires supérieures*, date officially from 1833 and actually from some thirty years ago. In 1907 they numbered 360, with 87,000 students of both sexes. The latter, called *Écoles pratiques de commerce et d'industrie*, are much more recent. In 1910 they numbered only 63, with 12,600 students. There are besides special schools for miners, clockmakers, etc., with about 2000 students. These figures do not amount to much, when we reckon that there are more than 600,000 young men and women employed in industry.

There are lively disputes among the representatives of these two classes of

The best solution would appear to be a combination of apprenticeship in the workshop for the practice of the trade, with general technical teaching. But it is evident that, if a two-sided training is to be arranged for, the difficulties of the problem will be doubled.

The organisations, both of working men and of employers, especially if they came to an understanding with one another, might perhaps revive apprenticeship again, and thus continue the best tradition of the ancient crafts and guilds on their best side. This is one of the points on which the interests of employers and employed are one. For, if it is very useful to the employers to raise the quality of their labour, it is no less useful to the unions; their coalition is strengthened when they include among their numbers "qualified" workmen who cannot be replaced at a moment's notice.

CHAPTER III : CAPITAL

I : THE TWO CONCEPTIONS OF CAPITAL

No economic conception save that of Value has given rise to so many theories as that of Capital. This is because the word capital is susceptible of two very different meanings. Let us examine these.

Of all the authors who have told stories of "Crusoes," and have proposed to show us man wrestling single-handed with the necessities of existence, not one has omitted to endow his hero with some instruments or provisions saved from the wreck. They knew very well, indeed, that, without this precaution, their story would be brought to an abrupt end, their hero not being able to live beyond the second page. And yet, had not all these Crusoes the resources of their labour and the treasures of·a rich, though virgin, soil? True, but there was nevertheless something lacking, something which they could not do without. The author had therefore to arrange by some artifice or other to provide them with it. This indispensable thing was Capital.

schools as to which gives the better results. Statistics seem to show that the first are more of the nature of small *lycées*, and draw the sons of the better-off working classes in the direction of public offices. But the second class, too, up to the present have turned out only a small number of working men.

There are also a large number of evening technical classes, organised by municipalities, labour exchanges, and philanthropic societies.

There is, however, no need to go to the example of a Crusoe, in order to be convinced of the utility of capital. The situation is exactly the same in our civilised societies. No problem in this world is more difficult than that of acquiring something when we possess nothing. Take any one of the proletariat, a working man, *i.e.* an individual who has no property. What will he do in order to produce what is necessary to keep him alive, to earn his living, as it is called ? A little reflection will show that there is not a single productive industry which he can undertake ; not even that of poacher—for which he would need a gun or at least snares ; or of rag-gatherer—for which he would need a hook and a basket.[1] Unless, as wage-earner, he can enter the service of a capitalist who will provide him, under certain conditions, with the raw material and instruments necessary for production, he is as miserable, as powerless, and as surely condemned to die of hunger as a Crusoe who has saved nothing from the wreck.

Animals, no doubt, when providing for their wants, have to be content with their labour and with Nature. Primitive man was, of necessity, in the same situation. It is quite evident that the first human capital must have been formed without the aid of any other capital. Man, more helpless on this earth than Crusoe on his island, had perforce, some time or other, to solve the difficult problem of producing the first wealth without the assistance of pre-existing wealth. It was by the strength of his arm alone that he had to set going the immense wheel of human industry. But, once started, the worst was over, and the slightest impulse has since been enough to give it an ever-increasing speed. The first stone man found to his hand, the first flint from which fire was struck, served as auxiliary forms of wealth by which he was able to create new ones under more favourable conditions. The power to produce increases in geometrical progression to the quantity of wealth already acquired. But we know that, though a geometrical progression increases with great rapidity after it reaches a certain point, at the beginning the rate of increase is slow. Thus our modern societies, living as they do on the accumulated wealth of a thousand generations, make light of multiplying wealth in all its forms. But they ought not to forget how slowly and precariously the first wealth must have been

---

[1] Intellectual production is no exception. The professions of barrister, doctor, magistrate, etc., presuppose the existence and utilising of a certain quantity of wealth, not merely in the form of instruments of work, libraries, surgeons' cases, a laboratory, a carriage, dress, etc., but more especially in the form of advances of money during the years of study and the early days of the career.

accumulated, nor during how many centuries the earliest human societies dragged their obscure way through the Stone Age before they formed their first capital. Many must needs have perished in this narrow pass. Only to a small number of chosen races has it been given to come out triumphantly and to rise to the rank of truly capitalist societies, *ad augusta per angusta.*

This, then, is the idea óf capital always given in treatises on Political Economy, and it is an essential one. There is, however, another and a more usual one.

In everyday language, capital does not mean the instrument of production, but *all wealth which brings in a revenue to its possessor independently of his labour,* all wealth, that is to say, which *produces income.* But this definition, it is evident, presupposes certain economic and social conditions : in particular the fact that wealth can be lent at interest, or can be usęd to secure the labour of poor people, who are only too glad to hire themselves out for their living.

It obviously takes for granted the existence of property, and, although it is as old as private property itself, it has become much wider in its application since credit has multiplied the ways of investment and increased the mobility of capital (see *infra, Associations of Capital*). What characterises this second conception of capital, then, is not *productivity,* but what we might call *rentability* ;[1] not the power to produce as an instrument of labour, but the power to command the labour of others—consequently to procure an income without personal labour, or at least with no other labour than that of watching one's investments and of gathering in their fruits.

This is why socialists emphasise this second meaning of capital alone. They will not admit that the bow of the savage or the plane of a Crusoe can be quoted as examples of capital. It is clear, indeed, that neither the savage nor Crusoe could have made " incomes " from them ; therefore they were not capital. They flout what we might call the *naturalistic* conception of capital, and substitute for it the *juridical* conception.[2] Capital for them is only a " historical category " which appeared in its due time, and will at its appointed hour disappear.

---

[1] The word is Dühring's. And Rodbertus, in his *Capital,* points out that it is impossible to appreciate rightly most of the problems of economic science, in particular the situation of the working classes, until we have seized and mastered the distinction between these two conceptions.

[2] This is the expression used by M. Chatelain, see *Le Capital économique et le Capital juridique, Revue d'Économie politique,* 1905, p. 673. In the former editions I used the expression *historical conception,* which is not so good.

What has created a violent opposition between these two theories is the attempt which has been made to use them as weapons, the first to justify, the second to discredit, the rôle of capital. Those who adhere to the first theory exclaim, " What a useful servant capital is, since even a Crusoe cannot live without it ! " Those who hold the second, reply, " What a tyrant capital is ; since it can exist only on the labour of others ! " These, however, are points of view which we shall discuss when we come to consider the distribution of wealth. The one point which we have here to make clear, is the true function of capital in production.

Now, there is no necessary contradiction between these two theories : each lays stress on one of the powers of capital. The one looks at the natural, permanent, and economic characteristics of capital ; the other at its acquired, relative, and juridical characteristics.

It is certain that the rôle of capital has changed with economic evolution. At first the modest instrument of the manual labourer, it has gradually passed from his hands into those of the rich, or even of the idle. From a simple instrument of production, it has become an instrument of gain. It is no longer merely an aid to labour ; it commands labour. It is this new social *régime* which socialists call *Capitalism*.

Nevertheless, even when this *régime* has disappeared, capital, as a means of production, will still remain. In our view, therefore, the definition of the economists is nearer the truth precisely because it looks to the necessary and essential characteristics of capital, while the other sees only those which are conditional and transient.

The fact that no wealth can be produced without the aid of some other pre-existing wealth, is an economic law the importance of which cannot certainly be exaggerated. Just as fire, under ordinary conditions, cannot be lighted without some bit of igniting matter (a match, an ember, a steel) ; just as an explosive mixture cannot go off without the help of a small piece of explosive matter called a fuse ; just as a living being cannot be produced without the presence of some pre-existent bit of living matter (germ, cell, protoplasm), so no wealth can be produced, under normal economic conditions, without the presence of a certain amount of pre-existing wealth. We must surely give some name, then, to this pre-existing wealth which has so characteristic a function. Now, the name we give it is *Capital*. If socialists will not accept this name, let them propose another ; but until they do so, we shall keep to this one.

II : PRODUCTIVE CAPITAL AND LUCRATIVE CAPITAL

At first sight there appear to be two fairly distinct categories of wealth.

Under the one come all the forms of wealth which directly satisfy our wants, which provide us with some sort of enjoyment, fleeting or permanent. It is not necessary to enumerate them. All that we have in our houses, on our tables, all that constitutes our well-being, come under it. We may call these *consumption goods*.[1]

But, alongside of this first category, we find many other goods which, in themselves, are unable to procure us any enjoyment, and serve only to produce the goods belonging to the first category. They exist for that sole object—*e.g.* instruments and machines, vehicles, factories, farms, roads, bridges, ccal, raw material, and all products which are in process of transformation and have not yet reached their final form. It is for this second category that the name of *capital* has been reserved.

We must take care not to include under it the earth and natural agents. These constitute an original factor of production which must not, for fear of confusion, be entered under the heading of capital.[2] The characteristic of capital is that it is *wealth created* not for itself but in order *to create further wealth*. It is, as Böhm-Bawerk so well expresses it, an *intermediary wealth*.

This distinction between wealth that is capital and wealth that is not, appears to be quite clear. There seems to be a dividing line, we might even say a gulf, between the two categories. The distinction is not, however, so simple as we might think.

In the first place, we must observe that many objects possess more than one property and may serve a double end ; they are on

---

[1] Some economists call them *incomes*. But this word is deceptive, as it implies that they are eaten up or spent, whereas consumption does not necessarily mean this. A picture, silver plate, a castle, a house, are consumption goods, but are not incomes. An interesting but different concept of income has been skilfully advocated by Professor Irving Fisher, in his book on *The Nature of Capital and Income.*—Am. Ed.

[2] Still, so far as land may itself be considered a product—to the extent, that is to say, to which it has been built on or improved—the name of capital may be given to it.

If Nature must be kept distinct from capital, so also must labour ; and yet several economists call *acquired knowledge* capital, *e.g.* knowledge certified by diplomas, in the liberal professions or public functions. True, such knowledge may be a source of income, but this income will be none the less the fruit of labour. What we ought to say is, that this knowledge could not have been acquired, nor these diplomas won, save for the possession of a certain amount of money-capital, but that is quite another question.

the border line, as it were, and may be classed under either category according to the particular use to be made of them. An egg is both a germ and an aliment; it is therefore capital if its germinal properties are being utilised for hatching purposes, and an object of consumption if its nourishing properties are being utilised for a meal. Coal used to heat an engine is capital, but when used to warm one's feet it is an object of consumption. A carriage is indispensable to a doctor, but it may also be used simply for a drive.

On the other hand, there is no form of wealth, even among those which by their very nature can only be consumed personally and for the pleasure they yield, which may not be sold, hired out, or lent, and thus bring in an income or profit to its owner. Now, as the bringing in of income has become to-day the characteristic feature of capital, we must admit then that there is not a single form of wealth which may not become capital if its possessor, instead of using it for his personal wants, uses it for gain. A motor car, a seaside villa, a fancy dress, may be hired out and thus become capital; in fact, any article whatever of food, or clothing, or of amusement, may be used as an object of *commerce*, and thus become what is termed stock-in-trade— *i.e.* capital.

Houses, for instance, are by their very nature consumption goods only, since, like food and clothing, they are products desired in themselves to satisfy the wants of those who live in them; and it was as such that Adam Smith from the beginning classified them. But they may become lucrative capital for their owner if, instead of inhabiting them, he lets them; and they may even become productive capital if they are used, not for dwelling in, but for purposes of production (factories, farms, shops).[1]

Again, the forms of movable property (Government stock, bonds, mortgages) which, in the everyday sense of the word, constitute capital as opposed to immovable property, are after all only *lucrative* capital, in the sense that they are not really productive, their income being drawn from the pockets of the debtor and taxpayer. Only that form of movable property called "shares" represents productive capital actually existing somewhere or other in the form of mines, railways, factories, banks, etc.; and these shares

---

[1] We should, however, point out that this distinction is hotly contested. Many economists hold that a house is always capital, even when it is used as a dwelling, because it is always productive of an income, viz., shelter, comfort, or service. But, on this ground, the armchair in which I sit should also be counted as capital productive of income, because it also renders me services. Some economists, indeed, go even this length, in particular Mr. Walras and Mr. Irving Fisher.

are merely the legal titles to it—the signs of it, as it were. We must be careful, therefore, not to count them twice over in the fortune of a country, once as titles and a second time in the material wealth they represent.

As for money, which may become anything we wish, we may class it, also, under productive capital with as much right as weights and measures or railway carriages, if we look on it simply as an instrument and vehicle of exchange.[1] But money when lent becomes *the* form of lucrative capital *par excellence ;* while, if used as an ornament, like the sequins which Eastern women wear round their necks, it is not capital at all, being neither lucrative nor productive, but a *consumption good.*

The important thing to remember then is, that capital which is used for producing new wealth is one thing ; capital which is used for producing income quite another. The income in the second case is not a new wealth for society ; it is simply a portion taken from the incomes of the lessee, the borrower, or the buyer.

In order to mark this distinction we shall call wealth which actually serves the purpose of production, *Productive Capital ;* wealth which serves only to bring in an income to its owner, *Lucrative Capital.*[2]

But this necessitates some explanation as to what we are to understand by the productivity of capital.

III : WHAT IS MEANT BY THE PRODUCTIVITY OF CAPITAL

THE part played by capital in production gives rise to trouble-some misconceptions. It is usually said that all capital yields

---

[1] This way of looking at it has been criticised. M. Chatelain, in particular, sees in money no more than a form of lucrative capital, because money, of itself. can produce nothing, and has no other rôle, when invested or put into business. than to bring in a profit. But the scales and touchstone which the Chinese merchant carries at his belt do not produce anything either : their sole object is to test the value of the ingots of silver. Yet, if they are indispensable to trade, they are capital. Why, then, should not the little ingot of silver itself be capital ?

[2] M. Böhm-Bawerk, in his book on capital, already quoted, approves of this classification and terminology. He prefers, however, to give to productive capital the name of *Social Capital,* and to lucrative capital that of *Individual Capital,* meaning thereby that the former alone counts as capital for society, the latter being simply capital for the individual. This is very true ; still, the expression may be misleading, for, from another point of view, lucrative capital cannot be conceived of apart from society, while productive capital may exist even for a Crusoe.

income—this seems to be of its very nature; and it is taken for granted that it yields it in the same way as a tree gives fruit or a hen lays eggs. Income is thus looked upon as a product due exclusively to capital.

What helps to spread this false idea is the fact that capital is most familiar to us in the form of Government stock, shares, and bonds, from which we tear off the coupon representing income. For six months or a year, as the case may be, the coupon grows; the day comes when it is ripe and ready to be gathered, and with a snip of the scissors we cut it off.

Further, capital seems to follow the same law of growth and multiplication as the animal and vegetable world. For, just as from the egg comes a hen which will produce more eggs, and from fruit grows a fruit-tree which will bring forth more fruit, so, out of income, when invested, comes capital which will produce more income. In fact, the law of compound interest causes an increase far more marvellous than even the multiplication of herrings or microbes. A single halfpenny put out at compound interest on the first day of the Christian era would amount by now to some thousands of millions of gold spheres as large as the earth. This is a famous arithmetical problem.

But we must get rid of all this phantasmagoria which arouses, not without reason, the socialist ire. This mysterious productive power attributed to capital, this generative force that is considered part of its nature, is a pure chimera. Whatever the proverb may say to the contrary, money does not beget money, and neither does capital. A bag of crowns, as Aristotle pointed out, has never been known to produce a single crown, any more than a bale of wool the smallest tuft of wool, or a plough little ploughs. And if it is true that sheep produce more sheep—as Bentham remarked, thinking thereby to refute Aristotle—it is not because they are capital, but because they are sheep, and endowed, like all living things, with the power of reproduction. Capital, in its capacity of raw material or instruments, is nothing but inert matter, and of itself absolutely barren. When, therefore, we talk of " productive " capital in opposition to "lucrative " capital, what we mean is simply capital as *an instrument of productive labour.*

It is true, as we saw (p. 114), that labour also, under the present economic conditions, is unproductive without the aid of capital. We might therefore be tempted to conclude that they are both on the same footing, and, like the two sexes, equally barren apart and equally creative when united. But this is not so. Capital, as we saw

(p. 98), is itself only a product of labour. To say that labour is fruitless without the help of capital is therefore simply to say that *present labour* cannot produce without the help of *past labour*. The ploughman, with the aid of a horse and plough, will produce much more corn than with his right arm alone : and it is the additional quantity of corn which constitutes the so-called income from capital. Still, it does not come from the plough. It comes from the man *aided by the plough.* And the plough itself is the result of some man's labour, past or present. We might call to mind here M. Alfred Fouillée's fine thought of the inventor of the plough working unseen alongside of the ploughman.

What misleads us is, that we see quite a number of well-to-do persons living on their incomes and even growing richer, without doing anything ; we take their incomes therefore to be a spontaneous yield from capital. In reality this income is the result of labour, but of labour which we do not see. *Somewhere or other, far or near, there are men working with this borrowed capital whose labour is producing the interest, profits, or dividends, which the owner of it receives.* The interest coupons of the shares or bonds of a coal-mining company represent the value of the tons of coal extracted by the labour of the miners ; those of a railway company represent the results of the labour of the engine-drivers, railwaymen, station-masters, pointsmen, who have co-operated in the work of transport.[1]

Even when the capital borrowed has been squandered or consumed unproductively, the labour is still going on somewhere. The interest, in this case also, is the product not of the borrower's own labour, but of the labour of some other person further removed. For instance, coupons of Government stock do not, as a rule, represent wealth produced by the labour or industry of the State, seeing that the latter is in the habit of spending most of the capital lent to it unproductively ; but they represent the product of the labour of all the citizens, which, in the form of taxes, has been paid annually into the Treasury, and which passes thence into the hands of the stock-holders. So, too, when a young man of rich family borrows money to throw away, the interest which he pays to the moneylender does not, certainly, represent the product of his own labour ; but it may represent that of the farmers on his estate, or,

[1] It does not necessarily follow, however, as socialists maintain, that the portion appropriated by capital in the form of income (interest, profit, etc.) is a spoliation of the workers. The whole question is, whether this portion so appropriated corresponds to a service rendered, indispensable to society. This is a matter, however, to which we shall return when we come to deal with " Income " (see Book III, chapters on *The Capitalist Rentier* and *The Entrepreneur*).

E

if he is borrowing on his inheritance, the product of his father's labour. And long after the capital lent has been squandered in riotous living, or blown away in smoke on the battlefield, it will still remain as lucrative capital, *i.e.* as a credit claim in the hands of the moneylender or the fundholder.

IV: FIXED CAPITAL AND CIRCULATING CAPITAL

CAPITAL in a concrete form, as used in production, does not last for ever. As a rule, it does not even last very long; for the very act of producing is its destruction, whether that act be instantaneous or repeated indefinitely. According, however, as its life is long or short, it may be used for a greater or smaller number of acts of production.

Capital in the abstract form of *values*, on the other hand, lasts for ever; for it is continually being renewed by repayment or redemption. It may take the form (*a*) of a value lent to a borrower, who has to pay a perpetual interest on it (*e.g.* a perpetual State loan), or who has to pay back the integral sum when the date of expiry falls due; this allows of its being again lent out at interest, and so on *ad infinitum ;* (*b*) of a value put into industry or trade by its owner, which reproduces not merely an income, but a sufficient surplus to replace itself in case of loss. It is this which makes economists so often compare capital to Proteus, or to the phœnix rising from its ashes.

Capital which can be used only once, because it is consumed in the act of production, is called *Circulating Capital—e.g.* wheat that is sown, manure that is put into the ground, coal that is burned, cotton that is spun. Capital which can be used for several productive acts, from the most fragile instruments, such as a needle or a bag, to the most enduring, such as a tunnel or a canal—even though these can only last by being kept in good condition, *i.e.* by being constantly renewed—is called *Fixed Capital.*[1]

The use of long-lived capital is of great advantage in production. However considerable may be the labour spent to set it up, however small the labour annually saved by using it, sooner or later a moment must come when the labour saved will be equal to the

[1] Some economists, however, apply another criterion to distinguish *fixed* from *circulating* capital. *Fixed* capital, according to them, is capital sunk in productive enterprises ; *circulating* capital is capital which only brings in profit by being exchanged.

This classification does not by any means fit in with the first. According to it, coal burned by a machine would be fixed capital, while it is circulating capital according to the definition in the text.

labour spent. When this moment comes, the capital is, to use the recognised expression, *redeemed*—that is to say, the labour henceforth economised will be a net gain for society. From this time on, and for so long as the capital lasts, the service it renders is gratuitous. The progress of civilisation tends continually to replace short-lived by long-lived capital. Three points, however, must be borne in mind :

(a) *The more lasting the capital, the more labour will be required to form it.* In this case, therefore, we have to strike a balance. As a rule, however, the extra labour spent is less than proportional to the increase of durability obtained, and this is just what makes the use of lasting capital profitable.

(b) The formation of fixed capital requires an immediate sacrifice in labour or expense, while the remuneration which it brings in economised labour or expense is postponed, *the delay being as a rule greater in proportion as the capital is more lasting.*

If the construction of the Panama Canal, for example, is to cost \$375,000,000, and is not to be redeemed for ninety-nine years, we must put into the balance, on the one hand, an immediate sacrifice of this amount, and on the other a remuneration for which we shall have to wait a whole century. Now, to establish such a balance, we must be gifted with a considerable degree of foresight and enterprise and with an unfailing faith in the future—a combination of conditions found only in very civilised communities. For this reason, peoples whose social condition is not very far advanced and whose political constitution offers but slight security rarely employ fixed capital. All their wealth takes the form of articles of consumption, or of circulating capital.[1]

(c) If fixed capital is too lasting, *it runs the risk of becoming useless.* Great prudence, therefore, is necessary in such undertakings as the above. For, after all, the durability of the actual capital itself is not the main thing : what matters most is the permanence of its utility. Now, if we can count to some extent on the first, we can never count absolutely on the second. Utility, as we know, is unstable ; a utility which we once looked on as most permanent may, after a time, completely vanish. When we pierce a tunnel or dig a canal there is nothing to guarantee that, within a century or two, traffic will not take some other route. And if this happens before the capital sunk in the tunnel has had

---

[1] Compare, for example, the kingdoms of India and Persia, where all the treasures of the "Arabian Nights" are still to be found, but hardly any railways, public roads, mines, or machinery.

time to be redeemed, a great amount of labour will have been spent in vain. It is prudent, therefore, seeing the uncertainty of the future, not to build for eternity; and, from this point of view, the employment of capital that is too long-lived may be dangerous.

The same holds good even in the case of lucrative capital. No individual, no bank, no loan association, would ever consent to advance capital which could not be redeemed or paid back before the end of two centuries. Why? Because such distant results do not enter into human calculations. We may lay it down as a fact that, in practice, no capital will be invested which does not offer the prospect of being recovered within three generations.

V: HOW CAPITAL IS FORMED

CAPITAL, being a *product*, can be formed, like any other product, only from the two original factors of all production, Labour and Nature. We have but to run over in our minds all the kinds of capital we can think of—tools, machinery, engineering works, materials of every description—to assure ourselves that they can have had no other origin.[1]

There would be no need to dwell on so obvious a point, were it not that some have seen an agent of a special nature at work in the formation of capital—namely, saving.[2] There is even a popular proverb to the effect that one can grow rich only by " working and saving." Labour we know; but what is this new personage, Saving, appearing on the scene? Can it be a third primary factor of pro duction that we have omitted? Certainly not: it is impossible to conceive of any others than labour and natural forces. Is it, then, a special form of labour? Some have taken this view. But what is there in common between labour and saving? To labour, is to act; to save, is to abstain.[3]

It is impossible to conceive how a purely negative act, a simple

---

[1] Karl Marx's expression that capital is "crystallised labour" would be true if, like all socialists, faithful to the principle that all value is due solely to labour, he did not purposely omit the share taken by nature in forming capital.

[2] It was the English economist, Senior, who said, that the third original factor of production after Labour and Nature, ought to be called, not Capital—since rapital is but a product and consequently a second-hand, factor—but *Abstinence*.

[3] Courcelle-Seneuil nevertheless maintained that "saving is but a form of labour" (see the article under this heading in the *Journal des Économistes*, June 1890). It is true that saving is sometimes, though not always, a pain (see Book IV, chap. iii, *Saving*); but it is not enough for an act to be painful to make it labour. Not to drink when thirsty is very painful, but it is not labour.

abstention, can produce anything. Montaigne may say, if he likes, that he knows " no doing more active and valiant than this not-doing." This may be very true from the moral point of view, but it does not explain how this " not-doing " can create a single pin.

When we say, then, that capital is created by saving, what we mean is simply that, if wealth were consumed at the rate at which it is made, capital would never be formed. It is obvious that, if the farmer's wife never left any eggs in the nest to be hatched, there could be no chickens. All the same, if a child were to ask where chickens came from, and we were to answer that the only way of producing chickens was to refrain from eating eggs, he might justly consider this good advice, but a feeble explanation.

Now, the reasoning which makes saving the primary cause of capital seems hardly more satisfactory. It amounts to saying that non-destruction ought to be classed among the causes of production—which is somewhat curious logic.

The formation of capital, in fact, always presupposes an excess of wealth produced over wealth consumed. But this may come about in two ways : either production may have exceeded wants, or consumption may have been painfully reduced below their level. The first way is, fortunately, by far the more frequent, and it is in this way alone that, historically speaking, capital has been formed. Of course, if man had not, like the ant and other animals, the faculty of foreseeing his future wants, it is certain that all the wealth produced would have been consumed or wasted from day to day—as it is among certain wild tribes ; capital would consequently never have been formed. Let us say, then, by all means, that foresight, sobriety, and other moral virtues are indispensable conditions to the original formation, and even to the preservation, of capital. But the Classical economists, in putting forward saving as an efficient cause of capital (they even call it *abstinence* to emphasise its painful aspect), do so, consciously or not, with the desire of justifying interest on capital as the remuneration of this abstinence.

What has suggested and accredited the idea that saving is the mother of capital, has been the use of money as almost the sole form of wealth. For, if we go back to the origin of all money-capital, we always find a certain number of coins which have been *put aside—i.e.* shut up in some money-box or safe or savings bank. Also we are in the habit of thinking only of *lucrative* capital. Now, in the case of the latter, it is true, we lend or invest only that which we do not ourselves need ; consequently all loan or invest-ment presupposes an excess of income over expenditure—*i.e.* a saving. And we conclude that all true capital, the capital of production, must have had the same origin. But therein lies our mistake.

Is there a single form of wealth to which we can point as created by abstinence ? The first stone axe of the man of the Quaternary Age was fashioned by a few extra hours of labour after a more than usually successful day's hunting, which gave him some free time in which to create this first capital. Do we imagine that primitive tribes, before passing from the hunting stage to that of agriculture, had first to lay up a store of provisions for a year in advance ? Far from it. They simply tamed cattle, and this cattle, which was their first capital, secured them against want for the morrow, and gave them leisure to undertake long labours. But in what way, as Bagehot [1] very aptly asks, does a herd of cattle represent saving ? Has its owner gone without anything on account of it ? On the contrary, thanks to the milk and meat he gets from it, he is better fed ; thanks to the wool and leather it gives him, he is better clothed.

We would not by any means dispute the importance of saving. But, if saving plays a large part in consumption (under which heading we shall come upon it again), we must not class it under production. Everything in its own place. Saving acts on production only when it returns to it in the form of *investment*—that is to say, when it disappears into production.[2]

[1] *Economic Studies*, pp. 166, 167.
[2] See Book IV, chap. iii, *Saving*.

PART II: THE ORGANISATION OF PRODUCTION

CHAPTER I: HOW PRODUCTION IS REGULATED

I: OF BUSINESS ENTERPRISES AND OF THE COST OF PRODUCTION

So far we have been studying the factors of production separately, and we have seen that each, by itself, can do nothing. In order to be of any use they must be united, either in the same hand, or, at least, under the same direction. How is this combination brought about?

It is possible that the three factors may be combined in the hands of one person, who, while owning a certain amount of land and capital, does the necessary labour himself. The peasant cultivating his own land with his own horse and plough is the typical form of this first method of production. He is called the *autonomous producer*.

But more often the same individual does not possess the three factors. One man will have his own labour and his land but no capital: such is the peasant who borrows on mortgage. Another will have his own labour and capital but no land, and will be obliged to take the last on lease: such is the farmer who farms land, or the shopkeeper who rents a shop. Others, again, will have land and capital, but will be unable or unwilling to furnish the labour; these will hire labourers.

We may even suppose the case of a producer who is unable himself to furnish labour, capital, or natural agents, and who will have to borrow the whole. Mines, railways, and the Suez Canal are enterprises of this nature; the ground (soil or subsoil) is obtained by long leases, the capital by loans and the issuing of shares, the manual labour by the hiring of thousands of workers.

Now, in all those cases in which the initiator of production borrows the whole or a part of the means of production from outside, he is called the *entrepreneur*. And his rôle, which is moreover the most important one of all, is to combine these elements of production so as to obtain the best possible results from them.

Enterprise is therefore the pivot of the whole economic mechanism. Everything turns on it. It is the point towards which all the factors

127

of production converge ; it is also, as we shall see, the point from which all the incomes diverge. For all the various forms of income which go by the names of interest, dividends, rents of all kinds, wages, salaries, are simply the prices obtained for the letting out of capital, land, or manual labour. The *entrepreneur*, then, is at the same time the one who sets the whole going, and the one who distributes the results.

We know from our study of the factors of production that, in order to produce any wealth whatever, a certain amount of pre-existing wealth must be consumed : the sum-total of this wealth consumed is what is called by economists the *Cost of Production*, and sometimes, by business men, the *Cost Price*.

Take, for instance, the working of an iron mine. The *entrepreneur* writes down under his expenses of production :

(1) The wages which he pays to the workers whom he has hired.

(2) The interest and the sinking-fund which he has to lay aside for the capital he has borrowed.

(3) The rent on the ground which he occupies, if, as in England, he has to pay a royalty to the landowner.

Even if he himself owns the ground and capital, this makes no difference in his calculation, since he would still include, in his cost of production, the interest on his own capital which he has put into the enterprise, and on that which he has used to buy the ground.

If, now, we pass from the extractive industry, which we have taken as example, to the industries of transformation, and follow the raw material—in this case ore—as it passes through the hands of the iron-worker or the manufacturer of ploughshares or of needles, we see that the original cost of production will grow like a snowball by the addition of layer after layer of costs of production, but that these will always be the same—namely, the price of the hire of labour, of capital and of land—*i.e.* wages, interest and rent.[1]

The *entrepreneur*, then, creates a balance between the sum of values destroyed and the value created. Naturally he will only go on with the work if he calculates that the value created will outweigh the value destroyed. It is really a kind of exchange that he is making : he is exchanging that which *is* for that which *will be*. He may possibly make a miscalculation, but this is accidental. It has often been

---

[1] Other costs of production besides these three fundamental ones will also appear on the balance-sheet of the *entrepreneur*, such as *insurance* against fire and accident, and also *taxation*.

said, and some great economists have even taught, that *value is determined by cost of production.* This statement is quite unfounded. We might equally well, and with more reason, say that it is the cost of production which is determined by the value of the object we wish to produce. For, before he undertakes to produce a new article, the first rule of the *entrepreneur's* art is to ask himself at what price he will be able to sell it, and then to arrange not to spend more in the production of it than it will be worth, particularly if it be an article already quoted on the market. Anyone wanting to undertake the working of a coal-mine would say to himself : " Coal being worth so much a ton in this district, let me see if I can extract it at a remunerative price—*i.e.* at a price which will leave a margin of profit." Suppose he has calculated badly, and is obliged to spend more in extracting the coal than it is worth, his foolishness will not raise its value by a single farthing. It will only have the effect of ruining him and forcing him to close the mine.

Still, is it not the case that, in reality, the selling price of nearly all objects tends to approach cost price, or at least to follow it in its variations, as if there were some link or necessary interdependence between them ? True, but this may be explained in the simplest way. It is a case not of cause and effect, but simply of the action of an outside force, competition, which tends always, like a sort of atmospheric pressure, to bring together the *cost of production and the value of each product*—a pressure which increases as the gap between the two widens. For it is easy to see that, so soon as the margin between cost of production and value has become large enough to allow a considerable profit to the *entrepreneur*, competitors will rush in, and by greatly increasing the quantity of the product, bring down its value and its price.[1] We may even assert that, under

[1] Two exceptions must, however, be noted :

(*a*) The value of certain articles may remain permanently *far above the cost of production ;* this is the case in monopolies, where competition does not act, or where it exercises a pressure only up to the level of the heaviest cost of production, thus leaving a margin which, as we shall see later, is what economists call rent.

(*b*) The value of certain articles may fall *below the cost of production* without, however, production ceasing ; as when, owing to some progress in industry, the cost price of an object gradually falls. In this case competition continually brings back the price to the level of the cost, not of production but of *reproduction,* which, for the products of industry, is generally lower than the original cost. It is also possible that capital sunk in an enterprise may be unable to be withdrawn—*e.g.* capital invested in mines or railways. In this case, the enterprise will continue, even if it does not cover the interest on, and redemption of, the initial capital, if only it is able to bring in a little more than the cost of working.

E*

a system of perfectly free competition, there would be a perfect coincidence between value and cost of production. This is one of the most important laws of political economy, for, as we shall see in the next chapter, it is this law which automatically regulates production.

Here, however, we come upon a difficulty. If the value of all things tends to coincide with their cost of production, it would seem as if the human race were being tricked somewhat in the same way as the Danaïdes, who were continually filling a bottomless jar. For, if every act of production only reproduces, in the form of new values, old values which have been destroyed, wherein is the profit or the progress ? It is not easy to understand how civilisation could ever have developed, or humanity raised itself above the animal level, if production did not normally leave a net product over, to serve for the expansion of man's consumption and for the increase of his capital. It is clear that if man did not gather more wheat than he consumed for sowing, he would long ago have died of hunger.

To solve this apparent contradiction, it is enough, as in other difficulties of economic science, to distinguish between the *individual* cost of production and the *social* cost of production.

In the case of the individual *entrepreneur*, what he rightly calls his expenses, his costs, his sacrifices, are in reality the incomes of his collaborators. These are, as we have seen, wages, interest, rent — *i.e.* the incomes of the workers, capitalists and landowners. Thus even if, owing to competition, the value of the products were to leave nothing over and above these costs of production, this would be unfortunate for the *entrepreneur*,[1] but the enterprise would still be remunerative for all his collaborators, to whom it would be bringing incomes. For them the net income might be enormous, although there was no income for the *entrepreneur*.

Still, even for society as a whole, surely there must be a cost of production ? For society has not the faculty of being able to produce without consuming. True ; but, for society, the cost of production is made up solely of the values actually consumed in production, the raw material that has been destroyed, and the instruments that have been worn out, the time and life spent.

---

[1] We shall see later on, moreover, that, even in such a case as this, the *entrepreneur* would not be much to be pitied, since he would still get a share, if not as *entrepreneur*, at least in his threefold capacity of worker, capitalist and landowner ; only these shares are written down not under profits, but under costs of production (see *Profit*).

II : THE AUTOMATIC REGULATION OF PRODUCTION

HEALTH, for the social body as for all living bodies, lies in a right equilibrium between production and consumption.

Not to produce enough is an evil, since a certain category of wants must remain unsatisfied. To produce too much is another evil, not so great, perhaps, but none the less real. All over-production involves not merely a waste of wealth, but a waste of energy, and consequently a useless pain.

Where each man produces for his own consumption, like Crusoe on his island, or rather, as in the first phase of domestic industry, like the family of antiquity or the community of the Middle Ages, the equilibrium between production and consumption is easily established. Each of us individually (or each small group) is capable of foreseeing his own wants and—though his previsions may not be infallible—of regulating his production accordingly.

The problem is not quite so simple when the producer no longer produces for himself or his family, but for a customer, for others.; for obviously it is less easy to foresee the wants of others than our own. Still, even under the system of the division of labour and of exchange, it is not so very difficult to establish an equilibrium between production and wants so long as the producer works *to order*, or at least so long as the habits of each customer are known and his consumption is easy to foresee. The baker, or the confectioner, can calculate fairly exactly the number of loaves or cakes which he will sell in a day.

But where the problem becomes really difficult is under an economic *régime* like our own, where the market has become immense, and the manufacturer no longer takes his orders from the consumer but from shopkeepers, intermediaries, and speculators, who anticipate the wants of the public, and buy and sell *on credit*.[1]

And yet it was precisely on the advent of this new *régime*, that the legislator, abandoning all the ancient system of regulation, decided that liberty should be the only rule in production. It is well known that the French Revolution, by the celebrated law of

---

[1] It is this anxiety to regulate production according to wants that explains, in part at least, the rigorous regulation of industry in past civilisations ; whether we take the caste system, in which no person was allowed, on principle, to follow any other trade than that of his father ; or the guild system, under which no one could take up a trade without the King's leave (Esmein, *Histoire du Droit*). And this applied not only to trades but to agricultural production and to commerce, which were regulated to excess. It was forbidden, *e.g.* to turn corn-land into vineyard, for fear of a corn famine or of over-production of wine.

17 March, 1791, abolished the guild system—under which no individual could take up a trade unless he had fulfilled certain conditions—and proclaimed the freedom of labour, or the right of every individual to produce whatsoever he chose. This reform, which met with unanimous approval, was not long in being imitated throughout Europe.

But has not this liberty on the part of every one to produce what he likes added a new uncertainty to the anticipation of wants, and thus brought anarchy into production ?

Socialists, particularly those of the first half of the nineteenth century, assert that it has. Classical economists, on the contrary, have been overwhelmed with admiration at the sight of the order and equilibrium which reign in production.

It is, in fact, at first glance, a somewhat perplexing phenomenon, that hundreds of millions of men should, without any previous understanding, be able to find every day just what they want—those at least who are able to pay. What Providence, what occult force, thus regulates the production of wealth from day to day, so that there is neither too much nor too little ?

The explanation given by the Classical economists is quite simple. Production, they say, is regulated in a very sure, simple, and rapid way by the law of supply and demand, which may be put thus : articles are worth more or less, according as the quantity produced is more or less adequate to man's wants.

If some branch of industry has not enough workers or capital, the want to which it corresponds will remain unsatisfied, and its products will acquire a higher value. The producers, especially the *entrepreneur*, who is the principal agent of production and the first to benefit by a rise in prices, realise larger profits. Other producers, capitalists and working men, attracted by profits above the average, enter into the same line of business. The production of the articles thus increases until the quantity produced has reached the level of the quantity demanded.

On the other hand, when a larger quantity of any article has been produced than is wanted, its value is bound to fall. This has the effect of reducing the income of the producers, and in particular the profits of the *entrepreneur*—the man who feels most directly every consequence. He withdraws, therefore, from a path of miscalculation and loss, and the production of the article slows down until the quantity produced has fallen to the level of the quantity consumed.

Such is the fine harmony of the spontaneous organisation of

production so often praised by Bastiat. It is a sort of automatic self-regulating mechanism, far superior, say the economists, to any artificial regulation, however perfect.[1]

This law is undoubtedly true as a tendency, but, before it can be free to operate, many conditions are necessary which we rarely find fulfilled.

First, supply must answer instantaneously to demand. The factors of production must therefore be absolutely mobile and able to move with lightning rapidity from the points where they are in excess, to those where they ·are scarce. There must be one single world-market, or at any rate markets closely interdependent, like communicating-jars, so that once the level is disturbed it may be re-established almost at once. Now, though we may admit that the tendency of the economic world is towards such a state, we have to own that it is still far from being an accomplished fact. All agricultural or industrial production, indeed, involves the investing of capital for a longer or shorter period (see *supra*, p. 122, *Fixed Capital and Circulating Capital*), and this capital, by the very fact that it has become " fixed," ceases to be mobile. The wine-growers of France are told that they are producing too much wine and that they must turn to something else ; and it is quite probable that, in the end, the law of supply and demand will force them to do so, if only through the competition of Algerian wines. But what is to be done with the seven or eight billion francs of capital sunk in the earth in the form of plantations and cellars ?

Nor is this all. Just where its action has fullest play the law of supply and demand shows an utter lack of harmony. For we must not forget that value has no relation to utility in the ordinary and normal sense of this word. The law of supply and demand distributes products and professions, not according to man's real wants, but according to his desires and the price which he is able or willing to spend on satisfying them (see *supra*, *Utility*).

The result is that some of the most useful occupations, such as agriculture, tend to be neglected, while the most unproductive ones, such as shopkeeping in towns—not to mention the great number of parasitical public offices—are multiplied to absurdity. If we compare the French census of 1906 with that of 1866, we see that, within the short period of forty years, the number of agriculturists in France has scarcely increased, while that of shopkeepers has more

---

[1] They give wheat as an example ; and certainly, although the wheat trade is no longer regulated, famines have disappeared from most countries.

than doubled.[1] In the medical profession, again, there is an ample supply of doctors if only they were better distributed ; but they are nearly all concentrated in towns, where, from lack of patients, they are reduced to the worst expedients in order to live, while the country districts meanwhile are under-supplied. When an epidemic of smallpox broke out in Brittany, in January 1893, the newspapers pointed out that there was not a single doctor within a radius of nine miles.[2]

Lastly, we must point out that " demand " does not come directly from the consumers, but from intermediaries, shopkeepers and speculators : that it is based not so much on real and present wants, as on future and presumed ones, and that consequently it is liable to error. Speculators may possibly have counted on wants which will never exist, in which case there will be over-production. Or they may have under-estimated wants, in which case there will be a deficit.[3] We shall come to this presently in the chapter on *How Production is Regulated.*

III : COMPETITION

In order to have full play, the law of supply and demand pre-supposes freedom of labour ; and freedom of labour, in its active form, is called *competition*. Competition thus appears as the great regulator of the whole economic mechanism of our modern societies.

Formerly it was the rule in treatises on Political Economy to attribute the following virtues to competition :

(1) Competition adapted production to consumption, and thus maintained the *economic equilibrium*.

(2) It stimulated *progress* by the emulation to which it gave rise among competing industries, the unfit being ruined and thus eliminated.

---

[1] See M. March, *Résultats statistiques du Recensement général de la population,* vol. i.

[2] In Paris, the number of doctors to each quarter shows eloquently that they are distributed, not according to illness, but according to profits, the proportion varying from 1 in every 94 inhabitants in some of the wealthy quarters, to 1 in 6000 in the poorer quarters ; and in one district (St. Fargeau) 1 in 17,772 inhabitants.

[3] It must not, from this, be too hastily concluded that speculation, *i.e.* the act of anticipating future events, is necessarily an evil. On the contrary, the speculator who buys in anticipation of a famine, or who sells in anticipation of plenty, may have a salutary regulative influence on the market. But speculation, after all is very apt to make mistakes, especially when it turns to gambling.

(3) It caused a steady *lowering of prices,* thus resulting in *cheapness,* to the great advantage of all, especially the poorer classes.

(4) It gradually *equalised conditions,* reducing profits and wages to practically the same level in all industries.

And economists of the Optimist school, like Bastiat, were never weary of praising these " harmonies," no less wonderful to them than Pythagoras' music of the spheres. They saw in competition a *spontaneous* or *natural* organisation, and they concluded that it was perfect of its kind and final.[1]

To-day this enthusiasm has slightly cooled down. Closer observation of facts and the actual results of freedom have not justified this optimistic faith. We have come to realise that the system of competition is no more, as it is no less, natural and spontaneous than many other forms of organisation which preceded it ; family industry, for example, or the caste, or the guild, system—for these, also, were the natural outcome of historical evolution. As for its beneficent effects, they are somewhat questionable. We recognise, on the contrary :

(*1*) That so far as the equilibrium between production and wants is concerned, competition ensures it only in a very irregular manner, if it does not even at times imperil it (see p. 139, *Overproduction and the Law of Markets*).

(*2*) That if free competition as a rule stimulates producers by

---

[1] See the description of it, a very fine one, moreover, which Bastiat gives in his *Harmonies* (chapter on *l'Organisation naturelle*).

To show how ideas have since changed, we shall quote the high-flown expressions of the first *Dictionnaire d'Économie politique,* published in 1852 by Messrs. Coquelin and Guillaumin, under the word *Competition :* " The principle of competition is too inherent in the earliest conditions of social life, it is at the same time too great, too lofty, too sacred, and, in its general application, too high above the reach of the pigmies who menace it, to need defending. We do not defend the sun, though it sometimes burns the earth ; neither need we defend competition, which is, to the industrial world, what the sun is to the physical world." And J. S. Mill is hardly less categorical : ". . . I conceive that . . . every restriction of it is an evil, and every extension of it . . . is always an ultimate good " (*Principles of Political Economy,* Book IV, chap. vii).

To-day, the Mathematical school of economy has taken up this same attitude again, and points out how, of all imaginable modes of organisation, the system of free competition is the one which realises for each individual the maximum of final utility (or ophelimity), but it declares that this state is purely hypothetical. M. de Molinari goes still further : he professes that all these objections are due to the imperfection of the system of free competition, and would disappear if it were fully carried out. (See, in particular, his book, *Comment se résoudra la question sociale.*)

the spirit of emulation which it maintains among them, it hampers them in other ways—*e.g.* as regards the *quality* of the goods. Every competitor, in order to keep up in the struggle, taxes his ingenuity to the utmost to substitute raw material of an inferior and cheap quality for that of a superior and dear quality ; so that, of all progress, the most remarkable has been that which has taken place in the adulteration of food, which has become a veritable art, turning to account all the latest discoveries of science.[1]

The monopolist, on the other hand, finds it as a rule greatly to his interest to maintain the superior quality of his goods, and the reputation of his trade mark becomes almost a point of honour.

(*3*) That free competition does not always ensure cheapness and sometimes may even provoke a rise in prices.   True, wherever competition has free play, it tends to bring down the value of all articles to the level of cost of production. But how does it do this ? By two consecutive acts : (*a*) by increasing the number of producers ; (*b*) by causing a fall in prices owing to the struggle which takes place among them.   Now, very often, the first effect only is produced, and that to an extent far beyond what is required.   The second does not take place ; for the new additional producers come to an understanding, tacit or otherwise, with the old, to raise the price to a level which will allow them all to make a living. Thus only the hurtful effect of competition remains. The most striking example is that of two or three competing railway lines between two towns. The traffic, which remains the same, has obviously to support two or three times over the costs of construction and of working. Another good example is the baker's trade. The number of bakers is ridiculously large. Each baker, selling less and less as a result of competition, is obliged to make good the deficiency by earning more on each article. A new competitor cannot bring down prices, as they are already so low that the older producers can make only a bare living. On the contrary, he will force them up, as one more will have to live on the same quantity as was sold before.[2] As M. de

---

[1] There are innumerable examples of this. It is possible now to make drinkable wine without grapes, jam without fruit or sugar, butter without milk, milk without cows, even eggs without hens, and to manufacture silks which contain 5 per cent. of silk and 95 per cent. of mineral matter.

[2] Formerly the number of bakers in each town was fixed in proportion to the population and bread was relatively cheaper than to-day. In Paris, not more than thirty years ago, there was one baker for every 1800 inhabitants ; to-day there is one for every 1300 inhabitants, or, if we include the branch establishments, 1 for eve y 800. The consequence is, that in order to live, a baker

Foville very well puts it, the competition of shopkeepers forces prices up, just as that of trees in a lofty forest sends them skywards to dispute the air and light.

Monopoly, on the other hand, does not imply an absolutely free hand. Prices, under monopoly, are no more arbitrary than under the competitive system. In both cases they are subject to the general law of values, the price of an object being limited by the desires of the consumers for it and the sacrifices which they will make to obtain it. Without entering into the difficult question of how prices are determined under a system of monopoly,[1] we would simply point out that it is to the interest of every monopolist to reduce his prices in order to increase his sales, on the principle of the Bon Marché, " small profits, quick returns."

It is not certain, either, that competition will eliminate only the backward and unfit. If it were nothing more than a form of emulation, it would ensure victory to the most moral, the most conscientious, the most altruistic, in which case it would be a means of progress and of true selection. But, as it is above all a struggle for life, it gives the victory to the strongest and most cunning, and may thus cause a veritable moral retrogression, since, as the French proverb says, " we needs must howl with the wolves." It may quite well eliminate the honest—e.g. the scrupulous shopkeeper who will not adulterate his products or who shuts his shop on Sunday ; the manufacturer who will not reduce the wages of his workers or increase the length of their working day. We shall see further on that honest industry is hardly able to cope with the competition of the sweating system.[2]

(4) That competition does not necessarily equalise profits and

must make 12 centimes per kilo. of bread (this is the unofficial valuation pub-lished periodically by the Prefecture of the Seine), whereas the large co-operative bakeries can cover their costs with a gain of no more than two or three centimes per kilo.

No one has denounced the evils of competition, in particular its seemingly paradoxical effect of raising prices, in a more spirited fashion than Fourier. But even J. S. Mill, whose energetic remarks in favour of competition we have already quoted, admitted (in a declaration before a Commission of the House of Commons, June 6, 1850) that the middlemen come in for an extravagant part of the total produce of the labour of society, and that competition has rather the effect of distributing the sum total over a greater number and of reducing the share of each, than of bringing down the proportion of what the class as a whole obtains.

[1] On this question see the interesting chapters in Cournot's *Théorie mathé-matique des richesses*, and *infra*, the chapter on *Prices*.

[2] The word competition contains, in fact, two quite separate ideas, though these, as a rule, are not distinguished :

One is that of the *freedom of labour*, or the liberty for every man to follow the

fortunes, since it is after all a veritable war, giving victory to the strong by crushing the weak. Now, we do not find that political wars equalise the power of nations, nor that the " struggle for life " among the animal and vegetable species allows them to develop equally. On the contrary, it is the elimination of the less fit that this doctrine implies. It is in countries like the United States, where industrial competition is in full force, that the most colossal fortunes are made.

(5) Finally, the most curious and unexpected result of all is that the state of competition is not a stable state. Experience shows that it tends to destroy itself by giving birth to monopoly. For, by the very act of eliminating small in favour of large undertakings, it encourages the growth of giant enterprises which aim at suppressing all competition. And these large producers try, in turn, to combine themselves into gigantic national syndicates (trusts, as they are called in the United States, cartels in Germany), which control despotically, at least for a time, some one entire branch of production. These trusts render real services, as we shall see further on ; but, in order to guarantee the public against their power and their practical monopoly, there is a tendency on the part of the State to intervene, at any rate until consumers take their defence into their own hands and organise themselves into federations.

It is quite possible to imagine, and we are already beginning to see, a state of things in which agreements between manufacturers and their employees through their respective unions, and between producers and consumers through co-operative associations, will dispel most of the evils of competition without reducing us to the necessity of placing the freedom of labour under the yoke of official ιegulation.[1]

line which he prefers. In France, as we have said, it dates from the Revolution of 1789.

The other is that of the *struggle for life ;* a chance for every man to arrive first if he can. This second idea did not appear till much later, under the influence of Spencer and Darwin.

Under the first aspect, competition, although it has not all the virtues attributed to it, cannot but win approval. Under the second, however, it has more dangers than virtues and needs to be carefully controlled (see the chapter on *Co-operation*).

[1] Apart from economic considerations, there are moral and philosophical reasons for believing that *co-operation* is destined gradually to take the place of *competition*. Even in biology, there is a new school which inclines to the idea that association and mutual help may be as powerful a factor in the progress and amelioration of species as the struggle for life (see Geddes and Thompson, *Evolution of Sex ;* de Lanessan, *La lutte pour l'existence ;* Kropotkine, *Mutual Aid*).

IV: OVER-PRODUCTION AND THE LAW OF MARKETS

JUDGING by the poverty of the great majority of mankind, it would seem as if production always lagged behind wants, and as if all our efforts should be turned towards hastening it on as much as possible. This is in fact what we actually do, and yet, curiously enough, it is the opposite fear of an excess of production—of a general glut on the market, as the English economists call it—which torments manufacturers and business men, and which we hear so often expressed. How can we explain this ?

The Classical economists have never shared these apprehensions; the peril of a general glut is, in their eyes, altogether imaginary and absurd. They do not, indeed, deny that in some, or even in many, branches of industry production may outstrip demand, owing to miscalculation. But they deny the real possibility of *general* over-production, and attribute the semblance of it to an optical illusion, the cause of which, they say, is easy to understand. The producers whose articles have flooded the market, and are in consequence not selling well, make a great outcry ; but those whose articles are scarce, and are therefore selling well, say nothing. Hence we hear only of over-production, and we end by believing that it exists everywhere.

Further, the Classical economists hold that, given a glut in one branch of production, the very best remedy that can be applied is to push production forward proportionately in the other branches. A crisis due to abundance can only be cured by abundance, according to the device of a celebrated school of medicine : *similia similibus.* Thus it is to the interest of all producers that production should be as abundant and varied as possible. This theory is known as the Law of Markets (*la loi des débouchés*). It was first formulated by J. B. Say, who declared, with pride, that it " would change the policy of the whole world." It may be expressed as follows : *the greater the number and variety of products, the more markets will there be for each one.*

To understand this theory, we must first put money out of the question, and suppose that goods are exchanged directly for other goods, as under the system of barter. Take, for instance, a trader arriving at one of the great markets of Central Africa. Will it not be to his interest that the market there should be as well stocked as possible with all kinds of products ? It will not, of course, be to his advantage to find there a large quantity of the same merchandise as he himself is bringing, say rifles ; but it certainly will be to his interest to find as many other kinds of produce as possible—ivory, gum. gold dust, etc. Each new article put on the market means another opportunity for disposing of his own, or, as this theory calls it, an *additional market* for his own goods ; the more the better, therefore. And, even if our merchant has had the misfortune to bring too many rifles. the next best thing that can happen to him will be for others also to have brought too many goods to the market. In this case the rifles will not be in excess relatively to the other commodities ; for, as J. B. Say aptly puts it, " what best helps on the sale of one commodity is the production of another."

It is just the same, he says, under the system of purchase and sale. Each of us has a better chance of disposing of his goods in proportion as others have more money, and the more goods they produce the more money they will have.

The best, therefore, that we can wish for a producer who has produced too much of anything, is that others may have done the same ; excess on the one side will counteract excess on the other. Has England produced too many cotton goods this year ? Well, if India by good luck has produced too much corn this same year, England will find it more easy to dispose of her cottons there. Suppose that, owing to an extraordinary increase in mechanical power, an enormous quantity of manufactured goods is thrown on the market, while the products of agriculture, which has not kept pace with industry, have increased but slightly. The value of agricultural products, in relation to manufactured articles, will have gone up, and consumers, obliged to spend a great deal on their food, will not have much money left to spend on manufactured goods. Suppose, on the other hand, that, owing to an increase in agricultural production, the balance is re-established. Consumers, spending less on food, will have no difficulty in absorbing the surplus of manufactured articles.

Still, even on the hypothesis that the quantity of all articles increases simultaneously, it is quite possible for prices to fall, and articles to be sold at a loss. How do we account for this ? The answer is that there is one product, and only one, whose quantity has not increased, viz., money. The value-relation between money and goods in general has therefore changed. As money is relatively scarce, prices have gone down. But *if money could be multiplied in the same proportion as the other commodities* the evil would be cured ; for, in this case, the value-relation called price would not change and the crisis would not occur. This hypothesis therefore only confirms the law.

To sum up, then, we may say, that the theory of markets tends simply to prove that there is no danger in over-production, *so long as the increase in production takes place simultaneously and proportionately in all branches.* For, as in this case there is no change in the relation between the quantities exchanged, the economic equilibrium will not be disturbed.[1]

Unfortunately, increase in production never takes place as the theory of markets would have it. It could, no doubt, be demonstrated mathematically that there is not one chance in a million of its taking place simultaneously and equally in all branches of production. It is by fits and starts, locally and intermittently, that the increase in production manifests itself. Moreover, for the theory of markets to operate, countries must not be separated by partitions, in the form of protective duties, which prevent an excess of goods in one country from pouring over into another and render a general level of the world-market impossible.

This is why the law of markets, though true in principle, is not able to prevent the repeated disturbances of equilibrium in exchange which bring on crises. This is also why producers nowadays try to ward off such disturbances by commercial agreements (cartels, trusts), which are one of the most interesting phenomena of our time, and which we shall study further on. These consist in reciprocal engagements, on the part of producers of some one branch of industry, not to produce more than a certain fixed amount, according to the state of the market.

Can the State do anything to avert these crises of over-production or partial over-production ? Some interesting experiments in this direction have recently been tried by different Governments, as, for instance, that of the Brazilian Government in regard to coffee. In order to relieve the market in times of glut, the Government bought enormous quantities of coffee, which it kept in reserve to sell in times of scarcity. This proceeding, which has been called the " valorisation " of coffee, reminds one of that of Joseph in Egypt, when he caused the public granaries to be filled during the years of the seven fat kine in order to sell the corn during those of the seven

---

[1] Still, even so, would not production in excess of wants be an evil, since there would be a waste of productive forces ?   The Classical theory, however, will not admit the possibility of such a hypothesis, since, in actual fact, we are far from the point when all human wants will be satiated.

M. Aftalion nevertheless criticises the Classical doctrine, in a series of articles which appeared in the *Revue d'Économie politique,* 1909, and tries to prove that general over-production is by no means a chimera, but may actually come about as a result of the decrease in the final utility of all products.

lean kine. And the results seem to have been fairly good, though this is a disputed point.[1]

V : CRISES

The study of crises has often been presented as the pathological side of Political Economy. Crises, in fact, may very well be likened to diseases of the economic organism; they offer as varied characteristics as the innumerable ailments which afflict mankind. Some are short and violent, like attacks of fever, and manifest themselves by a high temperature followed by sudden depression; others are slow, " like anæmia "—to take the words of M. de Laveleye. Some are peculiar to one country; others are epidemic and go the round of the world.

But these are, after all, metaphors, and we must ask whether crises really are maladies leading perhaps to death or, at any rate, enfeebling and wearing out the social body; or whether they are not signs of growth, the manifestation of an exuberant vitality closely bound up with economic progress, perhaps even the necessary condition of it.

It is under one or other of these two aspects, pessimistic or optimistic, that crises have been considered by economists. But before looking for the causes of crises let us see by what symptoms they are revealed.

All crises are heralded by the same precursory signs: an increasing activity in business, sales, investments, discount, a rise in the prices of goods, in Stock Exchange quotations, and in wages. All these movements become more and more accentuated, until a critical moment arrives—the actual moment of the crisis—when they are reversed, and the rising or falling curves suddenly change their direction. What we then see is : in the case of goods, sale at a loss, a fall in prices, the failure of business firms; in the case of capital, a scarcity of money-capital, difficulty in obtaining it,[2] a rise

---

[1] The Greek and Portuguese Governments, in order to counteract the overproduction of raisins and wine, have forbidden, or limited, the planting of new vines.

[2] At the height of the crisis of 1907, in New York, even the wealthiest found it impossible to obtain money. There was a wild run on the banks, which forced many, though perfectly solvent, to suspend payment until £24,000,000 of gold could be brought over from Europe. And yet the quantity of coin had never been more plentiful (33 dollars per head, instead of 22 as in 1897). But the defective organisation of the banks prevented its being utilised (see *infra*, chapter on *Banks*).

in the rate of interest and discount, perhaps even the suspension of bank payments, involving the forced circulation of bank notes.

A period of calm follows ; economic life resumes its normal train until there is a renewed activity and another cycle begins. The most striking characteristic, therefore, of crises, is their periodic recurrence.

Stanley Jevons had noticed that, during the nineteenth century, crises had followed one another at almost regular intervals of ten years : 1815, 1827, 1836, 1847, 1857, 1866, 1873, 1882. And, if he had lived longer than 1882, he would have had the satisfaction of seeing the last two crises of the century appear exactly at the expected moment, one in 1890 and the other in 1900.

Such regularity could not be attributed to chance ; it suggested the idea of some astronomical cycle. So we find Jevons turning to the skies for an explanation, and believing he had found it in the periodic recurrence of sun-spots, the varying intensity of the sun's rays—corresponding to the maxima or minima of these spots—resulting in good or bad harvests, which again determine crises.

But this is mere romancing.[1] Not only has it not been demonstrated that sun-spots have any influence whatever on harvests, nor even harvests on crises, but the recurrence of the decennial periods does not seem to have the characteristics of a natural law. The twentieth century has given it a direct contradiction, as the first crisis occurred in 1907. Moreover, there is always something a little arbitrary in the enumeration and chronology of crises ; for, in the first place, it is not easy to fix the precise moment at which they break forth, as it varies from one country to another ; and, in the second place, there are crises and crises. Some are of the nature of cyclones ; some are simple atmospheric depressions hardly worth considering.

Having abandoned the astronomical explanation of crises, it was necessary to find another. Economists have been at no loss. A German writer, Mr. Bergmann, in 1895, counted 230 explanations, and there have been others since then. It is not much to be wondered at after all. Since, by definition, a crisis is a general disturbance of the economic order, it is not surprising that all the phenomena of economic life—prices, profits, discount, investments, issues of notes

[1] This theory has, however, been adopted again quite recently and adapted to later astronomical observations, by Jevons' son, in an article in the *Contemporary Review* (August 1909).

or of securities, trade, wages, etc.—should be affected and should seem bound up with the crisis either as cause or as effect.[1]

At bottom, all these explanations are closely connected ; they may, however, be classed under two categories, according as they offer for principal cause, either over-production, or under-consumption. But it is evident that over-production and under-consumption are simply two faces of the same phenomenon, namely, a disproportion between production and consumption, which, however, appears under a different aspect according to the side from which we look at it.

(a) The explanation of over-production rises naturally to the mind when we look at the vertiginous progress of industry. We see manufacturers, stimulated by competition and by the fall in profits which it involves, exercising all their ingenuity to escape it. To this end they anticipate wants and produce in advance ; and a moment comes when production, having far outstripped, if not potential wants, at least the power of the consumers to absorb the stock produced, the *débâcle* begins, and a general fall in prices follows.

---

[1] The latest and most complete account of the theories of crises and their causes will be found in M. Lescure's book, *Des crises générales et périodiques de surproduction* (2nd ed., 1910). Among others :

(a) Variations in the quantity of the medium of exchange, metallic or paper money (De Laveleye) ;

(b) The tendency of profits to fall, which discourages industry (Ricardo and Henry George) ;

(c) Excess of saving and the investment of it in unconsumable capital (Sismondi) ;

(d) Insufficiency of wages and the reduction of consumption which results from it (Karl Marx and all the socialists) ;

(e) Variations in savings, which are accumulated as a reserve and then dispersed in circulating capital, so that they are not available for the reconstituting of fixed capital (Tugan-Baranowsky) ;

(f) The necessity for creating new means of production before objects of consumption can be produced, an operation which requires a fairly long time, so that when, finally, the instruments of production are ready, there are more of them than is required (Aftalion) ;

(g) The rise in cost of production, which takes place more quickly than does a rise in prices, whereby profit disappears and production is stopped (Lescure). M. Lescure divides all these theories into two groups : one, which he calls *organic* theories, in which the explanation is sought in the evolution of the capitalist system ; the other, which he calls *inorganic* (mechanic might be a better word), in which it is sought in a disturbance of the equilibrium between production and consumption. We are not able to seize the opposition, as all the theories given imply a disturbance of equilibrium in the economic order. But it seems, according to the examples given, to correspond somewhat to the pessimistic and optimistic theories mentioned above.

Manufacturers, to avoid selling at a loss, try to obtain money by discount, or by selling their securities, whence results a rise in the rate of discount and a fall in Stock Exchange values. So that, by very reason of the superabundance of goods, money becomes scarce, and those manufacturers who are unable to obtain it, fail. All the manifestations of crises mentioned above are, therefore, asily explained.

So also is their periodic recurrence. For we can easily understand that this alternative movement, by which production now goes ahead of consumption, now lags behind it, is necessarily a rhythmic movement. After each crisis, industry requires a certain amount of time in which to make good its losses, renew its reserves, and equip itself again with a view to new wants.

Note that it is quite possible for the excess of production to be not real, but virtual, that is to say, to exist, not as yet in the form of actual products, but in the form of enterprises launched by speculators on the financial market. This is quite enough to provoke a crisis; it is, indeed, one of the most frequent causes. The speculator thinks that the demand for motor cars, india-rubber, phosphates, etc., is going to be enormous. A host of such enterprises is started; great quantities of capital are sunk in railways, mines, plantations, factories; all sorts and descriptions of shares are issued. The value of these rises for a time : then one day it is found that some one product will no longer sell. The scrip, which represents the money value of these enterprises and of so many anticipated incomes, or, as Professor Seligman has eloquently put it, " the capitalising of so many hopes," comes down with a run : one after another the shares fall like a house of cards, and the capital sunk, which they represented, has no further value.

Note, also, that it does not at all follow that the over-production is general. On the contrary, if it were altogether general and proportionately the same in all products (a most unlikely hypothesis), there would not be a crisis, as we pointed out in the last chapter. It is partial over-production—that is to say, over-production in a few industries—that first starts the crisis, which then becomes general.[1]

(b) The explanation of under-consumption is more obvious to those who look at the miseries of the actual economic state, i.e. to socialists and those in sympathy with them. They do not deny that crises are caused occasionally by over-production due to the

[1] Thus the crisis of 1907, which wrought such havoc in the United States, began by an abnormal rise in copper and in all copper and mining stocks, followed by a sudden drop in the same.

greed of capitalists who try to make up in quantity for a reduced rate of profits. But the fundamental cause, in their view, is the insufficiency of money among the great mass of consumers of the working class, of wage-earners, who have not the wherewithal to buy back the products of their own labour. For it is useless to say that human wants are unlimited, or capable of infinite expansion. To sell an article, it is not enough to find some one who merely wants it : we have to find some one *able to pay for it*. Now the income of the great mass of the people has not, on the whole, increased at the same rate as manufacturing production. And, as these two causes, opposite in nature but one in tendency— viz., the growing necessity, on the one hand, for manufacturers to extend their production, and, on the other, the increasing number of wage-earners and the insufficiency of their wages—are becoming more and more marked, the disturbed equilibrium, instead of readjusting itself automatically, as it has hitherto done, will, they say, become more and more unstable until the final crash,[1] when the capitalist system will be buried under its own ruins.

But this picture of crises looks too much to the gloomy side, and does not seem justified by facts. Crises are not produced by a general fall in wages, as this theory seems to imply. On the contrary, they are preceded by a rise in wages and, consequently, by an increase in the consuming power of the working class. Again, there is no indication that crises will become more and more frequent and serious ; on the contrary, they seem to be becoming less frequent and less serious as production is becoming better organised and as the science of foretelling crises progresses. Lastly, even admitting the theory at the basis of this explanation—namely, that the wage-earning class is receiving less and less of the product of its labour and thus being more and more despoiled by the possessing class— it is not easy to see why a *general* insufficiency of consumption should be the result. For why should not the despoilers consume as much as the despoiled ? There would be less consumption of articles of prime necessity and more consumption of luxuries, but it would all be profit for industry, which makes as a rule more out of the latter than the former.[2]

---

[1] " Nowadays, the ultimate cause of a crisis can always be traced back to the opposition between poverty, *i.e.* the limitation of the consuming power of the masses, and the tendency of the capitalist *régime* to multiply the forces of production " (Karl Marx, *Capital*).

[2] The objection might be raised, perhaps, that the rich would not use this income taken from the poor in consumption, but would put it into savings, so

In our view, then, it is certainly to over-production that we must look for the general cause of crises. We have seen how, in our modern societies, the equilibrium between production and wants is somewhat precarious. It would be a miracle, indeed, if an equilibrium, regulated solely by the play of supply and demand, were perfect. It is, in point of fact, very unstable.

But why are there not crises of *deficit* as well as of over-production ? May not the equilibrium between production and consumption be disturbed as easily by an insufficiency, as by an excess, of production ?

Assuredly. Formerly such crises commonly took the form of famines ; famines were, indeed, the only crises known. To-day they are found only in the agricultural and mining industries. They are not as a rule very hurtful, except in countries industrially backward. A failure of the wheat crop may cause terrible famines in poor countries like India or Russia, and the insufficiency of certain raw materials may throw factories idle. The disasters caused by the " cotton famine," which followed the Civil War in the United States, are still remembered in England.

A crisis of under-production, when it occurs in goods of prime necessity, may even produce the same effects as a crisis of over-production—namely, a general glut on the market and a depreciation of goods. As explanation of this, we have only to point out how, when a bad wheat harvest sends up the price of wheat, all the consumers of wheat whose resources are limited—that is to say, the great majority of mankind—are obliged to limit their expenditure on other articles of their consumption, and thus a large number of objects, no longer in demand, remain unsold on the market, or are

that there would be, not a simple transfer of consuming capacity from one class to another, but a real reduction in consumption. And some writers have sought the explanation of crises in the under-consumption, not of the poorer classes, but of the wealthy. This explanation seems to us inadmissible ; for saving and investment are, as we shall see in Book IV, simply modes of consumption, and a consumption transferred from the wealthy class to the working class.

Still, we do not deny that there may be crises of under-consumption, if, for example, a country is ruined by war, or simply impoverished by bad harvests, so that all its inhabitants are forced to cut down their expenditure. More often, however, these crises of under-consumption are simply a sequel to crises of over-production. It is after the latter have reduced manufacturers to bankruptcy, thrown wage-earners out of work, and impoverished numbers of well-to-do persons by depreciating their investments, that individuals begin to limit their consumption. The crisis of 1907, which began in America, resulted, in 1908, in a general decrease in consumption, which was clearly visible in the considerable falling-off in the figures for international trade, and in the taxation returns,

disposed of at a loss.   This is why famines in India, for example, nearly always make themselves felt by a fall in the prices of English manufactures and products.

Cases of under-production are very rare in industry, as industry is generally able to cope with consumption, save when a crisis of over-production has momentarily paralysed it.   Industry may, of course, be taken unawares by an unexpected growth of certain wants, the want, say, for automobiles, which is felt in the demand for india-rubber.   But such specific crises in particular products do not bring on general crises.[1]

There is, however, one product of unique importance, in the case of which any disproportion between production and wants brings on a general crisis which is felt in every other product without exception.   Here, however, the consequences are exactly the opposite of those which accompany crises in all other products ; for super-abundance of this particular product brings on a general rise in prices, and scarcity of it a general fall.   It is not difficult to guess that it is money to which we are referring.

Some authors, indeed, have seen in the superabundance or scarcity of metallic money, or its substitutes, such as bank-notes, the real cause of crises.   No doubt over-production from gold mines, as at present, or the over-issue of bank-notes, such as took place in former times, may provoke a general rise in prices (see p. 61), but it does not seem able to provoke the reversing of the movement which is characteristic of crises ; and it is difficult to see why these monetary inflations should have the rhythmic character which marks crises.   In any case, these monetary crises, if such they be, are the easiest to gauge and foresee.

Although crises must, on the whole, be considered salutary, since their function is to re-establish the disturbed equilibrium, it goes without saying that such shocks are distressing, and therefore much dreaded.   Fortunately, the consequences of crises are, at the same time, their remedy, acting somewhat after the manner of automatic regulators.

[1] Thus the wine crisis, in France, which lasted about ten years (1900-1910), although it provoked a number of riots in 1907, did not bring on an economic crisis in the true sense of the word.   Its cause was over-plantation, which coincided with a falling-off in the consumption of wine, at any rate in the middle classes.   But vine-growers preferred to attribute it to adulteration, in other words, to the over-production of artificial wines.   In either case, however, the explanation is over-production.   Numerous articles have been published on this crisis (among others one of our own in the *Revue d'Économie politique*, July 15, 1907).

For it is evident that selling at a loss, a fall in prices, difficulty in obtaining money, and the spectacle of bankruptcies, are the very best means to alarm producers, and cannot fail to check over-production. Only, no sooner have these cooling effects worn off, than the thirst for gain begins again ; hence the rhythmic movement so characteristic of crises.

Still, prevention is better than cure : and to diagnose crises we must first know their precursory symptoms. Not a few economists have set themselves to study these,[1] and we may say that, to-day, the science of foreseeing crises is more exact than that of foretelling the weather. It is reasonable, therefore, to hope that the ill-effects which they bring in the world of business will gradually diminish, as we become better able to calculate the moment of their return and to apply the brakes in time.

We have seen that production is regulated in a not too satis-factory way by the law of competition. But this is not the only law which governs industrial evolution. There are three, in particular, which we would do well to study separately :

The law of the division of labour ;
The law of concentration ;
The law of association.

---

[1] As far back as 1860, M. Juglar, in a book called *Des crises commerciales et de leur retour périodique*, tried to discover, not the causes of crises, but, what is more scientific, their precursory signs. He believed he had found them by instituting a comparison between the cash of banks and their bills and securities. When the cash, after a rapid rise, begins to fall and, at the same time, the bills and securities, after a fall, begin to rise, a crisis is about to occur.

This comparison may be considered as a sure prognostic, perhaps the best, since it is the result of an *ensemble* of very complex factors (see the chapter on *Banking*) ; but it needs to be completed by others.

In 1911, in France, a Commission of economists and financiers was created by the Government to draw up an Index Table for crises. It pointed out six signs . (1) the percentage of unemployment ; (2) the consumption of coal ; (3) index numbers ; (4) figures for foreign trade ; (5) the rate of discount : (6) the difference between the cash and the bills in the Bank of France, this last being no other than the comparison pointed out by Juglar.

CHAPTER II: THE DIVISION OF LABOUR

I: THE DIFFERENT MODES OF
THE DIVISION OF LABOUR

LABOUR that is quite simple, like digging, lifting weights, rowing, cutting wood, does not lend itself to any division. All individuals thus employed will go through the same movements. This is what we may call simple co-operation.

But in operations which involve varied movements, however slight their complexity may be, there is every advantage in breaking up the labour into a series of fractional tasks and assigning each to a different individual. This is what is known as the *division of labour*, or what we may call complex co-operation.

Adam Smith's *Wealth of Nations* opens with a celebrated dissertation on the division of labour.[1] This great thinker showed thereby the importance which he felt should be attached to this fact ; and ever since it has been looked upon as a law of increasing significance, not only. from the economic, but from the social, and even from the moral, point of view.

Let us begin, however, with the simplest case. Division of labour is, with saving, one of the few economic facts which we find among certain species of the animal world. Among human beings, the earliest known form of it is division of labour according to *sex*, and the different functions which, even from an economic point of view, sex involves. This form of the division of labour corresponds to the first industrial phase, that of family industry.

This division of labour is by no means in harmony with our modern ideas of the aptitudes peculiar to each sex, according to which the man undertakes the heavy labours and the woman the household duties. Far from it. Man appropriated to himself the noble labours, such as fighting, hunting, the charge of the flocks, leaving to woman the meaner labours, not merely of the household, of weaving, etc., but of transport (thus making of her a veritable beast of burden), and even the labour of cultivation. *Cura agrorum feminis delegata*, said Tacitus, speaking of the

---

[1] Professional division of labour and its social utility had, however, been pointed out in antiquity. Plato, in his *Republic*, makes Socrates say : " all things are produced better and with greater ease when each man works at a single occupation in accordance with his natural gifts . . . without meddling with anything else."
And the celebrated fable of Menenius Agrippa is to the same effect.

Germans,[1] and we find the same thing still among the native tribes of Africa. Woman was the first slave, and slavery, properly speaking, in the sense of captives taken in war, was for her the first step towards emancipation, since it freed her, among other things, from the crushing labour of grinding flour and turning the millstone.

In antiquity, we find the division of labour taking the *professional* form of differentiation into *trades*. Is this due to the natural aptitudes of individuals?[2] It may have been so in the case of the free worker. But we must not forget that free workers were rare and the slave simply did what his master ordered him. It is more than probable that even the free man had his task assigned to him for social, political, religious, or ritualistic, reasons—such, for example, as the caste system—rather than on account of professional aptitude, which would not come till later, through practice and hereditary transmission.

Under the guild system, the separation of crafts becomes more marked, each confining itself to a single kind of work and framing its regulations with the jealous intent of binding every man to his own particular calling. An industry may be subdivided either into its *divergent branches*, as when the wood industry, for example, is subdivided among joiners, carpenters, wheelwrights, etc., or into its *successive processes*, as when wood in its raw state passes from the hands of the woodcutter to those of the sawyer. Each of these constitutes a separate craft,[3] and these subdivisions and ramifications increase as wants increase, every new want giving rise to a new craft.

---

[1] According to Bücher, the man's duty was to provide the animal food (hunting, charge of the flocks); the woman's to provide vegetable food (fruit-gathering and, later, agriculture). And this division of tasks seems to have been in no way due to any special aptitude for these labours, but to have a purely religious origin. In any case, it would seem that it was not till fairly late, perhaps in Greek antiquity, that woman's sphere was confined to the labours of the household (see a very complete treatment of the prehistoric division of labour, in M. René Maunier's articles in the *Revue de Sociologie*, 1908). Even in our own day, in the Breton island of Sein, says M. Le Goffic, " the field of human labour is divided thus : the sea to the men, the land to the womenfolk."

[2] It is to the different modes of intellectual and artistic activity, that the first professions mainly owe their origin. The priest, the soothsayer, the doctor, the sorcerer, the singer, the dancer, each endowed with a peculiar talent, are the first to create a distinct position for themselves apart from the rest. As a rule, the blacksmith comes next, the other artisans following a long while afterwards (Bücher, *Studies, The Division of Labour*).

[3] On the historical development of the division of labour in the family, in industry, in agriculture, and in trade, see Schmoller's articles, *La division du travail étudiée au point de vue historique*, in the *Revue d'Économie politique* (1889 and 1890).

But it is not till we come to the manufacturing system, that the *technical* division of labour appears. As all industrial labour consists, as we have seen (p. 96), merely in a series of movements, this series is broken up into as simple movements as possible, assigned to different workers in such a way that no worker performs more than one of them, and that always the same one. It was this division of labour, as seen in a pin factory, which first struck Adam Smith, and inspired the admirable passage universally quoted.[1]

It must be pointed out that, in contradistinction to the two preceding modes of the division of labour which are natural and spontaneous, this last is the result of invention and combination, as, for that matter, are all the movements of labour.

While the division of labour was becoming intensified by being confined to the factory, it was at the same time expanding through the development of transport and international exchange, and becoming *international*, each nation devoting itself more especially to the production of what seemed best adapted to its soil, its climate or its peculiar racial characteristics. England turned her attention to her coal and her cotton goods, the United States to machinery, France to articles of luxury, Brazil to coffee, Australia to wool, etc.

We see that the term " division of labour " has expanded till it has broken through the definition which Adam Smith gave of it ; its meaning also has become somewhat too vague. As a fact, it is rightly used only when applied to labour which is actually divided up and distributed, as in a factory, where the manufacture of a boot or a watch involves fifty or a hundred different operations. It is not rightly used when it is made to denote the separation of crafts, where one shoemaker makes the whole shoe ; a better expression for this would be the *specialisation of labour*. And it is still less so when applied to what we have called the international division of labour—*i.e.* the localising of certain branches of production in particular regions ; here we should rather speak of the *localisation of labour*.[2] But the expression "division of labour," though inaccurate, is consecrated by use.

II : THE CONDITIONS OF THE DIVISION OF LABOUR

THE technical division of labour is most perfect when labour can be split up into a great number of separate tasks. But the number

---

[1] See also chap. xii of Karl Marx's book on *Capital*.

[2] See an article on the specialisation of industries, by M. Laurent Dechesne, in the *Revue d'Économie politique* (1902).

of workmen must, of course, correspond to the number of these distinct operations.[1] Now, the number of workmen a manufacturer can afford to employ depends on the extent of his production. And as this, again, depends on the size of the market, we may say that ultimately the division of labour is in direct proportion to *the size of the market*.

This is why, as has often been observed, a division of labour is to be found only in large centres and is unknown in the country or in small villages. There we find groceries, toys, stationery, small wares—all of which in a large town would be so many distinct trades —sold side by side in one and the same shop.[2] And the cause is obvious. In a village a man must turn to all trades for the good reason that a single one is not enough to give him a livelihood.

On the other hand, when an industry can have the whole world for its market, it can not only afford to specialise in the production of certain articles for which the want is very limited—the immense number of consumers making up for the smallness of their wants— but it can push the technical division of labour in this specialised industry to its extreme limit. This is one reason why countries are so anxious to secure a large export trade ; it enables their industries to obtain all the industrial advantages of an extreme degree of division of labour.

Another condition generally pointed out as indispensable to the division of labour is *continuity of work*. For, if work is intermittent, the worker, who cannot remain idle in the interval, must be given something else to do, and is thus no longer confined to a single occupation. This is one reason why, as we shall see, the agricultural industry does not lend itself readily to the division of labour. Still, this condition is not so indispensable as the first— viz., a wide market ; for a man may quite well turn to different kinds of labour, if they are not simultaneous and if they last for

---

[1] It would be quite a mistake to think that we could carry out the division of labour by employing a single workman for each operation. As a rule, a much larger number is necessary. Suppose that the manufacture of a needle involves three operations—the making of the point, the head, and the eye. Suppose that it takes ten seconds to make the point, twenty to make the head, and thirty to pierce the eye. It is clear that, to keep pace with the worker who makes the points, there must be two workmen for making heads and three for making eyes ; six, therefore, not three, workmen are necessary, or the first would sit with his arms folded part of the day.

[2] We might at first think that the large stores of big cities, such as the Louvre or the Bon Marché, are an instance of the same sort, since they sell all kinds of articles. But this is not the case (*cf.* what we say further on of the large stores).

F

fairly long periods, without losing the benefits that result from specialisation. We may even see in this a good corrective to some of the drawbacks of the division of continuous labour.[1]

III : THE ADVANTAGES AND DISADVANTAGES OF THE DIVISION OF LABOUR

DIVISION of labour increases the productive power of labour to an inconceivable extent. The reasons for this are as follows :

(*1*) It divides the most complicated task, as we have already explained, into a series of simple, almost mechanical and very easily executed movements, thus greatly facilitating production.

So simple may the movements become, that the intervention of man is no longer necessary, and a machine may do all that is required. Indeed, it is by this very " technical analysis " of labour that we have been able to make machinery execute labours which at first sight appear most complicated.[2]

(*2*) The diversity of the tasks thus created—varying as they do in difficulty and in the strength and attention they require—allows of their being distributed *according to the individual capacity of the workers.* In this way the natural aptitudes of each man may be used to advantage, and the waste of time, strength, and even of capital, avoided, which would result if all alike, weak or strong, ignorant or intelligent, performed the same task—the strong and capable perhaps working at tasks too easy for them, the weak and ignorant at tasks beyond their powers.

(*3*) *Constant repetition of the same movement* gives a man remarkable dexterity, just as continuous application to intellectual work singularly develops the mental faculties, and, as a result, the productive powers. Doctors, lawyers, painters, novelists, scholars, are all specialists nowadays; each finds it to his advantage to confine himself to one small corner of human knowledge, in order to dig deeper and obtain better results.

[1] The socialist, Fourier, declared that labour would become attractive so soon as it became : (*a*) *very much divided up ;* he urged division, indeed, to an extravagant point, advocating as many groups of workers as there are vegetable species (cabbagists, radishists, pearists, cherryists, etc.) and as many sub-groups as there are varieties of the same species ; (*b*) *very much diversified,* each worker being obliged to give only a very short time, say an hour or two, to each occupation. His system of " short sittings " as he called it, was to provide, if I may so put it, a very varied " menu " of labour. This was how he proposed to satisfy what he picturesquely called the " butterfly " passion in man.

[2] The invention of the principal machines (in spinning and weaving, etc.) coincides exactly with the apogee of the division of labour in manufacturing.

To these advantages of the division of labour three others of lesser importance are usually added :

(*4*) *The economy of time* which results from the continuity of labour. A worker who changes his work often will lose, not only a certain amount of time in turning from one operation to another, but a certain amount of time in starting work again.

(*5*) *Economy of tools*, which reaches its maximum when each worker uses but one single instrument and uses it all the time.

(*6*) *The shorter period of apprenticeship* required, apprenticeship being longer in proportion as the trade is more complicated.

But serious evils have long been pointed out as weighing against these advantages.

(*1*) The demoralising effect on the worker, who is reduced, by the constant repetition of a very simple movement, to the rôle of a mere machine, apprenticeship becoming henceforth unnecessary. How often has the saying of Lemontey been repeated : " It is a poor record of a man's whole life never to have made more than the eighteenth part of a pin." And a more illustrious than he, Adam Smith, the very man who revealed the importance and the benefits of the division of labour, used still harsher words when he declared, " the man whose whole life is spent in performing a few simple operations generally becomes as stupid and ignorant as it is possible for a human creature to become." (*Wealth of Nations*, Book V, ch. i, art. ii)

(*2*) The extreme *dependence* which the division of labour creates in the worker, who is incapable of doing anything beyond the one specialised operation to which he is accustomed, and who is thus at the mercy of stoppage or dismissal. Like the very pieces he makes, which are of value only when joined into one whole, we may say that the worker, too, is of value only as a wheel in the great machine —the factory : apart from it he is good for nothing.

It is easy enough to answer these criticisms. No doubt there are many degrading tasks in manual labour, but this is not because they are divided. It is because there are, unfortunately, a great many forms of labour which, though necessary, will always be, from their nature, unattractive. The labour of the street-sweeper, of the drain-cleaner, of the stone-breaker on the high road, is not divided ; but is it any nobler than that of a worker who makes nothing but screw-bolts ? And, as has been very justly said, do we really think that the worker who makes nothing but pin-heads would gain much intellectually and morally if he made the whole pin ? Moreover, whatever unpleasant effects the division of labour may have, as regards monotony, are counteracted and mitigated :

(a) By the general technical education of the working man, which gives him, while working at one specialised task, an opportunity of realising the place which he occupies in the whole, and, if need be, of changing his trade—technical education in this respect being superior to apprenticeship. (*See supra*, " Apprenticeship.")

(b) By the use of machinery ; for no sooner does a technical operation become so simplified that it is purely *mechanical*, than the worker is replaced by a *machine*, which is found more economical. Now, the direction of a machine is often tiring, not because of the muscular effort, but because of the nervous tension involved ; but it is not as a rule stupefying. The high-grade machinery of to-day requires picked workmen. As it becomes more automatic, the workman becomes less so.

(c) By the shortening of the working day, which leaves the worker leisure to occupy body and mind in different ways.[1]

(d) By the fact that, under the minute division of labour, many of the operations in one industry are very similar to, if not identical with, operations in other industries, thus enabling a man to pass easily from one industry to another.—AM. ED.

It must be observed, too, that the above criticisms bear only upon the *technical* division of labour. The *professional* division of labour—that is to say, into functions, occupations, studies, has never given occasion to the first objection, that of degrading the worker. Far from it. As for the second objection, that of dependence, division of labour after all creates no more than a mutual dependence ; and this we are inclined to look upon as an economic, and above all a moral, advantage rather than otherwise. Under the name of the *interdependence* of individuals, indeed, it has been made the basis of the law of solidarity. Division of labour, by the reciprocal dependence which it creates among men—resembling the physiological division of labour among the organs of a living body—makes, as it were, the members of a society into *the members of one single whole*, thus apparently carrying out the ideal of the Solidarity school. Many sociologists dwell lovingly on this analogy.[2]

[1] The system of the short working-day allows Fourier's ideal of short sittings and varied work to be to some extent realised. The miner who leaves the mine at 2 o'clock in the afternoon has time, after a bath, to work in his little garden, and even, if he wants to, to grow roses. The worker at the Brest or Toulon arsenal, after his eight hours' day, does odd jobs outside of his trade.

[2] M. Durkheim, in his masterly book, *De la division du travail social*, makes division of labour the fundamental law of society. He sees in it the very basis of morals ; for it is this differentiation among individuals which makes each incapable of being sufficient to himself and obliges him to give and receive

And yet, one cannot consider as ideal a nation in which each man would be a man of one trade ; where mind and body would bear the indelible traces of the daily task. The all-round development of the personality would, we believe, suffer. Even social progress would be affected ; for society would run the risk of becoming stereotyped, as under the caste system. We are quite willing to admit, with M. Espinas, that the " aptitude for isolation is a very inferior feature of individuality," nay more, that it is a trait peculiar to the savage— and certainly the savage is no longer the ideal type of humanity, as he was for the writers of the eighteenth century. Still, facility in changing from one profession or trade to another is a power which is of great advantage to a man. Most of the men who have reached the highest positions in the United States, have worked at a score of trades in their lifetime. To be able to turn its members to manifold uses is the mark of a dynamic and progressive society, and this can be achieved only (1) by a training which, even when exclusively technical, should be wide enough to open many paths to a man and to allow him to change from one to another ; (2) by *leisure* sufficient to allow him to apply his talents to various ends, and to exercise his activities in all the different spheres of the domestic, the civic, the intellectual, the religious, and the æsthetic life.

CHAPTER III: THE CONCENTRATION OF PRODUCTION

I : THE STAGES OF INDUSTRIAL EVOLUTION

WE saw in chap. i. how the equilibrium between production and wants is maintained—and sometimes disturbed. Let us now turn from the static, to the dynamic, point of view, and see how production

services, thereby creating mutual help. It is, according to him, the effect, and at the same time the corrective, of the struggle for life. The *effect*, because, as the struggle for life is more acute where individuals are alike and have the same wants, each tries to specialise in order to do something different from his neigh-bour ; the *corrective*, because the very possibility which it opens to individuals of escaping competition is a possibility of escaping ruin or death.

Still, we are somewhat reluctant to look upon the division of labour as the basis of solidarity, seeing that it implies the increasing *differentation* of indi-viduals, whereas true solidarity implies their increasing *likemindedness*. As the philosophers Charles Secretan and Fouillée said, to be " *solidaire* " is to realise the unity of the human race : it is to try to realise and to anticipate this unity by acting as if we were all one.—AM. ED.

manages to follow the continual upward movement of wants. To do so, it has had to pass through various forms.

To the Historical, particularly to the German school, belongs the merit of having first pointed out and discriminated between the successive stages of industrial evolution.[1]

It is generally agreed that there are five :

(1) *Family or domestic industry.* This is the type which prevailed not only in primitive societies, but throughout antiquity down to the beginning of the Middle Ages. Men are here divided into small groups, autonomous, from the economic point of view, in that they are self-sufficient, producing simply what they require for themselves. Exchange and division of labour exist only in an embryonic state. (See *infra*, " Historical Survey of Exchange.")

Each group is a family, but the word " family " must be taken in a much wider sense than it bears to-day. The patriarchal family was not only much more numerous than the modern family, but it was artificially swollen by the outside elements—slaves, later on serfs—incorporated in it. Slaves, in Rome, were known in law by the term *familia*. The villa of the wealthy Roman proprietor with its army of slaves working at all sorts of trades, and the seigniory of the feudal baron with its serfs, belong to this same economic period.

(2) The *craft* plied by the artisan. This second phase hardly appears before the Middle Ages. What characterises it is : (*a*) that the producer no longer works for himself and his own little circle, but for the public, for the *customer*—a new personage on the economic scene ; (*b*) that the worker, in the towns at any rate, is autonomous : he produces with his own material and tools [2] : he has become what

----

[1] Le Play in France, Roscher in Germany, and, more recently, Schmoller and Bücher. *Cf.* the interesting development of this subject in Bücher's *Studies.*

To get an exact idea of industrial evolution, we must place ourselves in turn at different points of view:

From that of the *condition of the worker* the stages are : slavery, serfdom, the wage-system.

From that of the *technique of production* the stages are : manual labour, machine industry.

From that of the *size of the market* the stages are : domestic industry, the craft, the factory.

From that of the *instrument of exchange* the stages are : barter, money, credit. (See Ely's *Evolution of Industrial Society.*)

Now, evolution does not proceed at an equal rate along these different paths, and the stages do not always correspond. We shall limit ourselves here to a general view over long periods.

[2] It often happened, however, that the artisan did not possess his raw material. This is the case even to-day in country places : witness the dress-maker, the knife-grinder, the tinker or basket-mender, who go from house to

was called, under the guild system, *a master;* (c) that he employs no wage-earning labour, but only that of his family or of apprentices.

True, the artisan as yet works only to order, or for the small market of his own village, which he jealously guards for himself. He is associated, for mutual aid and defence, with the workers of the same craft, and forms with them the corporations which played so important a part in the economic, and even in the political, history of the Middle Ages, their regulations being codified in the fourteenth century in the *Livre des métiers.*

(3) *Home industry,* which must not be confused with domestic industry, though both are carried on in the home.[1] The artisans gradually lose their independence. Instead of working directly for their customers or the public, they now produce for some great merchant, for an *entrepreneur.* Here is another new personage, a leading figure, appearing on the scene. The artisans work at home, and generally own their tools, but the raw material is now furnished by the merchant. In any case, the finished product does not belong to them ; it is the merchant who sees to the selling of it. How has this intermediary slipped in between the worker and the public ? The reason is that, as the small city market has been destroyed and replaced by the national, or rather the international, market, the artisans are too poor, too weak, and produce at too high a price, to supply the large market. Such is the position of the silk-weavers at Lyons, the *canuts* whose looms are their own property, but who receive from employers (wrongly called manufacturers, as in reality they are only merchants) the silk thread which they weave at home ; the stuff when made they bring back to their employers.

(4) *The manufactory.* The intermediary or *entrepreneur* brings these scattered workers together in the same premises. He finds various advantages in doing so ; in particular the power which it

house. This is also the position of the small miller who grinds the corn which the peasants bring him, except that he is sedentary.

The German historical school (see Bücher's *Studies,* already referred to) makes a special phase of this kind of work, the second in industrial evolution, under the name of "let" labour. This is a possible division ; but this kind of labour appears to us simply a variation of the "craft," for all those who let out their labour possess their own tools and work for the customer.

[1] Le Play, who first pointed out the importance of this form of industry, christened it *collective manufacture.* This is not, in our opinion, a very happy title, as it suggests the grouping of workers under one and the same roof— exactly the opposite idea from that which he intends to convey. What, on the contrary, characterises this industrial phase is, that a larger or smaller number of workers work for a single master, but each at his own home ; *dispersed manufacture,* so to speak.

gives him of organising a skilful division of labour among them, thereby increasing the productive capacity of the whole, and reducing at the same time the cost of production (see *infra*). But, in these new circumstances, the worker possesses neither raw material nor implements; he no longer works at home, he has become a *wage-earner*. It is the intermediary who owns everything and who has become the employer. Now, this manufacturer is bound to be a large capitalist, since his function is precisely to supply all the workers whom he employs with the capital they need in order to produce. The fourth phase, therefore, could not begin until large quantities of capital had been amassed and combined in the hands of great merchants.

This transformation began about the sixteenth century. It was not without a struggle that the more perfect organisation of the manufacturing industry . eliminated the guild system and conquered the market hitherto closed to it by guild regulations. In France, it was actually found necessary to resort to State intervention, the State—particularly under Sully and Colbert—creating manufactories with special privileges, some of which (Sèvres china, Gobelins tapestries) remain to this day State manufactures.[1] In England such intervention was not found necessary, as the export trade to foreign countries and to the Colonies was sufficient to enable new manufactories to be established and to break down the framework of the guild system.

(5) *The factory*, the characteristic feature of which is the use of the mechanical motor.[2] This is the typical form of modern industry, the phase in which we live. It began with the application of steam to industry—that is to say, at the end of the eighteenth century: for we can hardly count the hydraulic mills which came into use in the thirteenth century as inaugurating the factory era, still less the water-mills known from the end of the Roman Empire. This system has carried productive power to its maximum. And yet it has done little more than develop most of the features of the preceding period :[3] the crowding together of ever-increasing masses of workers

[1] See Germain Martin, *La Grande Industrie sous Louis XIV et Louis XV*.

[2] The factory ought, by rights, to be called *machine-factory*, as M. Vandervelde proposes, in order to distinguish it from the *manu-factory*.

[3] Hence the German socialists, who made the classification, refuse to consider the factory as a distinct morphological type, and treat it as a simple development of the preceding form, *i.e.* the manufactory. (They still make out five phases in all, as they count the phase of "let" labour separately.) In our view, however, the application, on a large scale, of natural forces to industry is a fact important enough to justify separate classification.

on one spot, night labour, quasi-military discipline, the employment of women and children. As the factory necessarily requires large quantities of capital, it is the characteristic feature of what the socialists call the *capitalist system*. The factory system has also its evils, which serve, too often justly, as a theme for the accusations levelled against the present *régime*—accidents, chronic unemployment, over-production and crises, the creation of colossal fortunes at one end of society, while at the other a starving proletariat is often forced to sell itself for a piece of bread ; finally, the rise of a special category of proprietors known as *shareholders*, not easily distinguishable at first sight from mere parasites. All these features we shall explain more clearly in the following chapters.

It would be a mistake to think that each of these forces absolutely eliminated the preceding ones : each in turn came to the front— that is all. Even nowadays, although the factory is the characteristic mode of industry, all the other forms are still to be found. We see traces of domestic industry in the peasants' houses where the wife bakes the bread and spins the flax for the household linen ; and in some of the provincial towns where jam-making, ham-curing and washing, are done at home and have not yet become industries. In all towns a large number of artisans may still be found plying diverse trades and working for their customers as in the Middle Ages. And there are still manufactories which employ only hand labour.

Indeed, by a surprising turn in the evolution of industry, one of these modes of labour—home industry—instead of gradually disappearing, as we should have expected, is taking on a new lease of life and developing to an unlooked-for extent. In the large towns, some great industries, particularly the tailoring industry, are carried on almost solely in this form. It is possible that this curious revival is only temporary, and due to the recent intervention of the legislator in the organisation of labour. As the new legislative regulations apply only to factories, many industries find it easier to evade them by giving out work to be done in the home. (See *infra*, p. 172, *Home Work*.)

II : THE LAW OF CONCENTRATION

WE have just seen that, in order to provide for man's increasing wants and to supply an ever-widening market, production tends to evolve from the humblest modes, that of the individual and the family, to those of large enterprise, where thousands of workers and millions of capital are grouped together. The tendency to group and to

F'

concentrate the maximum of productive forces at a single point
is called the *law of concentration*, or more simply " large production." [1]

Classical economists and socialists—this is one of the few points
on which they are agreed—attach great importance to the law of
concentration. They consider it as absolutely proven and as bound
to wield increasing power in the economic world.

It is beyond question that large production, by grouping all the
factors of production—manual labour, capital, natural agents,
situation—succeeds in economising—*i.e.* in producing the same
quantity of wealth at less cost, or, what is practically the same,
more wealth at the same cost. The coal consumption per horse-
power of a powerful steam-engine is relatively much less than
that of an engine of lesser power. Electric lighting is much more
economical than gas, but only when used on a large scale : on a
small scale it is more expensive.[2] The residues in manufacturing,
the by-products, can only be utilised in large industry, because in
small industry their quantity is so minute.

By manufacturing, in addition to his principal commodity, all
the intermediate products—a process known as the integration of
industries, of which we shall speak presently—a manufacturer avoids
paying the profits which he formerly paid to the industries which
produced them.

Large production as a rule admits consumers to the benefits it
realises, by reducing prices. Even to the worker, it more often than
not secures higher wages and better conditions of labour than small
industry can offer. The time is past when factories were called
" capitalist hulks." To-day the trade unions are generally in favour
of large workshops—if only because, by common labour, they create
a class-consciousness among working men.

[1] Concentration does not necessarily mean the bringing of all the workers and
machines together on the same premises : it is not incompatible with the home
manufacture of which we spoke in the last chapter. Still, it tends so to group them
whenever accidental causes do not work against it. (See *infra*, p. 172, *Home Work*.)
We often speak of the law of concentration, in connection not with production,
but with distribution, meaning thereby a tendency (not quite proved, however)
of wealth, whether in land or capital, to become concentrated in the hands of a
more and more limited number of persons, so that, through the disappearance of
the middle classes, colossal fortunes are created.
These two aspects of concentration must not be confused. They do not always
go together. For, on the one hand, the largest enterprises—the great companies—
involve the division of capital in the form of shares and bonds ; while, on the other,
the concentration of property is not incompatible with small production. A large
domain, for example, may be broken up into a great number of independent farms.

[2] The cost per horse-power may be put at four or five centimes per hour in
small industry, and goes as low as one or even half a centime in large industry.

The tendency to concentration is, therefore, easily explained by the advantages which it offers to *entrepreneurs,* and even to society ; for it is, after all, to every one's interest that the forces of production should be employed as economically as possible.

There is, however, the other side of the shield : for, if this movement of concentration were to continue without a break, we should see all those who work on their own account—small artisans, small shopkeepers, small proprietors, all *autonomous producers*—gradually disappear from the economic scene, to reappear in the character of salesmen and employees—as wage-earners in short—working for immense undertakings, directed by millionaire capitalists, or by limited liability companies.

Now, this is the very reason why the law of concentration is so dear to the hearts of the Marxian socialists, and why, up till quite lately, they made it the corner-stone of their doctrine. Their idea is that, so soon as the law of concentration has gathered together all the instruments of production into the hands of a few individuals and reduced all independent producers to the rôle of mere employees, the capitalist edifice will be like a pyramid resting on its apex. The slightest shock will suffice to overturn it. All that will be necessary will be to expropriate these few capitalists to the general gain, without any other change in the organisation of production.[1] Collectivists even welcome trusts, seeing in them, as it were, the milestones of a royal road leading directly to collectivism.

Further, they express a sovereign contempt for small production, for individual enterprise. According to Karl Marx, it is a system which excludes concentration, co-operation on a large scale, the use of machinery, the intelligent rule of man over nature, singleness and unity in the purposes, in the means and in the efforts of collective activity. It is compatible only with a strictly limited state of production and of society. To perpetuate the *régime* of isolated production would be to prescribe mediocrity in everything.

We take the liberty of appealing from this somewhat sweeping judgment.

[1] This reasoning errs from inaccurate observation. It takes for granted that concentration of production and of supervision is always accompanied by *concentration of ownership.* It presents large enterprise somewhat in the aspect of an octopus with a thousand arms and a single head, easy to cut off ; but this is to forget that, more often than not, large enterprise, evolving as it does in the form of shareholding companies, has as many heads as arms : concentration of production is accompanied by *division of ownership* in the form of shares and bonds.

John Moody estimates that in the United States the corporate wealth of the country (stocks, bonds, etc.) is diffused among three million owners. In 1905, the railroads of the United States had 327,851 shareholders.—AM. ED.

The system of small industry (we are not speaking of home industry, which is a very different thing, see *infra*) is more favourable to a good distribution of wealth and consequently to social peace.   By reason of its extreme simplicity it, precludes most of the conflicts which spring up to-day between the different classes which share in distribution, particularly between labour and capital.   It does not bring about absolute equality—a state which is hardly to be desired—but it knows no other inequalities than those due to the unequal fertility of land and of the instruments of production, or bound up with the vicissitudes of human life.[1]

Even from the productive point of view, small industry is not so powerless and unprogressive as is thought.   Autonomous producers may associate and adopt certain processes of large production and of the division of labour without sacrificing their independence, their initiative, their responsibility, and their personal interest, all of which are powerful springs of production which collective enterprise threatens somewhat to slacken.   This is already being done by the French peasants through their farming associations, and the German artisans who associate to buy their raw material and to sell.   It is possible also, that the modern method of bringing motive power to the home by means of hydro-electric power-stations will supply the machines of small industry with the means of producing cheaply, and may even give rise to new forms of small industry.   It does not follow that there is always competition between large and small industry ; there may be a division of labour between them.

Moreover, even in enterprises best suited to concentration, it has not been shown that evolution in the direction of large production goes on indefinitely.   It is probable, on the contrary, that it will not go beyond certain bounds.   The growth of social organisations, just like that of living organisms, seems to be restricted by nature within definite limits.   Large shops, like the Louvre, or the Bon Marché, appear to have reached the stationary state some time ago. This may be explained on economic grounds ; for, beyond a certain point, the proportion of general costs increases rather than diminishes and the economy resulting from large production disappears.[2]

In any case, facts, more decisive than arguments, point in no

---

[1] See Brants' very impartial and well-documented book, *La petite industrie contemporaine.*

[2] See Vilfredo Pareto, *Cours d'Économie politique.*

It is beginning to be recognised to-day that general costs are not much lower in very large, than in small, industry ; not that the causes of economy we have just indicated do not exist, but that they are counterbalanced by other causes, which act in an opposite direction—costs of advertising and supervision, leakage, etc.

way to the disappearance of small industry or small commerce ; still less, as we shall see, to that of small farming. So true is this, that a good number of the Marxian school have abandoned the famous law of the concentration of enterprises.[1]

III : SPECIALISATION AND INTEGRATION OF INDUSTRY

CONCENTRATION of capital and of manual labour is not the sole characteristic of large industry. There are two other distinctive and, it would seem, contradictory features. The first is the tendency of large industry to confine itself more and more to one particular branch of production ; the second is its tendency to absorb all the industries complementary to the special production on which it is engaged. These are known as the *specialisation* and the *integration* of industry.

The increasing specialisation of industry is neither more nor less than an application of the law of the division of labour, and is to be explained by the same causes. An *entrepreneur* who devotes himself to the production of one single article, will naturally be in a better position to push this production to the point of perfection. Thus, not only will clock-making become a distinct industry, but within this industry some will make only watches, some cuckoo-

[1] Bernstein, *Socialisme théorique et Social-democratie pratique* (French translation).

Statistics on this subject in the different countries give such confusing results that they may be used in support of almost any contention. In France, however, the number of shopkeepers and small manufacturers taxed under Schedule A increased from 1,176,140 in 1852 to 1,521,067 in 1905, a rise of 29·40 per cent. ; whereas the number of those taxed under Schedule C, which comprises mainly large manufacturers, increased from 153,610 to 194,962, a rise of 26·90 per cent., or slightly less than the other.

For retail commerce and agriculture see *infra*, pp. 171 and 180.

For industry, the French census gives the following figures (*Résultats statistiques du Recensement de la population*, vol. i, part ii, p. 121):

	1896	1906	Increase
Small establishments (1 workman at most)	290,748	317,933	9%
Medium-sized establishments (1 to 100 workmen)	297,964	307,628	3%
Large establishments (over 100 workmen)	3,649	4,649	28%
	592,361	630,210	6%

These figures show that the number of small workshops has distinctly increased although less rapidly than that of the large : it is the medium-sized workshops which have remained stationary.

clocks, some alarm clocks; and, even in the making of watches, one manufacturer will confine himself to the finer kinds, another to cheap machine-made watches. So also in commerce we find, in the large towns, one shop selling nothing but bronzes, another only basket-work, another trunks and articles of travel.

But, side by side with this marked increase in specialisation, we also see, singularly enough, some factories and shops taking apparently quite an opposite line and multiplying the branches of their industry.

In large industry the number of factories which are annexing all the operations preliminary to, or consequent on, the production of their particular commodities is daily increasing. The Standard Oil Company manufactures its own casks of wood or sheet-iron, its giant pumps, its reservoir-trucks, and possesses a whole fleet of its own for transport. A chocolate factory will have a joiner's workshop for the manufacture of its packing-cases; paper and printing press for the making up of its boxes and labels; perhaps even cocoa plantations abroad, and ships for conveying the cocoa. A woollen spinning factory will have a chemical mill for treating the matter extracted from the grease of the wool, and perhaps a soap factory to manufacture it into soap. The power to turn by-products to account is, as we have seen, one of the causes of the superiority of large industry.

This phenomenon becomes still more striking in commerce with the appearance of the large *stores*, where, as in the Louvre and the Bon Marché, the customer can find not only everything he wants in the way of clothing and furniture, but even, as at Whiteley's, in London (called the " Universal Provider "), an elephant, should he wish it.

The contradiction between these two movements is only apparent. Integration does not stand in the way of specialisation. Each work-room of the factory, each department of the shop, is specialised and has its own technical autonomy. In a large shop, there are separate departments for silk goods, linen goods, carpets, etc., each of which has its own staff and special " buyers." The only difference is, that these specialities, instead of being under separate control, are combined under one management and lend each other mutual support. The integration of production is nothing else than one step further in specialisation—co-operative specialisation.[1]

Specialisation must not be confused with *localisation* of industry, although there is a certain relationship between the two move-

---

[1] For fuller details on these subjects, see the articles by M. Dolléans, *L'Intégration de l'Industrie* (in the *Revue d'Économie politique*, 1902), and M. Dechesne, *La spécialisation et ses conséquences* (same review, 1901).

ments. Localisation is the tendency which certain industries have to settle in the same region : silk at Lyons, wool at Roubaix, watchmaking in the Juras, the manufacture of aluminium in Dauphiny, etc. So long as the factories of one industry are working for the local market, it is clearly to their interest to move away as far as possible from one another. But, so soon as they produce mainly for export, it is to their interest to come together, for their competition is not increased thereby, and they may, on the contrary, find various advantages in doing so, *e.g.* proximity to certain sources of raw material and power, or the creating of a large regional market which attracts more buyers.[1]

IV : THE LARGE STORES

THE general opinion is that it is in commerce that the law of concentration is most felt. This, however, is simply because it is in commerce, in the form of large stores, that it is most obvious to the general public ; it is here that the complaints of the small shopkeepers, crushed by the competition of these colossal enterprises, are loudest.

The economic superiority of the large store is due to the following causes :

(*1*) Economy of *labour.*

This first advantage consists mainly in the power which the large store has of pushing the division of labour to its highest point by creating as many departments as there are classes of goods. But it results also from the mere grouping together of the employees. In the small shop, the greater part of the time is wasted. There are often hours during which each seller is unemployed. Take, for example, a hundred firms, each employing ten workers. Combine these into one business ; obviously, to turn over the same amount as did the hundred houses separately, it will not be necessary to keep the thousand employees. There will be no need of a hundred cashiers or a hundred

[1] The American census for 1905 gives numerous instances of the localisation of industries in the United States ; for example, 89·5 per cent. of the collar and cuff industry is to be found at Troy (State of New York) ; 44 per cent. of the glove trade at Gloversville and Johnstown (New York) ; 41 per cent. of carpets and rugs at Philadelphia ; 50·6 per cent. of the clothing industry in New York City, etc. The principal causes of this localisation are: proximity to materials, to hydraulic power, or to markets ; the influence of climate ; abundance of manual labour or capital, or the fact that the industry had on some previous occasion been started there. But it must be admitted that the localisation of an industry is often due to chance causes, such as the happy initiative of some local person, *e.g.* the diamond-cutting and the pipe industries in the little town of St. Claude (Jura).

bookkeepers.   Each worker, moreover, being now able to work without stopping, will be able to do two or three times as much as before, and will thus, in himself, take the place of two or three workers.

(2) Economy of *space*.

In order to have a hundred times more room in a shop or factory it is not necessary to occupy a space a hundred times larger, nor to use a hundred times more material in the building of the premises. For, if the volumes of two cubes are to one another as 1 to 1000, their surfaces are as 1 to 100.   Now, it is the surface only that costs. Besides, apart from mathematics, experience has shown that neither the cost of construction nor the amount of rent increases in direct proportion to the space occupied.   The smallest shop in Paris, with a turnover of 500 francs a day, will pay 6000 to 8000 francs rent. But the Bon Marché, which turns over on an average more than 500,000 francs a day, thus doing a thousand times more business, does not by any means pay a thousand times more rent.   Its rent is calculated at one million francs at most, or not more than the equivalent of two days' sale.

(3) Economy of *capital*.

The circulating, or working, capital of a large shop may be much less than that of a small one, in proportion to the amount of business done, and this for two reasons :

(a) Because, by buying them in large quantities or by manufacturing them directly, the large shop does not need to spend so much in obtaining its goods.

(b) Because its money returns to it much more rapidly, as its goods lie only a few days or weeks on the shelves, instead of months or years.[1]   It is clear that a capital of a hundred is equivalent to a capital of a thousand, if it can be renewed ten times as quickly.   Moreover, the fact that the goods will be fresher and more up to date, owing to this quick renewal, is an additional attraction to the consumer.

(c) Lastly, the large undertaking has, as a rule, better credit than the small, and obtains its necessary capital at a lower rate.

These great stores play a large part in the life of the women of all classes.   It was under the Second Empire, in the middle of the nineteenth century, that they were first started in France,[2] but it is only

---

[1] In some American " department stores " the entire stock of one " department " or single line of goods is " turned over," or completely sold out, thirty times in a year.—AM. ED.

[2] It was in the year 1852 that Aristide Boucicaut founded the Bon Marché ; in 1855, Messrs. Chautard and Hériot founded the Louvre.   The Belle Jardinière dates from 1856 ; the Samaritaine from 1859 ; the Printemps from 1865, etc.

Zola, in a series of novels in which he aimed at depicting French society under

within the last twenty years that they have really overturned the economic organisation of retail trade. These stores have introduced three very happy reforms : (a) sale at fixed prices, thus doing away with the waste of time involved in the archaic and absurd system of· bargaining; (b) cash sales, thus suppressing the degrading custom of credit, ruinous for the shopkeeper and consequently for the customer, since prices have to be raised to cover the risk of non-payment; (c) rapid renewal of stock, by sale at a loss if necessary. The waste of wealth which change of fashion from season to season involves in consumption, particularly in clothing, may thus be to some extent counterbalanced : wise consumers, who care little for novelty, are given an advantage at the expense of those who covet it.

Other reforms of more questionable utility have been introduced by these stores and have contributed not a little to their fortunes. In particular : (a) the liberty which they allow the customer of returning the goods bought, an idea to which the founder of the Bon Marché attributes the greater part of his success, as it tempts the customer. The latter says to herself, "Take it, as in any case I can return it," and then cannot make up her mind to bring it back ; [1] (b) the commission or bonus given to the employee on the sale of the goods, which is larger in proportion as the goods are less saleable.[2] This results in the encouragement of sales from the side of the salesman, just as the liberty to return goods stimulates purchases on the part of the buyer ; (c) attractions of all sorts in the form of exhibitions, distributions of toys, sometimes concerts and fêtes, avalanches of catalogues with samples, hundreds of vans with a whole cavalry of horses used as much for advertisement as for delivery, all of which exercise such a fascination on the mind of the public—particularly the feminine public—that a special mania, known as kleptomania, has resulted from it. A regular staff of inspectors is necessary to prevent or to discover the thefts committed by persons in " good society." In virtue of these last features, the stores appear as ingenious psychological devices for inciting to consumption, and the so-called cheap-

the Second Empire, did not neglect this important fact. The duel between the small shopkeeper and the large store forms the subject-matter of his novel, *Au Bonheur des Dames.*

[1] Or, what is no better as regards its demoralising effect, the customer turns this liberty into a veritable fraud, wearing the hats, fans, etc., for a day or two gratis. The open entry to these large stores makes this temptation still greater.

[2] The bonus must not therefore be mistaken for profit-sharing, as it is often largest on sales made at a loss.

ness ends in the ruin of many a household. This cheapness is, besides, to a great extent lost in the end, owing to excessive outlay on general expenses, advertising, etc., all of which have ultimately to be covered by the price.[1]

On the other hand, the great stores exercise an all-powerful and, in some respects, disastrous control over producers. As they are the largest, and often the sole, client of the manufacturer—for they sometimes buy only from those who undertake not to sell elsewhere—they hold him in their hands and are able to dictate prices to him. The large manufacturers may perhaps defend themselves, but the small ones are speedily reduced to the condition of home wage-earners, only too glad to work for the price offered, and unable to dispute it. In this way the large stores have contributed their share in the untoward evolution which is pushing the autonomous producer into the ranks of the wage-earning class.

Further, if we point out that the armies of employees in these shops are recruited in part from the small shopkeepers who have been eliminated, in part from the sons and daughters of the rural population, and that, on this side too, the large stores are tending to reduce the number of independent producers and to swell the proletariat in the large towns, it will be realised that their economic action is perhaps more alarming than reassuring, as regards the future of society.

Still, we must not generalise too much. It might be supposed, and some have even prophesied, that this evolution of the large stores would result inevitably (a) in the disappearance of the small trader ; (b) in a reduction in the number of the large stores, either by competition among themselves, till only one survived, or by the combination of the largest of them into a trust ; and that the law of concentration would thus lead from a system of utterly relentless competition to a system of the most absolute monopoly. But this somewhat too sweeping prophecy shows no signs of coming true. Facts reveal, on the contrary—and it is in some respects an unexpected lesson : first, that this development of the large stores has taken place only in fancy articles and, to a smaller extent, in

---

[1] It has been calculated that, in order to obtain 5 per cent. of net profit, the large store must make at least 16 per cent. of gross profit, the difference being absorbed by general costs. This does not prevent it from being able to sell cheaper than the small shop, since, however great its general costs may be, by spreading them over enormous quantities, it is able to reduce the percentage on each to a very small figure. This the small shop cannot do ; nor can it be content with a net profit of 5 per cent. In order to exist, the small shop must raise the cost price of its articles by about 30 per cent.

groceries. Elsewhere, for example in the baking trade, similar efforts have failed. The result is, therefore, that on the whole the number of small shops, instead of diminishing, is increasing.[1] Secondly, that the large shops stop short after they have reached a certain point in their development, or at least do not hinder the establishment and growth of similar shops in other quarters of the town.[2] So that here, if anywhere, the law which Vilfredo Pareto taught seems to hold good, that the growth of economic units, like that of living organisms, is limited by certain inflexible laws.[3]

It must be observed that it is in France that the large stores have spread most widely. This is probably due to the fact that retail trade in France had multiplied to such an extraordinary extent that it had degenerated into an exploitation of the public.

[1] We must, however, point out: (1) that the small shops which are increasing in number are mostly those with which the large ones do not compete. It is only natural, *e.g.* that there should be a number of pastrycooks in the vicinity of a large store, but we should hardly expect to find shops for fancy articles ; (2) that where the small shops have to meet the competition of the large, they are obliged to resort to deplorable methods, of which the principal are, in France, the *sou* per *franc* given to domestic servants, sale on credit, *primes, i.e.* presents distributed to those who spend above a certain sum.

The following are the figures for France (*Résultats statistiques du Recensement des professions*, vol. i, part ii, p. 121) :

	1896	1906	Increase
Small shops (1 employé at most) .	126,909	156,626	23 per cent.
Large shops (2 to 100 employés) .	106,072	120,667	13 ,,
Very large shops (over 100 employés) .	143	273	90 ,,
Total	233,124	277,566	19 ,,

We see that in the short space of ten years the number of small shops increased considerably, although less rapidly than the number of large shops. It is the medium-sized shops which increased least. This table leaves out of account the enormous number of establishments kept by a single person or a family ; these also have increased.

Statistics do not prove that the law of concentration is not at work here, but they show that small commerce is not being swallowed up by large.

[2] In 1900, the turnover of the Bon Marché was estimated, on an average, at over half a million francs a day, and it was thought that it would swallow up its great rival, the Louvre. Since then this figure does not seem to have increased, and not only is the Louvre holding its own, but a dozen or so other stores have sprung up in Paris which seem destined to make equally large fortunes. The check in expansion is perhaps due also to the fact (as indicated, p. 164, note 2) that, beyond a certain point, general costs tend to increase more rapidly than the turnover.

[3] These large stores take the form both of private enterprise (*the Louvre, Dufayel*) and of shareholding companies (*Le Printemps*). The *Bon Marché* has an organisation entirely its own. It is an ordinary shareholding company

Is not the evolution which created the large stores tending now to replace them by a higher form—that, namely, of co-operative societies for consumption ?   We shall consider this question in Book IV.

V : HOME WORK

THE expression home industry, though much in use to-day, is ambiguous : *home wage-earning* is what we ought to say.   For we are not speaking here of the home industry, the second social category to which we referred under the " Stages of Industrial Evolution " (p. 158), of those autonomous producers—the shoemaker, locksmith, bookbinder, painter, farrier—who ply a trade and are called " artisans."   These also work at home, but they work for themselves, on their own account, with their own capital, and sell to the customer.   When we speak of home industry we mean workers who work at home, but for an employer, and with raw material supplied by him.

Now, though the situation of the independent artisan is in some respects enviable, and theoretically—though allowance must be made in practice—may be considered the ideal working man's existence, that of the home wage-earner is as a rule pitiable.   There are, however, different degrees of home industry which we must distinguish :

(*a*) If the home worker possesses his own tools, say his loom, and deals directly with the employer or manufacturer, he resembles somewhat the artisan.   He differs, however, from the latter in that he does not possess the raw material, and sometimes not even tools : [1] above all in that he does not sell his product directly to the public, but to the employer.   On the other hand, he is not a wage-earner pure and simple, for he sells his workmanship to the employer.

with this reservation, that only employees of the firm (in theory at any rate) can be shareholders.   This is not sufficient, however, to confer on it the character of a co-operative society, as it is sometimes called ; for the profits are distributed after the capitalist manner, *i.e.* in proportion to shares, not to wages.

[1] As a rule, the home worker is supposed to own his tools and machines, and to hire his own motive power, if necessary.   This is the case with the weavers of Lyons and St. Etienne.   Sometimes, however, the employers lend the machines to the workers, as, for instance, in the linen industry ; they have often good reason to regret it, as the machines are in this case very badly kept.   (See the Inquiry made by the *Office du Travail, Enquête sur le travail à domicile,* vol. i).

In Switzerland some of the commodities that play an important part in export trade—such as embroidery, watches, and silk goods—are still very largely produced in the homes of the workers.—AM. ED.

He still feels independent, and we can only conclude that the advantages of independence outweigh the disadvantage of a wage lower than the average, since we find the workers themselves— for instance the weavers of Lyons and St. Etienne, and the clock makers of the French and Swiss Juras, etc.—preferring this system to that of working in the factory.

(*b*) It is for the worker who works for a middleman that home labour becomes so terrible. This sort of labour is very common. It is the form resorted to in most of the ready-made clothing industries.

For, when an enterprise becomes of any importance, the employer has neither the time nor the means to go out and engage every workman he needs ; he cannot do without intermediaries. Now, the intervention of these intermediaries generally means a reduction in wages, as it is out of the wages of the worker that the middleman is paid. Nor does he necessarily make a fortune. Often he works as hard as, and makes scarcely more than, his workers.

(*c*) Lastly, if the middleman employs the workers at his own house, it is no longer home labour for them : it is labour in a workshop, and in a workshop narrow, sordid, a nest of consumption and infectious disease, deprived of all the protection of labour legislation.[1] This is where home labour degenerates into what is known as the *sweating system*, the system of sweating all that can be got out of the worker.

Why is home industry always characterised by a lowering of wages ? It is, in the first place, because, in this industry more than in any other, the workers are exposed to the competition of the worst-paid labour, that of women, foreigners, inmates of philanthropic institutions, and, up till quite lately, of convents ;[2] that is to say, of all persons who, having some other occupation or some small income, ask of this accessory labour only a small supplement to it. Secondly, because these workers, being scattered, are unable to combine to form a union or coalition, and compete in a homicidal way with one another.[3]

This is why the question of home labour has of late stirred

---

[1] Sometimes the worker is not only lodged but also fed by the middleman, who takes from him, in return for miserable food and still more miserable lodging, as much as, or more than he would give him as wages. Here, so to speak, is the lowest circle of this hell ; and it is the situation of thousands of immigrants— Jews, Russians, and Poles—lost in the slums of East London.

[2] The Inquiry referred to (p. 172, n. 1) reveals the curious fact that the dissolution of the religious "congregations" has slightly raised the rate of wages in the linen industry in France.

[3] See M. Gemähling's *Travailleurs au rabais. Les concurrences ouvrières.*

public opinion so strongly,[1] more especially as the risks which customers run from products coming from these dens have been brought home to them. Numerous remedies have been suggested, unfortunately of doubtful efficacy. The one which appears most simple, viz., regarding these workshops as similar to factories, as regards legislation and inspection, is not very practical; for, not only would the number of inspectors have to be enormously increased, but they would often find it impossible to distinguish the workshop of the middleman from that of the family, which must nevertheless be respected as much among the poor as among the rich.[2] In any case, even were the inspection of home workshops possible, it could remedy at most only two of the evils of this kind of industry—the insanitary condition of the workshops and the excessive hours of labour—but not the third, viz., the low wages. The remedy for this last should, it seems, be sought, either in the organising of the workers into trade unions—but their scattered and isolated condition militates against this—or in the fixing by law of a *minimum wage*. Unfortunately, the fixing of a legal minimum wage might have the effect of depriving unskilful workers of their whole wage. We shall return to this question in the chapter on "Wages." Possibly a more modest and perhaps more effective remedy, though it results solely in a moral suasion, would be that applied by English law, and by a Bill recently proposed in France, which obliges an employer to register the names and addresses of the workers to whom he gives out home work, the wages he pays, and other conditions of employment. The social leagues of buyers might also do something (see Book IV, chap. i).

It is evident that home industry is an exception to the law of concentration. Here we have industries which not only have not evolved towards factory production, but have even, by an unexpected regression, returned to the home, the factory dispersing, as it were.

It is more particularly in the clothing industry (ready-made clothing, hosiery, gloves, laces, etc.),[3] and in a few others, such as toy-

---

[1] Eloquent exhibitions of the products of sweated industries, with a notice of the wages paid, and the hours of labour, have been held in London, Berlin, and other large towns.

[2] French law does not allow an inspector to enter a family workshop, unless a mechanical motor is used there, or unless the industry is one classified as unhealthy. Even in this case, his intervention is limited to precautionary measures regarding hygiene and accidents.

[3] See in this connection the facts quoted, and the conclusions drawn, by Aftalion in his book, *Le développement de la fabrique et de l'industrie à domicile dans l'habillement.*

making, that this method of production still continues, and, according to some, is on the increase. And yet the clothing industry would seem to be one of those best adapted to the use of machinery and the division of labour, for which, consequently, the factory method appears the most suitable. There is reason to believe, indeed, that the factory will ultimately win the day. On the other hand, the obstinate resistance of home industry to absorption by the factory may be easily explained by the following facts :

(1) Its products are generally small—clothes or parts of clothing —and their production does not require either much room or much mechanical power. Consequently they can be made quite well in a room by hand, by sewing machine, or by a small gas or electric motor of a quarter h.p. or less. The clothing industry must not be confused with the textile industry.

Division of labour, moreover, is quite compatible with home industry, the different pieces being distributed to the workers and put together afterwards.

(2) Production at home is appreciated by many workers owing, as we remarked before, to the independence which it allows them. So precious is this that they do not shrink from paying for it by a large diminution of wage. To earn as much as they would do in a factory, they are obliged, as a rule, to work much longer, but at least they may work when they will. For women, especially, there is the great advantage that home work allows them to look after their households and their children.

Sometimes among these home workers may be found persons enjoying a certain competence—pensioners, *concierges*, workers in the State arsenals—who take in work for their spare moments, asking only an auxiliary wage wherewith to eke out the family budget.[1] These persons ought to realise the deadly competition they are waging against the genuine worker whose only resource is this home labour.

(3) Employers on their side find immense advantages in it : (a) They are saved the expense of building a factory with its costly equipment ; (b) they escape all the laws regulating labour, and the surveillance of the inspectors whose duty it is to see that they are applied ; (c) they are able to pay lower wages for the reason given above. These advantages are occasionally even greater than those which result from large production in factories,

---

[1] Even the wives and daughters of employees or small officials in fairly good circumstances sometimes take in home work, and do it in secret. See the volume published by the *Direction du Travail, l'Industrie à domicile.*

and are enough to explain the survival, and sometimes the spread, of this method of industry.[1]

VI : INDUSTRIAL EVOLUTION
IN AGRICULTURAL PRODUCTION

Do the laws of concentration, of the division of labour, and of integration, which characterise industrial evolution, apply also to agricultural production ?   The answer used to be in the negative. It was said that agriculture was a distinct branch (see p. 80), in that it set to work nature, and the little understood forces of the earth, the sky and, most mysterious of all, life, which only imperfectly obey the will of man ; because it was subject to the law of diminishing returns, etc. It was pointed out in particular :

(1) That the law of concentration cannot apply to it, since the capital and labour employed have to be spread over the whole area of the ground cultivated. A large farm is not more concentrated than a small one ; as a rule it is less so, particularly when it takes the form of the *latifundia* so common in countries of large property.

(2) That the law of the division of labour and specialisation cannot apply to it, since the different natures of different pieces of soil and the rhythm of the seasons render work so varied and so intermittent that the agricultural labourer cannot confine himself to one single task. It is impossible to organise work on a farm in the same way as in a workshop, by giving one worker sole charge of the sowing, another of the reaping, another of the pruning of the vines, &c. As each of these labours lasts only a few weeks, a worker who has specialised in one or other of them would be idle for about eleven months of the year.[2]

(3) That the law of integration cannot be applied, since the

---

[1] The reports of the labour inspectors during the last few years have frequently pointed out cases of factory industry transformed into home industry, and have attributed them to the above causes, particularly the second. Employers seem now, however, to recognise that, all things considered, factory production is more profitable. See some interesting evidence in the Inquiry referred to (p. 172, n. 1).

[2] There are, no doubt, some continuous occupations which might be given to one individual for the whole year—that of *carter, shepherd, gardener*. But the greater number of workers are undifferentiated. And even such specialisation of occupation as this has not much in common with the technical division of labour in the workshop.

As for the specialisation of crops—what is called *monoculture*—it is too risky for the agriculturist. The wine-growers of the South of France took it up whole-heartedly ; but since the wine crisis their ardour has been somewhat damped.

agriculturist has neither the machinery, the capital, nor the technical ability necessary to annex different industries to his agricultural exploitation,—to manufacture, e.g. on his premises the chemical manures or the casks he requires, to utilise the by-products of his harvests, to distil alcohol, to extract tartaric acid from the dregs of his wine, or even to grind his flour.[1]

These differences do not, however, prevent agriculture from following in some measure the trend of industrial evolution. This is what is meant by the expression the *industrialisation of agriculture*, the precise meaning of which is, that agricultural production tends nowadays to resort, so far as its natural and special conditions allow it, to the same processes as the manufacturing and commercial industries; and for the same reason, viz., to get the most possible out of the factors of production, and thereby to reduce cost price, a step which the fall in prices of farming produce towards the close of the nineteenth century rendered urgent.[2]

The principal ways in which this industrialisation of agriculture manifests itself are :

(*1*) In *intensive farming*, which consists in concentrating on a given surface the greatest possible amount of capital and labour in the form of manure and rotations.[3] Thus, in the cultivation of the vine, where, thirty years ago, 300 to 400 francs per hectare were enough, a thousand francs will now be spent : and, in market gardening in beds or under glass, ten times as much. Market gardening in the suburbs of Paris may be made to yield per hectare as much in value as 30,000 francs of gross produce, and as much food as will support thirty persons. And it is already specialised, some gardeners growing only strawberries, others only lilac, etc.

It may seem at first glance as if intensive cultivation, by increasing so enormously the outlay on production, is going counter to its aim as indicated above, viz., the lowering of the cost of production. But this is a wrong impression. Though the cost of production is greater for a given area, it is less for each unit produced. The cultivation of the vineyard may cost 1000 francs per hectare

---

[1] Nor must *polyculture*—where the agriculturist produces all that he needs on his farm—be taken as an application of the very modern law of integration.

[2] See M. Hitier's pamphlet, *L'Industrialisation de l'agriculture* (*Revue d'Économie politique*, 1902).

[3] Cultivation is said to be *extensive* when, as the word indicates, it is spread over a surface instead of extending downwards ; when it is satisfied with Nature's unaided co-operation ; when the surface of the soil is simply scraped instead of being manured ; when the land is allowed to lie fallow while Nature repairs the losses.

instead of 300, but the yield will be 200 hectolitres instead of 30, and thus the cost price five, instead of ten, francs. This is obviously the reason why the agriculturist adopts intensive cultivation.

(2) In the *use of machinery*, the object of which is twofold : (a) to economise manual labour and time by means of machine-driven threshing mills, wine presses, crushing machines, wine pumps, etc.; (b) to carry out operations which would be beyond the powers of man or his domestic animals, in particular, deep ploughing, the forcing up of water from rivers or subt erranean beds for irrigation, etc.

It must be borne in mind that these two ways of applying industrial methods to agriculture do not necessarily go together, and that their results are often quite opposite. Intensive cultivation results mainly in increasing the gross and, indirectly, the net product, by making the earth yield a larger quantity of subsistence. It can quite well be applied to small cultivation, *i.e.* cultivation concentrated on a small surface. The typical example of this is the cultivation of China, which, by dint of much manure and tending, is able to feed, one way or another, the densest population on the globe :[1] or, to come nearer home, the market gardening of the suburbs of our large towns.

Machinery, on the contrary, results in reducing costs and gaining time; it is well adapted to extensive cultivation, and is even compatible with a decrease in the gross return. The best type of this kind of cultivation is that of America, which has a smaller population to feed, and works mainly for export.

It is evident, then, that, though these two methods may be equally profitable to the landowner, as he looks only for gain, society has a much greater interest in the first. For intensive cultivation not only increases the amount of wages to be distributed, owing to its greater cost of production, but increases the actual quantity of foodstuff owing to its greater gross yield. The use of machinery, on the other hand, reduces wages and rarely increases the harvest. On a large scale it might even encourage the emigration of the country population. But if emigration already exists from other causes, the use of machinery in agriculture will, on the contrary, have the beneficial effect of supplementing the deficiency of rural labour.[2]

If now, looking to the future, we were asked whether large cultivation were destined to eliminate small cultivation, just as, it

[1] See Mr. E. Simon's curious book, *La Cité chinoise.*
[2] It is unlikely, in our opinion, that machinery will ever have as great an effect in agriculture as in industry. In industry, which is concerned solely with

is said, large industry and commerce are on the way to eliminate small industry and small commerce, we should have to reply that the question in these terms is not rightly put. For what is meant by *large cultivation?* If, as the words seem to indicate, we mean agricultural enterprises of larger and larger *surface extent,* our answer must be in the negative. Agricultural evolution is tending altogether in the opposite direction. We saw that, as a nation passes from the hunting to the pastoral and from the pastoral to the agricultural stage, the extended surface which it requires for exploitation gradually diminishes, and this, in the agricultural stage, is still further reduced as it passes from extensive to intensive cultivation, that is to say, from agriculture in the strict sense to market gardening. But if, by large cultivation, we mean the application of ever-increasing quantities of capital to a given surface, then our answer is in the affirmative. Evolution is tending in this direction. For we saw that, at each of the above stages of cultivation, as the surface cultivated becomes smaller, the effort and concentration applied become greater, and accumulate like the pressure of water in a reservoir, the sides of which are being gradually contracted.[1]

We may expect the agriculture of the future, then, to assume the form of exploitations—we may even say domains, though the

the displacing of matter or the changing of its form, motive power is almost everything ; in agriculture, where life has to be created, all it can do is to improve the environment.

[1] The example of the United States, which cultivates on the largest scale, is often put forward, and it is asked: "Is not this the cause of that superiority of theirs which enables them to come and crush out our European agriculturists on our own markets ?"

But their example proves nothing against our contention ; on the contrary, it justifies it. For although these colossal farms of the New World, these *bonanza farms,* are able to produce wheat at very little cost, they are able to produce only *very small returns,* hardly more than an average of twelve bushels per acre, or less than the poorest ground in France, whose average is sixteen bushels. This extensive cultivation is still possible in the United States, where there is any amount of land and where population is relatively scarce ; but so soon as the population becomes dense, as in France, the method of extensive cultivation will have to be given up, and labour and capital will be concentrated on smaller and smaller surfaces in order to increase the return. Already statistics show a considerable reduction in the size of agricultural exploitations between the census of 1850, when the average was 202·6 acres, and that of 1890, when it had fallen to 136·5 acres. True, the average has risen somewhat during the last ten years, being 146·6 acres in 1900 ; but this increase is due not to concentration of property, but to the fact that cultivation has been spreading into the barren and semi-desert regions of the West, which do not lend themselves to intensive cultivation. In the older States of the Atlantic and of the basin of the Mississippi, the size of the farms has steadily decreased.

words are not synonymous—cultivated more and more intensively, but becoming ever smaller and consequently more numerous, and united by the ties of co-operative agricultural association (which we shall study shortly). We often hear people speak of the technical superiority of large cultivation. But those who do so are, as a rule, misled by the intellectual superiority which the large agriculturist naturally has over the peasant. They see the large domains better kept, setting an example in the direction of agricultural improvements, and they attribute to a difference in the mode of exploitation what is really due to a difference in the social condition and education of the land-owners.[1]

CHAPTER IV: ASSOCIATION FOR PRODUCTION

I: ASSOCIATIONS OF LABOUR

"To-day, Good Friday," wrote Fourier in 1818, "I have found the secret of universal association." But he flattered himself somewhat; he certainly did not discover it, although he emphasised it with singular vigour. Association is not of the order of phenomena which need to be discovered. It stares every one in the face. It is probably the most general of all the laws of the universe. It is manifest not only in the relations of human beings in society, but in the relations which group worlds into solar systems,

[1] The following figures are given in the census for 1906 (compare those for industry and commerce, pp. 165 and 171):

	1896	1906	Incr. or decr.
Small exploitations (1 hired labourer) .	683,596	708,872	+36 per cent.
Medium-sized exploitations (1 to 50 labourers)	791,126	615,188	– 22 „
Very large exploitations (over 50 labourers)	233	201	– 14 „
	1,474,955	1,324,261	– 10 „

It will be seen that in the short space of ten years the number of small exploitations has increased very considerably. This is the more remarkable as the total number of agricultural exploitations has decreased. The proportion of large exploitations to small is less than 1 to 1000.

In the United States there was one farm for every 14 persons in 1850, and one farm for every 8·9 persons in 1900.

Bernstein, although a Socialist, says in his book already referred to : " There is no doubt that everywhere in Western Europe, as in the Eastern States of the American Union, the number of small and medium-sized agricultural enterprises is increasing, while that of the large and giant enterprises is diminishing."—Am. Ed.

cells and molecules into organic or inorganic bodies—even in the relations of logic by which men think. The very animals are conscious of the laws of association, and some animal societies—those of the bees, the ants, the beavers—have served from time immemorial as an inexhaustible subject of instruction and admiration for man.

Association may take place for any purpose whatever, but the only one which concerns us here is association with a view to production, using the word not in the ordinary sense of association by contract, but in the larger sense of a group of individuals working together for a common end. In this sense it is indispensable in all operations beyond the strength of the individual, if it be but the lifting of a weight, and in all those which, being interdependent, must be carried out together, viz., the labours of the sower and the plough-man who walks behind to cover the seed, or of the engine-driver and the stoker on the same engine. Division of labour, as we have seen, always presupposes conscious association.

The association of men has passed through three phases :

(1) In the beginning it was *instinctive*, as with the animals.[1] Men grouped themselves together as by instinct, not merely in their struggles, but in their work and their play. Solitary labour was as little to their liking as solitary play.[2] The sexual instinct, too, created the most natural and certainly the earliest association, namely that of the man, the woman, and the child. It will be said perhaps that such association is not of an economic character. But this is a mistake. Marriage, or rather the household, seems at the outset to have been an association mainly economic in character. When the North American Indians were asked why they married, they answered, " Because our wives fetch wood, water, and food, and carry our baggage." [3]

It is quite possible, indeed, that it was the economic nature of marriage which gave it the permanent character that the sexual, or even the paternal, instinct alone would have been powerless to impart.

---

[1] See the interesting description of these animal societies in M. Espinas' book, *Sociétés animales*.

[2] The socialist, Fourier, sees in association the chief means of making labour attractive. And Professor Bücher, in his Economic Studies, particularly the one entitled *The Community of Labour*, shows very clearly how " labour done in common excites emulation ; no one wants to remain behind " ; and also how the rhythm or cadence, which characterises many forms of labour, requires the co-operation of several persons.

[3] Eyre quoted by Starke, *La famille primitive*. Confirmation of this fact may be found, also, among the polygamous Arabs, the Basutos of South Africa, etc.

(2) Association next became *coercive*, first of all in the form of *slavery*.[1] We have already said (p. 158) that slavery should be considered as a simple expansion of the primitive family determined by economic causes, the need, namely, of forming a more powerful association. It is not surprising, when we think of it, that foreign workers should have been introduced into the family at a time when the wives themselves were often the fruit of conquest—viz., the rape of the Sabines. As a rule, these strangers ended by becoming adopted members of the family, as we see in Greek tragedies of twenty-five centuries ago, and in the accounts of travellers in Morocco to-day.

It was by means of this forced co-operative association that the men of a former time, yoked together in hundreds, and moving to the rhythm of a brass instrument struck by a kind of orchestral conductor, as we see on the Egyptian bas-reliefs, were able to raise the pyramids and to urge along galleys of three or four tiers.

With *serfdom*, association became less strictly coercive : the tie between master and man was a looser one. But the association between the worker and the land, on the other hand, became closer, the characteristic of serfdom being, as we know, the binding of the serf to the soil.

Association still had a semi-coercive character under the *guild system*. It was compulsory in the sense that no one might do a piece of work unless he were a member of the guild for that craft, and then only by conforming to the regulations laid down by the guild, or later by the Government. But here the obligation, instead of being a servitude, was a privilege. The advantage and honour of admission into this association of trades called the " Guild " was granted only after long apprenticeship, and a test of capacity, consisting in the execution of a masterpiece.[2] Later on, the payment of heavier and heavier entrance fees was substituted for the master-piece, and money, favour, or relationship to a master became a greater claim to admission than technical capacity. This was the

[1] Slavery, that is to say, the right of the strongest, is not the only force which gives rise to coercive association. Certain constraints of Nature may have the same effect. The regular overflowing of the Nile imposed on those living on its banks conditions of irrigation and ordered labour which were perhaps the oldest form of co-operation among men. (See Metchnikoff's *Grands fleuves historiques*.)

[2] It would be a mistake, however, to think that the guild system ever included all workers within its regulations. M. Hauser (*Ouvriers du temps passé*) has shown very clearly that such a general statement would be a great exaggeration. But he has perhaps, in his turn, gone to the opposite extreme, when he asserts that in the Middle Ages " free labour was the commonest form of labour,"

beginning of the breach which was to widen to a chasm between worker and master. The workers, *companions* or *varlets*, as they were called, saw the entrance to mastership—*i.e.* to independent production—closed, and found themselves condemned to remain simple wage-earners to the end. It was then that, over against the guilds which had become associations of masters exclusively, they set up associations composed solely of workers (*compagnons*) which were to play so large a part in the history of the working classes.

(3) The movement, then, which, in the Middle Ages, seemed about to unite capital and labour into one association failed. But it led to a new form of association, known to-day by the name of *enterprise*—the technical word for it in political economy—consisting of a fairly large group of persons in which one individual, the employer, finds the capital and the land, and the others, who are hired for wages, supply the labour.

Is not this, save for a few details which still need perfecting, the free and contractual form of association, the last stage, so to speak, in social evolution ? The Classical school holds that it is. Still, it is worth while noticing that there is no feeling among the workers that they are associated with the employer in a common cause. Although they are, in fact, associated for production, they are not in any way associated in management or in distribution. Not only are they not associates in the legal and strict sense of the word *society*, but it is questionable if they even stand to their employer in a relationship of contract at all. For the so-called labour contract is, after all, simply an engagement. This is the technical word for it.

We shall see further on,[1] however, that the law, by calling on the workers to participate in the drawing up of the " workshop regulations," and by awarding damages for the breaking of engagements, tends nowadays to give the wage-system the character of a synallagmatic contract. And the two parties, employers and employed, tend also to impart to it certain of the characteristics of association by adopting such combinations as *profit-sharing* and *co-partnership*, which we shall study later.

May we not, then, hope that this imperfect association, called enterprise; will give place in turn to a final phase of free and full association—association in management and in distribution as well as in production—wherein *each will have the distinct consciousness that he is a member of a collective undertaking and the firm resolve to co-operate in it ?*

---

[1] See Book III, *The Labour Contract*. We shall find that some authors, among them M. Chatelain, already see in this an imperfect contract of association.

It would seem so, for this form of association already exists under the name of *co-operative association for production*. It consists of associations of working men who produce by themselves for themselves, and who keep the whole product of their labour. But, as the object of this system is the abolition of the wage-system, we shall defer fuller discussion of it to a later chapter. We may simply say here that this method of enterprise is not very important as yet, and is spreading very slowly.

II : ASSOCIATIONS OF CAPITAL

FROM what has just been said, it would appear that there has hardly ever been a really free association of labour on this earth. It is not the same, however, with capital. Capital, in the form of money, enjoys a freedom of movement, which labour cannot possess, and the development of credit is increasing its mobility extraordinarily. Before working men or landowners can co-operate in a productive enterprise, this enterprise must be started on some particular spot, and can group together only persons living in the same locality. Labour can change its place only with the person of the labourer, and the labourer is not easily uprooted from the place in which he has grown up. As for land, it is immovable. Capital alone has the wings of an eagle and can fly from one end of the world to another wherever it sees some profit to be gained.

So soon as an enterprise becomes fairly large—and this, as we have seen, is the general tendency—the *entrepreneur* finds himself as little able to supply the quantity of capital necessary, in proportion to the number of workers, as he is able, of himself, to furnish the necessary amount of manual labour. A number of capitalists therefore unite to provide the capital required, and the enterprise is constituted in the form of a shareholding company, a form invented in Holland in the seventeenth century and spreading rapidly to-day, at any rate in commerce and industry.[1]

What characterises this form of company is, that the capital

---

[1] Although the two words, *association* and *society*, are commonly used as synonyms, French law draws an essential distinction between them. The word society implies that profit is the end in view; the word association, on the contrary, precludes a lucrative end, and consequently applies only to groups which aim at some social, religious, or political, interest. But the ordinary language of every day takes little account of this juridical distinction ; thus we speak of " *sociétés de secours mutuels*," although the end in view is mutual help, and " *associations de production*," although their object is to sell at the highest price possible.

Note, however, that, contrary to what we might at first expect, the legislator

necessary to the enterprise is divided into fractions, called shares, of very small value—as a rule 500 francs in France,[1] £1 in England, and $100 in the United States. These shares represent portions of ownership in the company.[2] Thus, a company with a capital of fifty million francs will issue 100,000 shares of the French type, 100,000 of the American, and 2,000,000 of the English; and each person will take as many as he wants, according to his fortune and the confidence he has in the enterprise. It goes without saying that the amount which he will get from the profits of the enterprise will be proportional to the number of his shares: this amount is called a *dividend*. But what attracts him above all to this kind of investment is, that his responsibility and risk are also limited to the amount of the shares to which he has subscribed. This is the essential distinction between the limited liability company and every other company, and in England the word " limited " must be affixed by law to every enterprise of this kind. This way of minimising risks has made the most venturesome undertakings possible. Had the limited liability company not been invented, railways would never have been laid nor the Isthmuses of Suez and Panama pierced.[3]

Besides the ordinary share, these companies have other methods of participation by which to attract capitalists, large and small. To prudent capitalists, seeking security of investment and regularity of income, they offer debentures, which differ from shares (though their value is generally the same, viz., 500 francs) in that they

has always shown himself very suspicious of associations that have not a lucrative object (in France they were even prohibited until quite recently—1901), while he has always favoured societies whose object is gain.

[1] In France, the share may by law be as low as 100 francs, and only a quarter of it, *i.e.* twenty-five francs, need be paid up. In the case of small companies, whose capital is not over 200,000 francs, the value of the share may be only 25 francs, and the amount paid up one-tenth, *i.e.* 2 francs 50 centimes. These are the societies usually known as " co-operatives."

[2] Legally, the share is not a portion of co-ownership in the capital of the company, for this capital is not the joint property of the members. It belongs to the legal person, *i.e.* to the company itself, not to be confused with the person of any one of the members. But this is only a legal fiction invented in order to facilitate the administration of the company: the capital of the company is, in reality, collective property.

For the American law and practice on this subject consult Lough, *Corporation Finance;* and Conyngton, *The Modern Corporation.*—AM. ED.

[3] No capitalist, however rich, would, or could, have promised the 1300 million francs laid out by the company created by De Lesseps for piercing the Isthmus o Panama, because of the risks involved; while the same risks divided up indefinitely did not frighten the smallest purse. Consequently, only a few persons were ruined by that immense failure.

give the right to a fixed income, called interest, which is always paid whether the year be good or bad. The debenture-holder is thus a real creditor who runs a risk only if the company becomes insolvent, and who, even then, is paid before the ordinary shareholder. To bolder capitalists, on the other hand, most companies offer founders' shares, which do not give a right to participate in the profits until these have reached a certain figure, and until the ordinary shares have been paid ; so that they suit only those who have firm faith in the future of the enterprise.

Shareholding companies have spread so rapidly in all countries that they tend now to become the normal mode of production. Thousands of them are created every year, bringing together billions of capital. These are not all, of course, new enterprises : many are individual enterprises converted into companies.[1]

The shareholding company is, as a rule, distinguished by another characteristic : it is *anonymous*, that is to say, it is not an association of persons, like the associations of labour or the "co-operatives" (see next chapter), but an association of capital. This capital has, of course, owners, but they do not count. Their names may perhaps be known if the shares are registered, but if the shares are "bearer shares," as they more frequently are, their anonymous character is complete. This is the perfection of the capitalist association—it is an association no longer of men, but of money-bags.[2]

[1] It is calculated that there are, in the world, about 600 billion francs of negotiable scrip, in the form of stocks, shares, bonds, etc., distributed as follows :

Great Britain .	.	.	.	.	140 to 142	billion francs
United States .	.	.	.	.	130 ,, 132	,,
France .	.	.	.	.	106 ,, 110	,,
Germany	.	.	.	.	90 ,, 95	,,
Russia .	.	.	.	.	29 ,, 31	,,
Austria-Hungary	.	.	.	.	23 ,, 24	,,
Italy	.	.	.	.	13 ,, 14	,,
Japan .	.	.	.	.	9 ,, 12	,,
Other countries	.	.	.	.	35 ,, 40	,,
Total .		.	.	.	575 to 600	billion francs

The figures are M. Neymark's (*Bulletin de l'Institut international de Statistique*, vol. xix, Book II, p. 222), and refer to the year 1910. But as regards Germany they were then, and are to-day, below the actual facts.

[2] There are in French law three main classes of companies :

(1) The *limited liability companies*, which we have been studying in this chapter, and which are by far the most important.

(2) *Partnerships*—firms suitable to enterprises of lesser importance which have no need of many capitalists. Sometimes there are not more than two

There must, of course, be some one to control it. There is therefore a small Board of Directors and a chairman, but the responsibility of its members does not exceed the amount of their shares. The Board is the representative government of the company. It is elected by a general meeting of shareholders, and is bound to give an account of its mandate not oftener than once a year, the shareholders having, moreover, no effective control over it.[1]

It is not only in the production of wealth that the shareholding company has caused a revolution, allowing colossal enterprises to be carried through by the concentration of capital. By an operation which, at first sight, appears exactly the opposite, that is to say, by dividing up the ownership of capital into an infinite number of shares, it is having an equally revolutionary effect on distribution. But we shall return to this in Book III.

From the point of view of the workers, these societies, or companies, offer as a rule better conditions of labour as regards wage, steadiness of employment, pensions, &c.[2] Even trade unionists and socialists see in them more favourable conditions for spreading their propaganda and for the development of labour solidarity.

Still, as may well be imagined, such powerful organisations are not without danger, especially when they take the form of trusts: danger to the public, which they tempt with the promise of profits and with limited risk. The ease with which the most extravagant enterprises are able to find credulous and enthu-

---

or three partners, often relatives or acquaintances, and the company bears their names. The bond of association is much closer here, as the members are all responsible jointly, and for the totality of the liabilities of the firm. The so-called " *civil society* " (*société civile*), *i.e.* a society of non-traders, say, *e.g.* of landowners, presents somewhat the same characteristics, except that all members are responsible for equal amounts, but not for total liabilities.

(3) The societies *en commandite*, which are a mixed type of the other two combined.

[1] Sometimes only the large shareholders have a right to vote at the general meeting. They, alone, have a right to be elected to the board of directors. Thus, in the large French railway companies, a shareholder must have 40 to 50 shares in order to attend a meeting of shareholders and 100 to 500 before he can be eligible for the Board. The value of the shares varies from 1000 to 1800 francs. The government is, therefore, quite oligarchical; but this is necessary in risky enterprises which have been turned into joint-stock companies.

[2] Thus, in 1909, the five large railway companies in France spent 80 million francs in benefactions of all kinds (including pensions) to their staff in proportion to the 143 million francs of dividends distributed. The share of the workers, therefore, over and above their salaries, represents 60 per cent. of that of the shareholders. There are few private enterprises which could support such a burden.

siastic subscribers is daily illustrated in comic and in tragic ways. Even in the case of really productive enterprises, the public is often taken in by the process of over-capitalising, *i.e.* stating the capital above its real value. A mining or electrical enterprise, for instance, the real value of which is a million francs, is offered to the public in the form of 10,000 shares of 500 francs, which represents 5 millions. In the United States, where this process is common, the capital is said to be *watered.* A frantic boom at the moment the shares are issued forces their prices up. For a year or two perhaps fictitious dividends taken out of the borrowed capital keep these going, until the founders of the concerns, having disposed of all their shares to the public, and pocketed their profits, let the crash come.

In France, and in other countries, there are Bills before Parliament to prevent these abuses. A league has even been created for the reform of the laws concerning shareholding companies. At present, practically the only precautionary measure consists in an illusory publicity. Among the numerous remedies proposed are the following :

(*1*) To increase the responsibility of founders and directors toward shareholders.

(*2*) To raise the value of the share to, say, 1000 marks, as in Germany, and to require that it be fully paid up. But this would be to protect small savings by shutting them out from lucrative investment.

(*3*) To constitute a body of controllers, as in Germany, or of auditors, as in England, to verify the sincerity of statements and the real value of the shares. This would be a better plan ; but it must not be forgotten, on the other hand, that every new form of control exercised over this mode of enterprise weakens its economic power.

In any case, we cannot share the hope of some economists, who believe that not only will the anonymous company become the typical mode of all enterprise, but that it will spread to all domains of human activity.[1] We cannot resign ourselves to seeing in it the form of the future. Its very anonymity, that is to say, the mere fact that it associates only *capital* and not *individuals*, thus doing away with all responsibility, is, in our view, a cause of inferiority, moral at least, if not economic. Our hope is rather that association

---

[1] M. de Molinari in particular has developed this thesis in his interesting book, *L'Evolution économique au XIX siècle.* In his view, public services, police, education, etc., even States themselves, the Fatherlands, are destined to become joint-stock companies

will become co-operative, uniting all collaborators, workers, capitalists, even customers, by a more close and personal tie.

III : TRUSTS AND CARTELS

THE associations of capitalists of which we have been speaking, are composed of non-producing capitalists, sleeping-partners in one single enterprise. But there are also associations consisting of several enterprises combined, which may, or may not, take the form of joint-stock companies. We refer to Trusts and Cartels, so called because the United States and Germany were their birth-places.[1]

The *Cartel* (charter, contract), or in French, the *syndicat de production* or *entente commerciale*, is the simplest form of association among producers. It grew out of a feeling of reaction against the ruinous competition which producers carried on among themselves. It does not affect the individuality of an enterprise or its internal autonomy, but groups enterprises together under the best possible conditions for the sale of their products. For this purpose it has recourse to different methods, all of which have the same object, namely, to avoid, or at least to regulate, competition.

These methods consist :

(1) In marking out a zone to be reserved for each member of the association, that is to say, in giving each a monopoly over a particular district ;

(2) In fixing a maximum of production for each member which must not be exceeded ;

(3) In fixing a sale price to which all must conform. This does not entirely do away with competition, but sets up, as the end in view, superior quality rather than reduction in price. As conditions of production vary greatly, however, from one enterprise to another, this equalising of prices is somewhat unpractical and often unjust ;

(4) As none of these three means has proved very effective, in spite of the guarantees and fines intended to enforce them, a fourth

---

[1] There is no end to the literature on trusts and cartels. We quote simply a few writers : Jenks, *The Trust Problem ;* Meade, *Corporation Finance ;* Ely, *Monopolies and Trusts ;* Ripley, *Trusts, Pools, and Corporations ;* Macrosty, *On Trusts ;* Souchon, *Les Cartels agricoles en Allemagne,* and, among the most recent, Martin Saint-Léon, *Cartels et Trusts,* 3rd edition, 1909, and Clark (John Bates and John Maurice), *The Control of Trusts.*

An excellent analysis of trust literature and of arguments for and against the trusts is given in Professor Bullock's essay on " Trust Literature," reprinted in Ripley's book referred to above.—AM. ED.

method has been tried, which does away with direct sale between members and customers, and places the cartel, as compulsory intermediary, between the producer and the public. It is the cartel which buys the products of the associated producers,—prices, and the quantities to be supplied by each, being fixed beforehand; and it is the cartel which undertakes to sell them to the best advantage. In this way it becomes a sort of co-operative association for production.[1]

With the *Trust*[2] we advance further along the road of concentration and monopoly. The agreement becomes a fusion. Trusts, like cartels, have tried very different methods; continually prosecuted by the law, they were obliged to assume one form after another. Three successive forms may be indicated:

(*a*) The first differed very little from the cartel. It consisted of an *entente* among large manufacturers, or large companies, with the object of regulating prices. But these *ententes*, called *pools*, were forbidden in the United States after 1890 by the Sherman Act, as combinations in restraint of trade.

(*b*) Recourse was then had to a system called *consolidation*, by which all the associated enterprises gave up their autonomy and were melted into one. For this purpose each business was valued,

---

[1] There are over 500 cartels in Germany, where they have spread rapidly, especially in coal-mining and in certain semi-agricultural industries, such as alcohol, sugar, etc. In some Swiss towns, at Basle for instance, each brewery has its own quarter reserved for it, so that it is very difficult for the consumer to get the beer he wants.

Trusts, in the strict sense, have not yet penetrated into France, nor have the large co-operative federations, the French being of an undisciplined nature, not lightly binding themselves into large organisations. In some industries there are, however, *ententes*, tacit or contractual. One of the oldest and best known is the *Comptoir de Longwy*, dating from 1889 (anterior, therefore, to the German cartels), which controls the iron industry. It includes among its members most of the local producers of pig-iron. It has nothing whatever to do with the manufacture of the iron, but centralises all sales, which must pass through its hands, and fixes the quantities to be delivered by each member, and the price. Members may sell, themselves, as much as they please of their iron *manufactured*, and have a right to sell abroad whatever quantity of their pig-iron the *Comptoir* cannot take off their hands. In spite of what has been said against it, the *Comptoir* does not seem to have raised prices nor to have brought its members excessive profits; and it has done some good in defending French industry against German competition which follows the same methods.

[2] The word trust is a very old English word meaning confidence. The representatives of philanthropic foundations, or others, are called trustees, almost as, in France, we should use the word *fidei-commissionaire:* so also are directors in trusts, since the interests of all are entrusted to them. Certain deposit banks of the United States are called *Trust Companies*, but these must not be confused with industrial trusts (see *infra, Banks*).

and the value paid to its owner in the form of shares in the new company, the trust. The directors thus held everything in their hands and governed this agglomeration of enterprises as they thought fit, eliminating, when necessary, those which did not appear very flourishing. But laws were passed against this form of monopoly also.

(c) Lastly came the system which prevails for the most part to-day. Nominally and legally each enterprise remains autonomous, but this autonomy is only apparent, since the majority of the shares in each of the enterprises are held by an outside company. As this company is all-powerful in the administration of each separate factory, it stands to reason that it is so in the administration of the whole combined. This is what is called the *holding company*. It was on this system that the famous Standard Oil Company, in order to be within the limits of the law, divided itself up into some twenty so-called independent companies. But almost all the shares are in the hands of one single company. These governing companies are themselves, more often than not, in the hands of large financiers, who thus well merit their titles of Oil, Steel, Railway Kings,[1] etc.

The Trust is distinguished from the Cartel not only by the fact that the bond between its members is much closer, but because it is more than a mere commercial organisation ; it is an organisation for production. It pushes to their extreme limits the characteristic features of large industry—concentration, specialisation and integration [2]—as also the abuses of the shareholding company, viz., over-capitalisation, etc.[3]

The Trust, the very name of which was scarcely known twenty years ago, and which we did not consider worth mentioning in the earlier editions of the *Principles*, has become the most symptomatic phenomenon of the modern economic movement. The increasing number of trusts, above all the colossal proportions they have already attained, astound even the most indifferent public. Petroleum, steel, meat, whisky, tobacco, railways, the mercantile marine—there is

---

[1] The inquiry of Congress into the Standard Oil Trust brought to light the fact that two men (Mr. Rockefeller and the late Mr. Pierpont Morgan) governed a totality of enterprises (railways, mines, petroleum wells, iron-works, banks, etc.) representing a capital of £5,000,000,000, either directly or through managers. Hence the pun of the Americans, who now speak not of the " organisation," but the " Morganisation " of industry.

[2] Thus the Steel Trust does not stop short at grouping ironworks together, but groups also the iron mines and even the railways and canals which transport the ore.

[3] Over-capitalisation, *i.e.* the issuing of shares above their real value, has for its excuse the anticipation of profits expected from the actual creation of the monopoly.

nothing which may not be made into a trust.[1] They are like some monstrous fauna suddenly engendered by the capitalist age, which socialists and economists of the Liberal school contemplate with equal curiosity but opposite feelings ; the first saluting in them the last stage of capitalist concentration, after which there remains only collectivism ; the second, troubled by the paradoxical results of free competition, but faithful to the hope that, in spite of everything, the liberty which gave birth to trusts will be sufficient to kill them or render them harmless.

For the rest, the question whether in this movement the good results outweigh the ill, or *vice versa*, has not yet been answered.

Two weighty arguments may be brought forward in favour of trusts :

(*1*) They reduce the cost of production, which is the true criterion of economic progress. One of the most remarkable examples of the reduction of costs, which trusts alone can realise, is to be seen in the network of pipe-lines laid over thousands of miles for the transport of petroleum. Another may be seen in the utilising of by-products in the same industry — more than twenty different products being extracted from petroleum by the Standard Oil Trust—and in the manufacture of accessories (see above, p. 165, *Specialisation and Integration of Industry*). We may mention, also, the suppression of, or at least the reduction in, the number of commercial travellers [2] and in the costs of advertising ; in a word, in all outlay necessitated by competition, which becomes unnecessary so soon as the industry is a monopoly and has no longer to run after the customer. Add to this, too, the elimination of badly situated factories and the localising of production at most favourable spots.[3] It must be observed that cartels, or simple commercial agreements, are powerless to accomplish these results.

(*2*) They maintain an equilibrium between production and consumption which the system of free competition has been unable to do,

---

[1] The Standard Oil Trust is the oldest and most famous of all. Created in 1872, by a fusion of 29 companies, it has distributed annually from 350 to 400 million dollars in dividends on an original capital of not more than 100 million dollars.

The United States Steel Company, created in 1901, surpassed the former in its capital, but not in profits. Its properties (mines, works, railways) are valued at 2,000,000,000 dollars.

[2] By 1892 the number dispensed with in the United States was estimated at 35,000.

[3] The Whisky Trust was no sooner constituted in 1890 than it shut down 68 out of 80 distilleries (see Rousiers, *Les industries monopolisées aux États-Unis*).

thus warding off crises and steadying prices. The advocates of trusts, indeed, deny that these have raised prices, and quote, on the contrary, numerous instances of a continuous fall.[1] It is the policy of trusts to avoid an exaggerated rise as much as a fall. Moreover, even if prices were to rise a little, the consumer, they declare, would find a compensating advantage in their steadiness. As a rule, too, trusts are careful of the quality of their products, and despise the petty processes of small commerce, which tries to pass off bad stuff for good. The refineries of the Standard Oil Trust are subject to the most rigorous control.

But, on the other hand, there is no lack of arguments against trusts.

It is no more likely in the economic, than in the political, order, that a power absolutely without counterpoise should not abuse its strength, or, at any rate, should not turn it to its own advantage. Admitting, therefore, that trusts have not always raised prices, granting even that they have benefited the consumer to a slight extent by the economies which they have brought about in the cost of production, it is certain: (a) That they have used the greater part of these in enriching their shareholders and in accumulating fortunes, like that of Mr. Rockefeller,[2] in the hands of a few of them. It is the trust which has created the previously unknown species of multi-millionaire. (b) That not only have they not always given the consumer the benefit of the reduced cost of production, but they have shown in certain industries—the meat trust, for instance—a cynical indifference to his interests, which came to light in the preserved meat scandals in Chicago. (c) That they tend to create a *de facto* monopoly in every industry, ferociously crushing out all competition, not only by their superior organisation and reduced cost of production—methods which would be legitimate and beneficent—but by processes which amount to sheer piracy, such as selling at a loss whenever a competitor appears,[3] or illegally forcing special rates from the railway

---

[1] Thus the price of petroleum fell from 24 cents a gallon in 1871, to 6 cents in 1906, or from 28 to 7 centimes a litre. The answer to this is, that without the trust the price would be lower still, but it is a point that is difficult to prove.

[2] The American newspapers estimate Mr. Rockefeller's fortune at £80,000,000 to £120,000,000.

[3] M. Martin Saint-Léon quotes a passage from an official inquiry into the Standard Oil Trust. The President of the Commission to the Vice-President of the Trust : " It is your rule, is it not, to keep your prices below cost price until your rival has disappeared ? " Answer : " Yes."

And the Meat Trust made no secret of its intention to kill off, on the London market, all importation from the Argentine Republic, by selling its beef there at 3d. per lb.

companies.[1] Now, without professing a blind faith in the virtues of competition, we may take it that industrial government by a few autocratic magnates would be a worse system. (d) That, from the political point of view, the rise of these giants, armed with all the powers of corruption that illimitable wealth gives, may put the whole of the forces of government out of order, particularly in democratic societies.

Is there any way of preserving the economic advantages of trusts while rendering them powerless for evil ? This is the somewhat contradictory problem which economists and governments are tackling. We know that the Presidents of the United States, Mr. Roosevelt and Mr. Taft, have had the task at heart, and that law proceedings have been taken against various trusts. But if the law is able to prevent companies from fusing into one, or railways from discriminating in their rates, how is it possible for it to hinder a few millionaire capitalists from acquiring control of these companies and railways, and from arranging matters among themselves ? The trust to-day is often no more than an agreement, and therefore escapes all control.[2]

[1] American law forbids railway companies to grant individual reductions in freights. but there are a hundred ways of getting round the law. Sometimes the company raises or lowers its rates suddenly, warning the trust in advance, so that it may profit first. Sometimes it despatches the goods of the trust before those of its competitors. A case is even quoted of a company which was to hand over to the trust a part of the railway receipts taken from its unfortunate competitors !

[2] The struggle between the American Government and the trusts during the last five or six years is a curious one. In 1911, the Standard Oil Trust and the Tobacco Trust were each fined 29 million dollars, and ordered to dissolve by the Supreme Court. But an opening was left to trusts in the wording of the sentence which, as President Taft pointed out (1912), made it clear that *mere size was no sin against the law.* It was only when an agglomeration resulted in the strangling of competition, rise in price or monopoly, that the law was violated.

The French legislator, following public opinion in this respect, was very severe on what was called *accaparement,* or " cornering the market." The " accapareurs " of wheat were the terror of the people until fairly recently. A survival of this repressive legislation is still to be found in Article 419 of the *Code Pénal,* which punishes with prison and a fine " all who . . . by coalition among the principal dealers in a commodity or product . . . tend not to sell it or to sell it only at a certain price . . . or who by fraudulent ways and means shall have brought about a rise or fall in the price of the product or merchandise." But jurisprudence and most authors admit, that this text affects only cases where fraudulent manœuvres, *i.e.* other than those of supply and demand, have been employed to cause the rise or fall, and that it does not apply to agreements among producers with the sole object of regulating or even limiting the quantity offered. Thus the Comptoir de Longwy (see above) was recognised as legal by the courts. In any case, the trust, properly speaking, could not come under this article, since the idea of *coalition* is incom-

Economists of the Liberal school are of the opinion that, if the protective system could be done away with, trusts, which up till now have thriven behind the shelter of customs barriers, would be sufficiently checkmated by international competition; and they point to England, where trusts have spread less than in other countries. There is, however, no ground for believing that in the United States, or in Germany, trusts and cartels would be the first to be killed by foreign competition. On the contrary, they are likely to stand the blow better than weaker enterprises. Universal Free Trade would probably have the effect, not of suppressing trusts, but of transforming them from national into international phenomena—which would make them by no means less formidable. Perhaps the best corrective for producers' trusts will one day be found in the buying federations of the co-operative societies, which are veritable consumers' trusts. However fanciful such a solution may appear to-day, considering the extreme inequality of the opposing forces, it is still a fact that, in England, in 1906, a soap trust which was already constituted was forced to dissolve owing to the campaign waged against it by the Co-operative Federation of Manchester.

IV: AGRICULTURAL ASSOCIATIONS

WE have spoken of the association of labour and the association of capital; why do we not speak of the association of land? It is because, of the three factors of production, land is obviously the one which least lends itself to association, since it cannot be displaced. We might, by a far-fetched metaphor, talk of association among the different pieces of land of a domain, where some are used for growing wheat, others for fodder for the live stock, and where, in general, a rotation of crops is established among them, and all are worked for one common end. But the agricultural association with which we are concerned is not an association of lands, but of landowners. Now

patible with that of fusion (see Dolléans, L'Accaparement, and Colson, Cours d'Économie politique).

The old-fashioned method of accaparement, which consisted in withdrawing a certain class of merchandise from the market in order to make it rise artificially, is called " cornering " in the United States, and may be quite as much the act of a single man as of a cartel or trust. In 1898, a young speculator, Leitner, made a celebrated corner in wheat in the United States, which failed, but not without having first thrown the market into confusion (see Dolléans, op. cit.).

On the other hand, a trust has just been started in Germany of an official, governmental and obligatory nature. It is the trust which embraces all the potash mines of the Empire   (1910.)

the association of landowners is not an easy matter ; we know no
example · of landowners associating their lands with a view to
exploiting them as one and jointly.   What is the reason of this
difficulty ?   In the first place, such an association could be useful
only in the case of estates actually bordering on one another.
And, as the old saying goes, " *Qui terre a, guerre a,*" the near neighbourhood of landowners is more apt to give rise to lawsuits than to
associations.   Landowners, moreover, would not find much advantage in association, since large production and the division of labour,
which are its main objects, do not give by any means the same results
in agriculture as they give in the manufacturing industry.   (See
above, p. 176.)

But although agricultural association does not exist for purposes
of common farming, it has, when restricted to certain special operations, developed so greatly in many countries that it is one of the
characteristic features of the present economic movement.   It is
by tens of thousands that agricultural associations have blossomed
forth during the last twenty years (25,000 in France and 26,500 in
Germany).[1]

These associations vary greatly in form and character, according to the specific ends they have in view.   They may be reduced,
however, to the five following types : [2]

(1) Associations for the *joint purchase of materials and instruments necessary for cultivation*.   These are the most numerous and
important.   They are known, in France, by the name of *syndicats
agricoles*, and their rapid development since the law of 1884, which
created them, is a matter of pride to French agriculturists.   They
number over 6000, with more than 900,000 members.

These associations have rendered French agriculture an inestimable service by spreading the use of chemical manures.   Before their
day these manures had been little employed, not only because

[1] It is very remarkable that the United Kingdom, the country which stands
foremost as regards association in its threefold form of trade unions, co-operatives, and friendly societies, is almost in the last rank as regards agricultural
associations.   This is no doubt due to the fact that farmers, as well as landowners, exploit on a large scale and have no need of them.   Lately, however,
such associations have been increasing rapidly and number about 1000, the
greater part of which, however, are in Ireland.

[2] A National Federation has been created, in France, with the object of grouping together all the different forms of agricultural association.   It is subdivided
into four sections : syndicates for purchase, credit, co-operative sale, and insurance, which correspond precisely to our classification with the omission of
No. 5, which has, in reality, a peculiar character of its own, and may be classed
apart.   For fuller details see our *Institutions de progrès social*.

their price was high and their efficacy but little recognised, but because they were subject to the most barefaced adulteration. Special legislation had tried in vain to put an end to the frauds. The syndicates succeeded, by acting as intermediaries of purchase, and by submitting the manures to analysis in their own laboratories. Sometimes, as in Italy, where such associations flourish under the name of *consorzio agrario*, they manufacture the manures directly themselves. This has, however, rarely been done in France. These syndicates have brought prices down considerably, to the great irritation of the middlemen.[1] They have also rendered great services to viticulture as regards the choice of plants and the treatment of diseases of the vine, and some smaller services as regards the use of agricultural machines.[2] Lastly, they are the hives, so to speak, from which the different associations of which we shall treat presently have swarmed, although their social virtues have perhaps been somewhat overrated.[3]

In spite of the similarity of name and legal form, the agricultural syndicates must not be confused with the working men's syndicates (trade unions), of which we shall speak when discussing wages. The agricultural syndicates are composed of landowners, and nothing is further from their intentions than class conflict. There is some inclination to-day to turn these associations into *mixed* syndicates, *i.e.* syndicates composed of landowners and agricultural

[1] It is worth remarking that, in terms of the law of March 21, 1884, which created agricultural, at the same time as working men's, and employers', syndicates, the object of the syndicate is solely *the defence of trade interests*, not the purchase of anything at all, *i.e.* a social, not a commercial policy. The working men's and employers' syndicates have, indeed, adhered to this policy, which has kept their hands full. But the agricultural syndicates, which are only rarely concerned in class conflicts, and are composed wholly of good solid proprietors, have thought, not unreasonably, that the best thing to do was to look for practical advantages, and have become manure merchants, seed merchants, etc. That is to say, they have turned themselves into co-operative societies. Although illegal, jurisprudence had tolerated the practice on the ground that associations which buy only for their own members are not performing a commercial act, the latter, by definition, consisting in *buying to sell*. A recent decree of the Court of Cassation, however, which caused a great stir, has laid down that henceforth, for all operations of purchase and sale, agricultural syndicates must constitute separate co-operative associations or federations.

[2] They would seem well qualified to buy collectively such costly implements as steam threshing-machines and ploughs for breaking up the ground. But the attempts made have not been encouraging. On the whole they have not been able to eliminate the middleman, who hires out these machines at a stiff price. The reason of their failure is the lack of co-operative spirit, all members wanting to be served at the same time.

[3] See M. de Rocquigny, *Les Syndicats agricoles.*

labourers, as it is thought that this may prevent the rupture which is beginning to manifest itself between the two classes and may, by fighting agrarian socialism, ward off strikes. But up till now nothing of importance has been done in this direction.[1]

(2) Associations for the *production or sale of certain agricultural products*. These are the least numerous, and a e far from giving the results hoped for ; and yet they seem to offer the best solution for the requirements of small farmers, procuring the economic advantages which enable them to compete with large exploitations, while, from the moral point of view, presenting a real remedy against the conservative individualism which dominates them. But this very individualism has so far stood in the way of any effective understanding. It must be added, moreover, that the elimination of the middlemen, who, up till now, have undertaken the work of transforming and selling agricultural produce, is no easy task.

True we have just seen that the syndicates for purchase have practically succeeded in abolishing the middleman, but sale, as every one knows, is a much more difficult matter. It requires business capacities and organisation which the agricultural associations so far have not been able to acquire.[2]

Still, the results attained are not altogether negligible. We may point, in the first place, to the associations of cow-owners in the mountains, for utilising milk and manufacturing cheeses. These *sociétés fruitières*, as they are called in the Juras, are the oldest form of agricultural co-operation, dating from the thirteenth century, and are very numerous (about 1800). To-day they are losing somewhat their co-operative character and tend to become simple milk-selling enterprises, in which the *entrepreneur* manufactures and sells the cheeses on his own account. Associations for the manufacture of butter, which started later, are, however, increasing considerably in number. In Denmark, which stands first, in Germany, Switzerland and Northern Italy, the milk depôts, *laiteries*, as they are called, may be counted by the thousand. In France there are about 200 of them.[3] They have brought the peasant a distinct increase of income. The production of wine has been

---

[1] There are, however, a few agricultural syndicates composed solely of country labourers (vine-growers and wood-cutters) which have the same character as the trade unions in the towns.

[2] Yet, it will be said, agriculturists nevertheless succeed in selling their produce. Yes, so long as merchants buy them. But the difficulty here is precisely to find a substitute for merchants.

[3] In France, the most important centres lie in the Departments of the Charente and Poitou, where there were, in 1912, over 130 *laiteries* and

successfully carried on in Germany by the wine-manufacturing associations of the Rhine wine-growers, and also in Italy and Austria; but in France, though this country stands first in vine-growing and wine manufacture, the results of association have been meagre, and the checks numerous. Some societies have succeeded fairly well in selling the wine of their members, but hardly any have gone in for co-operative wine manufacture, *i.e.* the transforming of the grape into wine in a common cellar, as is done by the German societies.[1] The sale of corn from common granaries, where it is deposited, looked after, ventilated, and where it may serve as guarantee for a loan on the warrant system (see below, *Crédit mobilier*), has given good results in Germany, but has not yet been tried in France.

We must mention, besides, as very important, the Danish agricultural associations for the sale of eggs and bacon, and the Swiss ones for the breeding of cattle and for the sale of a special breed of calves, registered in a Herd-book, which have been of great profit to the agriculturists of these two countries.

In France, apart from the *laiteries* and the *fruitières* mentioned above, there are about two hundred agricultural associations for various kinds of production, and several hundred co-operative bakeries. A law of December 29, 1906, has given a strong impetus to such associations, as it puts a considerable amount of money obtained from the Bank of France at their disposal (see below, *Agricultural Credit*) under the following conditions :

(*a*) That the associations be composed solely of agriculturists who are members of agricultural syndicates, or of agricultural insurance societies.

(*b*) That the said associations have in view only operations that are strictly agricultural.

(*c*) That they do not distribute dividends on the share-capital.[2]

74,000 members. They have introduced such improvements in the manufacture of butter, that 20 litres of milk are now enough to make 1 kilogramme of butter, where 30 litres were needed formerly. And the butter is sold at 3 instead of 2 francs per kilogramme.

[1] The association of the *Vignerons Libres* of Maraussan (a small village of Hérault) has, however, had a brilliant success, thanks to the support of the socialist societies of consumption, in Paris. It has been able, not only to sell its wine above the ordinary price, but to build a " social cellar " at a cost of 200,000 francs.

[2] They are not forbidden to make profits, but they must divide them in proportion to the sales and purchases of each member, not in proportion to his contribution in capital.

(*d*) That the loan from the State does not exceed twice the capital paid up by the members.[1]

(*e*) That it be repaid within a maximum period of twenty-five years.

(3) Associations for *mutual insurance against agricultural risks*, principally against the death of cattle, but also against fire, hail, etc.   They number over 12,000 in France, 9000 of which are against the death of cattle,[2] 3000 against fire and a few against hail.

(4) Associations of *credit* to obtain capital for agriculturists at a low rate.   These are the societies which have developed so enormously in Germany.   But we shall return to them in the chapter on *Credit*.

(5) Associations for the carrying out of *works of public utility*, such as protection against floods, the drying of marshes, draining of lands, building of railways, etc. Associations for the above objects have this quite exceptional characteristic, that they may be declared compulsory by law; that is to say, if the majority of the landowners concerned decide on these operations, the minority are obliged to agree, or, in any case, to pay their share of the cost.   (Law of June 21, 1865.)   However arbitrary such a measure may appear, it is justified by the carelessness of landowners, and might be extended with advantage to other works, such as afforestation, the utilising of watercourses for motive power or for irrigation, or even to the marking out of boundaries.   (See below, p. 502, *The Ownership of Land*.)

V. INDUSTRIAL CO-OPERATIVE ASSOCIATION

THIS mode of enterprise differs from the preceding ones in that it suppresses the *entrepreneur*.   Those for whom the enterprise exists, *i.e.* customers, manage the business themselves, on the principle that one is never better served than when serving oneself.   Buyers

---

[1] The total of the loans must not exceed one-third of the State's share of the profits of the Bank of France. And, as this share is generally six or seven million francs, it amounts to an annual subsidy of from 2,000,000 to 2,500,000 francs, which is put at the disposal of these associations for agricultural production.   This money is not paid directly by the State, but through special organs called *Caisses régionales* (see below, *Agricultural Credit*).

[2] In 1897, there were only 1484 ; their increase is therefore astonishing. But it must be added that the State subsidises them to the annual amount of one million francs, making, for the ten years they have existed, a total of over seven millions.

The Department of the *Landes*, alone, numbers over 1000 of these small societies (see p. 745, *Insurance*).

are their own merchants, borrowers their own bankers, and tenants build their own houses.[1]

A consequence which follows directly from the above is, that these enterprises do not aim at profit, but simply at obtaining food, lodging, credit or whatever may be the object of the enterprise, under the best possible conditions of cheapness and quality. It is for this reason they claim to represent something really new in economic organisation ; for it would be no small revolution if, henceforth, industry were to aim not at profits, but at satisfying wants, not at lucre but at service.

Three main categories of co-operative associations may be distinguished according to the want which they aim at satisfying : associations for *consumption*, for *building*, and for *credit*.[2] We shall come upon them again under the chapters which deal with these subjects, as also the comparison between the Co-operatist programme and those of the Socialist schools. For the moment, we shall limit ourselves to some general indications on the largest of the three co-operative organisations, one which occupies an increasingly important place in the commercial and industrial movement, namely, the association for consumption.

It was the socialist, Robert Owen, who originally inspired this form of association, closely connecting it with the main preoccupation of his life, which was the abolition of profit. But the real success of the movement is connected with the celebrated Rochdale Equitable Pioneers, founded in 1844. In England, in 1912, there were 1403 of these co-operative associations in existence, with 2,642,000 members, or, including the families, about 12 million persons—that is to say, about one-fourth of the population of the United Kingdom. The

[1] Co-operative societies differ from capitalist societies from the juridical point of view also ;

(a) Because they are societies of persons, not of capital.

(b) Because the capital and persons may change, which amounts to saying that there is no limit to the number of shares ; consequently the shares do not increase in value with the success of the enterprise, since all who want may have.

[2] There is a fourth well-known form, the co-operative association for *production*, which we do not include here as it does not come under our definition. The co-operative association for production, whether composed of agriculturists, as we saw in the last chapter, or of workers, as we shall see later, is not formed by customers to provide for their wants, but by producers anxious to get rid of the middleman, and to keep their whole profits for themselves. In a word, co-operative association for production represents nothing original as regards production, but only as regards distribution, and it is under this last heading that we shall find it.

business done amounted to over £74,000,000 per annum, out of which they made over £12,000,000 of profits, almost the whole of which is distributed among the members. Most of the associations are grouped into a great federation, called the Co-operative Union, and are kept in touch with one another not only by means of annual congresses, but by two large centres of common purchase (Wholesales), a bank, and a newspaper—the *Co-operative News*—with a circulation of 80,000 copies. The English Wholesale Society sells its 1200 adherent societies goods to the amount of £28,000,000. It keeps a small fleet to fetch its produce from all parts of the world, employs over 17,000 persons, and produces directly in its own factories £10,000,000 of various articles. Its bank does business to the extent of £140,000,000 per annum.

But more remarkable even than these figures is the fact that some towns are already entirely given over to co-operation, the local co-operative society including nearly the whole of the population, *e.g.* Basle with 30,000 families, or over 100,000 persons out of its 125,000 inhabitants, Breslau with 100,000 members, Hamburg with 60,000, Leeds with 50,000, etc.

In Denmark, Germany, Russia, Austria, and Italy, also, co-operative societies for consumption are numerous, and are increasing rapidly in number, though they have not reached the same degree of organisation as in England. In France there are more of these societies than in any other country.[1] Unfortunately, most of them have only a small number of members, do but little business, and are divided against one another. They have, however, after great efforts, succeeded in creating a large federation for common purchase (1913).

Most of these societies are constituted after what is called the Rochdale pattern, characterised by the following four features :

(*1*) Sale *for cash* only, never on credit.

(*2*) Sale at *retail price*, not at cost price, in order to have a surplus.

(*3*) Distribution of the greater part of this surplus among the members *in proportion to their purchases*, not in proportion to their shares, which give a right only to a small interest.[2]

---

[1] In 1912, the *Bulletin de l'Office du Travail* counted 3000 co-operative societies for consumption in France (1200 being bakeries), with 850,000 members and 300 million francs of sale. See our book, *Les Sociétés co-opératives de consommation,* and also the series of *Almanachs de la Co-opération française,* published since 1893.

[2] This seems a contradiction of our definition of this mode of enterprise, which involved the abolition of profit. But this surplus really represents, not profit, but the difference between the price which the buyer has paid for an article and its cost price. Members of co-operatives, however, it must be admitted, often do not realise the distinction.

(4) The setting aside of a part of this surplus for works of social utility, such as education of members, funds for mutual help, propaganda, fêtes, excursions, etc.[1]

The immediate advantages of these institutions are :

(a) *Saving without privations*, if the Rochdale system be followed and the surplus distributed in bonuses at the end of the year—or an *economy* in the cost of living, if the societies be such as sell at cost price.

(b) More healthy and more abundant food, since no one has any interest in *adulterating* food, or in selling under weight or measure.

But the ultimate effects of this movement, if it develops in the future as it has done during the last half-century, will amount to nothing less than a transformation of the whole economic organisation of society, of which the characteristic features will be :

(a) The gradual elimination of the shopkeeper. We have said that some of these societies, in England, in Germany, and in Switzerland, have managed to include in their membership almost all the inhabitants of the town, and have thus overthrown the local trade, which naturally fights desperately against them.

(b) The abolition of advertisement with the enormous costs involved—the displaying of goods, the " selling off," and all the other forms of commercial fraud—whereby the moral level of business life will be raised.[2]

(c) The gradual absorption of industrial enterprises and the suppression of profit and dividends in proportion as the co-operative societies for consumption undertake themselves to produce all that they require. Only a small number are in a position as yet to start factories, but, through their Federations, it is becoming easier to do so.[3]

---

[1] In Belgium the co-operative societies, particularly the well-known " *Vooruit* " of Ghent, devote the greater part of their profits to socialist propaganda, and the shares distributed to members are given not in money, but in coupons exchangeable for goods at the co-operative stores.

[2] M. Georges Sorel, in his *Introduction à l'Économie*, says : " The large co-operatives have all the vices of democracies: frequent dishonesty and incapacity in their managers, thoughtlessness in the great mass of members, the formation of parties which imprudently follow their own personal ends." This portrait is, unfortunately, only too often true to life in France, but not in other countries. It simply proves how difficult it is for these societies to escape the action of the environment which it is their ambition to transform.

For the connection between co-operation as a programme of social transformation and socialism, see *infra, Co-operatism*. We would call to mind that co-operation is not a *class* organisation, but an association of all for all.

[3] For, in spite of their name, these societies for consumption are trying to

(d) An adjustment between production and consumption and the disappearance of crises, since the associated consumers will no longer produce more than they require.

CHAPTER V: PRODUCTION BY THE STATE

I: THE DEVELOPMENT OF STATE
AND MUNICIPAL ENTERPRISES

WE have spoken of production in the form of individual enterprise and in the form of association.   We have now to speak of production as organised by the State, meaning by the word State not merely the central government but municipalities and public powers in general, including even public institutions.[1]

The State may intervene in production in two very different ways : either as *entrepreneur*, substituting itself for private enterprise, or as *legislator*, regulating or stimulating private enterprise. In this chapter we shall confine ourselves to the first of these.[2]

The State as *entrepreneur* is not an entirely new phenomenon, some of the national manufactures of France dating back to the time of Colbert.   Nevertheless, the tendency of State, and still more of Municipal, enterprise to extend, is characteristic of the present time, and is due to three causes :

(1) The first, a fiscal cause, is the necessity for finding new resources to provide for ever-increasing expenditures of government

become societies for production, producing all the goods which they consume. For that, however, a high degree of organisation is necessary.   The English societies for consumption already produce in their own factories nearly one-third of what they consume, about £24,000,000.

[1] Institutions which, while having an official character as organs of the State, have nevertheless a distinct function and an autonomous organisation, such as Poor Relief (*Assistance publique*).

We may also quite well conceive of enterprises of international interest managed by a group of States.   The Suez and Panama Canals, submarine cables, etc., might come under this heading.

[2] Instead of devoting a special section to the legislative intervention of the State, it will be more methodical to study it in connection with each of the special cases which calls for it.   This is the plan we have followed in regard to shareholding companies, trusts and the different forms of association.   As the numerous laws to-day regulating factories and the inspection of labour have in view not the interest of the consumer and the public, but that of the worker, we shall return to them when we come to the question of wages, and the protective measures which constitute what is called *Labour Legislation*.   We may, however, refer, in passing, to the laws which regulate certain industries styled unhealthy,

without crushing the taxpayer. The latter, exasperated by the growing demands of the Treasury, turns on the State and says, " If you need so much money, do as we.do, and earn it." In this way the State is urged to become a manufacturer and a trader. The profits which it can make by so doing are enormous. The Russian State draws £68,000,000 annually, or two-thirds of its whole budget, from the sale of brandy and from its mines and estates ; the Prussian State makes £36,000,000 by its railways ; the French State over £16,000,000 from the sale of tobacco ; and the municipalities of different countries make hundreds of thousands from their various enterprises. This is a tempting prospect for States and towns burdened with debt.

(2) The second, a social cause, is the hostility felt towards capitalism, and the idea that the profits and dividends of the large companies are stolen from the people and should be given back to them. Now, surely the safest way of doing so is for the people themselves, as represented by the State or the local government, to take over the working of these lucrative enterprises. Indeed, the name by which this tendency is generally known is that of State Socialism or Municipal Socialism; although, as a matter of fact, in the instances in which we find it most fully worked out—those of the Prussian State and the British municipalities—it has certainly not been inspired by a socialist, or collectivist spirit in the ordinary use of these words.

(3) The third, a political cause, is the desire of the government to extend its functions in order to increase its power and stability, and to have a hold over a greater number of voters. In countries of universal suffrage, like France, this is perhaps the most potent of the three causes indicated. It is easy to understand that it is no

---

and subject them to various conditions, which forbid them, for instance, to be carried on without the previous authorisation of the State. In some countries, such as Switzerland, the permission of the State is required before any factory can be started.

State regulation of production is losing, rather than gaining, ground. We have only to remember how numerous and minute were the regulations by which the artisans of former times were bound, even in matters purely technical. Their products had to conform to a fixed type, and landowners were forbidden without leave to turn their wheat-land into vineyard, or their wine into brandy, or to begin the vintage before the ban had been declared, or to hold back their wheat harvests in their granaries. On the other hand, the State itself sometimes took over the provisioning of its citizens, at least in wheat, and exacted terrible penalties from those whom it considered engrossers.

Nowadays this tutelage of producers has been almost wholly abandoned. But, in the sphere of circulation, we find the State still exercising control in a very varied and active manner over commerce, transport, money and banks.

small matter for a government to enrol 300,000 railway employees in its service.

The tendency toward State or municipal enterprise is more marked in some industries than in others.

The undertakings which best lend themselves to it are naturally those already existing in the form of monopolies, which by their very nature cannot be other than monopolies : posts and telegraphs, coinage, railways, town water-supplies and lighting, tramways, etc. For what actually takes place · when enterprises such as these are started ? Seeing that they can be kept going only if invested with a legal monopoly, the State or city grants them this privilege for a certain length of time. "Why not," it thereupon says, " grant myself this privilege ? Why hand over in this accommodating way to shareholders the profits which I might quite as well keep in my own coffers ? If monopoly there must be, why should not mine be as good as that of any private company ? "

In undertakings which by their nature are not monopolies, but which are carried on as a rule under conditions of free competition, the tendency is less marked. There are indeed greater difficulties here, for one of two things must happen :

Either the State will accept the condition of free competition, in which case it will put other similar enterprises in a singularly unequal and even unfair position. For the State will compete with them not only with all the prestige which as a rule attaches to anything bearing an official character, but without having to trouble about the risks of loss or bankruptcy, and drawing on capital which, as it comes from the ratepayers, is taken in part from the very producers with whom it is competing.[1] It can hardly be called a fair fight, where one of the parties provides the other with the very weapons to be used against it. And if, in spite of all these inequalities, the State is beaten, as has happened more than once, its rôle will appear somewhat ridiculous.

Or else, realising how intolerable this situation is for its competitors, the State will convert the undertaking into an artificial monopoly, as it has sometimes done with tobacco, matches, telephones, and as

---

[1] For this reason the *Conseil d'État* in France has always refused to allow municipalities to start commercial undertakings which would compete with private enterprise. Thus, in 1892, it refused the town of Roubaix permission to set up a municipal pharmacy, although the latter was to sell medicines at cost price and might be considered as doing a charitable work. The *Conseil d'État* has, it is true, authorised other towns to create baths, to build letting houses, and even to undertake the gas-lighting (at Tourcoing), which would seem to prove that its jurisprudence is a little uncertain.

it may do, in France, with the sale of alcohol. In this case, however, it will be bound to expropriate with a fair compensation the undertakings already existing. This will be a heavy burden on its budget, and, from the financial point of view, will constitute a great risk; for the profits may not be enough to cover the cost of the transaction.

But these objections, though serious, are not altogether final. We can understand that they may be set aside in the case of undertakings of distinct general utility—those, for instance, which concern public health, such as pharmacies, public baths, burials, disinfection, markets, slaughter-houses ; or, again, though this is somewhat off our subject, in regard to the construction of cheap and hygienic dwellings (for nothing is more vital to the health, not only of the tenants but of all the inhabitants of a town, than housing) and the milk-supply—so useful an agent in the fight against infant mortality ; or, lastly, in the case of bread and meat, if it ever happened that the people were not properly supplied with these, either as regards quality or price. In such a case the municipalities would have to be allowed the right to open bakers' and butchers' shops. And this would perhaps be a better system than the tax on bread and meat—the sole weapon wielded by the municipalities in France for over a century, in their effort to protect consumers against the abuses of these two great trades.

But the march of events is not so logical, and the movement in the direction of State and municipal enterprise has developed in a somewhat haphazard way.

The following are the industries in which it is at present most advanced :

First, as regards *State enterprise*, we find the Post a state service in every country ; overland telegraphs [1] in almost every country (except the United States); telephones only in some countries (in France, where subscribers do not congratulate themselves on it, and in England, where they have recently been taken over). Railways are owned by the State in Germany, Russia, Denmark, Belgium, Switzerland, Italy, Holland, and, for part of the system, in France. Besides these large services, State enterprise takes other very varied forms. In Prussia, the State has mines, foundries, vineyards, porcelain factories, the whole bringing in considerable revenues. In Italy, the State has just monopolised life insurances. In Russia and Switzerland it has the monopoly of alcohol. In France, apart from the large fiscal monopolies of tobacco, matches, and gunpowder, the State has a few unimportant industries : Sèvres

---

[1] Submarine cables belong to private companies.

china, Gobelin tapestries, the Louvre engravings, national printing works, etc.   And in many countries (Italy, Spain, and several of the German States) we must add an industry—little to be recommended, but very lucrative—State lotteries.

Second, as regards *Municipal enterprise*, we find it an established fact, in most towns, in the matter of water-supply, burials, slaughter-houses, markets, disinfection, etc.   Lighting, whether by gas or electricity, is a municipal service in over 500 towns in the United States, and in a large number of towns in Germany, and is tending to become so in Great Britain, Switzerland and Italy.   In France it exists, as such, in only a dozen or so towns (among them Grenoble, Tourcoing, Valence [1]).   The municipalisation of tramways is highly advanced in England (174 municipal against 122 private enterprises in 1911); it is tending to become general in Germany and Switzerland, and is developing greatly in Italy.[2]   Municipal housing is proceeding apace in England, and somewhat more slowly in Germany and Switzerland. The town of Geneva distributes motive force in private houses. Finally, in England, attempts are being made to extend municipal enterprise in the most diverse and unexpected directions, not only in the providing of baths and sterilised milk for infants, but in the manu-facture of artificial ice and the utilising of by-products extracted from household refuse.[3]   There are municipal bakeries at Catania, Palermo, Verona, Leipzig and Buda-Pesth, and municipal slaughter-houses at Lisbon and Zurich.[4]

---

[1] The City of Paris exploits one of the sectors of electric lighting, that of the *Halles*.

[2] In Italy, a law of 1903 enumerates the enterprises which may be munici-palised, subject to the permission of the central authority, and, what is more interesting, to a referendum of the electors of the locality.   Nineteen enterprises, mostly those indicated above, are enumerated.   The construction of houses is not, however, among them.   This law, which lays down the general rules of municipal enterprise, has given a strong impetus to the movement.   There are over 3000 municipal enterprises in that country.

[3] In England, in 1910-1911, the total loans borrowed for municipal services reached the enormous figure of £410,000,000.   If we deduct the expenditure for schools, hospitals, asylums, prisons, high roads, canals, ports, cemeteries, drains, and keep to strictly industrial enterprises, the total is still nearly £170,000,000. For further information in connection with this chapter, see M. Milhaud's review, at Geneva, *Les Annales de la Régie directe*.   In England also there is a considerable literature on the subject.   See E. W. Benies on *Municipal Monopolies*.—AM. ED.

[4] In the North of Italy a plan is under consideration by which a syndicate of towns would buy fish from co-operative associations of fishermen on the Adriatic and sell it themselves in the markets.   These municipal syndicates would aim at buying not fish only, but all that is necessary for the working of their monopolies : coal, water and gas pipes, iron and copper wires.

II : THE DANGERS OF STATE AND MUNICIPAL ENTERPRISE

It goes without saying that the movement which we have just been indicating rouses the lively apprehension and sharp criticism of economists of the Liberal school. M. Yves Guyot lays it down as an economic formula, that " neither the State nor the Communes should ever do what may be done by an individual." [1]

This *a priori* principle is based on the financial results of State enterprises and on their economic and social consequences. The classical arguments against State enterprise and municipalisation are :

(*1*) The alleged incapacity of the State (or of any political body) to exercise the functions of *entrepreneur*, for which, says M. Paul Leroy-Beaulieu,[2] it has neither the *spirit of initiative*, in that it has no competition to stimulate it ; nor the *competency*, in that it is not organised to that end ; nor the *spirit of continuity*, its representatives being subject to all the vicissitudes of politics and of elections. The consequence is, that the State will produce at greater cost than private enterprise ; in other words, its action will be exactly contrary to the hedonistic principle of maximum satisfaction at minimum cost.

(*2*) The contradiction between the two ends pursued, the one being fiscal and the other socialist.

To gain its first end, which is to obtain resources by a more convenient method than taxation, the State ought to charge as much as possible for its services, as the French State does in the case of tobacco. To gain its second, which is to arrive gradually at a state of communism, the State ought to give its services for nothing, or, at most, at cost price, as it does in almost all countries in the case of the Post Office and education. Socialists certainly count on the day when not only water, but tramways, and perhaps even bread and the theatre, will be gratuitous for all ; when we shall come back, as it were, to the *panem et circenses*. But we are bound to choose between these two ends, and there is every reason to believe that the second will prevail, and that, under the pressure of the mass, a pressure irresistible in a country of universal suffrage, the continued lowering of prices will ultimately cancel the receipts.

(*3*) The political danger of an ever-increasing *officialdom*, which will end by enlisting nearly all citizens in its ranks, since all the

---

[1] *La gestion par l'État et les municipalities*, Yves Guyot, 1913.

[2] *Précis d'Économie politique.* For fuller details, see his book on the State, *l'État.*

different economic activities will gradually be converted into offices to be carried off by competitive examination, or, worse still, by nepotism and influence : a Saint-Simonism minus the maxim " To each according to his works." It is to be feared, moreover, that, in State or Municipal enterprises, the number of offices will be regulated, not by the needs of the public service, but by the number of persons seeking offices.

In answering these objections we must distinguish those of the political from those of the economic order. The latter do not seem conclusive.

In the first place, the contradiction between the fiscal and the social aims will settle itself. In the case of services useful to every one, or at any rate to the great majority of citizens—consumption that is necessary or desirable—the tendency will probably be to give them free ; while, in the case of services which affect only the minority—the consumption of luxuries—high prices and profits will be maintained. There would be nothing really objectionable in devoting the extra charge imposed on tobacco smokers, or alcohol drinkers, to providing water, transport, lighting, and perhaps even heating and motive force, to all citizens below cost price.[1]

As for the argument concerning the losses and mismanagement in State enterprise, it would be convincing only if we could draw up a corresponding balance-sheet for private enterprise. This we are unable to do; for the losses which private undertakings encounter pass unperceived, while those of public administrations make a great commotion. And the public, which bears with admirable composure, particularly in France, the daily annoyances inflicted on it by its tradesmen, is indignant when this purveyor is the State. This is as it should be ; only this exacting attitude towards State enterprise is an indirect homage on the part of the public. We cannot perhaps expect from the State the qualities peculiar to private enterprise, but there seems no inherent reason why the State should be more incompetent than any other collective organisation—company, trust, or co-operative society. For, mark well, the alternative lies, not as a rule between State enterprise and industrial enterprise, but between State enterprise and collective enterprise ; and there is no apparent reason why the boards of administration of State enterprises—of the railways, for instance—should not be composed of as competent men as are those of the big railway companies. The engineers, in any case, are the same in both. State enterprise, no

---

[1] Glasgow follows a simpler rule, viz., that each service should be self-sufficient, i.e. making neither profits nor losses.

doubt, will not aim at profits; but provided it tries to satisfy the public, so much the better. The ideal of a good economic organisation should be, not profit, but the satisfaction of wants.

This is precisely the programme of the co-operative societies for consumption. Those who, like ourselves, believe in their future cannot disregard Municipal enterprise; it is, in reality, simply a co-operative association, with the object of satisfying, at the lowest possible cost, the most necessary and general wants of all its members.

But, if the State is so constituted that its economic working only reflects its political working, if the administrative boards of its enterprises are only so many parliamentary committees, if its posts serve merely to give employment to sons of influential persons, it is likely enough that its undertakings will turn out badly. Here, however, we are passing beyond the sphere of economics. The whole question of the part which the State should play in production belongs, in fact, rather to the political than to the economic order : no general answer can be given. We may easily be in favour of the taking over of the railways by the State in some countries, e.g. Germany and England, whi!e against it in others, e.g. France, Switzerland or the United States. For the most democratic countries, those in which the extension of the economic functions of the State is most favoured, are the very countries where it is most difficult to put it in practice, municipal and State enterprises being too often subordinated to party interests.[1]

We may, however, obviate the political difficulties to a certain extent by conforming to the following rules :

(1) By conferring on State, or Municipal undertakings an autonomous organisation, a distinct legal personality, a board of directors recruited from outside of the political body, or at any rate on which members of the political body would be in the minority (and forbidden, as well as their near relatives, from holding any post in municipal enterprises); by giving them a special budget of their own, and by imposing on them the same book-keeping regulations as apply to private companies.

(2) By making room on these boards for representatives of consumers, on the one hand, and employees on the other, so that these State enterprises may be true co-operative societies both for

---

[1] It was a saying of Gambetta: "We govern according to parties, we administer according to capacities." But the danger is that the party in power may not know how to separate administration from government. This is the peril of State enterprises. See above, *State Socialism*, pp. 26-30.—AM. ED.

consumption and for production. This would perhaps be sufficient to prevent them from becoming crusted with officialism.

(3) By making these undertakings, whether State or municipal, responsible under common law, like those of private individuals. This is a condition without which the extension of the economic functions of the State would become unbearable tyranny. It is an abuse of power to make the State, as a governing body, cover the State as an industrial body, by saying that they are one! They must be quite distinct ! [1]

Failing principles, what may we learn from facts? Do State and Municipal services, where they are organised, work well? Do they bring in large profits to the towns, or at any rate satisfaction to the consumers? Nothing is more contradictory than the answers given, which proves what we have just said, that it depends entirely on circumstances, on the nature of the industry, and on the political organisation of the State.

From the consumers' point of view the results of Municipal enterprise seem as a rule fairly satisfactory. Those of State enterprise are more uncertain. In France, for instance, the postal and telegraph services work fairly well ; railways, in spite of all that is said, at least as well as those of the private companies,[2] while the telephone service leaves much to be desired.

From the point of view of receipts, we find from the Local Government Board's report, that the English municipalities produced, in 1910–1911, a net result of £360,000. But, as the capital invested cannot have been less than £160,000,000 (see note 3, p. 208), this corresponds to the ridiculous interest of 2 per 1000. The depreciation fund, moreover, is next to nothing—1½ per 1000. If it were raised to 2 per cent., the minimum in any private enterprise, their small profit would be transformed into £2,000,000 of loss. From the monetary point of view, therefore, Municipal enterprise is not very encouraging. This does not prove that well-administered towns may not find in these undertakings important sources of

---

[1] The State has been known, as a penalty, to suspend telephone services to subscribers against whom it had grounds for complaint, without feeling in any way bound to refund them their subscriptions. By a decree of the *Conseil d'État* of 1908, claims for the recovery of sums paid to the French State by telephone subscribers have been declared inadmissible, the price of subscription being assimilated to indirect taxation—a fine example of the detestable confusion between the economic and political functions of the State !

[2] It must be remembered that we are speaking here of the interests of the travellers, not of the budget or the taxpayers.

revenue; it only proves that the municipalities which can do so are as yet few and far between.[1]

III: THE DIFFERENT METHODS OF STATE ENTERPRISE

WHEN the State, or the public powers, intend to enter upon new undertakings they have recourse to one of the following methods :

(1) The *régie*. This is the simplest mode : the State works directly by means of its own agents. It is the mode which we have been discussing up till now, and we have seen its advantages and disadvantages.

(2) The *concession*. If the State does not care to undertake the enterprise on its own account, it may give it as a concession to a private *entrepreneur*.[2]   This is the method which has been almost solely in use up till now, and is still much the commonest. Concession does not mean that the State no longer has any interest in the enterprise.   The State retains control over it in various ways.   (a) It inserts in the schedule of charges certain conditions to be fulfilled regarding the execution of the work, the protection of the workers, the satisfaction to be given to consumers ; a tariff always accompanies a concession.   (b) It reserves a share in the profits.   This stipulation was made by the French Government in the case of the railways, and is usually made by towns when conceding such undertakings as gas, electricity, tramways or

---

[1] In gas-lighting the English municipalities made, as a whole, between 1898 and 1902, a gross income of 5·4 per cent., but a net profit of only 0·6 per cent. The houses built by the London County Council have cost (up till 1911) nearly £3,000,000, and bring in about £200,000, or 7·20 per cent.   But deducting interest, sinking-fund, reparations, taxes, etc., there remains little as net income.   The city of Geneva draws from its municipal enterprises over one-half of its revenues (28 francs per inhabitant), while it demands in taxes no more than 22 francs 25 centimes per head.   The gas supply brings in over £200,000 net in Berlin, and £80,000 in Brussels ; the tramways give £60,000 in Manchester, etc.

[2] In the case of undertakings that are not intended to bring in revenue—the making of a road, the piercing of a tunnel, the construction of some building or other—the word used is not concession, which implies a lucrative enterprise of long duration, but " public enterprise."

In these last there are also schedules of charges.   The undertakings must, on principle, be put out to tender, *i.e.* given to the lowest bidder, whereas, in concessions, this condition is not compulsory, nor even usual.   The system of concessions thus gives rise only too often to the " gratuities " (*pots-de-vin*) which have provoked, especially in the United States, such disgraceful scandals, and which it is the precise object of the system of " tender " to avoid.

metropolitan railways,[1] etc. (c) It puts a time limit to the franchise, reserving to itself the right of reversion at the end of the term, as in the case of the French railways, the Suez Canal, and many other enterprises. The fixing of such a limit to concessions is necessary, but is not without undesirable results, since, as the term approaches, the holder, unless he is able to obtain a renewal of the franchise, has no longer any interest in the good management of the business, and is concerned only to get the most he can out of the time that remains. (d) The State sometimes subsidises the enterprise; this generally takes the form of guaranteeing the interest, as was done in the case of the railways in France, and as is often done in starting industries in new countries.

Between the system of the *régie* and that of the franchise or licence there are two intermediate forms of State enterprise :

(3) The State may assign a share in the profits to the employees of the enterprise : this is the system of *participation*, or, as it is called in France, the *régie intéressée* ;

(4) Or it may stipulate for a fixed payment, standing as it were in the relation of a landowner to his farmer : this is called " farming " (*la ferme*).

This last system, much in use formerly, when the collecting of taxes was also an enterprise undertaken by wealthy contractors called *fermiers généraux*, is to-day almost entirely abandoned, since it sacrifices too much the interests of the public.[2] The *régie intéressée*, on the contrary, is a system that will most likely develop, since it minimises one of the serious objections to the *régie* by giving the employees an interest in the successful working of the business.[3]

Where it can be applied, this system, by means of ingenious combinations, allows the interests of the four factors of economic life to be associated ; (1) the State or town : (2) the *entrepreneur—i.e.*

---

[1] In France we may quote the Bank of France, as the State, in the concession, reserved to itself a share of the profits (see *infra*, the chapter on the *Bank of France*). In the case of the mines, the State takes 6½ per cent. of the net produce. This sum is so small that it can hardly be called a share in the profits. It is simply a tax. There is some talk of raising it greatly.

[2] The farming system is, however, still practised in some of the large Belgian towns (Liége, Ghent, Ostend) in the case of the tramways, gas, electricity ; and in some English towns in the case of the tramways only.

[3] The expression *régie intéressée* is a curious one, for surely it is the simple *régie* that is most " interested," since under it the State takes everything. The word, however, is applied not to the State, but to the *entrepreneur* and employees. It means that the latter, instead of being simple wage-earners, are interested in the business.

capital; (3) the workers—*i.e.* labour; (4) the consumers—the three first by means of profit-sharing, the last by a reduction of price.

Unfortunately, it can be carried out only in enterprises which can bring in profits; and this is not the case with all municipal undertakings.

BOOK II: CIRCULATION

In our *Principles* we included circulation in the same book as production. We had been struck by the fact that circulation is not an end in itself; wealth does not circulate merely in order to circulate. *Exchange* and *credit*, the two essential parts of the circulation of wealth—which, moreover, as we shall see presently, are but one—appeared to us simply as modes of the *organisation of labour*, with exactly the same end in view as association and the division of labour, namely, the facilitating of *production*.

If, in spite of this, we have decided to adopt the classical division and to give exchange and credit the honour of a special section of their own, it is not because it is more convenient for teaching purposes to make symmetrical divisions, nor because such a division corresponds to the ordinary distinction between commerce and industry. It is because these new modes of the organisation of labour carry us really into a different domain. Wealth is by this time created, and the question now is its transference. It is not its *form*, but its *owner* that will now be changed. Wealth will be no longer the object of technical transformation: it will become an object of *contract*.[1]

CHAPTER I: EXCHANGE

I: HISTORICAL SKETCH OF EXCHANGE

EXCHANGE occupies an enormous place in modern life.

To obtain some idea of it we have only to observe that almost all the wealth in the world has been produced simply to be exchanged. Take the harvests in the granaries, the clothes in the workshop, the

---

[1] We shall, however, find in this book not only the modes of *transfer* but the modes of *transport*, although these are purely technical and economic in character. This is because they cannot in reality be separated.

In J. B. Say's classical treatises, circulation is also included under *production*. But in more recent treatises there is a tendency rather to include it under distribution, for the reason indicated in the text, namely, that circulation implies a transfer of ownership, a contract of exchange or of credit. Now the modes of distribution from which all incomes, such as wage, farmer's rent, interest, etc.,

shoes at the shoemaker's, the jewels at the jeweller's, the bread at the baker's, and ask how much of all this wealth the producer intends for his own consumption. None, or at least very little. These things are simply merchandise, that is to say, objects intended for sale. Our industry, our skill, our talents, also are, more often than not, destined to satisfy the wants of *others*, not our own. Do we find the barrister pleading his own cause or the doctor treating his own ailment ? They too look on their services only from the point of view of exchange. This is why, when we estimate our wealth, we value it not according to its utility to us, but solely according to its exchange value, that is to say, its utility to others.

We must not imagine, however, that it has always been so. Exchange is not so simple a process as association, or the division of labour. These two, indeed, are so simple that even some of the animal species are able to practise them. Exchange, far from being instinctive, seems at the outset to have been repugnant to human nature. Primitive man regarded his products as a part of himself. Hence the strangely solemn rites with which alienation is surrounded at its origin, *e.g.* the *mancipatio* of Roman law. Curiously enough, donation seems to have been practised before exchange, and, in the guise of a reciprocal gift, is even said to be the origin of exchange.[1]

We might at first think that exchange must have preceded the division of labour, since, historically, no individual could specialise in a single task unless he knew that he could obtain from his fellow men the wherewithal to satisfy his other wants. And this is what Adam Smith said. The truth, however, seems to be just the reverse. It was division of labour that came first, since it may quite well take place, without exchange, in the family, or even in the tribal community, while it is hardly possible to conceive of exchange taking place without the division of labour, that is to say, without a certain specialisation of production.[2]

It is evident that, in the first phase of industrial organisation, that of the family, there could be no exchange with the outside world, as each group formed an independent and self-sufficing

are derived are themselves simply modes of exchange or of credit. And much may be said in defence of this way of looking at this matter. (See, in particular, Mr. Pierson's excellent treatise, *Principles of Economics*, translated from the Dutch into English.)

[1] In the second volume of Pantaleoni's *Varii Scritti delle Economia politica* there is a long and curious discussion on the origins and primitive forms of exchange. See also *L'Origine des villes*, by René Maunier.

[2] See, however, for the other point of view, Bücher, *Studies*.

H

organism. It was solely by the labour of its members and of its slaves, and, later on, by the tasks exacted from its serfs, that the family, the tribe, the manor, or the convent provided for its wants. Exchange took place only for a few exotic products brought by foreign merchants from abroad (see *infra, Merchants*). So that, although the word is somewhat grandiose as applied to such small groups, we may say that international exchange was the earliest form of exchange among men. At first irregular and accidental, it gradually became periodic, and markets were set up on the frontiers of countries, or at any rate outside of their fortified boundaries.

In the second phase, that of corporative or guild industry, exchange necessarily appeared with the separation of trades. It was, however, confined within the town walls, producer and consumer meeting as fellow citizens on the market, which became the centre of the city. Outside merchants—" forains " as they were called—were excluded, or only succeeded in gaining admission under rigorous conditions.[1]

In the third phase, that of the manufacturing industry, the market widened and became *national*. It was then that exchange and commerce really began. It has been pointed out that the establishment of the national market was coincident with the formation of the large modern State, as also with the substitution of the national system of fortification, introduced into France by Vauban, for the simple system of city fortification, a manifest sign that economic, political and military evolution everywhere follow parallel lines.

The market grew wider still when it became colonial, and the great commercial companies—*e.g.* the East India Company—which were to play so large a part in the eighteenth century, appeared on the scene.

Lastly, in the fourth phase, that of mechanical industry and railways, the market became in the true sense *world-wide*. Commerce thenceforth assumed the large proportions which have so profoundly modified the economic relations of our ancient Europe, and which have made international trade one of the most important questions of our time.

---

[1] Outside merchants were not as a rule allowed to sell in the towns unless on condition: (1) of paying a tax ; (2) of not selling retail, *i.e.* of selling not to the public, but only to the merchants of the locality ; (3) or at least of not selling save at certain times of the year and on certain fixed spots. (See Ashley, *Economic History*.)

II : THE BREAKING-UP OF BARTER
INTO SALE AND PURCHASE

WHEN exchange takes place directly, commodity for commodity, it is called *barter*, and is one of the most inconvenient and unpractical of operations. For, before barter can be successfully effected, the possessor of a commodity must not only find some one *willing to acquire the object he possesses*, but, a double coincidence not easy to achieve, some one able and willing to give him in return precisely *the object he wants*. Nor is this all. Even supposing this happy encounter takes place, *the two objects to be exchanged must be of equal value*, that is to say, must correspond to two equal and opposite desires. This is a third improbability.[1]

The invention of an *intermediate commodity* does away with these inconveniences. It presupposes, of course, an express or tacit convention, among men living in society, that each will consent to receive this commodity in exchange for his products. Once this is agreed on, everything becomes easy. Suppose silver is chosen for the purpose. In exchange for the commodity which I have produced and which I want to dispose of, I am willing to accept a certain quantity of silver, although I can do nothing with it. Why ? Because I know that, when I wish to acquire some object I want, I shall only have to offer its owner the same quantity of silver, and he will accept it, for the same reason that I did myself.

It is clear that every operation of barter is in this way broken up into two distinct operations. Instead of exchanging my commodity A for your commodity B, I exchange my commodity A for silver, in order later on to exchange this silver for the commodity B. The first operation is called *sale* and the second *purchase* (at least, when the third commodity takes the form of money strictly speaking). This would appear to complicate rather than to simplify matters.

[1] Lieutenant Cameron in his African voyage (1884) relates the shifts he was reduced to in order to obtain a boat : " Syde's agent wished to be paid in ivory, of which I had none ; but I found that Mohammed Ibn Salib had ivory and wanted cloth. Still, as I had no cloth this did not assist me greatly, until I heard that Mohammed Ibn Gharib had cloth and wanted wire. This I fortunately possessed. So I gave Ibn Gharib the requisite amount in wire ; whereupon he handed over cloth to Ibn Salib, who in his turn gave Syde's agent the wished-for ivory. Then he allowed me to have the boat " (Verney L. Cameron, *All Across Africa*, vol i).

And barter is still more difficult when it is services that are wanted. The Almanac of the Basle Missions of 1907 relates how, in Greenland, at Godhab, among the Esquimaux, there is a paper issued by the missionaries the subscription to which is *one wild duck* per quarter and *one seal* per annum.

But a straight line is not always the shortest road, and this ingenious detour saves, on the contrary, an incalculable amount of trouble and labour. What made barter impracticable was, as we explained, the necessity for the producer, Primus, to meet, as co-exchanger, another person, Secundus, able and willing : (a) to take the thing which Primus wanted to dispose of ; (b) to give him in return the very thing which Primus wanted to acquire. Henceforth Primus will still have to look out for a man who will take his goods, but he will no longer have to ask him in return for the goods which he himself wants. For these he will be able to apply to some other person, at some other time, in some other place. It was the *indivisibility* of the two operations which made them difficult. Once the knot that binds them is cut, each separately becomes fairly simple. It will not be very difficult to find some one who wants your goods, that is to say, a buyer ; it will be still less difficult to find some one disposed to give you the goods you require, *i.e.* a seller.

It must be remarked that, in exchange in the form of barter, it is very difficult to fix the values of objects, so that this form of exchange gives rise to the worst kinds of exploitation. In the trade with the natives of Central Africa, the value of the guns and cotton given in exchange for native rubber and ivory is often as 1 to 8, and this is still an honest rate. In many cases the ratio is 1 to 100. Money, therefore, in this connection may be called a blessing, and has been an instrument of morality and justice.[1]

But it must not be forgotten that the two operations, although henceforth separate, still form one whole, and cannot be conceived of apart. We are too much inclined, in our ordinary daily life, to think that sale and purchase are independent operations, and can stand alone. This is an illusion. *Every purchase implies a previous sale ;* for, before we can buy, *i.e.* exchange our silver for goods, we must first have exchanged something, our labour, our services, our products, for silver. *Vice versa, every sale implies a future purchase ;* for, if we exchange our products for silver, it is only in order to be able later to exchange this silver for other goods; otherwise what use should we make of it ? Of course, as silver may be kept unused for an indefinite time, a long interlude, years or even generations, may elapse between the two acts of the play, the

---

[1] All the philanthropists who have denounced the exploitation of the negroes in the Congo States have indicated, as one of the most effectual reforms, the abolition of payment in kind and the introduction of money, both in payments made to the natives for their goods and in the taxes exacted from them.

sale and its complement the purchase. But these two acts should be held together in our minds; for, in spite of the intervention of the third commodity and the complication which it introduces, every man in our civilised societies still lives, as did his primitive ancestors, by exchanging his past or present products and services for the past or present products and services of others. No one, not even the idle man of means, can spend, unless some one of his ancestors, or his debtors, has sold the product of his labour and handed on to him the money received. For *money* is the name given to this third commodity, by means of which barter is resolved into sale and purchase. The part which money plays in economic science as well as in daily life is enormous. We shall be obliged to devote several chapters to it.

III : EXCHANGE VALUE OR PRICE

ADAM SMITH and the older economists, to go back even to Aristotle, distinguished two values : *value in use*, which would be better called "individual value," and *value in exchange*, which would be better called "social value." And they showed that these two values might differ very greatly. A pair of spectacles, for instance, is of untold value in use to a short-sighted scholar, although their exchange value may be very small ; while diamond earrings, whose exchange value may be very great, have hardly any value in use for him at all.

What is the reason of this contradiction ? It is because the value in use of a thing is determined solely by the wants and desires, by the personal appreciations of a particular individual. It has no other basis than *subjective utility* for this individual ; it varies according to his wants and caprices, and has no general character or social import-ance. Value in exchange is more stable because it is determined by the wants and desires of all the persons in a country, perhaps in the whole world, who are willing and able to acquire the thing. A family portrait may have great value for me, but that confers no exchange value on it if it happens to be a mere daub. If, however, it is by Van Dyck, or by Rembrandt, it has an international exchange value determined by the desires of all picture-lovers.

It is evident that, for human beings living in society as we do, the exchange value of an object is far and away more important than its value in use.[1] Although value in use may exist without

---

[1] We have already pointed out that a coin—say a twenty-franc piece—has not the same value in use (*utility*) for a millionaire as it has for a poor man (see p. 38). And yet it is obvious that, in the hands of the rich man,

value in exchange, the converse does not hold good. All value in exchange necessarily implies great value in use, exchange in itself being a use of wealth that is of great importance to the possessor of it, and the possession of an object of value, quite apart from the possibility of selling it, being a cause of great satisfaction. In the example given above, it is probable that the owner of the Van Dyck portrait lays more store on it than on the portrait of his grandfather.

Exchange value, being, as it were, an average of the desires of a large number of persons, has a general character, a *rate*, as it is called, which, though formed by the aggregate of individual appreciations, imposes itself on each individual separately. Buyers and sellers must, as it is put, " follow the market rate."

Value in exchange is also called *price*.[1] Value and price are not, however, the same thing, since price is, as we saw, only one of the thousand possible expressions of value. Value is a relation established between any two things : *price is a relation in which one of the two terms is always money.* It need not necessarily be coined metal or paper money ; for in Africa, where pieces of cotton, or glass beads, are used as money, the value of the goods thus expressed is also their price. But the word price implies a common measure, a standard of comparison.

Having made this observation, there is no objection, however, to our conforming to custom and using the word price as the normal expression of exchange value.

Let us look, then, at the conditions which exchange value, or current price, must fulfil :

They may be put as follows:

(*1*) There can be only *one price* on the same market at a given moment for similar products. This is what Jevons called the *law of indifference*, meaning that, whenever two or more objects are identical, so that it is a matter of indifference to us which we choose, *i.e.* whenever we have no motive for preferring one to the other, we will not pay more for one than for the other.

We might at first think the contrary. Suppose, for example, that, on a given market, there are ten wheat sellers, each seller wanting a different price for his sack of wheat. Suppose, on the other hand, there are ten buyers, each attributing a different value to the wheat

it has the same value in exchange as in those of the poor man, all twenty-franc pieces being alike.

[1] The word prix is even used, in French, to express the value in use of things that cannot possibly be exchanged. We often hear the expression, " J'attache un grand prix à tel souvenir." But this is a mere manner of speech.

which he wants to buy.   Why should there not be as many different prices as there are pairs of exchangers, the buyer who is prepared to pay most coming to an agreement with the most exacting seller, while the buyer least pressed by necessity arranges with the least exacting seller for a much lower price ?   The reason is that no buyer, however great be his desire to buy, will consent to give a higher price than the rest are giving ; and that no seller, however easygoing, will consent to give his wheat for a lower price than his fellows.   Both, therefore, wait until the market price is fixed.

It is this unique market price, at a given moment, that is called the *current price*.[1]   This current price is quoted in special newspapers for all the most important goods—wheat, wines, coal, cotton, wool, copper, etc.—as well as for movable values and government stock, and serves as basis for all commercial operations.

(2) This one price must be such as to *cause the quantity offered and the quantity demanded to coincide.*

The two quantities are absolutely bound to coincide : it is absurd and contradictory to suppose that more sacks of wheat can be sold · than are bought, since they are one and the same sacks.

But this coincidence does not come about immediately.   It is only after a series of oscillations between the quantities offered and the quantities demanded, corresponding to oscillations in price, that equilibrium is established and the current price appears.   Take, for instance, our ten wheat sellers who are offering their sacks of wheat to ten buyers, but are asking 22 francs each for them.   Some of the buyers, finding the price too high, withdraw, and only five, say, remain.   The ten sellers, foreseeing that their wheat will be left on their hands, undersell each other in order to obtain the preference of the five buyers, and come down to 20 francs.   This price brings back three of the buyers who had left, and there are now eight buyers ready to take eight sacks.   If the ten sellers are determined to sell at any cost, they must resign themselves to reducing their price still further, say to 18 francs, in order to bring back the two most timid buyers and to make demand rise to the level of supply, *i.e.* to ten sacks.   But two of the sellers may possibly prefer to take away their sacks rather than go below 20 francs.   In this

----

[1] *Market* in the economic sense of the word must be understood to mean not any particular place or premises, but the whole of a region in which the movement of goods and the communications of buyers and sellers are rapid enough for a single price to be established.   The size of the market will vary, therefore, with the nature of the merchandise.   France is practically one single market for wheat ; the whole world is a single market for gold.

case 20 francs will remain the market price, for at this price there are eight sacks sold and eight sacks bought. Each demand finds its counterpart and the necessary coincidence is realised.

(3) The market price must be such as to *give satisfaction to the greatest possible number of pairs of buyers and sellers* present on the market.

To illustrate this let us put buyers and sellers over against one another on the wheat market, and express their claims in order, on a descending scale, beginning with the seller who asks the highest price and coming down to the one who is content with the lowest, and the buyer who offers least down to the one who is content to pay the most:

S^1 asks 22 francs	B^1 offers 18 francs
S^2 ,, 21 ,,	B^2 ,, 19 ,,
S^3 ,, 20 ,,	B^3 ,, 20 ,,
S^4 ,, 19 ,,	B^4 ,, 21 ,,
S^5 ,, 18 ,,	B^5 ,, 22 ,,

Suppose that S^1 opens fire by asking 22 francs. At this price there will be only one buyer, B^5, inclined to close with him, since none of the others is prepared to give the price asked. At this price, therefore, only one bargain would be made and only one sack sold. But B^5 will not be so simple as to give 22 francs, the maximum price, if he can get the wheat for less. He will wait, therefore, until other less exacting sellers have stated their prices. Then comes S^2, who asks only 21 francs. This demand brings forward a second buyer, B^4. There are now two buyers ready to come to terms, but, on the other hand, there are three buyers who will not go so high.

Lastly comes S^3, who asks only 20 francs. Three buyers out of five, that is to say, the majority, are disposed to close with this price, and, as there are exactly three sellers ready to accept it, there will therefore be three couples satisfied out of five. No other price would give the same result. This is the price, therefore, which will be the law of the market. For, if we suppose for a moment that S^4 were to consent to sell at 19 francs, there would no doubt be four buyers content with this price, but the three first sellers would refuse to sell and would withdraw. There would remain therefore only two sellers as opposed to four buyers. And the buyers who could not get served at 19 francs would hasten to recall the sellers who were on the point of starting off to look for better prices.

As for S^1 and S^2 on the one hand, and B^1 and B^2 on the other, if they will not compromise they will simply leave the market and will take no part in fixing the price.[1]

IV : THE LAW OF SUPPLY AND DEMAND

AT one time, in classical treatises on Political Economy, all that could be said on value and price was supposed to be summed up in the apparently quite simple and clear formula : *Value in exchange varies in direct ratio to demand and in inverse ratio to supply.*

[1] The price thus determined on the market is the price which satisfies the largest number of exchanging couples ; but it obviously gives them unequal amounts of satisfaction. For S^5 and S^4 find that they are selling at 2 francs and 1 franc respectively above the price which they had intended to ask. In the same way B^5 and B^4 find that they are paying 2 francs and 1 franc respectively less than the price they were willing to pay. And it is S^3 and B^3, the two co-exchangers who, by their agreement, have fixed the current price, who obtain the least advantage, since each of them only gets the exact price below or above which he would not have closed the bargain.
This is easily understood. Of the three sellers who found customers, S^3 was evidently the least keen to sell, seeing that he kept his price the highest ; and of the three buyers who were satisfied, B^3 was obviously in the least hurry to buy, since he offered least. Now it is quite logical that it should be *the two parties least impatient to conclude a bargain who should fix the price, since they are the ones whose opposing claims stand the best chance of coming together.* At first sight, we might be tempted to think that the seller who is most anxious to sell and the buyer who is most eager to buy are the ones who would come first to an understanding. But we must remember that, just because the one is impatient to sell and the other to buy, their claims will not coincide. In the above figures, the one asks 18 francs, but would like, all the same, to have more ; the other offers 22, but would prefer, if possible, to give less. They remain therefore in a state of expectancy until those who are in less haste have linked the two prices together.
The Austrian school gives the name of marginal-pair to the two parties whose competition determines the price.
This same school connects the theory of value in exchange with that of final utility, but not without difficulty ; for we must point out this curious fact, that value in exchange really coincides with final utility *only in the case of one single buyer and one single seller.* This seems truly a case of the exception proving the rule. (See this criticism more fully developed by MacFarlane, *Value and Distribution.*)
Those who care to see how a subtle mind can juggle with these difficulties should consult M. Böhm-Bawerk's *Capital* (vol. ii, Book IV) and Prof. Smart's very complete *résumé* in his *Introduction to the Theory of Value.*
We would add, moreover, with all due deference to the ingenuity and truth which lie at the basis of this psychological analysis of the mechanism of exchange, that prices are really determined by much more complex causes. As M. Brouilhet well expresses it, in a study on prices (in the review *La Vie Contemporaine*, April 1908): "The forming of prices is essentially a collective phenomenon, and reflects much more the capricious variation of crowds than the cold calculations of economists."

H'

This formula is perhaps somewhat too much discredited to-day. Various objections may, indeed, be urged against it :

(*1*) As a mathematical assertion it is contrary to fact. A reduction of *one-half* in the quantity offered does not necessarily *double* the price. If the supply of wheat in a country cut off from foreign trade were to be reduced by one-half, the price would much more than double : it might rise five times as high.[1]

(2) It mistakes the effect for the cause. If increased demand sends the price up, it is clear that a rise in price will in turn send demand down ; and if an increase in supply sends price down, it is clear that a fall in price will in turn tend to restrict supply. In other words, instead of saying that supply and demand regulate price, we might as well say that price regulates supply and demand. Take *e.g.* any security on the Stock Exchange, say three per cent. government bonds, and suppose them to stand at 100 francs. A certain quantity of bonds is always being offered and demanded. Suppose that, on the opening of the Stock Exchange, the quantity of bonds demanded is double that offered. Does anyone imagine that the price will *double* and reach 200 francs ? Yet this is what ought to happen if the above formula is true. In reality, the price quoted for these bonds will not rise more than perhaps 1 franc, for the simple reason that most of those who would have bought at 100 francs withdraw so soon as the price is raised. It is clear that, if the demand for these bonds diminishes as the price goes up, the supply, at the same time and for the same reason, increases. The time, therefore, is bound to come when the demand, which is decreasing, and the supply, which is increasing, will be equal ; and at this moment they will be in equilibrium. But a rise of *a few centimes* is enough to bring about the same result.

(*3*) It gives no intelligible meaning to the words *supply* and *demand*. We may perhaps understand by the word supply the quantity of goods, the stock, existing on the market; although in many cases a purely imaginary shortage of supply, such as the fear of a bad harvest, produces the same effect. But what are we to understand by demand ? The quantity demanded is absolutely undetermined, since it depends precisely on the exchange value or price of the object. At 5 centimes a bottle the demand for Bordeaux

---

[1] An English economist of the seventeenth century, Gregory King, in a celebrated law which bears his name, explained, as follows, the relation between the quantity of corn and its price : to a deficit of 10, 20, 30, 40, 50 per cent. there corresponds a respective rise in price of 30, 80, 160, 280, 450 per cent. This law, though true at the time when England was a closed market, has to-day lost all practical importance since the trade in cereals has become international.

wine would be almost unlimited.   At 100 francs a bottle it would be
next to nothing.   We are reasoning, therefore, in a vicious circle.

To escape from it, the Classical economists have given up the
vain attempt to find out whether it is supply and demand which
determine price, or price which determines supply and demand,
and try simply to determine the relations which exist between these
different facts.   This analysis has been carried to its limit by
contemporary economists.[1]

They lay down first of all the absolutely general law that
whenever prices rise demand falls, until a price is reached at which
demand disappears altogether.

They illustrate this law by
a very simple diagram.   Take
any commodity whatsoever.
Draw a horizontal line, and
mark off at equidistant intervals the rising prices by
conventional figures, 1, 2, 3,
4, 5 . . . 10, etc., which represent the prices quoted on the
market in centimes, francs or
livres.   Let the quantity demanded at one franc be represented by a vertical line of a
determined length, and the
quantities demanded at 2, 3,
4, 5 . . . 10 francs, etc., by

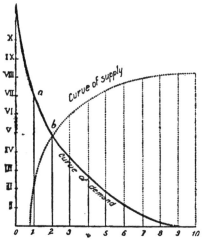

other vertical lines on the same scale.   These vertical lines will
be seen to diminish till they reach zero.   Join the tops of all these
vertical lines by one single curve.   This curve, which descends more or
less rapidly, but which always ultimately disappears at some point
or other in the horizontal line, shows, in a striking way, how demand
varies in relation to price.   It is called the *curve of demand*.

It is not without reason that this line is called " the curve."
If it were ever found to be straight, it would mean that demand was
varying exactly in proportion to price, a very improbable event.
As a rule demand decreases more quickly than price rises, for the
simple reason that there are a great many more poor than rich, and
that a small rise in price is enough to put an article beyond the

---

[1] It will be found in the books already referred to, of M. Colson and M. Landry,
as also diagrams representing the most complicated cases, which we do not
think it necessary to reproduce here.

reach of the masses. This gives the curve its concave form. But the curve will vary with each different commodity. With some it will fall—or rise if we prefer to look at it so—very rapidly, especially in the case of articles of luxury. If the price of a motor-car were to fall by one-half, the number of buyers would increase tenfold. In this case the fall of the curve would be much steeper than in our diagram. There are other commodities, on the contrary, objects of prime necessity, the demand for which would be but little affected by a rise in prices. Very little less bread would be consumed even if its price were doubled, and not much more if the price were to fall to one-half, bread being an ordinary ration, eaten for necessity rather than pleasure.

Sometimes, then, the curve is concave, sometimes convex; sometimes it is irregular, now rising, now falling. No two curves are alike. Thus a well-informed economist might say, simply by looking at a curve, and with no other knowledge whatever, " This is coal," or " That is copper."

And what meanwhile is supply doing? Supply varies, of course, inversely. *At each rise in price the quantity offered increases*, and the curve of supply is no less curious than that of demand.[1] It is, indeed, much more variable; for, when all is said and done, supply depends on production. And according as the production in question is strictly limited, as in the case of curios and famous brands of wine; or is subject to the law of diminishing returns, whereby its cost increases at a greater rate than its quantity; or is of such a nature that its cost decreases with increased output, as with most industrial products, will the curve rise more or less sharply.

Let us, then, make a third diagram, based on the text, where the two curves of supply and demand, which we have already traced, cross. This they are bound to do, as they run in opposite directions. Their point of intersection is of capital importance, for it marks the precise psychological point at which the quantities offered and the quantities demanded are equal, and exchange takes place instantaneously, like a chemical combination. If from this point we drop a vertical line to the horizontal line on which the prices are marked, it will indicate, like the pointer of a pair of scales, the current or market price—2 francs.

---

[1] As a rule supply begins by increasing rapidly so soon as prices rise, but after reaching a certain point it slows down, however high prices go, since production gets, as it were, out of breath. This is represented, as we see on the diagram, by a curve which begins to ascend rapidly, but which gradually slows down till it becomes nearly horizontal.

"But what does all this lead to ?" sceptics will perhaps say. "Will all these curves enable us to foresee when coffee or bread will go up in price ?" Alas, no ! And yet it is something to be able to put into precise and elegant formulæ notions which formerly were mere approximations.

Hitherto we have assumed an indefinite number of buyers and sellers, a condition equivalent to a state of free competition. But suppose there is only one single seller or one single buyer, conditions are at once changed. The case of the single buyer is rare,[1] but that of the single seller, i.e. monopoly (monos, alone), is very frequent.

Let us take the case, then, of the single seller, and, like Cournot, who first studied the law of prices under monopoly, let us take the owner of a mineral spring which has unique healing virtues. We might think that, in this instance, it depends on the owner to fix any price he likes, and that consequently there is no law of prices at work. Nothing of the sort, however. Even under monopoly the fixing of prices is not arbitrary. It is still determined by demand, although no longer by supply. Let us suppose, to begin with, that an inexperienced monopolist tries the price of 10 francs a bottle ; he will soon find that he is selling few bottles and making but little money—selling perhaps 1000 bottles, bringing in 10,000 francs. He therefore reduces the price to 1 franc and sells 100,000 bottles, making 100,000 francs ; for he immediately finds a market among the great mass of the middle classes. Suppose that, encouraged by this, he reduces his price to 40 centimes a bottle. As the number of sick persons is limited, and mineral water is after all not taken for pleasure, he will sell only twice as much—200,000 bottles—and will be disagreeably surprised to find his receipts fall to 80,000 francs. He will hasten then to raise his price until he finds the *price which, when multiplied by the quantity sold, will give the maximum return :* in this instance a franc a bottle.

We must be careful not to misinterpret the above formula and say that the monopolist will fix a price which will allow him to dispose of the whole quantity produced—in this particular instance the whole of the water. If we suppose, as we have just done, that the price he finds most remunerative is 1 franc, which gives him a sale of 100,000 bottles of 1 litre, while the spring can yield 300,000 litres, he will certainly not try to dispose of these 300,000 litres ;

---

[1] We may quote the large store as monopoliser of the products of small factories.

for in that case he might have to lower his price to 10 centimes, which would bring him in only 30,000 francs. He will prefer to lose the 200,000 litres. It was for a similar reason that a certain publisher is said to have destroyed a number of copies of the *Grande Encyclopédie*, and that the Dutch East India Company used to burn part of their spice crop, when harvests were large, in order to get a better price for what remained. If, during the great wine crisis in the South of France, the wine-growers could have come to an agreement with one another, they would not have hesitated to do the same.[1]

These remarks bring us to the question whether the system of competition or that of monopoly is the more advantageous to the consumer. The Classical economists, as we know, asserted that monopoly meant dearness and competition cheapness, so that the mere asking of the question would have seemed to them absurd and pointless.

The answer is not altogether simple. For, if it is true as a general rule that competition secures the minimum price, that which is nearest the cost of production, it is not always true, since, we saw above (p. 136), that a very great increase in the number of producers or sellers may result in sending up the cost of production and consequently price.

On the other hand, it is generally true that the monopolist keeps prices higher than they would be under free competition, since, as we have just seen, he aims solely at the price which will bring him the maximum profit, not the price which will enable him to dispose of the largest possible quantity of products. He may even find it to his interest to suppress part of his production, in which case his interest is in conflict with that of the consumer—the general interest. Still, we have seen how inaccurate is the idea that the consumer is at the mercy of the monopolist, who may fix prices at his own pleasure. The latter, on the contrary, is obliged to inform himself most carefully as to the desires and resources of

---

[1] To-day, however, monopolists employ less barbarous methods ; they do not destroy the excess produce, but simply refrain from putting it on the market and keep it in reserve for bad years.

Thus, to stop the fall in coffee, the State of San Paolo, in Brazil, which is the largest producer of this article, bought in 8 million bags, in 1906, in order to take them off the market and keep them back until the rate was normal again. At the same time it prohibited all new planting. This gigantic operation, called the *valorisation* of coffee, for which the Government had to advance £18,000,000, has been severely criticised as anti-economic. It does not seem, however, to have been altogether unsuccessful in keeping prices stable.

consumers. He cannot maintain high prices without injury to himself, unless his products are of such a nature as to appeal only to the wealthy, or to the few, *e.g.* the *Grande Encyclopédie*, or the works of celebrated painters. But in these cases the public interest does not suffer from it.

V: VARIATIONS IN PRICE

PRICE is the quantity of money which must be given to obtain some good or service. It is evident that the greater the value of the object, the greater will be the quantity of money which must be given to obtain it; or, what comes to the same thing, the smaller will be the quantity of the object which can be obtained with a given sum of money.

Price, therefore, like value, of which it is no more than an expression, is simply a relation. Now, we know that if we change one of the two terms of a relation the relation itself is changed.

If, therefore, for some reason or other the value of money changes, price must also change. Suppose, for instance, that the value of gold or silver has changed between yesterday and to-day. Clearly the value of every object measured by this gold or this silver will be found to have changed, that is to say, its price will have varied, and varied in inverse ratio to the value of the precious metals.

If, owing to some contraction of the earth, the length of the metre, or rather of the earth's circumference, of which the metre is a subdivision, were to shrink to-morrow to one-half of what it is to-day, all the objects henceforth measured by it would appear longer or higher, since what before was counted as one metre will now be counted as two. Yet, in reality, this would be no more than an optical illusion produced by the shortening of the unit of measure. Similarly, if gold and silver, owing, say, to their superabundance, were to lose half their value, it is clear that the price of all objects, *i.e.* their value as expressed in money, would appear to have doubled.

We may therefore formulate the following law : Every variation in *the value of money* involves an *inverse and proportional variation in prices*.[1]

It would, however, be inexact to reverse the formula and say that every variation in the price of an object necessarily implied an inverse variation in the value of money. It might do so ; but it is also possible that the variation in price might have its cause in the object itself, as in the case of corn after a bad harvest. Clearly, as

---

[1] See Irving Fisher, *The Purchasing Power of Money* (1911).—AM. ED.

price is a relation between the value of money and the value of some object of merchandise, everything which affects one of the two terms of the relation will affect the relation itself, and cause it to vary. Consequently, whenever we are met with a rise or fall of prices there are two categories of causes to be studied:

(a) Those which act on the value of the merchandise which is being bought.

(b) Those which act on the value of the unique merchandise called money.

(a) The specific causes which act on the value of goods elude all general classification. Every article of merchandise has its own innumerable causes which affect it, and there is hardly an event not only of the economic, but of the social, and even the moral, order, which is not felt in prices. If there is a rise in the price of corn, india-rubber, house-rent, pictures of eighteenth-century masters, the causes, in each case, must be sought separately and need have no necessary relation with one another.

(b) If we look at the other term of the relation—money—we are able to formulate general rules which apply to all cases, since money is the common denominator of all prices.

Now we find four causes which may make the value of money vary, three acting in the same direction and the fourth in an opposite direction.

(a) Quantity is the principal element which affects the value of money.[1] A second formula may therefore be laid down: Every variation in *the quantity of money* involves a *directly proportional variation in prices*. If, e.g. the quantity of money in a country were to double, we may take it for certain that, other things being equal, prices would rise considerably, although it would be rash to assert that they would exactly double.

This formula, known as the Quantity Theory of money, the discovery of which constituted one of Ricardo's claims to fame, is much discredited to-day.

It is the fate of all the so-called classical theories. Received at first with admiration, they are found later to be only rough approximations to the truth; eventually come the critical economists

---

[1] Economists who think that the value of articles is determined by their *cost of production*, think, logically, that the cost of production of money, *i.e.* of the metal (for the cost of mintage is trifling), is the principal cause determining its value. But, as we have rejected this doctrine in general, we cannot admit it in this particular instance, save to the extent of allowing that the greater facility in extracting the gold from the ore tends to increase its quantity.

who show that they are quite untrue. Such was the fate of the famous theory of Supply and Demand (p. 226). Still, the latter had so much truth in it that we can hardly avoid constant reference to it in ordinary language ; and the same is the case with the quantity theory of money. No doubt, if we take it in an absolute sense and assert, for example, that every time the quantity of money in a country doubles, prices will double also, we run the risk of being flatly contradicted by facts. For the quantity of money is only one of the many factors which act on price.[1] Still, it cannot be denied that it is a factor, and the most important one. The economist has a perfect right, like every other experimentalist, to look at only one of the causes of a phenomenon and to abstract all the rest. To make this formula strictly true, then, all we have to do is to add the reservation " other things being equal " ; and it was this that was meant by those who first gave expression to it. They were not so blind as to fail to see that other causes were also acting on money— quite apart from those which act directly on goods—and that these causes might possibly neutralise one another.

It is, however, a fact almost universally recognised that, wherever the precious metals are abundant, prices are very high. In the neighbourhood of gold mines, for example, prices are fabulous ; and whenever, in history, we find a sudden increase in the quantity of gold, we always find at the same time a sharp rise in prices, as, for instance, in the sixteenth century after the discovery of America, and in the middle of the nineteenth century after the discovery of the Californian and the Australian mines. And most economists to-day admit that the great and universal rise in prices which is stirring the public at the present moment is due, in part at least, to the increase in the output of the gold mines, which has almost quintupled during the last twenty years. How could gold fail to lose some of its value ?

(b) *The greater or lesser rapidity with which money circulates* is equivalent to a variation in its quantity, and consequently produces the same effect. It is evident that, if a railway company can make

---

[1] We may here repeat the remark which we made in connection with the law of supply and demand. If the quantity of money acts on prices, the rise or fall of prices reacts in turn on the quantity of money. For suppose that money, being too abundant for our wants, depreciates. Its quantity will decrease for a twofold cause : (1) as the value of the precious metals is diminishing, there will be less profit in producing them, consequently mining production will slow down ; (2) as the value of the coined metal is diminishing, while its industrial value continues to follow the general rise in prices, part of the money stock will be converted into plate or jewelry.

its carriages cover twice the distance in the same time, it is as if it had twice the number of carriages. This is why one steamship counts as three sailing ships of the same tonnage. In the same way, if a gold piece can be used for twice as many exchanges during the day, it is as good as two gold pieces.

The rapidity with which money circulates depends in turn on the density of population. The same coin by the end of the day will have passed through many more hands in a large town than in the country. This is why prices are always higher in the town than in the country. Still, this cause of the depreciation of money—namely its rapid circulation—is, in great part, counterbalanced by the number of acts of exchange, as we shall see under heading (d).

(c) *The degree of perfection in the methods of credit* which enable us to do without money, and consequently render it less useful and less in demand.

As regards paper money and bank-notes, the issue of these is equivalent simply to an increase in the quantity of metallic money. We must remember to deduct, however, from the value of the paper money issued : first, the quantity of coin stored in the coffers of the bank which the notes are only replacing in circulation; secondly, the quantity of coin that the paper money may have driven abroad.

It is through cheques, clearing-houses, and the like that credit mainly takes the place of money.[1] Without these powerful auxiliaries, money, in spite of the new gold mines, would never have been able to suffice for the great increase in commerce, and we should probably have seen an enormous rise in its value and a corresponding fall in prices—exactly the opposite of what has actually taken place.

(d) *The number of acts of exchange* (sales, loans, discounts, payments of wages, etc.) also influences the value of money, but in the opposite direction to the foregoing. That is to say, the more exchanges there are, the greater is the demand for money and the higher does its value rise. And as this is happening in all countries to-day, this increase in the demand for money keeps up its final utility and acts as a force to maintain its value, or at least to prevent depreciation when its quantity increases. If there had not been an enormous growth in industrial activity these last years, the depreciation of gold, and the consequent rise in prices, would have been much greater than it is.

The question of the causes of variation in prices has occasioned heated discussions and numberless controversies during the last few

---

[1] In connection with this paragraph, see *infra*, *Credit*, and, in particular, the chapter, *How Credit enables Money Payments to be dispensed with.*

years, owing to the great rise in prices which has taken place in all countries since 1907. Public opinion has been much stirred, particularly among the working classes, as the rise in prices has far out-distanced the rise in wages.[1]

In our view, the explanation of this crisis is to be sought nowhere else than in the enormous increase in the output of the gold mines which took place at exactly the same time,[2] in which we see a striking confirmation of the " quantitative " theory referred to above. The said output has quintupled in twenty years. It would be a miracle if it had had no influence on the value of gold. (See *infra*, p. 291.)

We must, however, point out, that a good number of economists, and nearly all business men, reject this explanation and look for the reason of the rise not in the depreciation of money, but in causes peculiar to various articles of merchandise. And, as these are unlimited, each observer indicates a different cause, one seeing it in protection, another in the increase of taxation, others again in incessant strikes, labour legislation, the weekly day of rest, trusts, or in the multiplication of middlemen, the growing taste for luxury, the Russo-Japanese War, etc.

But we should like them to tell us whether any one of these causes is universal enough to explain a phenomenon which has been felt at the same time in all the countries of Europe and America, in Australia, and in the Far East ; in Free Trade countries as well as in Protectionist countries ; and in countries like Japan [3] which know neither trade unions, strikes, nor trusts ?

[1] In France, from 1902 to 1907, the prices of all household articles rose in proportions varying from 15 per cent. to 50 per cent. (bread, 15 per cent. ; beef, 22 per cent. ; macaroni, 20 per cent. ; cheese, 25 per cent. ; coal, 34 per cent. ; fish, 50 per cent. ; and wine, even 100 per cent.). (See *l'Économiste français*, January 1910.)

The rise became accentuated in 1911–1912. The well-known restaurant firm of Duval, in Paris, noticed, for the year 1911 alone, a rise of 7 per cent. in the price of the food-stuffs which it buys. In Switzerland, the *Union des Syndicats* has published a well-substantiated pamphlet, *La vie chère*, showing practically the same rise in prices : 30 per cent. for meat, butter, cheese, and eggs ; 18 per cent. for bread ; 18 per cent. for sugar ; 10 to 15 per cent. for clothing ; on an average, $17\frac{1}{2}$ per cent. for food-stuffs ; 10 to 15 per cent. for industrial products ; and 20 per cent. for housing. A movement is on foot in the United States looking towards the appointment of an International Commission to study the high cost of living.—AM. ED.

[2] This is also the opinion of Professors Irving Fisher and Daniel Zolla. For the opposite view see M. Lescure, *Revue d'Économie politique*, 1912.

[3] In Japan, according to the paper *Osaka Asahi*, starting with the Index Number 100 in the year 1900, prices rose to 142 in 1912, and as high as 155 if we take food-stuffs only.

So far as a general cause of variation in prices is concerned, there can be only one : that, namely, which acts on the standard of prices, on money.

The resistance with which so simple an explanation meets may be attributed, among economists, to the discredit into which the quantitative theory of money has fallen ; among the general public and business men, to the difficulty of understanding that the value of money may change.

We may, perhaps, be asked why, if the rise in prices be due to the increase in the output of gold, it has not been proportional to this increase, the output, as we said, having almost quintupled. Our answer is : (a) because this annual output of gold pours, as it were, into a reservoir of over two milliards sterling, the level of which rises slowly (at the rate of about 3 per cent., corresponding fairly exactly to the rise in prices) ; (b) because the increase in the output of gold is partly counterbalanced by the general increase in the demand for it (notwithstanding the development of the cheque system and of credit transactions) ; (c) because a growing proportion of the output of gold and silver is absorbed, as by a sponge, in India and in the hoarding countries of Asia and Mussulman Africa, whence it does not return.

Variations in price cause great disturbances and thereby much suffering. When they take the form of a rise in prices they make living difficult for all who have to live on a fixed income, officials, fundholders, and working men—although in the case of the last, the wage, after a time, follows the rise in prices. When they take the form of a fall in prices, it is the agricultural and industrial producers who find their incomes diminishing, and are exposed perhaps to bankruptcy. A fall in prices intensifies competition among them, and is not slow in making itself felt in wages, through the slowing of business or the shutting down of factories.

Is there no means of preventing a rise in prices, or, at least, of rendering it harmless ?

For rises in particular categories of merchandise there is no general remedy. It is for consumers to organise themselves into buyers' leagues, or societies for consumption, and fight the rise. But, for a general rise in prices which is due to variations in the monetary standard, the remedy is simple enough, in theory at least, All that need be done is to regularise the value of the money-standard, by varying either the quantity of coins, or the weight of each coin. so as to counterbalance the rise or fall in the value of the metal.[1]

---

[1] The system of varying the *weight* of money in direct ratio to its depreciation is the simplest in theory, but is almost impossible in practice. The State could.

Another way would be, not to try to prevent variations in the value of money, but to take account of them in fixing prices. This system, however, would not be very practicable for daily purchases and could not apply to the settlement of debts. (See *supra, Index Numbers.*)

VI : THE ADVANTAGES OF EXCHANGE

THE following are the advantages of exchange :

(*1*) Exchange enables *wealth which would otherwise remain un-utilised to be used to the best advantage.*

Without exchange, what would England do with her coal, the Transvaal with her gold, Tunis with her phosphates, Brazil with her coffee and quinine ? In analysing the notion of wealth, we have shown that the indispensable condition for an object to be considered wealth is that it can be utilised (p. 42). Now, before this can be, exchange must first put it into the hands of the man who is to use it ; quinine into the hands of the fever patient, phosphate into those of the cultivator, coal into those of the manufacturer. Suppose that to-morrow exchange were to be prohibited by law, and that all men and all countries were forced to keep for themselves the whole of the wealth they produced. What an enormous quantity of wealth would at once be rendered useless and good for nothing but to be left to rot ! Without exchange, indeed, not only would most wealth be useless, but it would never have been produced at all. Exchange, therefore, creates an increase of utility, and often creates utility itself.

We must look on exchange as the last in the series of acts of production which begins with invention, also an immaterial act,

not recall all the coins in circulation whenever it struck new ones, and unless it did so, by virtue of Gresham's Law, the weak coins would drive out the strong.

The system of varying the quantity of money in direct ratio to its depreciation, so that, when prices doubled, only half the number of coins would be minted, has been proposed.

This proceeding has always seemed to us theoretically possible on condition of having, not a metallic money, but an international paper money, the quantity of which would be scientifically regulated, quite independently of the output of mines, by an international convention. See, in particular, *A More Stable Gold Standard*, by Mr. Irving Fisher (*The Economic Journal*, December 1912). On Mr. Fisher's system, the weight of the dollar would not be altered, but the dollar could be changed at any time in a State Bank for a weight of gold which would vary according to the indications of the Index Number. For instance, if the Index Number showed a rise in prices of 10 per cent., the dollar would be exchanged for a weight in gold one-tenth more than its real weight, which would raise its value by the same amount.

and which continues through the whole of the agricultural, manufacturing and transport operations, pushing the products along stage by stage towards their final destination—the hands of the man who can use them. Change of *form*, change of *place*, change of *hands*[1] —all three are equally indispensable in order to reach the final result.

There are, it is true, certain operations of exchange or credit, such as the sale of houses or of Stock Exchange securities, or of curios and furniture at salerooms, which may be reckoned by millions, and which cannot be said to constitute acts of production ; for what can it matter to production whether a particular share, stock, bond, picture, or house, belongs, to Peter or to Paul ? These are purely juridical acts of transfer, and concern the lawyer, not the economist. It is with the first category alone, that of exchanges which are bound up with production, that we are concerned.

And, yet, we are right in saying that sales and leases of definite products, or of capital, or land, even although these operations do not constitute acts of commerce, may be considered *creative of utility*, and consequently acts of production, in the sense that the objects sold or let acquire a greater utility by the very act of sale or lease, since they are more desired by the buyer than by the seller or lender. This is evident on the face of it ; for if it were not so, the seller would not have sold nor the lender have lent them.[2]

---

[1] May it not be objected that change of hands does not necessarily imply an *exchange* in the juridical sense of the word, *i.e.* a change of ownership ? Under a communist system no doubt this would be true : the transfer from one person to another would take place just as, actually, in a factory, the products pass from one set of workers to another. But under the system of private property, change of hands necessarily implies a transfer of ownership, or at least a transfer of some right or other.

It is certainly by a series of acts of sale that the raw material passes from the hands of the mining *entrepreneur*, or the agriculturist, to those of the successive manufacturers who transform it and bring it to its finished state ; and finally from the hands of the last holder—the retail shopkeeper—into those of the consumer.

[2] It is an old and much-debated question whether exchange should be considered as productive of wealth. The Physiocrats denied it. They professed even to prove that exchange could bring no gain to anyone. For, all exchange, they said, if just, presupposes *the equivalence of the two values exchanged*, and consequently implies that there is neither gain nor loss on either side. A man may, it is true, be taken in, but in this case the one man's profit is exactly counterbalanced by the other man's loss, so that in any case the final result is zero.

This was a pure sophism, long ago confuted by Condillac. If exchange never brought gain to anyone, or if every exchange necessarily presupposed a victim, it would be difficult to understand why men should have persisted in practising

(2) Exchange enables *persons and their productive capacities— which, without it, would remain inactive—to be used to best advantage.*

Observe that if exchange did not exist, each man would have to give up his time to producing his own necessaries. His production would be determined *not by his aptitudes, but by his needs.* Suppose, for example, that he needed ten different things, he would have to work at ten different trades, whether he did them well or ill. So soon as exchange is practised, the situation is completely reversed. Each man, certain now that he will obtain all that is necessary by exchange, turns his attention solely to the things which he can do best. Henceforth he regulates his production *not according to his needs, but according to his aptitudes,* or his means.

We may say that the advantages of exchange much resemble those of the division of labour. They are in fact the same, only on a larger scale. If it were not for exchange, workers would have to come to a previous agreement among themselves before there could be any association and division of labour. Exchange, dispensing as it does with the necessity for this previous agreement, enables the division of labour to pass beyond the narrow circle of the workshop, or the family community, and to spread to the very ends of the earth. Every one now, far or near, will produce according to his natural or acquired aptitudes, according to the nature of the region where he lives ; he will be able to devote himself entirely to one single operation and to put always the same article in the market, in the certainty, thanks to the ingenious devices which we shall study later, of being able to take away in exchange any other article that he may need. It has often been remarked that each one of us consumes in a day the combined result of the activity of hundreds, perhaps thousands, of workers, all united by the bond of a very real, though unconscious, association.[1]

it for so many centuries. In reality, what I give in exchange is always less useful to me, less desirable, *worth less,* than what I acquire, otherwise it is evident that I should not give it up ; and my fellow co-exchanger reasons in the same way. Each of us, in the exchange, thinks he is *receiving more than he is giving,* and, however strange it may seem, each is right. There is no contradiction in these opposite judgments and inverse preferences, since we know that the utility of everything is purely subjective and varies according to the wants and desires of each one (see above, p. 48). When, therefore, we say that, in every exchange, we are giving equal values on either side, what we really mean is, that both objects are of the same value as measured by a common standard, money. As value in exchange they are equal ; but, as value in use to the two co-exchangers, they are inversely unequal.

[1] There is a story to the effect that the American millionaire, Mr. Carnegie,

Exchange would be almost impossible if it had not created for itself certain indispensable agencies :

(1) *Means of transport* to facilitate and accelerate the movement of goods.

(2) Depôts called *markets,* to enable the possessors of different objects to meet.

(3) Agents, called *merchants* or *traders,* to serve as intermediaries between producers and consumers.

(4) Instruments, called *weights and measures,* to measure the quantities exchanged.

(5) An intermediate commodity, known as *money,* to break up barter into sale and purchase.

We shall study these in order in•the following chapters, passing rapidly over numbers (2), (3) and (4), and making a detailed study of numbers (1) and (5).

CHAPTER II : TRANSPORT

I : THE DIFFICULTIES AND THE COST OF TRANSPORT

WE may quite well conceive of exchange without any displacement of matter, as, for example, in the case of immovable property, or in simple speculations in goods. But displacement is an essential characteristic of that form of exchange for which practice and legal language reserve the name of *commerce.* Every invention which facilitates the means of transport will, to this extent, facilitate exchange and in doing so will stimulate production itself. How many products there are which would never have seen the light of day, had not the means of transport rendered them utilisable, to go no further afield for an example than the vineyards in the South of France ! Hence the history of commerce is, to a certain extent, the history of the development of communication by land and sea. And not merely the movement of exchanges, but the progress of

---

at a splendid banquet which he offered to the members of the Pan-American Congress of 1890, declared proudly that almost the whole world had contributed to the menu served. No doubt, but the wonderful thing is that a poor man can say just as much of his dinner ! As M. de Laveleye says · " The poorest working man consumes the produce of the two worlds. The wool of his clothing comes from Australia ; the rice in his soup from India ; the wheat in his bread from Illinois ; the oil in his lamp from Pennsylvania ; and his coffee from Java " (*Éléments d'Économie politique,* p. 198).

civilisation itself, is, in no little measure, determined by the great highways of communication.[1]

The difficulties of transport are due to various causes :

(1) *Distance.* Man has no command over distance. He can neither suppress nor reduce the space which separates two points on the earth. But the question of distance turns itself, for him, practically into a question of time ; and human invention has been very successful in overcoming this obstacle. If, in France, the time required to cover a given distance is twenty times less to-day than it was in the thirteenth century, we may say, in all accuracy, that the result is as if France were to-day 400 times smaller than she was in the thirteenth century (surfaces varying in proportion to the square of their linear dimensions). Now, thanks to railways, this hypothesis has become a reality. Progress in rapidity of communication results, therefore, in reducing indefinitely the area of the earth's surface.[2]

(2) *The nature of the commodities.* A live ox is not so easily transported as vegetables, nor are vegetables so easily carried as coal, nor coal as gold. The *delicacy,* the *difficulty of preservation,* the *bulk,* the *fragility* of the object are all so many obstacles. True, the rapidity of transport, of which we have been speaking, allows us to a great extent to overcome them. Cattle, alive or dead, could not have been brought over from America or Australia at the time of navigation by sail so well as they can to-day, thanks to the short length of the voyage. Fish, early fruit and vegetables, game, could not have been sent from the provinces to Paris as they now are daily, the journey being under twenty-four hours. On the other hand, the various inventions for the preserving of food-stuffs— such as refrigerating processes, the economic importance of which is increasing daily—have greatly helped. Recent discoveries, indeed, have brought these processes to so high a pitch of perfection, that fresh meat can now be brought from the antipodes. But, the difficulty, or, what amounts to the same, the cost, of transporting certain objects has still very vexatious economic consequences.

(3) *The condition of the ways of communication.* This is the most

---

[1] See M. Demolins' book, *Comment la route crée le type social,* in which this influence is set forth, not without exaggeration.

[2] Without going so far back as the thirteenth century, we find at the end of the eighteenth century Turgot's diligences, the speed of which was the wonder of his contemporaries, taking thirteen days to go from Paris to Marseilles ; nowadays we allow twelve hours, or twenty-six times less.

M. Cheysson has drawn up a series of maps of France in which the area of the country is gradually reduced from the time of Louis XIV to our own day, making this phenomenon clear at a glance.

serious obstacle, but it is also the one over which human industry has most successfully triumphed.

By sea the road is ready made, or, rather, there is no need of a road. Water will carry any weight indifferently, and the flatness of its surface allows ships to move freely in any direction. The feeblest motive force—gratuitous if it be the wind—is enough to move enormous masses. It is not surprising, therefore, that the sea has from all time been the great highway of commerce, and that peoples separated by a thousand leagues of sea have been nearer neighbours in reality than those separated by a hundred leagues of land. Even to-day, in spite of the progress in overland routes, transport by sea is infinitely less costly, from which the inference may be drawn that it represents infinitely less labour.[1] The cost of transport per ton per kilometre, by sea, is hardly ever more than 2 centimes, and is very often as little as $\frac{1}{2}$ centime, or less, while that of transport by railroad is 4 or 5 centimes.

By land the difficulty is greater. The rough surface of our planet rarely admits of the transport of merchandise without the making of artificial roads.[2] Transport by caravan, *i.e.* on the human back, as in Africa, or by beasts of burden, as in Asia, may be carried on over simple tracks, that is to say, natural roads made by the passing of foot-travellers or animals, but vehicular transport cannot. Now, the making of a road is a very costly business, and the more perfect the road, *i.e.* the harder and more level it is, the more costly it is to make. The railway is a perfect road, but it is also the most expensive, costing about 400,000 francs per kilometre in our European countries, and 100,000 francs at least in the places where it can be built at minimum cost. There is therefore an enormous quantity of capital sunk in railways, and the sum necessary to cover the interest and

[1] At Marseilles, coal which comes by sea from England through the Straits of Gibraltar, and which has travelled 2000 miles, is sold cheaper than the coal which comes from the mines of the Grand'combe by rail and has had to travel only 110 miles.

[2] There are three aspects from which we may view the gradual progress that is taking place in the means of transport on land and on sea : progress of the *route* : on land—macadamised roads, railways, bridges, tunnels ; and on sea—the tracing of the great sea routes according to the direction of winds and currents, the building of the Suez, Panama, Corinth and Kiel Canals ; progress of the *vehicle* : on land, the marvellous invention of the wheel, and on sea, the substitution of iron for wooden ships ; progress of *motive power* : on land, the change from the horse to the steam, electric, or oil engine, and on sea, from the labour of mankind in galleys propelled by oars, to wind and steam-driven paddles, and finally to the screw and the turbine. And, we may add, in the air, the petrol motor of airships and aeroplanes.

redemption will obviously be put on to the transport of the goods. In spite of this, if there be plenty of traffic, the railway is able to make transport very economical, not to speak of its regularity, ease, and rapidity. To develop force equal to that of the locomotive of a goods train, we should need at least 1000 horses on an ordinary road, and then they would do ten times less the distance. Compare this again with transport by carriage on the human back as in Africa, where it is imposed as a compulsory task on the natives and has become a worse scourge than the slave trade. Each new railroad in Africa is a deliverance for them.

It is perhaps somewhat premature to speak of the air road. This is not likely ever to become *economical.* For though, like the sea route, it has the advantage of needing no construction, it requires, on the other hand, an enormous expenditure of force to overcome weight and wind. This will probably prevent it from ever being used for the transport of goods.

The various obstacles which transport meets with are, of course, translated into costs. These costs must be broken up into two elements :

(1) Those which come under the heading of *mileage*, and are intended to cover the expenses of constructing the roads (overland, rail or water), that is to say, the interest on, and redemption of, the capital invested in them.

(2) Those which come under the heading of *traction* and *exploitation*, and are intended to cover the upkeep of horses, carriages, and the men who drive them ; or of ships and their crews ; or, in the case of railways, wages, the cost of coal, of renewing the rolling stock, etc.

It is a matter of great difficulty to decide the exact price which a transport business should, or can, make its customers pay. We can see that it is not so simple a matter as that of a grocer selling his goods. The question here is not simply of delivering an article, but of rendering a service, and a service made up of very complex elements : distance, speed, weight (in the case of goods), comfort (in that of travellers), etc. There is no more complicated part of a large transport business than the fixing of the rates, as it is called.

And if the transport business has a monopoly, legal or *de facto*, as is generally the case, the difficulty is greater still, since there is no pressure of competition to fix the maximum limit. There is only the rate imposed by the State, which is quite arbitrary. The maximum limit is, of course, the price at which a customer will refuse the transport of himself or of his goods ; but the difficulty is how to find it, especially as this utility-limit varies with each individual and each act of transport, while the rate has to be a general, not an individual, one.

When the construction of the road is undertaken by a company or by private contractors, it goes without saying that they will not do it for nothing. They will undertake the enterprise only if it will pay them something over and above the interest and redemption of the capital invested. The cost is therefore laid on the road. Thus the roadways in England, not more than half a century ago, bristled with turnpike tolls. The same plan is followed in the case of railways and tramways, a few suspension bridges, and the large maritime canals. The passage through the Suez Canal was at one time 10 francs per ton (which was to be gradually reduced to 5 as receipts increased). But the saving realised in the cost of insurance alone by ships which took the Suez instead of the Cape route, was equal to that sum, and the economies in coal, food and wages of the crew were ten times as much.

Where the construction is undertaken by the State, the latter as a rule writes off the cost, and charges nothing for the use of the road. This is what was done by France in the case of her magnificent system of overland roads (600,000 kilometres of national, departmental and parish roads, which cost $4\frac{1}{2}$ milliard francs for initial outlay, and require over 200 millions for annual upkeep). And the State is buying up the remaining toll bridges, in order to abolish the toll. Why is it doing this ? Obviously this present which it is making is only an apparent one, for the State does nothing gratis. It is simply exempting those who use the road from the cost of its upkeep by laying this cost on all citizens in the form of taxation. Now, is this just ? If my occupation or tastes keep me at home, why should I pay the costs of the man who wears out the road with his motor-car ? Is not this just as bad as the privilege which many more or less important personages have of travelling free on the railways at the expense of all the rest ?

It is evident that this would-be gratuity amounts simply to making the taxpayers pay instead of the consumers. And, whereas the consumers used to pay in proportion to their consumption, the taxpayers as a rule pay in proportion to their means, so that the basis of contribution is completely changed.

Now this mode of taxation may be justified in the case of *services which are really of public utility, i.e.* which minister to the wants of the great majority of the citizens and by which even those who do not make use of them benefit indirectly.[1] It may be answered, for instance, that, as roads are of general utility even to those who use them least—since they serve for the transport at any rate of the produce which these sedentary persons consume—a tax is a much less vexatious form of contribution than the stopping, by a toll, of each passer-by. The toll is, in this way, transformed into a kind of annual subscription.

But, if the means of transport are *of use to only a small number of persons*,[2] or if they are *restricted to one particular region*, there is no longer any reason for giving them for nothing. It would be unjust, for example, for the State to establish free telephones in towns, as this would be making the country populations pay for a means of communication which they never have occasion to use. It would be less unjust for each commune to buy up and work its own tramways for nothing, even although all the inhabitants of the town did not use them equally. Some economists have criticised free canals, holding it unfair that the State should take hundreds of millions of francs from the taxpayers in order to dig and maintain navigable highways which are of use to only a limited number of citizens—as a rule those living near their banks.[3] It may be said in reply, however, that owing to the heavy merchandise, particularly coal, which they transport, and to their competition with the railways, they are of benefit even to those who do not directly use them.

What are we to say of railways ? Do they fall under the first or second category ? We may certainly say that, if at one time only a small number of persons used this mode of transport, there is no reason why, as railways spread and become universal, they should be under a different system from ordinary roads. Thus, theoretically at least, the abolition of mileage would be quite justified wherever the railways belong to the State. Practice is, however, another matter. The enormous sacrifices which the State would have to incur, especially where it had bought up the railways—a sacrifice which it would be obliged to shift on to its citizens in the form of

---

[1] It would be excellent, for instance, to apply it to the consumption of water in towns. As water, in France, is paid for according to consumption, each person can consume only according to his means, and it is deplorable that the poor should be deprived of it for want of money.

[2] As is the case at present with the owners of motor-cars. A special toll for motor-cars would be quite justified, both for this reason and because of the enormous dilapidation they cause to the public highway.

[3] See the full treatment of this question in M. Colson's *Cours d'Économie politique*, Book IV.

increased taxation [1]—hardly allow us to count on the abolition of mileage for a long time to come. It is not, however, improbable that, in time, railway service may become free, first for mileage, so soon as the capital employed in constructing the lines has been redeemed, and perhaps later for traction; or that, at any rate, it may be paid for by a small annual subscription, such as the 10 francs a month which members of Parliament in France pay.

II: RAILWAYS

THE construction of railways was the most important economic event of the nineteenth century.

It was about the year 1830, in England first of all, and later in the United States and France,[2] that the first trains drawn on rails by locomotives were run. By 1840 there were 3000 kilometres of railway in Europe, more than half of which were in England.

By the year 1900, some 800,000 kilometres of railway were in operation, or twenty times the circumference of the earth: 300,000 of these were in Europe, somewhat more than this in the United States, and the remainder in other parts of the globe, and a little over 260 billion francs of capital had been invested in them.[3] This formidable system is increasing at the rate of about 25,000 kilometres per annum, and covers to-day over a million kilometres.[4] In Europe

---

[1] The abolition of mileage would cause a reduction of only about 40 per cent. in the prices of seats, as the remaining 60 per cent. goes to pay the costs of traction and exploitation.

[2] It was on August 26, 1838, that Queen Amélie opened the railway from Paris to St. Germain, M. Thiers remarking: "It is a plaything which will amuse the Parisians." And yet, from 1832, railways had been running in the mining centres, particularly from St. Étienne to Lyons.

[3] The cost of establishing a railroad varies, of course, very much. The average cost in France is 468,000 francs per kilometre, but it is almost double in England, and not more than a quarter of this in new countries and colonies where expropriation is not necessary.

[4] In 1910 there were 1,045,000 kilometres of railway distributed as follows:

Europe	. . . 349,000	Asia	. . .	102,000
North America	. . . 454,000	Africa	. . .	37,000
South America	. . . 72,000	Australia	. . .	31,000

In Europe, France, with 55,000 kilometres, stands third after Germany with 71,000 and Russia with 60,000. Great Britain has 39,000. But, in proportion to population, France has more than any other large European country.

The total gross receipts amount to 3700 million francs for Germany; 3100

and the United States the system is almost complete, but in many other parts of the world it is scarcely yet begun. The railroad is to-day one of the most powerful instruments of colonisation. In new countries it is not used, as in the old, merely to complete a network of overland roads, and to unite centres of population already existing. It penetrates right through bush and virgin forest ; and from it there come gradually forth, as from the trunk of a living tree, branches in the shape of roads, and fruit in the shape of towns.

The advantages which railways have brought to mankind are incalculable. We may perhaps give a rough idea of them when we say that the transport of one ton per kilometre costs about 4 centimes (4·3 in France, including, however, a tax of 12 per cent., and very nearly the same in the other European countries ; less than 3 centimes in the United States), while cartage costs about 30. If we multiply the 26 centimes saved by the 20 billion tons per kilometre transported in France, we may estimate the annual economy at 5 or 6 billion francs. This calculation, however, means nothing, since it is evident that without railways these billions of tons would not have been transported at all, nor the greater part of them even produced.

Only a little more than one-half of this price represents the cost of transport properly speaking. The other half represents mileage, *i.e.* the interest on, and redemption of, the capital spent in constructing the road. Mileage is abolished to-day on overland roads since the cost of these roads has been written off, and, in all probability, as we have already said, when the railways belong to the State mileage will be abolished on them also.

The question to whom the railways should belong, and how they should be exploited, is a difficult one. There are three possible solutions :

(1) *Free competition.* The railway is after all only a transport enterprise. Why not then leave it under the ordinary *régime* of all enterprises ? This method has been followed in England and in the United States, where it certainly cannot be said to have hindered the development of railways.

Still, there are numerous objections to it. The comparison with free enterprise is only a fiction. In the first place, the railway is not a mere transport undertaking ; it involves the making of a road, and, for that, the right of expropriation—a right which can be given only

millions for England ; and 1891 millions only for France. These figures are proportional to the density of the population and the wealth of each country. (Colson, *Statistique des Transports, Supplément au Cours.*)

by law and which is too responsible to be handed over to private enterprise without serious safeguards.[1] Further, the construction of more or less parallel lines between two towns, which is the sole way in which competition can be exercised, necessarily means an investment of double the capital, and is therefore altogether contrary to the hedonistic principle of the greatest good at least cost. Even supposing a single line were not enough for the traffic, it costs much less to double or quadruple the tracks than to construct a rival railway. Lastly, from the consumer's point of view, it is impossible for competition in this case to produce the desired end, namely, cheapness. For, even supposing competition forces the two companies to lower their tariffs to cost price, the cost price will obviously be higher where there are two lines than where there is but one, since embankments, stations, tunnels, bridges, etc., will have to be duplicated. Moreover it is easy to foresee that the two competing companies, after doing their best to drive each other out by lowering their respective rates, or even by transporting at a loss (some have even been known to offer refreshments gratis), will soon tire of this game and come to an agreement, thus sending up their rates again, so that the so-called competition will end in a monopoly. The experience of the United States fully confirms what we say. Agreements under different forms among railway companies, though prosecuted and condemned by law, end, in spite of everything, by leaving the railways in the hands of a few multi-millionaires and by conferring on these " railway kings " a quasi-sovereignty over transportation. They have become one of the great national problems—no longer merely economic, but political. In England the competing enterprises long ago came to an agreement to divide the country into sections, somewhat resembling those of the six large French companies.

(2) *Operation by the State*, or, as it is called in French, *en régie*. This is the system practised already in many countries (Germany, Austria-Hungary, Russia, Belgium, Roumania, Switzerland, Italy, Japan, etc.—over about 300,000 kilometres), and it is gaining ground. In the last three countries the railways have been bought up quite recently by the State. In France, a small portion of the railway system was worked by the State as long ago as 1878, and this has

---

[1] American legislation, however, provides few safeguards. In the United States anyone may construct a railway on condition solely of forming a society of twenty-five persons and of subscribing 628 dollars per kilometre, only one-tenth of which need be paid up. In return for this it is *incorporated* and may issue shares to a fantastic amount, expropriate, etc.

been increased by the purchase of the *Compagnie de l'Ouest* in 1909.[1]

The question of the exploitation of railways by the State has given rise to the liveliest discussions.[2] The Liberal school, of course, condemns it altogether. Apart from the matter of principle (see p. 209), it would seem as if the experiments already made in so many countries ought to be decisive, and that it should now be possible to settle the question one way or the other. But this is not the case, as the results have a different aspect according to the standpoint which we take.

From the point of view of the public, the *consumer*, State railways seem in no way inferior to those of the private companies either in comfort, security, or facilities of all sorts. On the contrary, the carriages of the German State railways are, if anything, better than those of the large French companies; and in France, even when the traveller passes from the system of the companies to that of the State, he has not as a rule anything to complain of. It is not easy to see, moreover, why the private administration of railways should be superior to that of the State, since the same engineers from the same schools are employed by both. As for the disadvantages of bureaucratic organisations, they are to be found in all large railway exploitations, whether State or private. The working of a railway like that of the Paris-Lyon-Méditerranée, with about 10,000 kilometres of line and 70,000 employees, has necessarily all the characteristics of a public administration. On the other hand, it is evident that, while the first concern of a private company is the interest of its shareholders—the services it renders to the public being only a means and not an end—the State administration, on the contrary, having no dividends to distribute, will concern itself only with the interests of the public. It is, moreover, much more directly under the control of public opinion and the press.

If, however, we take the business point of view, that of receipts, in particular that of *net income*, it is quite evident that the advantage lies on the side of private management. A company has to make its

---

[1] The law of July 13, 1908, authorised the purchase and that of December 21, 1909, ratified the conditions and the price.

The State railway system was thereby more than doubled, covering to-day over 8925 kilometres, *i.e.* more than any other company save the Paris-Lyon-Méditerranée, which covers 9562 kilometres.

[2] Léon Say wrote in the *Journal des Économistes* (October 1882): "It is easy enough to-day to see that the State exploitation (of the railways) is one of the most colossal errors that could have been committed. . . . It is a disaster." For the opposite point of view, see M. Milhaud, *Le rachat des chemins de fer.*

capital pay and must distribute dividends to its shareholders. As it cannot look, for profits, to a rise in the price of transport—its rates being generally fixed by law—it is obliged to find them in a reduction of cost, that is to say, by constantly improving its methods and economising in its administration. State exploitation, on the contrary, has no other control to submit to, as regards its working, than that of a committee of functionaries or politicians. And though, no doubt, the Minister of Finance has an interest in obtaining resources from the railway for his always needy budget, he will certainly not have the same solicitude as a board of shareholders who have a part of their fortune sunk in the business.

It must be added that the State constructs at greater cost than private enterprise ; that favouritism and parasitism, against which even the companies have difficulty in defending themselves, have here full scope ; that, as the employees of all degrees look on themselves as true officials, we can expect from them only the minimum of labour with the maximum of complaints ; [1] lastly, that it is more difficult for the State than for a private company to defend itself against the constant demands of the public for reduced rates,[2] a more generous distribution of free passes, more numerous and rapid trains (which must nevertheless stop at the smallest stations), an increase in the number of employees solely to give employment to a larger number of applicants, the construction of costly lines without any possible traffic, solely to satisfy electoral or military interests. So that the administration is caught, as it were, between the hammer and the anvil, between a continual increase of expense on the one hand and an inevitable reduction of rates on the other. Under such conditions it is not surprising that in all countries the net product is less, or rather the coefficient for exploitation is higher, on State railways than on those of private companies.[3]

[1] The general railway strike of 1910, in France, found some of its most ardent promoters among the State employees.

[2] In France, a campaign has been carried on for ten years to obtain for all army officers on the reserve, i.e. for about 100,000 persons, the quarter-price fare. Hitherto the companies have resisted valiantly, but if the officers of the reserve had been dealing with the State only, the latter would have been forced to yield at once.

[3] Thus, in Switzerland, since the acquisition of the railways by the State, i.e. between 1903 and 1910, the number of employees and the total of their wages have increased 50 per cent., while receipts have increased only 30 per cent. Also the figure for working expenses has risen from 65 per cent. to 73 per cent. It is the same in France. This is due in both countries to political influences.

In Germany the figure for exploitation on the State railways (i.e. the propor-

The question then of the State exploitation of railways cannot be decided on principle alone. The railway system will be worth what the administration is worth.

In spite of all its disadvantages, State exploitation of railways will become more and more common. This is because political, rather than economic, motives are at work here. They may be summed up as follows :

(*a*) The unwillingness of a government to leave in the hands of private companies, directed by large capitalists, the powerful economic, social, and even political influence which these big enterprises involve.

(*b*) The growing needs of the Treasury, for which the regularly increasing receipts of the railways are a splendid windfall. For although, as we said, the net revenue of the State railways is less than that of the companies, it is by no means inconsiderable. In Prussia it forms a notable part of the receipts of the Treasury.[1]

tion of cost of exploitation to gross return) is higher than that for the French companies (69 per cent., as against 56 per cent.). And yet the much greater density of population, as also the lesser cost of coal, ought to bring in to the German railways a better return than the French obtain. (See Colson, *Cours d'Économie politique*, Book VI). It is true that the fitting-up of the railways, the large stations, the uniforms of the employees, carriages, etc., are much more magnificent and have to be paid for.

In France, the gross receipts per kilometre and the figures for working are as follows :

Nord	77,000 francs	58·3
P.L.M.	56,000 ,,	53·8
Est	52,000 ,,	57·4
Orléans . . .	37,000 ,,	55·2
Midi	34,000 ,,	56·5
État	32,000 ,,	80·7

The State line therefore stands lowest as regards receipts and highest as regards cost of working. But it must be pointed out, that the north-western region through which it passes is not industrially wealthy.

It is to be feared, on the other hand, that individual complaints on the part of the public will have less chance of being listened to in the case of State railways than in that of private companies, either because the State will limit its responsibility, as it has already done with the posts and telegraphs, or because the law courts will hesitate to give judgment against it. It would be necessary, therefore, to see that the responsibility of the State was established.

[1] In Germany the railways bring in over £34,000,000 net to the Treasury, three-quarters coming from Prussia.

In Switzerland the federal administration of the railways keeps all the profits itself and must employ them in improving the service. Between it and the Treasury there is, as it were, an impassable barrier. But such disinterestedness on the part of the State is rare, and is to be explained perhaps by the existence of a certain jealousy between the cantons and the federal government.

(c) The interests of national defence, which require that all the railways should be in the hands of the Government for purposes of mobilisation.

(3) *The system of concessions.* This is a mixed system between the other two, and is the one practised in France. Though much decried there, it has been a matter of admiration in other countries. It is very complicated, but we may sum up its characteristics briefly as follows :

(1) The railways are considered as forming part of the public domain. The State, however, instead of operating them directly itself—*en régie*, as it is called—turns over the working of them to companies, as it does with its mines.[1] But, while in the case of the mines the concession is perpetual and equivalent to a complete surrender of the right of ownership, in the case of the railways it is only temporary, although the term is long—ninety-nine years. Once this term is completed, the State will enter into full ownership of the railways. As the conventions with the six large companies, among which the State had divided the French territory, were made between 1830 and 1860,[2] it will be between the years 1950 and

---

[1] The railway system in France is the result of two series of agreements made between the State and the companies.

The first took place in 1859 under the Second Empire. The main lines existed already and were beginning to bring in profits. But when the question arose of opening up secondary lines, the companies were unwilling to proceed to this without a guarantee of interest of 4 per cent. (4·65 counting the sinking fund).

The ingenious system of pooling was then hit upon. The lines in each company were divided into two groups, the old and the new. The State guarantee was not called on in the case of the new groups until after the companies had turned over into them the surplus receipts from the old groups. The sums given as guarantee of interest were, moreover, to be paid back when profits passed the limit fixed ; and they were in fact paid.

The second agreements of 1882, substituted for the earlier ones, have provoked sharp criticism, and have even been stigmatised as " scoundrelly." They were due to the same causes as those of 1859. There was a question, in order to complete the French system and carry out Freycinet's plan, of constructing 10,000 kilometres of third-class lines—those which run through no important centre. The State had begun by constructing them itself, but seeing that the operation was becoming ruinous it asked the companies to take it over. The latter accepted only on condition that the State would refund the expenses (with the exception of 25,000 francs per kilometre, which they took upon themselves) and that it would guarantee the interest on their loans, *i.e.* on the bonds which they should issue and even the dividends of their shares. The State, on the other hand, was allowed a share in the profits after they reached a certain sum.

[2] It was in 1842 that the general plan of the main lines was laid down, but the beginnings were difficult. The Revolution of 1848 did not help matters, and under the Second Empire the whole had to be reorganised.

1960 that they will terminate, and the State will then enter into this magnificent heritage which already·represents about 750 million francs of net revenue, or more than the interest on the enormous national debt.

(2) The State is the partner of the companies : it co-operates in establishing railways in two different ways :

(a) By *subsidies, i.e.* by undertaking the construction of the whole or part of the lines. Thus, after the great companies were formed, the State took over the whole of the making of the lines. And at the time of the conventions of 1882, when thousands of kilometres of railway were decided on—very costly, since they passed over rough ground, and not very paying as the region was a poor one—the State had to take on itself almost the whole cost of the construction of the lines.[1] In all, it has contributed 7424 million francs, or a little over 39 per cent. of the total cost of the French railways, which amounts to 18,874 million francs.[2]

(b) By *guarantees of interest,* calculated so as to secure the interest on loans issued by the companies for the building of their lines. Since the conventions of 1882, the dividends on the shares are also guaranteed and can fall no further ; but, as all surplus profits must be handed over to the State, it is almost equally impossible for them to rise, so that these shares have in fact become veritable bonds.

This measure had to be resorted to first, after the construction of the great lines, when others of secondary importance were proposed—the new group, as it was called ; and again later when, to satisfy the electors, or perhaps from some feeling of national solidarity, the Government started a third class of lines without any apparent prospects—one of which, as some one ingeniously put it, " was crossing the Cevennes incognito." It is to the guarantee of interest that recourse is had when railways are built in the colonies.

These guarantees of interest have often been called upon, and for considerable sums (100 million francs in the ill-omened year of 1893). The companies of the Nord and the P.-L.-M. have never needed to resort to them, but the Midi and the Ouest have accumulated such a mass of debt that it is doubtful whether they will ever be able to repay it.[3] Other companies have already begun

---

[1] See note on preceding page.   [2] Colson, *Statistique des Transports.*

[3] In the case of the Ouest, the State, balancing the debt owed by that company against the compensation due to it, was able to buy it back at a small cost.

to pay back. For it must be observed that these supplements of interest are only advances made by the State, and that the companies have to refund them in good years when their net product is more than enough to pay their bonds and shares.

Further, if the net revenue is above a certain amount, the State has a right to two-thirds of the profits. This happy day, supposed to be near at hand at the time of the conventions of 1882, has been long in coming. Still, in 1906, the State began to receive a share in the profits of a few companies. It could, of course, have done so much sooner had not new laws regarding pensions for employees, the weekly day of rest, improvements of the service, etc., greatly increased running expenses. But the State can hardly avoid sacrificing its own interest to that of its employees and the general public.[1]

There is in fact a kind of current account between the State and the companies. Sometimes one pays, sometimes the other, according to circumstances; at present the balance is in favour of the State, which is creditor to the amount of some hundreds of millions.

(3) The State has control over the railway rates. The companies are unable to raise or lower their rates without having their action ratified by the State.[2] The latter has also control over the management, and readily acts as organ for the complaints of the public.

(4) Finally, the State has the right at any time to purchase the railways. In this event it is bound : (*a*) to pay, during the remainder of the time that the concession has still to run, an annuity calculated on the revenue of the seven previous years (deducting the two worst), but never less than the net proceeds of the last year. The bonds and shares of the companies are thus transformed into State stock, though this hardly affects them. (*b*) To pay the estimated value of the rolling stock of the companies. The sums due to the State, however, by the companies must be taken into account.

---

[1] The State imposes a number of obligations on the companies, such as the gratuitous transport of the posts (an enormous and rapidly increasing charge), the transport of soldiers and a host of officials at reduced prices, etc., the whole working out at an economy of 110 million francs, not counting the 190 million francs of taxes. These advantages may be considered a sort of profit-sharing.

[2] We can easily understand why the companies should not have the right to raise their rates, without leave, the maximum rate in this, as in all concessions, being the price paid for a privilege ; but why not allow the companies to lower their rates at will ? Because the power to differentiate tariffs is a dangerous weapon in the hands of companies : in the United States, for example, it has been greatly abused. Though such a power may be of great service in facilitating transit or the transport of goods of small value, it may also be used to favour one industry at the expense of its competitors. When applied to products imported from abroad, differentiation is called, in France, *tarif de pénétration*.

Those who oppose the purchase of the railways by the State urge, in addition to the above arguments based on principle, the practical objection that, as the State, in less than fifty years, will have all the railway systems for nothing, it would be mere extravagance to take them over to-day just in order to enjoy them a little sooner. The answer given to this is, that it might be a very good national investment. For, as the State would pay for the railways on the basis of their present revenues, it would have the benefit of all subsequent increases, instead of leaving these for another fifty years in the hands of the companies. This answer would hold good if a progressive increase in the net revenue of the railways were certain. But, for the reasons given above,[1] their very transfer into the hands of the State might have the effect of checking the increase.

III : THE MERCANTILE MARINE

IT is not indispensable for a nation to have a large commercial fleet in order to do a great deal of commerce. Belgium, for instance, who, in relation to her population, occupies the first rank in commerce and has one of the largest ports in the world, Antwerp, takes almost the lowest place as regards her mercantile marine. Still, nearly every country, rightly or wrongly, holds that a large merchant fleet is indispensable both to its economic development and to its political power ; and the well-known remark of the Emperor William II, " The future of Germany is on the sea," is but the expression of a feeling shared by the governments of all nations.

From the point of view of national defence, it is thought that a navy can only recruit its *personnel* and keep up its material so long as there is in the country a nursery, so to speak, of professional sailors from which to recruit, and dockyards for maritime construction. But this argument, which was formerly very strong, has lost much of its force now that battleships and their armaments have become such extremely complicated machines, requiring the professional knowledge of engineers rather than of sailors.

From the point of view of commerce, it is believed that " trade follows the flag " : *i.e.* that not only does national industry find

---

1 On the companies' lines profits have ceased to rise and have, in fact, been decreasing so much the last few years that a possible raising of the rates has been announced. Gross receipts continue to increase, but expenses increase faster still, owing as much to technical improvements as to the rise in wages, old-age pensions, the weekly day of rest, etc. All these causes will act with still more force when the railways belong to the State.

the display of the national flag a most effective advertisement in foreign ports, but that, if a country allows its goods to be transported by foreign vessels, buyers will believe that they come from the transporting country and will transfer their custom to the latter. To obviate this danger, however, a country need only send its own subjects abroad to represent its commerce, as the Germans are so quick, and the French so slow, to realise. The nationality of the commercial agent abroad is much more important than that of the transport vessel.[1]

But if a large mercantile marine is not indispensable to the greatness, or even to the prosperity, of a nation, it is beyond all dispute that maritime transport is a lucrative industry, and that à country which, like Holland in former times and England to-day, transports the goods of all other countries will find profit in doing so ; while the country which has to apply to other countries to transport its own products must evidently pay the price. Thus France, who transports only a small proportion of her exports and imports, has to pay over £12,000,000 annually to foreign shipowners ; while England, who transports two-thirds of the tonnage of the whole world, and who also builds ships for all nations, gains by this twofold commerce over £80,000,000 per annum.

France would assuredly have gained much by developing this branch of industry. Nature, indeed, seems to invite her to do so, by the privileged situation which she has given her at the extremity of the European continent, with one large frontage on the Atlantic and another on the Mediterranean, a maritime population second to none in its love of the sea, and the second colonial empire in the world.

The falling-off of France in this respect is of recent date. For a long while France came next to England, and, although some distance behind, held nevertheless the second rank. In 1870, she was still third, after the United States ; to-day she is only fifth.[2] The causes of this decline, though they have been the subject of much inquiry, are not very clear.

[1] The Free Trade answer to this argument is, that it may be much more advantageous for a country to have its goods transported cheaply by other countries better equipped for the purpose, than to do it itself. This is the law of the division of labour. It is, no doubt, true ; but the question is, whether it would not be good for a country as favourably situated as the others to do it itself.

[2] The following table, according to Colson's *Statistique des Transports* (Supplement to his *Cours*), shows the position of the principal countries as regards their mercantile marines in 1911 :

(1) The best explanation seems to be lack of freight. French industry devotes itself more to finished articles, or articles of luxury, than to heavy goods. It does not, for instance, export such a commodity as coal, which in itself represents over 88 per cent. of the total weight of export from England. It does, it is true, import some, but not a great deal.[1] France is one of the countries which, owing to the variety of her produce, is most self-sufficing, and although this

	Steamships	Sailing-ships	Total Fleet
England . . .	18,122,000 tons	1,118,000 tons	19,240,000 tons
Germany . . .	3,893,000 ,,	433,000 ,,	4,326,0C0 ,,
United States .	1,955 000 ,,	1,305,000 ,,	3,260,000 ,.
Norway . . .	1,533,000 ,,	654,000 ,,	2,187,000 ,,
France . . .	1,471,000 ,,	470,000 ,.	1,941,000 ,
Italy . . .	1,040,000 ,,	372,000 ,,	1,412,000 ,,
Japan . . .	1,202,000 ,,	171,000 ,,	1,373,000 ,
Other countries .	6,753,000 ,,	1,630,000 ,,	8,383,000 ,
Total . .	35,969,000 ,,	6,153,000 ,,	42,122,000 ,,

We see that France stands only fifth, being beaten even by Norway and closely pressed by Japan. Japan indeed would come before her if the large fleet of native junks were included in the figures given.

It is evident that a steamship ton represents much more transport power than a sailing-ship ton. The superiority, therefore, of England, the United States, and Germany is still greater than appears at first sight from the figures for total tonnage. If, in France, the proportion of steamships is much smaller than in these countries, it is owing to the blundering law for the protection of the marine, of which we shall speak later, which encouraged the construction of sailing-ships. The new law will, we hope, remedy this.

Statistics for the mercantile marine seem often to give very divergent results and need to be carefully examined. Tonnage figures may, in fact, vary enormously according to the method of calculation:

(1) According to whether we count all the ships in existence, or exclude small vessels of under 100 tons (among these all fishing-boats). In the figures given above only steamships of over 100 tons and sailing-ships of over 50 tons are given.

(2) According to whether we count maritime navigation only, or include, like the United States, the internal navigation on rivers and great lakes: in this case the United States far surpasses Germany, and ranks second. In the figures given above, however, the maritime fleet only is counted.

(3) According to whether we count gross tonnage or net tonnage (*i.e.* deducting, particularly in the case of steamers, all the parts not used for transport).

(4) According to whether we add together sailing-ships and steamships without discrimination, or count a steamship, since it can do three or four times as many voyages in the same time, as equal to three or three and a half times a sailing-ship.

[1] We must remember that every ship has to make the return as well as the outward journey, and that to do so with profit it must find goods to transport both ways. If, one way, it has to go on ballast, this works out very costly. If French ships had to go empty to America, India, or Australia, in order to bring back corn or wool, they would be doing very poor business.

internal autonomy, which it is her object to develop by a protective system, may be considered an advantage in some ways, it is evident that, from the point of view of freight for a mercantile marine, it is a drawback.

Still, it may be said, the maritime trade of France, imports and exports combined, amounts to quite a good tonnage, and represents a larger movement of navigation than even that of Germany.[1] Why does the French marine carry only a quarter of it, leaving the rest to foreign fleets ? The reason is that French articles, just because they are generally dear, cannot wait. They are sent by rail whenever possible, and where they are obliged to go by sea they take the first ship that passes. Now, more often than not, this is a foreign ship. For the geographical situation of France, at first so favourable, ceased to be so when Germany and Central Europe became great centres of production. The French ports, from being termini for goods from overseas, became no more than mere *stations* of passage. Foreign ships find it convenient to touch at them in passing, to take in extra freight or to discharge some of their cargo ; but for the bulk of their shipments they prefer to load and unload in the ports of Antwerp, Rotterdam and Hamburg, more especially as these are free ports where there is always freight to be had.

(2) Another cause of inferiority lies, according to French shipowners, in French legislation, which imposes heavy charges on them that other countries have not to support, namely : (*a*) the obligation to have three-fourths at least of their crew of French nationality (this results in a kind of monopoly for the crew, so that they become more exacting, demand higher wages, more expensive food, and do less work, whence the necessity for employing more men on board) ; (*b*) social burdens, such as the obligation to repatriate sailors who, from illness or any other cause (save desertion), have been put ashore in foreign countries, and the recent compulsory weekly day of rest, which has just provoked violent strikes.

It has not been shown, however, that the situation of sailors in other countries is very different ;[2] and even were this charge proved,

[1] The movement of navigation for France, in 1910, was 29 million tons as against 22 millions for Germany, and 66 millions for England.
Now, out of this imposing figure the French flag flies over no more than 22 per cent., or less than one-quarter, of its imports, and 48 per cent., or less than one-half, of its exports, while the German flag and the English flag carry two-thirds of their maritime trade. (*Annales du Commerce extérieur*.)

[2] As regards the obligation for the majority of the crew to consist of French subjects, this rule is found in Spain where the proportion is four-fifths, in Italy,

we have only to point out that it is amply compensated for by the millions of francs which, as we shall see, the State grants shipowners in the form of premiums, and by certain privileges as regards the coasting trade, including the exclusive right of transport between France and Algeria. It is only just that the protection given to shipowners should extend also to sailors.[1]

When the causes of an evil cannot be diagnosed, it is difficult to find a remedy. Thus almost everything has been attempted without much success.

Protective duties were first tried. Indeed we may say that the protection of the mercantile marine was the starting-point of the whole protectionist system. Cromwell's famous *Navigation Act* (1651), excluding all oversea goods imported under any other flag than the English, was passed to protect the English marine and to wrest from Holland the empire of the seas ; and it is generally admitted that it contributed not a little to this result. Colbert's no less celebrated *Ordonnance*, of 1681, was also for the protection of the mercantile marine. Without analysing this method, which is now only of historical interest, we would simply point out that this protection took the form of increased duties on goods imported in foreign ships (*surtaxes du pavillon*), of duties on the foreign ships themselves (*droits de navigation*), and lastly, of a monopoly for the French flag of all commerce with the colonies and of the coasting trade.

where it is two-thirds, and in Greece and Russia where it is three-fourths. In Germany it applies only to the ships of subsidised companies, on which, however, no foreigners are allowed. In England it does not, it is true, exist in law (except for officers), but in actual fact the proportion of foreigners is much lower than that allowed by French law. English and German shipowners, again, complain on their part of burdens of their own.

[1] This monopoly, as it were, conferred on French sailors is, moreover, one of the fundamental articles of what is called *maritime inscription*, a system which dates from Colbert and which has been completed by subsequent laws. All youths inhabiting the coast-line are bound to serve for a certain time in the navy, in compensation for which they are allowed various privileges, the most important of which are :

(a) The monopoly of the merchant service.

(b) The right to a retiring pension, varying in amount according to the years of service and rank.

This monopoly in favour of inscribed seamen has called forth lively protests of late, as the organised sailors of Marseilles took advantage of it several times to stop navigation between France and Algeria, and to force shipowners to satisfy their claims ; and there has been some talk of abolishing it. There seems indeed to be no longer any object in it ; but there are very complex military and political interests involved.

But these measures, abandoned almost everywhere else, had to be given up by France also, either because they provoked reprisals, or because they were too injurious to national commerce and to the colonies.[1]

In 1860, following close on the famous free trade treaties with England, the policy of *laisser faire* was tried. This experiment, which lasted twenty years, gave no better results so far as the merchant service was concerned.

Lastly, recourse was had to the method always employed when a country is unable or unwilling to establish protective duties, and when nevertheless an industry must be helped—namely, *bounties*.[2] This has been the system followed since 1881.

The problem is the more complicated in that there are two industries which have here to be protected—the industry of ship-building and that of transport, or shipowning—whose interests are divergent, since the shipowners' object is to get their ships as cheaply as possible. Thus, in the last twenty-seven years, four systems have been tried under the laws of January 29, 1881, January 30, 1893, April 7, 1902, and April 19, 1906.

In the case of shipbuilding, subsidies are intended to compensate for the difference between the cost of production in France and in other countries, taking Great Britain in particular as term of comparison. But such a calculation is necessarily very arbitrary. The most recent law, that of 1906, grants a bounty of 145 francs per ton for steamships,[3] which seems quite excessive, since it is more than half of the cost per ton in England. This presupposes a difference of 60 per cent. in cost of construction, whereas ship-builders themselves admit that the difference is not more than

---

[1] All that remains of this system to-day is : (1) the monopoly of the *coasting trade* on the coasts of France, including Algeria ; (2) that of the coast fisheries ; (3) the *surtaxes d'entrepôt, i e.* a moderate increase in the customs duties on goods imported even under the French flag, when, instead of coming direct, they have put into foreign ports on their way.

[2] See chapter entitled *Bounties on Production.*

[3] In addition, a premium of 27 fr. 50 per 100 kilogrammes is allowed for the engine. A steamship of 3000 tons receives 435,000 francs for the hull and over 100,000 francs for the engine, *i.e.* a present of 550,000 francs !

For iron sailing-ships the premium is 95 francs per ton, and for wooden sailing-ships only 40 francs.

It is true that this premium is not promised in perpetuity ; it is to diminish year by year until 1916, when it will not be more than 100 francs per ton for steam-ships and 65 francs per ton for sailing-ships. This is in order to stimulate French builders. Further, the State has fixed a maximum of 115 million francs, which it is not supposed to exceed.

20 per cent. French shipbuilders, we should think, might at least acknowledge these favours by selling their ships cheaper than English ones. Nothing of the sort, however : they ask 50 per cent. more for them and take two or three times as long to build them.[1] The excuse they give is that, being too numerous, they have few orders and are overburdened by general expenses. But if they have few orders it is because they ask too high a price : they are thus reasoning in a vicious circle.[2]

In the case of navigation, the law gives bounties, now called *compensations d'armement* (shipowners' *compensations*), in order to make it quite clear that they have nothing to do with profits, but are solely compensation for charges. They are fixed according to the number of days during which the ship has been in active service, and on condition that it shall actually have performed a minimum journey and transported a minimum quantity of goods. This stipulation was introduced by the law of 1906 to prevent the incredible abuses of the previous system, which gave the subsidy solely in proportion to the voyage accomplished, so that ships were to be seen careering across the seas with no cargoes, merely to obtain the bounty.[3] These bounties are enormous. A ship of 6000 tons may obtain 60,000 francs a year for twelve years.[4]

As these bounties are given to shipowners in compensation for their alleged disadvantages as compared with foreign shippers, we might be inclined to think that they would enable French shipowners to offer as cheap rates to their merchants as do foreign vessels. Not at all. The phenomenon which we saw in the case of the shipbuilders is repeated here. Shipping is

[1] Declaration of the managers of the shipbuilding yards of the Loire, reproduced in a report of M. Charles Roux on the Budget of Commerce for 1898.

[2] In France there are a hundred or so shipyards, which cost a large sum, and half are always empty. In addition, as the French shipbuilding yards only work to order, they have on every occasion to turn out different models, while the English yards manufacture ships " ready made," as a " department store " does costumes.

[3] Some maritime companies were able to distribute dividends simply out of the bounties they received ; others refused freight because the time lost in loading and unloading would have reduced their bounties.

[4] The bounty (or compensation) per ton per day of *armement* (this is not quite the same thing as per day of *navigation*) is 4 centimes for steamships up to 3000 tons ; 3 centimes for those between 3000 and 6000 tons ; 2 centimes for ships of larger tonnage. The bounty may be received by the same ship for not longer than twelve years, and only for ships registered up to 1916 ; which simply means that in the case of shipowning, as in that of shipbuilding, the State did not want to bind itself beyond ten years.

much dearer in France than in other countries, and hundreds of millions of francs of merchandise are sent to Antwerp, Rotterdam and London to be shipped.[1] Yet French shipowners complain of lack of freight ! It is a repetition of the vicious circle which we pointed out in the case of the shipbuilders.

In order to stimulate shipowners to keep pace with the times, the subsidy is raised 30 per cent. for vessels which exceed sixteen knots ; it is reduced by 17 per cent. in the case of those which do not exceed ten knots, and entirely abolished in the case of those which do not exceed nine knots.

That shipowners may not be entirely at the mercy of French shipbuilders, the law allows them not only to buy their ships abroad but to benefit by the bounties when they do so, provided that they nationalise the ships and that these ships be not more than two years old—a somewhat rigorous condition.[2]

All this is certainly very ingenious. The legislator of 1906 did his best to avoid the mistakes of his predecessors ; and there has in fact been notable progress of late years. The French merchant fleet, which had remained almost stationary at the figure of one million tons during the second half of the nineteenth century, began to increase after 1900, and stands now at over 2,000,000 tons.[3] But it is doubtful whether this improvement is due to legislation, as the year 1900, the date at which it began, does not coincide with the application of any of the successive laws for the protection of the marine, and as there has been a simultaneous improvement in countries which did not practise the system of subsidies.[4] It is still

---

[1] Antwerp sends out in an average year 400 million francs' worth of French goods.

[2] Under the law of 1881 shipowners obtained only half a bounty in the case of ships bought abroad, and under that of 1893 none at all. This obliged them to have their ships built in France and to submit to the conditions of the French shipbuilders.

There is a duty on the nationalisation of foreign ships, but it is insignificant, viz., 2 francs per ton.

[3] This is *gross* tonnage. For steamships the *net* tonnage is about one-third lower, as the space for the machinery, coal-bunkers, etc., must be deducted. (Colson, *Statistique*.)

[4] The following are some figures for the last twenty-five years, steamships only (Colson, *op. cit.*):

	England Tons	Germany Tons	United States Tons	France Tons
1886 . . .	6,544,000	602,000	502,000	744,000
1911 . . .	18,122,000	3,893,000	1,955,000	1,471,000
Increase . .	177 %	546 %	289 %	98 %

The smaller rate of increase in the British marine is explained by the fact

more doubtful whether the result is at all commensurate with the enormous sacrifices made, as, since 1881, over 400 million francs have been thrown into the sea, without preventing the French marine from falling from the second to the fifth place.

Perhaps when the twelve years' term fixed for this new experiment has run out, a last attempt will be made by trying free ports (see next chapter); perhaps nothing will be done at all.

There is another kind of bounty, which consists in subsidies granted to great maritime lines on condition that they keep up a regular service between certain fixed points, and undertake to convey the mails and a few other State transports. Here the subsidy may be considered the price of a service rendered. It is very useful for a country, from the political as well as from the commercial point of view, to have regular means of transport over the great world routes, if it be only with its colonies.[1] This is somewhat similar to the system adopted towards the railways, and is followed in most countries.[2] The subsidised lines in France cost, it is true, relatively more than those of other countries, since, having little traffic, they can continue working only with the help of large indemnities. Their cost in 1910 was 26 million francs, which, added to the 35 millions of subsidy, makes a total of 61 millions.

IV : PORTS

THE question of ports is inseparable from that of the mercantile marine. Ports have been called the stations of the maritime highways. And it is clear that a country cannot hope to see the big maritime lines touch its shores if it offers no large stations. Formerly the only ports were natural ones, and if a country were well endowed by nature in this respect it was a great factor in its development. Nowadays, however, ports are becoming more and more artificial, since there is hardly one in existence well enough

that the growth of anything which has reached a certain degree of development necessarily slows down. England has, for long, been far ahead of the other nations, but she cannot remain so for ever. As it is, however, her fleet is still nearly five times as large as that of Germany.

[1] The three great subsidised French companies (*Messageries maritimes, Compagnie transatlantique, Chargeurs réunis*) represent nearly 800,000 tons, or almost half the total of the French merchant fleet. Were it not for them, many countries would never see the French flag.

[2] England herself gives 21 million francs, Italy more than 17, Germany and the Argentine Republic more than 15, and a dozen other countries from 1 to 10 millions.

adapted by nature to receive the colossal ships that are being built, requiring as they do a depth of 8 or 10 yards to come alongside, several miles of quay, slips 300 yards long for repairs, hundreds of acres of roadstead in which to turn, and dozens of wharves at which to discharge their cargoes.

Enormous expenditure is therefore required to construct ports for the entrance and repair of ships of all sizes.[1]

It is not easy to find the means of paying for these immense works. The State is not in a good position to do so, not only because its budget is always heavily burdened, but because the feeling of national solidarity is not sufficiently strong for the representatives of a hundred ports to consent to set apart a large share for one single port. To obtain satisfactory results from the large programme for public works of 1879, in France, the entire £20,000,000 of credit set apart for ports ought to have been devoted to two only, Le Havre and Marseilles, or at most to five. They were divided, however, over seventy ports in order to content each one, and the result is that nothing of any value has been done. It is here more especially that the law of concentration should be observed. Germany has only two large ports (Hamburg and Bremen), Holland one, and Belgium one.[2]

[1] The port of Hamburg, which has 10 miles of quay and 1000 acres of dock, cost £12,000,000; that of Antwerp about £8,280,000, and £2,280,000 have been pledged for new works. For Le Havre, after twenty years of shilly-shallying and of works executed slowly and found inadequate before ever they were finished, it has been decided to undertake new ones to the extent of some millions sterling. A still larger sum is to be spent on Bordeaux.

[2] The following is the tonnage of the principal ports (1911) from Colson's *Statistiques*, to which we have already referred. The tonnage given here is that of *ships* (under cargo or ballast) which have entered the ports, and may differ greatly from the figures for tons of *merchandise*, particularly if, as is sometimes done, the number of ships which have entered and cleared be taken, even though these are, necessarily, the same ships :

France				Other Countries		
Marseilles	.	9,770,000 tons	..	London .	.	19,663,000 tons
Le Havre	.	4,959,000 ,,	..	Liverpool	.	14,713,000 ,,
Bordeaux	.	2,916,000 ,,	..	Antwerp .	.	13,350,000 ,,
Boulogne	.	2,639,000 ,,	..	Hamburg	.	13,176,000 ,,
Dunkirk .	.	2,408,000 ,,	..	Rotterdam	.	11,194,000 ,,
Rouen	.	2,282,000 ,,	..	Genoa .	.	7,149,000 ,,

We do not include Paris, though it might stand at the head of French ports with 10 million tons, as, unlike London and Rouen, it is almost entirely a river port. Cherbourg has a higher tonnage than Bordeaux, but this is due to the fact that the large German passenger steamers call there.

We have given only the European ports in this list, but Hong Kong and New York are level with Antwerp and Rotterdam. Marseilles is therefore only eighth on the list of large world-ports.

The problem as to who should bear this enormous expenditure is a difficult one. There are three possible solutions :

(*a*) The State might take over the cost of the ports as it does that of the national roads and canals. This has hitherto been the policy in France; but the State is no longer equal to the burden.

(*b*) Private enterprise might undertake these works at its own risk and peril. This system is much in use in Eastern and African ports : in Morocco, for instance, where local resources are not sufficient. It is also to be found in England.

(*c*) The towns interested are naturally willing to make sacrifices, and the Chambers of Commerce of the respective ports are even better qualified to undertake the works, but their resources are, in both cases, quite inadequate. There is, however, another method—that of borrowing the necessary capital and making the navigators, that is to say, those who profit by these works, pay sufficient port dues to cover the interest and redemption of the loan. And this is in fact what is done ; but a certain amount of prudence is necessary in drawing up the tariff, or ships may be driven away to other ports and all the labours have been undertaken in vain.

Under this system the management of the port is confided not to the municipality itself, but to a special body. It is the system of *autonomy*. The British ports (London, Liverpool, Glasgow) are, as a rule, administered by boards or trustees, some of the members of which are nominated by the municipal council or the government, and the majority by shipowners, proprietors of docks, and others concerned. At Genoa this board is called a *censorio*, at Barcelona a *junte*.[1]

The most interesting question in connection with ports is that of *free ports*; that is to say, ports where goods in transit can be unloaded, stored, sold, manipulated, and even freely transformed without having to pay customs duties.[2] Formerly it was the whole town that was thus put outside of the customs boundary : Hamburg was free always, Marseilles at various periods of her history. Nowadays it is the port alone, or sometimes only a portion of it, which constitutes the free zone. It is separated from the rest of the town by walls or railings to prevent smuggling. Within this reserved

[1] For this and the preceding questions, see a small book by M. Lecarpentier, *Commerce maritime et marine marchande.*

[2] The three large ports of Germany—Hamburg, Bremen and Stettin—are free ports. Copenhagen was made a free port in 1894. In France, Bordeaux, La Rochelle, Marseilles (with certain reserves), and above all Algiers, are demanding freedom. It is probable that Algiers as a free port would become the first port on the Mediterranean.

space no one is allowed to live or to consume, but traders may do what they will, and manufacturers may even set up factories.[1]

The freedom of the port is a great factor in the development of the town on which it is conferred. Hamburg, for instance, certainly owes a large part of her wonderful fortune to her freedom. But it acts besides as a useful corrective to protection. Goods which are voyaging across the seas, knocking everywhere against customs barriers, find in these free ports little isles of liberty where they may rest, and they flock thither from all quarters of the globe. They cannot, of course, penetrate into the interior; but it is a great thing for them to be able to wait for favourable opportunities, to consider the direction they will take, to be exchanged, or even transformed in order to start off in some new direction. Colbert, whom protectionists will not challenge, had created, as a complement to his celebrated system, five free ports: Marseilles, Saint-Jean-de-Luz, Bayonne, Lorient and Dunkirk; and never was the French marine more prosperous.[2] It is really incredible that, in the present state of distress of the French mercantile marine, this remedy has not been tried, particularly as shipbuilding yards might be set up within the free zone, unhandicapped by duties on iron and other building materials. Subsidies for shipbuilding (p. 260) would thus become superfluous. There has been in fact some thought of trying it, and several bills were drawn up in regard to it. But they have been sleeping for many years in the parliamentary archives.

It is true that, like all reforms, it has called forth objections:

(1) It is unnecessary, it is said, since goods intended for re-exportation have already all the facilities they require under the system of *bonded warehouses* or *temporary admissions*, and pay no duties. True, but the goods which enter the bonded warehouse have to undergo as many formalities as if they paid the duties, or even more. They are always under the eye of the customs officer, whereas this annoying personage may not penetrate into the free port. Moreover, the free port is a *market;* the bonded warehouse is only a depot—quite another matter. As for temporary admission, it is simply a favour given to a particular industry and has no influence on the general movement of international trade.

(2) It would be dangerous, it is said, since these free ports would

---

[1] Thus within the free zone in Hamburg there are some 100 industries, employing over 10,000 workers.

[2] British ports may be said to be free ports by nature, Great Britain being altogether a "free island." And almost as much may be said of the Belgian ports like Antwerp, customs duties being insignificant in Belgium.

serve as refuges for industries which might compete with home industries if not on the home, at any rate on foreign markets; or for suspicious operations by which products might be adulterated and exported as French goods to the great detriment of French industry. But surely it would be better for competition to be carried on in our own ports than abroad. As for falsification, this is indeed a curious scruple. Would such counterfeiting be carried on any the less outside of France than within the French ports? Should not French industry fear rather to see its good products sold under foreign marks than foreign products sold under French marks? This, on the contrary, would be an excellent advertisement for it.

(3) It is impossible, it is said, since if, after unloading in the free port, the foreign goods wanted to enter the country, it would no longer be possible to know their origin, nor consequently whether to apply the maximum or the minimum tariff. There are two simple solutions to this difficulty. The more liberal one, adopted by Germany, is to apply to all goods entering the country from the free port the most favourable tariff without distinction. This would be another powerful attraction to the port. The other, less liberal, proposed in the French bill, is to apply the maximum tariff, unless of course the goods have been previously brought from the interior.[1] This would obviously deprive the port of some of its advantages: probably only goods intended for re-export would thereafter enter it. But even that would be something.

V: CANALS AND NAVIGABLE WAYS

THE navigable highways of countries have exercised a paramount influence on their destinies. Putting aside Egypt, which has been in the strictest sense of the word a creation of the Nile, the economic importance of rivers like the Mississippi in the United States, or the Rhine in Germany, cannot be exaggerated. They are, as Pascal eloquently expressed it, roads that move and cost nothing. Unfortunately, the rivers which offer the necessary conditions for good navigation—a slow current, a fairly constant level without too many bends—are somewhat rare. France, for example, is rather badly situated in this respect. Her large watercourses, instead of being parallel as in Germany, branch out from an almost unproductive central plateau. This arrangement of her rivers, which was good at the time when commerce was carried on by small boats, and which the geographer Strabo had reason to praise, is

---

[1] As also the *surtaxe d'entrepôt* (see note, p. 260).

somewhat unfortunate to-day. The Loire is too irregular; the Seine has too many curves;[1] the Rhone is too swift. After an expenditure of over 50 million francs on improving the course of the Rhone, there is some talk to-day of replacing the river by a lateral canal, at a cost of 400 millions.

Artificial waterways or canals can render much the same services as natural watercourses, the inconvenience of locks being compensated for by the absence of the tidal rise. True, the making of them involves great cost, but as a rule the original outlay is less than for railways, and the cost of upkeep much smaller. Lastly, haulage by canal properly speaking, whether by horses, towing-chains, or tubs, requires much less force for an equal load, and consequently costs much less than traction by land or by railway.

For some years past there has been a decided movement in France in favour of canals, as it was thought that they were one of the principal factors in the economic development of Germany; and the most imposing schemes have been the order of the day. Thus it has been suggested that a sea-to-sea canal should be made between Bordeaux and Narbonne (costing 700 to 800 million francs); a canal from Marseilles to Lyons and from Lyons to Geneva; a canal from Paris to the sea; that the Loire should be made navigable, etc. But the example of Germany does not prove much. It is her rivers, more especially the Rhine, rather than her canals, and also the wealth of her mines,[2] which cause the prosperity of her internal navigation. Now, France has neither the one nor the other. The milliards which such works would cost might, therefore, find a better use.[3]

[1] And yet it is the best navigable waterway in France, since, thanks to it, Paris has become the first port in France and one of the largest in the world (over 10 million tons).

[2] Of the 14,000 kilometres of navigable waterway in Germany, much more than half consists of natural watercourses. When we compare the Rhine with the Rhine, and Marseilles with Rotterdam, as some Marseillais have done with characteristic southern fervour, we forget that not only has the Rhine a larger, more regular and less rapid flow than the Rhone, that it is navigable up to Basle, while the Rhone ceases to be navigable before Geneva, but that, above all, it waters one of the richest and most thickly populated industrial basins of the world, including even a part of Switzerland; while the basin of the Rhone is narrow, thinly populated, and devoid of all industry, with the exception of Lyons, whose main industry (silk) stands in no need of river navigation.

[3] The canal which is being made at present from Marseilles to the Rhone will cost at least 100 million francs for a length of 80 kilometres, one part of which is underground, and it will probably see no more boats than the canal already made from the Rhone to Saint-Louis.

On natural navigable ways, *i.e.* on streams and rivers, free traffic is the rule. Everywhere they are common property and part of the public domain. The works undertaken, often at great cost, to level their courses do not change their character, since, precisely because they pertain to the public domain, they are always at the charge of the State and are written off.

In the case of watercourses made by the hand of man, *i.e.* canals, it is not necessarily the same. Waterways may be established under the same conditions as railways, *i.e.* under the system of concession, or even under that of free competition. This has been done in the case of a certain number of canals in England and in the United States.[1] In France, however, and in most countries, the State undertakes the building of canals, as the returns from these enterprises are not enough as a rule to tempt private enterprise. The State, in this case as in that of the rivers and the high roads, makes no charge for mileage. The boatman has therefore only the costs of haulage to pay—not more than about a quarter of the price by rail.[2] In France, the State has written off the 1600 million francs set apart for the making of canals, and does the same with the 20 million or so for annual upkeep.

It is more particularly for heavy goods, where rapidity of transport does not much matter, that the use of the waterway is so profitable. Thus, in France, wines from Spain, Algeria, and even from the departments on the shores of the Mediterranean, come by way of Rouen, which is becoming a great wine centre, although none is produced in the region itself.

The competition of the navigable waterways has this advantage for the public that it forces the railways to reduce their rates. Indeed, not only are the railways resigned to doing so, but they would gladly reduce them until all transport by canal were annihilated if the State did not interfere officially to maintain a certain margin between them (in France at least 20 per cent. of difference).[3]

[1] As well as the large international canals—Suez, Corinth and Panama—which were built by private companies. But it is well known that, since the failure of the French company of the Panama, the United States Government has taken over the enterprise. It would have been better if it had been undertaken by a union of all the American nations.

[2] *One centime* per ton per kilometre, as against 4 centimes by railway. Even if the costs of original outlay are included, 1 centime more (*i.e.* 2 in all), according to M. Colson, would be enough to cover this.

[3] The 11,400 kilometres of navigable waterways in France transported in 1910 over 5 milliard ton-kilometres, and the 40,000 kilometres of railways a little over 22 milliards. The amount of transport is, therefore, proportionally almost the same on the canals as on the railways.

VI: MODES OF THE TRANSMISSION OF THOUGHT

HUMAN beings had formerly but three ways of communicating with one another:

(1) *Speech*, which is of use only between persons present on the same place;

(2) The *letter*, which must be transmitted by a carrier and cannot therefore go faster than he does, and which besides only reaches an individual consignee;

(3) Certain *signs*, visible from afar, which allow of fairly rapid communication between distances—*e.g.* beacon fires—but the meaning of which can only be very limited.

During the second half of the nineteenth century the progress which took place in these three means of communication as regards speed, regularity and power, was so great that it is not easy to imagine how they can be further improved.

(1) Speech is now transmitted long distances by telephone and a man in any civilised country to-day may sit in his armchair and speak with some one miles off at the other end of a wire, itself fast becoming unnecessary. There are towns in Switzerland and the United States where already one out of every twenty inhabitants has a telephone.[1]

(2) Letter-carrying is now undertaken by a special agency called the Post Office, which has in its service the swiftest means of transport—trains and steamers. Millions of letters are daily transported in special carriages by the most direct routes to the ends of the earth at a uniform, fixed, and absurdly small price, not exceeding 25 centimes to any part of the world.[2]

Thanks to printing, the letter has been able to take the form of

---

[1] Subscribers to the telephone in different countries are as follows per 1000 inhabitants:

United States	.	.	81	Germany.	.	.	16
Denmark	.	.	35	Great Britain .	.	.	14
Sweden .	.	.	34	Holland .	.	.	11
Norway .	.	.	26	France .	.	.	6
Switzerland	.	.	21	Belgium	.	.	6

France stands low on the list mainly because the State, which has the monopoly of the telephones, charges a high price for a service which leaves much to be desired.

[2] The system of fixed postage for any distance whatever has been extended to goods by means of the *parcel post*. This mode of transport has developed enormously, and may possibly one day be extended to all goods. In France it is the railways, not the Post Office, which have charge of this business.

a *newspaper*, and thus to speak to millions of persons ; while the technical improvements in printing have enabled newspapers, containing as much matter as a large volume, to be issued in a few hours and sent to hundreds of subscribers for a few centimes.

Besides printing and mechanical inventions, there were two other important factors in this revolution : one was the invention of the postage stamp, introduced in England by Rowland Hill, in 1837—a curious instance of social solidarity equalising what is apparently most unequal, namely, the enormous difference in distances ; the other was the creation in 1875 of the Universal Postal Union,[1] which to-day transports over 20 billion letters and postcards.

But it is in the third means of communication, viz., signs, that progress has really been miraculous. Synchronic movements, transmitted by electricity, as distinct as speech or writing, have enabled news to be flashed more swiftly than the nerves transmit thought in the human body. For this purpose electricity borrows the aid of nearly two million miles of overhead wires or submarine cables, but it is already preparing to throw down these aids in order to fly more freely.[2]

It would be waste of time to indicate the consequences, not only economic but political, intellectual, and moral, of these means of communication which tend to make the whole world one single market, one single city—dangerous consequences too, for the unity which they create is not always that of affection, but sometimes rather that blind unity which gives such force to crowds.

Owing to their outstanding importance, governments have every-

---

[1] The *Universal Postal Union*, like many other international unions, has its centre at Berne, where a handsome monument commemorates its inauguration. It has established the uniform 25 centime postage (or its equivalent in each currency) for all countries adhering to it, *i.e.* for almost the whole world. And it has just instituted, not as yet an international stamp—since the differences in the monetary systems of different countries still render this impossible—but an international *order* which gives the right to a stamp for reply in all countries belonging to the Union.

The only country of any importance which still remains outside the Postal Union is China. Abyssinia has just joined it.

In France, 1400 million letters and penny postcards (leaving out of account those at 5 centimes) were carried in 1910, making an average of 36 per inhabitant. This is a lower figure than that for other countries, the figure for Germany and Switzerland being twice, and that for England and the United States three times, as high. Italy and Spain, on the other hand, have an average of only ten per inhabitant, and Russia five.

[2] In France, the number of telegrams sent is only 64 millions per annum, or less than 2 per inhabitant, which is a very low figure.

where monopolised them. Only the telephone in a few countries, and the telegraph in the United States, are still worked by private enterprise. Not that the administration of these great services by the State fails to give rise to lively recrimination,[1] particularly in the matter of the responsibility of the State in cases of error ; but the State has this advantage over private enterprise, that it does not aim at profits. For a long while the Post Office service, like the coinage, was a source of profit to the State. The tendency now, in both of these services, is to sacrifice fiscal interests to the public good and to sell at cost price—sometimes, indeed, as in the case of the Post Office, at a loss.[2]

CHAPTER III : MERCHANTS

I : THE HISTORY AND THE FUNCTION OF MERCHANTS

To transport products is not enough to make them exchangeable, that is to say, to make them *merchandise*. Intermediaries called *merchants* are as a rule necessary, and places of exchange called *markets*.

Commerce did not, as we might be tempted to think, begin among neighbours and gradually spread. There was too great conformity of habits and needs among the members of one family or one class, division of labour was too undeveloped, for a regular movement of exchanges to arise. It was between scattered peoples in far-apart regions, whose products and customs were quite different, that exchange was first practised. Commerce was international before it was national ; it was maritime before it was overland. The first merchants rose, like Venus-Aphrodite, from the sea. It follows, then, that the earliest merchants must have been voyagers, adventurers, such as we read of in the true history of Marco Polo, or the imaginary one of Sindbad the Sailor.

---

[1] In France, especially, the working of the telephones by the State has provoked real irritation, and given rise to a league of subscribers, who defend their interests against the State. The State service is both very dear and very slow: it is for this reason that the number of subscribers is comparatively small.

[2] In France, Post Office expenses for 1910, including telegraph and telephone, amounted to 279 million francs as against 378 millions of receipts, leaving 99 million francs of apparent profit. But to make the account exact, we should add the considerable costs which the railway companies incur for the carriage of letters and printed matter, estimated at 70 millions, part at least of the subsidies to the maritime companies, and the pensions of superannuated postmen.

As commerce was carried on between strangers, that is to say, enemies—for the two words were synonymous to the ancients—it everywhere made its appearance accompanied by fraud, ruse, and often violence; and it was with no sense of incongruity that Mercury was accepted by the public conscience as the god of merchants and of thieves.[1]

Merchants must, then, from the very beginning have been great personages, envied and feared, forming a veritable autocracy, above the artisans and agriculturists. It was not till fairly recently that small retail trade made its appearance.

Two phases may be pointed out in the history of the merchant:

(1) The first is that of the *itinerant merchant.* All countries where trade is little developed, *e.g.* Africa, are still at this stage: commerce is carried on by means of caravans. We find traces of it in the pedlar of our modern village, and the hawker who makes the streets of Paris ring with his cries.

But this system of the merchant travelling about with his wares is possible only in the case of products that are easy to transport. It is besides very costly, since each article must bear an enormous proportion of the general expenses. The profits of the merchants who go by caravan in Central Africa must be at least 400 per cent. to be remunerative.

(2) Wherever commerce is at all developed, the travelling merchant speedily gives place to the sedentary merchant, or *shop-keeper.*[2] Whereas before it was the merchant who went to look for the customer, now it is the customer who comes to look for the merchant. But the merchant must attract the attention of the passer-by. This he does by *sign-posts,* of which a trace is still to be seen in the barber's pole, the wooden pipe above the tobacco-shop, or the iron hat over the hatter's door; by the *display* of the goods themselves in resplendent shop windows; by announcements, advertisements, circulars, catalogues; or by commercial travellers. Commercial travellers differ from the travelling merchants of a former time in that they carry with them samples of the goods, not the goods themselves.

[1] It is somewhat curious to observe that the word *market* has the same etymological origin as the word *march* in the sense of *frontier,* since it was on the limits of the tribal territories that exchanges were wont to take place. Even to-day, in certain islands of the New Hebrides, the natives lay their produce on the ground, at the frontier, and withdraw, while the other tribe deposits its produce and exchanges if so inclined.

[2] At the beginning, however, there was a conflict between the travelling merchant and the sedentary merchant (see p. 218, *note* 1).

The advantages which society derives from the existence of merchants are as follows :

(1) They act as *intermediaries* between producer and consumer, saving each the time he would otherwise lose in looking for the other.

(2) They buy goods *wholesale* from the producer and sell them *retail*, saving the trouble which would inevitably result if the *quantity* offered by the producer and the *quantity* demanded by the consumer did not coincide.

(3) They keep goods *in stock*, and thus obviate the difficulties which would arise if the *moment* when the producer wished to sell and the *moment* when the consumer wished to buy did not coincide.

(4) They *prepare* goods for consumption by sorting them (corn), cleaning them (coffee), mixing them (wines), cutting them (cloths), etc. etc.

These are, no doubt, real services, but we must consider what they cost. For various reasons, the first being the easy nature of the work and the attraction which it has for many people, especially in France, the number of these intermediaries, particularly of retail merchants, or shopkeepers, is quite out of proportion to the need for them.

From 972,793 in 1866, their number rose to 2,068,620 in 1906.[1] It has therefore more than doubled in forty years, and for a population which has increased during the same period only 3 per cent. If the progression were to continue at this rate, in less than 200 years all the inhabitants of France would have become tradesmen ! As these 2,000,000 traders represent, with their families, about 8 million persons, we may say that one Frenchman in every five is in trade, which does not by any means imply that France is the first trading country in the world. Far from it. This state of affairs makes itself felt not only in the whole economy of France, but in its politics and its mentality. Along with the artisans, who are hardly to be distinguished from them, since they too sell to the public, these small traders form the *petite bourgeoisie*, which has had so great an influence in the history of France.

Thirty years ago, in Paris, there was one baker's shop to every 1800 inhabitants : to-day there is one to every 1300, and in some towns the proportion is larger still (one to 500 in Lyons, one to 380 in St. Étienne). The result is that the kilogramme of bread is sold, at lowest, at 10 centimes above cost price, meaning by that the

[1] *Statistique du Recensement de la population*, published by the Ministère du Travail, 1910, vol. i, part ii, p. 57.

price at which the co-operative societies can sell it. As the average consumption per head in France is 550 grammes per annum, the total annual consumption is over 7 milliard kilogrammes. So that this extra 10 centimes per kilo, due to the unnecessary multiplication of middlemen, costs the French population 700 million francs per annum for bread alone (the peasants who make their own bread must be deducted, but they are becoming more and more rare). Now multiply this figure by all the other articles of consumption, and we get some idea of the tribute which these middlemen levy. It is probably *more than twice the amount paid to the State in taxes*. Socialists and economists are at one, indeed, in protesting against this vice of our social organisation, particularly Fourier, who, as far back as 1822, foretold and denounced the abuses of the commercial organisation with a precision and spirit which have never been surpassed.[1]

This multiplication of middlemen, reducing as it does the amount of business done by each, ends in burdening every article with an enormous proportion of general cost, and prevents the natural fall in prices from being felt in retail commerce (*cf.* above, p. 136). The middlemen therefore tend to become veritable parasites.

If in addition we take into account the adulteration of produce, which is becoming a real peril to public health, and the lying advertisements which are likewise an effect of the keen competition among tradesmen, we are bound to ask ourselves whether the services rendered by these intermediaries are not nowadays too dearly paid for, and whether we could not find some other way of organising exchange which would be less costly for society.

The real remedy would evidently be to bring producer and consumer into direct touch with one another by doing away with intermediaries, or at least by reducing their number to a minimum. The great difficulty lies in the fact that the producer is not very well able to sell retail, while the consumer is still less able to buy wholesale. An attempt is being made to-day to overcome this difficulty by means of association in its two forms : that of producers who agree to sell directly to the public, *e.g.* the *agricultural associations* (*cf.* above, p. 195) ; that of consumers who agree to buy directly from the producers, *e.g.* the *co-operative societies for consumption* (see Book IV).

---

[1] *Œuvres choisies de Fourier*, ed. Guillaumin.

II : STOCK EXCHANGES AND TIME BARGAINS

FROM all time, in all countries, even in the most primitive societies, men have been accustomed to come together on certain days, in specified places, to exchange their products. These meetings are what are called *markets* or *fairs*. Markets are held at shorter intervals than fairs, generally once a week ; they are smaller and are as a rule urban. Fairs were formerly of great economic importance. The fair of Beaucaire dated the maturity of contracts over the whole of the South of France, and at the present day the fair of Nijni-Novgorod does 400 million francs of business, and brings together from two to three hundred thousand persons from all ends of the Old World.

Fairs and markets are, however, falling into disuse. Such intermittent mechanism is no longer sufficient for the requirements of modern life. Thus their place has been taken by Exchanges or Bourses, institutions where exchange is carried on in a more permanent and continuous manner. Commercial Exchanges (*Bourses de Commerce*), where actual goods are exchanged, are not the same as Stock Exchanges (or Bourses properly so called), where movable values are bought and sold. Stock Exchanges are the theatres of colossal operations and of feverish activity. The prices of securities, or of goods, are marked up on the official list every moment. This is what is called the *quotation*, and as this quotation has a decisive influence on the whole movement of exchanges, the fixing of it is subject to minute regulations. Operations, moreover, cannot as a rule be carried on except by special intermediaries, called *dealers* (in French, *courtiers*), or, in the case of securities, *stockbrokers :* these last, like solicitors, are invested with a legal monopoly.[1]

Formerly, goods, commercial effects, and movable values were all sold together on the exchanges, and the same agents undertook all the operations.[2] It was not till towards the beginning of the eighteenth century, after Law's crisis, that the Stock Exchange was

---

[1] It was the Edict of 1572, in the reign of Charles IX, which gave official investiture to dealers, in the words : " Créons et établissons à titre d'office tous courtiers tant de change et de deniers que de draps de soie, laine, toile, cuirs, et autres sortes de marchandises."

[2] In France stockbrokers alone have the right to negotiate securities inscribed on the official list, and they alone authorise this inscription. In return for this privilege they are subjected to a tariff for brokerage and are held responsible as a body to their clients. Neither the tariff, however, nor the responsibility, prevents them from making enormous profits, since each post is worth 1,500,000 francs and there are seventy of them.

separated from the Commercial Exchanges, and that stockbrokers were distinguished from other dealers.[1]

Exchanges are made either *for cash* or *for account*, but the latter operations are much more frequent.

The seller, for example, sells to day *at the current rate* a certain quantity of wheat *to be delivered at the end of the month.* Possibly he does not possess a single grain of wheat. But this is no obstacle : when the moment comes to deliver the wheat he will have no difficulty in finding some on the market.

If the commodity happens to have fallen in price before the end of the month, if, for example, the wheat sold at 5 francs now sells for 4¾, the seller for account does a good stroke of business ; for, in order to fulfil his contract, he has only to buy at 4¾ francs the wheat which he sold at 5 francs. He gains therefore the difference. This is, of course, what he was counting on. Every seller for account looks for a fall in price. Supposing, on the contrary, the price of wheat had gone up, say, to 5¼ francs, clearly he would have made a bad bargain.

The situation of the buyer for account is, of course, exactly the reverse. He has bought at 5 francs for delivery at the end of the month. If the price of wheat goes down to 4¾ francs he has done a bad stroke of business ; he has paid ¼ franc too much for his haste. But if it rises to 5¼ francs he has made a good bargain and gains the difference, ¼ franc. Every buyer for account, then, looks for a rise in price.

It is for this reason that, in the opinion of the public, and even in that of the government, the seller for account is a suspicious personage, suspected of trying to create a fall in price, since it is to his interest ; while the buyer for account is *persona grata*, always the herald of good weather. In reality there is little ground for either of these estimates. It is quite impossible for merchandise or securities to rise indefinitely, and, even if it were possible, it would not be a good thing. Rises and falls can be nothing more than rhythmic oscillations, neither of them better nor worse than the other, and both indispensable to the economic equilibrium, since, as we have seen, it is through them that production is continually being re-adapted to wants. When too much of a commodity has been produced, or when securities have gone up above their true value, a fall is very useful.

What we really ought to wish for is, that the swing of the

---

[1] All that we shall say here, however, regarding Commercial Exchanges, *i.e.* Exchanges of goods, applies equally to Stock Exchanges pure and simple, *i.e.* Exchanges of movable values.

pendulum, in exercising its salutary influence, should cause as little damage as possible, that is to say, should not be more abrupt than can be helped. Now, sale and purchase for account have this twofold effect : in the first place, they announce fifteen days or a month ahead the variation in prices and the direction which it will take. For sellers and buyers for account are, as it were, the vanguard of the great army of sellers and buyers for cash, and a rise or a fall in prices for account simply anticipates a rise or a fall in cash prices. Secondly (and this is still more useful), they lessen the effect of variations in price ; for every crisis that is foreseen is discounted, and its intensity diminished to this extent. If a fall in wheat is anticipated within a month, all wheat that is sold between now and then will be so much the less on settlement, and the market will be lightened by this amount. If, on the contrary, wheat is expected to go up, all that is bought from now during the month will reduce by so much the demand at the end of the month. Production, too, warned by the variations in the rate for account, will quicken or slow down its pace according to circumstances. Sales and purchases for account cannot, of course, prevent rises and falls due to natural causes, such as the failure or over-abundance of the wheat crop, but they can spread the effects over a longer time and a larger area, levelling the incline, as it were, so that commerce may roll along without too many jolts.

Let us go a step further. It may be that the seller for account not only has not the goods in his possession at the time, but knows that he will not have them even when the date of expiry comes; and that the buyer on his side has not the slightest intention of ever acquiring them.[1] Possibly they are neither of them merchants, but simply some lady or gentleman buying and selling wheat or wool, who have never seen a grain of wheat or a lock of wool in their lives. This is quite often the case. What then is this strange operation which consists in selling what will never be possessed ? It is simply a bet on the rise or fall of goods or securities, exactly like a wager on the race-course.

But when the settling day comes round, will not the seller have to deliver the goods and the buyer to pay the price ? Not at all. If there is a fall, the seller says to the buyer, " You will not require me to deliver my wheat ; you would be very much embarrassed if I

---

[1] It is in such a case as this—that is to say, when the sale is fictitious—that it is called a sale for account, or, more exactly, a *time bargain ;* when, however, the sale is real, and it is the delivery only that is deferred, perhaps because the goods are *en route,* then the expression " for future delivery " is used.

did, for you have no use for the wheat and no particular desire to pay for it. I will buy it back from you ; but, as it is only worth 4¾ francs now, I shall buy it at the present price. You bought it from me at 5 francs. You owe me, therefore, simply the difference, *i.e.* ¼ franc."

If wheat has gone up, say, to 5¼ francs, the same thing takes place, except that it is now the buyer who sells back to the seller, at 5¼ francs, the wheat which he had bought at 5 francs, and it is he who gets the additional quarter of a franc.

The whole business therefore is regulated, or, to use the technical expression, is *settled*, by paying the *differences* without the goods being either delivered or paid for.[1]

The societies which act as middlemen between sellers and buyers are called, in France, *Caisses de Liquidation*, their position being that of buyers over against sellers, and sellers over against buyers. As both operations are equal, the Caisse has nothing to disburse— and the possible insolvency of any one of its members is covered by guarantees. But what purpose do these *Caisses* serve ? In the first place, they act as a sort of clearing-house, making the passing of coin unnecessary ; further, by creating a community of interest between all parties, they eliminate any disturbance which might arise from individual circumstances, leaving only variations due to economic causes. These variations, therefore, have free play and are more clearly seen.

Sale and purchase for account, or, as it is also called, *uncovered*, is therefore neither more nor less than gambling. Ought it not to be prohibited ? This is the serious question with which we are faced.

On behalf of operations for account, it may be said that, even

---

[1] It is possible, however, that one of the two parties may wish to " continue " instead of going through the operation called settlement. The buyer, *e.g.* may find that the rise which he expected has not taken place, but thinks that it will next month : he wishes to remain a buyer for account. But if the seller, on his part, wants to close the account, what is to be done ? Even in such a case as this the buyer is in no difficulty. There is, in fact, a crowd of capitalists ready to lend him the money which will enable him to wait or carry over and who even make a sort of profession of it. The " contango," indeed, constitutes an invest-ment much sought after by free capital, for it is a loan on securities and for a short term. It is guaranteed by the goods or securities which the buyer gives the capitalist as pledge (or, to speak more exactly, sells him for cash and buys back for account).

If, on the contrary, it is the seller who wishes to continue, while the buyer wants to settle, he, too, has only to borrow the goods or securities he wants (or, rather, to buy for cash and sell for account). This operation is, however, less convenient, as a rule, than the other.

when fictitious and never actually carried out, they may render exactly
the same services as real sales for account—that is to say, they may
indicate in advance the variations of the current price, and, by
anticipating, moderate them. But, in order to render this twofold
service, these operations must be done by professionals, or at least
by persons able to foresee events. If they are done by just anybody
they amount to no more than mere bets on rises and falls, like wagers
on the race-courses.[1] Unfortunately, this is what only too frequently
happens. The gambling rage is now so great that men of all sorts,
men of the world, military men, concierges, etc., may be seen speculating in wool, leather, or any other value that an advertising financial
paper may recommend.[2] The evil becomes greater if the current
price is made to vary artificially by false news. Then, speculation, instead of preventing panic, which is its true rôle,
creates it.

The problem, then, is to distinguish between speculation based
on foresight, which is one of the highest forms of economic intelligence, and speculation based on chance, which is one of the most
deplorable forms of contemporary demoralisation. Now, the
legislator is hardly in a position to draw this distinction. He might,
however, prohibit all operations for account by non-professionals,

---

[1] A form of gambling all the more inviting in that a means has been devised for
limiting risks in the case of prudent persons, or those whose purses are limited, by
what is called the *option*. This is a sort of insurance by which the speculator,
if the operation turns out badly, may withdraw from it by paying a stipulated
forfeit. At the worst, therefore, he is safe to leave only a few feathers behind.

[2] We ourselves have received not only circulars, but visitors, inviting us to
go in for operations for account on sugar and alcohol. Here is a curious extract
from these circulars :

" By reason of the frequency and importance of financial obligations at a time
when the diminution of income is forcing every one to increase his resources,
we think it useful to popularise the operations carried on on the commercial
exchange. These operations, of which the great majority of *rentiers* are ignorant,
are, in our opinion, the only rational and logical ones : judiciously managed, they
may bring in the maximum of profit on the capital invested, with the minimum
of risk.

" Rise and fall are, in fact, governed solely by the law of supply and demand ;
production on the one hand, consumption on the other. No tricks. Our
business transactions are in goods which have an *intrinsic value*, which they
cannot lose under any circumstance. Where is the risk in buying an article for
about its cost price to be delivered in six months ? Is it not legitimate to expect
that within such a space of time you may profit by a favourable rate to settle,
i.e. to make a profit ?

" This kind of operation appeals to the cool, deliberate mind, which prefers a
commercial operation to speculations the success of which is nearly always a
question of heads or tails."

or by persons on their own account.[1] Still, it would not be easy to check them in practice. The best remedy would be for the Commercial Exchanges, which are officially constituted bodies, to do their own police work.[2]

III : WEIGHTS AND MEASURES

A SYSTEM of weights and measures is indispensable to exchange. Men are not long content to exchange one specific unit for another, say a gun for an elephant's tusk, and so soon as they begin to exchange quantities of things they must, in order to value them, determine beforehand the quantities to be exchanged. The balance is not only the classical symbol of Justice : it is also that of Commerce. For measures of length, man borrowed the necessary standard from his own body (the hand, the thumb, the foot, the step) ; for weight and volume he had to invent arbitrary measures. Among primitive peoples measuring operations are sometimes very extraordinary. It is told that, in exchanges between the Redskins and the Hudson Bay trappers, the unit of measurement for skins was the length of a gun, whatever it might be, and this was the reason why long carabines only came to be used by the trappers.

The French *savants* of the Revolution prided themselves on having

[1] Certain exchanges in France, particularly that of Roubaix, the great centre of the woollen operations, had, indeed, on their own initiative, restricted such dealings to traders. This does not seem, however, to have been sufficient to do away with the abuses, as the Government has recently appointed an extra-parliamentary commission to look into the matter. (See M. Sayous, *Les Bourses de commerce en Allemagne.*)

[2] In France, for a long time, law, or at least jurisprudence, assimilated time bargains to gambling, and therefore refused all legal redress to a creditor. But the law of 1885 has done away with this method of avoiding the payment of one's debts, which in no way hindered operations for account, but simply allowed dishonest persons to benefit now and then.

In Germany, a law of June 22, 1896, which made a great stir, established these two principal rules : (1) the right to undertake operations for account is reserved on pain of nullity, to those who are inscribed on a special register ; (2) operations for account are absolutely prohibited in the case of certain merchandise, notably cereals and mining values. But this law has been very badly received by business men : the greater number of them refuse to inscribe themselves on an official list which has somewhat too much the appearance of a police register. A new measure is about to suppress the register and to make the qualification of trader the only requisite.

This campaign against the exchanges is led by the agriculturists, who accuse sellers for account of causing falls, especially in wheat. Thus, after having been accused for centuries of having caused rises in wheat in order to starve the people, speculators are now accused of causing falls in order to ruin agriculturists !

taken the globe itself as their standard of measurement, or at any rate a definite fraction of it (the forty-millionth part of its circumference). In reality this standard is more imposing than accurate. The earth's circumference can never be exactly known, as the size of the earth itself varies. It has already been proved that the metre adopted is too short by one-fifth of a millimetre. It might have been better to have taken the length of the pendulum which beats the second at the latitude of Paris, or even the wavelength of the rays of some fixed light. The real standard, however, of the metric system is a bar of an alloy of iridium and platinum which was adopted by the International Conference of 1875,[1] and deposited in a safe at Saint-Cloud, of which three countries have the key ; and no one thinks any more about the earth.

What gives the French, or metric, system its advantage over the others, and has caused it to be adopted in a large number of countries, is not that its standard is superior, but that its divisions conform to the numerical decimal system—a system which simplifies calculation—whereas most systems of weights and measures are established on the duodecimal system.

The unknown inventor of the decimal system was evidently influenced by the fact that man counted on his ten fingers, but the service he rendered mankind would have been infinitely greater if, instead of creating ten digits, *i.e.* nine digits and zero, he had created twelve, *i.e.* eleven digits and zero. For the number 10 is a poor number, which can only be divided conveniently into two, while 12 can be divided into halves, thirds and quarters. It is because these simple fractions are much more convenient for the purposes of everyday life that some nations, such as England, have preferred to keep to their old systems of weights, measures and moneys, although they do not fit in with the numerical system. Even in France, many regions still remain faithful to the ancient measures of the pound, the arpent, etc. The metrical system will, however, soon be universally adopted.

---

[1] The " Bureau international des poids et mesures " was founded in 1875. It has charge of the international prototype of the metre and the measures derived from it. It undertakes the stamping and comparison of all the geodesical rulers, standards of length, weight, capacity, etc.

It has just succeeded in its demand that the carat (measure of weight for precious stones), which used to vary in different countries from 191 to 212 milligrammes, should be fixed at the uniform weight of 200 milligrammes.

Humbler functionaries are the verifiers of weights and measures, whose rôle is to inspect shops and see that they do not use false measures.

CHAPTER IV : METALLIC MONEY

I : HISTORICAL SKETCH OF MONEY

IT was not by virtue of any express convention, any social contract, that certain objects were able to become the medium of exchange ; it was the advantages they possessed which induced men to choose them and predestined them, as it were, to this high office.

The difficulties of barter (see above, p. 219) forced men to choose a third commodity in every exchange. They naturally chose the one most familiar to them and in most common use. Primitive peoples, for example, chose rough implements of hewn flint. In patriarchal societies cattle seem to have played the rôle of third commodity, and most of the Indo-European languages, even the Basque, have handed down the memory of this primitive form of money in the names which they have given it.[1]

Many other commodities, according to circumstances and countries, have played the rôle of third commodity : rice in Japan, bricks of tea in Central Asia, furs in the Hudson Bay territory, cotton stuffs called " guineas " and bars of salt in Central Africa. But there is one class of objects which early attracted the attention of men and was not slow in ousting all other commodities in all societies, however slightly civilised. I refer to the so-called precious metals, gold, silver and copper.

Thanks to their chemical properties, which render them relatively insusceptible to change, these are the only metals found in nature in their pure state—gold more so than silver, and silver than copper. Man was therefore able to recognise them and use them before his knowledge of metallurgy allowed him to recognise or make use of other metals, such as iron. It is worth observing that the old legend of the four ages, the age of gold, of silver, of copper, and of iron, ranks the four metals exactly in the order in which they were known by man. Their physical properties, their brightness, colour and malleability, which made them early sought after for ornament or for industrial purposes, would be enough to justify the

---

[1] The best known instance of this is the Latin word *pecunia,* which originally meant cattle, the herd. Even in Homer we find values (*e.g.* the armour of Diogenes and Glaucus) estimated in terms of oxen. Hence the expression " to put an ox on his tongue," meaning to buy a person's silence, which appeared so absurd in Leconte de Lisle's translation of Æschylus.

great rôle which they have played at all times and among all peoples.

These natural properties involve certain economic consequences of the greatest importance and give the precious metals a very marked advantage over all other commodities. They are as follows :

(1) *Facility of transport.* No other object has so great a value in so small a bulk. The weight which a man can carry on his back is about 30 kilogrammes. Now, 30 kilogrammes of coal is worth barely a franc ; of wheat, 7 to 8 francs ; of wool, 30 to 40 francs ; of copper, 50 to 60 francs ; of ivory, 700 to 800 francs ; of raw silk, 1500 francs ; of silver, 3000 francs ; and of pure gold, 100,000 francs.

The importance of this first characteristic is enormous, and much greater than we might at first sight think, for the following reason :

It is clear that, if the difficulty of transport could be overcome for any commodity, if the commodity could be made ubiquitous so that the whole world were one single market for it, its value would be exactly the same at every point in the world (see p. 223, note 1). For, if its value were less at one point than another, men would immediately transport it from the first to the second, and as, by hypothesis, transport would offer no difficulty and no cost, the slightest difference would be enough to make this operation profitable. The equilibrium therefore, even if disturbed, would be re-established instantaneously, like the level in the case of a perfectly fluid liquid.

Now, as precious metals are, of all commodities save precious stones, those which combine the greatest value with the smallest bulk, they are also the commodities whose transport is easiest and whose value in consequence will most rapidly regain its normal level. For 1 per cent. of its value (freight and insurance included) a mass of gold or of silver may be transported from one end of the world to the other,[1] while, for the same weight of corn, 20 per cent., 30 per cent. up to 50 per cent. of its value, according to distance, would have to be paid. It would seem to follow from this that the value of the precious metals must be the same, to about 1 per cent., all the world over. Such a conclusion would, however, be exaggerated. The value of the precious metals is not the same everywhere, being in fact lower at the places where they are produced than elsewhere. This explains the incredibly high prices so often found in gold-mining districts—in Australia half a century ago, and in the Transvaal and Klondike to-day. Still, we may say, on the whole, that the value

[1] See *infra, Foreign Exchanges.*

of these metals satisfies fairly well the first condition of a good measure of value—namely, invariability over space.

(2) *Indefinite durability.* Owing to their chemical properties, which render them resistant to almost every combination with air, water or any other body, gold and silver are able to remain unchanged indefinitely. There is no other form of wealth, in nature, of which so much may be said. Animal and vegetable products go bad, and even metals, like iron, finally oxidise and crumble into dust.[1]

This property is almost as important as the first. It produces the same effect in time as the other does in space, securing at least a relative invariability of value from one period to another. Owing to this durability, which makes it possible for the same particle of metal to be coined and recoined and to pass down through the ages, a mighty reservoir of these precious metals has gradually accumulated,[2] into which the annual production pours like a small stream and on which any accidental variation of the annual output has no more effect than a flood in the Rhone would have on the Lake of Geneva.

How different from wheat, for example, which is consumed at its first use. When each new harvest comes round, the barns are practically empty. If the wheat crop were one year to double over the whole world, it would mean that the stock also was doubled, and the fall in prices would be frightful. Now, within less than twenty years the annual output of the gold mines has increased more than five times over, rising from 500 million francs to $2\frac{1}{2}$ billions. As this production, however, represents only a small portion, about 5 per cent., of the stock of gold and silver in existence, the effect produced is trifling.[3]

Still, variations in the output of the precious metals make themselves felt in the long run, as, at the present rate of output, the stock of gold should be doubled in twenty-five years. If the value of the precious metals, then, offers a sufficient guarantee of stability over short periods, it is far from doing so over long periods. Hence serious disadvantages to which we shall have to return later.

(3) *Identity of quality.* Metals, being elements, are throughout self-identical. A skilled dealer would be able to distinguish between

---

[1] Copper keeps fairly well, owing to the fine layer of carbonate which covers and protects it.

[2] Some 80 billion francs to-day, 50 of these being gold. The United States, France, Russia, Germany and England hold more than half of this.

[3] Moreover, not more than one-third to one-half of this annual output falls into the monetary reservoir. The rest is directed into industry, or is absorbed by the hoarding nations of the East.

Odessa wheat and Minnesota wheat ; between a lock of wool from an Australian sheep and one taken from the back of a Spanish merino ; but the most skilful goldsmith or chemist, armed with the most powerful reagents, will find no difference between Australian gold and gold from the Ural mountains.   There is no need here for samples.

(4) *Difficulty of counterfeiting.*   The precious metals may be recognised by their colour, their ring and their weight, and are thus easily distinguished from all other bodies and even from all other metals.[1]

(5) *Perfect divisibility.*   By this we do not mean divisibility in the mechanical sense only—gold and silver being indeed extraordinarily divisible by way of threads or sheets—but in the economic sense of the word also.   Divide an ingot into a hundred parts, and its value is in no way changed ; the value of each fragment is exactly proportional to its weight, and the value of all the fragments put together is exactly equal to that of the original ingot.[2]

It is one thing to use the precious metals as an instrument of exchange and quite another to use them as money, properly so called.[3]   The use of the precious metals, as money, passed through three distinct stages :

(a) The precious metals were first used in the form of rough ingots.   In every exchange therefore these had first to be *weighed* and then *tested*.   We still find traces of the time when the instrument of exchange, silver or bronze, was weighed, in the legal forms of ancient Roman Law, such as the *mancipatio* and the *libripens*.   Not long ago in China, where coined money is not used, merchants might still be seen carrying a pair of scales and a touchstone at their belts.

(b) Weary of having to perform this double operation at every exchange, men conceived the idea of using cut ingots, the weight and standard of which were determined beforehand,[4] and, if necessary,

---

[1] Silver coins, for example, give quite a different feeling to the touch from nickel coins.

[2] Precious stones, which, in one respect, offer an advantage over precious metals, namely, greater value in smaller volume, are inferior in every other, since they are very variable in quality, susceptible of imitation, and, above all, cannot be divided without losing their value.

[3] " Great and powerful empires like Egypt, Chaldæa and Assyria existed for thousands of years in wealth and prosperity, with as extensive commercial relations as those of any people of antiquity, and constantly using precious metals in their negotiations, while absolutely ignorant of the use of money " (*Monnaies et médailles*, chap. i). The Egyptians used the precious metals chiefly in the form of rings.

[4] This, of course, presupposes the invention of a system of weights and measures, as we saw in the preceding chapter.

guaranteed by some seal or official stamp. The legislator who had this ingenious idea may justly claim the glory of having really invented money, for, from that time, ingots were no longer *weighed*, but *counted*, and this is the characteristic of money. The first money was probably coined between 650 and 700 B.C. by a king of Lydia, a successor of Gyges. Specimens of it may be seen in the British Museum. It is neither of gold nor of silver, but is an alloy of the two metals, known to the Greeks as " electrum " : it is not yet disc-shaped, but has the form of a bean, and bears simply the traces of a few lines and three stamps. The Chinese ingots until recently were very similar, bearing frequently the mark of certain business houses intended to certify to their weight and standard.

(c) One more step remained to be taken. Not only was the cubic or irregular shape of the ingot inconvenient, but, in spite of the stamp on it, nothing was easier than to clip it without leaving any trace. To be sure of its value, therefore, it was still advisable to weigh it. It was to remedy this practical difficulty that the form of coined money, familiar to all civilised peoples, was adopted, *i.e.* a small disc stamped in relief on both surfaces and on the edge, so that the coin cannot be tampered with without destroying the design.

This is the type of the coin properly so called, which has not been sensibly altered for centuries, and for which we may adopt Jevons's definition : " Coins are ingots of which the weight and fineness are guaranteed by the government and certified by the integrity of designs impressed on the surfaces of the metal." [1]

II : WHETHER MONEY RANKS ABOVE OTHER FORMS OF WEALTH

IF we were to consult public opinion, there would be no doubt as to the answer to this question. At all times and in all places, save among savages, money has held the first place in the preoccupations and desires of men, who have considered it, if not the only, yet by far the most important, form of wealth. Indeed, men seem to value all other forms of wealth simply by the quantity of money for which they can be exchanged. To be rich is to have either money or the means of obtaining it.

It would be curious to trace through history the various manifesta-tions of this idea which confounds gold with wealth : the attempts

[1] Jevons, *Money*, p. 57.

of the alchemists of the Middle Ages to transmute metals into gold, and thus to accomplish the *magnum opus*—by which they meant not so much a chemical discovery as an economic revolution ; the enthusiasm which seized on the Old World on the arrival of the first galleons from America, and the conviction that in that country of *Eldorado* would be found the end of all its woes; the complicated systems devised by all governments during the sixteenth and seven· teenth centuries to bring money into the countries which had none, or to prevent it from leaving those which had plenty ; and, to this day, the anxiety with which statesmen and financiers watch the coming-in and going-out of money, caused by the differences between exports and imports. The famous financier Law wrote, as late as the beginning of the eighteenth century : " An increase in coin adds to the value of a country." [1]

But if we were to turn to economists, the answer would be very different. It was, indeed, as a protest against this very idea, which it terms a prejudice, that Political Economy first revealed its existence. It had barely seen the day and was still at the incoherent stage, when Boisguilbert (1697) declared : " It is quite certain that money is not in itself a form of wealth and that the quantity of it has nothing to do with the opulence of a country." And since his time there is not an economist but has treated coined money with perfect disdain, insisting that it is only a commodity like any other, inferior, indeed, to others since it is incapable in itself of directly satisfying any want or of procuring any enjoyment, and is, in consequence, the *only form of wealth of which it may be said that its abundance or scarcity is of equally small consequence.* If there are few coins in a country, each will have a larger purchasing power ; if there are many, each will have a smaller purchasing power. What then can it matter?

---

[1] *Considérations sur le numéraire.* It was not because he saw in coin wealth capable, in itself, of satisfying the wants of man, but because he saw in it the indispensable aliment to productive labour. "An additional quantity of money will employ more individuals or the same number to greater advantage, and this, by increasing exports, will establish a balance favourable to the country. If, on the contrary, the quantity of coin diminishes, a certain number of workers hitherto employed will fall idle . . . production and manufacture will be reduced."

Law's statement was not, in our opinion, wrong, but the demonstration which he gives of it proceeds from a confusion between coin and circulating capital. It is this last only that is indispensable to keep labour going. Workers might quite well be paid in kind, as agricultural labourers sometimes are. The confusion between money and capital was the more dangerous in that Law, making another leap, assimilated metallic to paper money.

These two opinions, however contradictory they may appear, may be quite well reconciled. The public is right from the *individual* point of view, the only one which concerns it ; the economists are right in putting aside the individual point of view. And the explanation is as follows :

Every coin should be looked on as an order drawn on the sum total of existing wealth, giving the bearer a claim on some portion or other of that wealth, up to the value marked on his coin.[1]

It is clearly to the interest of each of us to possess as many as possible of these " orders " ; the more we have, the richer we shall be. We are not so stupid, of course, as to think that the orders in themselves can satisfy our hunger or quench our thirst. Long before economists had refuted this error we had seen it in the ancient legend of King Midas, dying of hunger in the midst of the wealth which his foolishness had transformed into gold. But we still hold that it is infinitely more convenient to possess these " orders " than any other form of wealth, and we are perfectly right in thinking so. For we know that, given the present organisation of society, anyone who wants to obtain an object which he has not himself produced (and the immense majority are so situated) can do so by the double operation which consists : (1) in exchanging the products of his labour, or that labour itself, for money, which is called *selling ;* (2) in exchanging this money for the object he wants, which is called *buying.* Now, the second of these two operations is quite simple : with money it is always easy to obtain what one wants. The first operation, sale, is, on the contrary, much more difficult ; it is not always easy to exchange an object. even of great value, for money. The possessor of money, therefore, is in a much better position than the possessor of goods. For, in order to satisfy his wants, he has only to go through one stage, and that an easy one, while the latter has to go through two, one of which is often very difficult. As has been well said, a particular commodity allows us to satisfy only a special and determinate want, whereas money allows

---

[1] An order, however, which has this advantage over ordinary credit documents, that it carries its own guarantee with it ; since a coin is guaranteed, in part at least, by the value of the metal contained in it. " If you can read with the eyes of the mind the inscription on a crown piece, you will make out these words quite distinctly : ' Render bearer a service equivalent to that which he has rendered society, a value which is ascertained, proved and measured by the value that is in me ' " (Bastiat, *Maudit argent*). We would add, however, some reservations to the optimistic postulate that every coin represents *a service actually rendered.*

us to satisfy any want whatever. The possessor of even a very useful commodity may not know what to do with it. The possessor of money is never at a loss ; he will always find some one ready to take it, and if by chance he cannot make use of it at once, he will at least have the option of reserving it for a better opportunity. With other commodities this is not always possible.

Besides being the *sole direct instrument of purchase,* money possesses another important function : it is the *sole instrument of payment of debts.* No other form of wealth has this singular virtue ; for law, as well as custom, recognises no other instrument for paying debts than money. There is no one in the commercial or industrial world who is not a debtor for more or less considerable sums. Now, though the trader or manufacturer may possess more goods in stock than the amount of his debts—and it has happened more than once in a failure that the assets have in the end been greater than the liabilities—unless he has at the given moment enough of this special wealth called money with which to honour his signature, he is declared bankrupt. Is it surprising, then, that such importance should be attached to a commodity on the possession of which our credit and our honour may at any moment depend ?

But if, instead of considering the situation of one individual, we consider that of the total number of individuals who constitute society, our point of view is changed. The proposition of the economists, that the quantity of money in a country is a matter of indifference, becomes more exact. It matters little to me, indeed, that the quantity of money I have in my possession is multiplied by ten, *if the same thing happens to all the other members of society.* On this hypothesis I shall be no better off than before, wealth being a purely relative thing. Nor shall I even be able to obtain a larger sum of satisfaction than in the past ; for, as the total sum of wealth on which these " orders " are drawn has not increased, each " order " will henceforth only give a right to a portion ten times smaller : in other words, each coin will have a buying power ten times less, or, all prices will have been multiplied by ten—and my situation will be the same as before.

And yet, *in their relations with one another,* countries, like individuals, find it to their interest to be well provided with money. If the quantity of money in France were to increase tenfold, this would not probably alter in any way the relation of Frenchmen to one another, (supposing the increase proportional for all), but it would greatly alter the situation of France in relation to foreign countries ; and economists have sometimes made the mistake, in combating the mercantile system, of seeming to deny this obvious fact. It is, of course, true, that money, by reason of its very abundance, would depreciate in France ; but it would retain intact its buying power on foreign markets, and France, by buying foreign goods with it, would be able to obtain an increase of satisfaction proportional to the increase in her money.

The thesis of the economists, therefore, that the quantity of money is a matter of indifference, is only absolutely true if we take into consideration not merely some individuals or some countries, but *all mankind*. It then becomes perfectly accurate to assert that the discovery of gold mines yielding a hundred times more than those which are worked to-day would bring no advantage to men. It would, if anything, be rather an untoward event, since gold in this case would be of no more value than copper, and we should have to burden our pockets with as cumbersome a money as that which Lycurgus wanted to impose on the Lacedæmonians.

III: WHETHER METALLIC MONEY IS DESTINED TO FALL INDEFINITELY IN VALUE

THE continued depreciation of metallic money is a fact demonstrated by all historical documents for at least a thousand years. This depreciation has been enormous.[1] At the time of Charlemagne the value of silver was about nine times as great as it is to-day ; it was about six times as great on the eve of the discovery of America, and twice or thrice as great at the time of the French Revolution. It seems therefore only logical to predict that it will fall indefinitely. Human industry is becoming daily more ingenious at discovering the hiding-places in which nature has buried her treasures, and more skilful in exploiting them economically. Neither silver nor gold is

---

[1] See Leber, *Appréciation de la fortune privée au moyen âge*, and d'Avenel, *Histoire des prix*. The fall was not, however, regular, and often the value of money went up again. The following are the maxima and minima of the historical curve according to Avenel :

850	9
1375	3
1500	6
1600	2½
1750	3
1890	1

The most striking fact brought out by these figures is the enormous fall in the value of money during the sixteenth century, following on the discovery of America.

so rare as it is believed to be; both exist everywhere [1]—in infinitesimal quantities, to be sure, but the progress in metallurgy is continually lowering the limit below which the extraction of ore ceases to be remunerative. It is probable, therefore, that the precious metals will become more and more abundant and will consequently continue to depreciate.

It might perhaps be urged that, owing to the growth of population and the development of exchange, there will be enough demand for these metals to counterbalance the increasing supply. But we must remember that this demand is, in turn, more than counterbalanced by the rapid progress in methods of credit and of communication. In the great financial centres, metallic money has been replaced, as we shall see, by ingenious systems of clearing houses and credit.

Is this increase in the quantity of money and consequent depreciation of its value a matter for congratulation or for regret? What difference can it make, some will perhaps ask? No one will be either the richer or the poorer for it; the only result will be that our money will grow heavier and heavier in relation to its value, as if gold had been turned into lead. And even this prospect need not trouble us much, thanks to the use of the bank-note and the cheque. Besides, if the so-called precious metals were one day to become cheap, other rarer metals would most certainly be found to replace these dethroned potentates.[2]

Yet it is not a matter of indifference. In reality the continued depreciation of the monetary standard is a phenomenon of great social importance, the effects of which should, in our opinion, be regarded as beneficent.[3]

[1] In the commonest bodies, such as sea-water and clay. Sea-water contains 40 to 50 milligrammes of gold per cubic metre, *i.e.* enough to endow each inhabitant of the globe with 100 million francs. It is known that the interior of the earth is composed of much heavier elements than the surface, probably, therefore, of metals. And as gold is one of the heaviest known metals, perhaps the earth has a kernel of solid gold!

[2] There are metals more precious than gold. Platinum is worth nearly twice as much; lithium, zirconium, and vanadium cost twenty and forty times as much, not to speak of radium, which is worth (1913) £26,000 *per gramme*. It is true that the Bohemian mine which, up till now, has had the monopoly of it, can produce annually no more than 2 or 3 grammes.

[3] Mr. Herckenrath, in the Dutch translation of this book, has criticised the doctrine we uphold in this chapter. Like his fellow countryman, Mr. G. Pierson, he does not consider the depreciation of the precious metals always beneficent. Ihering, too, declared in his *Kampf ums Recht* that "to sympathise with the debtor is the most potent sign of the weakness of an epoch," and we shall show further on (*Historical Sketch of Loans at Interest*) how nowadays the lender can

In the first place, the ordinary consequence of the depreciation of money is, as we know, a rise in prices.[1] Now, a rise in prices is a useful stimulus to production : it keeps up the spirit of enterprise and is favourable to a rise in wages ; it acts as a tonic, and is a symptom of sound economic health.

The public also is unconsciously glad of it, even when it has no reason to be. In the countries of South America, for example, where the inconsiderate multiplication of paper-money has provoked an enormous rise in prices, producers and manufacturers congratulate themselves on the rise, and are, as a rule, hostile to the financial measures which would put a stop to it, such as the withdrawal of the paper-money.

The depreciation of money, moreover, is favourable to debtors inasmuch as they are able to discharge their debts by giving a smaller value than they received. To repeat a famous expression applied to the discovery of mines in the New World, it is a new way to pay old debts. It acts in the same way as a fall in the rate of interest, or, better still, as an automatic redemption of capital. Now, it is very good for old debts to be redeemed, and not to weigh on generation after generation. Particularly important is it in the case of States, which are the largest debtors and the only really perpetual ones.

It is true, to the degree in which the depreciation of money is favourable to the producer and the debtor, it is unfavourable to the consumer and the creditor. But this effect is in itself good. For the consumer, if he be also a producer, will easily make up for his increased expenditure by a higher profit or by higher wages.[2] If he consumes without producing anything, so much the worse for him : the rise in prices will fall on him justly. As for the creditor, if his credit is for a short period, such as is usual in commerce, the depreciation of money will not affect him ; while, if it is for a long period, or in perpetuity, say in the form of investment in State stock, land rent, long-term railway or municipal bonds, it is only right that

---

be as deserving of sympathy as the borrower, *e.g.* the small capitalist who invests in large companies. Nevertheless the *growing power of money* constitutes always, in our view, a social danger, and the depreciation of the metal seems to us a happy corrective to this.

[1] On the question, called the *quantity theory* of money, as to whether every variation in the quantity of money involves a proportional increase in prices, see above, Book II, chap. i.

[2] Unfortunately, where the workers are unorganised, wages are slow to follow the rise in prices ; but they are quick to overtake it wherever they are kept up by trade unions.

the gradual reduction of his income should warn him that he is playing the part of a parasite in this world, and that if he would keep his social position or transmit the same to his descendants, he would do well to exert himself, or at least to teach his children to take an active part in life.   Lafitte, the great financier of the Restoration and anything but a socialist, said, long ago, in speaking of the *rentier* : " He must either work or cut down his expenditure. The capitalist has the idle rôle : his penalty must be economy, and it is not over-severe."[1]

As an illustration of what we have been saying, let us suppose our forecasts regarding the fall in the value of the precious metals are not fulfilled—and after all they are by no means infallible.   We should see exactly the opposite effects taking place: viz., a constant depression of prices weighing upon industry and discouraging enterprise ; States overwhelmed by their ever-increasing debts and driving straight to bankruptcy ; capitalists getting richer more surely by their idleness than the other classes of the community by their labour.   Nothing could be better fitted to provoke a social revolution. We ought, therefore, to rejoice at the depreciation of the precious metals, so long as it lasts ; it is like oil in the bearings.

IV : THE CONDITIONS WHICH OUGHT TO BE FULFILLED BY ALL GOOD MONEY

All legal money ought to have a metallic value strictly equal to its nominal value. This is the governing principle in the matter of money.

We know that money performs a twofold function : it is the sole instrument of purchase and it is the sole instrument for payment of debts (see above, p. 290).   Both of these functions originate in custom, but both require to be sanctioned by law.   For law alone can oblige a creditor or a seller to receive a particular kind of money in payment.   It is this privilege which constitutes what is called *legal tender.*   But the quality of legal tender presupposes the condition mentioned above.   Here, say, is a 20-franc gold piece.   By engraving on this coin the figure " 20 francs " along with the arms of the State, the Government intends to certify that it really has a value of 20 francs, and that every one may accept it in all confidence.

---

[1] Moreover, the intelligent *rentier* has many ways of escaping the effects of depreciation in the value of money : he may, *e.g.* buy shares " below par " (*i.e.* below the price at which the debtor has promised to repay them) or put part of his fortune into *shares* in industrial companies, securities which, unlike bonds or government stock, follow the rise in price of products.

If the coin has not the value attributed to it, the State is committing a veritable perjury. Unfortunately, for centuries monarchs had but few scruples in this respect ; to-day, however, it has become a question of dignity and good faith in which no government would dare to be found wanting.

Every piece of money must, then, be considered in two aspects : *as a coin it has a fixed value inscribed on one of its faces ; as an ingot it has a value identical with the market price of the metal.* For there are markets and quoted prices for gold and silver just as for corn and cotton.

Whenever these two values coincide—whenever, for instance, the small ingot of 6 grammes 451 milligrammes (nine-tenths fine), which constitutes the French 20-franc piece, has a market value of 20 francs (corresponding to a price of 3100 francs per kilo) [1]—we may say the money is *good*, or, to use the technical expression, that it is *sound*. We have still to find out how to ensure and maintain this perfect coincidence.

Case I. If the value of the ingot is greater than that of the coin, if, for example, when the coin is legally worth only 20 francs the weight of the fine metal which it contains is worth 21 or 22 francs, the money is said to be *heavy*.[2]

This is a good fault, but it is none the less a fault, and one which may, as we shall see, have somewhat serious consequences. Still, there is not much ground for fearing such a contingency. For, in the first place, it will only be through inadvertence that a government will strike too heavy a money, since this operation will be done at a loss. To coin gold pieces which are worth only 20 francs

[1] We are speaking of the kilogramme of gold nine-tenths fine, which is the standard of French money ; for it goes without saying that the kilogramme of pure gold is worth one-ninth more, *i.e.* 3444 francs 44 centimes.

[2] But ought not the coined ingot of gold to be worth always a little more than the uncoined ingot, for the reason that every object is worth more when it has been manufactured than in its raw state, the difference being equal to the cost of coining ? True, but the cost of manufacture is here so slight that it causes no sensible difference. The Paris Mint charges 7 francs 44 centimes for transforming a kilogramme of gold into money, or about 2 per 1000 (that is to say, it pays for a kilogramme of pure gold only 3437 francs, instead of 3444 francs 44 centimes, which is its real value, retaining the difference to cover its exp nses) ; or, m other words, it pays only 19 francs 96 centimes for an ingot with which it will manufacture a coin worth exactly 20 francs. The State might, if it wished, avoid this slight difference by transforming the ingot into money gratuitously, that is to say, by taking the cost of coinage on itself. This is done in England and the United States. Thus the English sovereign and the American gold dollar are the types of a perfect money : their legal value is absolutely identical with their commercial value.

from ingots which are worth 21 or 22 would be as ruinous an operation as if a manufacturer were to make rails at 100 francs a ton with steel which was worth 110. And, in the second place, even if a government, owing to circumstances which we shall discuss later (*e.g.* a subsequent rise in the price of the metal),were to find itself with too heavy a money, it would not be for long. For, no sooner would the public know that the coin of 20 francs was worth 21 or 22 francs as an ingot, than every one would hasten to realise this profit by considering his money as a commodity and selling it by weight. And the operation would continue until the gold pieces had completely disappeared. We shall see that this situation arises not infrequently in countries which are under bimetallic systems.

Case II. If the value of the ingot is less than that of the coin, if, for example, when the coin is legally worth 20 francs the weight of the metal which it contains is worth only 18 or 19 francs, the money is said to be *light*.

This contingency is much more to be dreaded than the previous one, for two reasons. In the first place, it is of the nature of a temptation to a government.[1] To make 20-franc pieces out of ingots which are worth only 18 or 19 francs is a fairly attractive operation for a needy and not over-scrupulous government, and not a few governments have given way to the temptation. We have only to call to mind the name of *faux-monnayeur*, which public resentment attached to the memory of certain kings of France. In the second place, once such a money has entered into circulation it does not disappear, as does heavy money, by force of circumstances. It comes to stay, and there is, as we shall see when we study Gresham's law, the greatest difficulty in getting rid of it.

To maintain equivalence in value between the ingot and the

---

[1] It is well known that the monetary unit under the *ancien régime* in France was called the *livre* (pound). But it is not generally known that it derived its name from the fact that originally, at the time of Charlemagne, it represented the weight of a pound of silver (the Carlovingian pound was 408 grammes only) ; that is to say, a weight equal to that of 82 francs to-day. How did it gradually fall to 5 grammes, which was practically the weight of the livre at the end of the *ancien régime*, and which is now that of the franc ? Simply by a continued series of issues of weaker and weaker money. One monarch after the other clipped a little off the weight of the old *livre*, while trying at the same time to maintain its former legal value. The history of the English pound is very much the same, though a little more honourable for the English Government, since, starting from the same point, it stopped short in its fall at its present value of 20s. See Landry, *Les mutations des monnaies*, for the debasement and forced currency of money under the kings of France.

coin, it is the rule under every good monetary system—and this is a principle of capital importance—to allow anybody the right to have metal coined, not at home of course, but at the Mint. This is what is called free coinage. So long as it exists the equivalence of value is guaranteed. For, if the value of the gold coin were ever to rise above that of the ingot, every one would hasten to take advantage of the gain to be made by turning gold into money. Ingots would be bought and taken to the Mint to be coined, until the scarcity of metal and the increase of coin restored the equality of the two values. Good money can be melted down without losing any of its value.[1] Here we have an instance of the economic axiom that whenever two objects may be transformed into one another they must necessarily have an equal value.[2]

There are, however, in all countries certain kinds of coin which do not fulfil the preceding condition, that is to say, their intrinsic value is more or less below their legal value. These are called "token" money (monnaies de billon). They are usually copper coins of small value, though sometimes also silver, and are not as a rule used for important payments, but simply as subsidiary money. In the case of these the legislator may, without objection, depart from his strict principle of equivalence of value. But in so doing he must sacrifice at the same time the characteristics of good money : (1) He must refuse to token money the character of legal tender : no one must be compelled to accept it in payment.[3] (2) He must suspend the freedom of coinage in the case of token money, otherwise every one would bring the metal to be coined into token money, in order to gain the difference between its metallic value and its legal value. The government reserves to itself alone the right to issue what quantity it judges necessary.

V : GRESHAM'S LAW

In every country where two kinds of legal money are in circulation, bad money always drives out good.

Such is the wording of one of the most curious laws of Political Economy, named after a Chancellor of Queen Elizabeth, who is said to have discovered it nearly four centuries ago. But long before

[1] This accounts for the picturesque English saying, "Good money stands the fire," in memory of the fire test used in mediæval procedure.

[2] See p. 222, *The Law of Indifference.*

[3] Thus, in France, no one is bound to accept copper coins save for sums below 5 francs, and, in the case of small silver, below 50 francs.

Gresham, Aristophanes had pointed out, in his *Frogs*, the curious fact that the men of his time preferred bad money to good.[1]

What makes this law at first sight paradoxical is that it seems to be stating that men *always prefer* bad money to good. Now, this looks absurd. Economic science rests entirely on the postulate that mankind under all circumstances will prefer the better of two articles, and facts daily confirm.it. Of two fruits, we prefer the one which has more taste ; of two watches, the one which goes better. Why, then, should we act in exactly the opposite way with money ?

The real truth is, however, that we are not acting differently. We are doing the same with money as with any other object. *When it is a question of keeping it for ourselves* we prefer good money, but when it is a question of giving it to a tradesman or to our creditors, why give good money if bad will do equally well, *i.e.* if it cannot be refused in payment ? And this is the hypothesis on which Gresham's law rests. It presupposes two moneys, both legal tender.[2]

All this explains why bad money remains in circulation, but does not explain why good money disappears. What becomes of it ? We employ it whenever we can turn it to better account than bad money, that is to say, in the three following ways, which are, as it were, the three vents by which good money escapes : in *hoarding*, in making *payments abroad*, and in *selling it by weight*.

(1) *Hoarding.* When people want to put money aside for possible contingencies they are not so foolish as to pick out the bad coins. As it is for their own use, they choose the best, since these offer most security. The panic-stricken persons who wanted to hoard money during the French Revolution did not waste their time in laying by *assignats* : they laid aside good *louis d'or*. Banks do exactly the same. The Bank of France is very careful to keep a large reserve of gold. In this way quite a quantity of the best money may disappear from circulation. This first cause of the disappearance of good money is, however, only temporary.

(2) *Payments abroad.* These have a more important effect.

---

[1] "We have often remarked that in this city [Athens] we treat our best citizens as we do our old money. The latter is without alloy, the best of all, the only money well struck, the only money which is current among Greeks and barbarians ; but, instead of using it, we prefer vile pieces of copper newly struck and alloyed with bad metal."

[2] It must be observed that Gresham's law applies even to counterfeit or demonetised coin : most persons who have the misfortune to find it in their pockets are in such a hurry to pass it on that the more suspect it is the quicker it circulates.

Although a country never has to pay more than a small part of its imports in coin, there are always remittances in specie to be made abroad. Now, although we may have the legal right to pay our debts to our fellow countrymen in bad money as well as in good, provided both are legal tender, this alternative is not open to us when paying for purchases from the foreigner. As the foreign creditor is not in any way bound to take our money, and will accept it only for the quantity of fine metal it contains—that is to say, for its real value—we cannot send him the light money. We keep the latter, therefore, for home use, since it is as serviceable here as the other, and reserve the good money for our foreign trade.

(3) *Sale by weight.* But what causes good money to disappear most speedily is *sale by weight.* This is surely a singular and not very useful operation! Yet it is very simply explained. So soon as a rise in the value of gold sends the metallic value of a coin above its legal value, so soon as it is worth more as an ingot than as money, it is obviously to our interest to stop using it as money and to use it as an ingot. We withdraw it therefore from circulation and send it to the market for precious metals. If the value of bronze were to rise considerably, it is almost certain that a number of bronze objects, bells, cannon, statuettes, etc., would be melted down in order to realise the value of the metal which they contain. When alcohol, for instance, rises in price, large quantities of wine are sent to the distillery to be converted into alcohol. So, when the precious metals rise in value, the coins struck from them lose their character of money and become merchandise which we hasten to realise, *i.e.* to sell.[1]

This, then, is the explanation of Gresham's law. It applies to the three following cases :

(1) Whenever a *worn* money is in circulation along with a newly coined money.

It was under such circumstances that the law was observed by Sir Thomas Gresham. In the reign of Elizabeth a new money had been struck to replace the one in circulation, which was greatly depreciated, more by clipping than by actual wear and tear ; and it was seen with dismay that the new pieces were fast disappearing, while the old ones seemed to be more abundant than ever.[2]

---

[1] M. Paul Leroy-Beaulieu has summed up this whole phenomenon very well in the formula : *local* money drives out *universal* money.

[2] In the case quoted by Aristophanes it was exactly the reverse ; the new money was chasing out the old. But this was because the situation was also reversed, the new money having been struck on a lower standard.

A government, then, must resort to frequent recoinages, or it will encounter great difficulties in replacing its old money by new.

(2) Whenever a *depreciated paper money* is in circulation along with a *metallic money*.

In this case, if the depreciation of the paper money is at all considerable, coin is driven out on a very large scale. Not many years ago we saw the whole of the Italian metallic money emigrate into France. In vain did the Italian Government take measures to bring it back, even prevailing on the French Government to forbid its circulation in France. It would never have succeeded had it not gone to the root of the evil and suppressed the paper money, or at least deprived it of its quality of forced currency. In the same way the United States and Russia, the two greatest producers of the precious metals, were entirely unable to keep their money at home, although they were supplying the raw material of it to the whole world. It was useless to strike it from the gold of their own mines. Their depreciated paper money drove it out inexorably.

(3) Whenever a *light* money is in circulation along with *good* money, or even whenever a *good* money is in circulation along with a *heavy* money.

In this instance the weaker of the two moneys drives out the other. This is the most interesting case: it occurs in almost all the countries which have adopted, at the same time, both a gold and a silver money. But the examination of it brings us to the question of monometallism and bimetallism, which we shall discuss in the following chapter.

CHAPTER V : MONETARY SYSTEMS

I : THE NECESSITY FOR EMPLOYING SEVERAL METALS AND THE DIFFICULTIES WHICH RESULT THEREFROM

THE discussion which has long been waged on this famous subject does not turn, as we might suppose, on the question whether a country should employ several metals for its monetary equipment, or be content with only one. This point does not even arise; for it is evident that every civilised country is obliged to employ simultaneously coins of gold, silver and copper, or some similar metal.[1]

---

[1] In France there are as many as four metals in circulation: gold, silver, nickel (for the 25-centime piece only) and bronze, which is however to be replaced totally by nickel.

These metals are distributed in very unequal proportions in circulation.

How could we possibly use nothing but gold, for instance ? The gold 5-franc piece, as it is, is inconveniently small; a gold sou would be an almost imperceptible atom. Copper only, unless we would return to the early days of Rome, would be worse still, since a 20-franc piece in copper would weigh a dozen kilogrammes. Even silver, though less inconvenient than the other two, as its value lies between them, would be impossible, the silver 5-franc piece being already too large, and the 20-centime piece too small, for current use. It is absolutely necessary to employ at least three metals at once.

But it is not necessary to employ all three as *legal tender*. One of them, copper, we know has never had this quality. It is always token or subsidiary money. There remain then silver and gold. Are we to confer on both of these the character and attributes of legal tender, or only on one ? This question, formerly known as that of the " single or double standard," is now more accurately referred to as the problem of *Monometallism* or *Bimetallism*.

If we confer the title of legal tender on *one only* of the two metals, gold for instance, there is no difficulty. Silver money, like copper, is relegated to the rank of token money, the value attributed to it is purely conventional, and no one is obliged to receive it in payment. Gold money is the only one which has legal currency : it is also the only one for which there is any need to maintain a perfect equivalence between legal value and intrinsic value.

If we confer the quality of legal tender on both moneys at once, the situation becomes much more complicated. To understand these difficulties better, let us take the French system, which may be considered the type of bimetallism, and let us go back to the time when it was being entirely reorganised by the law of 7th Germinal, Year XI (March 28, 1803).

The unit of money was the old *livre* (pound), transformed into a franc. It was a silver piece ; silver was therefore taken as legal money. Indeed, at that time no one would have dreamt of contesting its right to the title. But it was impossible not to give this title to gold as well.

For greater clearness, let us take the two similar coins which are found in the French monetary system, the silver 5-franc piece and the gold 5-franc piece. We want both of these to be legal money : they must both therefore have a metallic value rigorously equal to their legal value : this is, as we know, the *sine qua non*. It is not

Partial censuses taken from time to time of the cash used in public offices give approximately the following result : Gold, 65·8 per cent. ; silver, 32·4 per cent. ; copper and nickel, 1·3 per cent.

hard to fulfil this condition, so far as the silver piece is concerned. Silver is worth, or rather was worth at the time of which we are speaking, 200 francs per kilogramme: an ingot of 25 grammes, therefore, was worth exactly 5 francs; thus if we give our 5-franc silver piece a weight of 25 grammes the required condition is fulfilled. But what weight are we to give the 5-franc gold piece ? The kilogramme of gold was at that time worth 3100 francs (of the same standard as silver, nine-tenths fine): if, then, we strike 620 pieces from a kilogramme of gold, each will be worth exactly 5 francs (for 620 × 5 = 3100), and each one will weigh 1·613 grammes; in this case also the condition will be fulfilled.

Let us put these two coins in the scales of a balance ; we shall find that, in order to balance the silver 5-franc piece in the one scale, we shall have to put fifteen and a half gold 5-franc pieces into the other; or, in order to balance two silver 5-franc pieces, we shall need thirty-one gold 5-franc pieces. This proves that the operation has been well done. For the kilogramme of gold at that time was worth exactly fifteen and a half times as much as the kilogramme of silver (3100 francs, the gold kilogramme, against 200 francs, the silver kilogramme). We must bear in mind this relation of $15\frac{1}{2}$ to 1. It is the legal ratio between the values of the two metals. It is as celebrated in Political Economy as the famous relation of the diameter to the circumference, $\pi = 3\cdot1416$, in geometry.   So far, then, everything has gone splendidly.   But wait !

In 1849 the gold mines of California are discovered ; in 1851 those of Australia. The annual output of gold is therefore quad-rupled.[1] On the other hand, silver becomes scarcer, owing to the development of trade in India, which absorbs large quantities of it. The result is that the relative value of the two metals changes : to obtain 1 kilogramme of gold on the market for precious metals, it is no longer necessary to give $15\frac{1}{2}$ kilogrammes of silver; it is enough to give 15.   In other words, gold has lost almost 3 per cent. of its value.   Henceforward it is clear that these little ingots of gold which constitute gold coins have undergone a proportional depre-ciation : the gold 5-franc piece is no longer really worth more than 4 francs 84.

What is to be done to restore equilibrium ? Evidently we must add a little more gold, about 3 per cent., to each gold piece. To restore the equivalence between the intrinsic value and the legal value, the silver 5-franc piece should now be equal in weight to

---

[1] The production of gold from 1841 to 1850 was estimated at an annual average of 184 million francs only.   From 1850 to 1860 it was 700 millions.

15 gold 5-franc pieces, not 15½ as before. This means recoining the whole of the gold money ! But not so fast.

Twenty years later, in 1871, there is a change in the opposite direction. The output of gold, owing to the exhaustion of the Australian and Californian mines, falls by one-half : the output of silver, on the contrary, owing to the discovery of the bonanza mines of Western America, increases by one-half. At the same time, Germany, adopting the gold standard, demonetises her silver money, and floods the market with her thalers which she no longer wants. Once again the relative value of the two metals changes, but this time in the opposite direction. With a kilogramme of gold we can obtain on the market for precious metals, not 15½ kilogrammes of silver as before, but 16, 17, 18 and up to 20 kilogrammes ; in other words, silver has lost more than a quarter of its value in relation to gold. It is clear that, henceforward, each ingot of silver which constitutes a silver coin has undergone a proportional depreciation. The 5-franc silver piece is in reality worth no more than 3·50 francs. What should be done to restore equilibrium ? Evidently much more silver must be put into each silver coin : its weight must be increased by one quarter, in order that the 5-franc silver piece may weigh as much as twenty gold 5-franc pieces. The equivalence between the metallic value and the legal value would thus be restored ; but this would mean recoining the whole of the silver money !

If, then, we would maintain the character of our two moneys as good, *i.e.* if we would maintain a strict equivalence between their intrinsic value and their legal value, must we be for ever recoining now one and now the other to keep their weights in relation to the variations in value of the two metals ? This is the conclusion we seem forced to. But it is impracticable and absurd.[1] We shall see in the next chapter what expedient has been devised.

[1] A little reflection will show that it would be quite enough to vary the weight of one only of the two metals, taking the other, which would remain invariable, as unit : for example, to take the silver franc of 5 grammes as unit, and to vary the weight of the gold pieces now above, now below the legal weight, according to the variations in the value of gold metal. But this, in spite of its simplification, would be scarcely more practicable.

We might also, on the same hypothesis, leaving the weight of the gold pieces invariable, efface the indication of legal value engraved on them, and allow their value to move up and down freely according to the laws of demand and supply, just as in some countries, Indo-China *e.g.* the value of the piastre varies. The legislators of Germinal, Year XI, when organising the French monetary system, had quite clearly foreseen the difficulties which might result from it, and had actually proposed this method. And some economists to-day look on it as the only possible solution. But in this case gold coins would no longer be really

II : HOW IT IS THAT BIMETALLIST COUNTRIES
REALLY HAVE BUT ONE MONEY

As we have just seen, the serious drawback of every bimetallist system is the difficulty which it has in maintaining, for both of its moneys at once, the equivalence between intrinsic and legal value which ought to be the characteristic of all good money. According to the variations in value of the two metals, one or the other is for ever becoming too heavy or too light.

• Such a drawback may perhaps be considered theoretical rather than practical. What does it matter, it will be said, whether our gold or silver pieces have a legal value a little above or a little below their real value ? No one notices it, and in any case no one suffers from it.

This is a mistake. There is a very real disadvantage—more than that, a peril—in such a situation. For the lighter will gradually drive the heavier money out of circulation, till every country that is nominally under the two-standard system will find that it can keep only one of its two moneys in circulation, and that precisely the worse. A periodical ebb and flow will carry off the metal which is high in value and leave that which is low.

This is nothing more nor less than a case of Gresham's law, which we have already studied; but the history of the French monetary system during the last fifty years offers a marvellous demonstration of it.

When, under the Second Empire, owing to circumstances mentioned in the last chapter, gold began to fall, silver money began to disappear and to be replaced by a gold money—those fine" napoleons" —to which people were at that time but little accustomed. This gold money was greatly admired, and courtiers hailed it as a sign of the wealth and brilliance of the new reign ; but its abundance was in reality due to the fact that it was made from a depreciated metal. This phenomenon of the transmutation, so to speak, of the metals is very easily explained.

The London banker who wanted silver to send to India naturally tried to buy it where he could find it cheapest. In London he could not obtain more than 15 kilogrammes of silver for 1 kilogramme of gold. But by sending his kilogramme of gold to the Mint in Paris

money ; they would be mere ingots, circulating like any other merchandise. There would be a current price for 20-franc pieces as for cottons and wheat, and they would vary in the same manner. What a complication this would be in business and what a pitfall for the simple !

he was able to have 3100 gold francs struck, and to exchange them again for 3100 silver francs, which weighed exactly 15½ kilogrammes (3100 × 5 grammes). Thus for his kilogramme of gold he had managed in the end to obtain 15½ kilogrammes of silver.[1]

It is easy to see that, thanks to this kind of transaction, a certain quantity of silver money left France and was replaced by an equal quantity of gold money. This is the very way in which Gresham's law acts : strong money gives place to weak money. Shiploads of silver coins were exported from France to India. They were bought by weight to be sold to the mints of Bombay and Madras, and there converted into rupees. During this period these mints turned over two billion French francs into Indian money.

A veritable famine of silver money was not slow to follow. In former days prohibitive measures would certainly have been resorted to in order to stop its flight, and perhaps penalties inflicted on the persons who exported the silver coin. Economic science, by pointing out the cause of the evil, made a much more effective remedy possible. Silver money was disappearing because it was too heavy ; all that was necessary, therefore, to clip its wings and make sure that it would fly no more, was to lighten it by reducing its weight. or the proportion of fine metal in it. This was done, of one accord, by France, Italy, Belgium and Switzerland by the Convention of December 23, 1865.[2] The standard of all silver coins, *except the 5-franc piece*, was lowered from $\frac{900}{1000}$ to $\frac{835}{1000}$, which deprived them of a little over 7 per cent. of their value. *All these coins then became, and have since remained, token money*, and, according to the invariable principles on this matter, they lost from that day their character of legal money, and have since been accepted only as auxiliary

---

[1] The operation could also be reversed. A Paris banker could collect 3000 silver francs which weighed exactly 15 kilogrammes (3000 × 0·005 = 15) and send them to London in exchange for 1 kilogramme of gold, since 1 to 15 was the market value of these two metals. He would then have his kilogramme of gold struck at the Paris Mint into 3100 gold francs. The gross gain on this opera-tion was 100 francs, or a little more than 3 per cent., so that, even deducting the cost of mintage and transport, it was still very lucrative.

[2] This is what is called the *Latin Union*, although Spain and Portugal are not included. Greece joined it shortly after. At the beginning it was agreed that the coins struck in any one of the five countries should have the right to circulate in all. But this freedom of circulation was withdrawn in 1893 in the case of the divisionary silver money (*i.e.* pieces smaller than the 5-franc piece) of Italy and, quite lately, of Greece. This measure was taken, not against these countries, but at their own request, as exchange that was unfavourable to them drew away their small coins. (See *infra*, p. 440, *Foreign Exchanges*.)

money.[1] Why was an exception made in the case of the 5-franc piece ? There was no good reason for it, but France insisted on it. To turn all the silver coins into token money would have meant the entire abandoning of silver as legal money. It would have meant openly accepting gold monometallism, like England, and such a revolution in the monetary system alarmed the French Government. The 5-franc piece was therefore maintained with its weight and standard and character of legal money. Of course it continued to disappear, but it could be more easily dispensed with than the smaller money, and could always, if necessary, be replaced by the 5-franc gold piece.

From 1871 on, as we saw, the relative values of the two metals were reversed, and the French monetary system found itself disorganised. This time it was the gold money which was too heavy and in consequence began to emigrate ; the silver money which was too light and began to flood the circulation.

The operation explained above began again, but in the opposite direction. In order that there may be no obscurity, however, on this essential point we shall repeat our explanation.

A banker at Paris would collect 3100 francs of gold, either in 20- or 10-franc pieces. That made exactly 1 kilogramme of gold. He would send them to London, where, on the market for precious metals, a kilogramme of gold was worth 20 kilogrammes of silver. He would buy, therefore, 20 kilogrammes of silver, have them sent back to Paris and coined at the Mint. As the Mint had to strike forty 5-franc pieces (*i.e.* 200 francs) out of every kilogramme of silver, it would hand over to our banker $20 \times 200 = 4000$ francs, in pieces of 5 francs. Gross profit, therefore, 900 francs. Deducting the costs of transport, coinage, etc., and also the premium necessary to obtain gold pieces when they became scarce, the operation still remained a lucrative one. Clearly, for France, it meant a decrease of gold money and an increase of silver money. Repeated indefinitely, this operation would inevitably result in the complete substitution of silver for gold money in circulation.

It was necessary, therefore, for the Powers which had formed the Latin Union to plan together to avert this new danger. Just as, in 1865, they had stopped the flight of silver money by weakening its standard, so here too they might have stopped the flight of the gold money by weakening its standard or by reducing its weight.

---

[1] Up to 50 francs between individuals, and 100 francs (though in actual practice there is no limit) in Government offices. It is only right, in fact, that the State should not be able to refuse the money which it itself issues.

But this continual recoining first of one money and then of the other would have ended in disorganising the whole monetary system. A more simple expedient seemed preferable. *The Convention of November 5, 1878, suspended the coinage of silver money.*[1] Since that date the operation we have just described has become impossible. There is no longer any profit in buying silver ingots abroad, for they can no longer be coined into money in France.[2]

This measure, indeed, was entirely successful in preserving for France her fine stock of gold metal, which had not as yet been perceptibly encroached on.. But, as may well be imagined, the Convention, by closing to silver a market of nearly eighty million men and restricting to this extent its sale, only hastened its depreciation and aggravated the evil.[3] Silver, which up till then had lost scarcely more than 10 to 12 per cent. of its value, fell gradually to below 100 francs per kilogramme, or to less than half its legal value of 200 francs (corresponding to a ratio of 1 to 31 between the value of the two metals).[4] In other words, the 5-franc piece is no longer worth more than 2 francs 50, and the franc, owing to its lighter standard, is worth barely 45 centimes.

Under these conditions, the free coinage of silver money has not been resumed, and no one can tell whether it ever will be. We may therefore say that, although the countries of the Latin Union are

[1] In the case, at least, of the 5-franc pieces, the only silver money that was legal currency. For in the case of the smaller silver, each State reserved the right to coin a quantity, determined by the number of its population (first 7 and later 16 francs per head).

[2] The danger is, however, not entirely averted ; for we must provide against the possibility of the clandestine manufacture of silver money—not false money, but good money of legal weight and standard—which would still bring the coiner the enormous profit of 100 per cent. which the State makes to-day on its coinage. It is certain that this illicit operation does actually take place, and probably to a larger extent than we think. The quantity of silver money in circulation must therefore be a little over the quantity struck.

[3] Since then many other countries have given up the silver standard for the gold standard (see next chapter).

[4] In 1903 it touched its lowest point, its ratio to gold being 1 : 40, which corresponds to 77 francs as the price of the kilogramme of silver. The ratio afterwards rose to 1 : 26, corresponding to 118 francs per kilogramme, and fell again, in 1912, to 1 : 30.

The value of silver is always quoted in English ounces and pence : the ounce represents 31·103 grammes at the standard of 925 thousandths, and the penny 10¼ centimes; or, to put it more simply, when silver is at the value of 200 francs per kilogramme (the legal ratio of 15½ to 1) the English quotation is practically 54¾ pence per ounce. At the time we are correcting these proofs (March 1913) it is quoted at 27 pence, which corresponds to 100 francs (less a few centimes) per kilogramme.

still legally under the bimetallic system, in practice they have become almost gold monometallists. *Of all their silver coins only one is still legal money, and that one is no longer coined !*

III : WHETHER IT IS ADVISABLE TO ADOPT THE MONOMETALLIST SYSTEM

IT would seem, after the foregoing explanation, that there could be no room for hesitation.   The monometallist system is infinitely more simple : it cuts short all the difficulties which we have pointed out.   Why not, then, adopt it ?

This is what most countries have already done, beginning with England in 1816, Portugal 1854, Germany 1873, the Scandinavian States 1875, Finland 1878, Roumania 1890, Austria 1892, Russia 1897, Japan 1897, Peru 1901 ; and the Argentine Republic is about to follow.   Almost the only remaining bimetallist countries are the so-called Latin Union (France, Italy, Belgium, Switzerland and Greece), Holland, Spain, the United States, Mexico, and India.[1]   And even among these bimetallist countries the principal ones—France, the United States and India—are in fact gold monometallists in this sense, that they use gold alone for international exchanges.

As regards the Latin Union, we have just seen how weak, almost nominal, is the tie which binds it to legal bimetallism.   The same is true of the United States, where for a long time a powerful party, the Silver Men, carried on a campaign to establish legal bimetallism at home and even abroad.   They went so far as to secure the passing of a famous law, that of 1890, obliging the Government to buy 5 million dollars of silver bullion each month.   They were, however, defeated at the elections, and the law of March 14, 1900, expressly stated that the *gold* dollar was to be the standard unit of value : the silver dollar still retains the quality of legal tender, but its coinage is limited.[2]

[1] The States of South America are, in fact, under the system of paper money.

The countries of Asia are, as a rule, silver monometallists, except India, which since 1893 has been bimetallist, the English sovereign and the silver rupee both being admitted as legal money, in the fixed ratio of 15 rupees to the pound.   China, by a decree of 1910, adopted the silver 5-franc piece, the *yuan*, as standard.

[2] The United States did not adopt the same ratio between the value of the two metals as did the Latin Union ; the relation between their gold dollar and silver dollar being 1 : 16.

Mexico in 1904 followed the example of the United States, by adopting the

Why, then, do these States not cut the slender thread which still binds them to bimetallism, and adopt monometallism as the other nations have done ?

There are two difficulties in the way, one a matter of practice, the other of principle.

(1) The practical obstacle is that the adoption of the gold standard involves the demonetising of silver. If the 5-franc piece is no more to be legal tender, it will have to be withdrawn from circulation. Now, it is calculated that in France these 5-franc pieces represent two billion francs, nominal value, which, if sold by weight, would be worth only one billion. This operation would therefore cost a billion francs, and probably much more, since it would bring about a further fall in the value of the silver metal.[1]

(2) The objection on principle is, that fluctuations in prices are much more to be apprehended with a single standard of value than with a double standard.

We know that every variation in the value of money results immediately in an inverse variation in prices (cf. above, p. 231). Now, when there is only one money, it is to be feared that such variations would be more frequent and abrupt, throwing the whole commercial organisation out of gear and provoking frequent crises.

When, on the contrary, two moneys are used for measuring values, *a kind of compensation is set up between them*, very favourable to stability of prices and consequently to prosperity of trade ; for in business stability is of first importance. This phenomenon of compensation is somewhat difficult to explain, but it is possible to obtain a rough idea of the way in which it works.

We have only to bear in mind that the principal cause of the superiority of the precious metals, in so far as they are measures of value, lies in the fact that variations in their quantity are insignificant compared with the total amount of them in existence (cf. supra, p. 236). Now the greater the total stock and the more varied the sources which supply it, the more stable will the value of the metals be. If the stock consists of two metals, there will be, to begin with, a double quantity of it, and as it is unlikely that the causes which bring

gold standard, leaving, however, to the silver piastre its legal currency. She adopted the ratio, more in keeping with fact, of 1 to 32·58.

[1] It will be said, perhaps, that the State might leave those who had the 5-franc pieces in their possession to bear the loss. But this would not be a very honourable proceeding on the part of State, which has guaranteed the value of these coins by its own stamp ; moreover, it would be the ruin of the Bank of France, which has in its coffers about 700 million francs in silver, and would lose 350 millions, *i.e.* nearly double its share capital.

about an over-production of either one or other of the metals will act simultaneously, the variations will be less felt. A river is not so liable to sudden and dangerous floods if its tributaries are numerous, its sources far apart and very different in their geological and climatic characteristics. The risings of the Seine, whose tributaries come from all directions, are generally harmless,[1] while those of the Loire, or the Garonne, whose main tributaries all rise in the same region, are disastrous. It is preferable, therefore, for our reservoir of metal to be fed from two sources of different origin, gold and silver, than from one single source And if there were three or four, the level would be still more steady, so that, theoretically, *poly*metallism would be better than bimetallism. Indeed, if there had been no metal but gold, the discovery of the gold mines of California and Australia would have caused a most profound disturbance, through an excessive rise in prices ; and this may still one day be the effect of the Transvaal and the Klondike mines. The exhaustion of these mines, again, would cause a still more formidable disturbance. It matters little whether prices are high or low : what matters greatly is that they should not rise or fall suddenly. The ideal of a good monetary system is *stability of prices.*

Bimetallists are not only unwilling to give up their system, but are anxious to convert gold monometallist countries to it. They declare that none of the dreaded difficulties would arise if the system were established by an *international agreement* among all the Great Powers, on the basis of 15½ to 1, or any other ratio that might be determined by them.

This statement comes as a shock to economists of the Classical school. The fixing of the relative value of gold and silver, *ne varietur*, cannot, they say, depend on the will of any government, nor even of all governments combined, any more than can the relative values of sheep and oxen, or of wheat and oats. The value of things is fixed

---

[1] The floods of January 1910 only confirm this rule ; they were so disastrous just because so unexpected, having had no precedent for two centuries and a half (1658).

Leaving metaphors aside, this is but a particular instance of the *law of substitution* (see above, pp. 39 and 222), according to which, whenever, in consumption, one product can be substituted for another, their values necessarily tend to become equal. If electricity can be substituted for gas for lighting purposes and *vice versa*, the price of gas will necessarily be regulated by that of electricity. Now, there is no more perfect case of substitution than that of the silver franc for the gold franc, or *vice versa*, under a true bimetallist system ; that is to say, where there is a free coinage of the two metals. So long, therefore, as one may be used for the other indifferently, it cannot be worth more or less than the other.

solely by the law of demand and supply, and is quite beyond the reach of the legislator; that of the precious metals is no exception to the rule.

This reasoning of the Classical school is, in our view, too absolute. Gold and silver, for the very reason that they are used principally for money, are not goods of the same sort as sheep and oxen, or any other commodity. When we speak of the demand for the precious metals we mean almost exclusively the demand made by a dozen or so large States for their Mints. Now, there is nothing absurd in the idea that, if this dozen or so of buyers were to agree among themselves to fix the relative prices of gold and silver, they could succeed in doing so. If they were to declare that they would all buy the kilogramme of gold on the basis of 3100 francs, and the kilogramme of silver on that of 200 francs, it is more than probable that they would make this the law of the market.

It would be absurd, says the Classical school, to decree that an ox shall always be worth ten sheep, or that a quarter of corn shall always be worth two quarters of oats. True, no doubt, since the market for these goods is immense, and each one of us, by his individual purchases, helps to regulate its current price. But if there were only a dozen persons in the world who had any use for sheep and oxen, it is quite probable that by combining they could fix their prices at the rate of 1 to 10, or at any other rate which pleased them. Similar results have often been obtained under less favourable conditions, by coalitions of large merchants in commercial speculations.[1] (See *Cartels and Trusts.*)

This conclusion must not, of course, be pushed to an extreme. It is obviously beyond the power of governments, even if unanimous, to decree that gold and silver shall be on an equal footing, or that their relation shall be reversed and a kilogramme of silver be worth 15 kilogrammes of gold. Such a decision would remain a dead letter, because the industrial use of the precious metals, though less important than their use as money (absorbing at present

---

[1] There are, indeed, numerous proofs of the influence of the legislator on the prices of the precious metals : for example, the stability of the ratio between the value of the two metals which lasted nearly three-quarters of a century, thanks to the French law ; the fall in silver produced by its demonetisation in Germany, aggravated later by the convention which suppressed its coinage in the Latin Union and hastened recently by a similar suppression in India ; or, again, the stability which the British Government has maintained for some ten years in the latter country. The Government has established a legal relation between gold and silver (sovereign = 15 silver rupees), which it maintains by suspending the coinage of the metal which has fallen and coining that which has risen in value.

about 40 per cent. of the total output), cannot be neglected, and would be enough to prevent the fixation of so extravagant a ratio. All the governments in the world could not make silver worth the same as gold : men and women would never pay as much for a silver watch as for a gold one.[1]

Within reasonable limits, however, we do not hesitate to believe that an international agreement would be quite effective in fixing the respective values of the two metals, and in eliminating the principal drawback to bimetallism, viz., the disappearance of one of the two moneys. For where would it go, since in every country it would be subject to the same law ?

Is such an international agreement actually possible ? That is another question. It does not appear so, in view of the fact that every country holds it a point of honour to adopt the gold standard. The British Government in particular, whose co-operation would be indispensable to the re-establishment of bimetallism, has always rejected the idea. And even the nations which have established a legal ratio between the two metals have fixed on quite different ones (the United States 1 to 16, Austria 1 to 18·22, Russia 1 to 23·25, Japan 1 to 32·33, etc.).

It would seem better therefore for bimetallist countries simply to keep their *status quo*.[2] Such a policy might have been dangerous more than ten years ago, when the production of gold was becoming remarkably scarce, so that there was doubt as to whether there would be enough gold for all the States which wanted to adopt it as standard, or whether those which delayed might not come too late. But, in the closing years of the nineteenth century the output of gold more than quadrupled, and there is some ground for thinking that it may one day increase at as great a rate as, or even at a greater rate than, that of silver. The difference in value between the two metals will probably, therefore, diminish, and we may see a movement in the opposite direction from that of the years 1870–1895. The annual production of gold, which, in 1882, had fallen to almost

---

[1] Let us add that if, on this hypothesis, we were able successfully to keep the values of gold and silver at the same level, the gold mines would soon be abandoned for lack of profit—the cost of production of gold being normally greater than that of silver—while there would be an over-production of silver. This measure would end sooner or later, then, in suppressing the production of gold.

[2] A commission of delegates from the United States and Mexico was sent to Europe, in 1903, to see if an agreement could be come to for resuming the coinage of silver. The very interesting report of this commission, which was, however, unsuccessful, has been published (*Introduction of the Gold-Exchange Standard,* 1903–1904, Washington).

150,000 kilogrammes (500 million francs) has reached over 700,000 kilogrammes (2400 million francs) to-day (1912).   And auriferous soil is being found to some extent everywhere.[1]

It is true that the production of silver has also greatly increased, rising from 2,150,000 kilogrammes in 1875 (worth at that time at par 430 million francs) to over 7,000,000 kilogrammes in 1912 (a quantity which, however, in view of the fall in the value of silver, represents only about 700 million francs).   Still, the output of silver is increasing less rapidly than is that of gold (311 per cent. as against 466 per cent.) and the relation between the annual outputs of the two metals is now no more than 1 to 10.   The present ratio of value, 1 to 30, does not therefore at all correspond to their respective outputs.   Thus, if the gold source continues to flow as abundantly as ever, we have no doubt that the value of silver will rise once more, and it is not at all impossible that it may one day return to the old legal ratio.

The question of bimetallism has, then, lost much of its acuteness. There is no risk for bimetallist nations in remaining as they are ; and if they should at some future time decide to adopt gold monometallism the step will be less costly than to-day.   The solution of the problem is becoming daily easier and, at the same time, less urgent.[2]

Only, as gold has become in practice the only international money, bimetallist countries must take care that they have a sufficient stock of it.[3]   Otherwise they will be obliged to resort to the costly expedient of buying it, in order to make their payments abroad.   (See *infra*, p. 440, *Foreign Exchanges*.)

[1] The average for the five years, 1881–1885, was 152,500 kilogrammes, worth 625 million francs (with a minimum of 516 millions in 1882).   It was 697,000 kilogrammes in 1911 and 707,600 kilogrammes in 1912.   True, all this gold is not coined, and about 40 per cent. is employed in industry.   India also is now hoarding gold rather than silver.

[2] The crisis of 1907 provided a new argument for bimetallism.   Thanks to bimetallism France was able to face the reaction of the crisis unshaken, and was even in a position to lend effective help to England.   The Bank of France was, in fact, able to defend its gold reserve, without having to resort like all the other banks to a rise in the rate of discount, simply by discounting in silver instead of in gold.   And it was able to lend some millions sterling to the Bank of England and to the United States (see *infra*, p. 413, *Banks*).

[3] It was with this very object that Russia some years ago required the customs duties to be paid in gold, and Spain and Portugal are following the same policy to-day.

CHAPTER VI : PAPER MONEY

I : WHETHER METALLIC MONEY CAN BE REPLACED BY PAPER MONEY

IF we did not know already, by daily experience, that paper money can be substituted for metallic money, we should have some difficulty in believing it possible, and the question at the head of this chapter would appear somewhat strange.

Obviously it is impossible to substitute for wheat, coal, or any other form of wealth, mere pieces of paper with the words " 100 bushels of wheat " or " 100 tons of coal " written on them. Pieces of paper can neither feed nor warm us. And even if our only use for coins were to hang them round our necks, as the daughters of the East wear their sequins, it is clear that bits of paper of different colours could not take their place. But we know that money is not like any other form of wealth, and that, in our civilised societies, its utility is not of a material nature. A coin is no more than an *order* giving us a right to claim, under certain conditions, part of the wealth existing in the world (see p. 289). Now, this function may equally well be undertaken by a piece of paper, in fact better, as regards facility of circulation. The financier Law, though he led France to bankruptcy by his premature experiments, had at least the merit of perfectly understanding and demonstrating this. And the best proof of it is the increasing use of paper money. Already, in France, nine-tenths (in value) of the sum total of payments are made in notes, and coins are used only for small daily expenses. To make the matter clearer we must distinguish between three different kinds of paper money :

(*1*) *Representative* paper money, which merely represents an equivalent amount of metallic money deposited somewhere, say in the safes of a bank, where it serves as guarantee.[1]

When the public, for instance, finds the silver crown pieces too cumbersome, the bank keeps them in its safe and replaces them in circulation by certificates and cheques, which, just because they are of paper, are more easily handled. This first form of paper money can present no difficulty.

[1] During the crisis of 1907 in the United States, the banks issued cheques not payable in money, and *certificates*, guaranteed solely by securities, which were taken eagerly by the public.

(2) *Fiduciary* paper money, which takes the form of a credit document, or a promise to pay a certain sum of money. It is clear that the value of this promise depends solely on the solvency of the debtor ; if there is full confidence in his solvency, if, as is sometimes said in business language, " the signature is as good as gold," there is clearly no reason why this piece of paper should not circulate as easily as metallic money. Bank-notes generally fall under this second category, except in a few particular cases which we shall discuss later on.

(3) *Conventional* paper money, which represents nothing at all and gives no right to anything. It is for this form that the name *paper money* in the strict sense ought to be reserved. It consists of pieces of paper issued by a State which has no coin. These pieces of paper bear, it is true, such inscriptions as " note for 100 (or for 1000) francs," and thus have the appearance, like the other kinds of paper money, of a promise to pay a certain sum of money. But it is well known that this is a pure fiction and that the State will not redeem them, since it has no money with which to do so. It is in this third form, more particularly, that the substitution of paper for metallic money is difficult to understand. And it is not indeed an easy matter to bring about. Still, experience in all countries has shown that, under certain conditions, such substitution is possible, and that the public submits to it readily enough. Russia, and the republics of South America, have been under this system for some generations. And why not ? If by law and general consent —which ought always to ratify, in a measure, the declaration of the legislator—these bits of white or blue paper are invested with the power of being able to pay purchases, debts and taxes, what is to prevent their circulating just as readily as white or yellow coins ?

Yet we must admit that between the value of metallic money and that of paper money there will always be serious differences. Paper money will always be more *precarious*, more *restricted*, more *variable*.

(1) The value of paper money is *precarious* because it depends solely on the will of the legislator, and the law which creates it can also annihilate it. If the law were to demonetise paper money, there would be nothing left in the hands of the holders of it but a worthless rag ; for when paper money has lost its legal value it has lost everything. It is not quite the same in the case of metallic money. Apart from its legal value metallic money has also a natural value which it owes to the industrial properties and to the scarcity of the metal of

which it is composed. No doubt, if gold and silver were to be demonetised *in all countries*,[1] metallic money would lose the greater part of its value : we must not be under any illusions in this respect.[2] The very fact that the demonetising of silver money in a few countries alone caused a considerable fall in the value of the metal is a sufficient proof of this. But even so, the precious metals would still retain a certain utility, since they could be put to industrial uses. And as these uses would become more important and more numerous as the value of the metal fell, it is possible that the fall would not be so great as some think. Suppose the precious metals fell to two-thirds or three-fourths of their present value. The holder of demonetised coin would still possess a certain value which the law could not take away, probably a higher value than would have remained had any other commodity been chosen as legal money.

(2) The value of paper money is more *restricted*, for, as this value is conferred on it by law, it cannot extend beyond the limits

---

[1] We say "in all countries," for if it were demonetised only in one, its value would not be sensibly diminished. And that is just wherein the greatest security of the holder of metallic money lies.

[2] Many economists are, however, under this illusion, or at least do not sufficiently put their readers on their guard against it. Most of them imply that the State seal imprinted on gold and silver coins merely states their real value, as do the prices marked on goods. But the declaration that the piece of gold of 6 grammes is worth 20 francs is not simply a *declaration ;* it is, in part, an *attribution* of value. It is because the will of the legislator—ratified, if you will, by that of the people—has chosen gold and silver as money, that these metals have acquired the greater part of their value. And they would lose at least half, and probably more, so soon as this law or convention were to disappear. This is what Aristotle saw clearly when he said in his *Ethics :* "It was by a voluntary agreement that money became the instrument of exchange. It is called *numisma* from *nomos*, signifying law, because money does not exist by nature ; it only exists by law, and the changing of it or depriving it of its utility depends on us " (*Nichomachean Ethics*, Book V).

But we must not conclude from this, as some economists (notably Cernuschi) have done, that the value of the precious metals is *purely conventional*. For an object to have any recognised utility and value, the will and choice of men must come into play ; but if this will and choice are determined by *natural* causes, the value which results will itself be natural and not at all conventional. The choice which men made in singling out the precious metals was in no way arbitrary. It was dictated by the very real qualities that these metals possess. Even wheat owes its value, in great part, to the fact that most civilised men have adopted this cereal out of so many others for their food ; and if they ever replaced it by another, there is no doubt that its value would vanish. Still, no one would dream of saying that the value of wheat is conventional. The same holds good of the precious metals. The only difference is, that it is easier to find a substitute for the precious metals as money, than to find a substitute for wheat as food.

of the territory subject to that law.[1] Paper money cannot, therefore, be used in settling international exchanges The value of metallic money, on the contrary, as it is regulated by that of the metal, is almost the same in all civilised countries ; metallic money can therefore circulate everywhere, if not as coined money, at least as bullion. This is why metallic money is essentially a universal and international money, while paper money by its very nature remains a national money.

(3) Lastly, the value of paper money is generally more *variable* than that of metallic money, for the reason that the quantity of paper money depends on the will of men, while the quantity of metallic money depends on natural causes, such as the discovery of new mines. The one is issued by governments, the other by nature. It is therefore within the power of a short-sighted legislator to depreciate the paper money by issuing too great a quantity, and this happens only too frequently ; whereas it is not within the power of any government to depreciate metallic money to the same degree.

It is true that the discovery of exceptionally rich mines may at any moment throw a large quantity of the precious metals on the world's market, and thus bring down the value of metallic money. It is also true that, when a period of depression follows on a period of activity, a country may find that too much metallic money has been drawn into it. This has happened more than once ; but, since these variations extend over the whole surface of the civilised world, they never have the far-reaching nor the fatal consequences that variations in the quantity of paper money involve. Sought after and accepted everywhere, the precious metals, if they are in excess in one country, are not slow to flow of themselves into other countries. But sudden increases in paper money, being always confined within the limits of a particular country, which forms, as it were, a closed reservoir out of which there is no outlet, are disastrous.

Such are the disadvantages which render paper money so imperfect an instrument of exchange compared with metallic money. But they would be greatly minimised if all civilised countries were to bind themselves by an international agreement :

(1) To give legal currency to one single paper money.

(2) Not to increase the quantity of it, or to increase it only in a

---

[1] No doubt a Bank of France note will be accepted abroad by a money changer or by anyone who knows the Bank of France, and knows what its signature is worth. But in this case it is received, not as money, but as a credit document, that is to say, with the intention of having it cashed, just as a note signed by the Rothschilds would also be accepted in every country.

proportion fixed beforehand, calculated for each country according, say, to the increase of its population.

In this case the value of paper money, although still conventional—artificial, if you will—would have a basis as large as, and more stable than, that of metallic money itself, since it would rest on the unanimous consent of nations. For if, as we said a little while ago, metallic money is issued by nature and paper money by governments, it must be remembered that nature is blind, while governments must not be so. Nowadays, as we shall see, their means of obtaining information are quite sufficient to enable them to regulate the issue of paper money according to the needs of circulation. This being so, the quantity of paper money would be regulated by scientific foresight, not by mere chance, and its value would be less likely to vary It is probably this form that the money of the future will take.

The fact that paper money is artificial is by no means a sign of inferiority. Quite the contrary. The chronometer is an artificial instrument for measuring time, while the sun is a natural one. But this does not prevent the chronometer from being much better for the purpose than the sun. The substitution of artificial for natural instruments is the very characteristic of progress—the gun for the stick, the locomotive for the horse, the electric lamp for the light of the sun and the stove for its heat.

II : WHETHER THE CREATION OF A PAPER MONEY IS EQUIVALENT TO THE CREATION OF WEALTH

THE men who first had the idea of creating paper money [1] flattered themselves that they had thereby increased the general wealth just as if they had discovered a gold mine, or brought about the permutation of metals, the *magnum opus* dreamed of by the alchemists.

---

[1] We do not know who invented paper money. It was known in China from time immemorial, and the traveller, Marco Polo, brought back a description of it in the fourteenth century. Antiquity has left us many specimens of moneys, if not of paper, at any rate of leather or of some purely conventional value, which were called *siege money*, because, as a rule, they were issued in besieged towns to make up for the lack of metallic money.

It was the financier Law who first issued paper money on a large scale, in 1721 ; it is well known to what a catastrophe his system led. The notes issued by Law's bank were really bank-notes repayable in metallic money, and continued so up to the day when the excessive issue of shares in colonial enterprises and enormous loans to the State obliged the bank to establish forced currency. The assignats of the Revolution, on the other hand, of which we shall speak presently, were purely a paper money.

Their idea, in this form, was evidently absurd, for it assumed that wealth could be created *ex nihilo*. And yet it has been too much ridiculed. For it is quite true that the issue of a paper money may increase, in a certain measure, the quantity of wealth existing in a country. It was Adam Smith who first explained how. He pointed out that the metallic money circulating in a country is unproductive capital, and that the substitution of paper money, by setting this capital free, allows it to be utilised for productive purposes. Thus, in a comparison which has become famous, he likens metallic money to roads, and declares that if we could find a way of travelling in the air we might restore to cultivation and production all the surface of the soil now occupied by the roads.

Adam Smith's ingenious comparison, however, leaves our minds in some obscurity. It is easy to see that, so soon as we no longer need roads or railways, the ground which they occupy might be cleared and given over to cultivation and production—in France alone this would amount to about a million acres—but it is not so easy to see what could be done with metallic money so soon as we had discovered how to do without it. Should we melt it down for plate or for earrings ? There would be little to gain by that. No, we should employ it in purchases or investments abroad : this is where our profit would come in. France has a capital of over 7 billion francs in the form of gold and silver money. This enormous capital brings her in nothing. Suppose some means were found of substituting paper money for it, she would immediately have 7 billions to invest abroad in stock, railway shares, land, ships, or in introducing improvements in industry and agriculture, which in one way or another might bring in 5 to 10 per cent., *i.e.* 500 to 600 million francs of income.

Families who possess very valuable silver plate or jewels sometimes act on this principle, replacing these by imitation metal or false stones, and realising the capital thus invested so as to increase their incomes; also well-advised individuals, who, knowing that money brings in nothing so long as it sleeps in their pockets or in their safes, keep no more than they need at home, and invest all the rest. The richest people are often those who have the least money in their houses. The economical peasant has a secret drawer full of gold and silver coins, but the millionaire has only a cheque-book with which to pay his tradesmen.

Nations do the same. While France uses 7 billions of coin, England, more expert as regards credit, is content with three. She is not the poorer for that; quite the contrary. When therefore the question is asked, " Can a State, or can banks, by issuing paper money, really increase the wealth of the country ? " we must not answer with an unqualified negative. The thing is, in reality, feasible ; paper money may increase the wealth of a country, *but only up to the quantity of the existing metallic money.* If France were to replace the 7 billions of coin which she possesses by an equal sum in paper money, she might increase her wealth to the extent of 7 billions, but not a penny more. And this, again, is a theoretical maximum, for in actual practice it would be very risky to go right to the limit.

It is important to note that this gain cannot be realised by all nations at the same time. One country may utilise its supply of metal productively by selling it abroad, but, if every country were to do the same, clearly none would succeed. Gold and silver specie, offered by all the countries that were trying to get rid of it and demanded by none, would become a drug on the market and of no further value. It is here, in our opinion, that Adam Smith's comparison errs somewhat. For if we could find a way of doing without roads, all countries would benefit *at the same time* from the new utility and productiveness of these lands hitherto given over to transport. Still, even on this hypothesis of a universal paper money, the human race would always find some advantage in doing without the precious metals. For it would henceforth save all the labour annually expended in maintaining its metallic stock ; in turning bullion into money ; in filling up the gaps daily caused by friction and accidental loss ; above all, in keeping the quantity of it up to the level demanded by an ever-increasing commerce and population. And this is no small labour. Extraction from the mines, smelting, transport, coinage, exchange, etc., represent the labour of hundreds of thousands of workers—quite an army. Do away with the use of metallic money, and all these workers will be free for some new form of production ; the productive force of humanity will be increased to this extent.

In short, the answer to the question at the head of this chapter is very different from what it used to be. We must no longer say that paper money increases the wealth of a country *to the extent that it increases its monetary stock,* but, on the contrary, *to the extent that it allows this to be reduced.*

Such is the *economic* advantage which the issue of paper money may bring to a country. But it is of interest only to economists, and is not the motive which determines governments to issue paper money. The aim of the latter is a more practical and simple one, viz., a *financial* advantage. When a government finds itself short of money, the creation of paper money is a very convenient method of paying its contractors, its officers, and its stores, *without being obliged to borrow and consequently without being obliged to pay interest*. When a government is in this situation, its credit is probably not of the best, and if it is forced to borrow, the rate of interest will be very high. Here is a case where paper money is an economy by no means to be despised. Many States have resorted to it and have been none the worse, provided, of course, that they did not issue beyond the limit we mentioned, viz., the quantity of metallic money in circulation.[1] Every issue beyond this limit results only in depreciating the paper money and in inflicting on the country and on the State itself a much greater loss than any economy gained.

III: OF THE DANGERS WHICH RESULT FROM THE USE OF PAPER MONEY AND OF THE MEANS OF PREVENTING THEM

The advantages of paper money, either to a country or to a government, are real enough, but they may be too dearly bought, more dearly than they are worth. Thus, paper money has even been referred to as " the greatest curse of nations; it is in the moral sphere what the plague is in the physical." [2]

But it is worth while noticing that these evil effects are due more to the imprudence of governments than to the nature of paper money itself. They only appear, in fact, when the government has tried to go beyond the limit of which we spoke and to issue a greater quantity of paper money than there is need for. For the need can be quite sufficiently measured by the quantity of

[1] During the Franco-German War the French Government needed money and issued 1500 millions of francs in notes. If it had borrowed them it would have had to pay about 6 per cent., or 90 million francs per annum. If it had been willing to issue this paper money directly, it need have paid nothing at all except the expenses of manufacture. But it preferred, and with good reason, to do so through the Bank of France, to which it paid a commission of 1 per cent.: this cost it only 15 millions per annum. The country, in this case, gained too, as the money in circulation was quite insufficient, having been either exported for the purpose of buying arms abroad, or, what is more likely, hoarded away. The issue of these notes was therefore a benefit all round. Indeed, the quantity issued was a good deal less than the demand, since several private banks were obliged to associate to issue small notes below 5 francs to meet the public convenience.

[2] Circular of October 25, 1810, of M. de Montalivet, speaking in the name of Napoleon I.

metallic money usually in circulation. Unfortunately, the temptation to overstep this fatal limit is very great in the case of impecunious governments; many have done so and have ended in bankruptcy.[1]

It may however safely be said that, in the present state of economic science, a government which oversteps the limit is really inexcusable. For there are certain signs, familiar to the economist and the financier, which allow us to recognise the danger even from afar, and which give surer indications than sounding-lead or bearings give the pilot.

(*1*) The first of these signs is the *premium on gold.* No sooner has paper money been issued in excess than, according to the constant law of values, it begins to depreciate, and the first effect of this depreciation, the first sign which indicates it, while it is as yet invisible to the eyes of the public, is that metallic money is at a premium. Its unchanged value stands out, in the general depreciation of paper money, as rocks emerge in the outgoing tide. Bankers and money-changers begin to collect it, in order to send it abroad as

---

[1] Every one knows the lamentable history of the *assignats*, which were issued by the Convention and the Directory. The first *assignats* were issued in August 1789. At the outset the depreciation was fairly slow, and by the end of 1791 was still no more than 8 per cent. But by the end of 1792 the *assignat* of 100 *livres* had fallen to 72 francs, and in 1793 to 22 francs. There was a moment's pause. Then, in 1795, it fell to 2 francs, and in March 1796 to 30 centimes ! And yet these *assignats* had the confiscated property of the emigrants and of the Church as guarantee. The quantity issued was, however, far in excess of the value of the property, viz., 45 billion francs, or about twenty times the quantity of the coin actually existing at the time. Even if this issue had been of good gold and silver, it would have caused a considerable depreciation of the metallic money, since it would have been twenty times greater than what was required. We can imagine, therefore, what the depreciation of a simple paper money must have been. A pair of boots was known to sell for 4700 francs.

Even in buying national property, or in paying taxes, only a certain quantity of these *assignats* could be utilised, as the government itself would no longer accept them at their nominal value, but only at a value calculated according to official scales of depreciation which were constantly changing and diminishing.

Without going so far back as this, in Colombia, in 1903, the paper piastre which was worth, at par, 5 francs, fell to less than 5 centimes. An egg sold for 2½ piastres (12 francs 50) and a mule for 30,000 piastres (150,000 francs).

Experience has shown that when the issue of paper money is confided to banks instead of being undertaken directly by the government, it operates, as a rule, with much more moderation and presents fewer dangers, as bankers are more vigilant in the defence of their interests, or at least those of their shareholders, than is, alas ! the Treasury in the defence of public interests. Most governments to-day resort to this method. See the chapter on Credit, *The Difference between the Bank-note and Paper Money.*

bullion, and pay a little extra to obtain it. This, then, is the moment for the financier to open his eyes.

(2) The second is *a rise in the rate of exchange.* Bills payable abroad, *i.e.* foreign bills of exchange, are bought and sold in great quantities in all the large commercial centres of the world. Like every other commodity, they h. ve a quoted price, called the rate of exchange. Now, these bills or claims on foreign countries are always payable in gold or silver, more often in gold, as it is the international money. If, therefore, France were under the *régime* of paper money and this paper money were depreciated, we should immediately see the bills on foreign countries, on London *e.g.*, rise in price like gold itself, since they are in fact worth gold. Thus, if the 20-franc gold piece were at a premium of 2 per cent. and selling at 20 francs 40, the bill of exchange of 25 francs on London would rise to an equal premium and would sell at 25 francs 50. (See p. 440, *Foreign Exchanges.*)

(3) The third sign is the *flight of metallic money.* However slight the depreciation of paper money may be, if this depreciation is not immediately checked by the withdrawal of the excess notes, the small remaining quantity of metallic money will quickly disappear from circulation. This phenomenon is a sure characteristic, and is seen in all countries where the system of paper money has been abused—in the whole of South America, for instance, although this is the home of gold and silver mines. We have explained this in detail in connection with Gresham's law and need not repeat it here (see p. 297).

(4) The fourth is a *rise in prices.* This appears only later, and indicates that the evil is already serious and that the permitted limit has been far over-passed. So long, indeed, as the depreciation of paper money is slight, say, for example, 2 per cent. or 3 per cent., prices, except those of gold and silver bullion, are hardly affected. Neither retail nor wholesale dealers will raise the price of their goods for so slight a difference, and even if they did so the public would not feel uneasy. But so soon as the depreciation of paper money reaches 10 per cent., 12 per cent. or 15 per cent. all the tradesmen and producers raise their prices in proportion. The evil, which till then was latent, now breaks forth and shows itself in the light of day.[1]

---

[1] Business men and producers are by no means averse to a rise in prices. So readily do they adapt themselves to it, that they even become attached to the system of paper money and oppose its abolition, as this would result in restoring the old prices. When the United States was under the system of

(5) Lastly, we must note that the old prices do not change for those who are still able to pay in metallic money. Metallic money, indeed, far from losing in value, has gained. We see, then, the curious spectacle of a *duplication of prices*. Each article has now two prices, one payable in metallic money, the other in paper money. The difference between the two prices exactly measures the depreciation of the paper money.

So soon, then, as a government perceives the premonitory signs, viz., a premium on gold, or a rise in the rate of exchange,[1] its first duty is to forbid absolutely any further issue of paper money: it has in fact reached the limit at which it must stop. If it has had the misfortune to go beyond the limit, if it is now faced with the ominous symptoms of a rise in, and a duplication of, prices, it must retrace its steps and destroy all the paper money as this returns to the treasury, until the right proportions are reached again. Such an heroic remedy, however, involving as it does the partial sacrifice of State revenue, is not within the power of all governments. It can be applied only where governments have a surplus in their budgets, or are able to give up a part of their revenue.

IV: THE CHEQUE

THOUGH paper money has the advantage of economising metallic money, it is, as we have seen, only at the price of serious drawbacks and even of great dangers. If, therefore, some means could be found of economising metallic money without having recourse to so dangerous a substitute, this would indeed be a great boon.

Now, such a means does exist, more radical and at the same time less harmful. It does not force metallic money out, but dispenses with the necessity of using it. We refer to the *cheque*. Although the following explanations would be better understood after studying credit, the chapter on money would be incomplete if we did not indicate the means by which to-day we are enabled

paper money there was a distinct party, significantly called "Green-backers," which did all in its power to maintain paper money; and the same party is to be found again to-day in the Argentine Republic. For the explanation of this fact, see p. 293.

[1] When, after the war of 1870, France was under the paper-money system and all her gold was passing into Germany to pay the war indemnity, the premium on gold rose for a moment to $2\frac{1}{2}$ per cent. (50 centimes on a gold 20-franc piece). This was not much, but it was enough to put the government on its guard, and the danger was averted.

to dispense with money. The cheque is not, strictly speaking, an
,instrument of credit ; it is an instrument of payment.

For the juridical and economic nature of the cheque is such
that it always presupposes a sum of money, a *provision*, as it is
called in French, at the bank. It is distinguished in this from credit
documents, which we shall study later, from the bill of exchange,
and even from the bank-note, none of which necessarily presupposes
an equivalent sum in money in the coffers of the bank.[1]

This is what takes place in practice, in England, let us say.
Whenever an Englishman has to make a payment of any sort, even
for his current expenses, *e.g.* to a tradesman, he gives him a cheque—
that is to say, an order to pay, on his banker. This order, of course,
presupposes a deposit of money made first of all at the banker's.
The tradesman does not take the trouble to cash the cheque, but
sends it to his own banker, who very often does not cash it either.
For, as all the bankers in England are reciprocally debtors and
creditors for enormous sums, their correspondents in London have
only to come to an understanding and to balance their accounts.
This they do in the *Clearing House* (established in 1773),[2] where, by
means of simple entries in bank books, business to the amount of
over 14 billions sterling per annum, or over 40 millions sterling per
day is done. The Clearing House of New York liquidates still more
colossal sums (over 20 billions sterling, since Stock Exchange
operations are also included).[3] In settling the differences of these

---

[1] Still, in actual fact, the cheque is on the boundary line which separates
money from credit, for it is often paid by the banker when he has no corresponding
sum to his client's account, if the latter has a current account with him. And, in
any case, the creditor who receives a cheque in payment takes it on faith, for he
is never certain of being paid ; it is quite possible that there is no balance at the
bank, or that the signature is forged, or that the cheque has been stolen.

The cheque is used for the largest payments as well as for those of household
expenditure. When China paid her war indemnity to Japan in 1896 an instal-
ment of £8,250,000 was paid by the Chinese ambassador to the Japanese
ambassador by means of a simple cheque on the Bank of England, without a
single penny passing. Similarly, after the Russo-Japanese War in 1906, a
cheque of £4,840,000 was remitted by the Russian Embassy in London to the
Japanese ambassador.

[2] They do not all meet together, of course. Twenty-eight of them come,
bringing the cheques of all the other bankers, their correspondents. Each one
writes down what he owes and what is owed to him, and the differences are finally
settled in a draft on the Bank of England, where the whole transaction is
centralised.

[3] In France this system is not nearly so much used. The Bank of France,
however, acts as Clearing House, and delivers to those of its clients, particularly
bankers, who wish to use this method of payment, special cheques called *mandats*

enormous operations only a trifling amount of metallic money is required (about 3 per cent.).

This system is facilitated by the use, particularly in England, of the *crossed cheque*. The crossed cheque must be paid, like all cheques, through a bank, but it must besides be paid to the banker to whom it is crossed, *i.e.* whose name is written between the lines drawn obliquely across the cheque. This banker himself never cashes it, but settles it at the clearing house with his colleagues. The crossed cheque, therefore, is a cheque which can be used for settlement only by way of the clearing house, so that it has been humorously defined as a cheque drawn never to be paid. The German law of 1908 makes it possible, indeed, to prevent the cheque ever being paid in money by writing on it the words " To be carried to account." As the crossed cheque is of use only to the banker whose name it bears, it matters little if it be stolen or lost, since the illegitimate possessor would not be able to do anything with it, unless he had himself a current account with the banker to whom it was crossed, and had the audacity to have it carried over to his credit. Even in this case the fraud would soon be discovered.

In France the crossed cheque is little used. The ordinary cheque is much used in business, but not very often for daily expenditure. The middle-class Frenchman as a rule keeps his securities at home, cashes his dividends directly, and pays his tradesmen himself. He has therefore no need of cheques. Moreover, the use of the cheque implies a certain education on the part of the public. A tradesman can accept a cheque in payment only from a trustworthy person, 'for there is no guarantee that it will ever be paid.

We might perhaps go even further and do without the cheque altogether. Suppose all Frenchmen without exception were to open an account at the same bank, which undertook to register each client's receipts and expenses. Under such a system money might be dispensed with to the last farthing. Every time I made a purchase, instead of paying my tradesman, I should simply authorise the bank to place the sum to the debit of my account and to the credit of my tradesman : he, in turn, every time he bought supplies, would do the same. If I were making an investment, the proceeding would be exactly similar. The bank would place to my debit the sum representing the value of the security bought, and an equal value to the credit of the company which issued it, or of the holder who had sold it to me. At the end of the year the bank would send each

rouges to the annual amount of over 8 billions sterling. There is a clearing house in Paris, but it clears barely 800 millions sterling.

person his account, which would be closed by a balance either in favour of the bank, or in favour of the client. This balance would be carried over to the next year, to the debit of the client in the first case, to his credit in the second, and so on. It is clear that, if this system were generalised, it would be possible, theoretically, to regulate the sum total of transactions by a few lines of writing. Such a bank, in fact, would not be very different from the one of which Proudhon dreamt and which he tried to realise in his famous *Banque d'Échange*.[1]

If it is an impossibility for all Frenchmen to be clients of the Bank of France, there is an institution of which all Frenchmen are necessarily clients, which might undertake the function, viz., the Post Office, which has branches in every commune, whose postmen go from house to house, and which takes and carries for every one. There has been some suggestion of profiting by this situation and of making the Post Office play the part of universal banker. All that it would need to do would be to open a current account for any one who wanted it, and give him a cheque-book. Thereafter the debtor would only need to pay in, at the nearest Post Office, the sum due to his creditor and the Post Office would undertake to write it to the credit of the latter. If the creditor had no current account at the Post Office, the debtor in this case would send him a cheque, which the latter would cash like an ordinary postal order. This system might therefore theoretically dispense entirely with money as an instrument of exchange, and would meanwhile render great service by doing away with the troublesome and costly collecting of subscriptions, bills, etc.[2]

[1] See *Histoire des Doctrines économiques*, by Gide and Rist. Only, what made Proudhon's bank Utopian was the fact that it did not limit itself to balancing commercial operations already settled by cheques, but balanced operations not yet settled in the form of bills of exchange, with all the risks of insolvency which these involve.

[2] This is no mere dream. The postal cheque already exists in Austria-Hungary, Switzerland and Germany, and there is a bill before Parliament for its adoption in France. As we may imagine, the opponents of State intervention look with no favourable eye on this new function of universal banker which the State would assume. They hold that the Post Office has enough difficulty in carrying on its own business without adding to it another enormous one, necessitating an army of employees—who might shortly form a trade union and perhaps strike.

It must not be forgotten that the Post Office is already a Savings Bank. Private Savings Banks dread the competition of this new Postal bank, particularly as deposits would not be limited to the sum of 1500 francs. Competition would be avoided if the funds deposited in the Postal Bank brought no interest, or only a very low interest, such as the ½ per cent. allowed on deposits in ordinary

V: HOW THE IMPROVEMENTS IN EXCHANGE
TEND TO BRING US BACK TO BARTER

THE evolution which we have just described has shown us metallic money in process of being eliminated by paper money, the bank-note, and the cheque.[1] But these credit instruments still assume the existence of metallic money in the coffers of the bank. Metallic money is, as it were, always behind the scenes in all settlements made by bank-notes or by cheques. Economic evolution goes a step further when transfers and contra-accounts are the only means used for settlements. It tends, as Jevons remarked, by completely suppressing the instrument of exchange, to bring us back to the direct exchange of goods for goods—in short, to barter. There is, in fact, a curious resemblance between the ingenious and complicated processes which are the last word of economic progress, and the primitive methods of still barbarous societies. It is not the first time in its historical development that the spirit of mankind, after reaching the end of its career, has found itself back, apparently, near the starting-point, describing, if not one of the great circles which so struck the imagination of Vico, at least a curve in the form of an ascending spiral.[2]

It would really be a kind of barter that we should come to, under the above hypothesis of a single bank which had all the inhabitants of a country as its clients. There would be no use for money simply because every one would pay the products and services he consumed with his own products and services.

It *is* really a kind of barter that is carried on in that wonderful institution, the Clearing House. For the monstrous bundles of cheques, bills of exchange and commercial effects, which are ex-

banks. But the French bill, imitating in this Austria-Hungary, allows a rate of 2 per cent. And this seems quite without reason, since the money is only deposited with a view to payments.

[1] Even in France enquiries made periodically by the Minister of Finance show that, on an average, 87·4 out of every 100 payments are made in notes, and only 12·6 in metallic money ; and this is not for want of gold, as with some countries, since there are over 3 billion francs of gold in the coffers of the Bank of France.

[2] It is a phenomenon somewhat analogous to the modern tendency to suppress the shopkeeper, so that producer and consumer may come into direct contact.

No less curious examples are to be found in the other social sciences : the literal formalism of primitive legislations tends to come to life again in the modern methods of writing everything in detail ; the direct government by the people, in the cities of antiquity, reappears in the *referendum* of modern constitutions ; compulsory military service for all citizens brings us back to the condition which preceded the institution of standing armies, etc.

changed and balanced against one another daily, are only symbols of the chests, bales and casks which have actually been exchanged ; and, for the seeing eye, the Clearing House has the aspect of a colossal bazaar, somewhat resembling the markets of the African tribes or of the cities of antiquity, the sole difference being that, instead of goods, it is the titles representing them that are exchanged.

And international exchange, as we shall see in the next chapter, tends always to take the form of barter, each country importing as much as it exports and *vice versa*.

True, the precious metals, though they may be losing their function of instruments of exchange, still retain their function of measures of value; for it is clear that the value of all these documents, bank-notes, etc., rests ultimately on metallic money. Only this basis is becoming daily narrower relative to the enormous edifice which credit is building on it. The system has been likened to a pyramid resting on its apex and growing larger and larger, or to a top turning with lightning rapidity on a motionless metallic point, so unstable in its equilibrium that, so soon as the motion ceases, it falls.

We cannot even be certain that the precious metals may not one day lose their ancient privilege as measures of value. It is quite possible to conceive of a social state in which the unit of value for regulating accounts is purely nominal, and corresponds to no existing coin in circulation. History shows many moneys of account of this nature : the *mark banco* of mediæval bankers, the *livre tournois* of the *ancien régime* in France, and the English guinea of to-day.

Not until money has become a pure abstraction will the social State which we indicated in the last chapter be fully realised, and the economic relations between men regulated by simple book-keeping, through a bank with which all the inhabitants of the country have a current account.[1]

[1] Such a possible future state of society has been the object of numerous interesting studies by Solvay, Hector Denis and de Greef, in the *Annales de L'Institut des Sciences sociales* of Brussels, 1897.

It is impossible to understand this chapter without referring to the section *How Credit enables Money Payments to be dispensed with*, under the chapter on *Credit*.

CHAPTER VII : INTERNATIONAL EXCHANGE

I : WHAT MUST BE UNDERSTOOD
BY THE BALANCE OF TRADE

THE *balance of trade* is the name given to the relation between the value of imports and that of exports. Statistics show that the exports and imports of a country are hardly ever equal : the balance of trade lies sometimes on the side of imports, sometimes on that of exports. The former is the more frequent case.

Take France for example. The following are the figures of her special trade for the five years : [1]

	Imports	Exports
1908 . .	5641 millions	5051 millions
1909 . .	6246 ,,	5718 ..
1910 . .	7173 ,,	6234 ..
1911 . .	8066 ,,	6077
1912 . .	7951 ,,	6636
Total	35,077 ,,	29,716 ,,

It appears from these figures that, within a period of only five years, France bought from abroad 5361 million francs worth of goods more than she sold, representing an annual excess of imports over exports of 1072 millions.[2]

---

[1] By *general trade* is meant the movement of all goods which enter or leave France, even those which only touch in passing ; by *special trade*, the movement only of the goods which have been produced within the country or which are to be consumed there. Special trade does not, therefore, include either goods in transit or goods temporarily admitted. The figures for special trade are necessarily less than those for general trade, the difference between the two in France being 2 to 3 billion francs. In some other countries, *e.g.* Belgium and Switzerland, it is larger, owing to their geographical situation. But the figures generally given are those for special trade. The values of the exported and imported goods which are used as a basis for these figures are fixed every year by a special commission of business men. The variations given in the statistics do not therefore always indicate the variations in *quantity ;* if prices go up, trade seems to be increasing, although there has been no change in the movement of goods.

[2] The following, for the sake of comparison, are the figures given in the first edition of the *Principles :*

Must we conclude, then, that France is obliged to pay abroad over 1 billion francs annually in money? This is scarcely probable, since the most superficial observation shows that the quantity of money in circulation has not perceptibly diminished. It has, in fact, increased. The customs houses which register the exports and imports of goods register also the comings and goings of the precious metals; and the following are the figures which they give for the same period: [1]

	Imports	Exports
1908 . .	1173 million fr.	184 million fr.
1909 . .	540 ,,	361 ,,
1910 . .	406 ,,	390
1911 . .	455 ,,	285
1912 . .	528 ,,	320
Total	3102 ,,	1540 ,,

The stock of metallic money in France has therefore increased during this period by 1562 million francs, or over 300 millions per annum.[2]

If we take England, the figures are still more surprising. The

	Imports	Exports
1876 . .	3988 million fr.	3576 million fr.
1877 . .	3670 ,,	3436 ,,
1878 . .	4176 ,,	3180
1879 . .	4595 ,,	3231
1880 . .	5033 ,,	3468
Total . .	21,462 ,,	16,891 ,,

In comparing these two periods of five years, thirty years apart, we shall see: (1) that the total trade, exports and imports, has considerably increased (about 69 per cent.); (2) that the increase is greater in exports (76 per cent.) than in imports (63 per cent.); (3) that, in consequence, the balance of trade has become less unfavourable (in the sense in which we shall define it), since the relation of exports to imports, which was 78 to 100, is now 85 to 100.

[1] We give the figures for gold only, as it is the international money and the only one whose increase or decrease in a country matters. But even if we were to give those for silver, the above results would not be perceptibly altered.

[2] No doubt the customs returns are not absolutely accurate, since they do not include the money which travellers carry in their pockets. But as the omissions are probably about the same for imports and exports, the relation between the two will not be much affected.

Moreover, bank cash reserves offer the same proof. That of the Bank of France, for instance, has increased without a break for thirty years, and has risen from less than 2 to over 4 billion francs. The gold reserve alone has increased from 1880 millions, in 1899, to 3246 millions, in 1913, i.e. an increase of over 1300 millions in the last fourteen years.

annual excess of imports over exports in that country [1] are enough
to drain it of all its gold within a few months. Yet nothing of
the sort takes place. On the contrary, here, as in France, the
imports of precious metal are as a rule greater than the
exports.

What is the key to this enigma ? It is simply this. In order to
find out whether a country will have to export or to import money,
we must consider not merely the balance of its exports and its imports,
as is usually done by the public, but the balance of its credits and its
debits. Now, the *balance of accounts* is not the same thing as the
balance of trade. For, though export is the principal way of putting
foreign countries in our debt, there are others. And although
import is the principal way by which we become indebted to foreign
countries, it is not the only one.

What, then, are these international credits or debts, distinct
from exports and imports, which have been aptly termed *invisible*
exports and imports ?

They are numerous,[2] but the principal ones are the following :

(*1*) The *cost of transport* of exported goods, that is to say,
freight and insurance. If the exporting country itself undertakes
the carriage of its goods, it acquires a claim on foreign countries which
certainly will not figure in its exports, since the claim comes into
existence only after the goods have left the port and are on the way

---

[1] The following are the Board of Trade figures for England's special trade
during the last three years :

	Imports millions	Exports millions
1910	£574	£430
1911	577	454
1912	632	487
	£1783	£1371

Thus, in the short period of three years, the excess of imports over exports is
£412,000,000 ; and if we had taken the figures for general trade it would have
been more. But the value of the money existing in England is estimated at not
more than £120,000,000.

It is the same with Germany and most countries. There are practically only
three—Russia, the United States and the Argentine Republic—whose exports are
notably greater than their imports.

[2] We must take care not to include exporters' profits among them, as do
so many treatises on Political Economy, since these profits are already included
in the value of the exports, and this would therefore mean counting them twice
over. The value of exports is fixed by a Commission of the Customs according
to the current price of goods ; now this current price corresponds to the sale price
of the goods, and includes, naturally, the profits of the manufacturers.

to their destination.   Under this heading a country, like Great
Britain, has an enormous claim on foreign countries, estimated by
the Board of Trade at over £80,000,000 per annum.   For not only
does Great Britain carry practically all her own goods, but most of
the goods of other countries as well, and naturally she does not do
this for nothing.[1]

France, on the other hand, has a debt under this category,
calculated at 300 or 400 million francs, as she carries in her own
ships less than half of her exports and less than a quarter of her
imports.

(2) *The interest on capital invested abroad.*   Rich countries invest
a large part of their savings abroad, and receive annually under this
head considerable sums from abroad in the form of dividends and
coupons, or even rents and profits in industrial or commercial
enterprises.   The tribute paid to England in this form by foreign
countries, and by her colonies, is estimated at over £160,000,000.
For not only have India and the Australasian colonies negotiated
almost the whole of their loans in London, but Englishmen direct,
or own shares in, innumerable enterprises all over the world.   In
the United States they have become possessed of a territory as large
as Ireland.   France, too, has considerable claims on foreign countries.
These were estimated some years back at nearly £1,200,000,000
in capital and over £45,000,000 in revenue ; but the annual income
to-day must be at least 60 or 80 millions sterling.

Germany also is a creditor under this head, though probably to a
smaller amount ;   not because she is less wealthy, but because she
saves less, or at least finds investment for her savings more easily
at home.   Still, her investments abroad are rapidly increasing.

---

[1] The additional value which the cost of carriage adds to the value of goods
explains the following fact, which, at first, appears unintelligible.   If we take the
total exports and imports of all countries in the world we find a constant excess
of imports over exports.   Thus, according to the " *Office de Statistique univer-
selle* " of Antwerp, in 1904, the total value of the world's imports was 67 billion
francs, while that of its exports was only 63 billions, *i.e.* 4 billions less.   Now
if, instead of comparing the values of the goods coming in and going out, we
compare their *quantities*, it is evident that the two totals must be equal, for
clearly there cannot be *throughout the whole world more goods coming in than have
been sent out*, unless we suppose that they multiply *en route*.   Indeed, as some are
lost on the way by shipwreck, damage, etc., the goods arriving ought really to
be somewhat less than those going out.   But as we are considering their values,
not their quantity, and as these values increase *en route* precisely because of the
expenses of carriage, it is not surprising that the goods imported—that is to say,
goods at their destination—represent a greater value than the goods exported—
that is to say, goods at their starting-point.

Russia, on the other hand, Spain, Turkey, Egypt, India and the republics of South America figure as debtors. It must, however, be remarked that when debtor countries raise a loan—and for so long a time as this loan is not fully paid up—the rôles are reversed : it is they who become, for the time being, creditors of the countries which take up their loan. Every year France makes new investments abroad, and has therefore to send out money which we must deduct in our calculations from that which comes in to her as interest from her old investments. It may even happen some year that she has to send out more than she receives.

(3) *Tourists' expenses.* As the money which foreign visitors living in a country spend is not the product of their labour, but is drawn from estates or from capital invested at home, all countries frequented by wealthy foreigners find in their expenditure a continuous stream of claims. This has been estimated at £14,000,000 for Italy and £8,000,000 for Switzerland. It should be at least £16,000,000 in the case of France. Paris, Nice, Pau, etc., are the residences of a considerable number of well-to-do foreigners.[1]

The United States, England and Russia, on the other hand, are debtors under this head for hundreds of millions of francs. It is a form of tourists' expenses which they have to pay for their country-men.

(4) *Bankers' commissions,* when bankers extend their operations abroad. Banking centres like those of London, Paris, or Berlin, receive orders and carry on operations for the whole world, and, as they do not do it gratuitously, these countries are creditors under this category for considerable sums.

(5) *Sale of ships.* Ships bought do not figure in the customs returns either under imports or exports. Now, England, which builds ships for all countries, is creditor under this head for an enormous sum;[2] while France is in this respect rather a debtor than otherwise.

If we could know exactly the total amount of credits and debts of each country—including, of course, exports and imports—we should know what balance remained to the credit or the debit of

---

[1] From 400,000 to 500,000 foreigners are registered annually in the hotels and furnished rooms in Paris (550,000 in 1900 the Exposition year). Suppose that this is the total number of foreigners who come to France, although, in reality, there are many who never come to Paris; suppose that each of them spends no more than 500 francs during his stay—an absurdly low estimate, since some spend this sum daily—this still makes a sum of 250 million francs.

[2] Since 1899, however, the exports of new ships have been included in the British returns.

each, and we should find that the quantity of money which entered or left was equal to this sum.

Thus, to take France, the fact that during the last five years she has had an annual excess of imports of over 1 billion francs, and yet has received over 300 million francs per annum in money, shows that the balance of her credits over debits on foreign countries was at least $1000 + 300 = 1300$ million francs.

II : HOW THE BALANCE OF ACCOUNTS IS MAINTAINED

WE must abandon, then, the old and absurd idea—still so often repeated in prominent newspapers—that a country is going straight to ruin when it imports more than it exports. The problem, however, is only moved one step further back, since, substituting the words " balance of accounts " for " balance of trade," we have to put it thus : " Is not a country on the way to ruin if, when its accounts are finally settled, it has to pay to the foreigner more than it receives ? "

The economists of the Classical school answered boldly, " No." And they gave a very plausible demonstration in support of their statement.

Suppose, they said, in the case of France, the want of balance between credits and debts involves a continual drain on the precious metal. The flight of the metal will result, if the quantitative theory of money be true (see above, p. 232), in an increase in the value of money, and consequently in a general fall in prices. But if prices go down, this will be a great stimulus to export, since foreigners will have every inducement to purchase from us—the buying trade always makes for the cheapest market—and at the same time it will be a powerful drag on import, since foreigners will no longer find it profitable to sell to us, and our countrymen will be able to obtain goods henceforth more cheaply at home. We are as likely to see rivers flowing backwards to their sources as to see goods going from places where they are dear to places where they are cheap. In the last resort, then, this situation must tend towards *increasing exports* and *reducing imports*. This is precisely the remedy required. And in the end the money will come back just as it went out.

Suppose that France issues paper money to replace her coinage, the result will be the same, only accentuated. Metallic money will be at a premium in France, and the larger the quantity of paper money issued, the higher will be the premium. French producers will find it greatly to their interest to sell to foreign countries, since they will be paid in a money which is at a premium, and this premium will give them a profit. The export trade will therefore be greatly stimulated. The import trade, on the other hand, will be reduced, for foreigners do not care to sell in a country with a depreciated paper money, or can do so only by raising their prices, which again reduces the number of their customers.

Indeed, to reverse the current of imports and exports it is not even necessary to wait for a fall in prices. A subtler mechanism, viz., a *rise in the rate of exchange*, will produce the same effect, stimulating export and restricting import. (See *infra, Foreign Exchange.*)

In short, there is an automatic play in the balance of accounts which allows this balance to recover of its own accord its lost equilibrium. The current can no more persist in one direction than can the sea-tides. Sooner or later it turns, and brings back the coin it has taken away.

It was Ricardo who worded the demonstration in a striking formula, when he said that *international exchange always tends to take the form of barter* as among savages, save of course for the superiority of the methods employed. Every debt to a foreign country is paid for in an export of goods to that country, and, *vice versa*, every credit on a foreign country is paid for in an import of goods from that country, just as if money did not exist at all.[1]

Further, says the Classical school, experience has proved that whenever, as a result of a commercial treaty or any other cause, a country has found its imports increase very greatly it has never failed to find its exports increase simultaneously. Thus if, by means of a protectionist tariff, it succeeds in reducing its imports, it should expect to see its exports diminish proportionally.[2]

This theory certainly finds some confirmation in facts, since

---

[1] Mr. Herckenrath, however, in his Dutch translation of this book, points out that in the case of countries, as of individuals, exchange is not necessarily of *goods* for *goods*, but may consist of *goods* for *services*, or *vice versa*. This is true : when, for example, Switzerland, in exchange for tourists' money, gives the *sight* of her cascades, or Italy that of her pictures, these countries do not need to give any goods in return. We must therefore take the word barter in its widest sense, as including services as well as goods.

[2] We must be careful to add, all things being equal. For it must not be concluded from this that, in the commercial history of a country, the curves of export and import are necessarily parallel. Under the influence of causes peculiar to them they converge or diverge.

statistics show that coin is used only to a very small extent (about 3 per cent. to 4 per cent.), in the settlement of international trade.[1]

We must therefore admit that the balance of accounts is regulated automatically, and that credits and debts tend towards an equilibrium. This is what was called by Bastiat's school " an economic harmony."

Still, we are not so dogmatic about it to-day, and we are more ready to allow that it is an undesirable situation for a country to have—we do not say an unfavourable balance of trade, which really means nothing—but a balance of accounts which leaves it in debt to foreign countries.

For the decrease in a country's stock of money implies an impoverishment, if not within the country itself, at least in its relation to other countries; and the fall in prices, taken along with the fall in wages which it will involve, even suppose it be the remedy required, is none the less an evil. All producers know something of this.

On the other hand, this debit balance, apart from its consequences, is often the revelation of an unpleasant situation. It shows, either that the country cannot suffice for its needs nor pay with its labour what it demands from abroad, or that it has to pay tribute for its absentee citizens who go abroad to consume their incomes.

And if a country issues paper money to take the place of its vanishing coin, it is at once on the slope leading to bankruptcy. It is worse still if, having no money wherewith to pay its debit balance, it *borrows to clear itself*, like prodigal sons who are continually renewing the bills which they have signed. In this case it is going straight to bankruptcy. Such has been the history of more than one State.

---

[1] The following are the figures for France giving the movement of goods and of the precious metals during the last three years, exports and imports taken together :

			Goods	Precious Metals
1910	.	.	13,407 million francs	796 million francs
1911	.	.	14,143 „ „	740 „ „
1912	.	.	14,587 „ „	848 „ „
			42,137 „ „	2384 „ „

The precious metals represent not more than 5·7 per cent. of the value of the goods. And, as a large proportion of these precious metals is bullion intended for industrial uses, and is therefore a veritable commodity, we must not count more than two-thirds of these figures for the movement of money properly speaking. This gives, therefore, about $1\frac{1}{2}$ billions of money as against 42 billions of goods, *i.e.* $3\frac{1}{2}$ per cent. only.

III : WHEREIN CONSIST THE ADVANTAGES OF INTERNATIONAL TRADE

THE advantages of international trade have been looked at, curiously enough, from two entirely opposite points of view.

The Classical school lays it down as a principle :

(1) That international exchange is necessarily of advantage to both countries; for, if it were not, why should it take place ? The country which was losing by it would in that case be playing, willy-nilly, the part of dupe.

(2) That the advantage of the exchange for both countries lies in *import*.[1] It is importation that is the sole end and reason of international exchange : exportation is but a means, the only means which a country has of acquiring the goods which it imports—the price in kind with which it pays them. And the higher value of the goods imported over the goods exported measures exactly the advantage which international exchange brings it. To obtain, for example, a sum of imported goods worth 5 billions in exchange for exported goods which are worth only 4 billions, is an operation which represents 1 billion of gain for the country. The less one has to give in exchange for what one wants, the more profitable is the exchange.

According to this theory, when England and France exchange, say, a ton of coal for a hectolitre of wine, England compares the cost of producing a ton of coal with what the cost of producing a hectolitre of wine would be. And as this latter cost would be far greater—for how could England produce wine ?—the conclusion is, that the advantage of exchange to her would be immense. The advantage is, perhaps, less in the case of France, who has coal mines as well as vineyards, but it is nevertheless real, since the cost of production of coal is greater in France than in England.

(3) That the advantage is greater for the country which is least favourably situated by reason of poor soil, inferiority of productive forces, or absence of industry, etc., since for this country the effort and the cost saved by exchange are greater.

On the other hand, the Protectionist school, and even public opinion, in weighing the advantages of international trade, look solely to the side of *exports*. In these alone consists the true profit of international trade. Imports appear only as a necessary evil to which a country must be resigned when it cannot itself produce all that

---

[1] J. B. Say deplored the " erroneous opinion of governments who persuade themselves that they are doing harm to their country in admitting the products of other countries " (*Cours*, part iv, chap. xix).

it requires, but which it must try to reduce as far as possible, since they constitute an expense for it. Exportation alone represents increased wealth, receipts. The advantage therefore of international trade is measured by the excess of exports over imports, of receipts over expenditure. If France were to export 5 billions of goods in return for 4 billions of imports, we should consider this a gain of 1 billion for the country.

These two methods of reasoning proceed from an over-simplified point of view: from assuming that the situation of a country is similar to that of an individual. Now, we cannot compare a country, as do Free Traders, with a savage who finds in barter-exchange the sole means of obtaining what he needs; nor, as do Protectionists, with a merchant buying only to sell over again, and finding his profit in the excess of sale price over buying price. One country does not sell to another country. A country consists of thousands of individuals, each of whom buys and sells with no thought of the rest. And there is no conscious connection between exports and imports. Here it is not a case of a savage giving ivory *in order to* have a gun, or a merchant buying *in order to* sell again. The French manufacturer of motor-cars, who sells to England, does not do so with the intention of getting coal in exchange, nor does the Englishman who buys the motor-car think of reselling it. No doubt there are, as we have seen, general laws which govern the mass of individual acts and bring imports and exports to a certain equilibrium. But only the optimist can believe that these laws are conspiring for the good of all countries, particularly of those least well off.

The advantages of international trade are not such as can be calculated by arithmetic. They cannot be measured in money; they are complex and must be looked for, according to circumstances, now on the side of imports, now on the side of exports.

Let us look first at the advantages of imports. They are:

(1) *Increase of well-being*, whenever the goods imported are such as the importing country, owing to its climate or its soil, cannot itself produce: colonial produce in the case of European countries, wine or raisins in that of England, salt of Norway, coffee of France, coal of Switzerland, etc. This advantage is beyond dispute.

(2) *Additional food-supply*, where the land is too limited to feed the population. England, in her narrow island, in order to feed her increasing millions, is already obliged to demand over £280,000,000 worth of foodstuffs in imports, amounting to about *one-half* of what

she consumes in cereals, meats and drinks. So, too, Germany has to ask a large part of her food-supply from foreign countries.

This is a general fact which is becoming more and more accentuated with time. As their populations increase, European countries are obliged to obtain larger and larger quantities of provisions from abroad. This advantage is rather a lesser evil than a positive good. Obviously, it is better for a country to import its bread from abroad than to see a portion of its population dying of hunger; but, although it is no disadvantage for a single individual to have to rely on others for his daily bread, it is easy to understand that such a course is not without danger in the case of a nation.

(3) *Economy of labour* in the case of wealth which could be produced at home, but only at a higher cost than abroad.[1] France, for example, could very well make her machines herself, and does make very fine ones, as, for instance, the motors of her automobiles and aeroplanes; but she often finds it more profitable to obtain them from England and the United States, since these countries are better provided by nature with iron and coal and better equipped with mechanical appliances.[2]

This advantage of international exchange usually presupposes

---

[1] This is the main advantage of international trade admitted by the Classical school. Bastiat puts it in these words: "To obtain an equal satisfaction with less effort," and J. S. Mill, in slightly different words, referred to it as a way of "obtaining a more useful employment of the world's productive forces." It is, indeed, the advantage of exchange among individuals, as we have explained it (see p. 239); it is a kind of extension of the division of labour. But this point of view is insufficient, if not erroneous, in the case of *international exchange*, since each country, far from trying to carry out a more and more detailed division of labour is seeking to realise as far as possible its economic autonomy.

[2] It is evident from the above explanations that the costs of production of the exchanged products (estimated in labour or money, it does not matter which) may be very different in each of the two countries; in other words, there is no necessary connection between them. This may appear surprising, since the ordinary rule in exchanges between individuals, under free competition, is that the costs of production of the objects exchanged are equal. Why? Because if the object A, costing only ten hours of labour, may be regularly exchanged for B, which costs twenty hours, every one prefers to produce A rather than B, and the abundance of A and the scarcity of B soon bring down the value of A and raise the value of B until *two* A's have to be given for one B. But this levelling process does not take place from one country to another, because the displacing of capital and the labour which it involves is difficult, well-nigh impossible. Even though the production of wine were more profitable than that of coal, we should hardly find English miners coming to settle as wine-growers in France, nor the wine-growers of Languedoc going to become miners at Newcastle. Countries are not like communicating jars in which the water always finds its

productive inferiority on the part of the importing nation. Yet such is not always the case. A country may find it advantageous to import certain forms of wealth, *even when it is able to produce them under more favourable conditions than the country which is exporting them.* Suppose that the Antilles are able to produce corn under more favourable conditions than France, say with *three* days' labour per quintal instead of *six;* would it not be more to their advantage, in this case, to produce their own corn than to import it from France ? And yet it is quite possible that they may find it pay to import it. They have only to find a means of paying for this French corn with a commodity which they can produce still more cheaply than corn. bananas say, which cost only *one* day's labour. Obviously, it will be a more profitable operation for the Antilles to raise bananas and import corn, since they will obtain the same quantity of corn with three times less labour than if they were producing it themselves.

A country may therefore be in a position to produce everything at less cost than its neighbours and yet find it profitable to import their products. For, even in this case, it will gain by devoting itself to the production of the goods which it is best fitted to produce, and by selling them to its less privileged neighbours, in return for produce which it is well fitted to produce, but not so well fitted perhaps as for some other things. In this case export is no more than a means of obtaining import—a *do ut des.*[1]

As for exportation, its advantages are as follows :

(*1*) It utilises natural forms of wealth or productive forces which

own level. They are separated, as it were, into closed compartments almost hermetically sealed.

What, then; determines the relation of the quantities exchanged ? Who says how much wine France is to give in exchange for a ton of coal ? The play of supply and demand, *i.e.* bargaining. Of two countries, the one whose produce is most sought after by the other will succeed in giving the least possible, and consequently in obtaining more advantages than the other. This is what is somewhat pompously termed the *law of international values* of Ricardo and J. S. Mill. See *Histoire des Doctrines*, by Gide and Rist, and also Cournot (*Principes mathématiques de la théorie des richesses*, chap. xii) and Bastable (*Theory of International Trade*).

[1] It was Ricardo first, and later J. S. Mill, who drew attention to this curious fact, which might be called an economic paradox ; for it is not normal that, if A can do a thing more easily than B, he should think of buying it from B. Still, this phenomenon, although rare, is not peculiar to exchange between countries ; as Ricardo remarked (and also M. Herckenrath in his Dutch translation of this book), it may also be found in the case of individuals. A professor of botany or a doctor may be a very clever gardener and nevertheless find it to his advantage to give the care of his garden to a less expert gardener, in order to devote all his time to his studies or to his patients.

would be turned to no account if they did not find an outlet abroad. Without exportation, Peru would not know what to do with her guano and her nitrates, Australia with her wools, California with her gold, Spain with her wines.

(2) It serves to buy the products, raw material and foodstuffs, which are lacking in the country or which exist in too small a quantity. It is thanks to their export of manufactured articles that England, Belgium and Germany are able to supply their industries and their population with raw material.

(3) It brings down the cost price of industrial products and thereby develops national industry. For we know that division of labour and progress in large production depend on the size of the markets (see above, p. 153). If England had not exported to the whole world, she could never have pushed her industrial appliances to such perfection as she has done. To take an example which we have already quoted, it is because her shipbuilding yards work for the whole world that England is able to build ships more cheaply than any other nation.

IV: WHY INTERNATIONAL TRADE IS NECESSARILY DETRIMENTAL TO SOME INTERESTS

IT must not be concluded, from what we have said, that international trade has only advantages and no drawbacks. This would be a mis-understanding of its consequences. It is evident from our explanation that importation aims at, and results in, the economy of a certain amount of labour. Now, as our modern societies are founded on the division of labour, it is impossible to economise labour *without throwing a certain class of labourers out of employment.* The silk trade with China is advantageous to French consumers, as it allows them to obtain silks with less expenditure of money and labour ; but the agriculturists and workers of the Cevennes, who used to live by this industry, find themselves to some extent expropriated.

It is quite true, as we explained (see p. 336), that every new import tends to call out a corresponding export, and that the Chinese silks will be paid, for example, by articles of Parisian manufacture which will have to be produced for the purpose. But it must not be forgotten that the silks imported from China represent a *smaller* value than the French silks which they have supplanted, otherwise they could not have superseded them on the market. They repre-sent, say, 100 million francs, while the French silks represented a value of 120 millions. To meet this import by an equivalent counter-export it will be enough for the Parisian industry to send to China (or elsewhere) 100 million francs' worth of Parisian articles. The final result therefore will be a decrease of 20 millions for the home production, representing a corresponding decrease in employment.

Were this displacing of labour the sole result, it would still be a serious injury to certain classes of the population. The silk manufacturers of the Cevennes, unable to turn their spinning mills into factories for *articles de Paris*, would have to lose the fixed capital sunk in their works ; and, as the spinners whom they employ are not able to start making tops for the Chinese, it is by no means certain that they will find another trade. The result is ruin for the former and unemployment and misery for the latter.

We may, however, point to some extenuating circumstances. It may be said that international trade, like machinery (see p. 87), increases indirectly the quantity of labour which it began by diminishing, and that in two different ways :

(*1*) The fall in prices which results from free exchange will bring about an *increase in consumption*, and consequently an increase in production. The fall in the price of silks, for example, will induce us to buy more. Even supposing this increased demand is only for Chinese and not for French silks, still an increased export of *articles de Paris* will be necessary in order to pay the growing import trade ; and this may amount, not merely to the 100 millions mentioned, but perhaps to the 120 millions as before.

(*2*) The fall in prices, by lessening expenditure in one particular article, will allow consumers to *transfer the economy thus realised to other expenditures or to invest it*. Consequently, all that is taken from labour in one direction will return to it by another, and, in the form of savings and new expenditure, will go to support other industries. It is quite probable that in the end the quantity of national labour employed will remain the same.

Export, as well as import, may have undesirable effects. Countries like Russia, which regularly export their corn and their fodder and do not repair the exhaustion of their soil by chemical manures, impoverish and rob it of all its fertilising elements. It is as if they were exporting little by little the soil itself. Peru, who has already exported all her guano and is now in the act of exporting all her nitrates, is exhausting her future reserves, whatever be the momentary gain.

CHAPTER VIII : COMMERCIAL POLICY

I : HISTORICAL SKETCH OF INTERNATIONAL TRADE

DURING antiquity and the Middle Ages, international trade was not so universal as it is to-day. It was in the hands of a few small countries—Tyre and Carthage in ancient times, the Italian republics and the Hanse Towns in the Middle Ages, Holland at the beginning of modern history—which, owing to their maritime situation, had monopolised trade and transport. The other peoples played an entirely passive part. They received the foreign traders with a certain kindliness, much as the negro tribes of Africa to-day receive Mussulman, or European, merchants, since they obtained through them goods which they could not themselves produce ; they even sought to attract traders by granting them special privileges.[1] In return for these, they exacted certain dues as a kind of profit-sharing, in much the same way as the small African kings to-day levy tribute on the caravans which cross their territories. Customs duties, if we may so name them, were, therefore, at the beginning, purely *fiscal* in nature, and in no way protective. For what, after all, could they have protected, since there was no national industry ?

With the formation of the large modern States, in the sixteenth and seventeenth centuries, the matter assumed a different aspect, and for two reasons :

(*1*) Because these large States set up the pretension of forming national markets, of becoming self-sufficient.

(*2*) Because the opening of the great maritime routes of the world gave international trade an impetus beyond anything hitherto known. International competition, which could not exist so long as trade was limited mainly to objects of luxury—Tyrian purples, Venetian brocades, sword-blades from Toledo, spices—began to be active so soon as trade was well enough equipped to transport articles of ordinary consumption, such as cloth from Flanders.

It was then that a body of doctrines was formed, and to a certain

---

[1] When Louis XI, far ahead of the ideas of his time, tried, in 1482, to organise a protective system and to keep out foreign merchants, he met with strenuous opposition from the representatives of the merchant class in all the towns of France, assembled together at Tours, who wished to attract " *toutes nations estranges* " (see an article by M. de la Roncière in the *Revue des questions historiques*, July 1895).

extent put into practice, known nowadays by the name of the Mercantile System.

Until not so very long ago this system was set forth as follows. The Mercantilists, it was said, believed that money was the sole form of wealth, that, consequently, the important thing for a country was to obtain money; that a country, when it had not the luck to possess gold or silver mines of its own, had no other means of obtain-ing money than by selling as much as possible to other countries and draining their gold and silver away from them little by little. If it were so imprudent as to buy from abroad, it was thereby robbing itself of its coin. To export as much as possible, to import as little as possible—in a word, to aim always at a favourable balance of trade—was the conclusion of the mercantile theory.[1]

To-day this way of presenting the mercantile theory is considered somewhat of a caricature. In its over-simplification it applies rather to the precursors of mercantilism, sometimes called *bullionists*, because of the importance which they attributed to the precious metals, an importance not so childish as we may think, at a time when gold and silver were perhaps rarer than they have ever been in history; when the increasing requirements of trade, the growth of industry, not to mention the budgets of newly fledged States, were causing a veritable famine in money; and when the methods of credit which were to allow of its being more profitably used were barely invented. If the discovery of the mines of the New World dazzled the men of that time and provoked such great covetousness, it was not without good reason; the discovery came at the psychological, or, as Bastiat would have said, the providential, moment.

But the Mercantilists, while attributing a legitimate importance to coin, did not confuse it with wealth or capital, nor did they assert that the sole commercial policy of nations should be to obtain the greatest possible quantity. Their aim was to create national industry. In this they were collaborators of the statesmen who created the modern States of which we spoke, and precursors of the men who are to-day called "Nationalist" economists.[2] Customs duties, moreover, and prohibitions were not the only measures which they advocated. The first national manufactures

---

[1] *England's Treasure by Forraign Trade*, 1664, by Thomas Mun, a rich London merchant, marks the apogee of mercantilism. We may mention for France the *Traité d'Économie politique*, 1615, by Montchrétien.

[2] Still, we cannot call the Mercantilists the precursors of economic science, for, though they were economic politicians, they did not introduce into the science the idea of natural law which was the Physiocrats' title to fame (see *supra*, p. 9).

M

were founded by them, and they sought above all to attract good workmen, whom they considered a form of wealth no less precious than gold.[1]

Still, it is true that they had the idea of making customs duties serve to keep out foreign competition and to develop national industry. These duties in their hands lost the *fiscal*, and took on a *protective*, character. Cromwell, in England, and Colbert, in France, were the first statesmen to create a true and complete protectionist system. That of Colbert had three distinct objects :

(*1*) To prevent the import of manufactured goods by means of protective duties.

(*2*) To encourage, by a reduction of duties, the import of raw material and of all that serves for manufacture.

(*3*) Above all, to favour the export of national products by encouragements to manufacturers, or by bounties.

This system, generally known as *Colbertism*, reigned supreme till the appearance of the " Economists." We know that the Physiocrats ruthlessly demolished all the mercantile theories. Taking exactly the opposite standpoint, they hoisted the device "*Laissez-faire, laissez-passer*," and fought no less energetically for freedom of exchange against the protectionist system. than for freedom of labour against the guild system. But the French Revolution, which led to the triumph of their ideas in regard to the freedom of labour, failed altogether in regard to the freedom of trade. It is true that the twenty years of European war which followed were not a very good preparation for the advent of Free Trade.

In England, however, the ideas of Adam Smith had borne fruit. England, indeed, had never been very protectionist, except in so far as to secure her maritime trade and the monopoly with her colonies. The famous Methuen treaty with Portugal, in 1703, and Eden's treaty with France, in 1786, would to-day be considered Free Trade treaties. And, so soon as the wars with Napoleon were ended, she began to lower her duties on industrial products. In regard to grain the English government was for a long time obdurate ; for this touched the interests of the English aristocracy, from which the House of Lords was recruited. It was against these protective

---

[1] To mark, shortly, the difference between Bullionists and Mercantilists, we have only to remember that the former tried to prohibit the efflux of coin, and that more than once severe penalties were inflicted by governments for exporting it ; while the latter tried to hinder the efflux of skilled workers, and severe penalties likewise sanctioned this system. Thus at Bordeaux, in 1726 and 1752, the clothworkers and ropemakers who tried to go to Spain were caught and imprisoned.

duties on corn (the *Corn Laws*) that Cobden, in 1838, began his memorable campaign at Manchester, destined to overturn the whole of the protective system. It was, indeed, a particularly odious sight to see the English lords, owners by right of conquest of almost all the lands of the kingdom, shutting out foreign corn in order to sell their own at a higher price, and profiting by the growing needs of the population to obtain higher and higher rents. The House of Lords was in no position to resist the movement of indignation let loose by the League, and, in 1846, on the signal conversion of the Minister, Sir Robert Peel, it was obliged to yield. The duties on corn once abolished, the rest of the protectionist edifice, including Cromwell's famous Navigation Act to which the maritime greatness of England was attributed, fell to the ground.

In France, a league founded by Bastiat, in 1846, on the lines of the English Anti-Corn Law League, failed, as social conditions were there entirely different. But the Emperor Napoleon III., whose policy was based on the alliance with England and whose instincts were fairly democratic, took advantage of the power which he had reserved to himself by the Constitution, to sign a commercial treaty with the British government without consulting the Chamber. This famous treaty of 1860, submitted to somewhat reluctantly by France, caused considerable stir in Europe, and was immediately followed by treaties between all the European Powers; so that it was held to mark the end of the century-long system of Protection and the beginning of the final era of Free Trade.[1]

But the reign of Free Trade was not to last long. In the first place, the United States had remained outside of the movement. This last country, the home, so to speak, of Carey and List (though the latter was a German), the two greatest theorists on the side of Protection, had always been protectionist in doctrine as well as in fact, one of the principal causes of its revolt against the mother-country being that it was not allowed to " make even a horseshoe." It was only natural then that its first thought should be to reconquer its industrial autonomy. But the protective duties, very moderate at the beginning, became heavier and heavier as time went on, and always for some new reason. First it was to protect the infant industries—this was List's system; after 1866, it was to pay the costs of the Civil War. Later this reason too fell through; for, when the larger part of their debt was paid off, the States did not

---

[1] A very relative Free Trade at best, for free import was allowed only in the case of raw materials and agricultural produce. For manufactured articles, the duties were about 15 per cent. *ad valorem.*

know what to do with the money from their customs and were reduced to distributing £40,000,000 of pensions to persons ostensibly injured in the war. The reason thereafter alleged for maintaining the duties was to defend the high prices and high wages of America against the low prices and low wages of Europe.[1] The celebrated McKinley tariff of 1890 was severe enough ; the Dingley tariff of 1897 was more stringent still ; and the Payne tariff of 1909, which was to reduce the duties, only aggravated them.[2] It must, however, be remembered that the United States is a Union of forty-eight States, some of which are as large as France, and that between them there is perfect Free Trade. It is as if all the States of Europe were to band together in a Zollverein and raise a customs barrier against American products.

In 1872, on the close of the Franco-German War, France, under the government of M. Thiers, tried to follow the example of the United States and to throw on foreign products the burden of the new taxes which she was obliged to create in order to pay for her defeat. But this attempt failed, owing to the treaties still in force at the time. It was Germany who, in 1879, on the initiative of Prince Bismarck, was to inaugurate. in Europe the return to a resolute policy of Protection.[3]

Germany followed a very opportunist policy in commercial matters, and one which answered her purpose very well. In 1833 she paved the way for her political unity by a Customs Union among the different German States. When the Free Trade period came she stood wholly for it ; but her political unity once accomplished, she was ambitious to become a great industrial power, and wheeled round towards Protection. When, having rapidly succeeded in her aim, she was forced more recently (1892–1894) to seek markets

[1] In 1879 General Grant, ex-President of the United States, at a reception in Manchester, where it was hoped to convert him to Free Trade, pointed out ironically that England had followed the protectionist policy for two hundred years ; that she had pushed it to an extreme and had found advantage in so doing ; that it was undoubtedly to that system that she owed her industrial power ; that, after these two hundred years were over, England had thought fit to adopt Free Trade because she could get nothing more out of Protection.

[2] The duties amounted on an average to 57 per cent., but in the case of some goods they were much higher. The new President, however, Dr. Woodrow Wilson, who represents the Democratic party, has now carried through a measure for lowering the tariffs.

[3] In date Austria was the first, by her tariff of June 27, 1878 ; but her example had much less influence. For details and history, see Lexis, *Revue d'Économie politique*, 1895.

abroad, she adopted the mixed system of commercial treaties, outlining, as it were, a new Zollverein embracing the whole of Central Europe.

In 1892, France, free by this time from the commercial treaties which had been concluded under the Empire and had afterwards been renewed, became protectionist again, and has since gone steadily on in the same direction (see *infra*, the special chapter on France).

Even in England, the classical land of Free Trade, this last system is beginning to be somewhat shaken. It was Mr. Chamberlain, Colonial Secretary during the Transvaal War, who inaugurated the campaign against the old Manchester school. This neo-Protection first took the form of *imperialism*; that is to say, it was inspired by a political motive, that of uniting by ties of common interest all the peoples who make up the immense British Empire. To bring this about it would be necessary for the colonies, for the most part already strongly protectionist, to grant reductions of duty to the products of the home country ; and for England, on the other hand, to allow free entry to the products of her colonies, which would involve the creating of duties on foreign products. The first part of this programme would not be so very difficult to carry out, for already the Dominion of Canada, South Africa, and New Zealand give favoured treatment to English products, in the form of reductions varying from 25 per cent. to 33 per cent., and Australia seems about to follow suit. It is the second part of the programme which, up to the present time, has been the stumbling-block, as England is not anxious to compromise her trade with foreign nations for the benefit of the colonies, her trade with the latter amounting to only one-quarter of her total foreign trade. Still, apart from the imperial reason, there are other forces at work to-day pushing England, like other countries, in the direction of Protection. One of these is the necessity of obtaining resources for the enormous increase in her military expenditure and expenditure on social insurance, particularly old-age pensions (see Book III, chap. v).

With the exception of England, then, there are in Europe, at the present time, only a few small countries, Holland, Norway and Denmark, which have remained faithful to Free Trade, their areas being too small to allow of their being self-sufficient. Everywhere else, even in Switzerland, customs barriers have been set up again, and tariff wars have taken the place of commercial treaties.

There must have been some general causes at the root of this sudden, irresistible and spreading epidemic of Protection, but it is not very easy to discover them, or at least to locate them. Perhaps

it is due, at bottom, to a reawakening of the nationalist spirit, somewhat analogous to that which created the mercantilism of the
sixteenth century. The principle of nationality created, in the second
half of the nineteenth century, two great States in Europe, and
awakened the ambitions of many others. Every country, provided it
has a certain area, now aims at becoming self-sufficient, and sees in its
economic independence a condition of its political independence.
Further, nothing is so contagious as Protection; so soon as one
country adopts it, the others follow suit for fear of being
worsted. Add to this the fact that, since the examples of the United
States and of Germany have shown that Protection is quite as able
as Free Trade to lead a country to industrial supremacy, the faith
in the latter has been distinctly shaken. When the McKinley tariff
was promulgated, an English economist said: " If this tariff is to
succeed, our political economy is founded on a colossal error which
will bring about our ruin as a nation." Now, the tariff has succeeded
excellently, so far as the United States is concerned. How then are
we to avoid a certain feeling of scepticism, or refrain from asking
whether Protection and Free Trade are really so powerful for good
or for evil as their partisans and their adversaries claim ? As a fact,
it is our opinion that the industrial prosperity of a country depends
on other causes; that the customs system is one of the smallest
factors in this, and that its importance has been singularly
exaggerated.[1]

[1] As proof, we give below the progression of international trade in five
countries since 1880, a date which practically marks the beginning of the reaction
in favour of Protection (in millions of francs, round numbers). (*Annuaire
statistique du Ministère du Travail*, 1908.)

	England	France	United States	Germany	Belgium
1880	17,600	8,500	7,500	7,100	2,898
1910	30,576	13,407	16,879	20,347	7,671
Increase	74 %	57 %	125 %	174 %	165%

We see that the trade of Protectionist Germany and that of Free Trade Belgium
have increased in about the same proportion, while Free Trade England has
remained far behind Protectionist Germany and the United States, and Protectionist France stands last of all. But these inequalities are easily explained by
other causes than the customs system.

In the case of England, it is evident that a country which has reached the
height of its commercial evolution cannot increase so quickly as relatively new
countries, like the United States and Germany.

In the case of Belgium (and one might add Holland) the relatively high figure
for commerce is due partly to the fact that it includes the precious metals and
transit, but mainly to the size of the country. For the smaller a country is,
the more important, relatively, is its foreign trade. And this stands to reason.

The violent reaction which has manifested itself in our day against the Classical school, although not bearing directly on the question of Protection, has contributed nevertheless to shake our faith in absolute principles; and those, in particular, who stand for the Historical, or Realist, school admit that the commercial system of each country ought to be appropriate to its particular situation.[1] Still, the reaction in favour of Protection is not so marked in theory as it is in trade policy. We may even say that the greater number of economists have remained faithful to the Free Trade doctrines, although List (German)[2] in 1841, and Carey (American)[3] in 1859, made a breach in the Manchester doctrine at the very height of its fame. According to List—who is a direct descendant of the Mercantilists in that, for him, Protection is only a means of developing national industry and is destined to disappear so soon as its object is attained—every nation should aim at rising from the agricultural to the industrial system, in order to turn its resources to best account and to gain economic independence, Protection being indispensable at the critical age which marks the transition from the first to the second phase. He would therefore protect, not agriculture, but industry, and that only during its infancy; and he approves of England having emancipated herself from Protection. Nowadays List would be considered more a Free Trader than a Protectionist,[4] as Protection to-day is based rather on the " nationalist " —we might even say " imperialist "—idea.

A State which consisted of only a single town, like Venice or Tyre in olden times, would be obliged to live almost solely by its foreign trade.

As regards France, the relatively small increase in her foreign trade which has brought her down to the last rank, does not indicate a weakening of her industrial and commercial activity, but is due to the stationary state of her population. For if we divide the figure of trade for each country in 1912 by the figure of its population, we obtain the following figures, which represent the amount of trade per head, and show that France comes second in rank among the great countries :

Belgium	1030 francs
England	665 ,,
France	344 ,,
Germany	308 ,,
United States	177 ,,

[1] See Cauwès, Cours d'Économie politique.

[2] National System of Political Economy. According to List, a nation ought to pass normally through five stages : (1) savage ; (2) pastoral ; (3) agricultural ; (4) manufacturing ; (5) commercial. This last, which co-exists with the two preceding ones, and is consequently a more complex economy, is the one to aim at.

[3] Principles of Social Science.

[4] See Histoire des Doctrines, by Gide and Rist.

Why does international trade involve what is called a problem ? And why is it that it has stirred up more controversy, caused more volumes to be written, and even more shots to be fired than any other problem ?

Is not the trade of one nation with another in all points just like that of one individual with another ? Is it not, like private trade, an ordinary and normal form of exchange ? And if this is so, why a special theory of international trade ? If exchange is in itself a good thing, why should it become dangerous from the purely accidental circumstance that the two parties to it are separated by a frontier ?

This, in fact, is the point of view of classical Political Economy. It does not admit, nor understand, that international trade may be regulated by different principles from any other trade. For it, this celebrated problem is not a problem at all and need not take up our attention. Exchange is only a form of the co-operation and the division of labour concerning the marvellous effects of which we have spoken ; the advantages it brings are reciprocal and equal for each of the two parties. What does it matter, then, whether those who are exchanging belong to the same country or to different countries ? Free Trade between all nations of the world will be the last stage in the evolution which has gradually substituted the city market for the domestic market, and the national market for the city. market. And all the advantages which we pointed out in connection with exchange, viz., the better utilising of men and things, simply increase as the field of exchange widens.

But public opinion does not profess this superb indifference. It is indeed so divided on this momentous question that our best plan will be to set forth both sides objectively and impartially.

II : THE PROTECTIONIST POSITION

PROTECTIONISTS do not deny that Free Trade may be preferable from the theoretical point of view, nor even that it may be more in conformity with the general good of mankind. They do not by any means give themselves out as enemies of international trade, as they abundantly prove by the efforts which they make to secure it, and by the subsidies which they give to the mercantile marine and to the large commercial ports with a view to developing them. Only they want to keep the profits themselves. They hold that nations, and those who govern them, have not the right to speculate on the general welfare of mankind : they must confine themselves to the particular interests of the country in which they live. They consider, rightly or wrongly—and this is the crux of the whole question—that international trade, left to itself, is liable to ruin the industry of a country, to restrict or even to stifle its productive forces, and thus indirectly to endanger its national existence. In their view, international exchange not only does not confer equal and reciprocal advantages on the two parties, but, on the contrary, may ruin one by enriching the other, and it behoves a nation not to be the one that suffers.

Far from considering international trade as a form of the *division of labour* and of *co-operation*, they look upon it as a state of warfare ; a form of the *struggle for life* among nations. And just as the whole art of warfare consists in invading and occupying the enemy's territory while preventing him from invading or occupying our own, so the tactics of international trade should consist, according to them, in invading foreign territory with our exports while prohibiting foreign imports from entering our own. What a country must aim at, then, is to establish a national industry, vigorous enough to keep out foreign goods, and even to fight them on their own ground. This has been the problem of Protection for some centuries : a problem which it is trying to solve by means of the most elaborate tactics.

The following, briefly, is the Protectionist line of argument :

, (*1*) As international trade has, in our days, assumed the form of a struggle for existence, it is bound to produce the ill-effects inherent in competition, even competition among individuals, viz., the *crushing out of the weak*. The United States, for example, owing to the size of its agricultural exploitations, the fertility of certain regions which renders manuring unnecessary, the low price of land, and the moderate taxation, is able to grow wheat under much more economical conditions than our European countries can. Now, if the importation of American wheat prevents French cultivators from any longer growing wheat, what are they to do ? Produce wine, it may be said. But Spain and Italy are able to produce wines much more alcoholic than the French, owing to their climate, and much cheaper, owing to the low price of labour. And France is in the same inferior position with regard to silk as compared with China, wool as compared with Australia, and meat as compared with the Argentine Republic. Are French cultivators, then, who represent half the population of France, to abandon the land and crowd into the cities ? Such a displacement would menace not only the prosperity, but the public health, morality, political stability and military force of the nation—its very future. And who is to guarantee that this population, driven from the country, will find more remunerative work in the towns ? May not the manufacturing industry in turn succumb before the import of foreign goods ? If a country has the misfortune to be inferior to foreign countries in every branch of production, it will be dislodged from one industry after another, until the only course left to it will be to transport its remaining population and capital to the countries which are carrying on this victorious competition, in order to benefit by their better conditions.[1] If France is no longer able to compete with America, let her emigrate to America. This would be the logical consequence of a system which sees in international trade no more than the best method of drawing the most out of the earth and the men on it, without taking into account the fact that these men are divided into nations, and that each of these nations has a will and a right to live.

We can understand a convinced Darwinian sacrificing the individual for the good of the race ; but we can hardly expect a country to let itself be sacrificed for the good of humanity. It would be the more absurd, as there is so much more at stake than mere commercial superiority. A nation has another rôle to play in this world than the simple economic one of producer.   Are we to run the risk of some new Greece being one day eliminated from among the nations because its barren soil has not allowed it to produce as cheaply as its rivals ?

Still, Protectionists disclaim the desire to suppress international trade altogether, in order to get rid of foreign competition ; they simply believe that equality in competition must be restored. If a foreign country, say America, owing to its natural resources in the way of virgin soil, or to the fact that its budget has not to support the consequences of a burdened past, is able to produce wheat at 18 francs per quintal, while the French agriculturist can produce it only at an average cost of 25 francs, it is but just that a *compensatory duty* of 7 francs should be laid on imported

---

[1] Observe that this is exactly what takes place in the home trade between the different parts *of the same country*. Is it not the very freedom and ease of communication between the Cantal or the Basses Alpes, and Paris that is causing the depopulation and industrial decay of these departments ? Here, one part of France gains what the other loses, and there is no need, from the national point of view, to interfere. But if the Cantal were an independent country and wanted to remain so, it would have good reason to be uneasy and to try to fight the attractions of Paris.

wheat to equalise the charges, just as jockeys are handicapped according to their unequal weights.[1]

(2) Even supposing that no country went under in the international struggle, that each found a branch of production in which it could keep its supremacy and into which it could turn all its productive forces, would this be a desirable state of affairs ? The Free Trade school answers in the affirmative, since it sees therein a vast application of the law of the division of labour. It is its pleasure to consider the whole world as an immense workshop, in which each nation does the one thing which it is best fitted by nature to do, and where in consequence we find all the productive forces of our planet, and of humanity, used to the best possible advantage. France will produce only fine wines, ladies' hats and silk goods ; England, machinery and cotton goods ; China, tea ; Australia, wool ; Russia, wheat ; Switzerland, cheeses and clocks ; Greece, raisins.

But here again the national interest is absolutely sacrificed to a supposed general welfare which is a pure abstraction. An ideal such as this, if it could be realised, would mean the demoralisation of all countries, and consequently of the whole human race ; for the race has no existence of its own apart from the nations which constitute it. And if it has been admitted that specialisation in one form of labour is fatal to the physical, intellectual and moral development of an individual (see p. 155), what are we to say of its effect in the case of a nation ! A country in which all men followed the same occupation would be no more than an amorphous mass, without organisation. Biologists teach us that the development of an organism and its position in the scale of life are in direct proportion to the variety and multiplicity of its functions, and the differentiation of the organs which perform those functions. It is exactly the same in the case of a nation. If it would rise to a rich and intense life, it must try to *multiply all its forms of social activity*, all its energies, and must be on its guard lest foreign competition destroy them one after the other.[2]

(3) The importation of foreign products, if not counterbalanced by a corresponding exportation of home products, is liable to ruin

[1] This argument is often presented from the side of the working man. Protection, he is told, is the best insurance against the unemployment which is inevitable under a system of free importation of foreign products. This argument had a great effect on the working class in England during the last electoral campaign of the Tariff Reformers.

[2] This is what M. Dupuy, Minister of Commerce, meant when he said in the Senate (March 11, 1910): "The customs tariff is one of the conditions of the independence of a nation."

a country : *first by taking away its coin,* and secondarily by *reducing it to the position of debtor.* The importing country pays with its money so long as it has any, and when it has none left it is reduced to borrowing, often from the very country that is selling to it. Its situation thus goes from bad to worse, since, to the debt resulting from its imports, there must now be added the interest which it has to pay.[1] It is thus hastened on its way to bankruptcy. Such was the history of Portugal, Turkey, and the South American Republics.

(4) Customs duties are the best of taxes, since it is the *foreigner who pays them.* A country need not hesitate therefore to resort to them, since it *not only protects its industries thereby,* but procures resources which cost its citizens nothing.[2]

(5) Lastly, they say, *national security* is of itself enough to justify the protectionist system. On every hand we see nations striving hard, at the cost of heavy sacrifices, to create fortresses, war fleets, armament factories. But the industries indispensable to the security of a country are not simply this or that factory of arms or of biscuits ; there is coal, without which trains cannot go and mobilisation is impossible ; there is iron, there are horses, wheat, meat, cloth, leather—all the things that are necessary to feed and clothe millions of men in time of war.

If England can allow herself to import half of her food supply from abroad,[3] it is because she is mistress of the great maritime routes, and spends colossal sums to maintain her supremacy in time

---

[1] This is what Cato the Elder meant when he said : " *Patrem familias vendacem, non emacem, esse oportet* " (*De Agricultura*). The Mosaic Law said (Deuteronomy xv. 6) : " Thou shalt lend unto many nations, but thou shalt not borrow; thou shalt reign over many nations, but they shall not reign over thee." It is true that these words refer to loans, not sales, but, say the Protectionists, it amounts to the same, since the selling country becomes in the long run a creditor.

[2] M. Méline, leader of the Protectionist party, said before Parliament (February 28, 1898) : " It is the foreigner who pays the customs duties."

After the Civil War in the United States, Mr. Lawrence, Controller of the Treasury of the United States, spoke to the same effect (quoted by *l'Économiste français,* 1882, vol. i, p. 411).

[3] It has been calculated that the quantity of foodstuffs imported into England per annum is enough to keep the population for about six months, and into Germany for about three months ; in other words, half of the population of England and a quarter of that of Germany is fed from abroad. This is not the case with France, as her population is not dense and her soil is very fertile.

Not long ago Switzerland, learning that Germany intended to give a bounty on the export of flour, a proceeding which would have killed her flour-mills, was so alarmed at the thought of her bread depending on foreigners that she had some idea of making the flour trade a State monopoly !

of war. But if ever she had reason to fear that her communications were cut, there is no doubt that she would take measures to increase her agricultural production, by artificial processes if necessary. Given the monstrous form of modern warfare, which arms the whole population of a nation and absorbs all its economic resources, there is not, so to speak, a single industry which may be said to be unnecessary for the national defence.

Such, in short, are the arguments which have been brought forward for centuries in favour of the protectionist policy. The method that has been most generally employed in all. times for carrying out this policy has been the putting of more or less high duties on imported goods. This, however, although the most effective, is not the only method. We shall see presently that Protection may be exercised without resorting to protectionist duties. (See *infra*, p. 378, *Bounties on Production.*)

III : THE FREE TRADE POSITION

FREE TRADERS as a rule begin by refuting the arguments just enumerated.

(*1*) The argument drawn from the danger of competition is, they say, very effective ; but see what singular aberrations it has undergone, and to what contradictions it leads.

Formerly it was said that we must protect the weak against the strong, the young against the old ; this is what was called the *infant industry argument.* It was pointed out that infant industries have to contend with great difficulties. It is not easy for them to withstand the competition of old-established enterprises in possession of vast markets, and able, by reason of their extensive production, to push the division of labour and large-scale methods to their highest perfection. The struggle is all the more difficult that, in these new countries, wages are higher and workmen less experienced. It is well known that young trees cannot easily be grown close to old ones, since the latter have already taken possession of the light above and the sap of the soil below, leaving but little room for the young ones in which to stretch out their branches or their roots.

The argument, they say, appeared plausible. It seemed to be borne out by the experience of new countries, such as Australia and Canada, which, though nurtured on the pure doctrine of Free Trade, did not hesitate to raise, as by instinct, a protectionist rampart even against the mother-country herself.

The United States, too, have always been invoked as a standing example for Protectionists. Would American industry, it is said, have grown so rapidly if it had had to fight English manufactures from the beginning ? Would it not have been crushed at the outset by its powerful rival ?

Perhaps so ; but now that the United States have brilliantly accomplished their economic evolution and have become one of the first manufacturing countries of the world—now that their industries are great and powerful—have they renounced the shelter of the rampart which protected their infancy ? Far from it ; they continue protectionist still, spurning as an indignity the " infant industry " argument. Taking entirely different ground, they declare to-day that a country, rich and advanced in civilisation, paying its workers high wages, must protect itself against the more backward nations where wages are low, meaning by this our ancient Europe. For, say the American economists, just as Europe and Asia lower our civilisation and our standard of life by sending us their starving emigrants, so they work towards the same result by sending us their cheap goods. We must defend both our civilisation, and our high wages, against the invasion of cheap labour, and the products of cheap labour.[1]

Again, when they talk of restoring equality in competition by means of *compensatory duties,* we must know on which side the disadvantage lies. France, for instance, declares that compensation ought to be given against America as having more natural resources, a soil not yet exhausted by twenty centuries of cultivation, and a lighter budget. The Americans, on the other hand, claim that compensation should be made against Europe, because the lower wages and longer hours of labour of our workmen, as well as the greater value of our money, enable us to produce at much lower prices than they can.

What, then, are we to conclude ? To whom is Protection really necessary ? To the young against the old, or to the old against the young ? To the weak against the strong, or to the strong against the weak ? And who are the strong, and who are the weak ? What are we to think of an argument which may be used equally well by either side ? [2]

[1] This violently nationalistic argument is set forth in a scholarly manner by Patten (*Economic Bases of Protection*), who contrasts " dynamic " societies like the United States with the " static " societies of Europe.

[2] The argument for the equalising of taxation by compensatory duties is based on the idea that the customs duties are paid by the foreign producers. But if, as we shall see, these duties fall back more often than not on the home

Let us dispose also of the foolish fear that a country can ever be depopulated by international trade. This dreadful picture of a nation dislodged from one branch of production after another by foreign competition, reduced to leaving its land uncultivated and to seek an asylum on the very territory of its conquerors, is fantastic. It is not likely that a country will ever find itself so poorly endowed by nature as to be inferior to all other countries in every single branch of production. And if it were, it would be absurd to think that the exclusion of foreign products could improve matters or prevent capitalists and workers from seeking happier lands elsewhere. A customs barrier cannot serve as a prison wall, nor is it advisable that it should.[1]

There is no country, however poor, but will find something to produce, something to give in exchange to other countries which are better off. And if a country be reduced to such an extremity that it has nothing to give, the Protectionists may rest more reassured than ever ; for all imports will immediately cease. Foreign products will be stopped more effectually than by any prohibitive duty, by the fact that they will no longer be paid for. For we know (p. 336) that imports, in general, are paid for by exports. If a country, then, has nothing to export, nothing to give in return, how can it buy anything from abroad—unless we admit such an obvious absurdity as that a foreign country will send its goods for nothing ? In this case, indeed, the importing country is more to be envied than pitied.[2]

(2) The fear of specialisation to the death and of the consequent demoralisation of a country seems equally unfounded. No doubt every country has a right to develop all its latent energies, not

consumers in the form of a rise in prices, we may appreciate the irony of this so-called compensation, which, under the pretext of equalising the struggle, puts a double weight on the shoulders of the one who is already the most heavily burdened.

[1] Can we suppose, for instance, that in the departments of the Cantal or the Basses-Alpes had been surrounded with a customs barrier, this would have made them richer or would have prevented their inhabitants from emigrating to Lyons or to Paris ?

[2] We would ask those who persist in believing that it is with its *money* that the unendowed country pays its imports, where it gets its money from, if it has nothing to sell. There is only one condition on which a country can import without exporting ; that is, if foreign countries are in its debt to such an extent that it can pay by way of contra-account (p. 393). But how can a country which, by hypothesis, is unendowed by nature be in this position ?

Even in the case quoted of the South American republics, the cause of their scarcity of metallic money must be sought rather in the abuse of paper money than in foreign imports (p. 393, note 1).

only in agriculture, but in industry; to make the best possible use of its soil, its climate, and the aptitudes of its race. This goes without saying. But what is the best system for awakening and developing these energies ? Is it not precisely international competition, by the rough discipline which it imposes on a nation, constraining it either to do better than, or differently from, the rest ; dislodging it from positions already occupied in order to force it to create new resources elsewhere ? Do we really find industry less diversified in free trade countries like Holland, Belgium or England than in protectionist countries ? By no means.

(3) The inferiority or ruin prophesied to the nations which resign themselves to being buyers, as compared with those which are able to remain sellers, is but an empty prediction.[1] No doubt it is better for nations, as for individuals, to be rich than poor ; but the mistake lies in believing that the position of buyer is necessarily inferior to that of seller. Do we, for instance, as consumers, consider ourselves inferior to our tradesmen ? The importing nation is after all the one which makes other nations work for it— paying them, of course. This is surely not a sign of inferiority or of poverty.

The reasoning, again, which makes out that every importing country ends by getting into debt rests on a false analogy between a country and a spendthrift buying on credit. International exchange is carried on by bills of exchange at several months' date. It is a kind of barter, and nothing resembles buying on credit less than barter. A nation may, it is true, ruin itself by borrowing—although as a rule it is more likely to ruin its creditors—but this is quite another matter and has nothing whatever to do with its purchases.

(4) It is absurd to make out, as a general doctrine, that protective duties are paid by the foreigner, and that, instead of constituting a burden on the nation, they bring in additional revenue to the government. It would really be too convenient if a country could obtain its revenues by taking them from the pockets of neighbouring States. And even if Protection had this magic power, since each country in turn would hasten to profit by it and make its neighbours

---

[1] As Protectionists insist above all on nationalist and patriotic considerations, it is interesting to confront this opinion with that of various foreign economists, given in a recent book by M. Ludwig Lang, professor at Buda-Pesth (*Hundert Jahre Zollpolitik*). The author does not criticise the protectionist policy of France, because he admits " that she, more easily than any other nation, may be self-sufficient," but he believes that " by her customs policy France is doomed little by little to lose the rank which she once occupied in the world."

pay its taxes, it is evident that none would be any better off in the end.

By virtue of a law, known in taxation as the " law of incidence " (*répercussion*), nearly every tax paid by a producer or a trader is transferred by the latter to his invoice, and shifted finally on to the consumer. The foreign producer will certainly not fail to do the same.[1]

But even admitting the whole force of this argument, and supposing that foreign producers consent to take the protective duties on their own shoulders, what will be the result ? The price of the foreign products will not be raised : consequently their competition, and the depressing influence which they exercise, will not be lessened. In the end, then, home industry will gain neither the exclusion of the foreign products nor the rise of prices for which it hoped. And we shall have to add a last, and still more decisive, criticism to the system of protective duties—that *they are useless*.

(5) Finally, as regards the possibility of war and the necessity of being prepared for it, should we not rather ask ourselves whether Protection has not the effect of creating the very danger against which it claims to defend us—whether tariff wars are not liable to provoke real warfare ? The idea that a country can grow rich only by export is much more likely to lead us to seek markets by force and by war. And, though this policy may now be out of favour between civilised nations,[2] it is still practised towards those less advanced. The colonial expeditions, and even the wars against China, had practically no other origin.

On the other hand, experience shows that commercial relations

---

[1] The foreign producer may, however, occasionally bear the duties in certain exceptional cases pointed out by J. S. Mill. Every rise in price involves a reduction in consumption. The foreign producer has therefore to ask himself whether it is not to his interest to make a sacrifice and reduce the price of his article by a sum equal to the amount of the duty, in order to be able to sell at his old price and thus keep his customers. The duty which falls on his produce forces on him the disagreeable alternative either of *reducing the number of his sales* or of *making a sacrifice in the price*. It is not impossible that, all things considered, his interest may induce him to choose the latter course and to take on himself the whole or part of the duty. Thus, during the Franco-Swiss tariff war of 1893 to 1895 many French manufacturers, in order not to lose their Swiss customers, bore all, or part, of the duties fixed by the new tariff.

Only, before foreign producers resign themselves to this extremity, two conditions are necessary : (1) their cost price must admit of their doing this ; (2) they must have been unable to find another market for their goods.

[2] At a banquet given in his honour in London (January 28, 1910), the German ambassador said : " It is a fact that a market cannot be conquered by brute force. . . . How could the conqueror make a customer of those whom he had ruined and killed ? "

between nations are a very effective obstacle to war. It is probable that they have more than once within the last century staved off a war between England, France and Germany. Montesquieu wrote: " The natural effect of trade is to produce peace." [1]

In any case, if Protection is to be put forward as a military necessity, it must be presented as an *additional expense* in the war budget, and not as a source of revenue. An American economist calculated that a certain spinning factory had cost his country more than an ironclad cruiser. This was frankness indeed! Far better declare openly that protective duties and tariff wars are no less costly than armed peace or real warfare, but no less necessary to the existence of a nation which demands its place under the sun. Protectionists, however, do not like to make this admission ; they prefer to delude themselves by the prospect of imaginary gains.

Free Traders are not content merely to refute the arguments put forward by Protectionists. They take the offensive and enumerate the disadvantages of protective duties.

(1) From the point of view of *consumption*, protective duties tend undoubtedly to raise *the cost of living*, or at least to prevent it from falling. Most articles of large consumption, those which the workman consumes, are cheaper in free trade countries like England than in France or Germany. Very careful official inquiries, made on the spot by the British Board of Trade, show that the cost of living of the working man in France and Germany is 18 per cent. higher than in England and Belgium ; and this can hardly be attributed to any other cause than the customs duties on foodstuffs.

. The duties paid on entrance end as a rule by being added not only to the price of the goods imported, but to the price of all similar goods consumed within the country ; so that the public is really paying out of its pockets, in the form of augmented price, ten times more than the State receives. Suppose, *e.g.* that France imports 10 million quintals of foreign wheat, worth 20 francs per quintal at the port of arrival. Owing to the competition of this foreign wheat, the whole 80 million quintals of wheat —the average production of France—are also sold for 20 francs per quintal. This is precisely the grievance of the French producers. Suppose now that a duty of 7 francs is put on the foreign imported wheat, the State will receive from its customs officials, provided the duty has not reduced the quantity imported,

[1] *Esprit des Lois*, Book XX, chap. xi.

70 million francs. But turn now to the consumer : not only will he pay 7 francs more for each quintal of foreign wheat, but, as the French producers will naturally try to sell their wheat at the same price as the foreign producers he will pay 7 francs more for every quintal of home-produced wheat, *i.e.* $80 \times 7 = 560$ million francs. In the end, then, these protective duties will have brought 70 millions to the State and 560 millions to the home producers, but they will have cost the consumers 630 millions.

This question as to the influence of Protection on prices is the crucial one ; and if it were proved that Free Trade meant cheapness, and Protection dearness, the latter cause would certainly be compromised. But facts are more complicated. As a rule what takes place is this. Protective duties, by increasing the profits of the producer, cause an increase in national production. This increase in production, however, which sometimes amounts to over-production, causes a fall in prices on the home market which may be equal to the amount of the duty. The duty in this case is no longer effective. Indeed, it seldom acts to the full extent. The difference in price between French wheat and foreign wheat on the London market is rarely 7 francs, or the full amount of the duty : more often it is 3 or 4 francs. This means that the competition of French producers among themselves does not permit the current price of wheat to rise to the highest level of the dam raised against foreign wheat.

Well, say the Protectionists, so much the better. The home production has been increased ; the country no longer needs to apply to foreign countries for its bread ; the money which it paid to them is now paid to French agriculturists, and the price of wheat has been kept within reasonable limits.

Yes, but we are between the Scylla of deficit and the Charybdis of over-production. When a bad harvest comes the pressure of home competition will cease, and the price of wheat will rise to the maximum of the protective duty—or even beyond ; so that public outcry will necessitate the suspension of the duty. If, on the other hand, within the kindly shelter of the customs barrier, production degenerates into over-production—which happened in the case of wines in France—it will involve a heavy fall in prices. Is it any better for France to be flooded by her own wine and wheat than by those of foreign countries ? In our view, the over-production thus called forth in the home country is worse than that which comes from abroad ; from the latter it is easy to defend ourselves by buying no more than we want, but, when the over-production is at home, a refusal to buy more at a given moment would ruin the home producers. Stability of prices is the great advantage of Free Trade.

(2) From the point of view of *distribution*, protective duties give rise to injustice; for their effect is to guarantee a minimum income to the producers of protected goods, an injustice the more glaring as the law refuses to guarantee a minimum wage to the workers.[1]

The advantage resulting from them is, besides, much greater for the rich than for the poor. Protective duties aggravate the inequalities already existing. Here is a duty of 7 francs per quintal on wheat, which is to raise its price from 20 to 27 francs. The landowner who cultivates poor land, or who has not very adequate resources, and who produces only 10 quintals per hectare, will gain no more by the duty than an additional 70 francs of income, which will not perhaps be enough to cover his costs; but the landowner already favoured by nature, or employing more up-to-date methods, who reaps 30 quintals per hectare, and who, by very reason of his privileged situation, might well do without protection, will gain on the contrary an additional income of 210 francs per hectare.

(3) Even from the standpoint of *national production*, which it is the aim of Protection to encourage, protective duties do undoubted harm by *raising the price of raw material and the equipment necessary for production*. Hence the perpetual and interminable conflicts between the various branches of production. When an attempt was made to put duties on the entry of silks, in order to protect the cocoon producers in the Cevennes and by the banks of the Rhone, the most violent protests were raised by the silk spinners of Lyons. If duties are put on the entry of woollen, silk or cotton yarn, the spinning industries which use them as their raw material are ruined, etc. True, to remedy this, complicated methods of "temporary admission" have been invented, but these are but insufficient palliatives (see *infra*).

---

[1] M. Méline, the chief author of the present customs tariff in France, put it in so many words: "The philosophy of our customs tariff is to maintain current prices in such a way that those who see their profits decreasing may keep up their prices at a remunerative level."

But then justice should make us do what is being done in Australia at this moment where very high protective duties have been established, but where a law has just been passed declaring that, if the manufacturer does not pay his workers the trade-union wage, or if he raises his sale prices, he will be subjected to a tax calculated so as to absorb the whole or part of the benefit of the protective duty. And though the law has been declared unconstitutional and has not as yet been applied, it is none the less significant.

(4) From the point of view of *commerce*, it must not be forgotten that protective duties, by reducing imports, *tend by that very fact to reduce exports*, and thereby run directly counter to the efforts which are being made to facilitate communication between nations by piercing mountains, cutting isthmuses, subsidising steamship lines, laying telegraphic cables, opening international exhibitions, establishing monetary conventions, etc. Can we imagine anything more absurd than to spend hundreds of millions of francs on piercing tunnels under the Alps at ever-increasing cost, only to put customs officers at both ends to stop the passage of as many goods as possible ? Hundreds of millions have been spent on the Seine, the Rhone, the Gironde, and thousands of millions on canals ; there is even some idea of digging a railway under the Channel. And why ? Simply to lower by a few centimes the cost of transport on goods coming that way from abroad. And yet, at the same time, for very fear that they may come, their prices are raised 20 or 30 per cent.by customs duties ! [1]

(5) As to *industrial progress*, Free Traders maintain that protective duties slow down its rate by removing or weakening the stimulus of outside competition. Bismarck, in one of his speeches, referred to the pike which are put in carp ponds to keep the carp moving and to prevent them from tasting of the mud. The comparison is quite appropriate here. If a country is to keep its rank as a great industrial and commercial Power—and this is the object of Protectionists—it must be forced continually to renew its equipment and its methods, unceasingly to eliminate its worn-out or antiquated organs, as the serpent renews its youth by changing its skin. Now, as such an operation is always very disagreeable, it is doubtful whether producers would carry it out were it not for external pressure.

(6) Lastly, from the *fiscal* point of view, protective duties may increase revenue at the beginning, but they *reduce or suppress it in the end by drying up its source, viz., import.* McKinley, when President of the United States, in presenting his famous tariff, declared categorically that its object was not to increase revenue, but, on the contrary, to reduce it, and finally to suppress it

[1] David A. Wells, in his *Primer of Tariff Reform* (1885), calculated that a duty of 20 per cent. was equivalent to a bad road; a duty of 50 per cent. to a large and deep river with no means of crossing it ; a duty of 70 per cent. was a vast morass on either side of the river ; a duty of 100 per cent. a band of thieves who rob the merchant of almost everything he has, and who make him feel lucky at having escaped with his life. *See* Bastiat's equally clever pamphlets on the same line.

when the duties had reached a high enough level to attain that end.

When, on the contrary, duties are of a fiscal, not of a protective, character, such as those which England imposes on exotic products— tea, coffee, sugar, tobacco and wines—which she does not herself produce, it is to the interest of the government to make them sufficiently low to encourage the import of the taxed products; and since, as a rule, the lower a tax the greater its yield, the Treasury may find in these taxes a considerable source of revenue.[1]

IV: THE SYSTEM OF COMMERCIAL TREATIES

IT should be our ideal to establish the same relations between nations as between individuals. Now, the ideal relations between individuals are not those of competition, nor even of simple exchange, but of co-operation.   This fact of itself is enough to set us against the protectionist systems in so far as their aim in regard to nations is "Each for himself, each to himself."   But this is not to say that we are free to consider absolute Free Trade, the principle of *laisser-faire*, *laisser-passer*, as altogether desirable; for this is only an anarchical form of competition.

The system among nations which most nearly approaches the association of individuals is that of the *commercial treaty*, whether in the form of a reciprocal contract between two countries, or, better still, of a *commercial union* between several countries.   There is a tendency at present in this direction; and it is, in our view, the line which the future will take.   The policy of commercial treaties, by the curb which it puts on exorbitant pretensions, by the mutual interests and bonds of solidarity which it creates between the contracting nations, seems to be the wisest policy that can be adopted; and moderate Protectionists and Free Traders are, as a rule, at one in recommending it, though from different motives.

To Free Traders commercial treaties offer the following advantages :

(*1*) They guarantee *fixity* of tariffs over a long period of time (generally ten years), which is a great advantage in commercial operations. True, on the other hand, they bind down the contracting countries, and deprive them of the power to modify their tariffs

---

[1] Customs revenues are not by any means proportional to the amount of protection. Thus, England draws about £34,000,000 from her customs, while France draws from £20,000,000 to £24,000,000, according to the year.

according to circumstances; but this should be considered a good, not a bad, effect, since manufacturers are thereby able to calculate and fix their prices for a fairly long period. The main grievance of foreign, especially of English, manufacturers against the French commercial system is that, owing to the power which the French Government reserves to itself of modifying duties at will, they can never count on the morrow.

On the other hand, this very fixity was the main objection which French producers had to the system of commercial treaties. They were unwilling to be tied down, or deprived of the power of raising duties whenever they thought fit. And France, as we shall see, abandoned the system of commercial treaties over fixed periods for *commercial agreements*, revocable at the will of either party. This is, in reality, not only a very anti-social but a very unpractical attitude to take. So much so, indeed, that, in spite of the protests of French manufacturers, the government was obliged, in certain cases, to *consolidate* the duties in order to be able to negotiate with other countries—that is to say, to bind itself not to modify them, as in the case of the duties on corn from Russia.

(2) They create a solidarity of interest between other countries, as well as between the two contracting parties, by what is known as the " most favoured nation " clause—a clause which it is customary to insert in all treaties—in virtue of which *every concession made by one country to another is extended by right to all countries with which the conceding country already has treaties.*[1]

(3) They lead gradually to a *more liberal system*, owing to the mutual concessions which the contracting parties wrest from one another at each renewal of the treaties ; whereas experience has proved that, once a system of Protection has been set up in a country, it tends to become aggravated and to spread, one industry after another coming forward to claim its share.[2]

(4) Finally, they strengthen friendly relations between nations and diminish the risks of war. A treaty of commerce between two countries is almost as good as an alliance.

---

[1] But this clause, owing to the interdependence which it creates, makes the negotiation of new treaties very difficult. It was owing to it that the recent agreements between France on the one hand, and the United States and Canada on the other, were nearly wrecked.

[2] It is in this that the so-called " infant industry " argument, which recommends Protection as a temporary state, indispensable for new countries, but destined to disappear when they reach their economic majority, is belied by experience.

Commercial treaties, on the other hand, satisfy certain demands of the Protectionists.

(1) They presuppose, virtually at least, the existence of a general tariff and of protective duties, since every treaty is a reciprocal contract, and every contract implies the exchange of advantages. Now, what advantages can a country, which has no duties on imports, offer in exchange for those which it claims ? It may threaten to shut its door perhaps, but it must first see that it has a door to shut. If there is free entry, there can be no basis for a treaty. This is why England finds it difficult to conclude treaties, and why, in order to provide herself with this power of negotiation, one of her political parties is now inclined to establish duties. For treaties necessarily imply the principle of *Reciprocity*, or, as it is called in England, of *Fair Trade*, as opposed to *Free Trade ;* that is to say, the opening of the door to countries which open theirs, and the shutting of it to those which shut theirs.

Economists of the Liberal school do not trouble much about reciprocity. No doubt, they say, it is very desirable that the door should stand wide open on both sides, but, if it is shut or half shut in one country, this is no reason for shutting it in the other. Better one door open than both shut ! If, for example, Europe puts duties on American products, she inflicts an injury on the United States ; but she inflicts one on herself as well, and the damage done to our neighbours cannot be considered as compensation for the damage done to ourselves.

This is quite true ! *Retaliation*, as it is called, is absurd as a remedy, but it may be justified as a measure of war, to force the aggressor to change his methods. In any case, the aim of the commercial treaty is precisely to avoid these retaliations and tariff wars.

(2) Commercial treaties *save industries* the ruin of which would cause too great a disturbance in the country, or the continuance of which is desirable from the political, as well as from the economic and social point of view. If France, *e.g.* judges that her mercantile marine should be kept up at any cost for purposes of national defence, or her wine-growing industry because of the enormous amount of capital invested in it and the amount of wages which it distributes, commercial treaties enable this to be done.

(3) They permit of a *differentiation* of duties, so that the respec tive situations of countries, and of the industries in each which appear to be most threatened by competition, may be taken into account ; whereas the general customs tariff is necessarily uniform,

and cannot draw distinctions between the countries from which the goods come, or can do so only as a measure of war.

True, this differentiation of duties is often rendered of no effect owing to the most-favoured-nation clause; but not always. For, as the clause extends only to products that are identical, the favoured product may be specified in such a way that the favour cannot be extended to others : for example, the favour granted to wines from Champagne will not be extended to sparkling wines in general. This is called *specialisation*, and has been so often resorted to by Germany, in order to evade the clause of the treaty of Frankfort, that France is now threatening to follow suit.[1]

(4) They are opposed to the acts of artificial competition by means of which a country tries to push its products into foreign markets, *e.g.* bounties on export, such as the late sugar bounties ; or the selling of articles abroad at a lower price than that at which they are sold in the home country—a process familiarly known as *dumping*.

But, it may be asked, where is the harm in this ? Thanks to the bounties which sugar-producing countries were so obliging as to give to their manufacturers, England had her sugar for next to nothing ; thanks to dumping on the part of German syndicates, Russia was able to get her rails cheaply.[2] This was a happy windfall. Yes, because England had given up making sugar. But Russia does not intend to give up making rails ; and it is not good for the industry of a country to find itself thus at the mercy of foreign Powers. When a State, rightly or wrongly, considers that it needs to protect some industry or other, it cannot allow this protection to be annihilated

[1] The following words have been attributed to Herr von Bülow, when Imperial Chancellor: "The strength of our new tariff is that it now includes 946 articles, and is in consequence highly specialised, which means that on any one article we may make concessions to Austria, Russia and to Italy without these concessions applying to France. Between the French article and the analogous Russian, Italian and Austrian article, differences will easily be found which, though very small, are in reality sufficient to admit of the application of two different clauses " (quoted by M. Blondel, *Bulletin de la Fédération des Industriels*, 1905). This declaration has been disavowed, but it certainly sums up the system.

For example, to give Swiss cattle an advantage over French cattle, and to evade the clause of the treaty of Frankfort, the German-Swiss treaty declared that only bulls raised at an altitude of over 300 metres above sea-level, and grazing in summer at an altitude of over 800 metres, could benefit by it. Again, in order to favour Italian wines, Marsala has been made a special class.

[2] According to a diplomatic note of the Russian Government in 1902, the German syndicate for the manufacture of rails sold its rails at 115 marks per ton in Germany and 85 marks abroad.

by the foreigner by means of an artificial reduction in the price of competing products, with the sole object of forcing the door.

Such then are the advantages of the system of commercial treaties. They would be greater still if veritable Customs Unions could be established. But this does not seem to be the tendency of the age. Still, if Great Britain were eventually to constitute a Customs Union of her whole immense empire, and if the United States were to succeed in constituting a Customs Union including all the republics of America—in face of these two Zollvereins, occupying one-third of the world each, a third union would have to be created, embracing all the States of continental Europe.[1]

V : THE TARIFF LEGISLATION OF FRANCE

WE have said that the commercial system of France, as it results from the law of January 11, 1892, was inspired mainly by a spirit of antagonism to the commercial treaties of 1860 (see p. 349). The following are its characteristic features : [2]

(1) It establishes an *autonomous tariff—i.e.* duties fixed by *a law*, which can be modified only by a new law.[3] The country, instead of having its hands tied by a treaty—by a reciprocal contract—reserves the right to modify tariffs when, and only when, it thinks fit. In consequence, the customs tariff is promulgated in the form of a law, each category of goods being enumerated in detail with the specific corresponding duty.

(2) Still, the antipathy of France towards commercial treaties does not go so far as to refuse to negotiate with any country ; such isolation might have serious drawbacks. France therefore will conclude, if not treaties, at any rate *commercial agreements*, which, instead of being for a fixed period of time, are always revocable at

[1] See articles published on this subject by M. Peez in the *Revue d'Économie politique*, 1891–1892.

[2] See Nogaro and Moye, *Les régimes douaniers.*

[3] In certain cases of urgency, however, the government may establish duties by simple decrees. It may, for instance, decree *surtaxes* on goods coming from countries which would impose differential duties on French goods, and *compensatory* duties against bounties on export and dumping.

It may, in particular, in the case of foodstuffs, decree the *anticipated* application of the duties which it proposes to create or raise, since, so soon as it is seen that a new duty is about to be established, trade hastens to buy and thus to escape, for a time at least, the payment of these duties. This measure of safety is called the *padlock*. Its utility is, however, very doubtful, as it is unlikely that the large makers are not aware of what is coming, and, even if taken by surprise, the sudden raising of prices which will follow may be disastrous.

the will of either of the two parties on a six months', or a year's, notice. The autonomy of the tariff is thus safeguarded.

(3) But if there were only one single tariff for every product, commercial agreements would be impossible; for what would be the use of negotiating and bargaining where there was only one fixed price ? The system of 1892 comprises therefore not one, but two tariffs for each article.[1]

The one, called the *minimum tariff*, is fixed according to the difference between the cost price of a product in the home country and its cost price abroad. The duty is supposed to be calculated in such a way as to restore an exact equivalence between the two articles and to allow them to compete on equal terms. Note, in passing, that such a calculation is impossible. For we know (p. 222) that, though on a given market there is only one sale price for similar articles, there are as many cost prices as there are articles. It is here, as we shall see (Book III), that rent comes in. There are no two industries, any more than two pieces of land, whose costs of production are the same, even though they manufacture the same articles. There is not, therefore, *one* French cost of production and *one* foreign : there are thousands of both.

The other, called the *maximum* or *general tariff*, is generally 50 per cent. higher, and is intended to serve as a weapon in the hands of the negotiator, in order to obtain concessions from the other party, or to be able to hit back in case of refusal.

The negotiator will be able to say, " If you do not reduce the duties on such-and-such an article, or if you do not give me the most-favoured-nation treatment, I shall apply the general tariff to you." This maximum tariff may be said to exist in all countries, in the sense that every country has a general tariff, and that the object of negotiation is always to obtain a more moderate conventional tariff. Only, in other countries, the possible concessions are not fixed in advance ; whereas, under the French system, the minimum tariff cannot be touched—it is *taboo;* it is the sacred boundary which must not be crossed, since, by definition, it is the minimum of protection which a specified industry can accept without perishing.

Now, this innovation on the part of France, though it has been imitated by other countries, does not seem to us of a nature to render negotiation more advantageous. If, in a sale, the buyer knows before-hand the lowest price to which the seller can come down, while the seller does not know the price to which the buyer may be willing

---

[1] There are, however, certain articles, corn in particular, for which there is only one, and this a maximum, rather than a minimum, tariff.

to rise, the seller is surely at a disadvantage. It is as if the French negotiator were able to move his pawns over two squares only, while his opponent is able to move over a hundred. The former will certainly lose the game. For remark, that the system of minimum and maximum tariffs allows of no intermediate duty.

And France, moreover, does not seem to have been very successful in her negotiations. She has been obliged sometimes to grant all that the foreign country asked ; sometimes to resort to tariff wars, as with Italy and Switzerland—unfortunate from the political, as well as from the economic, point of view. Finally, she has been forced to make some fairly serious breaches in her tariff wall :

(a) By lowering her would-be inviolable minimum tariff, on discovering that there was no other means of obtaining concessions from the other party. She was forced in this way to reduce nine articles of the minimum tariff in order to treat with Russia, and fifty-four to treat with Switzerland. There were lively protests, but the Chamber and the Senate, hard pressed, had no other course open than to vote these reductions.

(b) By undertaking not to alter the duties on certain specified articles. For we can understand that countries to which France, in return for numerous concessions, granted her minimum tariff, might say, " But what good will this concession be to us, if you withdraw it to-morrow by altering the law ? " [1] To relieve their quite natural apprehensions, the government took upon itself on several different occasions to *consolidate* the duties ; that is to say, it undertook not to alter them so long as the agreement lasted. Russia, in particular, by the convention of 1905, exacted and obtained the consolidation of the duties on grain and petroleum, and she had great interest in doing so. Consolidation does not suppress the power of denouncing an agreement, but it means that the whole agreement must be denounced at once ; and this, as we can understand, is a guarantee. French autonomists, however, protested bitterly against the new concession,[2] and the government has been congratulating itself lately on being able to avoid it in its agreement with Canada.

---

[1] And this apprehension is well founded ; for, even before the general revision of the tariff, in 1910, Parliament had already several times voted rises in the minimum tariff ; in particular on corn, wine, meat, etc. Between 1892 and 1907, the duties on forty articles were raised and on five only reduced.

[2] The *Société des Agriculteurs de France* declared that, considering that this convention took away from them the liberty over their tariffs . . . that it put in question the whole economic system inaugurated in 1892, that it injured most seriously the interests of French agriculture . . . it protested energetically against this convention and demanded that it be not ratified.

We must distinguish four different situations in which France stands in her commercial relations with foreign countries :

(*1*) There is one country, Germany, to which France is bound by a veritable treaty, a treaty which, as distinct from ordinary treaties of commerce, has no time limit and cannot be dissolved save by common consent—or by a new war. The reason is that this treaty is an integral part of the political treaty of Frankfort, which closed the war of 1870–1871. As a matter of fact, it is not a convention, but simply an article (Art. 11) stipulating that the commercial relations of the two countries shall henceforth be based " on the system of reciprocal most-favoured-nation treatment." This clause was not imposed by the conqueror, but demanded by the French Government.[1]

(*2*) With all the countries of Europe, except Portugal, and with a certain number of countries outside of Europe, she has conventions by which she grants her minimum tariff *en bloc* and benefits by the most-favoured-nation treatment. To free trade nations such as England, Belgium, and Holland, the same favour is given without a formal convention.

(*3*) To a fairly large number of countries outside of Europe she grants her minimum tariff for certain articles only, in return for concessions which are also specified. This is the case with the United States, China, and Brazil.[2]

(*4*) Lastly, there are a few countries to which the maximum tariff is applied—Portugal, Peru, Chile, Bolivia, the British Colonies, etc.

It is not easy to sum up the results of this system, even after eighteen years of trial. Protectionists declare that the experiment is decidedly in their favour, as the balance of trade is less unfavourable, and agricultural production in France has greatly increased. Free Traders, on the other hand, answer that the progress in agriculture is due to quite other causes than the customs duties, in particular to the development of large agricultural syndicates and to the increasing use of chemical manures ; and they point to the fact that, in spite of this, the cost of living and of raw material is higher in France than in free trade countries (see p. 362).

[1] It does not apply to all the conventions that either country may enter into, but only to those concluded with one of the six neighbouring countries—Belgium, Holland, Russia, Austria, Switzerland and England. Indirectly Italy is also brought in, as, owing to the Triple Alliance, she has a right to the same treatment by Germany as Austria has.

[2] On the occasion of the agreement of 1910, the United States claimed the benefit of the minimum tariff, on penalty of applying their maximum tariff, which is prohibitive. In the end a compromise was made.

The system laid down by the law of 1892 was completely modified in a strongly protectionist direction, in 1910, the minimum tariff being raised on a large number of articles, so that France might have something to hold out in treating with other countries. The best excuse that can be given for this is that other countries have already proceeded to do the same, in particular Spain and Switzerland. And the current of the world seems to be running in this direction.

Let us look shortly at the way in which customs duties are fixed. There are two methods :

(1) The first is to fix the duty at so much per cent., according to the value of the goods. This is the duty *ad valorem*; it has the great advantage of simplicity ; the whole tariff may be condensed into a single page. But if this system has the simplicity of the income tax, it has also the same drawback—*i.e.* it is practically impossible to prevent fraud without recourse to very vexatious measures. For the mere declaration of the parties is no guarantee to the Treasury. The declared value, says the American law, must correspond exactly to the price marked in the schedules, and the invoices must be checked by the consul in the exporting country. Any understating of value involves the payment of a double duty, and sometimes the confiscation of the goods. But, in reality, the United States fixes an official price according to valuations which are always arbitrary; it even goes the length of organising a veritable espionage.[1]

The most ingenious, and least inquisitorial, method of control which has so far been devised is the *right of pre-emption*; that is, the right given to the customs authorities to acquire the object at the declared price. But it is evident that this right is a threat more than anything else, for the Administration cannot turn itself into an auction mart.

(2) The second method is to fix the duty according to the nature of the goods—a separate duty for each article, like sale prices in shops. This is what is called the *specific duty*. It is a very complicated system, since, in order to get more nearly at the value of an object, it is necessary to multiply the categories. Thousands of articles have to be catalogued in detail, with so many subdivisions, that large volumes are necessary to contain them, and it is no small task to find one's way among them, especially as, in spite of all his efforts, the legislator has not been able to foresee

---

[1] In particular for diamonds bought by Americans in Paris.

everything. It is not merely Egyptian mummies which have embarrassed the customs officials ! This system has the advantage, however, of almost entirely suppressing fraud,[1] and, by reason of its very complexity, it gives a better handle for bargaining in the negotiation of commercial treaties, and for differentiating duties according to the kind of industry. It is this last method which has been adopted in France and in most other countries.

Not all imported goods are subject to customs duties. There are two categories which, in conformity with the spirit of the protectionist system, ought to be exempted :[2]

(1) Products which are *not grown in the country*, in the case of which there is no home industry to be protected, *e.g.* exotic products.

Still, even these hardly ever escape the customs. As a rule, they are taxed for fiscal purposes, as articles of luxury—though this is often an ill-founded presumption, as in the case of coffee, the real value of which has fallen to 80 centimes per kilogramme and which pays in France frs. 2.20 of duty. It is from such exotic products that England obtains most of her £32,000,000 of customs revenue. Or, more often than not, they pay duty for protectionist reasons on the ground that they compete indirectly as substitutes with home products. Thus, in France, petroleum and pea-nuts pay as competing with colza and olive oil. It is on the same ground that the brewers in England are asking for an increase in the duties on wine.

(2) Products which serve as *raw material* for other industries, a duty on which would react in the form of increased cost of production. As these industries would be placed at a disadvantage over

---

[1] We say " almost," as it is still possible to find a way of transferring an object from one category to another less heavily taxed.

[2] In addition it would seem as if we ought to exempt from protective duties :

(a) Products which a nation is able to produce so cheaply that it does not need to fear foreign competition—wine in France, machinery in the United States, wheat in Russia, oranges in Spain, etc.

(b) Products which satisfy such pressing and general needs that every rise in price causes injury to all, the typical example being wheat.

Yet, it is rare that even the products under these two headings find favour with the Customs. In the first case, it is said that a nation is never able to produce so cheaply as to defy all competition. In the second, that the primary utility of these products is one more reason for protecting them. It is just because a nation cannot do without bread that the agriculturist who produces corn must be kept alive. And thanks to this line of reasoning, wheat, which up till 1885 paid only 60 centimes per 100 kilogrammes, has since been subjected to duties of 3, 5, and finally 7 francs, or about one-third of its value !

against foreign industries, Protection would thus be working counter to its own object.[1]

But exemptions of this nature are difficult to carry out. For where these raw materials—wool, silk, leather, linen, iron, coal, etc.—are also produced in the home country, those who produce them claim the same right of protection as their fellow citizens. An ingenious system of compromise has therefore been devised which consists in exempting from the duty only those raw materials which are intended for re-export in the form of manufactured articles, and will have to compete with foreign goods on the international market. This is what is called *temporary admission*. To prevent fraud, the importer has to sign an undertaking to pay the duties, with surety—hence the name *acquit-à-caution*—and under penalty of a heavy fine, if within a certain time he has not re exported these raw materials transformed. A duty is sometimes exacted in the first instance and refunded later, on re-exportation : this is what is called the *drawback*.[2]

This system is not very convenient to apply if the raw materials that are re-exported in a manufactured state are to be the very same as were imported ; the verification of their *identity* involves vexatious measures for the manufacturer. And if we must be content, as is generally the case, with *equivalence* of the quantity re-exported to the quantity imported, we open the door to all sorts of combinations for evading the law. Take for example a miller at Marseilles who imports Russian wheat, but who works only for home consumption. He has no right to demand temporary admission, and pays therefore the import duty—no light one—of 7 francs per 100 kilogrammes.

[1] The official classification, moreover, distinguishes : (I) foodstuffs ; (2) raw material ; (3) manufactured articles. It is counted a sign of progress when imports under (1) and (3) decrease, while those under (2) increase. This is the point of view of the Colbertists.

In the case of coal, which, if not raw material, is at least instrumental and necessary to industry, the duty is very moderate—1 franc 20 per ton.

[2] The system of temporary admission applies to a fairly large number of raw materials : wheat intended for grinding, iron, silk thread, etc. In all, there are 135 million francs of exemptions. The *drawback* is used for hardly anything but salt intended for salting meat, and only to the low figure of 1 million francs.

Temporary admission must not be confused with the system of the *bonded warehouse* in which goods are stored provisionally while awaiting re-exportation, and in which they may not undergo industrial transformation, but only commercial manipulations ; nor with *transit*, when foreign goods simply pass through France in closed and sealed trucks. Goods which pass through the bonded warehouses, and goods in transit represent enormous sums, about 1½ billion francs. This is what causes the difference between general and special commerce. (See above, p. 330 n.)

But he bethinks him that there is a miller at Lille in exactly the opposite situation, *i.e.* who wants to export flour to Belgium, because he has too much. The Marseilles man says to the man of Lille, " I will get exemption from the duty by saying that I work for export : I shall send you my *acquit.* When you export, you will get it signed for me." It goes without saying that the miller at Lille will not do this service for nothing. They will go shares, according to supply and demand, in the profit of 7 francs per 100 kilogrammes.[1] The favour granted by the State is here a useless sacrifice.

Nor is it the Treasury only which suffers. What is a more serious matter, the producers of wheat and the consumers of bread may be affected too. For it is obvious that, if an importer can sell his *acquit* for 5 francs, this amounts to his having paid a duty of only 2 francs. Now, such a large reduction of duty will artificially encourage the import of wheat at Marseilles, and thus possibly cause a fall in the price of French wheat, to the detriment of the agricul- turists of the South ; while, in the North, as the export of French wheat is encouraged by what is practically a bounty of 7 francs (less the price paid for the *acquit*), this may cause a rise in the price of wheat to the detriment of the consumers in the working towns of the district.

A more or less successful effort has been made to remedy these abuses by requiring that the transformed material be exported from the port at which it entered (this is what is called the system of *zones*) ; or by having it escorted to the factory where it is to be transformed. But this involves costly and vexatious control.

In Germany, the system of temporary admissions has been replaced by that of *import orders,* which, in spite of their name, are more of the nature of bounties on export. Every exporter of cereals (the " order " is only given on these) receives a certificate which may be given in payment for the customs duties (on the import either of cereals or of a certain number of specified goods), and is therefore a bounty on export, save that, instead of being paid in money, it is paid in a paper money which undergoes an " agio," varying with supply and demand.

---

[1] In practice, this proceeding resolves itself into a sale of *acquits.* Their current price varies according to the law of supply and demand, *i.e.* according as the exporters who wish to buy them, or the importers who wish to sell them, are in the majority.

N

VI : BOUNTIES ON PRODUCTION

SINCE protective duties have so many drawbacks, is there no system which could be substituted for them—what one might call Protection without protective duties ?

There are several systems. We would point out in particular : (1) the *differential railway rates* in Austria-Hungary for encouraging the export of certain products ; (2) the *guarantee of interest* for capital invested in new industrial enterprises, often resorted to in South America and Mexico ; (3) the *exemptions from, or reductions in, taxation* granted to new industries which a government wishes to acclimatise, of which there are many examples in Hungary, Roumania, etc.[1]

But the system most in use is that of *bounties on production*, where the State grants a sum of money under certain conditions to the producer.[2]

This method does not seem to present any of the disadvantages of import duties, and it is far superior to them, in theory at least, for the following reasons :

(*1*) Bounties put no obstacle in the way of foreign trade, while they allow the full development of imports, since they leave free

---

[1] In Roumania the law grants to new industries free concessions of land, exemptions from customs duties or the refunding of them in the case of their raw material and equipment, reductions in taxation, etc. In return, however, after a period of five years, three-quarters of their employees must belong to the country, and they must take on whatever number of apprentices the administration thinks fit.

[2] These bounties *on production* must not be confused with *bounties on export*, which were common enough in former days, but are now rarely given. They were recently granted to the sugar industries in Germany, Austria and France, with the curious result that sugar could be sold cheaper abroad than at home. They were abolished, however, by the International Convention at Brussels (March 5, 1902), where it was agreed : (1) that the import duty for sugar in all the contracting countries should be the same (6 francs per 100 kilogrammes, or about 10 per cent. of the value, not counting, of course, the internal taxes, which in France amount to 25 francs per 100 kilogrammes) ; (2) that if any country granted a direct or indirect bounty, the customs duty would be raised by all the other countries to an equal value. Volumes might be written on the history of sugar production.

In France, however, there is still a bounty on the export of codfish. There has been some talk of resorting to export bounties—but intermittently—in order to remedy crises of over-production, by allowing a producer to get rid of his surplus abroad, or to enable him to sell cheaper abroad than at home, since he would be able to make an abatement equal to the amount of the bounty. The *import orders* in Germany of which we spoke are of this nature ; they differ from the bounty only in that the State, instead of paying them in money, receives them in the place of money due to it.

entry to foreign goods and do away with all barriers. Customs duties, on the contrary, require a costly administration, and create the powerful and demoralising industry called smuggling.

(2) Bounties are, in consequence, far less likely to provoke international conflicts.

(3) They cause no loss to consumers, since they do not raise the price of products. On the contrary, producers are able to sell more cheaply, owing to the supplementary profit which bounties allow them.

(4) They are no hindrance to production, since they do not raise the price of raw material nor the cost of production. They may, indeed, be so graduated as to stimulate the progress of the industry they are protecting.

Thus the bounties granted to the mercantile marine vary, as we have seen (pp. 260–262), according as the ship is a sailing-ship or a steamship, built of wood or of iron, and according to speed. So too, the bounties given by the law of 1891 to silk spinners are in proportion to the degree and perfection of their machinery, as are likewise those given for sugar, which have contributed to improve not only the production of sugar but the cultivation of the beetroot.

But all of these advantages are outweighed by the capital objection that bounties are a form of *expenditure*, while customs duties are a form of *receipts*. Now States, being as a rule in debt, are naturally more inclined to accept money than to give it away.

And yet, from the purely theoretical, and even from the moral, point of view, we might look upon this frank acknowledgment that bounties are expenditure as a sign of their superiority rather than otherwise. There is no pretence that they are other than they appear to be—namely, a sacrifice imposed on the country for the sake of public utility. This form of Protection gives rise to no uncertainty : the public knows that it is paying for it and exactly the price which it is paying. Customs duties, on the contrary, keep up a mischievous illusion, *making the country regard as a gain what is in reality a burden*.

There is, however, another objection to bounties : they have too personal a character. The advantage resulting from a customs duty is always more or less anonymous ; no one knows exactly who profits by it. Now, the manufacturer who is to get a bounty is known, and also the amount which he receives. This is the reason why such a system will never be popular. It exposes in too glaring a light the sacrifices which it asks of all and the privileges which it grants to a few, thereby offending the spirit of equality. We must add that it requires a discernment and an impartiality which can hardly be expected of any government, and that where it has been practised it does not seem to have given any appreciable result. This is not very encouraging.

A government, therefore, does not resort to bounties unless it has no other course open to it; that is to say, unless it is unable to resort to protective duties, either for fear of injuring some other national industry—this was the reason why bounties were granted to the silk producers, the silk manufacturers of Lyons protesting energetically against duties on their raw material; or for fear of exposing itself to retaliation on the part of foreign countries—this was the reason why bounties were resorted to for the protection of the mercantile marine.

In France, these bounties constitute a somewhat heavy burden on the budget, amounting to about 13 million francs for the producers of cocoons, linen, hemp, oil, and for silk-spinning; to which must be added 61 millions for the mercantile marine (see above p. 263). Yet our marine is progressing much more slowly than are those of other countries; and as for silk growing and spinning, they are rapidly losing ground.[1]

The system of bounties would be useful if it could be abolished once the experiment was ended and so soon as it ceased to give results. But experience shows that this never happens.

VII: TRADE WITH THE COLONIES

THE question of the commercial relations between a country and its colonies constituted for centuries one of the most important chapters of economic history. It used to be thought that colonies had no *raison d'être* save to bring advantages to the mother-country, by buying her manufactured articles as dearly as possible and selling their colonial produce at the lowest prices.[2] With this idea a complete and complicated system was elaborated, called a *colonial compact*,

---

[1] Particularly silk-growing, in spite of the fact that the bounty is considerable—60 centimes per kilogramme; and the kilogramme of cocoons is only worth 3 or 4 francs.

[2] See above, p. 90, *Emigration and Colonisation*.
Montesquieu himself said "the object of these colonies is to carry on commerce under better conditions than is possible with neighbouring peoples, between whom all advantages are reciprocal. It was decided that the mother-country alone could trade with her colonies, and that *with good reason*, since the object of such settlements was the extension of commerce, not the foundation of a town or a new empire." (*Esprit des Lois*, Book XXI, chap. xxi)

which may be summarised in the following five articles : (1) colonies may buy only from the mother-country ; (2) colonies may sell only to the mother-country ; (3) colonies may not start manufactures, for fear of being tempted to consume their own products ; (4) colonies may not receive or despatch goods except under the flag of the mother-country ; (5) and as a sort of offset to the lion-like clauses of this so-called compact, the mother-country undertook to receive colonial products duty free, or with reductions of duty.

The surprising thing is that all colonies were not killed outright by this system. Many, it is true, were ; others, like those of the two Americas, were able to revolt in time.

This famous question, which formerly caused so many conflicts, has not yet lost all its importance. The relations between mother-countries and their colonies may be classed under three headings :

(1) The system of *autonomy*. The colony fixes its own customs duties : this is the English system. The colony may put duties on the products of the mother-country just as on those of foreign countries ; or it may give them preferential treatment. The most important British colonies, Australasia and Canada, have given a proof of their independence by adopting, against all home traditions, an ultra-protectionist system. Still, under the influence of the imperialist idea, several of them have lately granted reductions of duties, to the amount of a quarter or even a third, on products from the mother-country—with no hope of reciprocity, however, since England, as she has no protective duties, cannot differentiate between the imports she receives (see above, p. 368).

Several French colonies also—those of Africa (with the exception of Algeria and the Gaboon) and of the Pacific Coast (with the exception of New Caledonia), the five French towns in India, and Saint-Pierre-et-Miquelon, in America—enjoy commercial autonomy. As a rule, like the British colonies, they give the home country preferential treatment.

It goes without saying that, on this system, the mother-country preserves the same independence as she allows her colony. She may, therefore, either tax its products at the same rate as those of foreign countries, or grant them preferential treatment.[1]

[1] In principle the products of autonomous colonies benefit, in France, by the minimum tariff and even by a certain number of total exemptions. This is the case with most of the products which come from Tunisia. As, however, these products, which are very much the same as those of France (wines, corn, olive oil, etc.), offer a dangerous competition to the similar products of the mother-country, an attempt has been made to reconcile the interests of the Tunisian colonists and the French agriculturists by fixing each year a limit to the quantity

(2) The system of *assimilation*. The colony is considered as forming a part of the mother-country, and is in consequence enclosed within
the same customs boundary. The products of the mother-country
enter therefore duty free, while those from other countries are
subject to the same duties as on entering the mother-country.
This is the system applied to most of the French colonies. It is
deplorable. Even admitting that it might be justified in the case
of colonies near at hand, like Algeria, it is sheer folly to force
colonies at the other end of the world—like Indo-China, Réunion,
the Antilles, Guiana, Madagascar, the Gaboon, and even New
Caledonia—to supply themselves with French goods and to keep
out by exorbitant duties the foreign products which are perhaps
at their doors. It can have no other effect than that of enormously
increasing the cost of living in these colonies, of isolating them artificially from the environment from which they might draw their
nourishment,[1] and ultimately of decreasing their buying power ;
leaving out of account the fact that the exclusion of foreign
products renders foreign governments very hostile to the extension
of the French colonial empire. The trouble in Morocco had no other
cause than this. As the colonies of Great Britain, on the other hand,
are open to all, the colonising work of this country provokes much
less distrust. This system of assimilation, under the cloak of solidarity
among all the members of one and the same body, is a survival,
pure and simple, of the old egoist colonial system. And French
manufacturers, although they have not read Montesquieu, have
no hesitation in saying openly that " the aim of colonisation is to
procure markets, not the foundation of a new empire."

Such a system indeed is worse than the colonial compact ; for,
unlike the latter, it does not offer the compensation of reciprocity in
the form of free admission of colonial products into the mother-
country. In practice, it is true, these products are not subject to

of each category which may be imported. French viticulturists would put
the same restriction on wines from Algeria.

[1] This system has also the unfortunate result of suppressing by quasi-
prohibitive tariffs the importation of foreign goods, and with them the customs
duties which form the larger part of the colonies' budgets—a paradoxical result,
but none the less real.

For the rest, the absurdity of this system is so evident that the law of
January 11, 1892, which created it, allowed the colonies to ask for reductions
of duty on the foreign products which are most useful to them. But these
reductions must be authorised by the *Conseil d'État*, and are seldom granted.
In 1911, foodstuffs were allowed free entry, and a Bill has recently been laid before
the House to allow assimilated colonies the right to modify their tariff according
to their needs.

protective duties ; but as nearly all colonial produce, sugar, coffee, cocoa, spices, etc., are more or less articles of luxury, they rarely escape the fiscal duties. It is only with great difficulty that certain French colonies have been able to obtain a few reductions.[1]

An additional unfairness is that the mother-country obliges the colonies to abolish their export duties—which constitute an important resource for their budgets—in the case of products intended for her consumption, in order to keep down their prices.

(3) The system of the *open door*. The colony is open to imports from all countries by virtue of international conventions. This does not mean that the colony may not establish customs duties ; but such duties must be purely fiscal in character ; there must be no difference in treatment between the mother-country and other countries, and, in general, the duties may not exceed 10 per cent. of the value. This system, which was unknown formerly, and is spreading to-day, is imposed on the colonising country by other countries as the price at which they put their recognition of its conquest. The vast Belgian and French colonies in the Congo are under this system, by virtue of the convention of Berlin of 1885, as is also the French Protectorate of Morocco, by the Franco-German Treaty of 1912.

Although this system seems hard on the colonising country, which has to bear all the costs of colonising without keeping the profits, it is one which has our approval. For, in the first place, it is a guarantee for the natives of the new colony and, as it spreads, it will greatly diminish the chances of international conflict over colonies, so menacing at the present day.

Although the system of assimilation applied to the larger part of the French colonial empire has greatly reduced the trade of its colonies with foreign countries, it has not, owing to the force of circumstances, been able to eliminate it entirely. Foreign trade still represents (exports and imports combined) about 57 per cent. of the total trade of the colonies. The exceptional cases of Algeria and Tunisia, where the proportion is only 20 per cent., are easily explained by their proximity to France.

[1] A duty is about to be laid on foreign cassava. That of the colonies has been provisionally spared ; but the President of the Customs Commission in the Chamber has warned them : " What we want is that you should bring us what we lack ; what we do not want is that you should compete, as does foreign cassava root at the present moment, with our potato, our maize, our barley, our beetroot." This is the colonial system of the eighteenth century, pure and simple.

As for the trade of France with her colonies, it amounted, in 1910, to nearly £68,000,000 (or about 15 per cent. of her total trade), nearly £50,000,000 of which was with Algeria and Tunisia alone.[1] It is still far behind that of Great Britain and her colonies, which amounts to £480,000,000.

CHAPTER IX : HOW CREDIT IS ONLY AN EXTENSION OF EXCHANGE

I : MEANING OF CREDIT

CREDIT is only an extension of exchange—exchange in *time* instead of in *space*. It may be defined as the *exchange of present for future wealth*.

For example, I sell you wool. But you have not the wherewithal to pay me ; that is to say, you have no present wealth to give me in exchange. No matter. You will give me the future wealth you propose to create with the wool ; that is to say, an equivalent value in cloth when made.

Here the fact of exchange is visible to the naked eye : this is indeed a sale. The only difference between it and an ordinary sale is that it is made *on credit* instead of *for cash*. But this difference, which appears of so little importance, has enormous consequences. It is no small thing to bring the future into the sphere of contracts.

There is another method of credit, where the act of exchange, although virtually present, is less easy to see. Instead of selling, I *lend* you corn ; that is to say, you will pay it back to me at the next harvest. You will not, of course, give me back the same corn, since you will have used it for sowing your field, but other corn taken from your harvest. The Roman lawyers very rightly said that, in a loan, the ownership of the thing was transferred completely ; this is why they called it the *mutuum* (from *meum-tuum*) ; and that the same was the case with the similar thing given back in payment. If, instead of corn, we take as example a sum of money, which is to-day the usual object of a loan, it is no less evident that here again there is an exchange of present for future wealth.[2]

---

[1] For details, *see* M. Girault's book, *La Colonisation*.

[2] When a particular object is lent, which the borrower must return as he got it—say a house or a piece of land (renting or leasing), or a horse or a book (hiring)—the definition which we have given does not hold good ; there is no longer exchange, there is *letting* ; but, for that very reason, there is no *credit* in the strict sense of the word.

Now, these two operations, the *sale on credit* and the *loan*, constitute precisely the two essential forms of credit.

The essential characteristics of credit are therefore : (1) *the consumption* of the thing sold or lent ; (2) the *waiting* for the new thing that is to replace it. For whereas, in the letting of a house or a piece of land, the one who lets knows that it will be restored to him, and never loses sight of it for an instant in the hands of the borrower, the man who lends a thing intended for consumption knows that he is depriving himself of it for ever ; he knows that it is bound to be destroyed. The borrowed wheat must pass under the millstone before it can become flour, or be buried in the furrow till the next harvest comes round. The borrowed bag of crowns, no matter to what use it is to be put, must be emptied to the last coin before the money that it is expected to bring in can be gained. Now, this is a truly disquieting situation both for the person who borrows and for the person who lends, for see what it results in :

(*1*) The lender, in the first instance, is exposed to considerable risk. No doubt he is counting on an equivalent wealth which will replace that which he has lent, but after all *it does not yet exist ;* it has to be produced, and everything that is future is, by that very fact, uncertain. Legislators have done their best to safeguard the lender against all dangers, and the precautions which they have devised on this score constitute one of the most important branches of civil legislation (the guarantee, collective liability, mortgage. etc.). Nevertheless, there must always be a certain confidence on the part of the lender, an act of faith, and this is just the reason why the name " credit " has been applied to this particular form of loan (*creditum, credere*—to believe). And credit is being called on more than ever to justify its high title, since, as we shall see, personal credit is tending more and more to take the place of real credit, both in the current accounts of banks and in societies of mutual credit. This, it will perhaps be said, is a return to the past, to the ancient times of Rome, when the creditor had no other guarantee than the actual person of the debtor ; but there is a great difference. Then, it was the actual body of the debtor which served as guarantee— a body which could be imprisoned, struck, even cut in pieces (*partis secanto*, said the Law of the Twelve Tables) ; whereas to-day, in trade or in societies of mutual credit, personal credit has no other guarantee than the trustworthiness of the debtor—not his physical, but his moral person.

(*2*) As for the borrower, his obligation does not, like that of

N

the tenant or lessee, consist simply in preserving the thing lent and in keeping it in good repair, so as to restore it at the end of the term fixed.   He must, after having used—that is to say, destroyed—it, make another equivalent to it, in order to pay it back when it is due. *He must therefore take great care to employ this wealth in a productive manner.*   If he is foolish enough to consume it unproductively, in personal expenditure, for example, or if he simply does not succeed, for some reason or other, in reproducing a sum of wealth at least equal in value, the result is ruin.   The history, in fact, of all countries and all epochs is a veritable martyrology of borrowers who have ruined themselves by credit.

Credit is therefore an infinitely more dangerous mode of production than any which we have so far considered—a mode which can be used only in societies whose economic education is highly advanced.

II : HISTORICAL SKETCH OF CREDIT

CREDIT is much the most recent of all modes of economic organisation. Presupposing as it does the accumulation of capital in money form, it was too complicated to have come into existence in primitive societies.   It was, however, practised to some extent in the form of cattle-hiring.

But surely, it will be said, the loan, or at least the sale for account, played an important part in antiquity and in the Middle Ages. True ; but it was looked on as a kind of assistance given to one's own family or class, or as a method of exploiting strangers or persons of different social standing,[1] rarely as a method of production. Hence the opprobrium so justly attached to this form of contract, the riots which it provoked, and the repeated demands for remission of debt, sometimes granted by popular governments.   The canonists of the Middle Ages, in trying to distinguish productive loans, where they admitted interest as legitimate, from unproductive loans, where they condemned it as usury, did not reason so badly, and the attention which they gave the subject was fully justified by the necessities of the times.[2]

Credit, as a mode of production, only really came into existence when future wealth, which is its true object, was materialised and put into commerce in the form of *negotiable securities*.   This was a

---

[1] " Unto a stranger thou mayst lend upon usury ; but unto thy brother thou shalt not lend upon usury " (*Deuteronomy* xxiii, 20).

[2] See Ashley, *Economic History*, and below, *Interest*.

veritable economic revolution, dating back to the thirteenth century. Its history is somewhat as follows : [1]

At first the credit claim was not looked on in the light of wealth, since it did not bear on material objects : it was a personal relationship between the creditor and the debtor. As the commentators of the Roman Law significantly put it, the obligation adhered in the body of the debtor, *ossibus haeret*. And if the debtor failed, the creditor could not pay himself out of the goods, but only out of the body of the debtor. This is why, as we said before, he could imprison that body or even cut it in pieces. Under such conditions, the idea of *transferable* credit claims could not possibly arise.

It was not long, however, before the Roman jurists took an important step forward, assimilating credit claims to material goods (*bona*) and rendering them transferable by such devices as the *novatio* and the *litis contestatio*.[2] Nevertheless, the transfer of credit claims always remained more difficult than that of material goods, and even to-day requires somewhat complicated formalities, in particular the notification of the debtor.

But commercial law, ever in advance of civil law, had, even in the Middle Ages, adopted a twofold and admirable method of representing a creditor's claim by means of a written document, the *bill of exchange,* or *promissory note.*

The merchant of Venice, instead of sending 1000 ducats to Amsterdam, gave them to a fellow townsman who had dealings with Amsterdam and who gave him, in exchange, a letter ordering his correspondent at Amsterdam to pay 1000 ducats to the person who should present the letter. The merchant therefore simply sent the letter instead of money.[3] In the beginning, this letter could be utilised only by the man to whom it was addressed. It was not

---

[1] Bruno Hildebrand classifies economic evolution into three periods : (1) the *natural* economy characterised by the absence of exchange (the producer himself consuming his products), or, at most, by exchange in kind ; (2) the *money* economy characterised by sale and purchase ; (3) the *credit* economy characterised by the loan and sale on account, which, in our opinion, has not yet reached its full development, since we hold that it may one day render the use of money altogether unnecessary (see p. 329).

[2] See Paul Gide, *La novation et le transport des créances,* 1879.

[3] The *bill of exchange* runs as follows : If Paul has sold goods to Peter, he writes on a sheet of stamped paper : " Montpellier, January 1, 1911. Three months from date pay to James, or order, the sum of 1000 francs for value received," adding below, " To Peter at Paris," signed " Paul," and hands it on to James, and when James wants to transfer it, he will write on the back : " Pay to the order of William," signed " James," and so on.

There is another credit document, viz., the *promissory note.* Here Peter, the

till the fifteenth century that the idea occurred of making it nego-tiable by a simple endorsement on the back of the letter.

The endorsement was a great simplification, but it was still a formality, and by no means an unimportant one, since it involved the joint responsibility of all who signed. A further step was taken, and endorsement made unnecessary, by the creation of credit documents to bearer which pass from hand to hand as easily as money.

This was the last step in the evolution of credit. From that time on enormous quantities of wealth—not fictitious, but future wealth, a very different thing—were added to the mass of already existing wealth and circulated in the form of negotiable documents, or documents payable to bearer. These documents are now the object of a colossal commerce,[1] the merchants who deal in them being called bankers.

But where, it may be asked, is the great utility in representing credit claims by negotiable documents ?

It is this. If it is a great advantage for a borrower, or a buyer on account, to have some capital at his disposal during a certain time, it is, on the other hand, a great disadvantage for the lender to have to do without it during the same time. A manufacturer has to make purchases and pay wages every day. He can keep going only on condition of daily renewing his capital by the sale of his goods ; but if he sells his goods on credit, *i.e.* without being paid, it would appear impossible for him to continue his business.

What is he to do in this case ? The same capital cannot surely

---

buyer, writes : " Three months after date I promise to pay Paul, or order, the sum of 1000 francs for value received. This January 1, 1911—(signed) Peter."

The promissory note is, therefore, simply a *promise to pay*, given by the debtor to his creditor. The bill of exchange is more complicated : it is an *order to pay* addressed by the creditor to his debtor. An order to pay whom ? Not the drawer, the creditor, but a *third person*. Owing to this form the bill of exchange is used more particularly for settling distance or time operations. Its function is much more important than that of the promissory note.

It is a serious thing for a merchant debtor not to pay a bill of exchange to let it be *protested*, as it is called. He may, by so doing, be proclaimed bankrupt. If the man on whom the bill of exchange is drawn be insolvent, it is the man who has drawn it who is responsible. And failing him, it is one or the other of those through whose hands the bill has passed and who have endorsed it. The guarantee, therefore, which this document gives the creditor is perfect.

For the cheque, which is not, properly speaking, a credit document, see *supra*, p. 325.

[1] The quantity of negotiable documents, or, as they are called in French, "*effets de commerce*," in circulation in France is some 40 billion francs.

be at the disposal of two different persons, the lender and the borrower, *at the same time ?*

And yet this is what actually happens. And it is the negotiable security which allows this apparent impossibility to be accomplished.[1]

In exchange for the capital which he has handed over, the lender, or seller on account, receives a document, *i.e.* a piece of paper, which may take various forms—promissory note, bill of exchange, etc.— and this document represents a value which, like all values, may be sold. If, therefore, the lender wishes to come into his capital again, nothing is more simple : he has only to sell, or, as it is called, *negotiate*, his document.

III : HOW CREDIT ENABLES MONEY PAYMENTS TO BE DISPENSED WITH

THAT credit allows payment to be postponed is evident from the definition of it. But how it allows payment to be dispensed with altogether does not appear so clearly ; for surely, it will be said, sooner or later, when the time has expired, the sum will have to be paid up. Yet even that is not necessary.

This is what happens. In the first place, *sale for cash*, that is to say, the exchange of goods for money, gives place, as we have just seen, to *sale for credit*, that is to say, exchange of goods for a credit claim. I give you my goods and receive in exchange a promise to pay, in the form of a promissory note or bill of exchange.

Here, *e.g.* is a debtor A. Instead of paying his creditor B in money, he gives him a draft on X. B, who owes C money, instead of paying C, gives him the draft which A has given him ; C uses it in turn to pay D, etc. Supposing D is finally paid by X, one single payment will have sufficed to settle four exchanges ; and if X happens to be in A's debt, this payment will itself be unnecessary, and the whole series of exchanges will have taken place without the use of money at all.

---

[1] Léon Say, in his preface to Goschen's *Théorie des changes* (French translation), says : " This absolute representation of property by the security has removed all obstacles in the way of the exchange and the transference of rights. To-day, mills, factories, railways, all things, in a word, that can be possessed, are sent by letter from France to England, England to Canada, from Holland to the Indies, and *vice versa*. The thing itself remains immobile, but its image is ever being transported from one place to another. . . . The object is in one place, but it is enjoyed everywhere."

It should be added that, if the image may stand for the object, it is because it really has an *equal value*. See, however, what we say, p. 392.

Now, the extreme complexity of social relations, and the fact that each one of us, or at least each producer, is in turn buyer and seller, makes the use of these various modes of extinguishing debts much easier than might at first sight be imagined.

For example, suppose I am a barrister, and one of my clients, a wine-seller, owes me money. Instead of paying me, he writes me a promissory note. When I want to pay my bookseller I can give him this note in payment. If the bookseller happens to get his wine from this wine merchant, he in his turn will only need to give him this note in payment.[1]

Let there be three persons or three countries in the world, whom we shall call A, B and C. Suppose that A is in debt to B, who is in debt for the same sum to C, who again is in debt to A, a situation which we shall represent by the accompanying diagram.

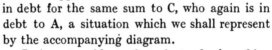

Is it not evident that, instead of making the sum of money respectively due by these three debtors to their three creditors go round the whole circle, it is simpler to settle the whole without paying a farthing ?

But, it may be asked, is it not very unlikely that C would be in debt precisely to A, and be just on the spot to close the circle ? No doubt; but if C is not in debt to A, he will perhaps be in debt to D, E, F, G, or H, etc., until we finally come upon some one—our X in the example above—who is A's creditor, and the problem is solved. The greater the number of persons in the game, the larger the circle, the *better chance there is of closing it.*

It was in international trade that men first resorted to credit in order to dispense with money. The difficulties and dangers of transporting large quantities of money great distances are supposed to have suggested to the Lombards the idea of the bill of exchange. Let us see how this works out in practice. Suppose that French merchants have sold 10 million francs of wine to England, and that they have sold on credit; that is to say, instead of getting money, they have drawn 10 million francs of bills of exchange on their English debtors. Suppose that the English coal companies, on their side, have sold 10 million francs of coal to French manufacturers, and have drawn bills of exchange to an equal value, payable in

---

[1] We have already seen (p. 324) how money may be dispensed with by the use of the cheque, but to pay with a cheque is, after all, to pay—the cheque, as we know, always presupposes a deposit, *i.e.* a corresponding sum of money at the bank ; in this case, however, we are trying to dispense with money itself.

France. When the French manufacturers want to make up their accounts, will they send 10 millions in specie ? No ; by means of bankers, whose business it is to find and sell such documents, they will simply get from the wine-sellers the 10 million credit documents payable in England, and will send these to their creditors, the coal companies, saying to them, " Get your payment from your own countrymen." Thus the absurdity of two opposite currents of money crossing the Channel at once will be avoided.

Our example, it is true, supposes two countries creditors and debtors to one another for an equal sum, which does not very often happen. But even where this is not the case, the same result may be arrived at in a more roundabout way. Suppose that France has bought 10 millions of tea from China, but has sold nothing to her in return. Here a contra-account seems impossible, since France has no credit claims on China. Will she not in this case have to pay in money ? It does not follow ; for though France has sold nothing to China, there are plenty of other countries in the world which have, and which therefore are her creditors. France has only to buy, on the world's market, drafts on China, paper payable in Shanghai or Hong-Kong. But will she not in the end have to give money for these drafts ? Not necessarily, since she may always pay for them with drafts on some other country. Thus, if she buys credit claims on China in London, she will pay for them with her own credit claims on England. And the tea bought by France from China will be paid for by the wine sold by France to England without untying the purse-strings.

Were it not for these ingenious combinations, international trade would really be impossible ; for if France had to pay in money 7 or 8 billion francs of imports annually, where would she get this immense amount ? She does not possess as much. In fact, as we said, the money which passes from one country to another is only a small fraction, one-thirtieth at most, of the value of the goods exchanged.

It is not in international relations only, but in the relations between inhabitants of the same town or district, that the credit document, in the form of the cheque, is tending to oust money. (See what we have already said, pp. 324–327.)

IV : CAN CREDIT CREATE CAPITAL ?

CREDIT has become so important in our modern societies that we are tempted to attribute miraculous virtues to it. By our constant references to the large fortunes founded on credit, by our tacit assumption that the greatest enterprises of modern industry are based on credit, we almost irresistibly persuade ourselves into the belief that credit is an agent of production quite as able as land, or labour, to create wealth.

This, however, is pure fancy. Credit is not an *agent* of production : it is—and this is quite another matter—a particular *mode* of production, just like exchange, or the division of labour. It consists, as we have seen, in the transfer of wealth or capital from one person to another ; but to transfer is not to create. Credit no more creates capital than exchange creates goods. As J. S. Mill admirably puts it, credit is only " the permission to use the capital of another person."

What fosters the illusion is the existence of credit documents. We have seen that all lent capital is represented by a negotiable document of equal value in the hands of the lender. Hence it appears as though the act of lending had the miraculous power of making *two* capitals out of one. For, the old capital of 10,000 francs which has been transferred to your hands, and the new capital represented in mine by a note for 10,000 francs—do not these make two ?

From the point of view of the individual this paper is indeed capital : but from that of the country it is not. For it is clear that it cannot be negotiated unless some other person will give me, in exchange, the capital which he possesses in the form of money or goods. This note, therefore, is not capital *per se ;* it simply gives me the opportunity *of procuring other capital in the place of that which I have given up.* It is evident, moreover, that, to whatever use I want to put this paper, whether it is to be devoted to production or to my own private expenses, I can turn it to account only by converting it into objects of consumption, or instruments of production already existing on the market. It is with this material wealth, not with bits of paper, that I shall produce, or keep myself alive.

If every credit document, that is to say if every credit claim, really constituted wealth, it would be enough for each Frenchman to lend his fortune to his neighbour to double the fortune of France, and to bring it from 250 billion francs up to 500 billions !

But, it may be asked, do not these documents represent *future wealth ?* Certainly. But it is just because the wealth is future wealth that it must not be counted ; it will be counted so soon as it comes into existence. Till then there will always be this marked difference between present wealth and future wealth, that the latter does not exist. We neither produce nor live on expected wealth. We might just as well, when taking the census of the population, include all who will be born within the next twenty years, on the ground that they are future members of society.

But, if credit cannot be termed productive in the sense of creating capital, it nevertheless renders eminent services to production by allowing the existing capital *to be used to the best possible advantage*.[1]

For if capital could not pass from one person to another, if each man personally were reduced to turning his own capital to account, an enormous quantity of it would remain unused. In every civilised society there are a number of persons who cannot themselves make use of their capital, viz. :

Those who have *too much* : for, so soon as a fortune exceeds a certain figure it is not easy for its owner to turn it to account by his own unaided strength, apart from the fact that in such cases he is, as a rule, but little disposed to make the effort.

Those who have *not enough* : for working men, peasants, servants who have laid by small savings, cannot themselves employ their tiny capitals. And yet their pence added together may amount to millions.

Those who, by reason of their *age, sex* or *profession*, are not themselves able to turn their capital to account in industrial enterprises : women and children, persons who follow the liberal professions, barristers, doctors, military men, priests, functionaries, and employees of all classes.

On the other hand, there is no lack in the world of promoters of enterprises, inventors, agriculturists, even working men, who would know how to make a good use of capital if they had any, but who unfortunately have none.

If, then, thanks to credit, capital can pass from the hands of those who cannot, or will not, make anything of it to the hands of those who are able to employ it productively, this will be of great profit to all concerned and to the whole country. The capital thus withdrawn from barren accumulation, or unproductive consumption and fertilised by credit amounts, in all countries, to millions sterling. It has justly been said that credit possesses the virtue of turning

---

[1] We refer here, as we are dealing with production, only to credit which is used to facilitate production ; but there is a form of credit still more perilous which is used to facilitate consumption. We shall come to it again under this latter heading.

capital in a latent state into capital in an active state.   Credit in fact performs the same function in relation to capital as exchange does in relation to wealth.   We have already seen that, by transferring wealth from one possessor to another, exchange does not create wealth, but helps it to be better utilised and enables the labour of production to be turned to better account (see above, p. 237).[1]

V : LAND CREDIT (*CRÉDIT FONCIER*)

CRÉDIT FONCIER, as it is called, is a form of credit *which takes land as security*.

The simplest and oldest form of this kind of credit is the loan on mortgage.[2] From the lender's point of view it possesses an advantage which has made it always much sought after by capitalists, viz., its almost absolute security, land being a pledge that can neither perish nor be stolen.   But alongside of this advantage, the loan on mortgage possesses great disadvantages for both parties.

It burdens the borrower very heavily, as the rate of interest is rarely under 5 per cent., while the income which he will draw from his land will generally be below this level.   If, as so often happens, the borrower applies the sum borrowed to enlarge his estate, he is going straight to ruin, for the lands he buys will bring in less profit than the interest he will have to pay, unless he cultivates them with his own labour.   It has often been said that credit holds up the landowner as the rope holds up the hanged man ; and though the saying is harsh, it is not exaggerated—save when the borrower is some large financier or some big company.

For the lender, also, the loan on mortgage has great disadvantages, inasmuch as, while it gives him full security for his money, it does not allow him to recover it quickly.   It is not easy for him to transfer his credit, and when the date falls due he has too often to resort to the extreme measure, as disagreeable for the creditor as it is deplorable for the debtor, of expropriation.   Thus it is only to usurers that the

---

[1] Credit also enables a certain quantity of metallic money to be dispensed with.   But we have already studied this function of wealth at length (see p. 389), and we shall return to it in connection with the bank-note.

[2] The sum total of mortgages in France is not exactly known.   M. de Foville puts it at 15 billion francs.   But this includes mortgages on houses as well as on land.   Now it may be calculated that the mortgage debt of rural property amounts to only one-half of this—7 to 8 billions.   Estimating the total value of the land at 80 billions (see *infra, Equal Division*), this represents a burden of 10 per cent.   In other countries it is much higher, being estimated at 58 per cent. in England.

loan on mortgage is a profitable business. If the number of landowners who have been ruined and expropriated in every country by the mortgage loan, were to be weighed in the balance with the number of those who have grown rich by it, this mode of credit would certainly appear in so odious a light that its abolition would surely be called for. In those countries in particular where it is practised on an ignorant and improvident population—in Algeria, the countries of the Danube, and in Russia—it does incalculable harm.

On this question of credit on land, the legislator finds himself between two opposite tendencies. On the one hand, efforts are being made in most countries to check the abuses of the mortgage loan by making the minimum of land indispensable to the existence of a family—the *homestead*—not liable to seizure. We shall return to this under landed property. On the other hand, there is a desire to help the country population to become small proprietors ; and how can this be done if not by credit, *i.e.* by giving them the capital necessary to acquire and work the ground ? This is the object of the recent French law, of March 19, 1910, which, subject to certain conditions, puts funds lent by the Bank of France at the disposal of the peasants. (See chapter on *Property*.)

Some ingenious improvements, however, in the mechanism of land credit have been introduced, which lessen the dangers of the borrower and the difficulties of the lender.

(a) The first consists in the creation of special banks, known in France by the name of *Sociétés de Crédit Foncier*. These banks act as intermediaries between capitalists and landowners. They borrow money from the former in order to lend it to the latter, and although they do not render this service for nothing, still they secure some important advantages to both parties. To the capitalist who lends the money, they offer securities as safe as mortgages, since they have the same guarantee, but much more easily realisable, as the guarantee is not one particular piece of land, but the entire funds of the society. And as the society is as a rule some powerful company, these securities circulate as easily as stocks or railway shares. When the possessor wants to recover his money he has only to sell them on the Stock Exchange. To the landowner who borrows money, they offer the threefold advantage : (1) of a long-period loan, *e.g.* for seventy-five years ; (2) of repayment gradually and without sensible burden by way of *annuity ;* (3) lastly, of a rate of interest, as a rule, relatively low.

Such banks exist in many countries. In France there is only one society of this sort, a powerful company, invested with a monopoly, since 1852, under the name of the *Crédit Foncier de France*. This great establishment lends over long periods. The interest is practically 5 per cent., but this rate includes an annuity calculated so as to redeem the capital within a period of seventy-five years (or fifty years when the interest paid is 5·34 per cent.), so that, when the term expires, the landowner finds himself entirely free from debt, having meanwhile paid a somewhat smaller interest than he would have had to pay to an ordinary creditor. On the other hand, if he is able to clear himself sooner, he may do so whenever he likes, a small indemnity of 5 per 1000 being retained on instalments already paid. In spite of these ingenious combinations, the services which the *Crédit Foncier* has been able to render agriculture are not very great : the sum total of loans made since its foundation reach, it is true, the imposing figure of over 6 billion francs (2 billions of which are still running), but most of this has been used for buildings in towns, and less than a billion has gone to rural property. It would be more appropriate, therefore, to call it the *Crédit urbain*.[1]

After what we have said, we should, indeed, rather congratulate ourselves than otherwise on finding it so little used, were it not that, unfortunately, many rural landowners resort to other worse forms of borrowing through the kind offices of solicitors.

(*b*) The second improvement consists in making mortgages negotiable by means of endorsement, just like any other commercial credit ; and this system, sometimes, though somewhat incorrectly, referred to as the *mobilisation* of landed property,[2] has been very skilfully organised in several countries. But it is very doubtful whether any system, however ingenious, will allow the holder of a mortgage to negotiate his scrip as easily as a commercial security. It would be contrary to the nature of things, for the mortgage must always partake, to a certain extent, of the immobility of the land on which it rests.

In Germany, the landowner may create mortgages in advance on his land, which he may then negotiate as occasion requires, in the same way as a banker draws cheques on himself. These are called *Handfesten*. The landowner thus carries his land in his pocket,

---

[1] The sums lent every year by the *Crédit Foncier* (on land or houses, but not including loans made to communes, which amount to almost the same sum) vary from 100 to 140 million francs. They show, however, a marked tendency to decrease, as in 1882 they amounted to over 300 millions. The yearly total of mortgages from all sources is estimated at 2 billions.

[2] In Australia, under the *Torrens Act*, the mortgage may be very easily transferred. See Book III, *Evolution of the Ownership of Property in Land*.

and can, as it were, coin it ; for he may divide a piece of land worth 10,000 marks into, say, ten mortgage notes of 1000 marks each, which he will use as required. These notes bear numbers ranging successively from No. 1, which has the whole land for guarantee and offers therefore every security, to No. 10, which, coming last, is somewhat contingent. They are therefore very unequal. Now, the curious thing is that the landowner may offer them in any order he likes. If he inspires confidence in other ways, he may give No. 10 as guarantee, and reserve the better and more secure ones for the bad days ; whereas, under the system of ordinary mortgage, the borrower is obliged to give the first claim to the first lender, and later, when his personal credit is lower, can only offer mortgages of the second, third, up to the tenth rank, consequently of small value.[1]

This ingenious system, first started at Bremen in 1860, had had a more modest precedent in the decree of Messidor 9, Year III, which created mortgage schedules (*cédules hypothécaires*) to be issued by the landowner, transferable by endorsement—an innovation which caused quite a scandal and was never applied. The Bremen system does not appear to have been much more successful. It is indeed unnatural to try to marry, as it were, the bill of exchange to the land. A mortgage investment, to be safe and lasting, cannot circulate rapidly. And we repeat, the more easy mortgage credit is made, the more dangerous will it become, and the more surely will the small landowner be delivered into the hands of the usurer.

In short, credit on land, as it is called, is really on the margin of credit : it is more of the nature of an investment.

---

[1] The landowner, however, has the right to issue these *Handfesten* only after certain formalities—verification of his titles by a special court, inquiry and advertisement in the papers, etc.

These *Handfesten* are worded as follows : " The Land Commission hereby witnesses that X has created on his immovable property situated at Y a *Handfeste* of 2000 marks." And if the title is not the first in order, the sum after which it is to rank is written at the top. Thus, in the example we have taken, if the document is No. 7, it will have the words " *after* 6000 *marks* " written on it. The lender in this way knows that he can claim nothing unless the land sells for over 6000 marks, this sum being due to creditors holding previous numbers. The landlord, of course, may himself hold these, but he cannot take advantage of this over the too confident lender as it would be an act of bad faith.

VI : AGRICULTURAL CREDIT

AGRICULTURAL credit, at first sight, is very much like credit on land. It differs, however, quite distinctly from the latter in its *economic end,* its *juridical character,* and *the institutions* which are its organs ; and it is, in our opinion, able to render much better service.

(*1*) In the first place, the object of agricultural credit is to provide not so much the capital necessary to acquire or start a farm as the floating capital necessary for *current working expenses.* It is applicable, therefore, not only to the landowner but to the farmer. It must be remembered that it is in the nature of agricultural industry not to give returns for a year or more. There is a picturesque saying among the peasants in the South of France that agriculture is the trade of the " year to come " ; but its expenses are continuous, the cultivator must be for ever making advances. Now, the precise aim of agricultural credit—and nothing could be more useful— is to provide these advances. They do not need to be for long periods, like the mortgage loans, but they must be for longer terms than industrial loans, which are generally represented by bills of exchange for ninety days.

(*2*) In the second place, agricultural credit does not rest on the land itself : it is guaranteed ;—(*a*) either by the working capital, the equipment of the farm, the cattle, the crops when brought in : it is, as the jurists say, a movable, not an immovable, credit ; (*b*) or, as is more often the case, by the personal solvency of the borrower, backed as a rule by the support of some other person who acts as security, or by membership in some association the members of which are liable for one another's debts. It is therefore *personal credit,* and marks, as we have seen, a great moral advance on real credit.

(*3*) Lastly, the institutions of agricultural credit are very different from those of credit on land. They fall into two different categories : (*a*) those which organise personal credit ; (*b*) those which organise credit on movables.

(*a*) The first are *co-operative credit societies.*[1] These consist as a rule of small landowners (the large ones having no need of such societies), who combine in order to obtain by association the credit which they could not obtain separately.

---

[1] They are also called societies of mutual credit. But this term is not exact and may lead to error. It implies that the members lend *each other* the capital they need. Now, this does not often happen : as a rule the capital lent to members is borrowed from outside.

The most complete type of these associations, and one which is spreading over the whole world, is that called after its founder, *Raiffeisen.*

It was in the year 1849 that Raiffeisen started his first bank. At his death, in 1888, there were 862 banks in existence. To-day there are about 4000, with 300,000 members.

These societies present in general the following features : (1) The members bring *no share capital* into the society, and as the society is thus constituted without capital there are no shares.[1] (2) They receive *no dividends* : the profits, if there are any, go to constitute an indivisible and perpetual fund, which, by continually increasing, will one day allow members to dispense with outside capital, and thus to lend without interest. This will be the free credit dreamt of by Proudhon. (3) Members are jointly responsible to the extent of all *their goods.* This is the characteristic feature which gives these societies a remarkable moral and educational value, but which, on the other hand, alarms persons of a tenaciously individualistic turn of mind, in particular the French peasant. (4) All offices are unpaid, except sometimes that of the cashier. (5) Lastly, these societies have generally a religious character (in Germany, France, and Italy), which allows them the more easily to impose the above obligations on their members, while exercising over them at the same time a severe selection. This tends to increase the credit of the association.

These societies have done incomparable good. They have veritably delivered the German peasant from the usurer who was devouring him. In Germany, in Italy, and even in France, the Catholic social school is actively and successfully at work in developing them.

There are besides, in Germany, 10,000 to 12,000 associations of agricultural credit which differ very little from the Raiffeisen type. The most important are the Haas Societies, so called from the name of their director. These follow the same rules : they are co-opera-tive, *i.e.* they lend only to their own members, but the religious, moral, and philanthropic feature is not so marked : the shares or quotas of the societies are higher, and administrative offices are not gratuitous, etc. In 1905, the two great federations became one

---

[1] This is the principle at least; but it has been necessary sometimes in practice to depart slightly from it, as the law does not, as a rule, recognise the existence of societies whose aim is economic, when they have no capital. In any case it is the rule that capital, in the form of shares or quotas, should be reduced to a minimum.

organisation, uniting nearly the whole of the 17,000 societies of agricultural credit, with 1,500,000 members. There is also the group called Schulze-Delitzsch, which, however, is occupied more especially with the working men of towns ; we shall return to it presently. In all, these societies lend to the figure of seven billion marks per annum.

France has been very backward as regards agricultural credit, the first society being founded in 1885. Agriculturists would have preferred to have recourse to the Bank of France, like traders and manufacturers. But they need long-term loans, as a rule for a year, and the Bank of France can lend only for short periods, 90 days at most. The State, however, when renewing the privilege of the Bank in 1897 made it contribute to the organisation of agricultural credit by taking from it a loan of 60 million francs without interest,[1] 40 millions of which are put at the disposal of the societies of agricultural credit. These societies at first availed themselves of but a small part of this fund. As it is becoming better known, however, it is being drawn upon more largely.

The societies of agricultural credit in France are divided into two groups :

The first comprises the societies which are connected with the syndical movement, which were formed by a law of November 5, 1894. They may consist only of syndicated landowners, or members of agricultural insurance societies, and can issue loans only for agricultural objects. It is for these societies that the 40 millions from the Bank of France have been reserved. The State does not, however, lend directly to them. It is too incompetent to do so, and too liable to political influences. Intermediary organs have been created for the purpose, called *Caisses régionales de crédit.* These are land banks—there are a hundred or so to-day—which receive the money from the State as a loan without interest, and which lend it in turn to the local credit societies at a moderate rate of interest. The maximum term of the loan is five years, and the sum lent must not be more than four times the subscribed capital of the members. The loans take more often the form of discounting the drafts drawn by agriculturists than actual advances of money. These societies of mutual credit differ from the Raiffeisen societies

[1] This loan must be repaid by the State when the concession expires (1920) unless the charter of the Bank be renewed. In addition, the Bank pays the State, as its share of profits, about 6 or 7 million francs per annum. These are also devoted to agricultural credit, but mostly to long-term loans : one-third being apportioned to agricultural co-operatives for production (see p. 200, n. 1) two-thirds to individual loans for developing small property.

in that they do not, as a rule, act on the principle of joint responsibility. Where would be the use of it, since the State already puts more capital at their disposal than they need, without asking any such guarantee ?

The second consists of societies which are a faithful copy of the Raiffeisen type, and are sometimes called *Caisses Durand*, after the individual who introduced them into France and is still at their head. They do not require their members to be syndicated ; nor are their loans, which take the form of advances, not discounts, restricted to purely agricultural operations. They exercise a paternal control over the employment of the sums they lend, requiring a signature as guarantee, and they emphasise the religious character of the society. They do not make use of the State advances, in the first place, because they do not want State aid or control, preferring to rely on themselves alone ; and in the second, because the State is not very willing to grant them loans, finding nearly always some pretext for refusing. There are about 1000 of these societies in all, but they are very small, each society containing under forty members, and extending barely beyond the village boundary, as it is preferred that all the members should know one another.

In all we may count from 3000 to 4000 societies of agricultural credit in France ; they do not, however, lend more than about 200 million francs.[1] The causes of the somewhat indifferent success of co-operative credit in France are not easy to find. They are to be sought, no doubt, mainly in the character of the French peasant, who is little inclined to throw in his lot with his neighbours, and does not like to have his affairs known, preferring, above all when it is a question of money, the discreet offices of the notary.[2]

(b) *Crédit mobilier* (movable credit) is organised for agriculturists in the form of loans on fictitious guarantee, that is to say, where the borrower is not obliged to give the lender the object pledged.

[1] The societies of the first (syndical) type number 3946 plus 97 regional banks. They have at their disposal for lending : (1) their capital (shares, deposits, etc.), 25 million francs ; (2) the money advanced by the State, 40 million francs. With this, in 1911, they lent to the amount of 134 million francs.

The societies of the second type (Raiffeisen) number 1600 with 30,000 or 40,000 members, and lend to the amount of 20 million francs.

[2] With agricultural credit we should put maritime credit for fishermen. Credit is as indispensable for them as for agriculturists, but, being poorer and more careless of their interests, they do not know how to make a right use of it. A recent law in France (March 25, 1910) has attempted to organise it on the same basis, and with the same resources, as agricultural credit, but so far without any result.

When a manufacturer wants to borrow on security, he deposits his goods in the establishments called *Magasins Généraux* (*general warehouses*), and receives in return a double title, the one attesting his ownership over the object deposited, which allows him to sell it when he thinks fit; the other, called a *warrant*, which enables him to borrow by giving this title as pledge to the lender.

But these ingenious combinations, which make borrowing such an easy matter for the manufacturer, cannot be adopted by the agriculturist. It would be an inconvenient and even ruinous proceeding for him to transport and store his corn or wine harvest such a long distance away, not to mention the nuisance it would be to the general warehouses, which are not prepared for such emergencies. The agriculturist, therefore, while keeping his harvest in his own barn or cellar, has obtained the right to pledge it in return for warrants which he may give to the lender. But supposing he were to sell part of his pledged harvest? In that case he would be punished by law. In spite of this, however, lenders appear to be really distrustful of this form of credit, and up till now it has developed but slowly. The best thing would be to create, for the agriculturist, something equivalent to the general warehouse of the manufacturer; to establish, that is to say, communal, or, better still, co-operative, barns and cellars in every village, which would receive the harvests, sheltering them probably better than their owners would, while offering every security to lenders.

Why, instead of resorting to advances and warrants, does not the agriculturist simply draw bills of exchange on his buyer, as the ordinary small trader does, and have them discounted at a bank? This is what the syndical credit societies and the regional banks generally do, discounting the drafts of the agriculturists, and, after adding their signature to them, getting them discounted at the Bank of France. But, before a bill of exchange can be drawn, something must first have been sold. Now, the agriculturist may need money before he has sold, perhaps to avoid selling at an unfavourable moment. Banks, again, lend in the form of discount only for very short periods, ninety days being the maximum at the Bank of France, while the agriculturist needs a much longer time. Banks may, it is true, renew the drafts, but it is a dangerous proceeding.

VII: POPULAR CREDIT

UNDER the influence of Proudhon's ideas, popular credit was very much in vogue towards the middle of the nineteenth century.

It was even held to contain the solution of the social question. Is not, it was asked, our object to put the instrument of labour, namely capital, into the hands of the workers? Now, there are apparently two ways of attaining this end : one, advocated by economists, viz., *saving;* the other by socialists, viz., the *expropriation* of the capitalist class. But between these two solutions, the first of which is impracticable, because the working man does not earn enough to acquire the capital which would make him free, and the second, no less impracticable, implying a general overthrow of society and inevitable injustice, there is another —namely, credit. If only we could find a means of lending the working man the capital he requires in order to produce on his own account, and lend it to him at the lowest rate of interest and in the form of a loan continually renewable, we should obtain the same result as by expropriation, without the necessity for resorting to such an expedient.[1]

To-day this form of credit does not appear in so imposing a light. We no longer look upon it as a means of emancipating wage-earners, but only as a means of preventing the independent producers, who still remain, from falling into the wage-earning class ; that is to say, we try to safeguard and develop the middle class of artisans and small shopkeepers.

The means adopted for doing so are the same as in the case of the peasants, viz., the *association of credit* and the system of *warrants,* or of making money, so to speak, on a commodity before it is sold. We shall not recapitulate this second method, which is of no use to the working man, and of little use even to the artisan or tradesman. But the first is of great importance, if not to wage-earners in general, at any rate to workers who want to become, or to remain, independent producers.

An isolated worker or artisan, however honest and hard-working, cannot offer a sufficient guarantee to a lender : illness, unemployment, and death threaten at any moment his best intentions. There is a well-known proverb, " Loans are only for the rich," and the experience of every day confirms it. But if these workers or artisans are grouped in tens, hundreds, thousands, and united by ties of collective responsibility, they will offer a more solid security, and will easily find credit without passing through the hands of the usurer. Their individual subscriptions, too, though

[1] Proudhon even thought it possible to lower the rate of interest till it became almost gratuitous, and thus to suppress the wage-earning system. See page 560, note 2.

small, will in time mount up and form an imposing fund, which the society will be able to lend to its members.

It is in Germany, under the inspiration of Schulze-Delitzsch, whose name remains attached to the institution, that these *people's banks* (also called co-operative societies of credit), the essential feature of which is the unlimited liability of all members, have developed to such an extraordinary degree.[1] The heads of these societies in Germany hope to give small industry the means of effectively fighting large industry, by providing it with the capital and equipment it lacks. This, if accomplished, will be an important result.

These societies, however, aim at more than merely developing credit ; they also try to encourage the habit of saving in the lower classes. This is why certain of their features are not, at first sight, very democratic. (1) The shares represent large sums (1000 marks, as a rule), payable little by little in instalments and so graduated as to oblige subscribers to economise ; (2) profits are distributed to shareholders in order to stimulate them ; and, (3) in order to have profits to distribute, a fairly high interest is demanded of the borrower, so that the borrower seems to be somewhat sacrificed to the lender. But this is of little importance, since the lender here is also a working man, and a working man whom the societies are desirous of turning into a capitalist.

In Italy, too, these people's banks, the first of which was founded at Milan in 1865 by M. Luzzatti, are very prosperous ; but in England, where co-operation in the form of consumers' societies is very highly developed, there are no co-operative societies of credit. The reason, no doubt, is that small independent industry, like small property, has given up fighting against the invasion of large industry and large property.[2]

---

[1] The Schulze-Delitzsch federation numbers to-day about 1200 of these banks (not counting a large number of consumers' co-operative societies and others, which form part of the same federation) and over 600,000 members. They have a capital (shares, deposits, and loans) of 1600 million francs, and, in consequence of the circulation of this capital, they manage to lend their members nearly 5 billion francs. The losses they suffer on this enormous sum are quite insignificant, 5 centimes per 100 francs. The profits realised are divided among the members according to the value of their *shares*, not, as would be more in conformity with the co-operative principle, according to that of the sums borrowed.

These Schulze-Delitzsch banks also give agricultural credit, claiming to do as much in this direction as the Raiffeisen societies ; but their standpoint is rather that of the capitalist than the philanthropist.

[2] In Scotland the ordinary banks play the part of popular banks, and succeed admirably, thanks to the enormous number of their branches, to the intimate

As for France, inconceivable as it may appear seeing that France is the country of the small bourgeoisie and small commerce, people's banks are even less developed there than is agricultural credit.[1] The reason for this lies perhaps in the fact that the small shop-keepers and artisans, in fighting the big stores, the large companies, and the co-operatives, prefer to resort to political rather than to economic action, bringing pressure to bear on members of Parliament to obtain laws and taxes which will harass and burden their competitors; a more convenient method, perhaps, so far as tactics are concerned, but very dangerous for the economic development of the country.

' The old ideal of popular credit as a means of abolishing the wage-earning system is still alive in France, but the form it now takes is that of furnishing capital to working-men's associations for production. Between 1860 and 1866 several loan establishments, with the significant title of *Crédit au Travail* (Credit to Labour), were created with this object, but failed.[2] To-day there is a *Banque des associations ouvrières de production*, which lends to the co-operative societies. It is through this bank that the State allots annually some hundreds of thousands of francs in loan to these associations. But we shall return to the co-operative associations for production under the chapter on *Profit*.

VIII : PUBLIC CREDIT—THE FUNDS

STATES, like individuals, live normally on their incomes. But, less wise than individuals, they often live beyond their incomes, and there is not one, at least among those termed civilised, which has not its national debt, large or small. A national debt, indeed, is the generally accepted sign that a country has emerged from barbarism, and has entered into what is elegantly termed the " Concert of Europe." National debts have increased at an alarming rate : the total, which was insignificant a century ago,

terms on which they are with the people, and to the high moral and economic level of education of the latter.

[1] In France people's banks, or urban co-operative societies of credit, are not at all numerous (14 only in 1912), and their clients belong rather to the small *bourgeoisie* than to the working class proper.

An effort is, however, being made by government, to create credit for small industry and small commerce by the same means as have been employed for small agriculture, *i.e.* local societies of credit, people's banks, and a central establishment of credit, the utility of which is not very clear.

[2] For an account of the efforts made at this time, *see* an article by M. Moride, *Le mouvement des coopératives de crédit vers* 1863, *Revue d'Économie politique*, 1910.

is estimated now for the whole world at over 160 billion francs. France enjoys the unenviable reputation of occupying far and away the foremost rank among these States, with a national debt which may be put at 33 billions at least.[1] The next largest debts, those of Russia and Germany, do not exceed 24 to 25 billion francs.[2] However enormous the figure for France may appear—and we would not think of denying its gravity—it must be remarked that the total income of France may be calculated at about 30 billions, almost the amount of her debt, and the total figure of her capital at 250 billions (see Book III). Now, suppose a private individual, a manufacturer, earning, say, 30,000 francs per annum, with a capital of 250,000 francs, had contracted a debt of 33,000 francs, no one would consider his situation desperate, nor even his credit much shaken.

When a State spends more than its income, it does what an ordinary individual does : it gets into debt and applies to capitalists for the sum it needs.[3]

[1] Constituted as follows (January 1, 1910):

3 per cent. perpetual	22 billions
3 per cent. redeemable	3½ ,,
Various annuities (due mainly to the railway companies)	6 ,,
Floating debt	1½ ,,

In addition, the communal and departmental debts amount to about 5200 millions—about half of which are for Paris alone.

[2] The following are the debts of the principal States and the percentage per head (see *Annuaire des porteurs français des valeurs étrangères*, by M. Boissière, 1912):

France . . .	33 billion francs	840 francs
Germany . .	25 ,,	380 ,,
Russia . .	24 ,,	144
Austria-Hungary .	19 ,,	373
England . .	18 ,,	400
Italy . .	14 ,,	400 ,,
United States .	14 ,,	150

It must be remarked, however :

(1) That to get at the real value of the public burden, it is necessary to deduct values possessed by the State, which, in some cases, are considerable : for Germany 9 to 10 billions for property in mines, railways, etc. ; for the United States 9 billions cash reserve in gold or bullion.

(2) That the burden per head means little, so long as we do not know the wealth of the country. It is certain, for instance, that, although the contribution per head is the same in Italy as in England, the burden is very unequal.

[3] The State may apply directly to the public by opening subscription lists, or it may make use of bankers. The first system is, as a rule, preferred for political reasons, because the effect is better if the loan is covered a great many times over ; but it is not more economical than the second, since, for the sake of prudence, bankers are always asked to guarantee the subscription.

National borrowings, however, differ from the borrowings of private individuals in three ways :

(*1*) The State (like cities and large companies, when they borrow from the public), instead of debating the sum to be borrowed and the rate of interest to be paid, offers stock for sale, bringing in a fixed interest, at a price determined beforehand, but which is fixed, of course, according to the market rate of interest, otherwise it would find no buyers. For instance, if 1 billion be the amount it needs, it will issue stock bringing in 3 francs per annum, and the price of this it will fix at a higher or lower figure according to the state of its credit and the expectations it has of an answer to its appeal.

(*2*) The State borrows, as a rule, by way of perpetual security— that is to say, the capital of the debt can never be claimed back—reserving the right to repay only if it suits itself.[1] We may be surprised at first to find lenders accepting such a clause ; but we have only to remember that the capitalists who lend their money to the State do not do so with the idea of having it refunded, but only with the object of investing it and of procuring a safe income. A certificate of irredeemable stock fulfils this condition admirably ; and, if the capitalist should want at a given moment to recover his capital, he has only to sell his stock on the Stock Exchange.

(*3*) The State borrows as a rule *below par*, that is to say, it acknowledges itself debtor for a larger sum than it has really received. For example, take a State able to find a lender at an interest of 5 per cent., but not below. It may issue stock representing a capital of 100 francs, bringing in an interest of 5 francs, and put this stock on the market at the price of 100 francs, *i.e. at par*. This would certainly be the simplest method, and it is the one followed by some countries ; but as a rule the French State has taken another line. It prefers to issue stock representing a nominal capital of 100 francs, bringing in an interest of 3 francs only. But, as it would not be able to find lenders if it sold such stock at 100 francs, *i.e.* at par, it offers it at 60 francs. Clearly, for the lenders, this amounts to the same as the first method, since to receive 3 francs of interest on 60 francs is really to

---

[1] This method of borrowing has an historical origin. It was invented as a way of eluding the prohibition of the loan at interest. Common law, like canon law, prohibited interest, on the ground that it was unjust for the borrower to have to repay the capital and to pay interest as well. But if the capital was *never to be repaid*, then the right of the lender to a *perpetual* annuity became quite legitimate. The State simply adopted this principle when it was reduced to borrowing in the sixteenth century.

invest money at 5 per cent. It is indeed much more profitable to the lender. For, though he has only given 60 francs, he receives in exchange a certificate the nominal value of which is 100 francs and the real value of which may one day reach this figure if the credit of the State improves. This is what has often taken place.[1]

It is on the part of the State that it is difficult to understand such an operation. For not only is it strangely complicated, but it is absolutely ruinous, and bears a close resemblance to the transactions by which prodigal sons write themselves debtors to the usurer for 1000 francs when they have really received only three-quarters of this sum. Of the 25 billions, which is the amount of the irredeemable debt at the present day, the State has probably not received more than 20 billions.

It must, however, be observed that, as the State is never bound to repay the capital—for we have said that the State borrows in perpetuity—it is of little consequence whether it binds itself to pay more than it has received or not. What matters is that the interest to be paid should be as low as possible. Now, the excuse for this singular proceeding is precisely that it enables the State to obtain more favourable conditions as regards interest. It is probable that the lender, *by very reason of the surplus value which he hopes to obtain for his stock, will be less exacting in regard to the rate of interest.* For instance, even supposing that at the moment when the loan is issued the credit of the State does not allow of a lower rate of interest than 5 per cent., the lender may still consent to pay 75 francs for a certificate of 3 francs of interest (which will mean for him an interest of 4 per cent. only), in the hope that it will one day rise to 100 francs.

Notwithstanding, borrowing below par ought to be condemned on principle. For it has the objection of rendering any future repayment of the debt impossible, or at least ruinous, for the State, thereby, as we shall see, making every future conversion very difficult.[2]

---

[1] The French 3 per cents rose above 100 francs from 1892-1902, but they have since come down 12 or 13 points below par. The English 3 per cents had risen above par long before this, but they stand now at no more than £74 (March 1913). It must be observed, however, that they have been converted into 2½ per cents.

[2] It is somewhat curious to see the French State, which arrogates to itself the right to borrow in the form of irredeemable funds, forbidding the communes and departments, in the interest of future generations, to do the same. The departments, and the towns may, in fact, borrow only in the form of bonds redeemable within the period of time fixed by the loan; in other words, by expressly undertaking to repay the loan gradually by annuities within a period of twenty, thirty, or forty years.

The American, Jefferson, said that a nation had a right to contract a national debt only on condition of repaying it within a generation, *i.e.* within thirty or forty years ; and he was perfectly right.[1] For it is iniquitous that one generation should be able to throw the burden of its follies on all those to come.

A wise government therefore should always borrow in the form of redeemable securities, that is to say, undertaking to repay the whole of the capital borrowed within a specified time, say the thirty or forty years mentioned above, never in any case more than a century. If the period of time is fairly long, a very small sinking . fund, $\frac{1}{2}$ per cent. of the capital for example, or even less, is enough to redeem the entire capital, thanks to the marvellous power of compound interest.[2] The burden of redemption therefore adds but little to that of the interest, and offers the inestimable advantage of keeping the future clear.

There is another system equally favourable to future generations, and still more advantageous to the State. The State, when borrowing, may declare that, not only will it never repay the capital lent, but it will pay interest only during a certain number of years— thirty, fifty, or a hundred. This is what is called the system of *terminable annuities*. When the due date comes round, the State finds itself quite clear of the debt. It is a method which has often been employed in England. This operation is not, however, so profitable to the State as at first sight appears. For it is evident that the State will not find lenders unless it offers them an annuity which will allow them to save enough annually to replace their capital before the term is up. Theoretically, the burden for the State is the same as if it were borrowing on redeemable funds. If, in spite of this, the State finds this form of loan more advantageous, it is because the lender does not always fully realise the burden of redemption, and allows himself to be tempted by the attraction of a higher interest to be obtained at the actual moment. The State thus speculates on the improvidence of fund-holders, and for that reason this method of raising a loan, though more profitable financially, is open to criticism from the moral standpoint. It is, indeed, rarely resorted to in France.

Even if a government is in the habit of borrowing in perpetuity,

[1] Unless the loan be one by which future generations will benefit ; the building of railways, schools, etc.

[2] The following is the method adopted. Every year a certain number of certificates drawn by lot are paid off. This number is small to begin with, but increases in proportion as the interest to be paid on the debt decreases with the reduction of the debt, leaving larger sums at the disposal of the State.

it ought to try so far as possible to extinguish, or at least to reduce, its debt. There are two ways of doing this. It may reduce the *capital* of the debt, which is called *redemption;* or it may reduce the *interest* on the debt, which is called *conversion.*[1]

(1) *Redemption.* The redemption of a perpetual debt differs from the issue of redeemable securities, of which we have just spoken, in that it is optional on the part of the State. The State, though never bound to repay, reserves the right to repay if it wants to. It may thus wait until it has money enough to pay off all, or part, of its creditors at its leisure.

Instead of repaying the holders of stock, the State prefers as a rule to buy up a certain number of certificates on the Stock Exchange at the current rate of the day and to cancel them.[2] As the State is thus both creditor and debtor, the debt is extinguished by " confusion." This operation is sometimes more profitable to the State than repayment would be, since the State is always obliged to pay back *at par, i.e.* to pay a sum equal to the nominal value of the stock; whereas on the Bourse it is often able to buy back below par.

If carried on energetically and consistently, this operation might bring about great results; unfortunately, it requires in the first instance a regular and continuous surplus in the budget. Now, as

---

[1] A third is sometimes mentioned—*consolidation.* Consolidation, however, does not reduce the national debt, but simply transforms a short-term debt into a perpetual debt, the capital of which consequently can never be demanded. Apart from loans in the form of redeemable stock, to which it resorts only on great occasions, the State is continually borrowing small sums for its current expenses, in the form of Exchequer bills (*bons du Trésor*), that is to say, notes repayable within four or five years. These, and other analogous bonds, constitute what is called the *floating debt,* which sometimes increases to such proportions that the State is barely able to meet its liabilities when the date falls due. In this case it transforms this floating debt into a consolidated debt, or, what comes to the same, it issues a perpetual loan to repay the floating debt; this is what is called consolidation. It is a financial expedient, often necessary, but not to be recommended.

[2] This was done, formerly, in a more complicated way. The sum set apart every year for redemption was put into a special fund, called the *Caisse d'amortisse-ment* (Sinking Fund). The stock bought by this fund was not destroyed, but was kept and the interest from it used in buying up more stock. It was hoped that, by the continual capitalisation of interest, wonderful results would be obtained. In actual fact the only result was the creation of a sort of reserve, on which the Government hastened to lay its hands so soon as occasion offered. This is what happened in England. Buying and cancelling stock may produce exactly the same effect as the capitalisation of interest, if the equivalent of the interest is employed every year in cancelling new stock, without leading the Government into the same temptation.

the budgets in most modern States show a deficit, this method of redemption is impracticable.   And if, nevertheless, it is practised, as it has been in France during the last few years, it is a mere delusion.   For what is the use of redeeming with one hand only to borrow with the other ?

(2) *Conversion.*   It is a pity, no doubt, for a State to have to give up the idea of extinguishing the capital of its debt ; but there is some consolation in the fact that this capital is, as we have pointed out, only a fictitious burden, and can never be claimed.   The only real burden in the national debt is the interest ; to reduce the interest is therefore as effective as to reduce the capital ; but how is this to be done ?   ·

The fundholder is not likely to accept with good grace a reduction in the rate of interest promised him.   The State, on the other hand, cannot reduce the interest of its own accord, against the will of the fundholder, for that would be to fall short of its word—a kind of bankruptcy.   It solves the problem therefore in the following way :

Take, for example, the last conversion of French stock, which took place in 1902, and which consisted in reducing to 3 per cent. the stock which previously stood at $3\frac{1}{2}$ per cent.   On the day on which this operation took place, this $3\frac{1}{2}$ per cent. was quoted at about 102 ; that is to say, it was selling on the Stock Exchange 2 francs above par.   The Government said to the fundholders: "We offer you the choice, either of accepting interest reduced henceforward to 3 per cent., or of being paid back the capital at 100 francs." For it must be remembered that, though the State is never *obliged* to pay back the capital of the debt, it has always the *right* to do so. This two-fold proposal of the State is therefore absolutely within its right.   But what is the fundholder to do, summoned thus arbitrarily to choose ?   If he decides for repayment he loses on the actual value of his stock, since it is selling on the Stock Exchange for more than 100 francs. He also risks losing on its future value, since it is probable that, if the credit of the State is maintained and increases, this stock, even at its reduced interest of 3 per cent., will be worth in future more than 100 francs.   Observe that, if the Minister of Finance knows his business, he will choose the moment for this operation when securities are going up, when, consequently, it is impossible for the fundholder to invest his money in good securities at more than 3 per cent.   Since, then, on the one hand, the fundholder cannot obtain a higher rate of interest on his capital than the one offered ; since, on the other hand, the repayment of the capital would mean a loss to him ; since, finally, if he accepts the lower rate of interest there is still the chance that his stock may rise in value,[1] he will accept the reduction of interest, though it may be with a bad grace. In the instance we have given, as in all the others, the great body of fundholders accepted the reduction unanimously. Now, as the interest to be paid per annum amounted to a total of 238 million francs, this reduction of ½ per cent. (or one-seventh) meant an annual economy of 34 millions.[2]

The total conversions, made since the beginning of the nineteenth century, have relieved the national debt of 160 million francs of interest per annum. True, the taxpayer has not noticed it, since, owing to the fact that expenditure has continuously increased, he pays quite as much as before, if not more. (See Book **IV**, *Public Expenditure*.) But the fact remains that, had it not been for these conversions, he would have had 160 millions more to pay.

From all that has been said, we see that every conversion pre-supposes, in the first instance, that the State funds which are to be converted are quoted *above par*. So long, indeed, as any fund is quoted below par, that is to say, below the price at which it is repayable, the State cannot think of summoning fundholders to choose between repayment and the reduction of interest. All would hasten to choose repayment, since this would give them more than the real value of their stock, and the State, obliged to pay back several milliards, which moreover it did not possess, would have to borrow this sum, probably from the very persons whom it is paying back—a feat no less disastrous than ridiculous.

Conversion requires, as a preliminary condition, not only a general rise in the stock, but a general rise in ordinary securities; in other words, a general fall in the rate of interest. For it is just the impossibility of investing his money at as profitable a rate as hereto-fore which will make the fundholder accept the rate of interest offered by the State.

[1] In reality, this additional value has not been realised, the 3 per cent. to-day being worth no more than 87 francs (April 1913). The fundholders of 1902, less fortunate than their predecessors, who had lost on their incomes but gained on their capital, find themselves losing both on their incomes and on their capital.

[2] It must not be forgotten that the 3½ per cent. was itself the result of a series of conversions of the original 5 per cent. stock, by which this had been reduced in 1884 to 4½ per cent., and in 1894 to 3½ per cent.; thus the fundholder who had kept the same stock since the loan of 1872 would have found his income reduced by two-fifths; his capital would, however, have been increased by about one-seventh. Further, the State guaranteed fundholders against a new conversion for eight years only: since 1910, there is nothing to prevent it, if the stock rises above par, from again reducing this 3 per cent. to 2¾ per cent. or 2½ per cent., as in England, but this is a fairly remote contingency.

Nothing can be said against the legitimacy of such operations. They constitute, indeed, a real duty on the part of the State, since the State ought never to impose a needless burden on its taxpayers.[1] But for these operations to be really useful, the State must cease its continual borrowing. Unless it does so, the fear of future conversions may make lenders exact a higher rate of interest, so that the State will find itself obliged to pay on its future loans all that it saved on its past ones.

CHAPTER X: BANKS

I : THE FUNCTIONS AND THE EVOLUTION OF BANKS

WE have seen that the exchange of goods is almost impossible without the help of certain intermediaries called merchants. In the same way the employment of capital would be almost impossible without the help of certain intermediaries called *bankers*.

Since the Middle Ages the history of banks has been closely bound up with that of commerce, and the creation of each great bank marks a new stage in commercial development. The earliest banks were those of the Italian Republics : Venice (1400 ?), Genoa (1407). Commercial pre-eminence then passed to Holland, and we next see the great and celebrated Bank of Amsterdam (1609), speedily followed by the banks of Hamburg and Rotterdam. Finally, the creation of the Bank of England, in 1694, apprises us that England is about to succeed to the commercial supremacy of the world. The Bank of France does not come on the scene till much later, not before the beginning of the nineteenth century. The financier Law had, however, founded a bank in 1716, remarkable for the time, but mainly celebrated for its disastrous end.

Bankers originally were simply merchants of money—*money-changers*, as we say to-day. In London, in the seventeenth century, it was the goldsmiths who undertook this business. To-day, the money-changer plays but a small rôle, mainly in frontier towns, or in large centres where foreigners need to change one money for another. In the Middle Ages, however, when each seigneur had the right to

---

[1] It was not States only, but all the large public borrowers—municipalities, railway companies, joint-stock companies of all sorts—which took advantage of the windfall which the fall in the rate of interest offered them, to resort to conversions on the largest scale. It is, however, possible that such favourable conditions may not recur for a long time, as the rate of interest has apparently ceased to fall, and is even beginning to rise.

coin money, the great number of different moneys and the frequency of false coinage—resorted to by the sovereign himself—made these shops, where every man could find good money by paying an *agio*, very important.

In Holland, where, owing to her great trade, the moneys of all countries accumulated, merchants found it greatly to their advantage to deposit their silver in the Bank of Amsterdam, which guaranteed that they would always receive back the same weight of silver, that is to say, a value equal to the sum deposited. Accounts were reckoned in an ideal money called Bank Money, and a credit on the bank represented always a value of 8 per cent. or 10 per cent. more than the same sum in current money (see Adam Smith's celebrated statement on this subject, Book IV, chap. iii).

Bankers are just like ordinary merchants. Merchants deal in goods, bankers in capital, in the form either of credit documents or coin. Merchants buy in order o sell again and find their gain in buying as cheaply as possible and selling as dearly as possible. Bankers borrow in order to lend, and get their profit by borrowing as cheaply as possible and lending as dearly as possible. But it is easy to see that bankers exercise a most important economic function. There is no more valuable merchandise, in modern times at least, than money; those who have money have the power, by granting or withholding it, to dispense fortune or ruin, or at any rate to paralyse the merchant, or the manufacturer. In business, the withholding of credit is death.

Borrowing and lending, then, are the two fundamental transactions of banking commerce, and, as borrowings by a bank usually take the form of deposits and loans the form of discount, banks are called as a rule banks of deposit and discount.

There is, however, a third very important transaction quite distinct from the other two, although, at bottom, it also is a form of borrowing. We refer to the issue of bank-notes. This operation, however, is not essential to banking commerce; more often than not it is an exceptional and privileged function, belonging only to certain banks, known as banks of issue.

Besides these three fundamental operations there are many others of less importance.

In the first place, there are other methods of lending money than discount, viz., the *overdraft*, which is a loan on the mere integrity of the borrower; the *advance on securities*, which is, on the other hand, a species of loan against pledge; the *sleeping partnership* (*commandite directe*) in industrial enterpris s—a dangerous operation from which the large banks in France usually abstain, but which is practised in Germany on an extensive scale, and which has doubtless contributed in no small measure to the industrial expansion of the country.[1]

There are the great operations of *foreign exchange*, that is to say, the commerce in foreign bills.

There is the *issue of securities*, that is to say, of shares and bonds in joint-stock companies, and of State loans, which amount to billions of francs every year and which bankers undertake to float and place.

There is the *custody of securities* belonging to the public, which is becoming more and more common, and is a source of considerable gain to the banker, not from the fee charged for keeping the securities, which is extremely small, but from the commission which the banker receives on each coupon he cashes and on the sale and reinvestment of the securities.

In banking, as in other commerce, division of labour creates specialisation. Some banks deal only in credit operations strictly speaking; others deal only in financial operations. These were formerly called, in France, (and still are in Germany) by the name of *crédit mobilier*, as distinct from *crédit foncier*, indicating that they undertook to furnish the necessary capital for industrial enterprises.

The law of concentration, also, is seen no less in banking commerce than in the commerce of goods. It is only natural that the movement which led to the large stores should lead also to the large banks. It is clearly visible in France, where, within the last thirty years, several banking establishments in the form of joint-stock companies—the three best-known being the *Crédit Lyonnais*, the *Société Générale*, the *Comptoir d'Escompte*—have spread their branches over the whole country and have carried on a crushing competition with local banks, which as a rule are private enterprises.[2] The same tendency is to be seen in other countries, especially in Germany, where seven large banks control some sixty other affiliated banks, grouping together a share capital of over 2 billion francs.[3]

The causes of this successful competition are very much the

---

[1] There is also the *mortgage loan* given by land banks. (See p. 394.)

[2] These three banks, whose share capital amounts to 680 million francs, have over 1000 branches (a certain number of these are abroad and in the Colonies), through which they receive over 3 billion francs in deposits.

[3] See M. Depitre, *Le mouvement de concentration dans les banques allemandes.* In England, twenty-six banks with over 5000 branches centralise almost all banking operations.

same as those which we have already pointed out in other spheres (see *The Law of Concentration*, pp. 161–165), viz., the credit and prestige of a powerful business house, the possibility of lowering prices (*i.e.* the rate of discount)[1] owing to the great number of transactions, the selection of capable managers by means of large salaries (an expenditure certain to be recouped from the salaries of subordinate employees, who console themselves with the hope of advancement), etc. Still, we must not generalise here any more than in the other branches of production, nor conclude too hastily that the small, or medium-sized, banks have disappeared. The latter have still enough attractions to retain certain classes of capitalists, in particular manufacturers of the neighbourhood, who can obtain credit more easily on the spot than from a distance, and men of independent means who like to change their investments often, and who find, in these local banks, more sound and friendly advice as to the reinvesting of their capital, as well as, sometimes, a more sure, because a more modest, asylum from the investigations of the Treasury. For these menace more especially the large credit establishments as representing capitalism, or what is called the " financial oligarchy." Save, then, for the issue of notes, of which we shall speak in the next chapter, concentration does not seem to be leading towards monopoly in the case of banks any more than in that of the large stores, nor even towards a trust or union of large banks. There appears, on the contrary, a distinct renewal of activity on the part of the local banks.[2] Here also Marx's famous Law of Concentration has not been realised.

For some time the large banks, or credit establishments, in France have been the object of vigorous attack. They are reproached with not fulfilling their chief economic function, which, it is said, should be to stimulate and support home enterprises ; and they are charged with draining away the national savings in order to invest them abroad. The answer of the banks is that it is not their rôle to be sleeping partners in industry, as their funds may thus be endangered. In any case the funds would be locked up for a long time and it would be impossible to pay back the deposits on call, which, for the three large banks mentioned above, amount to over 4 billion francs. It is,

---

[1] The rates of discount and the commissions were very high in local banks before the competition of the large credit societies. It is the same story as that of the local shops before the competition of the large stores. The *Crédit Lyonnais* (in its report for 1909) states that commissions to-day are not one-quarter of what they formerly were.

[2] Their number is estimated in France at nearly 1000 and their capital at 1 or 1½ billion francs. Some are starting branches within a limited zone.

they declare, this locking up of funds in industry which caused the ruin of most of the local banks, in spite of the fact that, being on the spot, they were much better situated for obtaining information. The rôle of banks, at any rate of deposit banks, should be limited to short-period operations, of which discount, as we shall see, is the perfect type. As for long-period loans to industry or to agriculture, these are the business of the establishments specially set apart for them, the *Crédit Foncier* and the *Crédit Industriel*, which, again, ought to obtain their funds, not by deposits, but by long-term securities.

This answer would be irrefutable if these credit establishments kept, as some do, strictly to the rôle of deposit and discount banks. But it is well known that many of the most important of them float securities of all kinds on a large scale, *e.g.* the Russian loans. It is not, of course, as a rule the funds on deposit that are used for this purpose. But the banks get their clients to subscribe, and the more easily as their influence extends over an immense *clientèle* composed mainly of small capitalists not much versed in financial matters and eager for lucrative investments. They answer, it is true, that enterprises are scarce and less tempting to the French public;[1] but may it not also be because they bring smaller profit to the bank, whereas the commissions on foreign government loans are enormous ?

II : DEPOSITS

THE first operation of the banker is to obtain other people's capital. He may, of course, use his own capital, or capital obtained by association, which in the large credit societies amounts sometimes to hundreds of millions. But if the banker worked only with his private capital, or with subscribed capital, he would make but little gain ; and the public itself, as we shall presently see, would not benefit much from his operations. The banker must carry on his transactions with the money of the general public, and to do so he must borrow it.[2] The somewhat blunt remark " Business is other people's money " is, in banking at any rate, no more than the truth.

[1] The *Crédit Lyonnais*, in its annual report for 1909, in replying to these criticisms said : " It may be a matter of complaint that owing to the stationary state of our population our industrial development is not greater ; but France is always in search of investment for her savings . . . and credit societies, in procuring for her foreign government stock, have simply bowed to necessity."

[2] Most of the large banks, indeed, never use their own capital in their transactions, investing it in immovable property or in stock, as a reserve or a guarantee for their clients. This is what is done by the Bank of France, for example.

But how will the banker borrow this money from the public ? Not after the manner of States, or towns, or industrial companies, which borrow for long periods in the form of stock, bonds, and shares. Such a mode of borrowing requires too high a rate of interest to allow of the banker making a profit. What he asks of the public is the circulating, or floating, capital which is to be found in the form of coin in its pockets or its safes. In every country there is a large quantity of capital in this form, not as yet fixed anywhere. doing nothing, producing nothing, and only awaiting employment. The banker says to the public: " Entrust it to me until you have found some use for it, I shall save you the trouble and anxiety of keeping it and will give it back to you as soon as you want it, on demand. `This is one service which I shall be doing you. In addition, I will give you a small interest of 1 or 2 per cent.[1] This is more than it is producing for you, since it is bringing you in nothing. Lastly, I shall render you the service of being your cashier and of paying your tradesmen as you instruct. These are great conveniences for you."

Wherever this language is heard and understood by the public, bankers are able to obtain a large amount of capital on easy terms, draining off, so to speak, not only all the loose coin in circulation, but a great deal more [2]—over £320,000,000 in France, over £1,000,000,000 in England, and over £1,600,000,000 in the United States, the deposit system being much more widely practised in those two countries.[3]

These funds kept in the banks, ready to be repaid at the will of the depositor, are what are called *deposits*.[4]

[1] He may even give no interest at all. Certain banks, such as the Bank of France and the Bank of England, give none, holding that they render depositors a sufficient service as it is ; and their contention is borne out by the fact that, notwithstanding, they receive enormous sums on deposit. Nay more, in former times deposit banks, such as the ancient ones we mentioned, made a charge for the safe keeping of the money, as in those days they did not employ their deposits and consequently made no profit by them. To-day, however, all banks try to employ productively the moneys deposited with them ; and most of them are in the habit of giving a small interest in order to attract deposits, the interest being slightly higher if the depositor undertakes not to withdraw his money within a certain time—six months, a year, five years.

[2] How can there be more deposits than there is money deposited ? The explanation is simple. The money deposited does not lie idle ; it circulates and is used for perhaps ten other deposits before it is withdrawn.

[3] The above figures do not include the sums deposited in savings banks, which have little in common with ordinary banks, and which, in France amount to about £240,000,000. (See Book IV.)

[4] This word *deposit* must not be taken in its juridical sense. The deposit in law is a sacred thing which the depositary should never touch. The deposit of

III : DISCOUNT

ONCE the bank has borrowed its capital at a low rate, its next business is to turn it to account by lending it to the public.

How is this to be done ? The banker cannot, as we have said, lend it for a long period, by way of mortgage for instance, or by entering into partnership in industrial enterprises. He must not forget that this capital is only on deposit in his bank and that he may be called on to refund it at a moment's notice. He must part with it, therefore, only for short-time transactions, which deprive him of control over it for short periods and which leave his capital in some measure within his reach and under his eye.

Can a loan transaction be found which fulfils these conditions ?

There is one which answers to them admirably. When a trader, who has sold his goods for deferred payment, according to the usage of commerce, happens to need money before the date on which his account falls due, he applies to his banker. The latter advances him the sum due to him for the goods sold, deducting a small amount for banker's profit, and obtains in return the bill of exchange on the purchaser of the goods. The banker keeps this bill till the date it is due, when he sends it to the debtor to be collected ; in this way he recovers the capital which he had advanced.

This process is called *discounting*. It is, we may say, a form of loan ; for it is clear that the banker who advances a merchant 985 francs in exchange for a bill of 1000 francs payable in three months, and collects 1000 francs from the debtor when the bill falls due, has in reality lent his money for a period of three months at 6 per cent. or a little more. This loan is always for a short term. For not only are the bills negotiated by the banker payable as a rule within three months at the outside, but this is a maximum term hardly ever reached. The holders of bills do not always negotiate them the very day after they have sold their goods. They may keep them until perhaps the very day before they mature. At the Bank of France, the average time during which bills of exchange remain in the bank's portfolio varies from twenty-one to twenty-five days. It is only, therefore, for quite a short time that the banker is deprived of the money he has on deposit.

money in a bank is a simple loan, which the banker proposes quite openly to use and which he only accepts for that purpose. It is quite a different matter when a man deposits securities at his banker's which the latter is to take charge of and cash. These he cannot dispose of.

Deposits are often formed automatically by the accumulation of income from securities left at the bank.

We see, then, that, if demands for the repayment of deposits are spread over a period of three or four weeks, the banker, thanks to his returns, will always be in a position to meet them. Now, it is very improbable that demands will be so frequent, in normal times at any rate. It is therefore difficult to find a loan transaction better adapted to the requirements of deposit.

There is, besides, the fact that discount is not only a convenient form of loan, but an extremely safe one, owing to the joint and several responsibility of all the co-signatories. For there is not one single debtor, the " acceptor," as he is called ; there are always at least two. And in the event of the acceptor failing, the drawer of the bill is responsible. If he hands over the bill to a third person, the latter, in case of non-payment, becomes responsible also, so that the debtor has practically as many securities as there are signatories to the bill. The more it circulates, therefore, the more signatures it obtains—sometimes it is even necessary to add a slip to it, as there is no room for further signatures—the better is its value guaranteed. The Bank of France exacts three signatures, that is to say, in addition to the drawer and the acceptor, there must be an endorser. It is a bank which as a rule undertakes this office. Now, the losses of the Bank of France from bad debts do not amount, on an average, to 5 million francs out of the 19 billions discounted, i.e. less than 26 centimes per 1000 francs.

Still, it is evident that at times of crisis the banker must run a considerable risk. If all depositors were to " make a run " on the bank on the same day to claim their money, the bank would most certainly be unable to meet their demands, since its money, or rather *their* money, is circulating in different businesses all over the world. It will not, of course, be long in returning ; but there is always this difference between the money borrowed by the bank in the form of deposits and that lent by it in the form of discount, that the former may be claimed at a moment's notice, while the latter can only be claimed after a certain lapse of time. . And this difference might be enough, some time or other, to cause bankruptcy.

Is this very problematical danger a sufficient reason for preventing banks from turning to account the capital deposited with them, and obliging them to keep it intact as a veritable deposit, after the manner of the old banks of Venice or Amsterdam ? Certainly not. Such extreme caution would satisfy no one.

(*1*) It would not satisfy the depositors ; for if the bank were to keep their money in its cellars, without turning it to account, obviously, instead of allowing them interest on their deposits, it

would have to make a charge for keeping them. It is better, therefore, for depositors to run the risk of waiting a few days for repayment than to keep their unproductive money at home, or to pay for
its safe keeping elsewhere.

(2) It would not satisfy the country ; for the economic function of
banks consists in combining scattered and unproductive capital and
turning it into active and productive capital. Now, this function
would evidently become impossible the moment banks were unable
any longer to make use of their deposits.

Banks, then, do not hesitate to use the sums entrusted to them.
But they are careful to keep always a certain metallic reserve, in order
to meet possible contingencies.

It is impossible to determine *a priori* what the proportion between
the amount of the metallic reserve and that of the deposits should be
(see later, *Organisation of Banks*). A bank with many large deposits,
or a bank whose credit is not very good, ought to keep a large cash
reserve, which it should strengthen in times of commercial crisis ; that
is to say, whenever it can foresee that depositors will be likely to need
their money.

We have said that discount is not the only way in which banks
employ their capital. They lend it :

(1) In the form of *advances on securities*, taking care that the
sum lent is a good deal below the real value of the securities.
Advancing on securities is one of the most important operations of
the Bank of France (amounting to over $5\frac{1}{2}$ billion francs in 1912).

(2) In the form of *overdrafts*, which they open with their clients.
Banks are said to give an overdraft when their clients may draw out
more money than they have deposited. This is obviously equivalent
to allowing them a loan. As this method of " uncovered " lending,
as it is called, is very dangerous and offers no real guarantee, and as
it requires on the part of the director of the bank a very exact appreciation of what each of his clients is worth, some banks refuse to
practise it. The regulations of the Bank of France forbid it absolutely.

IV : THE ISSUE OF BANK-NOTES

THE interest of a banker, like that of any other business man, is to
extend his operations as much as possible. By doubling his business
he doubles his profits. But how is a banker to do this ?

If he could create capital *ex nihilo*, in the form of coin, instead
of patiently waiting for the public to bring it to him, this would
surely be a very profitable proceeding. And, as it took some centuries

for the public to get into the habit of depositing its money at the bank, bankers had the ingenious idea of creating straight away the capital they required by issuing *bank-notes*, or simple promises to pay. Experience has shown that the method was a good one; [1] it has succeeded admirably.

In exchange for the commercial paper presented for discount, banks, instead of giving gold and silver, give their notes. It may seem surprising that the public accepts such an arrangement. Here, for instance, is a business man who comes to discount a bill of 1000 francs, and who receives in exchange simply another credit document in the form of a bank-note of 1000 francs. " Of what use is this to me ? " he may say. " It is money I want, not credit claims. Credit for credit, I might as well have kept the one I had." But a moment's reflection would be enough to show him that, although the bank-note is only a credit document like the bill of exchange, yet it is a much more convenient one, for the following reasons :

(*1*) *It is transferable to bearer*, like a coin ; while the bill of exchange is subject to the formalities and responsibilities of endorsement.

(*2*) *It is payable at sight*—this used, indeed, to be printed cn the face of the note itself; whereas commercial paper is payable only at a specified date.

(*3*) Precisely because it is payable at sight, it can give rise to *neither discount nor interest.* Its value, like that of money, is always the same and is not subject to variation. Commercial paper, on the other hand, varies in value according as its term is more or less distant.

(*4*) *It is always payable*, whereas credit documents cease to be valid after a certain date.[2]

(*5*) *It is for a round sum*, corresponding with the current money system, 50 or 100 or 1000 francs, while credit documents, as they represent commercial operations, have as a rule a fractional value.

---

[1] This ingenious invention is attributed to Palmstruch, who founded the Stockholm Bank, in 1656.

The ancient bankers of Italy and Amsterdam and the goldsmiths of London issued notes, it is true, in the seventeenth century, but these notes represented simply the coin which they had in reserve ; they were deposit receipts, not true bank-notes.

[2] And if it is never presented, as is the case with notes destroyed by accident (fire, shipwreck, etc.), it is not, in France, the bank that profits. The Bank, on the expiry of its privilege, has to give an account of them to the State. Twice already the State, pressed for money, has made it pay over in anticipation some million francs of an old issue of notes which seems definitely lost.

(6) *It is issued and signed by a well-known bank*, such as the Bank of France, the name of which is familiar to the general public, whereas the names of the signatories of bills of exchange are as a rule known only to the persons who have business relations with them.

The above considerations cause the bank-note in reality to be accepted by the public as ready money; it is a fiduciary paper money (see p. 315).

Banks as a rule derive great profit from the issuing of notes. They obtain in this way the resources they need for extending their transactions. Moreover, the capital which they obtain in the form of notes is much more profitable than that which they obtain in the form of deposits. For deposits generally cost them an interest of 1 or 2 per cent., whereas notes cost no more than the expenses of manufacture, which are insignificant.[1]

But we cannot conceal from ourselves the fact that, though this operation may bring in splendid returns to the banks, it may also lead them into grave dangers. For the sum total of notes in circulation, which may at any instant be presented for payment, represents a debt payable on demand of exactly the same nature as the debt resulting from deposits. The bank is therefore exposed to a two-fold peril : it may be called on to refund its deposits and its notes at one and the same moment.

If the necessity for a metallic reserve is imperative when the bank has to face only the payment of its deposits, it will be even more so when it has to face also the debt resulting from the notes which it has circulated. We can understand therefore why, in various countries, the law obliges banks, if they wish to have the right to issue notes, to lay aside a certain metallic reserve.[2] Prudence would dictate such a measure if the law did not. On the other hand, as money lying idle in cellars brings in nothing, it is to the interest of banks to reduce their cash reserve to a minimum. If the Bank of France were an entirely private bank, it is certain that the shareholders would protest against the locking-up in its cellars of 4 billion francs of hard cash, and would insist on this being employed in discount, or in some other lucrative operation.

---

[1] *Relatively* insignificant, for bank-note paper is made with the greatest care and the engraving also is costly. Still, the cost of each note of the Bank of France is not more, on an average, than seven centimes. The note remains in circulation for about three years, when, worn and dirty, it returns to the Bank and is destroyed.

[2] See *infra*, chapter on *Regulation of Issue*.

V: DIFFERENCES BETWEEN THE BANK-NOTE AND PAPER MONEY

BANK-NOTES and paper money resemble each other so closely that the public hardly understands the difference between them. Both of them take the place of money. In France, and England, the bank-note is even legal tender, like gold. It is, however, distinct from paper money issued by the State, and is superior to it in three ways:

(*1*) First of all, the bank-note, in principle, is always payable, *i.e. convertible into specie*, at the holder's will, whereas paper money is not. Paper money has indeed the appearance of a promise to pay a certain sum of money, and its holder may entertain the hope that the State will one day, when in better circumstances, redeem its paper; but this more or less remote prospect hardly affects those who accept these notes, as they have no intention of keeping them (see p. 315).

(*2*) The bank-note is issued *in the course of commercial transactions,* and only to the extent required by these transactions—as a rule up to the value of the bills of exchange presented for discount ; whereas paper money is issued by the government in order to meet its expenses, and this issue has no limit other than the financial necessities of the moment.

(*3*) Lastly, as the name indicates, the bank-note is issued *by a bank, i.e.* by a society whose principal object is to carry on business, and whose principal care is to preserve its credit ; whereas paper money is always issued by a State.

The bank-note is therefore quite distinct from paper money. It may, however, approach it so nearly as almost to be taken for it, if it happens to lose all, or some, of the characteristics which we have pointed out:

(*1*) If the bank-note is given forced currency, that is to say, if it ceases to be payable in cash, at any rate for a certain length of time. This has happened quite often, in times of crises, to the notes of almost all the large banks. Care must be taken not to confuse *legal tender* with *forced currency*. A note is legal tender *when creditors or sellers have not the right to refuse it in payment*. A note has forced currency *when its holders have not the right to demand payment in cash for it at the bank*. Forced currency always presupposes legal tender, but the converse does not hold good. Bank-notes are legal tender in France and in England, but they have not forced currency. Every one is bound to take them, but every one has the right to demand cash payment for them at the bank.

Even in the case of forced currency, there still remain the other two differences we mentioned between the bank-note and paper money, in particular the second, viz., that the quantity of bank-notes issued is neither unlimited nor fixed in an arbitrary manner, but is regulated by actual business necessities. This is a very solid guarantee.

(2) If the bank-note, besides being given forced currency, is issued, not in the course of commercial operations, but with the sole object of making advances to the State and of enabling it to pay its expenses, this is what takes place : the State, being in need of money, says to the bank : " Make us some hundred million bank-notes which you will lend us, and we will relieve you of the obligation of giving coin for them by giving them forced currency." This is what took place in 1870, during the Franco-German War. The government borrowed from the Bank on different occasions a total sum of 1470 million francs ; but, to make this loan possible, it first decreed forced currency.

In such a case as this the second guarantee in turn disappears. The issue of notes has no longer any other limit than the needs of the State.

Even so, there yet remains the third guarantee, viz., the personality of the issuer ; and this of itself is enough to render the bank-note much less liable to depreciation than paper money. So well has experience proved this, that governments as a rule have given up issuing paper money directly and have had recourse to the intermediary services of banks. For the public take for granted that banks will resist, so far as possible, an exaggerated issue of notes, knowing that it would spell ruin for themselves. And they believe—not without reason, alas !—that a financial company which has to watch over its own interests will be more alert and tenacious than a government, or a Minister of Finance, who has to think only of the public good.

VI : MONOPOLY OR COMPETITION—THE STATE BANK OR THE PRIVATE BANK

THE question [1] of monopoly or competition can arise only in connection with the issue of bank-notes. In regard to commercial operations, such as discount, the law of concentration may tend, as we have

---

[1] The question of *monopoly of issue* which we are discussing in this chapter must not be confused with that of the *regulation of issue* with which we shall deal in chap. viii. Free competition of banks is, as we shall see, quite compatible with very severe regulation as to issue, or, *vice versa*, monopoly is quite compatible with great liberty of issue.

seen, to reduce the number of banks. But we are still far from actual monopoly or from any idea of investing one single bank with a legal monopoly. The interests of commerce, indeed, require a great number of competing banks, in order that discount may be obtained at a cheap rate.

But the issue of notes is a somewhat different matter. It is not the interest of traders that is here at stake, but that of the public. It is no longer a question of obtaining advances on the best terms, but of obtaining a good paper money equivalent to the metallic money, and one which will give as much security. Now, we do not resort to free competition in issuing metallic money, since we know that, by virtue of Gresham's Law, bad money drives out good, and that competition would deliver the country over to the worst money coined. The minting of money is a monopoly in every country, and what is more, a State monopoly. Why should it be different, then, in the case of a money, like the bank-note, which is destined to replace metallic money, and which, like it, has legal currency ? A great multiplication and diversity of notes is, indeed, so inconvenient that countries such as the United States, in which free competition is allowed in the issue of notes, are forced in the end to impose the same note on all banks and to have it manufactured by the State. Thus we are brought first to a single bank of issue and ultimately to a *State bank*.

Monopoly of issue already exists legally in France, Austria, Spain, and Belgium in the form of more or less private banks ; and in Russia, Switzerland, and most of the South American States in the form of State banks. Even where monopoly of issue is not legally established, as in England and Germany, the tendency is towards monopoly *de facto ;* as, when the banks which still have the right of issue dissolve, or for some reason or other give up their right, they are not replaced, and the Bank of England and the Imperial Bank of Germany fall heir to their rights.

This step towards monopoly, particularly State monopoly, is, as we may imagine, looked on with anything but sympathy by the economists of the Liberal school.

They would be more willing to accept it if it were only a question of the issue of notes ; if the State bank were to be, like the mints of all countries, simply a workshop for the manufacture of bank-notes. But the issue of bank-notes cannot be separated from the banking operations connected with it. It is by discount, or lending, and in no other way, that these notes enter into circulation. How then could a State bank exercise its functions without discounting ?

Notes presuppose a metallic reserve ; the metallic reserve comes from the deposits : everything is bound up together. And this, moreover, is precisely what the partisans of the State bank, whether Socialists or Radical Socialists, intend. They will not allow the State bank to be reduced to the rôle of merely issuing notes over the counter. They intend it to be thoroughly equipped to fight what they call the financial oligarchy, with the large reserve necessary to serve as a war fund for the State, and the power, which control the rate of discount would give it, over the whole movement of business. Here again, therefore, we must expect to meet the well-known argument against the unfitness of the State to exercise industrial functions, particularly such a delicate function as the control of credit. It will be said :

(1) That a State bank will necessarily be more occupied with political than commercial ends ; that it will not refuse to discount the paper of influential friends of the government, while it will often refuse the paper of its opponents.

(2) That it will continually be forced to give popular credit, agricultural credit, relief for the poor, and to support public works to the detriment of its financial office.

(3) That it will be unable to refuse demands for money on the part of the State itself, and thus it will be led to inconsiderate issues which will end in the depreciation of the note.

(4) That, in the case of an unsuccessful war, the conqueror, who by the law of nations has hitherto respected private banks, will have no such scruple regarding the State bank, and will consider its cash as a lawful prize.[1]

(5) That when the State and the bank are one, instead of the credit of the State benefiting by the credit of the bank, it will be the credit of the bank which, in times of crisis, will suffer from any blow to the credit of the State. During the war of 1870-1871, the 3 per cent. French government stock fell from 75 to 50 francs, that is to say, it lost one-third of its value, while the bank-note of

---

[1] The head of the Imperial Bank of Germany said in the Reichstag (February 17, 1909) :

" What is of first importance is that the capital of the bank should be secure from political influences, as also from confiscation by the enemy in case of war. In 1870–1871, no one dreamt of claiming the funds in the Bank of France for the German Empire on the ground that they were public property. In 1806, the funds of the Society of Maritime Commerce, acting as the Bank of Prussia, were not confiscated because it was a joint-stock company. What is necessary above everything in the event of war is that there should be a bank with independent credit alongside of the State credit."

100 francs suffered a depreciation of only 50 centimes, which the public did not even notice. If the Bank of France had been the State bank, is it not probable that the note would have lost as much as the stock ?

(6) Lastly, that the State will not obtain in this way the profits which it hopes for, nor the financial power to which it aspires. Commerce will probably avoid dealing with this State bank, and, if pushed to it, may even find a way of doing without bank-notes altogether. The example of England proves that this is not so very difficult. The State bank will therefore remain empty and solitary in its official majesty, unless, to obtain clients, it arrogates to itself also the monopoly of discount and of all banking operations. Here we should find ourselves in frank collectivism.

This last objection, in particular, carries much weight. Credit and banking are inseparable, and it is quite possible that a State bank might not inspire the confidence which, more than any ordinary bank,' it needs, if it is to succeed. This, however, is not a question of principle, but of fact, which experience alone can determine.

But, if monopoly of issue is given to a *private bank*, the preceding arguments against monopoly no longer apply. Still, the Liberal school has some criticisms to level against this system also. A monopoly conferred on one bank, even if restricted to the issue of notes, reacts on all banking operations, and involves an inequality unjust towards competing banks, and prejudicial to the public. For monopoly of issue confers on a bank the right to discount with notes that cost it nothing. How can competition continue under such conditions ? This, they say, is how the Bank of France obtained a pre-eminence which was probably justified neither by its activity nor by its commercial capacities, and which has made all other banks its vassals. The Bank of France is praised for having nearly always maintained a lower rate of discount than the banks of other countries. But wherein is the merit in so doing, seeing that it discounts with notes which cost it no more than the expenses for paper and engraving ? Moreover, it is not commerce that benefits by this lower rate. For, to obtain discount at the Bank of France, three signatures are necessary. The business man is therefore obliged to apply to an ordinary bank, which discounts his paper for him at 4 or 5 per cent., and gets it rediscounted at the Bank of France for 3 per cent., thus profiting by the difference.

These arguments, in our view, have not much foundation. The instance of the Bank of France only shows what a mistake it is to think that monopoly of issue creates a privileged situation. The Bank of France, in 'fact, gains little by it. It does less discounting than the competing banks [1] and at the same time saves them the necessity of keeping cash in their safes. These banks, instead of accumulating money that will lie idle, fill their portfolios with *bankable paper*, that is to say, paper which the Bank of France will 'discount; and when they need money they simply apply there for it.[2] The Bank of France thus acts as their cashier. It is the bankers' bank.' In order to play this rôle of reserve for all the banks in the country, it must have an enormous amount of cash on hand. This does not allow it a large margin for the issue of its notes, nor, consequently, for exceptional profits, particularly if we take into account the numerous charges which the State imposes on it as the price of this privilege. In other countries, also, we do not find that the privilege of issue gives rise to much jealousy, proof being that quite a number of banks in Germany and in England, which still enjoy the privilege,· are giving it up voluntarily.

It would follow from our discussion that the best solution, in practice at least, would be to confer a monopoly of issue on one single bank—a private bank, but controlled by the State. This is what has actually been realised in the organisation of the Bank of France, a bank which has stood the test for a century, and has come victoriously through many a political and economic crisis.

Let us look a little more closely at the organisation of this bank— as well as at that of the national banks of the principal countries.

VII: THE GREAT BANKS OF ISSUE

THE great banks of issue are, as we have just said, either private, or State, institutions.

To know whether a bank should be called a State bank, or a

[1] In 1880 the amount discounted by the five large banks of deposit was only half of that discounted by the Bank of France. To-day (1909) it is more than three times as much. See Théry, *L'Europe Économique*, p. 125.

[2] By "bankable paper" is meant bills, or drafts, which will be discounted without difficulty by the Bank of France, thus allowing the banker who has them to obtain money whenever he wants it, and saving him the necessity of keeping it in stock. Paper, to be bankable, must have three signatures, and must be payable within ninety days and in a town where the bank has a branch.

Not only are bankers thus relieved from the necessity of keeping coin in their tills, but they throw on the Bank of France the costly duty of sending round to people's residences for the payment of small drafts, which may be as low as 5 francs. In Paris, out of the 8,910,000 papers discounted in 1912, 4,304,500, *i.e.* almost half, were for sums less than 100 francs.

private bank, we must ask to whom does its capital belong ? If it is the State which has provided it, wholly or in part, it is a State bank. Such are the national banks of Russia, Sweden, and Switzerland (Federal Bank). If, on the contrary, the capital has been subscribed by individuals, by shareholders, it is a private bank. The Banks of France, of England, and of most countries, are of this nature.

The question of the ownership of the capital is, however, a secondary matter. What is more important is the manner in which the issue is regulated.

Every one in France knows the large establishment which bears the name of the *Bank of France*, and knows that it alone has the right to issue notes. The Bank of France is not, as is sometimes thought, a State bank. It is a joint-stock company like any other company, the capital of which has therefore been contributed by individuals ; only, instead of being administered solely by its shareholders, it has a governor and under-governor nominated by the State.

The Bank of France, a creation of Napoleon I when he was First Consul, was founded on February 13th, 1800. But it was not till 1803 that it had the privilege of issuing notes, and, even then, only in Paris and in the cities where it had established branches. Other banks consequently received the same privilege for the principal towns of the provinces. Since the Revolution of 1848, however, and the crisis which forced the departmental banks to consolidate with the Bank of France, the latter has enjoyed the exclusive privilege of issuing notes ; the right has already been renewed for several periods of thirty years, and was extended in 1897 until 1920.[1]

The privilege is not conferred gratuitously on the Bank. It is subject to a number of conditions of which the following are the principal :

(*1*) The Bank is permitted to discount only bills which bear three signatures and are drawn for ninety days at the most.[2]

(*2*) It is not allowed to give interest on its deposits.

---

[1] Parliament, however, reserved the power to abolish the privilege by law at the end of any year.

[2] It should be added—and this is the obligation which stands most in the way of its making profits—that the Bank is obliged to charge the same rate of discount for every one, and has not the power, as have other banks, of charging its clients according to their solvency, or the importance of the paper they present. The object of this is to prevent it from charging the small tradespeople more than the large. And it is the small traders who are much the more numerous ! In 1912 the Bank of France discounted over 28 million drafts, but it accepts drafts from 5 francs upwards, and their average value varies from 600 to 700 francs.

(3) It may make advances on certain securities, or on bullion, but it must never make " uncovered " advances in its accounts with its clients—save to the government, to which, on the contrary, it is obliged to allow certain gratuitous advances.[1]

(4) It may not issue more than 6800 million francs of bank-notes.

(5) It has to make the State a payment, calculated both according to the sum total of its " productive circulation " and according to the rate of discount.[2] This is a sort of " profit-sharing " which the State arrogated to itself at the last renewal of the Bank's privilege.

This monopoly, like all monopolies, has been strongly attacked, and each renewal of privilege has occasioned heated discussions.

It is certain that the Bank, that is to say, the shareholders, find it profitable, for the value of the shares has multiplied about four times over within a century. But this surplus value is only in part due to monopoly, the shares of many other non-privileged credit establishments having also risen greatly.[3] It is, besides, of little importance whether the privilege is profitable or not to the Bank : what we must ask is whether it is profitable to the country. Now, that we are able to answer in the affirmative.

For this system has given excellent results, not only to the shareholders, but :

[1] The successive laws which renewed its privilege, laid it under the obligation to lend to the State, *without interest*, a sum amounting, to-day, to 200 million francs, including the 60 millions set aside for agricultural and industrial credit (see *supra*, p. 400), and to act gratuitously on behalf of the State in all movements of the Funds (about a dozen billion francs per annum).

[2] The calculation is somewhat complicated. The rate of discount is multiplied by the productive circulation and one-eighth of the result is taken.

What is " productive circulation " ? We might think it was the excess of notes in circulation over the cash reserve. In reality it is a little more complicated than that. It is the average figure of the loans made by the Bank in discount, or in advances on security. Thus in 1912 the average of discounts and advances, added together, was a little over 2 billion francs. Multiplying this by $3\frac{1}{2}$ per cent., the average rate of discount, which gives a little over 70 millions, and taking one-eighth of the result, we get 8,750,000 francs. This is the share of the State.

We know that this share is handed over by the State to the co-operative societies of agricultural credit (see above, p. 400).

[3] The profits of the Bank vary from 40 to 50 million francs, 25 to 30 millions of which are distributed to shareholders, the rest being absorbed by taxes, payments to the State, and costs of administration. If we compare this figure of 30 millions of dividend with the original capital, which is 182 million francs, we get a rate of $16\frac{1}{2}$ per cent. ; but if we compare it with the total figure of transactions, which varies from 30 to 40 billions (35,702 in 1912), it only amounts to the extremely low figure of 1 per *thousand*.

(*1*) To the public, since the bank-note of the Bank of France has always been worth gold, and sometimes more, and has passed through most formidable crises, such as the war of 1870, without losing its credit.

(*2*) To trade, since discount has always been at least as low as in other countries. During the crisis of 1907–1908, when the Bank of England and the national banks of other countries raised the rate of discount to 7 and 8 per cent., the discount of the Bank of France did not rise beyond 4 per cent., and that only for a short time.[1]

(*3*) To the State, since the Bank, on all momentous occasions, gives the government the support of a credit equal, or even superior, to that of the State, its war fund reserve amounting to over 4 billions. In addition it provides the State, in the form of profit-sharing and taxation, with over 12 million francs annually, *i.e.* one-third of the average dividends allotted to its shareholders.

The Imperial Bank of Germany is also private, its capital having been subscribed by shareholders ; but it is much more under the control of the State than is the Bank of France. In the first place, the State nominates all members of council and leaves no right of control to shareholders ; in the second, it takes a much larger share of the profits (three-quarters : 70 per cent. as against 20 per cent. for the shareholders) ; in the third, it reserves the right to buy it over. The Imperial Bank, moreover, has not the monopoly of issue for the whole Empire ; four banks issue notes for the four principal States.

The Bank of England, on the contrary, is altogether independent of the State, save that, at the start, it had to lend the State its capital, which now consists altogether of government stock, which it must keep in this form. It is a private company, governed by its own directors. It has no exclusive privilege for the issue of notes (except in London) : there are provincial banks which also issue notes. The system is not, however, one of free competition, for the number of banks which can issue notes is specifically limited. The only banks which have this privilege are those which already exercised it in 1844—the date of the famous law for the organisation of banks, which was due to the initiative of Sir Robert Peel. And, as these banks, which numbered at that date 279,

---

[1] During the last eleven years (1898–1909) the average rate of discount was 3 per cent. at the Bank of France, 3·61 per cent. at the Bank of England, 4·48 per cent at the Bank of Germany. But we must not be over-vain on this account (see what we shall say later, p. 448, note 2).

disappear, they are not replaced by others. The result is that, sooner or later, the Bank of England will find itself, *de facto* as well as *de jure*, invested with a monopoly of issue.

VIII: REGULATION OF ISSUE

IT was an accepted principle, in the flourishing days of the Liberal doctrine, that legal regulation of issue was useless, freedom here, as in other spheres, being sufficient. This is what is called the *banking principle*, as opposed to the *currency principle*, which we shall come to presently. On the former principle, circulation should be regulated solely by banking transactions ; on the latter, it should be regulated solely by the quantity of cash in the coffers of the bank. The struggle between these two principles is celebrated in economic history, and bulked large in the discussions of the first half of the nineteenth century.

What, ask the adherents of the banking principle, is there to fear ? An over-issue of notes ? This is an imaginary danger : the simple play of economic laws will keep the issue within right limits, even should the banks want to exceed them. For :

(*a*) In the first place, bank-notes are issued only in the course of banking operations, that is to say, in discounting or in advancing on securities. Before a bank-note can enter into circulation there must be some one who wants to borrow it. Issues therefore are regulated according to the needs of the public, not the desires of the banker. *The quantity of notes issued by a bank will depend on the number of bills presented for discount*, and the quantity of these bills themselves will depend on the movement of business.

(*b*) Again, bank-notes enter into circulation only for a short time : a few weeks after they have been given out they return to the bank. Here, for example, is a note of 1000 francs which is given in return for a bill of exchange. In a few weeks, in ninety days at the outside, when the bank cashes the bill, the 1000-franc note will return to it. Not the same note, of course ; but what of that ? As many notes will come in as went out.

(*c*) Lastly, even suppose a bank were able to issue too great a quantity of notes, it would be unable to keep them in circulation ; for when too many notes are issued they depreciate, and so soon as depreciation, however slight, begins, holders of notes hasten to return them to the bank and claim payment. It would be useless therefore for the bank to try to flood the public with its notes. It would only be flooded in its turn.

This line of argument contains a certain amount of truth, and experience has, as a rule, confirmed it. Banks have rarely succeeded in forcing more notes into circulation than business demanded.

Still, we cannot disguise the fact that absolute freedom of issue may give rise to grave dangers, at periods of crisis anyhow, if not during normal times. Now, crises are becoming more and more frequent in the economic life of our modern societies.

In theory, no doubt, it is true that the quantity of notes issued will depend on the public demand and not on the will of the banks. Note, however, that an unscrupulous bank, which aimed solely at attracting clients, could always, by sufficiently reducing the rate of discount, draw away the clients of competing banks and greatly increase the figure of its issues.

True, the notes, issued in too great a quantity by such an imprudent bank, would come back for repayment so soon as they depreciated; but depreciation does not make itself felt instantaneously. It may not be felt for some weeks; and if, during the interval, the bank has continued to throw into circulation an excessive quantity of notes, when these come back it will no longer be able to pay them, and will sink as it were under the ebb-tide of circulation. Of course, by its failure the bank will be the first to be punished for its imprudence. But what good will that be to us? Our concern is to prevent the crisis, not to punish the authors of it.

The system of absolute liberty, indeed, without any regulation of issue has never been practised in any country.

Four systems of regulating issue have been introduced in different countries.

(1) The first consists in *limiting the amount of notes in circulation*[1] *to the amount of the metallic reserve.*

Here the bank-note is no more than a representative money (see *supra*, p. 314). It offers absolute security; but, on the other hand, it is of little use save to take up less room in the pocket than gold and to economise the wear and tear of the latter. The bank, in this case, is no longer a credit establishment: it is simply a safe in which money is reserved for eventualities, a counter over which payment is made.

---

[1] Instead of saying "the amount of notes in circulation" we say, for short, the "circulation." The circulation is not quite the same thing as the issue; for a bank has always in reserve a stock of notes which are issued, *i.e.* manufactured, but which will not enter into circulation until they are wanted. So long as they do not circulate they are as if they did not exist.

This is the rôle of the Bank of France, against which, during its life of nearly a century, the only reproach that can perhaps be urged is that of a somewhat exaggerated prudence, its metallic reserve amounting often to nine-tenths of its notes. But this is due solely to economic circumstances, for the Bank is, as we shall see, subject to no regulation as regards the amount and proportion of its cash reserve.

This is approximately the system of the Bank of England, but the *currency principle* was here imposed by law, under Peel's famous Act of 1844. By the terms of this law, the Bank can issue notes only up to the amount of the metallic reserve *plus* a sum of £18,600,000. Why this margin? It is simply the capital of the Bank. A fictitious capital, however, £11,000,000 of it being an old claim on the State which has never been repaid, and the remainder being invested in government stock.[1]

To better ensure the observance of this regulation, the Bank of England is divided into two distinct departments: the *banking department*, which has charge of banking operations, deposits, and discounts, but which cannot issue any notes; the *issue department*, entrusted with the issue of notes, which cannot, however, transact any banking operations. It delivers its notes to the banking department as they are required; when it has handed over notes to the value of £18,600,000, it will deliver no more, unless in return for specie, or bullion.

Such a system in the case of any other bank than the Bank of England could not be regarded as offering any serious guarantee. The capital of a bank, in fact, is not a pledge which can be always and immediately realised, especially when, as here, it consists for the most part of a simple claim on the State.

Further, this automatic limitation of issue has, in practice, and precisely at critical times, such serious disadvantages that on three different occasions already it has been found necessary to suspend the law and allow the Bank to exceed the limit. It is easy to understand that, if the Bank happens to have £20,000,000 of gold in reserve and £38,600,000 notes in circulation, it will be obliged to refuse all discount. For with what could it discount the paper presented to

---

[1] When the government gave the Bank of England its charter in 1694, it took over all its capital in return, since when it has never paid it back.

This capital, and along with it the margin of issue, is gradually increasing, as whenever a provincial bank disappears, the Bank of England has the right to increase its capital by two-thirds of the circulation of the said bank. It must, however, deposit an equal amount of government stock. (See Andréadès, *History of the Bank of England*.)

it ? Not with notes, for the limit of £18,600,000 has already been reached ; nor with the specie it has in reserve, for if it were to reduce its reserve, were it only to £19,999,000, as the circulation of notes still stands at £38,600,000, the limit would still be exceeded. Yet the Bank of England cannot refuse discount without bringing bankruptcy on half the commerce of the world. Twice already, through unwillingness to suspend the law, in 1890 and 1908, it has had to fall back on the kindly offices of the Bank of France.[1] The difficulty is, that, as it is a case of suspending a law, it is the government and not the Bank which has to assume this grave responsibility.[2]

(2) The second system of regulation consists in *fixing a certain proportion* (generally one-third) *between the amount of the metallic reserve and that of the notes in circulation.* This method has been adopted by various countries—Germany, Austria, Spain, Switzerland, Italy, Holland, Russia, etc.—but, contrary to the general opinion, it has not been adopted by the Bank of France.[3]

It is a more elastic system than the first, but it has the same result, namely, of rendering all discount and even the repayment of notes at a given moment impossible, and of creating in consequence the very danger it would avert. Suppose, for instance, the metallic reserve is 100 million francs, and the issue of notes 300 millions.

---

[1] In 1890, the Bank of France sent over £3,000,000 to the Bank of England. In 1908, it simply discounted over £3,000,000 of foreign paper which the Bank of England could not discount.

[2] In the case of the Imperial Bank of Germany, as in that of the Bank of England, there is a margin fixed by law between the total of the metallic reserve and the total of circulation ; a margin which increases in proportion as the Bank of Germany succeeds to the right of issue of other banks (it stands at present at about 550 million marks). But there is this great difference between the two banks, that the Bank of Germany may encroach on the margin *when it thinks fit,* on condition (1) of paying an enormous tax of 5 per cent. on notes issued above the limit—a measure of public safety which is equivalent to the suspension of the Bank Act in England, but which is much more practical, as there is no need to call in the intervention of the legislature ; it is the Bank itself which quietly raises the barrier without excitement or panic ; (2) of having a reserve of specie equal to one-third of the total of the notes, the remainder being in bills of exchange of ninety days.

The banks of Scotland may be classed under this category. The law of 1845, which abolished their liberty of issue, limited their uncovered circulation to the maximum figure existing at that time, which was, for the dozen banks with the right of issue (there are only ten to-day), £2,676,000. All issue of notes beyond this limit must be covered by an equivalent in gold.

[3] In Austria and Italy the proportion is 40 per cent. In Russia, the circulation of notes may not exceed twice the metallic reserve, and the uncovered issue must never exceed 300 million roubles (£32,000.000).

The Bank is just within the limits fixed ; but at this point it is unable to cash a single note without bringing down the reserve below the third of the amount of the notes (for 99 is not one-third of 299). On this system, too, then, it becomes necessary to suspend the rule.

(3) The third method consists simply in fixing a *maximum of issue.*

This is the system practised in France, the maximum being 6800 million francs. But what safeguard is there in limiting the issue if the Bank is able to reduce its metallic reserve to zero ? Where is the guarantee for the public ? Solely in the prudence of the Bank, which will endeavour to maintain a wise proportion between the metallic reserve and the circulation. The Bank of France, indeed, has always acted as if subject to the *currency principle*, its metallic reserve being generally 80 per cent. of the circulation. But if we have confidence in the wisdom of the Bank, what is the use of imposing a legal limit ? [1] Why not trust ourselves entirely to the *banking principle ?*

[1] This limit does not, in fact, exist in the statutes of the Bank. A maximum was established, provisionally, during the war of 1870, when it was found necessary to resort to forced currency; but this maximum was to disappear along with the forced currency. It was maintained, however, though with no real ground, proof being that it has had to be raised five times, the last time to 6800 million francs in 1911. This is due to the fact that the public is gradually becoming accustomed to use bank-notes, and notes chase gold out of circulation back into the coffers of the Bank. Thus the metallic reserve of the Bank increases parallel with the issue of notes. In 1880, the metallic reserve was less than 2 billion francs. To-day it is 4 billions.

In 1912, the cash reserve of the Bank of France averaged 4028 million francs, for a circulation of 5323 millions. It represented, therefore, 75 per cent. of the total of the notes, or three-quarters. If we add to the cash reserve the éffects in the Bank's portfolio, amounting to 1333 million francs, we see that the notes are more than covered. True, on the debit side there are 671 million francs of deposit, but, as an offset to this we must include, among the assets, 685 million francs of advances on securities and 200 millions of advances to the State, not counting the resources of the Bank (over 200 million francs).

For several years now, the total amount of notes in circulation has been increasing, while the metallic reserve has been decreasing. This is generally the premonitory sign of a crisis (see *supra*, p. 149, n. 1).

For the purpose of comparison, we give the figures for 1909 and 1913 (middle of March) :

	1909	1913
Circulation	4982	5677
Metallic reserve	4487	3815
Proportion of the metallic reserve	90 per cent.	67 per cent.

Thus, five years ago, the metallic reserve was nine-tenths of the total of notes. At the present moment, it represents only two-thirds.

A figure of nearly 6 billion francs of notes in circulation, which may be raised to 6800 millions, is however excessive and dangerous, and is justified only by political considerations. The idea is that the Bank should have the strongest cash reserve possible in order to serve as a war chest; and it is evident that, if the Bank is not to draw on this for its discount and transactions, it must continue to issue notes. Five billions is seven times more than the ordinary amount of the circulation in England. True, France needs more paper money than England, since bank deposits, cheques, and contra-accounts are less used (see p. 319). But this again is a mark of inferiority.

(4) The fourth method consists in obliging banks *to guarantee the notes they issue by reliable securities*, as a rule by certificates of government stock, which must be equal at least in value to the notes.

This is the system practised in the United States.[1] Each " national " bank [2]—and there are over 7000 of them—must deposit in the Treasury a value, in certificates of government bonds, equal to that of the notes it intends to issue. The notes are handed over to it by the State, the bank not being allowed to manufacture them itself.

This system was devised by the government during the Civil War of 1863, as much to sell off the government bonds, which the State was obliged at that time to issue in billions, as to guarantee the notes; just as the French State obliges savings banks and public establishments to invest their funds in government stock. It was, moreover, a very good stroke of business for the banks, since their government bonds brought them in 7 per cent. To-day, as the debt is in great part repaid, government bonds have become scarce, and it is difficult for the banks, which are increasing in number, to find the necessary amount.[3] On the other hand, as the bonds no

[1] And also, it may be said, in England, as we have seen that the £18,600,000 which England may issue " uncovered " are represented by claims on the State, partly in the form of stocks and partly in the form of simple loan.

[2] These national banks are ordinary private banks, their title of " national " being due to the fact that they are governed by Federal laws. The State Banks not only do not issue notes, but do not as a rule carry on commercial transactions, their business being mainly in Stock Exchange operations. There are also *Trust Companies* (which must not be mistaken for the Industrial Trusts of which we spoke in Book IV), which deal mainly in mortgage and other investments.

[3] The Federal debt is now no more than £184,000,000, of which £144,000,000 worth of bonds are locked up as the deposits of the national banks, and the remainder is the property of the savings banks.

longer bring in more than 3 per cent., it is but a poor investment for the banks. Thus the issue of notes in the United States has become very difficult. There is no elasticity in the circulation. This is what aggravated the crisis of 1907. It was not gold that was demanded : the public would have been quite content with notes. But the banks could not issue them. An expedient had to be resorted to, and cheques not payable in money (that is to say, payable only by contra-account) and certificates pledged on movable securities were issued ; while the State had to issue a loan with the sole object of putting new stock at the disposal of the banks, for surety ! It had also to allow the banks to give it other securities as guarantee.

In normal times this guarantee in government stock is superfluous to ensure the credit of a bank ; and in times of crisis, just when the remedy is most necessary, it may easily prove insufficient. For, at such times, all Stock Exchange securities, government securities included, necessarily depreciate ; and if, to meet the demands for the payment of notes, the banks are obliged to realise the enormous quantities of stock held as security, the rate of securities will fall, and repayment will be impossible. In a word, bank-notes in the United States are only coined government stock, and the banks are simply the counters across which it is issued.[1]

These banks are subject besides to a great number of restrictions. They may not issue notes beyond the sum total of their capital ; they must keep a metallic reserve equal to about one-fourth of the sum total of their deposits, though the amount varies in different places ; they must deposit with the government, in cash, a sum equal to 5 per cent. of the sum total of their notes ; they must pay a tax of ½ per cent. on the value of the notes issued and another ¼ per cent. on the amount of the deposits ; they must show that they have a minimum capital varying according to the importance of the town, but not very high ($100,000 as a rule, and only $25,000 in localities of less than 3000 inhabitants, etc.).

We see, then, that, taking everything into account, no one of the systems hitherto devised offers an absolute guarantee for the redemption of notes. Banks, in fact, are, and ought to be, considered institutions of credit. If we will use credit we must put up with its disadvantages. To try to combine the advantages of credit with

---

[1] Since the crisis of 1907, however, the situation has been improved by a law (1908) allowing bills of exchange to serve as guarantee for the issue of notes, provided : (1) That the proportion so guaranteed does not exceed one-third of the issue ; (2) that the banks which wish to avail themselves of this faculty first constitute themselves into a federation of at least 10 banks (see M. Raphäel-George Lévy, *Banques d'emission et trésors publics*).

those of cash is simply to try to square the circle, for the two are mutually exclusive.

The example of the United States shows that, just where banks of issue are most numerous and competition is keenest, the regulation of issue is most severe. The example of France, on the other hand, shows a minimum of regulation where there is monopoly. And it is only natural that it should be so, for monopoly is, of itself, a very effective guarantee. There is good reason to think, indeed, that a bank occupying a unique position in a country, rendered powerful by history and tradition and with a strong feeling of its responsibility, will carry into the issue of its notes all the prudence that can be desired. Experience has confirmed this forecast in the case of all the large banks, particularly the Bank of France, which can only be accused of an excess of caution as regards its metallic reserve. And yet, we have seen that the Bank of France is subject to no regulation as to the amount of its metallic reserve, and to a limit only as to the amount of its issue. For this reason the idea of a Central Bank is gaining ground in all countries, even in the United States.

These large banks have, of course, relations with one another. We have said that twice already the Bank of France has lent some £3,000,000 of gold to the Bank of England to save the latter from raising her rate of discount. But we might imagine, in the place of such intermittent relations, a great international council, a sort of financial Areopagus, at which these banks would be represented, the function of which would be to send coin to the countries which wanted it, and so maintain monetary equilibrium and prevent crises. This is the imposing plan of which M. Luzzatti made himself the apostle in 1907.

IX: FOREIGN EXCHANGES

BY the word " exchange " we must not be understood to mean the operation which consists in changing the coins of one country for those of another—an operation which does not concern the economist. *Exchange is the commerce of bills of exchange.*

The portfolios of all the great banking houses, of those at any rate which have transactions abroad, are filled with bills of exchange to the value of millions sterling, payable in all parts of the world. They are the object of a very brisk trade, and are referred to as *paper on Berlin, New York, etc.,* according to the place at which they are payable.

The bankers who hold them and trade in them are obviously only middlemen. We must therefore ask ourselves from whom they buy this commodity, this paper, and to whom they sell it again.

In the first place, they buy it from those who produce it, *i.e.* from those who, for some reason or other, are creditors of foreigners, in particular from *home merchants who have sold goods abroad,* and who have, on the conclusion of the sale, drawn a bill of exchange on their foreign purchaser, say in Berlin or in New York. If this merchant happens to need money before the bill falls due, or if he simply finds it inconvenient to send abroad to collect his bill, he will apply to a banker who will buy it from him, *i.e.* will discount his draft.

To whom will the banker now sell it ? To those who have payments to make abroad—and they are not a few—in particular *to home merchants who have bought goods from foreigners.* If the home buyer, *e.g.* has not been able to induce his foreign seller to draw a bill on him, he will be obliged to send the amount due in pounds sterling to his creditor's residence. This is inconvenient and not always possible, as he may happen to be in a country where there is no gold money and where only silver or paper money is available. If, however, he is able to obtain paper payable at the place where his creditor is, he will have a more convenient and less costly method of settling his debt (see above, p. 390). This is what is called *making a remittance.*

It would seem as if this paper should always be sold or " negotiated " for the sum of money to which it entitles the holder. A bill of exchange of 1000 francs should always be worth 1000 francs, no more, no less. This is not the case, however. For, in the first place, it goes without saying that the value of the paper will ·vary according to the confidence placed in the signature of the debtor and the period of time which must elapse before the bill falls due. But, even putting aside such obvious causes of variation, and supposing the paper absolutely reliable and payable at sight, its value will vary daily, according to the variations of supply and demand, just like the value of any other commodity. These variations are what is called the *course of exchange,* and are quoted in the papers like Stock Exchange prices.

It is easy to understand what is meant by the play of supply and demand as applied to commercial bills. Suppose that, on account of her exports or for some other cause, the *claims* of France on some country amount to 3 billion francs. Suppose that, on account of her imports or for some other cause, her *debts* to that country amount to 4 billions. It is clear that there will not be enough paper for all who want it, since only 3 billions can be obtained while 4 billions are required. All who need this paper in order to settle their accounts will bid highly against one another for it, and the price of foreign paper will rise ; that is to say, a draft of 1000 francs payable at Brussels or at Rome, instead of selling for 1000 francs, will sell for 1002 or 1005 francs. It will be, as the expression goes, *above par* : it will *rise to a premium*.[1]

Conversely, if we suppose that the claims of France against foreign countries amount to 4 billions, while her debts abroad amount to only 3 billions, it is certain that the paper will be in excess. A large number of bills therefore will find no purchasers, and it will be possible to utilise them only by sending them abroad to be cashed. Bankers, then, will try to get rid of them by disposing of them even below their face value. Thus the draft of 1000 francs · on Brussels will be disposed of for 998 francs, perhaps even for 995 francs, *i.e.* it will fall *below par*.

Whenever, within a country, paper payable abroad is quoted *above par*, the rate of exchange is said to be *unfavourable* to that country. What does this mean ? That the course of exchange is unfavourable to the buyers ? But in that case surely it would be favourable to the sellers ? What is really meant is that the rate of exchange indicates that the *claims which the country in question has against foreign countries are not sufficient to counterbalance its debts to foreign countries,* and that in consequence, in order to settle the difference, it will have to send a certain quantity of coin abroad. The rise in the rate of exchange, in other words the dearness of paper payable abroad, is therefore an infallible warning that we must expect an *export of coin,* and it is for that reason that we speak of "unfavourable exchange." Conversely, whenever, in a country, the paper payable abroad is quoted *below par*, we may say that the rate of exchange *is favourable*, the reasoning being the same. A fall in the price of paper on foreign countries shows that, when exchange is settled, the

---

[1] The measuring and quoting of these variations in the rate of exchange has become a veritable science. The unit generally taken is the bill of exchange for 100 monetary units (francs, dollars, rubles, marks, florins, etc.), and enquiry is made to see whether it is quoted above or below its nominal value. Take a bill of exchange of 100 marks on Hamburg. As the mark is worth 1·25, the nominal value of this bill is 125 francs. In exchange on London, however, the unit taken is the bill of exchange for £1, the real value of which is 25 francs 22 centimes. Exchange on London is therefore *at par* whenever paper on London is quoted at exactly 25 francs 22 centimes on the Paris Bourse.

balance of accounts will be in favour of France and an import of coin may be expected.

We must not, of course, attach too great importance to the words " favourable " and " unfavourable." We know that, for a country to have to send coin abroad or to receive it from abroad, is neither a great peril nor a great advantage ; and that in either case the process will be only temporary (see p. 335). But, from the bankers' point of view, the situation is of great importance ; for, if coin has to be sent abroad, it will be the bankers' cash reserve that will be called upon. All signs, therefore, which point to such a situation are of capital importance to bankers, and they watch the rate of exchange as steadily as the sailor, who fears a storm, keeps his eye on the barometer. (See *infra*, *The Raising of the Rate of Discount*.)

We must, however, remark that variations in the price of bills of exchange are confined within much narrower limits than are those of ordinary commodities. In normal times (save for a few exceptions which we shall mention presently) the price of paper is never quoted much above, or much below, par. There are two reasons for this :

(*1*) First of all, we must ask, why does the French business man who owes money abroad try to obtain a bill of exchange ? Solely to save the cost of transporting coin and of converting French into foreign money. But it is clear that, if the premium which he has to pay in order to obtain a draft is higher than these costs, which are after all not very heavy, he will no longer have any reason to buy a draft. Again, the merchant who is a creditor of a foreign country, or the banker who acts as his middleman, tries to negotiate these bills of exchange only in order to avoid the trouble of sending them abroad to be cashed, and of having the money sent over. But, rather than dispose of these drafts at too low a price, the merchant or the banker will prefer the latter alternative. To sum up, then, as the only object of trade in paper is *to economise the costs of transporting coin from one country to another*, it is easy to see that this trade will no longer have any reason to exist so soon as it becomes more costly than the direct sending of coin, *i.e.* so soon as the variations in price exceed the cost of carriage. As this cost, even including insurance, is extremely small, variations in the rate of exchange must also be extremely small.

The rate of exchange beyond which it becomes more economical for the debtor to send coin than to buy bills is called the *gold point* (or specie point). The *gold point* is of great importance for the banker, for it is what announces the exodus of coin, and consequently the withdrawal of cash from the bank.[1] (See next section.)

(2) But there is also another cause at work limiting the variations in the price of paper, a cause at once more remote and more subtle, to which we referred when discussing international exchange (see p. 336). Suppose that in Spain, say, the price of foreign bills of exchange rises above par, that is to say, the Spanish seller who has drawn a bill of 1000 francs on Paris can sell it for 1010 francs : these 10 francs are clearly so much added to his profit on the sale. Instead of gaining 10 per cent. as he expected, he finds that he has gained 11 per cent. This additional profit, obtained by all those who have sold abroad, will induce a large number of merchants to follow their example ; in other words, *a rise in the rate of exchange acts as a premium on export.*[2] And as, on the contrary, the Frenchman who sells 1000 francs' worth of goods in Spain can only negotiate this draft by losing 10 francs, we may say that a rise in the rate of exchange acts as a protective duty.[3]

[1] There are always two *gold points*, which correspond to one another, like the two poles, the one above par, which marks the outgoing of coin ; the other below par, which marks the incoming of coin.

[2] After the war of 1870 there was for several years a great increase in French exports. Why ? Because the enormous payments which France had to make to Germany caused foreign paper to rise greatly above par, and the profits which French exporters of paper obtained from the paper which they drew on their foreign debtors were so great, that they could content themselves with a very small profit on the price of their goods and could even sell them at a loss. As a result, goods were sold to the foreigner, not so much for the profit on them, as to have the power of drawing bills on foreign debtors and making a profit on these.

The merchants who export from the South American Republics, or even from Spain, also gain enormous premiums and supplementary profits in this way. This does not mean that their countries gain by it. Thus, in Brazil, some years ago the price of coffee, owing to over-production, fell by one-half, or from 70 to 40 francs per sack (50 kilogrammes), on the home market. This meant ruin for the Brazilian producers. But, at the same time, the depreciation of paper money, due also, in part at least, to its excessive quantity, caused the millree to lose half its value. Ruin twice told for the planter, we might suppose. Not at all. For the bill of exchange of 40 francs, for which he obtained payment in gold in Paris, or London, was worth 70 francs of Brazilian paper. He obtained therefore exactly the same price as before. And the planters look with no great . favour on the measures that are being taken by the government to raise the value of paper money and, by burning the excess, to make exchange more favourable.

[3] This is not to say that it is good for a country to have the unfavourable exchange and the depreciated money, whether paper or silver, which leads to this result. As always, there will be a number of persons who will profit by it. But when a country has to borrow or to pay its interest, it will find itself burdened to the same extent.

But what is the final result ?   As sales for export increase, the number of bills of exchange to which the sales give rise increases also, and the value of these bills, according to the general law of supply and demand, gradually falls until it comes down again to par.

On the contrary, if paper falls below par, it is easy to show by the same reasoning that this depreciation will mean a loss to merchants who have sold abroad and will tend to curtail exports, and, as a result, the supply of foreign paper, until the value of the latter reaches par again.

. There is, in fact, nothing more at work here than the ordinary mechanism of supply and demand, which tends to restore equilibrium by increasing, or restricting, production.

We have said that in some exceptional cases the rate of exchange may vary to a great, or even to an unlimited, extent. For example :

(*1*) When the place on which the paper is payable is distant, or not within easy means of communication, the cost of sending the money will be much greater and the variations in the price of bills of exchange will be much more marked. It is clear that a merchant who has to make payments in Tibet, or in the towns which have newly sprung into existence on the banks of the Yukon, will deem himself lucky if he is able to find paper on these places, even if he has to pay 10 or 12 per cent. for it above its nominal value.   A creditor, on the other hand, who has to cash bills there will be glad to negotiate them even at 10 or 12 per cent. below par.

(*2*) But it is in the case of a country whose money is depreciated that variations in the rate of exchange may become excessive and, so to speak, unlimited. A bill of exchange on Rio de Janeiro will bring less than two-thirds of its nominal value in London and Paris, as the Brazilian millree, the nominal value of which is 2·83 francs, is worth at present (1910) only 1 franc 68.   A bill payable in depreciated money must necessarily suffer the same depreciation that the money has undergone. On the other hand, a bill of exchange on London, or Paris, paid at Rio de Janeiro in the money of the country, will bring more than half again of its nominal value.

The effect on exchange is the same when it is not merely the paper, but the metallic, money which has depreciated.   Silver money, for instance, has lost half of its value.   Thus all claims on mono-metallist countries with silver money, say the countries of the East, lose a third, or a half, of their value in exchange ; and *vice versa*, countries which have a silver standard benefit by an enormous premium when settling their claims with countries which have a gold standard.

It is enough, therefore, to read the rates of exchange, even if we have no other knowledge of the economic and financial conditions of different countries, to have a fairly exact idea of their situation; to know whether they buy more than they sell, or sell more than they buy; whether their currency is depreciated, and what is the amount of this depreciation.

(3) Lastly, whenever a debtor has difficulty in obtaining gold, either because his credit is limited, or because the banks make difficulties about discounting his bills, or because the balance of trade, or rather of accounts, has drained the country of its gold, the rate of exchange may possibly rise far above par. For example, on the payment of the indemnity of 5 billion francs to Germany, France would have had great difficulty in collecting enough gold to settle this enormous ransom. The French Government sought everywhere for paper payable in Germany, or even in London, in order to pay by way of *arbitrage*.[1] The result was that the rate of exchange on Germany, and even on London, continued for long above par, not only in France but elsewhere.

X : THE RAISING OF THE RATE OF DISCOUNT

THERE is one case in which banks run the risk of being obliged to redeem a great quantity of their notes, viz., whenever large payments have to be made abroad. As these payments cannot be made in notes, but only in coin, recourse has to be had to the Bank to convert notes into specie.

[1] Arbitrage is only a more complicated operation of exchange. Briefly, it is this. Paper on London is to be obtained not only in Paris but in all the commercial centres of the world. If it is too dear in Paris, it may be purchased in some other place where, owing to different circumstances, it will be cheaper. The operation of *buying paper where it is cheap in order to sell it where it is dear* is what is called arbitrage. The arbitrage brokers pass their time at the telephone ascertaining the rates from one place to another.

Arbitrage has the effect of enabling all nations to pay their debts by way of contra-account. If paper is dear in a country, it is a sign that its debts are greater than its credits, and that it cannot consequently clear itself by the simple balancing of accounts. By the paper, however, which its brokers buy abroad in places where the opposite condition prevails, *i.e.* in countries whose credits are greater than their debts and where paper is consequently cheap, the country is able to pay off the whole of its debts by contra-account, and equilibrium is restored. Indeed, if this method of balancing accounts were confined to two countries, it would in most cases be impossible, for it would be a mere chance if the exports between two countries coincided exactly. France, *e.g.* buys much more from Russia than she sells to her, and on the other hand she sells to England a great deal more than she buys from her.

If, after a bad harvest, some 20 million quintals of corn have to be bought abroad, we have straightway about £16,000,000 which must be sent to America or to Russia ; and the Bank may be sure that the greater part of it, if not the whole, will be drawn from its coffers. The cellars of the Bank are, as we have seen, the reservoir in which the greater part of the floating capital of the country accumulates in the form of coin, and the only fund which can be drawn upon in an emergency. This is a situation which may become perilous for the Bank if its metallic reserve, especially its gold reserve, is not very large. Happily, the Bank is forewarned of this situation by a surer sign than the barometer gives the sailor, viz., by the rate of exchange rising to the *gold point* (see last section, p. 443). For, if the rate of exchange becomes unfavourable, *i.e.* if foreign paper is negotiated above par, the Bank is bound to conclude that the number of debtors who have payments to make abroad is too great—greater, at any rate, than the number of those who have to receive payments—and that, as this will mean a balance which cannot be settled by contra-account, it will be necessary to ship coin abroad to pay the difference.

Even without a rise in the rate of exchange, the gradual increase in the quantity of commercial paper, coinciding with a decrease in the quantity of the cash reserve, points to a disquieting situation. It was from observing these two facts that M. Juglar deduced a method of foretelling economic crises and of representing them by diagrams. Two curves are traced, one indicating the quantity of drafts held by the Bank, the other the amount of the cash reserve. Whenever these two curves diverge rapidly a crisis is imminent ; on the contrary, so soon as they tend to come together again recovery is probable. For the rise of the first indicates that business is increasing and that resort is being had to credit ; while the fall of the second indicates that money is wanted. Experience has usually confirmed these ingenious forecasts. Once the danger is ascertained the Bank will take due precautions. To avoid having to make too large cash payments, it must take measures either to *increase its metallic reserve* or *to reduce the quantity of its notes in circulation*. To increase its reserve is not altogether within the power of the Bank ; but it is within its power not to put more notes into circulation, that is to say, *not to make any more loans to the public*, either in the form of advances or of discount ; for these, as we know, are the two operations by which the Bank puts its notes into circulation. Clearly, this will accomplish the desired effect.

For, on the one hand, the issue of notes is stopped, so that their quantity will not increase, and, on the other, the commercial effects docketed at the Bank gradually fall due. Thus every day brings back a considerable quantity, either of notes—which diminishes the amount in circulation—or of coin—which increases the metallic reserve.

The circulation of notes may be compared to that of water in a circuit of pipes. The notes flow into circulation by the valve of issue, *i.e.* by discount, and after circulating return to the Bank by the valve of " encashment." Now, if the Bank were to shut the valve of issue while leaving open the return valve, circulation would soon dry up.[1]

Still, such a complete stoppage of advances and discount as we have just supposed would be too radical a measure. On the one hand, by suppressing all credit, it would provoke a terrible crisis in the country ; on the other hand, it would injure the Bank by putting an end to its transactions and at the same time to its profits. But a bank may obtain the same result, in a manner less disturbing to commerce and more profitable to itself, by simply restricting the amount of its advances and its discounts. To do so, it is enough for it either to raise the rate of discount, or to be more exacting as to the paper it will discount, refusing paper of long maturity or paper the signature of which does not seem reliable enough.[2]

---

[1] Suppose, for example, that a bank has a billion francs of commercial bills in its portfolio, a million francs' worth of coin in its coffers, and two billion francs' worth of notes in circulation. If, owing to some sudden panic, all the holders of notes were to come and demand payment in specie, the bank would be unable to comply. So soon, however, as it has any reason to fear such a danger, all that it has to do is to stop discounting. And this is what will happen. As the bills of exchange which it holds fall due one after another, the sum of one billion is bound to return to it within ninety days at latest (in France twenty-three days on an average) (see p. 419). What will its situation then be ? If this billion has been paid in coin, it will have in its coffers two billions of coin, or exactly the amount of its notes. It has therefore nothing more to fear. If this billion has been paid in notes, it has no longer more than a billion notes in circulation or exactly the amount of its metallic reserve : it has nothing to fear in this case either. If this billion has been paid half in coin and half in notes, it will find itself with a metallic reserve brought up to 1500 millions, a circulation of notes reduced to 1500 millions, and in this case too it is safe. And so on through any number of combinations that we can imagine.

[2] The Bank of France has a much more simple way of defending its gold reserve : it simply uses the right which every debtor has, under the bimetallist system, of paying in silver (in 5-franc pieces, of which it has over 600 million). It has availed itself of this right whenever it has deemed it necessary, in particular during the crisis of 1907. Thus it was able to keep its rate of discount at 3 per cent. (for a short time only at 4 per cent.), while the Banks of England and

This measure, however moderately applied, is of course far from satisfactory to business men, as it renders coin more difficult to obtain at the very moment when it is most needed.   It has often been accused of provoking crises, and perhaps with some truth.   It certainly is a drastic remedy, but it is the one which the situation demands.   Experience has amply demonstrated its efficacy, and a prudent bank ought not to hesitate to resort to it in order to defend its cash reserve.   For not only has this measure the salutary effect of warding off danger from the bank, but it has a good effect on the economic situation of the country.

Suppose France foresees that she may have to send large remittances abroad.   The raising of the rate of discount at the right moment will reverse her situation, making her a creditor of the foreign country for considerable sums, and consequently causing an influx of foreign gold, or at least preventing the outflow of her own supply of coin.   This is what will happen.

The first result of the raising of the rate of discount is a *depreciation of all commercial paper.*   A bill of exchange of 1000 francs, which was sold in Paris for 970 francs when the rate of discount was at 3 per cent., will not fetch more than 930 francs when the rate has risen to 7 per cent. ; this is a depreciation of over 4 per cent.[1]   The bankers of all countries, in particular the arbitrage brokers,[2] will therefore purchase this paper in France, where it is cheap, and will thus become in debt to France to the extent of their purchases.[3]

The second result is *the depreciation of all Stock Exchange securities.*   Every financier knows that the Stock Exchange is very much affected by the rate of discount, and that a rise in the rate of discount involves nearly always a fall in the price of stocks.   This is because Stock Exchange securities, particularly those which are called international as being quoted on the principal exchanges of Europe, are often used by merchants, or at least by bankers, in place of

Germany were raising theirs to 7 and 7½ per cent.   It has been much extolled for so doing, but it was an easily won merit, since the other Banks had not the power, which it had, of refusing to pay in gold.

We can only say that this is an argument in favour of legal bimetallism as it exists in France, by which gold is used in normal times, while the paying power of silver is maintained as a resort in case of need.

[1] To make the calculation clearer we assume that discount is calculated for a term of one year.

[2] See *supra*, p. 446, n. 1.

[3] It is not only by way of arbitrage that foreign money will come into France. Foreign bankers will probably send money directly to their correspondents in France for discounting drafts, since this operation is very lucrative.   Money does not take very long to go where it can be invested at 7 per cent.

commercial paper [1] for paying their debts to foreign countries. So soon as they find that they cannot turn their paper into cash, or that they can do so only at a heavy loss, they try to obtain ready money by selling their stocks, or any movable securities whatever. These securities consequently fall and follow the fate of commercial paper. But, just as a fall in paper attracts foreign bankers, so a fall in Stock Exchange securities occasions numerous purchases on the part of foreign capitalists ; and thus France finds herself again the creditor of foreign countries to the extent of these purchases.

Lastly, if the rise in the rate of discount is great and lasts long enough, it will bring about a third result, viz., *a fall in the price of commodities.* We have just said that business men who need money begin by negotiating their commercial paper ; if this resource fails or is too expensive, they fall back on what Stock Exchange securities they happen to possess ; lastly, if they are at the end of their resources, they will have to sell or to " realise " the goods which they have in stock ; hence a general fall in prices. But this fall will produce the same effects as the preceding ones, and on an even larger scale ; that is to say, it will stimulate purchases from abroad, thereby increasing French exports and rendering France the creditor of foreign countries.

We may sum up all this by saying that a rise in the rate of discount creates *an artificial scarcity of money* [2] *and thus causes a general fall in all values ;* and though this, no doubt, is an evil, still the ultimate result is large demands from abroad, and consequently large remittances of money. This is beneficial, and is precisely the remedy the situation requires.

[1] To make a payment on London, the simplest way no doubt is to look for commercial paper payable in London, but Italian Debt coupons, Lombard Railway debentures, shares in the Ottoman Bank, the mines of the Transvaal, the Rio Tinto mines, etc., which are also payable in London, would do equally well. These are veritable international moneys and are continually used as such.

[2] We say an " artificial " scarcity, although it corresponds nevertheless to a reality, or at least to a contingency which tends to become real—viz., the flight of money abroad. The evil is cured by a like evil—the precept of the homœopathic school in medicine, *Similia similibus.*

BOOK III: DISTRIBUTION

PART I: THE DIFFERENT MODES
OF DISTRIBUTION

CHAPTER I: THE PRESENT MODE
OF DISTRIBUTION

I: THE INEQUALITY OF WEALTH

THE inequality of wealth has always given rise to bitter complaint. The quarrel between rich and poor is as old as the world.

The irritation is no doubt partly caused by a natural feeling of envy, which does not allow a man to suffer patiently that his fellow beings should have the advantage of him in fortune, talent, nobility of birth, mind, or even virtue. And certainly the evolution of our modern societies is making the inequality more and more painful.

This may be due primarily to the idea that inequality of wealth increases as wealth becomes more and more concentrated in a few hands. The multi-millionaires are a new economic fauna unknown in previous ages. But such an explanation is open to question. Karl Marx's pessimistic theory that wealth was bound to go on accumulating at the top of society and poverty at the bottom, so that the inequality would become more and more marked, has not been borne out by facts. The number of large fortunes is, no doubt, increasing rapidly, and the fortunes themselves are becoming larger, but the number of paupers, on the contrary, is decreasing.[1]

But there is a better reason for this painfulness, namely, the fact that inequality of wealth persists even after *all the other inequalities between men have been levelled one by one.* Laws have brought about civil equality; universal suffrage has conferred political equality; the spread of education tends even to create a kind of intellectual equality. The inequality of wealth alone remains and increases; and whereas formerly it was hidden, so to speak, behind other greater inequalities, now it appears in the foreground and draws all the indignation upon itself.

And economic inequalities are much more insidious than were

[1] Still, facts such as the following must be noted: In England, in 1911, out of the total of successions, one half belonged to 970 persons, the other being divided among 440,000. The division was, therefore, approximately one half to *one* as against the other half to 500.

the older inequalities, their social consequences more widespread, for good or for evil. They have engendered a host of new inequalities which aggravate their effects. Even the forces of intelligence, eloquence, ambition can now no longer do without the aid of wealth.

For wealth does not merely give luxuries to its favourites, which would be a matter of small importance ; it does not merely give length of life, health, independence, leisure, and higher culture, which would be a great deal ; it gives power in all domains. The "plutocracy" has always existed ; but it would seem as if the new dynasties which are starting up in the United States under the steel, cotton, petroleum, and railway "kings," are concentrating in their hands a more despotic power than ever was conferred by nobility or valour, knowledge or genius, on the men of a former time. And it is just for this very power that wealth is so ardently desired. It is, after all, more to the honour of human nature that wealth should be sought for the sake of *power* than that it should be sought for the sake of *enjoyment*.

Fortune, in dispensing or withholding her favours, changes the conditions of human beings much more now than formerly. At the time of Charlemagne, as to-day among the Arabs of South Algeria, the inequality between rich and poor did not open, as it were, an abyss of hatred between citizens ; for wealth was rare, and the enjoyments it could procure but little varied. Now that both have multiplied so enormously, the rich are able to draw overflowing handfuls from the bazaars of this Vanity Fair, while the poor can only look hungrily through the windows.

And again, if inequality of wealth meant only inequality of enjoyment l But statistics show that the average life is three times as long in the rich classes as in the poor ; so that, by a cruel irony of fate, the smaller the share of wealth which falls to a man, the greater is the tribute which he must pay to illness and death.[1]

---

[1] M. Leroy-Beaulieu, in his *Répartition de richesses* (chap. *du Sisyphisme et du Paupérisme*), tries to establish a sort of equivalence between the evils resulting from pauperism and those resulting from illness or moral suffering : "What is the number of paupers," he says, "compared with the number of human beings afflicted with infirmities of all sorts, incurable or organic illnesses such as scrofula and phthisis ? Above all, what is it compared with the still greater number of men tormented with sharp moral pains ? Poverty, no doubt, is an evil, but to the well-balanced mind it is still one of the mildest, one of the least widespread in civilised societies." The eminent economist forgets that poverty is, in itself, a cause of "very sharp moral pains," a very active cause also of "scrofula and phthisis," and that, consequently, it is not in the *two opposing* scales, but in the *one scale* that fortune seems to have placed the evils which afflict mankind. The

Worse still. The poorer the man, the greater the tribute he has to pay to vice and crime ; for statistics show, what reason itself has easily foreseen, that the criminality of the poor classes is greater than that of the well-to-do. Modern knowledge has therefore burst like soap-bubbles the old axiom about poverty going hand in hand with health and virtue. The poor have no longer even this consolation.

In explanation, or justification of these terrible inequalities, it is said that they are inevitable and, in some respects, beneficent. Inevitable, as consequences of the many other inequalities—physical, mental, moral—which Nature has given mankind. Beneficent, because, so long, at any rate, as human societies are at the stage of relative poverty, inequality of wealth acts even more than do wants, as a stimulus to production. By the prospect of advancement it keeps men on the alert from the bottom to the top of the social ladder ; it gives full scope to individual initiative by concentrating powerful quantities of capital in the hands of the boldest, and is a fruitful source of variety in human labour, thanks to the endless range of wants and resources which it establishes among men.

But this optimistic explanation does not seem to be justified by facts.

In the first place, inequalities of wealth appear not natural, *but artificial*. They seem to be not so much the chance result of good or bad opportunities as the intentional result of a certain social organisation, of certain economic institutions, such as property, or heredity, created and maintained by those who benefit by them.

If we had some means of measuring the inequalities of the intellectual and moral order, we should probably find that they rarely coincide with the inequalities of wealth. This is not to say that wealth is not often due to qualities of initiative, daring, perseverance—qualities which make conquerors and overcome chance. But more often than not, it is only those who are already well

figures for tuberculosis in the working-men's *faubourgs* of Paris are ten times higher than those for the Champs-Élysées.

According to the statistics of the city of Paris (*Annuaire statistique du docteur Bertillon*, 1912) the rate of mortality is as follows : Porte Dauphine, 79 per 10,000 ; Europe, 86 ; Champs Elysées, 90 ; Monceau, 93 ; Père Lachaise, 237 ; Belleville, 245 ; Charonne, 251 ; Salpêtrière, 335. In London it is still worse. According to the official figures, mortality varies from 11·3 per 1000 in wealthy houses to 50 per 1000 in very poor houses. At this rate a rich man has from four to five times as many chances of life as a poor man. Among the numerous and very varied causes of suicide, poverty stands always in the first rank.

equipped who can avail themselves of good opportunities. In any case, it is a common platitude that fortune is in no way proportional to the qualities and deserts of men. Still less is it proportional to the "trouble taken," since, on the contrary, as Mill somewhat bitterly remarked, the scale of remuneration seems to descend as labour becomes more painful, until a point is reached where the hardest labour is scarcely sufficient to provide for the bare necessities of existence.

In the second place, for the stimulating force of inequality on production to be really effective, the inequality ought to be proportional *to the wealth actually created, or to the services personally rendered,* and there should be equal opportunities at the starting-point. But this twofold condition is very imperfectly realised under our present economic system : we have just seen the reason why.

Accruing by inheritance from generation to generation, inequality of wealth creates the " social classes." It discourages those who are at the bottom of the ladder by depriving them of every chance of rising ; while it lulls to sleep those who are at the top with a feeling of permanent security. It breaks the bonds of social solidarity, creating between Lazarus and Dives an abyss which cannot be bridged. It brings labour to a standstill equally among the poor who are too poor to produce, as among the rich who are too rich to need to. It engenders the two evils which have afflicted our society for so long, namely, idleness and pauperism, and thus creates a class of parasites at the top and at the bottom of the social scale.

II : HOW DISTRIBUTION TAKES PLACE

IF every man produced in isolation, like Crusoe on his island, he would keep whatever he had made for his own use, and the question of distribution would not even arise. The rule *suum cuique* would hold good by sheer force of circumstances.

But such a system, which would of course exclude all exchange and division of labour, is incompatible with social life. Even among savages who live by hunting or fishing, such complete self-dependence is never found. And in our own societies the baker, or the shoemaker, would be disagreeably surprised if he were told, " You have produced so many loaves or pairs of shoes ; good, keep them. They are your share." Obviously, what each of us wants is not the actual product of his labour, in kind, but the just equivalent of the product of his labour. Now, is this desideratum realised in our present societies ?

In every civilised society, each individual is continually throwing values into the stream of circulation by selling his goods or hiring out his services, and drawing out *other values* in various forms of income. Each of us brings to market what he possesses: the land-owner his crops; the houseowner, house-room; the capitalist, capital in money; the manufacturer, the products of his factory; and the man who possesses neither land nor capital offers his labour or his intelligence. Each one naturally tries to sell his products, or to let out his services at the best possible price. This price does not, however, depend on him; for these products, or services, are sold on the market at a price fixed by the law of demand and supply; which is equivalent to saying that the price at which they are sold will be higher or lower according as they satisfy a more or less intense desire for them on the part of the public. It is therefore the public, the consumer, who, by the price which he sets on our products and our services, fixes the share which is to come to us; and it is these shares—under the different names of *wages, house rents, farm rents, interests,* or *profits on the sale of the products*—which constitute our income.

It is the law of supply and demand, then, which ultimately dispenses wealth.

Is this just? For the economists of the Classical school the question could not be asked. It is so, because it cannot be otherwise. There is no more ground for an economist, pure and simple, to ask if this distribution is just, than there is to ask whether the distribution of the light and heat of the sun over the globe is just, or the inequality between the torrid and the polar zones.

The Optimist school, however, takes up the discussion on the ground of justice and, turning the problem into the question whether or not *each one is drawing out of the total mass a value equivalent to what he has put in,* answers in the affirmative.

In their view the law of supply and demand, which maintains the equivalence of the values exchanged, is precisely the mechanism which will allow of each drawing out of the pool a sum of values equal to what he has put in. And this equivalence is measured in the most impartial and least arbitrary way, since exchange on the market amounts to free contract. The values received are, of course, very unequal; but surely it is quite in accordance with social utility and justice that the rarest and most desired goods, those which satisfy the most pressing wants of society and which do not exist in a sufficient quantity to satisfy those wants, should be paid for by the highest price. Is not commutative justice at the same time distributive justice ? We can only estimate the value of services rendered to society by the price which it attaches to them.[1] By giving a high price to my products or a low price to yours, does not the public measure exactly the degree of importance, the degree of social utility, which it attributes to our respective products and labours ? Society, you may say, is not a good judge. But who is a better judge than the consumer ?

Besides, they say, these inequalities in value will find a limit in competition, which tends always to correct the injustices that such a system may entail. For, if a product or a service be quoted at an exorbitant price, a host of rivals immediately throw themselves into the same industry or career, in order to profit by the windfall, and the increased supply of these products or services brings down their value to the level of cost of production ; that is to say, ultimately the value of everything *tends to be regulated by the amount of labour and expenditure it has cost.* Now, what better rule of distribution can we imagine ?

From the practical point of view, too, the present system of distribution certainly possesses a great advantage over all other imaginable systems in that it *goes of its own accord :* it works automatically. The law of supply and demand allows us to dispense with all authority ; the legislator does not need to give each one his share, like a mother dividing a cake among her children. Every one makes his own share for himself, and the legislator has to intervene only to prevent one from taking another's share.

In criticism of their thesis we would ask, how a mode of distribution can be just, in which the law of supply and demand is the sovereign dispenser of fortunes ? The law of demand and supply is, we admit, a natural law ; but precisely because it is a *natural* law it is as absolutely indifferent to aspects of morality and justice as the law of the circulation of the blood, which makes hearts beat for good and for evil, or that of the rotation of the earth, which, as the Gospel says, " maketh the sun to rise on the evil and on the good, and sendeth rain on the just and on the unjust." Here, *e.g.* is a street-sweeper who is paid 2 shillings a day for ensuring the public health and keeping off epidemics ; and here is a pianist paid £500 for playing for two hours at a concert. No labour (if we may so call it) is more remunerative at the present moment than that of boxing, which may

---

[1] We cannot but remember in this connection the answer given to the Empress Catherine, who complained to a certain singer that she was asking a larger salary than that of her ambassadors : " Well, then, make your ambassadors sing."

bring in £1200 per minute.[1] If we ask why the last act is paid a hundred thousand times more than the first, Bastiat's school will answer boldly : " Because it renders society a service a hundred thousand times greater, the *proof* being that society consents to pay a hundred thousand times more for it."

So be it ; but let us speak no more of social justice, since the products, services, and labours most useful and indispensable to man, from manual labour to that of inventors who have died of poverty, may have almost no value in exchange ; while acts which are merely the result of natural gifts or propitious circumstances, which give to a few rich persons the most fleeting, or it may be the most immoral, enjoyment, may be highly esteemed and may bring a fortune to those who are able to offer them at the right moment.[2]

As for competition, we can hardly count on it to correct these inequalities and bring back the level of remuneration of each person into some sort of relation with his trouble or merit. For competition tends to bring the price of the most ordinary labour and services lower still ; while rare acts—the so-called noble services—are always, by their nature, more or less monopolies. In the examples given above it is the street-sweeper, not the virtuoso or the boxer, who is most severely exposed to the law of competition.

If only this competition worked under conditions of *fair play*, if each one brought to market his own labour and services, we might, while pitying those who bring little and take little away, see in this merely the caprices of blind Fortune and accept it as good or bad luck in a lottery in which, if the lots are unequal, at least chances are equal.

But it must be observed, that those who come to market to exchange their products, or their services, come under extraordinarily

---

[1] Compare the following newspaper extracts :

" The illustrious Paderewski has just signed an engagement in the United States by which he will give a hundred concerts for £50,000 (or £500 per concert). He has just received £1400 for a single concert at Chicago." The famous Italian tenor, Caruso, declared recently that he made £48,000 per annum. A jockey, O'Connor, aged 21 years, makes £5000 a year regularly, not counting gratuities and bets. In a boxing match in the United States, in 1910, Johnson made £20,000 in fifteen minutes ; Jeffries, who was beaten, made £12,000.

[2] Mr. Herckenrath, in his Dutch translation of this book, remarks that these injustices in the law of values are due mainly to the fact that our estimates of values are unjust ; but that progress in the moral education of the human race may one day change this and bring our estimates into conformity with justice. This is quite possible ; we do not say therefore that the law of value is immoral, but only that it is non-moral. If all men became just, the law of values would perhaps become just too.

unequal conditions. The winning numbers are accessible only to those who are able to stake, in other words who already have some acquired property, and the chances of gain are proportional to the stakes. What a difference in their possibilities of making a fortune there is between the labourer who has only his right arm to offer —that is to say, a force of which there is an excess on the market, and which is consequently of little value—and the manufacturer who brings machines of thousands of horse-power, the capitalist who brings sacks of gold, the rural or city landowner who brings land indispensable to life. These last, no doubt, render immense services; for it is an incalculable service to furnish other men with the means indispensable to their work, or the lodging without which they can neither be born, live, nor die. But it is not very easy to see, in virtue of what principle of justice or social utility, certain men are thus privileged to render such precious and dearly paid services to their fellow beings.

It is evident that inequality of remuneration results mainly from inequality of contribution. The distribution of income is thus predetermined by the manner in which land and capital are owned. It is not enough to say, "Each person obtains the equivalent of what he has contributed." We must also know whence each one has obtained what he is contributing. How is it that some come into the market, and even into this world, already provided for, and almost certain beforehand to have the lion's share? And by whom have they been thus provided for? Has it been by their own labour? By law? By force? This is what we must now inquire into.

For we must not overlook the fact that, if this present system goes of itself, it did not create itself. If it goes of its own accord, it is because the mechanism is already there. But the starting of it, *i.e.* the creating of private property with its many attributes, rents of all kinds, interest, etc., took centuries of conquests, revolutions, laws—the whole power of kings, nobles, and parliaments. And this work of transformation is still going on, so that it is difficult to discover under the present economic order what remains of the so-called natural order.

III. THE BASIS OF THE RIGHT OF PROPERTY

As we have just seen in the last chapter, the right of private property is the mainspring of the whole mechanism of distribution in civilised societies. It is this which sets them all in motion: it is therefore necessary to know on what this right is itself based.

The utilising of things nearly always implies their *appropriation*. To utilise bread we must eat it ; to utilise clothes we must wear them ; to utilise a house we must live in it ; to utilise the earth we must cultivate it.

We may, however, enjoy the usufruct of a thing, as a tenant, borrower, etc., without being the owner of it. Property, indeed, does not make its appearance until appropriation has severed itself from the simple personal using of wealth. A man is not the owner of a thing unless he has the right either to keep it without using it himself, while at the same time preventing any one else from touching it ; or the right to turn it to account by means of others, that is to say, the right to dispose of it without conditions—the *jus abutendi*, as it is called. This, at least, is the most absolute conception of the right of private property, that which the Roman law has cast in bronze.

What are the ways of acquiring property ? The most important are : purchase, donation, and inheritance either by will or by intestate succession ; but we must remark that all these ways are *derived*, as the jurists say—that is to say, are second-hand. Each implies a transfer, which in the first three cases takes place at the will of the parties concerned, and in the last by law. They presuppose therefore the existence of constituted property. Now, what we want to know is how property as such was *originally* constituted.[1]

And here jurisconsults indicate only three modes, which may, moreover, be reduced to a single one, viz., *possession*.

(*1*) It is, in the first place, *occupancy* which figures as the initial fact from which the right of property is derived. " Appropriation precedes production, both historically and logically. Primitive races regarded, and often now regard, appropriation as the best title to property. . . . Priority of appropriation is the only title of right which can supersede the title of greater force." [2] Occupancy is, indeed, a better principle than the driving out of the weak by the strong : as a claim, it is morally superior to the right of conquest.[3] It

---

[1] We are not concerned here with such modes of acquiring property as *theft* or *chance*. Although in all countries these modes account for the transfer of considerable sums, their action is negligible on the sum total of transfers, except in the opinion of those who, like socialists, believe that theft is the origin of all property and that the owning of property is, of itself, according to a famous definition, theft.

[2] Graham Sumner, *What the Social Classes owe to each other* p. 68.

[3] In ancient societies property was founded on the right of conquest. The type of quiritarian property at Rome was property acquired *sub hasta*, by the spear.

implies the taking possession of something which belonged to nobody.
Still, so far as it, too, does not imply any act of labour—say, the
discovery of a treasure or the opening up of virgin soil—it has not
a sufficient economic or moral basis to justify its being made a
perpetual and exclusive right.[1]

(2) *Accession* or *incorporation* is a mode of acquisition founded
on the principle that the accessory follows the principal. It is this
mode which attributes to the owner of the soil the ownership of the
buildings, or plantations, raised on his ground by the labour of
others; and to the employer who has furnished the raw material
the ownership of the object manufactured by the worker.[2] It is
therefore only an extension, as it were, of the right of occupancy,
and can have no other virtues than belong to the latter.

(3) But these two modes of acquisition are insignificant compared
with the third, viz., *prescription* (or *usucapion*, as it was called in old
Roman law), which attributes the property of a thing to whoever
has possessed it for a certain length of time—in the case of movable
goods, indeed, a lapse of time is not even necessary. Prescription,
in the case of immovable goods, makes it superfluous to verify the
original fact of occupancy, which would be almost impossible; while
in that of movable goods, it dispenses with the necessity of verifying
whether or not there has been accession. It is thus the sole juridical
basis of property.

Now, this is nothing more, in the nature of the case, than a
bare fact destitute of all moral value. No doubt it is not impossible
for prescription and first occupancy to coincide with saving (see
infra), but legally there is no necessity for them to do so. We
can understand therefore that efforts have been made to find a
more solid basis for the right of ownership than the simple fact of
possession. Three propositions may be mentioned:

(1) *Natural right*. This is the Classical thesis—quite discredited
to-day. For if it is able to explain the right of ownership, so far as
this consists in utilising objects and turning them to the satisfaction
of our wants, it can hardly explain it in its other aspect, namely,
that of a power wielded over others (see the distinction drawn, p. 43).
Indeed, there is no more revolutionary theory than this; for, if
property is a natural right, what are we to say of the many who

---

[1] Occupancy is not mentioned in the *Code Napoléon*, but it is implicitly
admitted as respects hunting, fishing, and treasure-trove.

[2] Property in an object, whether movable or immovable, gives a right to all
that it produces, and to all that is connected with it accessorily, either naturally
or artificially. This right is called the right of accession Art. 546, French Civil
Code).

are without it and who demand it ? All that is meant, therefore, by the argument is this : property is an indispensable condition of personal independence, since the man who possesses nothing has to put himself at the service of others in order to live ; consequently the aim of social science must be to see that each man has a minimum of property.

(2) Great efforts have been made to prove that *Labour* is the basis of property. The Classical economists, and even Pope Leo XIII in his Encyclical Letter *De conditione opificum*, defined the right of property as " the right of a man to the product of his own labour." A man should, therefore, own all the things he has created by his activity. They are, as it were, the legitimate extension of his personality. But if anyone were to try to put this criterion into practice he would find himself singularly disillusioned. Take, for instance, an inventory of your possessions. Is this house the result of your labour ? No, it comes from my family. Are these forests or meadows the product of your labour ? No, they are the product of no man's labour. Are the goods which fill your shops, or the crops which fill your barns, the result of your labour ? No, they are the product of the labour of my workers and farmers. Then what about the definition given above ?

It is worth remarking that, in the definitions which they give of the right of property, neither the texts of the Roman Law, nor even the articles of the French Civil Code—although the latter issued from the Revolution—mention labour. We can understand that in ancient times labour could not have been a mode of acquiring property, since it was almost wholly servile, the worker himself being the property of the master. Alas ! even at this day labour *in itself* never constitutes a legal claim to ownership : the characteristic of the " labour contract," as it is called, being that the wage-earner has no right over the product of his labour. It is the man who gives him work, the employer, who acquires and retains the ownership of the product (see *infra*, *Wages*). And even where the worker, as an independent producer, say a peasant or an artisan, has the right to the ownership of his products, it is not because these are the fruit of his labour, but because, as owner of land and raw material, his right of property extends to all that comes from the former, or to all that is added to the latter (see above, *Accession*).

(3) *Social utility*. This is the fort within which the defenders of private property have taken refuge. And it is built upon a rock that can withstand assault. History and facts show us that private ownership has, up till now, been the best condition of

utilising wealth, the most energetic stimulus to production. No doubt there are cases in which the interest of the proprietor runs counter to the general good ; to wit, the classic example of the forest, which it is to the owner's interest to cut down and to the nation's interest to preserve.[1] But what is this compared with the much more serious and numerous instances of waste and dilapidation due to the absence of individual ownership ?

If social utility, however, be the ultimate basis of the right of owner- ship, it follows that property is no longer the fortress of individualism. The individual is no more owner for himself, but for society. Owner- ship becomes, in the noblest and most literal sense of the word, a public function. It will no longer be absolute in the old Roman sense of the word, but only to the extent to which sovereignty over things, and the right to dispose of them freely, are indispensable to obtaining the best results. The right of ownership will vary according to circumstances and environment. We may quite well admit that it must be absolute, say in the case of a pioneer in a new world—just as the *dominium ex jure Quiritium* was to the Roman peasant. But this absolute character must yield in cases such as the ownership of factories, mines, or railways. Such ownership is burdened by conditions created in the interests of the public. On this ground it becomes easier to admit expropriation for the sake of public utility.[2]

Let us now examine the objects over which the right of owner- ship may exist, the persons who may exercise it, and the powers which it confers.

IV: THE RIGHT OF PROPERTY IN REGARD TO ITS OBJECT AND ITS SUBJECT

AT the present day all wealth, with the exception only of such forms as by their nature are incapable of being appropriated—the sea, large rivers, etc.—may become the object of private property. In all the countries of Europe, in fact, nearly all the forms of wealth are already appropriated.

This was not always so. There was a time when the sphere of private property was extremely small. At the outset it com-

---

[1] See the detailed study of such antagonisms in M. Landry's *L'utilité sociale de la propriété individuelle.*

[2] Under the present system of owning property, expropriation by the State, or by towns, is so costly that enterprises of public health have often to be given up. This is due to the fact that, by French law, it is the proprietors themselves, formed into juries, who have charge of fixing the amount of the indemnity.

prised only a few forms of wealth, in particular two which have long ceased to be objects of property in all civilised countries—slaves and women. It included also objects of immediate personal use, jewels, weapons, horses, which, as a sign that they were private property, were buried in the tomb along with their owner, as were often the slaves and the women.

Gradually the right of ownership came to include the house —as family, if not as individual, property ; for the house meant the hearth, the household gods, and these belonged to the family.[1]

Later the right of ownership was extended to a portion of the land, beginning with that whereon were the ancestral tombs ; for ancestors, too, were a sort of family property. But, in spite of this first step, private ownership in the one and almost sole wealth of the ancients— land—was very slow in developing.[2] When we come to study income from land we shall see how, little by little, land has been occupied either by conquest, as in former times, or by colonisation and by clearing, as to-day. The time, indeed, is not far distant when the whole earth and all that it bears on its surface will be private property. At present only a few mountain-tops and forests still preserve their independence.[3]

One after the other, according to the epoch, this or that form of property took on a peculiar importance : cattle among pasturing tribes ; land under the feudal system ; coal mines when the era of the steam-engine began. Private property has, indeed, in our own times created for itself new objects unknown to the ancients. First, movable values, *i.e.* claims, or shares of property in the form of credit documents to bearer—pieces of paper which slip into a pocket-book and which to-day constitute the most convenient and most coveted form of wealth. Out of the 250 billion francs which constitute the total wealth of France, at least 100 billions come under this new category.[4] Secondly, the immaterial works of

---

[1] See *La Cité antique*, by Fustel de Coulanges.

[2] " According to Meyer, the Hebrew language has no expression for *landed property*. According to Mommsen, the idea of property among the Romans was not primarily associated with immovable estate, but only with estate in slaves and cattle (familia pecuniaque)." *Cf.* also the etymology of the word *mancipatio*, which evidently presupposed some movable object. Herbert Spencer, *Sociology*, part v.

[3] In a message to Congress (January 1910), Mr. Taft, President of the United States, expressed his fears in regard to the private appropriation of all the natural wealth. It was his desire that not only the forests but lands containing mines or waterfalls should be declared inalienable.

[4] As M. Jaurès remarks in his *Études socialistes*, " It is by reading his news-paper that the owner of to-day has news of his property." Certain it is that this

literature, science, and art have become objects of property in the form of copyrights and patent rights.

Possibly in the future private property may take other forms of which at present we can have no conception.

The same gradual expansion is seen in regard to the persons on whom property may devolve.

In the beginning their number was limited to the sovereign, and later to the head of the family. Slaves, strangers, and sometimes even women, were excluded.

Nowadays, not only is the right of property vouchsafed to every human being, but it has been extended even to fictitious beings called *legal persons*. The first to be invested with such a personality were the gods, who could thus possess wealth and inherit, to the great profit of their priests. They were followed by States and public bodies, such as towns ; and, later still, private associations were also able to own property.[1] The right of these last, however, was not admitted without some resistance on the part of the State. It was to associations of an economic character, to *firms* or *corporations*, as they are more often called, which pursue industrial or commercial

is a form of private property which bears but slight resemblance to the property of former times, and one which the men of a former age would hardly have appreciated.

[1] Until the last few years the right of associations to own property was explained by the existence of a juridical person, outside of, and above, the persons of the members. Some jurisconsults now reject this conception as anthropomorphic and mystical, and insist on seeing nothing more than collective property. Nevertheless, the conception of an independent juridical personality seems to us clearer and truer, at least in regard to associations which have not a lucrative object. In the case of " foundations," of which we shall speak presently, it is not easy to see, if we deny their personality, who can be the collective owners of their goods. Those who benefit by them, it has been said. The sick, then, in the case of hospitals, the great men chosen by the committee, in the case of the Nobel prize ? Persons to come, therefore, and as yet undetermined ? It is when the association is dissolved that the difference between the two points of view comes out most clearly. If it is this fictitious person who is owner, since this person dies without heirs, the estate will fall vacant, and the State will take possession of it. This is not a very pleasing prospect, it is true. But if, on the other hand, it is the members who are collectively owners, they will divide up the goods among themselves, and such a result seems to us much more contrary to the nature and aim of the association than the first. There is, however. a third and preferable solution, which consists in providing in the statutes of the society that, in case of dissolution, the estate is to devolve on some similar work. May we not consider this a veritable legacy by the defunct association to its nearest relative ? For the discussion of these difficult questions, which belong rather to the juridical than the economic sphere, *see* M. Saleilles's book, *De la Personalité juridique*, 1910

profit, that the right of possessing was most easily accorded. To associations without a lucrative object, which follow the higher and more disinterested ends of philanthropy, education, science, religion, and politics, this right, contrary to what we might expect, was long refused, particularly in France ; and to this day it is granted very unwillingly. There is an economic cause at the root of this ancient antipathy to what is called the "dead hand " (*main-morte*), the fear, namely, that property belonging to collective bodies will be badly administered, or at any rate withdrawn from circulation and commerce for an indefinite time. But there is a still stronger political cause at work, the fear, namely, of seeing these societies, once they become powerful, rise against the State and substitute themselves for it in the great social services. In French law, with the exception of a few privileged associations like the Trade Unions and the Friendly Societies, which may even inherit by legacy, no association may, on principle, acquire by donation or by legacy without first, a general authorisation on the part of the *Conseil d'État* giving it the power to inherit and, secondly, a special authorisation on the occasion of each new acquisition. Now, acquisition by gift is the sole channel by which these associations are able to obtain property, since, by definition, their aim is not profit, and they are thus debarred from carrying on industry or commerce.

This dread of the " dead hand," which may be traced back to the old French lawyers, is, in our view, quite obsolete. It is most desirable that part of the wealth of the world should be withdrawn from private interests and applied to disinterested ends. The economic objection to placing wealth outside of commerce may have some weight in the case of land, but it has none in the case of property in the form of securities, or of houses. We should agree, therefore, to restricting the right of ownership of " legal persons " in the case of land, since land, being limited in quantity, ought to be reserved for the living. But in the case of all other forms of property there is no reason for creating other restrictions than those which follow from the object aimed at by the association.

A further step has been taken to day, and the right of property granted not only to associations, but to institutions—we might almost say to ideas. These are what are called *foundations*.[1] A man, if he wants his work to continue after his death, has only to endow it with sufficient property for it, in fact, to continue, to possess in perpetuity, and even to become rich by new acquisitions. Here, it is true,

[1] As, *e.g.* the Nobel prize, for distributing 1,000,000 francs annually among five persons pre-eminent in some way or other.

French law is still more rigorous than in the matter of the " legal personality " of associations.   The State alone can sanction the existence of foundations, and it may withdraw its sanction as soon as there is no longer any reason for their existence.   It is easy to understand this.   An association is still, as it were, a living being that is continually renewing its lease of life, and dies when it is no longer of any use.   But a foundation is like a dead person who survives, embalmed, immutable, incapable of change, and consequently of adapting itself to changing circumstances. A foundation for the worship of Jupiter cannot last when Jupiter has no longer an altar, and foundations for Masses must necessarily cease in a country which passes from Catholicism to Protestantism.[1]   Other legislatures, however, in particular the English, are more liberal.   Private foundations, administered by *trustees* who may be replaced *ad infinitum*, are legal, on the sole condition that their object be of general utility and not a purely private one.[2]   They are watched over by the Charity Commissioners, whose business it is to see that they remain faithful to their object, and to modify this object when circumstances require.

V: THE RIGHT OF PROPERTY WITH REGARD TO ITS ATTRIBUTES—SUCCESSION

THE right of property, says Art. 544 of the *Code Napoléon*, is the right to enjoy and dispose of things in *the most absolute fashion.* Although this definition has ceased to be altogether true—for the law of property is nowadays subject to ever-increasing restrictions— it brings into sharp relief what ownership really is, an absolute right : (1) absolute, in that it embraces the sum total of the satisfactions which may be obtained from a thing, including even the stupid satisfaction of destroying it ;[3]   (2) absolute, in that it is not limited

---

[1] The case of the Faculty of Canon Law in Paris in the seventeenth century has been quoted, where there was only one professor left, who, in order to keep the revenues, obstinately refused to appoint himself colleagues. (Liard, *L'enseignement supérieur en France*, t. i. p. 71.)   *See also* M. Charmont's study on corporative property (*Le droit et l'esprit démocratique*).

[2] English law admits the foundation only as a *charity*, but jurisprudence interprets this word in the widest sense as all that can serve for the good of all. The famous British Museum is a charity.   A perpetual foundation for the upkeep of a tombstone would not, however, be sanctioned, as the interest here is only a private one.

[3] A proprietor, however, may not set his house on fire : this is the first restriction which we find to the right of property, and is due to the dangers which a fire would involve for the neighbours.

by time, or at any rate is limited only by the length of life of the object. *Perpetuity* and *free disposal* are, then, the two characteristics of the right of property.

(*1*) *Perpetuity.* When the right of property has for its object goods which perish in consumption, or which last but a short time, perpetuity is of no great economic interest, since it is not actually realised. But when the object appropriated is perpetual in its nature, or at least very long-lived, the right of property appears in its full force and with all its consequences.

Are there many objects that last for ever ? In the first place there is land, whose duration is limited only by that of our planet, or by the geological cycles which model its surface. For this reason property in land has always had an exceptional character, and we shall have to devote a special chapter to it. Houses, as mere buildings, have not the same character of perpetuity ; yet they partake of it so far as the ground on which they are built is concerned. Works of art, particularly when marble or bronze, may also acquire the character of perpetuity; and the same may be said of metallic money. But the frequent changes which force these forms of wealth into the whirl of circulation make perpetuity of ownership in their case a matter of small account, save in the case of hoarding.[1]

But if the object of the right of property is sometimes everlasting, the subject never is. He dies. This is a critical moment for the right of ownership. What is to become of it ? Since the right does not die, it must pass into other hands. Into whose ? Into

---

[1] Still, as money is depreciating, it is not, like land, conferring an increasing power on its owner. With works of art the case is different ; the enormous increase in their value during the last quarter of a century is truly phenomenal.

We might at first think that all fortunes, even those which consist of movable values, would be by nature everlasting, were it not for accidents. For is not capital for ever renewing itself ? (see p. 122). But there is a confusion here. Capital in kind, in the form of instruments of production, perishes, and that very rapidly. Capital in the form of movable values, securities, shares and bonds, mortgage claims, etc., is longer-lived, since, in reality, it does not consist of *things* properly speaking, but of the continually renewed products of an enterprise. The length of life of the products is, however, limited by that of the enterprise, which in the case of large companies, like the Suez Canal or the great railways, is not more than 99 years. It is only government stock which, theoretically speaking, has an unlimited life, and goes by the name of *rentes perpétuelles* (see *Public Credit*).

True, the arrangement is that bonds and even shares are paid back before the enterprise expires, so that their owners can reinvest their capital indefinitely. But this is only an apparent perpetuity resulting from continued renewal, like the repairing of a house as it deteriorates, until nothing is left of the original building.

Moreover, technically speaking, movable securities do not constitute property, since they are claims or shares.

those of the man appointed by the deceased ?   This would be quite in keeping with the law, although, as we shall see presently, it is a right which was not acknowledged without hesitation.   But if the deceased has not appointed any one, on whom will the right devolve ?   On the nearest relatives, the law declares.   What is the reason of this *intestate* devolution, as it is called ?

It is sought to justify intestate succession :

(a) *As a reasonable interpretation of the will of the testator when he has said nothing.*   It is natural, indeed, in the case of near relatives, to think that if the testator had intended to disinherit them, he would have said so explicitly : if he has said nothing it may be presumed that he intended to leave them his goods.   But, in the case of cousins, or even nephews, it is absurd to reason in the same way, and to interpret the silence of the deceased as constituting a right.   This interpretation, indeed, is inconsistent with the right of succession conferred by law on near relatives (the legal provision), even when the deceased has formally disinherited them, since this right is established precisely to oppose the will of the defunct.

(b) **As an application of the *right of aliment*,** sanctioned by nature and by all legislations towards certain relations—children, fathers and mothers, husbands and wives—*i.e.* towards those whom we have brought into life, or from whom we have received it, and towards him or her with whom we have shared it.   These are, no doubt, obligations which death cannot sever.   Still, the reason is insufficient, for, if the obligation of aliment is the sole ground of the legal provision, the latter ought not to exceed the limits of an alimentary pension.

There is, therefore, no sound argument for intestate succession, at any rate in the collateral line.   It is a survival from the time when property was still vested in the family, and when consequently, the rightful holder being a "legal person" who never died, there was no interruption nor transfer of property.   If it apparently passed from father to son, it was by *continuation* and not by succession, strictly speaking.   Thus the father had not the right to disinherit his family, nor had the sons the right to refuse the succession.[1]

Even from the family point of view the right of intestate succession cannot be said to strengthen family feeling, particularly when it goes the length of overriding the express will of

---

[1] Thus in Rome, even after the right of intestate succession, strictly speaking, had been established, the members of the family called on to inherit went by the name of *heredes necessarii*—compulsory heirs.

the head of the family. So true is this, that the school of Le Play, which aims at making the family the basis of the social order, demands that liberty of bequest be restored to the head of the family, or at least that the part reserved for heirs of the blood be strictly limited. Also, economically, its effect may be considered injurious rather than otherwise, in that it secures to the children a paternal inheritance which they have done nothing to deserve, thereby relieving them of all effort ; or allows a man to fall heir to the inheritance of some far-back relative in another corner of the globe, thus introducing the chances of the lottery into the legal devolution of fortunes.

Many economists therefore, even non-socialists, are inclined nowadays to abandon the principle of intestate succession, at least along the collateral line.[1]

The reason why it is still retained is the difficulty of knowing to whom to allot the unclaimed fortune. To the State ? But it is held, and not without reason, that to disappear into the immense gulf of the State budget would be the worst possible fate for it. Successions thus acquired by the State would require, at the very least, to be set apart for a specific purpose, say for old-age pensions or some similar object.[2]

(2) *Free disposal.* The other essential attribute of the right of property is, as we have said, the right of *free disposal :* the right, as the French Code defines it, to enjoy and dispose of things in the most absolute fashion. In this definition, as all law students know, it is the right of disposing—the *jus abutendi,* as the Roman law more forcibly expressed it—which is the only attribute characteristic of the right of property.

But this right " to dispose of a thing at will," which gives ownership the essentially absolute character without which we should not recognise it, did not always exist. It was only gradually that the idea of ownership widened, passing through the same progressive stages as the object of ownership. To have imparted to it this sovereign attribute—which it had lacked till then, and which it is beginning to lose again under the influence of modern ideas—was the Roman's claim to glory from the juridical point of view.[3]

---

[1] M. Colson, *Cours d'Économie politique,* vol. ii. p. 182, asks that the limit be drawn at the sixth degree. According to the French Civil Code, the right of succession goes to the twelfth degree. Collateral successions are not very numerous, and would be even less so if they reverted legally to the State.

[2] See, however, a solution suggested by M. Herckenrath in an article to which we shall refer later under *Equal Sharing.*

[3] See Charmont, *La transformation du droit.*

The following, so far as we are able to conjecture, is the order in which the right of private ownership acquired its essential attributes :

(*1*) Probably the first right of property was that of exploiting one's possessions, *i.e.* of turning them to account by the labour of others—slave labour in former times, the labour of the free wage-earner to-day. This was the most " noble " attribute, since it absolved the owner of property from personal labour.

(*2*) The right of *gift* seems to have been one of the earliest modes of disposing of wealth—at least in the case of " movable " objects— prior even to the right of sale (see above, p. 217). For, if the owner has the right to consume a thing for his own satisfaction, why deny him the right to let another person consume it ? If he has the right to destroy it, why deny him the right to give it away ? Is not the power to extend the benefit of anything to another the noblest and most enviable privilege of the right of property ?

(*3*) The rights to *sell* and to *let* do not seem to have appeared till much later—at least in the case of immovable property. Aristotle, in the fourth century B.C., declared that these were necessary attributes of the right of property, but does not speak as if they were at that time generally recognised. There were reasons enough, indeed, why they should not be. So long as property was vested in the family and was under the seal of religious consecration— which was the characteristic of property in antiquity—alienation was not possible : it constituted an impious act on the part of any member of the family. Further, as division of labour and exchange did not yet exist, each family was self-sufficient ; and as movable wealth was rare—each man kept his own, sometimes even taking it to his tomb with him—sale could only be an exceptional and abnormal act. Thus, when it first appears, we find it compassed with extraordinary solemnities : it is a sort of public event. The *mancipatio*, for instance, had to take place in the presence of five witnesses, representing the five classes of the Roman people.[1]

(*4*) The right *to bequeath*, *i.e.* to give by will, which has always been considered the most important attribute and the crowning feature of the right of property, prolonging as it does this right beyond death, was still slower in making its appearance.[2] The

---

[1] And it is the same in Germanic law. The Law of the Ripuarians in the sixth century declares that sale may take place only *in mallo*, *i.e.* in the assembly of the people.

[2] Maine considers that the right to bequeath freely indicates the greatest latitude ever accorded to individuals in the history of civilisation.

right to dispose of one's possessions at death ran counter to the principle of intestate succession, and is still in conflict with it in most of our modern legislations, particularly the French Civil Code. The difference becomes most apparent in the matter of the legal provision which gave certain heirs (*réservataires*) the right to a portion of the paternal fortune even against the will of the father of the family. Here there are two ideas at war with one another : that of individual ownership, which gradually expands until it includes the right of bequest ; and the ancient idea of family owner- ship and the preservation of property within the family. There is reason to believe that, even in Rome, where the idea of private property developed so actively, the father had not the right of bequest before the Law of the Twelve Tables (450 B.C.).[1] And the solemnity of the act, which had to be performed before the whole populace assembled as witness—partaking, as it were, of the sacred ceremonies in use at the promulgating of laws [2]—shows clearly enough that this was not an everyday affair. In allowing a will to be drawn up in the form of a *holograph*, *i.e.* a simple writing with no other formality than the date and signature, the law has to-day singularly reduced the majesty of this formidable right, which enables a man to decide for all eternity. The number of those fit to exercise such a prerogative is few. And even when the right of bequest serves to create useful foundations, enabling a man who has lived as an egoist to die as a philanthropist without much sacrifice, the good effects are often cancelled, or greatly reduced, by clauses imposed by the vanity of the deceased.[3] Ought the right of bequest, then, to be abolished, as we saw there was some inclination to do in the case of intestate succession ? Certainly not. For, in the first place, how- ever blind the will of the testator may be, it will always be less blind than chance, or intestate devolution. Further, we must take care not to weaken one of the most powerful springs of production by

[1] In Greece, according to Fustel de Coulanges, the right of bequest dates, in Athens, from the time of Solon (sixth century B.C.), and in Sparta not before the beginning of the sixth century B.C.

[2] " *Uti pater legassit ita jus esto*," says the Law of the Twelve Tables (*legassit* = has made the law !).

[3] It is for this reason we consider the jurisprudence of the *Conseil d'État* deplorable, which, in the case of legacies to foundations and associations, always reserves a large portion for the " family "—a care quite superfluous in France, where legacies to foundations are meagre enough as it is.

In the United States in 1907 gifts for works of public good were estimated at $42,000,000 in the case of legacies and $108,000,000 in that of donations—in all $150,000,000. In France they were estimated at $8,000,000. Few legacies are made in France save to the Institute.

depriving men of the right to dispose of their possessions. Goods which are not at our disposal, which we are forbidden to give, or to bequeath to whomsoever we choose, will lose a great deal of their utility : they will be *less desired* and fewer efforts will be made to produce them. For, to the honour of human nature be it said, the number of men who work and save for others rather than for themselves is very large. If forced to think only of themselves, they will work less and spend more. What a lot of wealth would thus be thrown into unproductive consumption by selfish dissipation ! How many years would be withdrawn from productive labour through premature retiral ! [1]

Here, then, with its four attributes stands finally constituted the right of private ownership. We shall find this right acting henceforth with irresistible force as an instrument of distribution.

Through the combined action of succession, gift, and bequest, it will render wealth independent of personal labour by transmitting it to those who have not worked ; it will crystallise it in permanent forms, and will create, on the other hand, a class of " disinherited." Many men will find themselves owners of wealth which they have not produced, but which is presumably the product of the labour of their ancestors in a more or less remote past. And the optimistic principle that each one in this world receives the equivalent of the products of *his own* labour will find itself severely strained.

The right to lend, lease, or let property will intensify the division we spoke of between the idle and the industrious, superimposing a new division of classes, that of creditors and debtors, which will be a menace to social peace.

By its power to exploit others, the right of property will create still another division of classes, that of wage-earners and employers— the former working in the service of the latter ; the latter taking, in appearance at least, the fruit of the labours of this wage-earning class. It will thus prepare the way for the struggle between labour and capital.

Lastly, the power to sell transforms the ownership of a product into the ownership of its value ; ownership thus becomes subject to

[1] We must not exaggerate, however. We do not mean that if men were only life-rented in their property, they would cease from working to become wealthy ; bachelors do not become less wealthy than fathers of families. But it is the case, in France particularly, that when a father has provided for his children, he often considers it unnecessary to increase his fortune, and retires from business.

all the fluctuations of demand and supply, the sport of chance, and assumes the unstable and contingent form which characterises wealth in modern societies.

CHAPTER II: THE SOCIALIST MODES OF DISTRIBUTION

As the existing mode of distribution seems in some ways so unjust, it is only natural that efforts should have been made to find a better one. Hence there have arisen the various socialistic systems.

We must, however, remark that it is not merely distribution and distributive justice that socialists want to reform, but the whole system of production and exchange. Fourier was not so much concerned with the better distribution of wealth, as with the means of increasing it. Karl Marx looks on all the present or past modes of distribution as simply the necessary consequences of the prevailing methods of production.

Still, a brief survey of the different socialist schemes is perhaps more in place under the heading of Distribution, as all of them at bottom turn on the eternal war of rich and poor.

We have already shown in our introduction (pp. 22–26) the general principles common to all socialist schools. We shall now set forth briefly the characteristics peculiar to the principal socialist systems, in particular those which answer to the four, and only, formulas of distribution which we can imagine:

To each an equal share.
To each according to his needs.
To each according to his deserts.
To each according to his labour.

I: EQUAL SHARING

THIS simple mode of distribution seems to have existed in a far-off past: all the ancient lawgivers whose names have come down to us in history or in legend—Minos, Lycurgus, Romulus—appear to have divided the land equally, if not by heads, at least by families. And as by the end of a few generations the original equality was, of course, destroyed, it was re-established by new divisions. Such a system was possible in primitive societies which numbered only a few cities and one single category of wealth—land. But in societies

like our own it would be absurd. Thus to-day, even among revolu
tionary socialists, there are no longer any advocates of equal sharing.

There still remains, however, something of the simplicity of this
idea at the root of the socialist systems. All of them take for granted
that, in civilised societies, there is more than enough wealth for
the wants of all ; and that if there are poor, it is simply because the
big have taken the share of the little. We have only, therefore, to
take back—by expropriation, say the revolutionary socialists, or
by progressive taxation, say the moderate ones—what the rich have
unduly seized. This, at all events, is the popular feeling.

But the rich in all countries are few in number.[1] Society has
often been compared to a pyramid whose point represents the
wealthiest, and whose base the poorest, citizens.[2] Thus, even if the
fortunes of the rich were to be distributed over the whole nation,
no one would be any the better off. If we were to take the top off
Mont Blanc and spread it uniformly over the whole surface of
France, the level of the soil would be raised by only a few centi-
metres. The sum of wealth accumulated in a country like France
may be put at 250 billion francs at most. If we divide this figure
by that of her population—39 millions—the result gives about
6400 francs per person. Supposing, therefore, that wealth in France
were equally distributed by families and a family consisted of four
persons, each would receive as its share 26,000 francs, of which
about 7000 francs would be in land, 5000 francs in housing, 11,000
francs in movable values or joint industrial property, 2000 francs in
furniture, and about 1000 francs in cash.[3]

But if, instead of throwing all fortunes into the general pool, as
we have done in the above calculation, *we were to throw in only those
of the rich*—which is what popular socialism means—we should
arrive at absurdly small shares. If in France, for instance, the
successions above one million francs were annually divided up among

----

[1] In Prussia, there are 14,000 millionaires (in marks) out of a population of
40 millions. In France they are estimated at about 20,000.

There are not more than 500–600 successions of over a million francs in
France in an average year.

[2] M. Vilfredo Pareto in his *Cours d'Économie politique*, by means of past and
present statistics, has drawn up what he calls " the curve of incomes," which
confirms the image of the pyramid, but corrects it by a mathematical calculation :
the geometrical figure which corresponds to his formula becomes a pyramid with
concave sides—an arrow-point.

[3] The sum total of the private fortunes in a country may be estimated in
two ways :

(a) By making a valuation of each class of goods separately, adding

all Frenchmen, the share of each would amount to only 40 francs. If, in England, all successions above £50,000 were divided up, it would amount to 81 francs. This result, disconcerting at first

them together, as the following summary and approximate table show for France :

Land (with agricultural implements)	80 billion frs.
Factories, shops (with plant and equipment) . . .	20 ,,
Houses	60 ,,
Movable values in the form of securities	120 ,,
Furniture, clothing, consumption goods	20 ,,
Money	8 ,,
State domains	3 ,,
Total	311 billion frs.

(b) Or, by multiplying the amount for inheritances and donations for any one year by 36, a rough estimate of the average number of years during which they are in the hands of one generation. The figure for successions and donations is calculated in France (average taken of the years 1910–1912) at 7 billion francs. Multiplying this figure by 36, we get 252 billions, a sum much below that obtained by the direct method. But if we take into account that the amount *declared to the Treasury* for inheritance tax is always about one-fifth less than the reality, we find we are justified in increasing our figure by 30 billion francs, so that the two methods arrive at almost the same total.

It must be observed, however, that, of the movable values, over 30 billions are government stock and claims on the State, and 15 billions are mortgage claims, making in all about 50 billions of wealth, which is fictitious, since it represents the claims of Frenchmen on other Frenchmen, or on the nation as a whole. We must not therefore count these. Again, part of the value of factories and shops which take the form of shareholding companies is included under movable values: 5 or 6 billions more must therefore be deducted, which leaves about 250 billions.

The wealth of the United States was estimated in the official report for 1904 at 107 billion dollars, *i.e.* 554 billion francs, or, dividing this among 82 million inhabitants, 6750 francs per head, or 27,000 per family. But this formidable figure, it appears, must be considerably reduced, since some wealth has been counted under two different headings. The monetary standard also has a smaller value in the United States than in Europe.

The wealth of Great Britain was calculated some time ago by Sir Robert Giffen at 375 billion francs, or, dividing it among the 45 million inhabitants, at nearly 9000 francs per head. But Mr. Chiozza Money put it at only 292 billion francs in 1902.

The fortune of Germany was calculated by Mr. Steimann Bucher, in 1912, at 350 billion marks, or over 6000 francs per head. Although the wealth of Germany has increased enormously of late years, this figure seems exaggerated.

The total fortune of Italy is estimated by Pantaleoni at not more than 55 billion francs, and by Nitti at 65 billion francs, which would give a result of 1880 francs per head or 7500 francs per family, more than one-half of which is in land.

sight, is explained by the *relatively minute proportion of rich persons* to poor.

We may make the same calculation for income. M. Vilfredo Pareto, in his book already referred to, calculated for Prussia that, if the limit of income were fixed at 4800 marks (6000 francs), a modest enough sum, and we were to take the surplus from all those whose incomes were above this limit and divide it among all the inhabitants, the income of each would be increased by only 100 marks.

It must not be thought that the income of a country is composed solely of the income from capital and immovable goods as given above, which would amount to less than 12 billions in the case of France, even at the rate of 5 per cent. The incomes from labour, about 25 billions, must be included, which will more than double the figure, bringing it to, say, 30 billions. Mr. Giffen calculates them, for England, at 44 billion francs. This would represent about 3000 francs income per family in France, and 4400 in England.

Well, it may be said, surely this is better for the great majority of the nation than the actual situation, particularly as, in addition to this share in capital, each one will have the income from his labour as well. Arithmetically, there is no doubt about it ; and those who seek to vindicate the actual economic *régime* by denying the reality of this fact are mistaken. At bottom, this is what gives the social revolution its prestige in the eyes of the masses. Only, we must know whether this division—which must be periodic, or else it will be of no effect—by preventing the capital from being concentrated in powerful hands and, still more, by precluding all possibility of making fortunes, may not have the effect of drying up the most abundant sources of social income, thereby reducing the total quantity to be distributed and the share of each. The economic, social, and psychological consequences of such a displacement of wealth are very uncertain. And if, in order to bring it about, we must resort to a general expropriation and a sanguinary revolution, we would venture to say that the game is not worth the candle, and to hope that this modest competency—hardly more than the " fowl in the pot " of Henri IV—may be obtained by more pacific means.[1]

---

[1] M. Herckenrath has revived this scheme, proposing (in an article in the *Revue d'Économie politique*, 1904, on *La question sociale et l'héritage*) to carry out the partition quite pacifically by dividing up all successions equally among all Frenchmen. He calculated that 6 billion francs of successions every year would mean 150 francs per person per annum ; and, carefully capitalised, these small annuities would bring every Frenchman, within twenty to twenty-five

II : COMMUNISM

An equal share for each man is impossible. Very good! Since every division would be neither more nor less than a cause of new inequalities, let us not share everything, but have everything in common among the members of society as among members of one and the same family. Let our principle be, as in the family, *to each man according to his needs*. This is, indeed, the simplest and most ancient of all socialist systems. It was, in fact, considered almost out of date and absurd when, quite lately, it was revived again by a new school, the Anarchist school, and restored to some of its ancient glory.

Not that the Anarchist school aims primarily at community of goods. Its true end is the development, free and entire and without restraint, of the human individual. But *Communism* appears to it the only possible way of attaining this end.[1] According to this school

years, a small dowry of about 6000 francs. To avoid dividing up each succession into infinitesimal fractions, they would be put wholesale into a central bank or into regional banks, after the immovable property had been sold, and the share of each person would be regulated once a year.

This system has the ingenuity, in theory, not of abolishing succession, but of making every one heirs. But such a confiscation of all possessions at death would call forth energetic efforts on the part of both large and small proprietors to leave no visible succession behind them. They would prefer to consume their wealth.

[1] The authors who have expounded communist theories are very numerous, from Plato in his *Republic* to Fénelon in his *Télémaque ;* but the most recent and best known are Gracchus Babœuf, Robert Owen, and Cabet.

Babœuf, who took the name of Gracchus because he thought that the Roman tribune who passed the agrarian laws was a socialist of the " one man one share " type, was the leader of the conspiracy of *les Égaux* under the Directorate, and was condemned to death and executed in 1797. He had drawn up a complete programme of social organisation, which began with the words : " Nature has given each man an equal right to the enjoyment of all things."

Owen, who was born in Scotland in 1771, and died in 1857, was what might be called a " paternal " communist, neither revolutionary nor democratic. He wanted reform to come from above. A rich manufacturer, he inaugurated, from the beginning of the century onwards, all the great philanthropic measures of our time : the reduction of the hours of labour, the prohibition of child labour, workmen's co-operative societies, savings banks, stores, even lay schools. Not content with this, he dreamt of organising communist societies, one of which he tried to found in the United States under the name of New Harmony, in 1826. The attempt was an utter failure. The co-operative movement, however, owes its birth indirectly to him (see *Histoire des Doctrines*, by Gide and Rist).

Cabet, author of the *Icaria*—one of the numerous novels written in imitation of Sir Thomas More's *Utopia*—founded in Iowa, in 1848, the society of Icarians. The existence of this society, incessantly agitated by internal quarrels, was never very brilliant. See the very complete study of it by M. Prud'hommeaux.

private property, however small, always implies a limit and an authority whose business it is to make this limit respected. The mere fact of being able to possess a thing privately, whatever it may be, will always be an obstacle to those who possess nothing and will be a means of exploiting them. The only mode of distribution, therefore, which this school will allow is, to use its striking image, the " taking from the heap."

Now, no one is so simple as not to admit that the formula " To each according to his needs " is the most agreeable ; [1] but, in order to apply it, there must be an unlimited quantity of wealth, or at least a surplus, so that, like air and water, each may take as much as he wants.

Unfortunately this is not the case ; the quantity of wealth is, and probably always will be, insufficient for our wants or our desires, since the latter increase in proportion to the very ease with which we can satisfy them. The " taking from the heap," therefore, is impracticable, and it becomes necessary to put people on rations.[2] Now, in the family, the authority of the parents is enough in giving each one his allowance. But what authority is there here to perform this delicate task ? None, since the programme of the new communists—the anarchists—is the suppression of all authority, all government, and their device " Neither God nor master." Everything, they assure us, will be arranged by amicable concessions and goodwill. But nothing justifies a hypothesis so contrary to all that we know of human nature.

Still, we would not assert, as is sometimes too hastily done, that the communist system is altogether chimerical. It has certainly existed, if not at the origin of all human societies, at least at the beginning of a great number of them. There is no doubt that on a small scale it is possible, since, not to mention a number of religious bodies, we see communist societies in the United States which have existed for nearly a century,[3] and new ones are continually being

---

[1] We do not say, as is sometimes said, " the most just " ; for why should more wants create more rights ? The sober would always be the losers by that game. Professor Schmoller says very rightly : " It is altogether a mistake to make our needs a rule of distributive justice, for our needs have necessarily an egoistic character ; it is labour, merit, acts, which alone can serve the human race and furnish a rule of distributive justice " (*Uber einige Grundfragen des Rechts und der Volkswirthschaft*, 1875).

[2] True, the Anarchists take for granted that all rationing will become unnecessary owing to the excess of wealth. (*Cf.* Kropotkine, *The Conquest of Bread.*)

[3] See Nordhoff, *Communistic Societies ;* and Richard Ely, *The Labor Movement in America.*

created. If they have not given very striking results, they have shown nevertheless, by their very existence, that community of goods is not altogether incompatible with productive labour, nor with a certain amount of real happiness. But even such relative success is subject to the following conditions :

(1) The societies must be very small, not exceeding some hundred, say, or perhaps a thousand members.[1]

This the communists themselves generally admit. Fourier fixed the maximum figure for his " phalanstery " at 1500 persons ; Owen at 500 to 2000 ; while, for the anarchists, the basis of communistic organisation is the autonomous *commune*, the State being abolished altogether. The reason for it is simple. As the number of members increases, the interest which each has in the association diminishes. When the association is very small, every one may hope to benefit to an appreciable extent by his personal efforts ; but, in a communistic society embracing all Frenchmen, each one would be interested only to the $\frac{1}{38000000}$ degree. This would be too minute a fraction to stimulate anyone's zeal.

Now, the political evolution of our modern societies does not seem to be leading us towards the autonomy of communes and the abolition of States, but rather to centralisation, to the extension of the powers of the State, to the erection of great nationalities, to imperialism. Further, even if the communist society were reduced to the size of the commune, there would be rich communes and poor communes, and the inequality of groups would be substituted for the inequality of persons.

(2) The societies must be *submitted to a very severe discipline*. For it is easy to see *a priori* that life in common and equal sharing are incompatible with any encroachment on the part of individuals who would consume more than their share, or with any attempt at evasion on the part of those who would shirk their tasks. Experience confirms this ; for establishments where common life is the rule—convents, barracks, or schools—are also those where obedience is indispensable.[2] It should not be overlooked that

---

[1] All of those existing in the United States have a very small membership.

[2] The history of the Republic of Icaria is full of instruction on this point : we find the neophytes continually trying to evade a rule which they find unbearable, and Cabet struggling vainly, in the interests of the community, to obtain dictatorial powers. See Regulations of the Colony of Icaria, 1856: "Art 4, Be prompted by your devotion to the community. . . . Art. 16, Bind yourself to perform the work assigned to you by the management. . . . Art. 26, Have no preferences or dislikes in the matter of food. . . . Art. 27, Bear with resignation the discomforts of life in common. . . . Art. 37, Bear whatever discipline is imposed."

religious feeling, pushed to fanaticism, has generally been enough of itself to maintain the discipline essential to the existence of these communities.   All the communist societies of the United States, save that of the Icarians, which merely vegetated, are religious sects; and the republics of the Jesuits of Paraguay—the only great example which, for size and permanence, we are justified in quoting—were a veritable theocracy.

In this the practice of communism is absolutely at variance with the anarchist ideal, which implies the abolition of all discipline and regulation, and which shows itself, in any case, quite irreconcilable with the tendencies of modern life.

III : ASSOCIATIONISM

WE refer under this somewhat awkward name to the socialists who see in the various forms of *free association* an adequate solution of the social question, without any need to resort to revolution, or to abolish property, interest, or the inequality of fortunes.   It is in France more particularly, and during the first half of the nineteenth century, that this socialism flourished under such leaders as Fourier, Saint-Simon, Pecqueur, Leroux, Proudhon, and Louis Blanc.   Although, after the appearance of Collectivist Socialism, it fell into discredit, and is now qualified as Utopian, it cannot be said ever to have died, and is being revived in new forms by the "solidarity" and "co-operatist" socialists.

It is certainly a mistake to count Fourier, of *phalanstère* fame, among the communists.   Fourier was a communist only in regard to consumption and production, and not in any way as regards the distribution of wealth.   Common life in the phalanstery was for him merely a means of organising production and consumption on a more economic basis, and had no such aim as that of establishing equality among men.   On the contrary, it was to leave untouched, as Fourier expressly declared, not only the inequalities resulting from labour and talent, but also those resulting from unequal contributions of capital.   Distribution was to take place on the following basis : $\frac{5}{12}$ for labour, $\frac{4}{12}$ for capital, $\frac{3}{12}$ for talent; which has nothing of the levelling spirit about it.   Fourier even promised the shareholders fantastic dividends and riches.   He looked, mainly, to *attractive labour* to solve the social problem, and he claimed to render work attractive by a complex organisation of it into *groups* and *series*.   In his bulky volumes the number of his really inspired ideas is only equalled by that of his extravagances.[1]

The school of Saint-Simon, now fallen into oblivion, exercised an extraordinary influence over a whole generation in France and outside of it.[2] Although it is now only of historical interest, we must say a word or two about it, as it offers a formula of distribution which is at first sight very attractive, namely, *to each according to his merits.*

This school takes seriously the oft-repeated principle that a man, by the very fact of directing an industry or even of possessing a fortune, exercises a " social function." It would turn this metaphor into reality by making all trades, professions, and branches whatsoever of human activity public functions in the strictest sense of the word, appointed and remunerated by the State.

Saint-Simonism is, therefore, a form of socialism, with this peculiarity, that it is an aristocratic and capitalist socialism. Far from proscribing manufacturers, large employers, or even bankers, this school confers on them the government of society, under the control of a *Chambre de savants.* It by no means objects to inequality, but it endeavours to replace artificial inequality by an inequality due to individual merit. This is what is meant by its celebrated formula, " To each man according to his capacity, to each capacity according to its works." The Revolution, it declared, was unable to succeed, since, when suppressing all political, fiscal, and civil privileges conferred by birth, it forgot one, the most exorbitant and absurd of all, namely fortune. Logically, it ought to have abolished succession in everything, particularly in the most important social functions, those, namely, of industrial organiser, landowner, and capitalist employer.

The *abolition of inheritance* is therefore the essential article in the programme of the Saint-Simon school. And this is only logical ; for, if economic functions are public functions, the power to transmit them by inheritance, like private property, would be absurd. The abolition of *intestate* inheritance may easily be admitted (see p. 468), although it was the rule with many of the public functions in aristocratic societies, royalty first of all. But, if there is little reason

---

[1] See *Œuvres Choisies,* which we published with an Introduction in the *Petite Bibliothèque économique.*

[2] Saint-Simon, who died in 1835, left behind nothing more than a politico-religious system, somewhat incoherent, though enlightened by flashes of genius. But he founded a great school which exercised a veritable fascination on the spirits of the most distinguished men of his age ; and two of his disciples, Bazard and Enfantin, developed his doctrine very fully, giving it more precision, particularly from the economic point of view.

for the transmission of social rank—even where heredity of blood may be held to transmit certain natural qualities, and where, in addition to the physical inheritance, there is the force of example and education to take into account—the case is a little different with *testamentary* succession, where the heir is appointed, not by the accident of birth, but by the father of the family. If we agree with the Saint-Simonians, that the possession of wealth is in itself a social function, is it not logical to conclude that the man who performs this function is the one best fitted to point out his successor ? [1]

And though we have admitted that the testator is seldom capable of filling so important a rôle, still it would be difficult to find anyone to take his place. For who, if not the father of a family, can be asked to point out the most capable or most worthy ? The government perhaps, which might nominate each individual in each different kind of labour, as it nominates its officials to-day, assigning them their rank and salary according to their presumed merit ? But would public feeling be less shocked at seeing fortunes distributed by the favour and arbitrary will of some power or other, than it is to-day at seeing it dispensed by law, or heredity, or the will of a testator ?

Again, if the suffrage of electors were to be substituted for the government, we may be sure that it would not be a *régime* of " capacity " that would result. If, finally, we were to fall back on a system of competitions and examinations in all the different labours and occupations, from the lowest to the highest forms, we should create the worst form of mandarinism.

The Saint-Simonians, after abolishing succession, are forced, then, in the end, to fall back on the priest as the " dispenser of fortunes " ; a priest very different, it is true, from what we understand by the word, viz., a couple, " man and woman," but after all a mystic and infallible authority.

It seems vain, therefore, to look to the abolition of succession as a means of carrying out the formula : " To each according to his

---

[1] It is quite possible that, where liberty of bequest exists, the father may fulfil Saint-Simon's ideal by leaving his fortune to the most deserving. Pullman, the well-known manufacturer of Pullman-cars, who died in 1897 leaving a fortune of $6,000,000, left his two sons only $3000 a year each, stating that, as neither of them had shown the sense of responsibility which in his opinion ought to be felt in order to make a good use of large properties and sums of money, he was obliged to his great regret, as he had explicitly told them, to limit what he left them to sums which would produce just the income he considered reasonable for their existence.

capacity, to each capacity according to its works"; or, at any rate, to imagine that this formula will give any better guarantee than the present system of competition. We may indeed ask whether, even supposing an infallible criterion of merits could be found, such a system would be just. It may quite well be argued, on the contrary, that intellectual superiority should no more be a claim to wealth than physical superiority. It is already in itself an enviable enough privilege, and has no need to be supplemented by an additional one, namely, the right to claim a larger share of material wealth.[1]

As for Louis Blanc, in his view the social evil lay mainly in competition, and the remedy in association for production—an association of working men, but backed by the State, somewhat similar to that which Lassalle demanded later in Germany. We shall return to it in connection with co-operative association for production.

Proudhon[2] would not willingly range himself alongside of the associationists, for he distrusted associations. He does not, strictly speaking, come under any heading. He called himself an anarchist, though he was in reality a good bourgeois and a friend of order. Still, his ideal certainly was to make the whole of society a true association, wherein the services rendered and received by each should be exactly balanced—hence the name, *Mutualism*, by which his school is usually known. Parasitical shares—shares, that is to say, which consist of more than has been given in return, *e.g.* interest, rent, farmer's rent, etc.—would thus disappear of themselves.

It would be a mistake if, remembering his famous saying, "Property is theft," we were to class him among the communists. Theft necessarily implies that property is legitimate. What Proudhon wanted to abolish was simply property that was a tax on labour. His idea was a property that should aid labour, taking nothing from it ; and this is why free credit seemed to him the true solution of the social problem.

IV : COLLECTIVISM

COLLECTIVISM is a milder form of Communism. It proposes to hold in common *the instruments of production only*—land, mines, factories,

---

[1] "If we were to consult public opinion, it would seem as if the cleverest and most skilful man is a natural creditor of ordinary mortals. But this is a serious misapprehension of the moral law." Renouvier, *Morale*, t. ii.

[2] The literary output of Proudhon is immense, turbid, and eloquent. His principal books, besides the memoir on *Property* (1840), which is not his master-piece, are his *Contradictions Économiques* (1846) and *La Justice dans la Révolution et l'Église* (1858).

banks, railways, raw material—and to leave consumption goods under the *régime* of private property, save that they are to be better distributed.[1] (For this distinction, *cf.* pp. 22–26, etc.)

To distinguish itself from the socialist systems which preceded it, collectivism calls itself *scientific socialism*, implying that it is not a *system* but a *demonstration*. It does not propose an ideal of justice or fraternity, but claims to represent the order of things towards which modern societies are actually tending, pushed thither, willy-nilly, by the law of evolution.[2]

Formerly, if property were private, it was because production also was private : there was a harmony between the mode of production and the mode of distribution. An instance of this is the small workshop of the Middle Ages. To-day, owing to the development of large industry, large commerce, large property, that is to say, the law of concentration (see p. 161), individual production is gradually giving way to collective production, *e.g.* the large factory, the mine, the railway company.

Yet distribution still continues on the basis of individual property. There is therefore a discrepancy between the system of production and that of distribution which must at some moment or other cause a disturbance of the social equilibrium, and the collapse of the present capitalist *régime*.

In the march of evolution, the existing forms of individual production are condemned one by one to disappear, and the day is bound to come when all the instruments of production will be " socialised," and all the small producers expropriated by the large.

But the wheel will continue to go round, and it will be the turn of the large expropriators next to be expropriated for the good of

---

[1] Collectivism is of fairly recent date. Colins, in Belgium, appears to have been the first to use this word (1850), but his collectivism was mainly agrarian. Pecqueur (1838) and Vidal (1846) were the first in France to draw the distinction between instruments of production, and objects of consumption, which is the characteristic feature of the system. But it was the *Manifesto of the Communist party*, issued by Marx and Engels in 1847, which first made it an aggressive doctrine. In his famous book on *Capital*, Karl Marx gave it its critical form, furnishing it with the arsenal of weapons with which it assails the present organisation of our modern societies. Finally, it was Cesar de Paepe in Belgium (who died in 1891) who first traced a general plan of collectivist organisation. Although collectivism is often referred to as " Marxism," after its most illustrious theorist, all collectivists are not Marxists. An increasing number are, indeed, breaking away from Marxism.

See among the innumerable publications on this subject *Les Systèmes Socialistes et l'Évolution économique*, by M. Bourguin.

[2] This conception of an evolution altogether determined by economic necessities is known by the name of *historical materialism*. See *supra*, p. 24 n.

society. Harmony will thus be established between production and distribution, and the logic of evolution will be borne out, whereby it is decreed that *to a collective mode of production there shall henceforth correspond a collective mode of distribution.*

How will this expropriation, this socialising of capital, come about?

Either legally, by the will of the majority of the nation, who will apply on a large scale the law of expropriation for the sake of public utility;[1] or by revolutionary means, if, owing to universal suffrage, to the parliamentary system, or to the resistance of the middle classes, a pacific solution is impossible. This, then, would be the last act in the class conflict which has been waged for centuries, and which, for Karl Marx, constitutes the most important fact of history, the keynote to all the others.

Expropriation once carried out, the instruments of production would be turned to account by the nation, or the commune, either directly or by means of trade unions. The proceeds would be put into the National Treasury, which, after deducting the amount required for social expenses,[2] would hand back the surplus to the workers to be disposed of absolutely.

We have said that collectivism differs from communism in that

[1] With or without compensation? With compensation, say the more moderate, if the property-owning class is willing to accept it with good grace. Only the compensation will not be paid as it is at present, in the form of capital which the expropriated person may invest, obtaining an equal or even greater income from it. This would not modify the economic situation in any way, as the capitalist producer would simply be replaced by the capitalist *rentier.* It will take the form of consumption orders which will disappear as they are consumed, like money that is put into a cash-box and drawn on until it is finished, the owner of which, once he has spent it, falls back into the rank of a simple citizen living by his labour alone.

A method more economical for the State has been proposed, which consists in confiscating inheritances progressively, so as not to disinherit completely until, say, the fourth generation, the *generation as yet unborn.*

Collectivism does not prohibit inheritance, as is generally thought. It has no objection to a man who has earned something by his labour leaving this to whomsoever he pleases, nor to the beneficiary living without working until he has consumed it.

This might surprise us at first sight, did we not know that the collectivist excludes from the domain of individual property, land and capital—*i.e.* almost the only forms of wealth that are productive and lasting, the only ones, consequently, for which inheritance has any serious consequences—and considers objects of consumption alone as private property. Restricted to these, inheritance is of but slight importance.

[2] These social expenses would be much greater than our actual taxes, as they would have to cover the maintenance of all children, old persons, invalids, insurance against risks of all kinds, and a depreciation fund for implements and buildings (as all these would belong to society); lastly, a *reserve fund* for

the latter aims at establishing community of all goods, while collectivism demands it only for the instruments of production, leaving consumption goods under the *régime* of private property. To be more exact, we should say that, at present, collectivism does not even demand that *all* the instruments of production should be held in common, but *only those which are already worked collectively, i.e. by means of paid wage-earners*. Thus the land cultivated by the peasant, the fisherman's boat, the artisan's workshop, would still be individual property and would remain so as long as they continued under the *régime* of individual production.[1]

On what principle will the products be divided among individuals ? On that of *every man according to his labour*. But this principle may be understood in two quite different ways : either, to each according to the result obtained, which is practically the same as that of the Saint-Simon school—to each according to his works ; or, to each according to the trouble he has taken. It is in this last sense that we must understand the formula of collectivist distribution : *To each according to the trouble he has taken, measured by the number of hours of labour which he has furnished.*[2] Those who are unable to work are guaranteed a minimum *allowance*.

Collectivism may therefore be summed up as follows : its aim is *gradually to socialise the instruments of production ;* its means, *the conflict of classes*—the working class against the capitalist class, the working man against the bourgeois.[3]

---

maintaining and increasing the national capital. True, on the other hand, these expenses would be reduced by the amount of the interest on the national debt, since it would no longer be paid, and the Army and Navy budget, since there would be no more fighting—or so at least it is hoped.

[1] We know already (p. 115) that the collectivists do not consider the instruments of production, as capital, so long as they are in the hands of the worker. They are therefore very logical in their programme.

It is thanks to this *distinguo* that for the last few years the collectivist party has been able to stand as the sole defender of the property of the small peasant, small artisan, and small shopkeeper. It is on this ground that it is able to reassure small producers and peasants whom the prospect of a general expropriation may have alarmed. By limiting expropriation *for the moment* to proprietors who employ salaried labour, *i.e.* to the rich, they reassure the rest, omitting sometimes to add that their turn will come later.

[2] " The quantity of labour is measured by its duration. . . . But the labour which constitutes the substance of values is equal, uniform human labour, the *expenditure of the same intensity of labour-power*." Karl Marx, *Capital.*

[3] This formula of " class conflict " does not necessarily imply armed fighting or civil war, any more than does the struggle between political parties, churches, or languages ; but it implies the ultimate elimination of the capitalist class. (See chapter *infra, The Social Classes.*)

Against this doctrine the following criticisms may be urged:

The so-called historical law, on which the whole structure of collectivism stands, viz., the gradual transformation of individual production into collective production, is a mere generalisation. It by no means covers all the facts of the case, and is even contradicted by many. We have already pointed out (p. 177) that in agricultural production, in spite of the assertions of the collectivists, there is no decisive proof of a tendency in this direction. On the contrary, land is becoming more and more divided up, and farms are becoming smaller and smaller as the population becomes denser and cultivation more intensive. The shareholding system has been applied to land only in a few quite exceptional cases. Even in industry, not only are small businesses not disappearing before large, but they are developing quite as rapidly.[1]

There is no proof, then, that a general expropriation of individual producers in favour of a small number of collective enterprises on which, when ripe, the nation will lay its hands, will ever be realised. The "logic of evolution" is thus at fault, and, consequently, the logic of collectivism.

On the other hand, the discrepancy between a mode of production which is said to be becoming collective, and a mode of distribution which is said to be remaining individual, is a mere verbal antithesis. In reality, the two are transformed at the same time. In every enterprise in the form of a shareholding company, property becomes collective at the same time as does production, in the sense that there are as many shareholders as there are workers, and often more.

Finally, the class conflict, although an undeniable fact, is much more complex than the Marxist outline of it would lead us to suppose (see infra, p. 498); and there is no indication that it is approaching an end. For the force of resistance which the possessing classes are able to offer against expropriation, that is to say, against the socialising of their goods, is growing, not weaker, as the collectivists assert, but stronger. The number of humble individuals, servants, country people, and also working men, who buy government stock, bonds of the Paris Municipality or the Crédit Foncier, even railway shares, is increasing daily; and they cling as firmly to their

---

[1] See above, The Law of Concentration.

This belief in the total concentration of production has given rise to lively polemics in the very bosom of the collectivist school. See the refutation of it in Bernstein's Zur Geschichte und Theorie des Socialismus, Berlin, 1901, which made a great sensation. He shows that in England, e.g. the number of well-to-do families with from £150 to £1000 a year has more than trebled within thirty years, and that the number of small shops (with one to ten workers) has almost doubled, etc.

securities as does the peasant to his field.[1] They would, of course, ask nothing better, in the case of equal division, than to add part of the wealth of the rich to their small shares ; but they would not be at all inclined to sacrifice the latter, however minute, for a vague and undetermined collective right on the national capital.

Collectivism does not give a pretext to most of the classical objections to socialism. It avoids the main objection, namely, the lack of personal interest and consequent disappearance of all activity and all production. It cannot be said that a system which aims at securing to each the just equivalent of the product of his labour by eliminating all parasitism, is sacrificing personal interest, or appealing to sentimentalism and altruism. At the same time, by refusing to sketch the lines of the future society and leaving that undertaking to evolution, it makes criticism difficult. Still, if it would apply its principles logically, collectivism will meet with serious practical difficulties, of which the following are the most important :

(1) The right of individual property which the collectivist school proposes to maintain, restricting it, however, to the products of personal labour, is only a delusion. For if this right of property were to be recognised, with all the attributes that constitute it— in particular the power to lend, to sell, or to turn to account— it would speedily restore inequality of wealth and the classes of creditor and debtor, employer and wage-earner, buyer and seller, *i.e.* the whole economic edifice which had been overturned. Collectivists therefore declare that in no case may the so-called proprietor sell or lend his share, nor employ it in making others work[2] ; he may only consume it, keep it, or give it away ; in other words, he is forbidden to turn it to any but *an unproductive use.* Now, in the first place, this opens anything but a reassuring prospect for the future of production. And as, moreover, the possessors of wealth are not likely to submit to such a mutilated form of property, and will probably make desperate efforts to obtain the most out of

---

[1] The collectivists say (see Vandervelde, *Le collectivisme et l'évolution industrielle ;* Jaurès, *Études socialistes*) that the development of joint-stock companies tends to make property " volatile." But remark that it tends in this very way (1) to democratise property by making it accessible to all ; (2) to make it, in its anonymous form of titles to bearer, a world commodity which cannot be seized either by the Treasury or the Collectivist State.

[2] Will he be allowed to turn it to account himself, independently ? Provisionally, perhaps, and so long as there are independent producers ; but logically he will not, since individual production is ultimately to be replaced by social production.

it, we may foresee measures in the future which will greatly hamper the liberty of the individual. In any case, the right of property, thus deprived of its most essential attributes, will be but a word, a shadow, and we shall fall back into communism, or something very like it.

It would seem then that the boast of the collectivists that their system is a happy mean between communism and individualism, is vain, and that collectivism cannot but end in one or the other.

(2) The plan of getting rid of all the captains of industry—employers, landowners, capitalists—and replacing them by managers chosen by working-men's unions, by federations, or by committees, is enough to awaken the liveliest apprehensions of all who have any knowledge of the small degree of economic training there is among the working classes. True, the same objection is urged against the co-operative system, in which we nevertheless believe; but, in the co-operative system, the elimination of property comes about by free competition, not by a stroke of policy; that is to say, it is effected within the bounds of possibility and social utility.

But the social class whose disappearance would, in our opinion, be most calculated to cause anxiety is that of the capitalists who save. There are in France millions of large and small capitalists, particularly small ones, who lay by with difficulty, year in year out, about 2 or 3 billion francs, and who thus keep going the source from which the fortune of the nation is maintained and renewed. They do it in their own interest, of course, but the result is of no less vital importance to the country. Now, under the collectivist *régime*, this marvellous spring—private saving—would dry up, for the following reasons : In the first place, once men know that their necessaries are secured, they are not likely to strive any longer to save out of the shares allotted to them. In the second, even supposing that some continue to save a part of their income in the form of labour coupons, they will keep these savings for their wants and will not think of investing them—a proceeding, indeed, which would be strictly forbidden. All they will have the right to do will be to hoard them up uselessly, in a way which will be of no advantage to society. But, as the national capital must nevertheless be maintained and increased, what are we to substitute for this private saving ? Public saving, we are told. The nation will do what all financial companies do at the present day : it will deduct from its revenues 10 or 20 per cent., which it will set apart for a reserve fund. Very good. But up to the present no government has been found that knew

how, or was able and willing, to save.   We must suppose therefore
that the collectivist government will differ from all its predecessors ;
that it will be economical, provident, in a word, by the mere fact
of becoming collectivist, will acquire all the virtues which are
characteristic of the " bourgeois."

(3) The suppression of the independent producer—society becoming the only *entrepreneur*—necessarily implies the *suppression of the
liberty of labour*.   The citizen will no more be able to choose his
employment than is the working man hired by the employer at
the present day.   Just as the wage-earner betakes him to the post
assigned him by his employer, so all will have to repair to the posts
assigned them by the great, the only employer—the Nation ; and
no one will have—what the worker to-day still has—the chance
of seeking another employer elsewhere.   This is a terrible prospect,
which the various collectivist writers try in vain, by ingenious
systems, to palliate.[1]

But, it may be said, the whole working class is already under
this very servitude that appears so alarming.   Alas, yes ; and it is
for that very reason we would seek a way of escape for those who are
actually suffering under it, not a way of extending it to those who are
to-day delivered from it.

(4) Lastly, the formula of collectivist distribution, " to each man
according to the number of hours of labour he has furnished," runs
up against great practical difficulties and an important ethical
problem.

Practical difficulties, because this mode of distribution is bound
up with the Marxist doctrine which makes labour the sole foundation of value.   Now if, as we have already explained, and as most
economists to-day believe, labour is only one of the elements of
value ; if final utility, or desirability, is really at the basis of
value (see pp. 53–57), the Marxist system of distribution is not in
harmony with facts.   I might quite well be given, in exchange for
my labour, a number of claims equal to the number of hours I have
worked ; but no one can guarantee that, in exchange for these
claims, I shall be able to obtain products representing the same
number of hours of labour ; for no one will ever be able to hinder a
rare object from being worth more than a common object, even if
it has cost the same number of hours of labour to make.   .

---

[1] Efforts have often been made (Thompson, Owen, Rodbertus, etc., see in
particular Georges Renard, *Le régime socialiste*) to find a mechanism which will
ensure an automatic distribution proportional to labour.

But no better automatic mechanism can well be imagined than the law of
Demand and Supply.   And Neo-Marxism to-day recognises this.

An *ethical* problem,[1] for is it really just that each person should be rewarded according to the trouble he has taken, the number of hours and minutes measured by the clock ? Would it not be more just to pay him according to the result obtained ? Is it not the work (*opus*) rather than the labour (*labor*) which should be the criterion of distributive justice ?

For the rest, this discussion is already somewhat ancient history ; for collectivism in its pure form, as summarised and criticised above, has profoundly changed during the last few years as regards both its doctrines and its actions.[2] It is no longer concerned with the question whether the present economic *régime* is based on surplus value, or on surplus labour, nor on what basis the society of the future ought to be organised. Socialism has become practical, and its whole effort is turned towards depriving the bourgeois class of economic government and handing this over to the working class. The *working-class* character of collectivism, which was its force, which gave it its superiority of propaganda over the preceding forms of socialism, has thereby been strengthened. But, in the bosom of this new socialism itself, there have arisen numerous divergences of tactics.

The most faithful followers of the Marxist doctrine, of whom M. Jules Guesde is the purest representative in France, would obtain possession of the public powers by putting socialists on the municipal councils and into Parliament.[3] In the meantime, with

[1] An ethical problem which the Marxist school does not ask itself; for it waives all moral considerations from its demonstration. We, however, must not pass it over.

[2] For the doctrines of " Neo-Marxism," see Gide and Rist, *History of Economic Doctrines* (English translation).

[3] Such a conquest of the political power is far from being realised in any country, unless perhaps Australia. But it is making rapid progress everywhere in the sense that the number of socialist members is increasing in all parliaments. True, these are not all working men. The following are the figures for 1910, which are somewhat curious :

Finland	.	.	.	.	84 members out of 300 = 28 per cent.
Sweden	.	.	.	.	36	,,	165 = 22	,, ,,
Denmark	.	.	.	.	24	,,	114 = 21	,, ,,
Belgium	.	.	.	.	25	,,	166 = 21	,, ,,
Austria	.	.	.	.	39	,,	516 = 17	,, ,,
France	.	.	.	.	76	,,	584 = 13	,, ,,
Germany	.	.	.	.	45	,,	397 = 11	,, ,,
Norway	.	.	.	.	11	,,	123 = 9	,, ,,
Italy	.	.	.	.	44	,,	508 = 8½	,, ,,
Great Britain	.	.	.	40	,,	670 = 6	,, ,,
Switzerland	.	.	.	7	,,	170 = 4	,, ,,

We see that, contrary to what we might expect, the French Republic is far

implicit confidence in the law of concentration, they count on the evolution of the capitalist system to prepare automatically its own end.

The revolutionaries attach little importance to political action. Instead of looking for emancipation to law and social reform, they look for it solely from the working class as organised into unions. This is what is called ' direct action." It is purely economic. This party is nowadays known as the *Syndicalist* party— the syndicate being, by definition, composed only of wage-earners— and has for its organ the *Confédération Générale du Travail*, the C.G.T. so often spoken of, which is simply a federation of all the unions. Its principal method of action consists in incessant strikes, as a preparation for the general strike which is to be the working-man's revolution. This movement has found some enthusiastic adherents among the intellectual classes, who have drawn from it a new moral and an ideal philosophy of their own.[1]

The *Reformists*, on the contrary, without disavowing the principle of class conflict or renouncing strikes, do not despise social reforms, particularly when these take the form of laws and not philanthropic institutions. They do not believe that the capitalist *régime* is nearing its end, nor, even supposing it were, that the working class is ready to take over the economic government of society. But they try to prepare the way for it to do so by various forms of association, particularly the trade union, as also by the co-operative societies for consumption, of which it remains for us to speak. Long disdained by socialists, these are beginning now to find a certain amount of favour.

V : CO-OPERATISM

THE word *co-operatism* is a neologism, beginning to be used by those who see in co-operation not only a means of improving social conditions, but a complete programme of social renovation. Co-operatism is directly descended from the Associationist Socialism of which we spoke above. It does not, however, like the latter, incur the epithet Utopian. It takes its stand on, and works within, the

from being in the first rank, and the Swiss Republic is far and away the last. This is perhaps because where democracy is already a political fact the people are less impatient to carry it out socially.

In Germany, since the election of 1910, the number has risen to 110, or 28 per cent.

[1] See, in particular, M. Georges Sorel, *Réflexions sur la violence*, and the review edited by M. Lagardelle, *Le Mouvement socialiste*.

existing economic framework; it is already carrying into practice some of the most important desiderata of Socialism; and, in the meanwhile, it is bringing about an immediate and very real amelioration in the conditions of those who practise it—a result by no means to be despised.

We saw that, at the beginning of the nineteenth century, Owen in England, and Fourier in France, held that mankind could be reformed by means of free association, and to this end devised more or less ingenious mechanisms which, however, did not succeed. But the practical necessities of life, more powerful than any theories, have caused diverse forms of association to spring up spontaneously in different countries : in England co-operatives for consumption ; in France co-operatives for production ; in Germany co-operatives for credit ; in Denmark rural co-operatives; in the United States building co-operatives, etc. These, although still of modest proportions, have already begun seriously to transform present economic conditions, and to open up a wider and more hopeful prospect. For each of these forms of co-operative association we must refer the reader to the chapter under which it falls.[1] We shall simply indicate here the features in which co-operatism resembles, or differs from, the other socialist programmes.

(1) All co-operative associations aim at the economic emancipation of certain classes of persons, so that they may dispense with intermediaries and be self-sufficient. Consumers' societies allow consumers to do without the baker, the grocer, or any other shopkeeper, by buying directly from the producer, or, better still, by manufacturing their necessaries for themselves. Credit societies allow borrowers to escape the clutches of the usurer by furnishing them directly with the capital they require, or by enabling them, through ingenious combinations of saving and mutual assistance, to create it for themselves. Producers' societies allow the worker to do without the employer by producing themselves on their own account, selling directly to the public, and keeping the whole product of their labour for themselves.

(2) All aim at substituting solidarity for competition, and the co-operative motto, " Each for all," in place of the individualist motto, " Each for himself." Individuals no longer compete, in

---

[1] For co-operative association as a new mode of enterprise, see *supra*, pp. 200–204 ; for consumption and for building, *see Consumption* ; for co-operative *Agricultural* for production, *see Profit* ; for co-operative association for credit, *see* association *Credit*.

principle at least, but associate together to provide for their wants ; and these associations in turn make it a rule to combine in order to form vaster organisations. Without denying the stimulating action of competition on production, they hold that the struggle for life has deplorable moral and even economic effects, involving a waste of productive forces (see above, *Competition*).

(3) All aim, not at abolishing private property, but at spreading it by making it accessible to every one in the form of small shares ; [1] while, at the same time, they aim at creating alongside of, and above, it a *collective property* in the form of impersonal funds, to be used for the development of society and for works of social utility.

This collective property, this lay *main-morte*, already amounts in the English co-operatives to nearly £4,000,000.

(4) All aim, not at doing away with capital, but at depriving it of its preponderant rôle of management in production, as also of the tribute which it levies for this *in the form of profit*. The suppression of profit, in all its forms, was the essential point in Owen's system.[2] Many societies are expressly forbidden by their statutes to make profits, or are obliged to put them into a reserve fund. Those which are allowed to make profits distribute them among their members—in proportion to their purchases when they are consumers, or to their labours when they are employees, but never in proportion to their shares, *i.e.* the capital which they contribute. The service done by share capital, like that of borrowed capital, is paid for by a small interest, never by a dividend ; and some societies go so far as to allow no interest on capital. When we remember that, in the limited liability company which is spreading so rapidly nowadays, it is capital which takes over all the profits of the enterprise as well as the management of the business, the worker being reduced to the rôle of a mere wage-earner, we shall understand

---

[1] True, during the last few years a certain number of Collectivists, and even of Anarchists, have been advocating and practising co-operation, without, however, giving up their ideal of the socialisation of property. Co-operation for them is a preparatory stage, paving the way for Collectivism, providing a framework and resources for the class conflict. For the Co-operatists, on the other hand, co-operation is an *end* in itself, that is to say, it contains the germ of the future society, to bring about which we have only to allow the small co-operative societies to evolve and multiply, just as we allow the grain which contains the fruit to ripen and increase.

[2] The economic system called *le morcellisme*, or sometimes *propriétisme*, is closely related to *coopératisme*, since it also aims at making property more accessible to all, thus putting an end to the wage-earning system (see M. C. Sabatier, *Le Morcellisme*, 1907), but it differs from it in that it is more individualistic in inspiration and aim.

how, by reversing the situation and making capital in turn no more than a paid wage-earner, the co-operative system is neither more nor less than a social revolution.

(5) All co-operative associations, then, possess a considerable educational value. They teach their members, not to sacrifice any part of their individuality or of their spirit of enterprise, but to develop their energies by helping others while helping themselves; to place the end of economic activity in the satisfaction of wants, not in the pursuit of gain; to raise the moral level by doing away with advertisement, fraud, the adulteration of food, the sweating system, etc.; to abolish all the methods by which men exploit their fellow men, and all causes of conflict. Indeed, it may be said that each great form of co-operative association marks the smoothing away of some conflict or other, some duel of opposing interests. The consumers' association does away with the conflict between seller and buyer; the building association that between landlord and tenant; credit associations that between creditor and debtor; producers' associations the conflict between employer and employed.[1]

Will these associations ever be able to carry out such an ambitious programme? It remains to be seen, as the oldest is not yet sixty years of age. Claudio Jannet, who was anything but a co-operatist, felt justified in writing that it was "the only social experiment of the nineteenth century which had succeeded." Unfortunately, in France, these associations are rapidly imbibing the vices of the mercantile environment which they aim at regenerating, and their object is now less to abolish profit than to get hold of it for themselves in the form of bonuses. The co-operative associations for production, on which the older French socialism had founded such great hopes, have had some brilliant but rare successes. But, in other countries, credit associations and, above all, associations for consumption are developing in a manner that is surprising not only their enemies but their friends. Credit associations aim at hardly more than defending the middle classes, but consumers' associations aim at absorbing all other forms of co-operation, and at bringing about a sort of co-operative commonwealth, in which the

---

[1] There are other forms of association which also aim at suppressing the conflict of interests : working-men's unions, and employers' unions, try to suppress competition among workers in the same trade or among employers in the same industry. But in these cases the conflicts arise from a rivalry of *similar* interests, whereas co-operative associations try to conciliate conflicts which arise from *opposing* interests.

whole control of production will pass into the hands of the consumers themselves. This would be a revolution of no small importance.

But even supposing such a programme could not be completely carried out, co-operation would at least have this advantage that it would not compromise the future by pouring human societies into one uniform and predetermined mould. The great superiority of the social *régime* which it would establish is that it is *optional ;* it does not practise the *compelle intrare*, nor resort to force, whether revolutionary or legal, to suppress the existing economic organisation. It simply turns against the latter its own weapons of competition and liberty.[1]

The attitude of socialism to co-operatism has singularly varied. At the outset, during the first half of the nineteenth century, socialism and co-operatism were one. On the appearance of Marxism, socialism declared itself resolutely hostile to co-operation, seeing in it nothing less than a bourgeois institution for capturing the working classes by the inducement of material advantages, and for instilling into them a taste for saving and for property. And it must be admitted that this was the light in which the Classical economists presented co-operation. But the example of the societies of consumption in Belgium, to which the creation of the socialist movement in that country is really due and which have been successfully imitated in France, has gradually reconciled socialism and co-operation ; and, to-day, socialist congresses do not hesitate to make a place for co-operation, alongside of syndicalism, as an effective mode of emancipating the working classes. Still, socialists do not admit that co-operation can bring about the socialist aim, namely, the collective ownership of the means of production : it only paves the way.[2] Their approval is limited, moreover, to the societies of consumption ; for, so far as production and credit are concerned, socialism persists in considering these as institutions which can but imbue the working classes with the bourgeois spirit.

[1] All the criticisms that may be urged against co-operation as " a social palingenesis " will be found in M. Leroy-Beaulieu's *Traité d'Économie politique* (t. ii, pp. 608–649). For fuller details, see our collection of lectures, *La Coopération*, and the small volume, *Les sociétés coopératives de consommation.*

[2] Thus at the International Socialist Congress at Copenhagen in 1910, one of the principal subjects discussed was the attitude to be taken towards consumers' co-operatives, and a motion was unanimously passed by which the " Congress, while putting workers on their guard against those who maintain that co-operation is in itself a sufficient end, urge all societies to participate actively in the co-operative movement."

PART II: THE DIFFERENT CLASSES
OF SHARERS

INTRODUCTION

I: THE SOCIAL CLASSES

WE have been considering the *principles* which govern the distribution of wealth, both those which regulate it at the present time and those which it is proposed to substitute for them. Let us now examine the *persons* among whom this wealth is distributed, and the share which each one claims. It goes without saying that it is not individual claims which we have to examine, but the claims of important groups, of *classes*, as they are called, *i.e.* of men who, united by a bond of common interest, base their claims to distribution, on the same ground.[1] As their claims are antagonistic, we must expect to find these groups in a state of permanent conflict. Even among individuals, though the rights of each one are minutely regulated by law, we know that the dividing of successions is a fruitful source of quarrels and lawsuits; much more will this be the case where the conflict is between formidable forces and where it is the actual laws themselves that are the object of attack.

Class must not be confused with *caste*. The caste system implies immovable barriers between different groups: its origin is political and religious, and it is sanctioned by law. Class creates only movable barriers, which do not prevent individuals from passing from one group to another; it is economic in origin and is sanctioned simply by custom. Political and civil laws no longer recognise inequalities among men—either in democratic or in undemocratic societies—and there are now hardly any outward signs left which distinguish them. It is difficult in a crowd of Americans, Englishmen, or Frenchmen to discriminate between the working man and the bourgeois. This does not mean that permanent differences between them do not exist: everyday language goes to prove that they do

[1] This, at least, is the simplest definition of " class," though there are many others. Some persons indeed hold that classes no longer exist, and that the word must be struck out of the language. The fact of possessing or of not possessing, professional solidarity, the difference in habits and education, even original differences of race, have been proposed as criteria of " classes " (see Cyr von Over-begh, *La Classe sociale*).

when it calls a man who has left his social *milieu* of his own will or perforce, a *déclassé*. The surest sign that classes still exist in our modern societies is the fact that intermarriage, the *jus connubii*, as the Romans called it, does not take place between them any more than it did in the Middle Ages, or in antiquity. Not only will a girl of the middle classes not marry a working man—unless perhaps in George Sand's novels—but even the daughter of a clerk will not willingly do so.

Socialists to-day see only two conflicting classes : those who possess and those who do not, *i.e.* Capital and Labour ; and, in their view, as we have seen, this century-long struggle will shortly end in the victory of labour. The expropriated capitalists will return to the ranks of the workers, and there will be an end to classes and to class struggles.[1]

Now, it is true that the struggle between capital and labour is in the foreground at the present moment. Still, it has been pointed out that the above division into those who possess, and those who do not, is somewhat too sweeping. The Classical economists distinguished not two, but three classes—workers, capitalists, and landlords—corresponding to the three factors of production, each claiming its share : *wage* for the first, *profit* for the second, *rent* for the third. And Karl Marx himself has acknowledged the exactness of this threefold division. Now, it makes a great difference in a fight whether it is between two parties or three. The presence of a third renders it less cruel, as it is usually to the interest of this third party that neither of the two adversaries should be completely wiped out, and it leans therefore now to one side, now to the other to keep the balance between them. This is precisely what has taken place here. The landlord and the capitalist have very different interests, as may be seen in the political life of all countries in the classical fight between Liberals and Conservatives, Whigs and Tories. If, at the present moment, the menacing force of working-class socialism is uniting them into an *entente cordiale*, it has not always been so. In England, at the time of the great fight for Free Trade, the manufacturers stood by the working men against the landowners to obtain the repeal of the duties on corn ; and later the landowners, in revenge, sided with the working men against the manufacturers to pass the Factory Acts.

---

[1] The *class struggle* must not be confused with *competition*, although both are signs of the struggle for life : the latter exists between likes, the former between unlikes. There is competition, but not a class struggle, between one grocer and another.

But are there only three sharers, three classes of interests ? By no means ; there are a great many more. In the first place, there are two distinct classes of capitalists—the *active* capitalist, *i.e.* the *entrepreneur* or employer, the chief actor on the economic stage, who directs and controls everything ; and the *passive* capitalist, the *rentier*, who does no more than lend his capital to the *active* capitalist to turn to account for him, who is never in any direct relation with the wage-earner. The manufacturer and the *rentier* have not the same interests, for the former is generally to be found among borrowers and the latter among lenders. In the second place, there are different sets of workers who are not always of one mind. There are working men in the strict sense ; there are employees ; there are public servants. All, it is true, have this in common, that they are wage-earners ; and we see at this moment a certain number of them claiming, on this score, the right to group themselves under the banner of the *Confédération Générale du Travail*. But this is only a small minority in each set.

Lastly, and above all, there are the independent workers, artisans, shopkeepers, men following the liberal professions, who have enough capital to keep them from becoming wage-earners, but too little to be able to take wage-earners into their service. There are millions of these independent workers in France, forming what is called the *middle class ;* and this middle class, precisely because of its mixed character, seems called upon to play a very important part in the conflict of classes, the part, namely, of buffer.[1] The principal cause of conflict among the other classes, viz., the separation of the worker from the instrument of his work, does not exist here. Each produces with his own capital and keeps the whole product of his labour for himself. If there were only independent producers in a nation, the great social problem of distribution would not exist ; even inequality would be confined within narrow limits, for it is only by setting a large number of persons to work that a large fortune can be made.

Unfortunately, this peaceable class is the very class whose exist-ence seems threatened by the law of concentration ; and not socialists alone, but the economists of the Liberal school declare that its days

[1] The federation of employees and that of retail shopkeepers, which number between them 600,000 members, at a congress (July 1908) disavowed the " stupid idea of class conflict " ; it has also been denounced by the *Confédération Générale du Travail* as the " most dangerous organisation for the future of syndicalism." An *Office des Classes moyennes* was created in Belgium in 1906, official in character, to collect all information on this subject and to organise periodical congresses in different countries.

are numbered. We have already said (see *Law of Concentration*) that this prophecy does not appear to be justified by facts. If the middle class is being eliminated in some spheres, it is growing fast in others, and on the whole is not declining in importance. All who have social peace at heart are doing their utmost to defend it. The question of the middle classes, as it is called, is one of the foremost problems in Germany, Austria, and above all in Belgium.

The following figures give approximately the distribution of the population among the different classes by thousands of inhabitants:[1]

I.	Employers	Industry 823		6,247
		Commerce. . . . 575		
		Agriculture and Fisheries 4,795		
		Liberal Professions . . 54		
II.	Autonomous Workers	Industry 2,051		4,149
		Commerce. . . . 554		
		Agriculture and Fisheries 1,356		
		Liberal Professions . . 188		
III.	Working men and Employees	Industry 4,273		8,092
		Commerce. . . . 874		
		Agriculture and Fisheries 2,705		
		Liberal Professions . . 240		
IV.	Domestic servants			1,012
V.	Public services			1,220

Total of the active population 20,720
Persons supported by the preceding classes: women without
   professions, children, students, patients in hospitals, prisoners   18,532

Total Population 39,252

[1] This table is drawn up from the *Résultats statistiques du Recensement de la Population en* 1906 (vol. i, 2nd part, in particular p. 182), the figures being given in a somewhat simplified form. We give a few additional explanations.

In the class of employers the number 4,795,000 for agriculturists seems very high. This is because it includes, besides landowners, all the farmers and *métayers* who employ any wage-earners, even if it be only one: thus many peasants are included who ought rather to come under Class II with the 1,356,000 small agriculturists, whose number on the other hand appears too small. It must be remarked, also, that husband and wife have often been written down as heads of the farm, which doubles the figures. The real number of agricultural exploitations is much smaller. (See below.)

The number of State employees (1,220,000) will appear exaggerated. This is because the figure takes into account the army on land and sea (600,000 men), and 77,000 workers in the State industries. There remain then about 550,000 functionaries strictly speaking. See an article by M. Fernand Faure in the *Revue Politique et Parlementaire*, May 1910: he gives, however, a somewhat higher figure, 702,000 for 1906, and 758,000 for 1909).

All the groups of the active population include a fairly large number of

Modern societies are therefore much more complex and diversified, their interests much more ravelled, than the rough image of two classes, one on the top of the other, might lead us to suppose. The class struggle may thus pass through many a vicissitude, and it is difficult to foretell the issue. The proud motto which Marxist Socialism has given the working class, since the Communist Manifesto of 1848, namely, " To look to itself alone for its emancipation," will probably not avail ; for history shows us, on the contrary, that the classes which have been emancipated have only been so by the help of the other classes of the nation, *e.g.* the slaves, the serfs, and even the Third Estate of '89·

It is impossible to examine here all the groups mentioned above. In fact, we shall not even keep to the classification of this table in our review of the different categories of co-sharers. For this classification is made solely from the professional point of view, the point of view of production. Now, the object of our present study is distribution and the conflicts of opposing claims. We shall consider therefore only the four typical classes : the landlord, who obtains rent ; the capitalist, who gets interest ; the wage-earner, who gets a wage ; and the *entrepreneur*, or employer, who gets profit.

We shall have, in addition, to consider two other co-sharers, paupers and the State. For each of these takes a by no means negligible share out of the general income, the first in *alms*, the second in *taxation*. Only these incomes are second-hand.[1] The State is represented in the above table under the heading of Public Services. But paupers do not appear in it for the good reason that poverty is not a profession, or, at least, is not recognised as one.[2]

women : 2,783,000 under employers ; 1,956,000 under autonomous workers ; 2,954,000 under wage-earners. The proportion varies from a minimum of 8 per cent. in transport and 22 per cent. in public offices to a maximum of 82 per cent. in domestic service (*Statistique*, p. 136).

[1] Income is said to be second hand when it is taken off wealth already created by another. There is no doubt of its being so in the case of the pauper. In that of the State, however, income cannot always be said to be second hand as the State may also create wealth. But this distinction between first and second hand income raises the whole social question, since, according to socialists, all incomes are second hand save those from labour.

[2] It will be noticed that the class of *rentiers* does not figure either in the above table. This is because, in the nature of things, it is outside of all professional classification. It does not belong to the active population. There is, however, in the *Statistique de la Population* (p. 142) a heading for persons living solely from their incomes and those with no profession, under which we find 565,000 *rentiers*, landlords, persons retired on pensions. But this figure is of little interest, since it includes only the smallest section of the capitalist-*rentier* class, which, for the most part, is scattered among the other social categories—employers, liberal

As for the middle class (p. 499), it does not need a special chapter since, for it, there is no question of sharing : it keeps what it produces. And we have already dealt with it in the chapters on concentration of production, agricultural and urban credit and elsewhere.

CHAPTER I : LANDLORDS[1]

I : THE OWNERSHIP OF LAND

NOT only is private property in land sanctioned by all legislations to-day, but landed property is considered the type of property *par excellence*. When we speak of property without qualification every one knows that it is landed property that is meant.

Still, we may hold it as certain, in spite of numerous controversies on the subject of late, that property in land is of relatively recent date, and that it was not without difficulty that it was established [2] (see above, p. 463).

We may distinguish, in the evolution of landed property, six successive stages which we shall briefly indicate : [3]

(*1*) It is obvious that landed property has no *raison d'être* among tribes who live by hunting, or among pastoral peoples at the nomadic stage. It can còme into existence only with agriculture. And, even

professions, public offices, etc. The *rentier* as *rentier* pure and simple is none the less an economic type of great importance, meriting certainly a separate chapter.

[1] The class of landlords is composed of three categories : those who work their lands by hired labour ; those who farm out their lands ; those who cultivate their lands themselves. These correspond to what we have called active capitalists (*entrepreneurs*), passive capitalists (*rentiers*), and the independent worker, although the separation between them is not rigidly marked. It often happens, for instance, that a landlord turns some of his land to account himself, farming out the rest ; or that a farmer possesses lands of his own.

[2] The recognition of absolute ownership in land was perhaps the most characteristic feature of Roman law ; and yet, even in Rome in early times, it is practically certain that individual ownership extended only to the house, and to a very limited area around it—half a hectare.

For the authors who incline to the collective origin of property, see de Laveleye, *La propriété et ses formes primitives ;* Viollet, *Du caractère collectif des premières propriétés ;* Esmein, *Nouvelle revue historique du droit*, 1890 ; and for those who take the opposite view, Fustel de Coulanges, *Nouvelles recherches ;* Guiraud, *La propriété foncière en Grèce.*

[3] The order here given is logical, not chronological. We do not mean that in all countries property has assumed each of these forms in succession. The *dominium ex jure Quiritium*, for example, a free and absolute form of ownership, preceded, historically, the feudal form of ownership, although logically it is an improvement on it.

in the early phases of agricultural life, property in land is not an institution. This is due to two causes : first, land is over-abundant, and no one needs to mark off his share ; secondly, agricultural methods being as yet primitive, the cultivator leaves his field as soon as it is exhausted for another. Land is cultivated, if not in common, at least without division ; it belongs to society as a whole, or rather, to the tribe. The fruits of it alone belong to the producer.[1]

(2) Gradually, however, population becomes more sedentary and more closely attached to the soil : it also becomes denser and has to adopt more productive methods of cultivation. The first phase then is succeeded by a second, that of temporary possession, together with *periodical redistribution.*[2] The land, though always considered as belonging to society, is divided equally among the heads of families. This division is not final, but only for a certain length of time. At first the period is a year, as this is the ordinary cycle for agricultural operations. As agricultural methods improve and cultivators require more time for the maturing of their labours, the periods become gradually longer. This system of the periodical division of the land is still practised in Russia. It is the community of the inhabitants of each village as a whole which owns the land and distributes it for use among its members by a periodical drawing of lots. The periods vary from one commune to another, but the most general is nine years. The assembly of the heads of families, the *mir*, has sovereign power over the distribution of the lots and the rotation of the crops.[3] The land of the commune is as a rule marked

---

[1] *Arva per annos mutant* (" they change lands every year "), says a famous text of Tacitus, speaking of the Germans. The meaning of this text has, it is true, been recently contested, and a new translation (somewhat paradoxical since it presupposes advanced cultivation), " they change their crops every year," proposed instead. In any case, this system of tribal ownership is still to be found in some places, particularly among the native tribes of Algeria.

[2] But it is very improbable that Rousseau's maxim has ever been realised, viz., "The fruits to all, and the land to no one " (*Discours sur l'Origine des inégalités des hommes*).

[3] For fuller details, see Kovalewsky, *Le régime économique de la Russie.* Contrary to what is generally taught, the *mir* is not a survival of an antique form of communal ownership ; it does not appear to be older than the sixteenth century, and it spread mainly during the eighteenth. The law abolishing serfdom, which tended to emancipate property, only consolidated the *mir*, since it fixed an annual payment as the price of the redemption of the land and made all the peasants of the commune jointly responsible for it. This forced them into a community. A recent law of November 1906 has virtually abolished the *mir*, allowing every inhabitant of the commune, who makes the application, to have the lot which he cultivates given to him as his own absolute property. At the outset not so many availed themselves of this right as we might have expected :

out into three concentric zones : (1) land which has been built on, along with gardens, which together constitute private property ; (2) arable land, which is parcelled out periodically into portions as equal as possible, according to the number of families ; (3) meadow land and the forest, which generally remains undivided both in use and ownership.

(3) A time comes when these periodic divisions fall into disuse. Those who have improved their lands do not willingly submit to an operation which, for the good of the community, deprives them at intervals of the surplus value due to their labour. Thus there arises the institution of *family ownership*, each family henceforth being the absolute owner of its share of land. This is not individual property, for the right of disposal does not yet exist. The head of the family can neither sell the land, nor give it away, nor dispose of it at death, since it is considered collective estate. This system may still be found in the family communities of Eastern Europe, especially the *zadrugas* of Bulgaria and Croatia, which number fifty or sixty persons ; but they are tending rapidly to disappear owing to the independent spirit of the younger members of the family.[1]

(4) The evolution of landed property passes also through a phase which, though accidental in its nature, has never been omitted in the history of human societies. I refer to *conquest*. There is not a single territory on the earth's surface which has not at some time or other been taken by force from the people who inhabited it and appropriated by the conquering race.[2]   The conquerors, it is true, just because they were conquerors and masters, did not trouble to cultivate the land. Appropriating simply the legal ownership, the

but the movement is progressing rapidly, over 2½ million peasants out of 12 millions having applied for lots. Unfortunately there are already complaints that the land is being bought up by engrossers.

[1] See *Les communautés de famille et de village*, by Laveleye, in the *Revue d'Économie politique*, August 1888.

[2] An Irish preacher, speaking to a congregation of small farmers who stamped with approval, said : " Walking one day over private ground, I was stopped by a landlord, who cried, ' Get out of here ! '—' Why ?   From whom did you get this land ? '   ' From my father.'   ' And your father ? '   ' From his ancestor.' —' And this ancestor ? '   ' He fought for it.'—' All right !   Now we are going to fight for it too ! '   And the preacher took off his coat.

As a proof of the influence which conquest has had on the evolution of landed property, Herbert Spencer makes the curious observation that the countries in which the ancient forms of collective property have been best able to maintain themselves are the mountainous and poor countries, the situations of which have enabled them to escape conquest.

" eminent domain," as it used to be called, they left the actual possession of the soil to the subject population, by way of *tenure*. This tenure was more or less akin to veritable ownership, but was always limited by the conditions under which it was granted to the cultivator, by the servitudes with which he was burdened, by the dues which he had to pay to his overlord, and by the fact that he was unable to alienate the land without the latter's consent. The Feudal System, as it was called, which was for centuries the basis of the social and political constitution of Europe, has left traces in many countries. In England, more especially, almost all landed property, in law at least, is still held in the form of a tenure, and is bound by fetters that are very hard to remove.[1]

(5) The growth of individualism and of civil equality, and the disappearance of the Feudal System, particularly in countries which came under the influence of the French Revolution, brought about a fifth phase, that which marks our own epoch. It is characterised by the final establishment of *free ownership of land*, with all the attributes which the right of ownership implies. Still, even this free ownership of land, as set forth, for example, in the Code Napoléon, is not identical in all points with the ownership of movable property. It differs from the latter in numerous features familiar to jurisconsults ; but the essential difference consists in the difficulties put in the way of transfer. We have only to call to mind the inalienability of the immovable estate of married women under the dowry system, the formalities required in transferring immovable property, and the enormous charges on such transfers.

(6) To assimilate the ownership of landed property to that of movable property, and to mark the final stage of this evolution, only one step remained. It consisted in making the ownership of land mobile, so that an individual could not only possess land, but dispose of it as easily as movable property. This last step was accomplished in a new country, Australia, by means of the celebrated Torrens system, according to which the right of ownership of land is represented by a simple entry on a register. A landowner is thus able, as it were, to put his land in his pocket in the form of a piece of paper, and to transfer it almost as easily as if it were a bill of exchange. A campaign has been carried on for some time with the object of introducing this system into the older countries of Europe ; it is probable that the logic of facts, and the natural course

---

[1] " Thus was established, in our English law, the cardinal maxim with regard to the possession of lands, viz., that the king is the sole master and the original owner of all the land in the kingdom." Blackstone's *Commentaries*.

of evolution which we have just sketched, will lead ultimately to its adoption everywhere.[1]

(7) We might perhaps expect a further stage in this evolution, a stage in which landed property would be represented by a share, *i.e.* by a registered title, or even a title to bearer. But, first, it would be necessary for agricultural enterprise, like industrial enterprise, to assume the form of the limited liability company. Now there does not appear to be any sign of this, nor can the experiments so far made in this direction be said to have succeeded.

The conclusion to which we are led, from this summary review, is that the ownership of land has passed gradually and steadily from the collective to the individual form, and tends to approximate more and more closely to the ownership of movable property and capital, even to the point of becoming practically indistinguishable from it.

What are the causes which gradually withdrew land from the ownership of the primitive community and gave it over to the free and absolute ownership of the individual, which have made it follow step by step the progress of agriculture and of civilisation ? They are as follows :

The right to the fruits of the earth carries with it the right to the earth itself, at least during a certain period of time. The man who has sown the seed must be allowed time to reap the harvest. Six or seven years must elapse before the man who has planted vines can gather his grapes, and half a century before the man who has sown acorns can cut down his oak trees. Even annual crops, where the methods of farming are at all advanced, require such labours as manuring, improving the soil, draining, irrigating, etc., labours which can be recouped only from the harvests of ten, twenty, perhaps fifty successive years. Now it is indispensable that the man who has done all these should be able to recoup himself : otherwise we may be sure he will leave them undone. In order therefore to stimulate labour it was felt advisable to give the cultivator a right not only to the produce of his land but to the land itself, as instrument of his labour—a right which was temporary at first, but, given gradually over longer periods as cultivation progressed and labours

---

[1] For fuller details of this system, see *infra, Systems for Breaking up Landed Property.*

The object of the Torrens system, as its author himself declared, is to rid landed property of all the impediments which hinder free access to it, like the portcullis, drawbridge, and moats which defended the approaches to the castles of our ancestors.

of longer duration became necessary, ended by becoming per-petual.

Given the more or less rapid but always continuous growth of population, it is more important to-day than ever before to choose the method of cultivating the soil which will provide food for the greatest number of persons on a given area. For this reason society, while claiming theoretically an eminent domain in the land, cannot do better, in the interests of all, than to delegate this right to those who are able to obtain the most out of the soil. Now, up to the present time it is individuals who have best succeeded in doing so, and, till we have proof to the contrary, there is every reason to believe that they are the best fitted to fulfil this social function.[1]

Still, if social utility be the sole end and reason for the existence of private ownership, we have some ground for thinking that this last has departed somewhat from its original aim.

(1) In the first place, it seems unnecessary to extend the right of individual ownership to lands which have not *undergone any actual labour*. Mussulman law, more faithful than our own to the principles of Political Economy, admits this right only in lands which have undergone effective labour. These are called " living " lands, as opposed to uncleared or " dead " lands, which remain collective property. " When a man has put life into dead land," says the Prophet, " it shall belong to none other, and he shall have exclusive right over it." It is owing to the application of this principle that, in certain Mussulman countries, Algeria and Java for example, collective ownership still occupies a very large place.

In France, however, out of about 50 million acres of unculti-vated land (woods, pastures, waste lands), *i.e.* two-fifths of the surface of France, only 15 millions still belong to the State and the communes ; all the rest have been invaded by private ownership.

(2) In the second place, if ownership is a social function, the recognition of the right of ownership ought to be subject to the

---

[1] This is the conclusion to which Herbert Spencer comes, after some hesitation, in his book on *Justice* (1891, Appendix B): " While I adhere to the inference originally drawn, that the aggregate of men forming the community are the supreme owners of the land—an inference harmonising with legal doctrine and daily acted upon in legislation—a fuller consideration of the matter has led me to the conclusion that individual ownership, subject to State-suzerainty, should be maintained."

Collectivists, it is true, assure us that the collective cultivation of the soil will give much better results, even from a technical point of view, than will individual ownership, since it alone is able to employ large-scale methods of production, and to reap the advantages thereof. See, however, what we said regarding large and small scale cultivation, p. 179.

effective exercise of the function. This is the rule usually followed
to-day in the colonies, in concessions, or sales of land. Residence
on, and actual cultivation of, the land are necessary conditions.
There is no reason, that we can see, why what is deemed good for
new countries should be held superfluous for old. And we should
be spared the scandalous sight of vast stretches of land left uncultivated by their owners, while agricultural labourers are emigrating
or dying of poverty for want of it.

(3) Lastly, we may well ask whether it was absolutely indispensable to make the right of ownership in land *perpetual*. It certainly
seems as if this perpetuity far exceeds the requirements of cultivation. Man, whose life is brief, does not need eternity in front of
him in which to accomplish even the greatest tasks. Railway enterprises, the Suez and Panama Canals, etc., are based on concessions of
not more than ninety-nine years. And in many colonies, now, the
"eminent domain" of the State is safeguarded, land being conceded
only for a fixed period.

Strict logic, perhaps, would appear to justify perpetuity ; for
surely the right of ownership should last as long as the object lasts.
Now, the object here is everlasting. Land is, indeed, the only
enduring form of wealth. Time, which destroys all else, does not
touch it save to renew its youth each spring. Nevertheless, logic
is here at fault. What lasts for ever is after all only the land and
its natural forces ; the transformations which result from labour,
even when they become actually part of the soil, last but for a short
time.

II : INCOME FROM LAND.—THE LAW OF RENT

THE first economists---the Physiocrats, Adam Smith, J. B. Say—
taught that land *produced rent* naturally, just as it produces fruits.
Why then is this liberality of nature not free to all men ? It would
be, if land were unlimited in quantity like air and light. But to-day,
in all countries, the land is already appropriated by private ownership.
The result is that the holders of land are able to draw income from
it, either by selling the gifts of nature at a high price, or by hiring
out the actual land itself. Land rent appeared therefore to the
Physiocrats as the *result of a monopoly*—a monopoly which they
did their best to justify on such grounds as the general interest of
cultivation, the money sunk in the land, etc.

Now, this explanation of the income from land implies the idea
that nature can create value, that is to say, a belief in the doctrine

which makes utility, in the material sense of the word, the basis of value.[1]

Such an explanation could not satisfy the subtle mind of Ricardo. As principal author of the doctrine that value is based on labour and cost of production, this great economist could not, without demolishing his own theory, allow that the value of land or its products was created partly by nature. Yet he had to admit that income from land represented something more than the labour of cultivation, since he saw that all over England land readily found tenants, that is to say, men who, after paying their way and the expenses of cultivation, still had enough left from the produce of the land to pay for the hire of it. It was to explain this difficulty that he conceived his theory of land rent, the most famous theory of Political Economy and one which has been for a century a bone of contention among economists.

This theory, or law, presents itself under two aspects which it is important to develop. In what we might call its *static* aspect, it becomes apparent in the process of fixing the prices of agricultural products on the market and explains the emergence of land rent. In what we might call its *dynamic* aspect it is seen in the gradual rise in land rent in economic history. It is in this second form that it has made its most striking appearance, but it is under its first aspect that it has contributed most to economic science. We shall therefore consider this first.

Take, for example, some hundreds of sacks of wheat on a market. Obviously · they have not all been produced under identical conditions. Some have been obtained by dint of toil and manure ; others have sprung up almost of themselves from fertile ground. Some have come from San Francisco round by Cape Horn ; others from farms near by. If each sack, then, were labelled with its cost of production, we should probably not find two alike. Suppose, for instance, there are ten sacks. The cost of production of sack A will be 10 francs, of sack B, 11 francs, of sack C, 12 francs, up to sack J, which has cost 20 francs.

But we have seen already (p. 222) that there can never be more than one price on the same market for similar products. The sale price therefore of all these sacks of wheat will be the same. But, as the cost prices are all different, how are the sale price and the cost price ever to coincide ?

---

[1] This is evidently what Adam Smith meant when he said, " In agriculture nature labours along with man " : the share due to her help " is seldom less than a fourth and frequently more than a third of the whole produce."

The answer is that the sale price and the cost price will coincide only in the case of the sack which has cost the most to produce, *i.e.* sack J, which cost 20 francs. And the reason is simple. The sale price must be enough to cover the expenses of the unfortunate seller who has produced wheat under the most unfavourable conditions, otherwise he would not bring his wheat to market. Now, we are taking for granted that the quantity of wheat offered is not greater than the demand for it, and that consequently the last sack cannot be dispensed with, nor the competition of this last producer.

We come to the conclusion therefore that, whenever identical products are sold on one and the same market, their value tends to coincide with the maximum cost of production.

Now, clearly this price of 20 francs will leave a differential gain to all the more favoured wheat-producers whose costs of production are less, viz., a gain of 10 francs to the producer whose sack has cost 10 francs, of 8 francs to the one whose sack has cost 12 francs, etc. It is this gain, or rather the income which results from these regular gains, which is, properly speaking, rent.

This demonstration satisfies the law of value, as conceived by Ricardo. The price of wheat is determined by cost of production, but only the cost of production of the worst unit. It implies that there is always one piece of land, at least, that which produces sacks of the J category, which gives no land rent—nothing more than the income of the capital and labour expended on it. It is this land *which is the decisive factor*, serving as standard for all the rest. As for the other lands, their incomes are due not so much to their fertility—for if they were all equally fertile they would give no rent (see next chapter, p. 512)—as to the lack of fertility of the lands with which they are competing; not to Nature's generosity, but to her niggardliness.

The owner of a fertile piece of land certainly possesses a privilege, a monopoly if you will, but a monopoly of quite a peculiar nature. For it consists not in the power to sell at an enhanced price, but in the power to produce more cheaply. A mere matter of words, you may say. Not so; for while the monopolist injures the public by unduly raising the price, the owner of the fertile land simply accepts the price fixed on the market by necessity. And even if, in a movement of generosity, all the owners of wheat land were to give up their rents, the current price of wheat would not be reduced one farthing; the landowners would simply be making a present to their farmers or to their immediate buyers.[1]

[1] Ricardo said, "Corn is not high because a rent is paid, but a rent is paid because

We see that, on this theory, there are only differential rents; that is to say, there would be no rents if all the lands were of the same quality. Now it is just at this point that Ricardo's theory seems inexact. For, even supposing all lands were identical, if there were not enough for man's wants, rent would still emerge. There is not merely differential rent. There is such a thing as absolute rent.

It has been urged that the phenomenon of rent is not peculiar to land, and is found wherever there is inequality of situation in production. True, and Ricardo himself distinctly said so. Whenever similar products, produced under very unequal conditions, are sold at the same price, the phenomenon of rent will necessarily appear to the advantage of the producers most favoured by circumstances. We shall see that *profit*, itself, is only a kind of rent.

Still, it is almost exclusively in landed property that the law of rent is in conflict with the general interest. Elsewhere, in industry for example, it manifests itself only temporarily, since the better situated producers are as a rule able of themselves to supply the market by increasing their production *ad libitum*. Rather than profit by their privileged situation to continue to sell at the old prices, it is their interest as a rule to lower prices, so as to undersell their competitors and drive them gradually from the market. They thereby gain less on each article, but they make up for this in quantity.

This explains why, in industry, although at a given moment the general price of the market is always determined by the maximum cost of production, *in the long run* it is determined by the *minimum cost of production*—a fact which is of great advantage to society. It is to be seen in the gradual fall in the rate of profits.

Quite otherwise is it in agricultural production, where, it is to be feared, prices are determined by an ever-increasing cost of production, which will be translated into a progressive rise in land rent.

Let us turn to the second aspect of Ricardo's Law of Rent.

corn is high." The same idea is expressed in the well-known formula, " *Rent does not enter into cost of production*." Wages and interest constitute the sole expenses of production, and thus indirectly, through the action of competition, the value of the product. And we come from this to the interesting conclusion, which has been utilised to the full by Mill and Henry George, that the total land rent of a country might be confiscated by taxation without affecting the price of wheat.

III : THE RISE IN RENT AND SURPLUS VALUE

AT first, said Ricardo, men need to cultivate only a small quantity of land and choose the best. In spite of the fertility of this land they do not, however, get a better return from cultivating it than they would from any other employment of their labour and capital. For, as there is more than enough land for every one, it is subject to the law of competition, which brings down the value of its produce to the level of cost of production. They do not therefore get *rent* in the strict sense of the word.

Increase of population, however, calls for increase of production. And, as all the best lands are appropriated, it becomes necessary to *bring less fertile land under cultivation*, that is to say, land on which the cost of production is higher. Suppose that land of the first quality yields 33 bushels of wheat per acre, at a cost of £5, or a little more than 3s. a bushel—land of the second quality will not produce more than, say, 22 bushels for the same expenditure, which brings the cost of production up to more than 4s. 6d. It is evident that the owners of these second-class lands will not be able to sell their wheat for less than 4s. 6d, as in such a case they would lose, and would stop growing wheat. Now, we are arguing on the assumption that the population cannot do without them. It is no less evident that the owners of the first lands occupied will not sell their wheat at a lower price than their neighbours ; they too will sell at 4s. 6d., but since this wheat costs them only a little over 3s. as before, they will make a gain of nearly 1s. 6d. a bushel or about £2 10s. an acre. It is this gain which, on Ricardo's theory and in the vocabulary of Political Economy, bears the name of *rent*.

As population continues to increase, larger and larger quantities of foodstuffs are required, and men are forced to cultivate lands less fertile still [1]—producing, say, only 16 bushels an acre. The cost price of the bushel thus rises to 6s. and, for reasons which we have just pointed out, raises every bushel on the market to the same price. From now onwards the owners of first-class lands see

[1] But why do we assume that men, in order to increase production, are continually obliged to extend their cultivation to new lands ? Can they not increase their production equally well by a better cultivation of the good lands ? No doubt they can ; but, owing to the law of diminishing returns, after a certain limit is reached, each increase in yield involves a more than proportional increase in expenditure and consequently a rise in the cost of production. The result is therefore exactly the same as if land of the second quality were cleared. See, in this connection, the chapter on *Diminishing Returns* (pp. 77–82), with which Ricardo's law is closely connected.

their rent rise to nearly 3s., while those of second-class lands gain in turn a rent of 1s. 6d.

This " order of cultivation," as Ricardo called it, may go on indefinitely *raising the price of food to the detriment of consumers and increasing rent to the profit of landlords,* who find their incomes swelled without any trouble on their part, and whose fortunes have their origin in the impoverishment of the rest of the community.

This is Ricardo's theory of rent. It has been said that historically it is untrue to facts, being no more than an *a priori* conception invented by Ricardo to support his doctrine of labour-value. And an American economist, Carey, claims with some reason to have shown that the order of cultivation was in fact the reverse ; that men began by cultivating the lighter and less fertile lands, as these are more easily cultivated, or lands situated on heights, as these are more easily defended ; and that it was only slowly and gradually that agriculturists, better equipped and trained, were able to clear the rich and fertile lands defended by their very excess of vegetation.[1]

But of what importance is this after all ? If Ricardo's " order of cultivation " must be rejected on historical grounds, the essential fact which his hypothesis brought out, namely, the spontaneous and in some sort inevitable increase in the value of land, both as regards capital and income, remains true. For, if we remember the three characteristics of land which no other forms of wealth unite in the same degree, namely, that (a) it satisfies the essential and permanent wants of mankind, (b) it is limited in quantity, (c) it is everlasting, we can easily understand how the value of land and of its products increases with time, at any rate in a progressive society, and how all the factors of social and economic progress contribute to raise it.

The principal cause which acts on the value of land is the growth of population, since naturally the more people there are, the more food-space and lodging-space are required of the earth ; but the phenomenal increase in wealth, the building of roads and railways, the rise of large cities, even the development of order and security, inevitably increase the surplus value of land—what the English economists call by the significant name of *unearned increment.* The increase in the value of the soil in America between 1905 and 1910,

---

[1] In reality each reasoned rightly from the *milieu* in which he lived. Ricardo lived in England, where the land has been privately owned for centuries, and where the value of the soil grows with the population. Carey had the spectacle of the New World before his eyes, where land was superabundant and only those lands most easily reached and worked were cultivated.

R'

as shown by the American census returns, was $7,200,000,000 ; so that, as M. d'Avenel pointed out, every sunset sees a rise in rural property of $3,400,000.[1] It is true that this enormous increment is not due entirely to social and natural causes ; part of it is due to the value put into the ground by the landowner.

There are only two causes capable of checking or reversing this upward movement.

The first is the competition of new lands following on great colonising enterprises and improvements in the means of transport. This cause has been at work with such intensity during the last thirty years that the value of land in Western Europe (particularly England, as being more open to wheat from America and the Indies) has fallen 30 per cent. This fall is not, as it is often taken to be, a contradiction of Ricardo's doctrine. On the contrary, it confirms it. For it is this very competition of new countries and colonies that has temporarily arrested the upward movement of rent in the old countries.[2] And it is probable, if I may say so, that it is a simple accident in economic history. During the second half of last century there was such activity in the clearing of unoccupied lands that the supply of farming produce exceeded the capacity of

---

[1] Henry George estimated that each immigrant raised the value of the territory of the United States by $400. As about 20 million immigrants have landed since the beginning of the last century, their very presence alone constitutes an unearned increment of $8,000,000,000 with which they have endowed American soil.

In older countries, where the above causes act with less force, and where the increase of population has slowed down greatly, as in France, the surplus value of the land is naturally less marked ; but it was great in the past.

In England, the average farm rent was valued, at the beginning of the nineteenth century, at 11s. an acre, and in 1877 at 29s. It had therefore almost trebled ; during this very time the population of England (not counting Scotland and Ireland) had likewise trebled, being 8,990,000 in 1801 and 24,850,000 in 1879. It was in 1880 that the surplus value of rent and, consequently, that of the land, reached its maximum. Since then land rent has considerably fallen in England ; the average farm rent per acre being 20s. (See the *Journal of the Royal Statistical Society*, December 1907.)

In France, the value of landed property, after rising considerably till the end of the reign of Napoleon III, fell on an average about 30 or 35 per cent. Since the beginning of the present century it has been rapidly rising. It must not be forgotten that, in France, except for building ground in a few large towns, the principal cause which determines the surplus value of land, namely, increase of population, is lacking.

[2] Mr. Herckenrath, in the Dutch translation of this book, remarks that if colonisation and means of transport bring down land rent in old countries, they send it up enormously in new. So that, taking the whole world into account, the values of lands tend to balance one another.

consumption at the time. In a little while, however, when these new countries are peopled, the law of land rent, momentarily interrupted, will continue on its way.

The second cause—which seems curiously paradoxical and is yet characteristic of Ricardo's theory—consists in *great and sudden improvements in the art of farming.* According to Ricardo, such progress would result in rendering the cultivation of bad lands unnecessary, or even in causing them to be abandoned, which would bring down rent. Without needing to resort to such a hypothesis, however, we have only to remember that all agricultural progress is bound, by multiplying products, to lessen their final utility, and consequently the final utility of the earth itself.

It must be pointed out that neither of these causes applies to building land. This explains why it is that no value has risen so amazingly as that of building land, and no expenditure has increased more than that of house rent.

IV: THE LEGITIMACY OF LAND RENT

FROM the explanations we have just given it follows :

(*1*) That the income from land is the result of a peculiar kind of monopoly.

(*2*) That this income is bound to increase, owing to social causes independent of the landlord.

At first sight, these conclusions seem hardly in favour of the legitimacy of land rent.

Still, it may be said, if the private ownership of land be considered legitimate, land rent must be so also, since it is a simple consequence of the other.

But if we turn from the question of the income from land to that of the right of ownership of land, we shall find that it also is not unchallenged. For not only does land offer, *sui generis*, the three characteristics mentioned (p. 513), which are enough of themselves to raise a question as to the legitimacy of its being privately owned, but it has another unique characteristic—that it *is not the product of labour.* Everything else is a product of labour but land.[1]

If, then, we admit, as not only socialists, but even Classical

---

[1] A diamond is not, one may say. But the diamond has no value until it has been *found* and taken out of the earth.

Some attempt to justify private property in land, and the income from it, by the following argument : " Property in land is legitimate because every piece of land has been bought and paid for in money ; consequently the income from

economists generally do, that labour is the basis of property, we must logically conclude that everything may become private property *but land.*

This distinction is very striking in its simplicity and logic. It is very ancient, going back, as we shall see in the next chapter, to the very origins of property. It is also very modern, rallying round it at the present day not only socialists, but a number of contemporary economists and philosophers.[1]

The Optimist school, however, absolutely denies it, asserting that land is just as much a product of labour as is the clay pot fashioned by the hand of the potter. Man did not, of course, it says, create the land, but neither did the potter create the clay. Labour never creates anything : it simply modifies the material which nature provides. Now, the action of labour is no less real and effective when applied to the soil than when applied to the materials drawn from its bosom. And the optimists refer us, for an example, to the lands which the peasants of the Valais or the Pyrenees literally transported on their backs to their mountain slopes. An ancient author tells how a peasant, accused of sorcery

land is simply the interest of the money thus invested." This is reasoning, however, in a vicious circle.

It is not because land is sold for £4000 that it brings in an income of £120, but, on the contrary, because it brings in £120 of income, independently of all labour on the part of its holder, that it is able to fetch £4000. Now what we really want to know is why it brings in the £120.

All that can be said in regard to this argument is that the landowner, like the holder of any office that has been bought, has a right to have the price refunded if he is expropriated. But that is quite another question.

1 In Belgium, Émile de Laveleye, in his book *La Propriété*, would fain return to the collective forms of primitive ownership. In Lausanne, Professor Walras has proposed an ingenious system for the buying back of the soil by the State, of which we shall speak later. In France, the philosophers Renouvier and Fouillée declare that, before the usurpation of private ownership in land can be pardoned, and, as compensation to non-landowners, the law ought to sanction the right to poor relief. In Germany, Professor Oppenheimer maintains that large landed property is the source of all social ills. In Italy, Professor Loria does not deny the legitimacy of private property in land, but points to the appropriation of the soil as the great monopoly which has vitiated the whole evolution, social, political, moral, religious and æsthetic, of human societies. He sees the solution of all problems in the return to " free land " without, how-ever, indicating very clearly the means for bringing this about (small property and association). In England, A. R. Wallace, and a school of Christian Socialists, teach that all private property in land is illegitimate, falling back on the words of the Bible, " The earth is the Lord's and the fulness thereof." In the United States, Professor J. B. Clark, who is certainly not a socialist, declares that the State is the creator of, and therefore the legitimate owner of, the value in the land.

because of the rich harvests he obtained from his land while his neighbours' fields remained barren, when called before the Roman proctor, pointed for all defence to his two arms, exclaiming : *Veneficia mea haec sunt* ("These are my sole spells"). Landowners have only to give the same proud answer for their defence.

Even if land were not a direct product of labour, it would, at least, according to this school, be the product of capital. The value of land and the increment accumulated through the ages are sufficiently explained by the improvements made by landlords and the expenditure these landlords have incurred. Indeed, if we were to add together the accumulated expenses of successive owners, we should find that there is no piece of land which is *worth what it has cost*.[1]

In spite of the element of truth which this argument certainly contains, it does not appear to us conclusive. No doubt man and the earth have been attached from earliest times by the tie of daily labour—labour even of the most toilsome kind, to which we owe the expression, "In the sweat of thy face shalt thou eat bread." The word labour itself originally referred to the tilling of the soil (*cf.* the French *labourer* = to plough). But if land is the *instrument* of labour, it is not the *product*. It exists before any labour of man. Man, of course, by his labour and expenditure is daily improving and modifying this marvellous instrument of production furnished by nature, in order the better to adapt it to his purposes. He is thus obviously conferring on it new utility and value. We recognise also that with every advance in the art of agriculture land tends to become more and more a product of labour. In market gardening, for instance, the mould is an artificial compound prepared wholly by the gardener. Still, it is always possible, in theory at least, to strike, under the accumulated layers of capital and human labour, the primitive value of the soil.[2]

[1] Michelet said, "Man has the best of claims to the land : that of having made it." The Physiocrats also based the right of property in land on the expenses incurred to create the domain, which they called "advances on the land."

[2] Bastiat's school, in order to prove that the value of land is due solely to labour, emphasises the fact that virgin soil is without value. The fact is true, but the conclusion drawn from it proves nothing. The reason why lands situated on the banks of the Amazon are without value is not, by any means, because they are virgin soil, but because they are inaccessible, situated where there are no men to utilise them, and where the very notion of wealth cannot arise. It is obvious that land had no value before the first human being appeared on its surface, and that it will have none again when the last representative of the human race has disappeared ; but the virginity of the soil has nothing to do with this. And the proof is that if, by the touch of a magic wand, we could

This original value appears to the naked eye in natural forests and prairies which have never been cleared or cultivated, and which, nevertheless, sell or let for high prices ; in the tracts of sandy shore, for instance, in the departments of Gard and of Hérault, which have been ploughed only by the sea winds, yet which made the fortunes of their lucky possessors so soon as it was discovered by chance that the vineyards planted there were free from phylloxera ; it is visible too in the building lands of great cities into which the plough has never penetrated, and which have none the less an infinitely higher value than the best cultivated land.

Even in the case of cultivated land, the natural value of the soil appears quite distinctly in its *unequal fertility ;* since, of two lots of land which have undergone equal labour and expenditure, one may bring in a fortune each year, while the other may barely pay expenses.[1]

As for the argument that no land is worth what it has cost in cultivation, it is based on a wrong method of reckoning.[2] We certainly do not deny that, if we were to add together all that has been expended on a given piece of land in France, from Druidical times when the first Celt cleared it down to the present day, the total would not be much larger than the present value of the land. But for our calculation to be exact we should have to add together on the other hand all the receipts from this piece of land, beginning from the same date. The sum, thus corrected, would certainly show that the land had given a permanent and regularly increasing rent

transport these lands to the banks of the Seine just as they are in their natural state, they would be worth as much as or more than the old lands lying round it, although these have been ploughed by the labour of centuries. Or, if this hypothesis is too fantastic, suppose some piece of land in France surrounded by a wall and abandoned for 100 years like the castle of the Sleeping Beauty, until all trace of human labour has disappeared and it has become virgin soil as at the beginning ; and let anyone say whether, in such a state, the land will have lost all its value and will find neither farmer nor purchaser. Ten to one, on the contrary, that even in this state it will be worth much more 100 years hence than to-day.

[1] Languedoc produces ordinary wines of a fairly uniform type, which sell at practically the same price. Now, on some of its lands called " *terrains de grès* " (sandstone lands) the cost of production per hectolitre, not counting interest and the replacement of capital invested, is estimated at 15 to 16 francs, while on the low-lying lands of the plains it is sometimes as low as 6 francs. This is a remarkable confirmation of Ricardo's theory.

[2] This argument is, moreover, absurd, for building land is always uncultivated

V: THE HIRING-OUT OF LAND

WHEN the owner of a piece of land is unable or unwilling to cultivate it himself, or by means of hired labour, he lets it out to a cultivator, called a tenant farmer, and the price for which he lets it is called farm rent (French, *fermage*). The farming lease is therefore a fixed contract (like the wage contract or the loan contract) by which the owner of the land gives up all right to the produce of it in return for a fixed annual sum in money—the *rent*.

The rent which the farmer pays does not necessarily coincide, as might be expected, with land rent in the strict sense, *i.e.* with that part of the income from land which is independent of the landlord and distinct from the income due to the labour or capital expended. The rent which the farmer pays is, as a rule, higher than land rent; either because it also includes the interest on the capital sunk in the land and let along with it, or because, under the pressure of necessity, the farmer is sometimes obliged to give the landowner not only the share due to natural and social causes, but part of the income due to his own labour. Still, it may sometimes happen that the rent paid is lower than the land rent, when, as is often the case in France, farmers are scarce and much sought after. In this case the tenant retains for himself part of the proceeds of the natural advantages of the earth.

The rent which the tenant farmer pays is governed by the same law as are wages and interest, that is to say, by the law of supply and demand. In new countries, where land is abundant and every one can find vacant lands on which to settle as landlord, tenant farmers will not consent to pay more rent than the interest on the capital which has been put into the land. On the contrary, where population is very dense, where the whole of the land is occupied, and where wealth is solely agricultural, as in Algeria or in Ireland, farm rents may rise till the tenant farmer can barely get his living.[1]

The hiring out of the land is a mode of obtaining income which is open, theoretically, to the most serious criticism. Although land-leasing, in law, is the same as that of the letting of a house, or the lending of money, from an economic point of view it is very different.

---

[1] In Algeria, the tenant farmer, called *khammes*, keeps only one-fifth of the harvest for himself ! It is well known that in Ireland the rise in farm rents was so great that part of the population died of hunger, others were obliged to emigrate, and what remains is in a state of permanent insurrection. And, since 1881, a complete agrarian legislation has been promulgated, intended, in the first instance, to bring rents down to a legal maximum, and recently to enable farmers to buy the land with money advanced by the State.

The most serious argument against the leasing of the land is, that it deprives private ownership of its *raison d'être*. We have seen that the private ownership of land exists not in virtue of some " divine right," but because it has been recognised as the most productive mode of exploiting the soil, the one most in keeping with the common good. We have taken for granted that no one was able to make a better use of the land than the individual landowner. This direct exploitation was the ground on which private ownership was justified. But what becomes of this argument when we see, as in the case of the lease, the owner of the land delegating the labour of cultivation, in order to be free to consume his rents in some large city or abroad ? If, as we said, landowning is a social function, it ought to be performed by the person who actually owns the land. To let out a function for hire is to become unworthy of it.

·The landowner who, instead of turning the soil to account, makes it an instrument of gain and a means of living without working, ill performs the social mission entrusted to him. It is difficult to conceive that the land has been distributed to certain men rather than others, simply to provide them with an income, *fruges consumere nati*, like the benefices and prebends which kings were wont to dispense among their favourites. The very reasons urged in defence of the right of private ownership in land turn, apparently, against the system of tenantry.

A second objection is, that this separation between the rôle of landowner and that of cultivator is fatal to the interests of cultivation. To obtain the best possible results from the earth, a man must love the soil and cling to it. Now, when the land is let out on lease, this love of the soil is bound to weaken both in the owner of the land, who no longer lives on it and sometimes even does not know it, and in the tenant, who is merely a bird of passage.[1]

On the other hand, we cannot but think that an institution so ancient as the farming-out of land, so widely practised in all countries, rests on some solid basis.

Thus, in favour of the system of farm tenure the following arguments may be urged :

[1] See what Michelet says of the peasant proprietor : " Thirty paces off he stops short and, turning round, throws a last look on his land, profound and sombre, but, for one who has eyes to see, full of passion, feeling, and devotion."

And compare this other quotation : " In Haute-Savoie it is not unusual, when the inferiority of the crops on certain lands is remarked on, to hear the observation, ' Oh, that is only hired land.' " (Report of M. E. Chevallier on Class 104 for the Universal Exhibition of 1900.)

(*1*) The system of farm tenure constitutes a division of labour quite consistent with the good organisation of production, since it is rare that even an absentee landlord is altogether without interest in his land. " The landlord," says M. Leroy-Beaulieu, " stands for the future and permanent interests of the domain, while the tenant represents only the present and passing interests." [1] This is all very well, but even supposing that the landlord looks on his function in this light, as the " present interests " and the " future interests " may one day clash it would be better for them to be in the same hand.

(*2*) The system of farm tenure allows many to enter into the agricultural industry who have not enough capital to become land-lords, but who have enough to make them unwilling to work as day labourers. A peasant with 10,000 francs considers it better worth his while to take on lease a domain of 10 hectares, than to buy one of two or three, since the first will yield him perhaps 10 or 20 per cent. on his capital, while the second may not bring even 3 per cent. This is true ; but his capital, if placed in the earth, would be safe, whereas what he puts into his farm is precarious. He ought, at least, to be guaranteed repayment of the money he has put into the soil. Now, this he is guaranteed neither by law, nor by jurisprudence, in France at any rate.[2]

(*3*) To prohibit the leasing of land would be to limit property in land, and thus to compel many landowners to sell their estates who, owing to age, sex, profession, forced absence, or the extent and number of their domains, cannot work them themselves. This is possibly true, but is it not an advantage rather than an objection ? Since these persons cannot effectively carry out their function as landowners, let them hand it over to others who can.

The conclusion to which we are brought, then, is not that the leasing of land should be prohibited, but that those who believe in the social utility of the private ownership of land, and who wish it maintained as an institution, should aim at restricting the system of farm tenure as much as possible. For, wherever it becomes general, it brings discredit on private ownership, and prepares the way for expropriation.[3]

[1] *Essai sur la Répartition des richesses*, chap. i.
[2] It is different in England, where an important law of 1875 admits the right of the departing tenant farmer to compensation for improvements which he has made, those at any rate which are specified by the law.
[3] Economic evolution seems, certainly, to be tending in this direction. Farm tenure, which for some centuries has been the most usual land system in all countries, is gradually losing ground. The United States appears to be an exception.

If the private owning of land is to be safeguarded, it must become a *métier*, a profession, a function; and we must aim, by all the means in our power, economic and even legal, to bring about a social condition in which only those will become landowners who are ready to exercise the function of landowning, *i.e.* who will work the land themselves.[1]

Civil law contributes to this end when, as in France, it facilitates the reconstitution of small properties.

It goes counter to it when, as also in France, it multiplies the conditions of the transfer of land belonging to minors, married women, or " legal persons." In this case it makes the leasing of land in a way compulsory, since it keeps the land forcibly in the hands of those who are unable to turn it to account directly. On pretext of safeguarding private interests, it compromises the very existence of private ownership.[2]

There, between 1880 and 1900, the number of agricultural exploitations under the system of lease, or *métayage*, increased 98 per cent., *i.e.* almost doubled, while the number of domains worked directly only increased by one-quarter (24 per cent.). The *Census*, however, explains that this increase in the number of farms leased is due solely to the bringing under cultivation of new lands, and is not found on the older lands.

[1] Our statement must not be taken as meaning the " land to the peasants." It is not necessary that all the land of a country should be held by those who drive the plough or wield the mattock. Landowners with capital, education, and leisure may usefully further agricultural progress, at any rate if they live upon their lands. If there had been no wine-growers in the South of France except the peasants, it is probable that the phylloxera would not have been destroyed. The peasants have simply followed—and after much resistance—the initiative of the large landowners.

[2] The following are the figures in France for tenant farming and *métayage*, (which we shall study in next section) giving the number of farms and their area, according to the agricultural statistics for 1892.

	Number	Area	Proportion
Cultivated by owner . . .	4,191,000	18,324,000 hect.	53 per cent.
Cultivated by tenant farmer .	1,078,000	12,629,000	36 ,, ,,
Cultivated by *métayer* . .,	349,000	3,767,000 ,,	11 ,, ,
	5,618,000	34,720,000 ,,	100 ,, ,,

The total area of France is 52 million hectares, the above table giving only the area cultivated. It is seen that tenant farming represents only one-fifth in numbers, and one-third in area, of the total of agricultural exploitations. Even if we add to this the figure for *métayage*, the proportion does not rise above one-fourth in numbers, and less than half in area. But there are many countries where the tenant system, either by itself or along with *métayage*, covers almost the whole of the land.

VI : THE SYSTEM OF *MÉTAYAGE*

Métayage, known in French legal language as the *colonat partiaire*, a name borrowed from Roman law, differs from farm tenure in that the rent, instead of being payable in money and invariable during the term of the lease, is payable in kind and consists in a proportion —usually half—of the harvest. The rent consequently *varies* with the harvest.

This contract is much in use in certain countries, particularly in Italy, Portugal, Russia, and the countries of the Danube. In Italy, out of the 11 million hectares cultivated, 5½ millions, *i.e.* one-half, are worked on the system of *métayage*. In France, as we have seen, it is not so common (see table, preceeding page).

The proportion of land under *métayage* seems to have been much larger formerly than at the present day. Arthur Young estimates it, for France on the eve of the Revolution, at seven-eighths, or 87 per cent. Its steady decline might lead us to conclude that *métayage* is an out-of-date institution condemned to disappear at no very distant date.

It is true that it is peculiarly adapted to poor countries, and that, as a country becomes richer and cultivation more intensive, the *métayer* tends to give place to the tenant farmer or to direct cultivation by the landowner. The tenant farmer is, after all, nearly always a small capitalist—in England sometimes a large one—while the *métayer* has, more often than not, no capital, and contributes only his labour, a few farming implements, and some- times half of the live stock. He works on the land himself with his family, and grows inexpensive crops. The landowner, on his side, does not care to invest much capital in the exploitation, as the equal division of the additional net product due to the application of this capital makes it a poor investment for him.

Still, if *métayage* is inferior to farm tenure from the economic point of view, it offers a number of advantages from the social point of view. And these have been sufficient to keep this institu- tion going in many countries, and to rally round it perhaps more partisans to-day than at any other time.

The social superiority of *métayage* is due to the following causes :

(*1*) It creates a common interest between the landowner and his tenant, whereas, under the system of farm tenure, their interests are antagonistic. For the landlord and the *métayer* share equally in good fortune and in bad : they are veritable partners. *Métayage* is to farm tenure what sleeping partnership is to the loan at interest, that is to say, a contract of association as opposed to a fixed contract. Those therefore who look to co-operation for the solution of the social question ought to look on *métayage* with no less favourable an eye.[1]

(2) It enables labourers who are too poor to become farmers, still less to become landlords, to cultivate the ground on their own account. The *métayer* is never at a loss for his rent, since he pays in kind and not out of his pocket. He gives the landlord much or little, according to what the land yields him. The farmer, on the contrary, obliged always to find money even when the land has given nothing, is often in straits, and sees in the landowner an exploiter and a kind of tax collector.

(3) The *métayer* is guaranteed against abusive exploitation, to which farmers, owing to inter-competition, are so often exposed, and which sometimes sends up rents to an exorbitant level. For *métayage*, fixing by usage the shares at one-half, keeps off the action of competition on prices, prevents any dispute as to the rate of the rent, and never allows the landowner to absorb the whole of it.[2]

(4) *Métayage* is better adapted than is farm tenure to ensure long leases. Under the system of farm tenure the landlord is always tempted to look for a new tenant who will give him a higher rent. But under the system of *métayage* the landlord, unless for personal reasons, has nothing to gain by a change of *métayer*, as the shares remain the same whoever cultivates the ground. *Métairies* in this way remain in the same family for generations. There are some in the Limousin which are said to date back 300 years.

(5) Under *métayage* the landowner necessarily takes much more interest in the rotation of the crops and in the success of the harvests —seeing that his own share depends on them—than under the system of farm tenure, where the rent he receives is fixed and paid in money. The landlord and the *métayer* are brought into closer contact, and the relations between them are more intimate and familiar.[3]

---

[1] *Métayage* must not, however, be confused with profit-sharing, which is rarely applied in agriculture. Profit-sharing implies that the landowner remains the employer and works the land himself, the profit-sharer being but a hired worker.

[2] The *métayer* is, however, often forced to give the landlord, in addition to half of the crops, certain rather burdensome and quasi-feudal dues called the *impôt colonique*.

[3] In certain regions of Central France, middlemen have come in between the big landowner and the *métayer*, called *fermiers généraux*, who rouse almost as

For all these reasons *métayage* may be considered an element of social peace, even a solution of some issues of the agrarian problem.

The contract of *métayage*, moreover, may be modified according to circumstances, and thus lends itself better than might be expected to progress in cultivation. We may, for example, conceive of a system of *métayage* where the *métayer* contributes a large amount of capital. In the wine-growing industry in the South of France, the landowner simply provides the ground ; the *métayer* or *vigneron*, as he is called, raises the plantations at his own cost, sinking considerable capital in them, and the harvest is divided between them after the fifth or seventh year. We may also imagine a system under which the landowner would advance the capital in return for a moderate interest ; this would solve in part the problem of agricultural credit. In a word, the ancient contract of *métayage* may be rejuvenated in various ways and adapted to new needs, while at the same time preserving its essential character wherein lies its whole worth—of a " society in losses and gains," as ancient French law put it.

VII : SYSTEMS OF LAND NATIONALISATION

THE essential character of the private ownership of land, as admitted by the Classical economists themselves—namely, that it is a sort of monopoly, justified in practice, but hard to justify on grounds of abstract right—was bound to give rise to efforts to bring fact into line with theory.

Not only out-and-out socialists, but quite lukewarm economists and philosophers who had little sympathy with socialism—some even of the Liberal and Individualist school—have admitted that the individual ownership of land is illegitimate, or at any rate needs to be corrected by a social co-ownership, somewhat resembling what the jurists formerly called the "eminent domain " of the State. And they have tried various ways of bringing about this social ownership.

The most important plans proposed are as follows :

(1) Perpetuity of ownership in land should be abolished and a system of temporary concessions substituted for it. The State, owner of the soil, should lease it to individuals to cultivate for periods of fifty, seventy, or even ninety-nine years, as is done in the case of railway concessions. At the end of the period the State

much animosity as did their namesakes of a former time in another chapter of history. They are accused, like all middlemen, of trying to get the most they can out of the *métayers*.

should enter into possession of the land (just as in France, in 1950, it will enter into possession of the railways), and should re-lease it for a new period, making the new lessees pay the equivalent of the unearned increment, either in a lump sum, or in annual rent. In this way the State, representing society as a whole, would receive all the unearned increment ; and this would ultimately bring it an enormous income, and perhaps enable it to do away with taxes.

Such a method need not be so incompatible with good husbandry as M. Leroy-Beaulieu asserts, particularly if care be taken to renew the concessions a good while before the end of the term. The greatest undertakings of modern times—the large railways and the Suez Canal, etc.—have been carried out on this system. Indeed, it ought to be more favourable to good cultivation than the one actually in vogue in most countries, where almost all the land is cultivated by tenant farmers who may be dismissed at a moment's notice.

But the execution of such a plan, if carried out, as it should be, with equity, would meet at the outset with an insurmountable obstacle in the preliminary buying back of the soil.[1] As the value of the land in France is estimated at 70 or 80 billion francs, the compensation of the landowners would be a ruinous undertaking for the State.

We ourselves suggested a long time ago[2] a less costly system of redemption, according to which the State would purchase the land for an *immediate payment*, the transfer not to take place *till ninety-nine years later*. Under such conditions the State could obtain the land for a very small sum. The landowner, balancing, on the one hand, dispossession at so remote a date that neither he nor his grandchildren would suffer from it, and, on the other, a sum of money immediately available, would hardly hesitate to accept the price, however small. We even calculated this price in annuities : 1000 francs to be paid in 100 years, *i.e.* in the year 2013, at the rate of 5 per cent. would be worth, to-day, 7 francs 98 centimes. Thus 80 billions—taking this to be the value of landed property in France —payable in 100 years, would be worth at the present moment only 638 million francs in cash. This would not be a very high price.[3]

---

[1] It is only just that those who bought their lands under the protection of the law should not be despoiled of them by the law. If society wishes to change its land system, the cost of doing so ought to be borne by all its members.

[2] *De quelques doctrines nouvelles sur la propriété foncière. Journal des Économistes*, May 1883.

[3] M. Paul Leroy-Beaulieu, while declaring this system of purchase " perhaps the most ingenious " of any ever proposed (*Collectivisme*, 1st edit. p. 176), nevertheless rejects it as impracticable. We are not inclined to press it, for the simple

(2) The second system, suggested by the two Mills, if not by the Physiocrats themselves, and brought into prominence again by Henry George,[1] consists simply in putting a progressive tax on landed property calculated so as to absorb all the land rent, the *unearned increment.* This system, in favour of which there are leagues in America, Australia, and even in England, is open to serious objections.[2]

(a) The confiscation of the income from land by taxation would have the same results as the confiscation of the land itself. It would greatly reduce the value of the land, leaving the landowner only the nutshell, as Henry George himself declares. Hence the necessity in justice—though Henry George absolutely denies it—of compensation, and practically the same fiscal difficulties as we mentioned above.

(b) Further, there is the great practical objection that, in the surplus value of land, there are generally two elements : one due to social and impersonal causes ; the other due to the labour of the landowner, or at least to capital advanced by him. In creating such a tax, great care would have to be taken not to touch the increase due to this second element, on pain not only of injustice, but of discouraging all initiative and progress in agricultural enterprises, which are, as it is, only too stationary. Now, the separation of these elements is practically impossible. The landowner himself could not do it accurately, much less an officer of the Treasury.

reason that a social reform adjourned for 100 years has not much practical value. Besides, as the rate of capitalisation has risen since our system was proposed, the bases of calculation would need to be seriously modified. At the present rate of $3\frac{1}{2}$ per cent., a much larger sum would have to be paid as equivalent of the 80 billions payable in 100 years.

The period might, perhaps, be shortened and the sum to pay yet remain the same, if the date on which the State was to enter into possession of the land were fixed to be on the death of the last child conceived when the law was promulgated, *i.e.* by setting as a limit the period of two or three generations.

[1] Author of *Progress and Poverty,* which had an enormous success. Henry George died in 1897. His system is known in England and the U.S. as the Single Tax, as, on his programme, it was to be more than enough to allow all other taxes to be abolished.

[2] One objection, which we ourselves were among the first to urge in the article referred to, is, that if society confiscates for itself all the gains on the ground that they are not due to the action of the landlord, it is only fair that it should bear the losses on precisely the same ground. . . . But we withdraw this objection on considering that, if the value of the land were to fall or disappear, the tax on land rent would also fall or disappear, so that the State, and not the landowner, would bear the losses. In fact, what this system amounts to is simply removing the landlord from all risk whether of *gain or loss.*

In our view, then, every system for nationalising the land is impracticable, so far as already established property is concerned. But it is not the same as regards future property, that is to say, concessions of new lands. In all countries and colonies, not more than a century ago, there was still an immense public domain, which has unfortunately almost disappeared owing to inordinate concessions at low prices to individuals and companies. Had these concessions been temporary, the States in question· would have laid up for themselves precious resources for the future, and would perhaps have done something towards solving the social problem for future generations.[1] But, just where it would be most easy to prevent the abuses of the private ownership of land, the necessity for doing so is least felt. Private ownership, indeed, in new countries like Australia and the Argentine Republic, and at an early stage, has only advantages and no drawbacks. As it exists only over lands which have been cleared, and as it spreads with cultivation, it has all the appearance of being consecrated by labour. As it covers but a small portion of the soil, and as land is superabundant, it does not in any way constitute a monopoly, and is humbly subject, like any other enterprise, to the law of competition.

It is only as society develops and population becomes denser, that we see the nature of private property in land begin to change and to take on little by little the character of a monopoly which may grow out of all proportion. By this time it is too late to buy back the land, but not perhaps too late to tax unearned increment, at least in towns.

VIII : SYSTEMS FOR BREAKING-UP LANDED PROPERTY

THE attention given to the preservation of small rural property where it already exists, and to creating it where it does not, is seen in the modern legislation of various countries, England, Germany, Denmark, Russia, the countries of the Danube—and even France, although in France there is less necessity for it than elsewhere. It is not, however, an easy thing to create small property. Where it exists, as in France, Belgium, and Germany, it is the result of a combination of political and economic causes which were at work for centuries, and which, in France, for example, existed long before the Revolution of 1789, to which small property is generally credited.

---

1 In old countries the mines at least might be nationalised. (See *infra, Owner-ship of Mines*.)

The seigniorial ownership of feudal times was gradually transformed into an " eminent domain," which finally left the peasant the absolute owner of the soil. Traces of the ancient ownership lingered simply in the form of dues, numerous and burdensome it is true, from which the Revolution—this was its special work—finally freed the land.

In England the movement was in exactly the opposite direction. The small freehold proprietor, the *yeoman*, as he was called in Shakespeare's time, appears to have been more numerous than in any other country. Gradually, after a century of legal usurpations, not unlike those by which the Roman patricians at the time of the Gracchi converted the *ager publicus* into private domains, the lords transformed their political rights into rights of property, and absorbed, by Enclosure Acts, the free lands of old. To such a point did this go, that, at the present day, almost the whole of the soil of the British Isles is in the hands of four or five thousand owners, and it is only with their dearly bought permission that forty-five million human beings can live thereon. The land question has thus become the great problem in England, and the Government is doing its best to undo the work of centuries.[1]

But ancient usurpations are not enough to account for such concentration of landed property as we find in England. The usurpation of common lands took place in other countries, even in France. It is the system of succession which, in England, has main-tained and aggravated this concentration. Not only has the *law of primogeniture* prevented the land from being divided among the children,[2] but the practice of *entailing* property has rendered domains to all intents and purposes inalienable. The twofold result is that, on the one hand, most of the citizens are debarred from owning land, and, on the other, the privileged few are actually unable to dispose of it, and find themselves in the position of usufructuaries.[3]

[1] There are 1,200,000 landowners in the British Isles, but the great majority, three-quarters at least, possess less than an acre with a little cottage and garden. To give a more accurate idea of the distribution of land in Great Britain and Ireland, we should say that half of England and Wales is possessed by 4500 persons, half of Ireland by 744 persons, and half of Scotland by not more than 70 persons.

[2] The law of primogeniture, introduced at the Norman Conquest, exists only in cases of intestate succession and for land.

[3] A recent law has improved this situation by allowing landowners burdened with entail to break it (exception being made of the castle and grounds) on condition of reinvesting the value realised in securities in the name of the heir.

How, then, may small property be created.? In three ways :

(a) The most direct is for the State to lend the agricultural labourer the money necessary for acquiring a small piece of land. This is the system adopted in a great number of countries. It answers to the desire of the peasant, who would like to see himself owner of the land which he has cultivated so long as day labourer, tenant farmer, or *métayer*, but who is unable to do so for want of money. There are, as we have seen, credit institutions (see pp. 394–397) for the purpose, but they are too dear and too dangerous to be recommended to the peasant. The State could offer better conditions.[1]

It is in England that such a measure is particularly desirable. There, the number of small peasant-proprietors cultivating their own lands is only 60,000 as against 3 or 4 millions in France.[2] A number of laws have, indeed, been passed recently with the object of helping small property, but their inspiration proceeds from two very different sources.

One, *conservative*, would create small property after the manner of France, or of Ireland since 1903, by giving advances to small agriculturists to enable them to buy the land, and, where no land is on the market, by resorting to expropriation on the ground of public utility.

The other, *socialist*, would increase, not the number of small landowners, but the number of State tenants. This was the source of inspiration which resulted in the Small Holdings and Allotments Act of August 1908, by which the County Councils are charged with the duty of buying the land, by expropriation if need be, and *letting* it to small farmers.

[1] In Roumania concessions are gratuitous under certain conditions. In Denmark the State requires that whoever would become landowner shall pay one-tenth of the price, but it advances nine-tenths at 3 per cent., with no redemption annuity during the first five years and a very small one thereafter. The peasant in this way becomes a landowner, while paying distinctly less than if he were a simple tenant farmer. The land thus acquired must not exceed 5 hectares in area and 4000 crowns in value.

In Germany the State advances three-fourths of the price, and repayment has to be made within sixty years at 4 per cent. These small domains are called *Rentengüter*.

In Russia small rural property is developing rapidly owing, first, to the creation of the Peasants' Bank, in 1882, which acts as intermediary in buying land ; and, secondly, to the law of 1906 authorising the dividing up of the *mir*, of which we have spoken (see p. 503).

[2] In Great Britain, there are 513,000 small holdings, but only 60,217 of them are cultivated by their owners, the rest consequently being leased. This represents but a minute proportion of the land.

Results, so far, have been meagre. The County Councils have great difficulty in obtaining land and are loth to resort to expropriation, either because of the cost, or for fear of displeasing the landlords, whose influence is great.[1] Co-operative societies, however, to the number of 100, have been formed to facilitate the buying and reselling of the land, and these have achieved good results.

In France a recent law (March 19, 1910) allows those who desire to purchase land, or who, having land, need capital in order to work it, to make use of the considerable funds at the disposal of the *caisses régionales de crédit agricole*.[2] We saw in connection with agricultural credit (p. 400) that these land banks had at their disposal 40 million francs advanced by the Bank of France, as well as about 100 millions granted by the State from its share in the profits of the Bank. But up till the law of 1910 these funds could be lent only for agricultural operations of short duration—for expenses of cultivation. Since 1910, however, they may be lent also for the purchase, equipment, transformation, and reconstitution of small rural holdings. The maximum time of the loan is fifteen years and the maximum value 8000 francs, and it must be guaranteed by a mortgage or a life insurance on the borrower. The interest is less than three per cent.

Before these systems can work, the State must obviously be able to find lands to purchase. This is not always easy, particularly where, as in England, the large estates are practically inalienable. And it is a serious matter to fall back on expropriation, since it amounts simply to turning out old landowners for new.

[1] At the end of 1911, of 26,741 requests received, it was possible to satisfy only 11,797, the size of the lots being, on an average, 12 acres.

At first allotments of not more than one acre were created, *i.e.* just enough to keep a cow. To prevent the tenant from alienating them, they were not given outright but were leased in perpetuity. As this was found quite inadequate, small holdings of as much as 50 acres were created, which could be bought outright and paid for by annuities in fifty years. The tenants may not alienate them until the whole has been paid for.

Small-holders are content, as a rule, to take the land on lease and keep their money for the better working of it.

In Ireland, results have been better. Already £60,000,000 has been spent by the State in buying back the lands, and it is expected that twice as much again will be spent. By that time, more than half of Ireland will have passed from the hands of the landlords into those of their tenant-farmers.

[2] This is the third time we find the State advancing funds for agriculture. The first time (p. 199) it was to the co-operative agricultural associations for production; the second (p. 400) was to co-operative societies of credit. And this time it is to develop small property by individual loans.

(*b*) A second way to create small property, is to impose by law equal division of the land at each transfer by succession, as was done in France by the Code Napoléon. The famous Art. 826, when laying down the law of equal division among the children, did not stop short at mere equivalence, but gave each child the right to claim his share in *kind ;* that is to say, each heir may claim his share of the smallest field, and, if division is impossible, the judicial sale becomes necessary, with all the enormous costs it involves. It is difficult for the father of a family to evade this by bequest, since he may dispose of only a limited portion by will.

There is no doubt that this system, though drastic, is effective, and that, if England were to adopt it, many of her immense estates would, after a few generations, be broken up.

It is, however, much more difficult than one might think to know the exact results which it has had in France. This is because, however humiliating the confession may be for statisticians, the number of properties is known only approximately ; not precisely enough in any case to allow us to measure the increase or decrease in their number.

If, for instance, we take the surveyor's unit of cultivation, the *parcelle*, which the landowner calls a field, *e.g.* a cornfield or a vineyard, the number of them is enormous—about 150 millions—and a single estate may contain hundreds of them. If we take the list of lands subject to taxation, we are better informed as to the number of properties, but hardly so as to the number of proprietors, since those whose properties are scattered may have to pay five or six different collectors, and are thus registered five or six times over. The lists, moreover, do not distinguish between rural ground and urban ground.[1]   Lastly, if we take the number of agricultural exploitations (5,505,000), we come nearer the truth ; although we must remember that a large estate divided into five or six farms,

[1] Fiscal statistics, which are usually fairly accurate, allow us to compare the number, and the distribution, of lands subject to taxation, with an interval of a century between.

The number of lands subject to taxation, which had been increasing from the beginning of the nineteenth century up till 1882 (from 10,296,000 in 1826 to 14,336,000 in 1882), fell to 13,466,000 in 1908—a diminution of more than 6 per cent. in twenty-six years. But this may be no more than apparent, and due to the fact that the administration is trying to group together lands belonging to a single proprietor—as also to the fact that the number of rural inhabitants is diminishing, both by emigration to the towns and by the reduced birth-rate.

Pieces of land of less than ten hectares make up 92 per cent. of the total in number, but only 35 per cent. in area (*Statistique Agricole* for 1882).

counts as five or six exploitations, while several small properties belonging to the same farmer, count as one single exploitation. The following figures give the number of agricultural exploitations in France, and their increase or decrease over a period of twenty-six years :

	1892	1908	
Small property (less than 10 hectares)	4,853,000	4,611,000	− 5 per cent.
Medium-sized property (between 10 and 40 hectares) . . .	711,000	746,000	+ 5 „
Large property (over 40 hectares) .	139,000	148,000	+ 6½ „
	5,703,000	5,505,000	− 3½ „

Although statistics vary somewhat and may be interpreted in different ways, we would seem justified in concluding :

(1) That the number of rural landowners in France is very great (about 5½ millions). Including the members of the family, this should represent nearly half of the French population. The number is, however, diminishing owing to emigration to towns and to the stationary state of the population.

(2) That, of these, the small landowners who possess less than 10 hectares far outstrip the rest in numbers, representing 84 per cent. of the total, but not in area, their property covering less than one-third of the whole.[1]

(3) That the number of independent cultivators, *i.e.* cultivators who are also landowners, is on the increase, while that of dependent cultivators on the one hand, and landowners who are not cultivators on the other, is on the decrease.[2]

(c) A last and more indirect way of creating small property, is to bring land on to the market, that is to say, to make it as easily

---

[1] The area of the three categories of property is distributed as follows :

Small property (up to 10 hectares) .	12,788,000 hectares	29 per cent.
Medium-sized property (10 to 40 hectares)	14,825,000 „	34 „
Large property (over 40 hectares) . .	16,270,000 „	37 „
	43,883,000	100 „

[2] These dry figures have been the subject of passionate discussion, since with them stands or falls the great theory at the basis of Collectivism, viz., the law of concentration (see pp. 163, 484).

What would be more interesting to know is the number and proportion of landowners cultivating their own lands, of *peasants* in the sense of autonomous producers. The following are the figures which we have been able to gather

transferable as any other commodity. This would be the surest
way of putting an end to the objections against the private ownership
of land. For what would it matter that landed property were by
its nature a monopoly, if every one could acquire it ? What would
it matter that this ownership were perpetual, if it remained in the
hands of each person for only a short time ? The inevitable surplus
value would no longer enrich one person and one family, but, scattered
and mobile, would benefit all. This would also be the best method
of attracting to the land the capital which it needs, as capital will
not readily come if it is to be buried in perpetuity.

This system has been actually put into practice in France.
Sales of land reach annually the figure of 2 million hectares. As
there are about 35 million hectares of private property, this means
that the whole of the land changes hands once every eighteen years
or so, or, in other words, that the land, on an average, does not
remain even for one generation in the hands of the same family.
It is very different in other countries, particularly England.

But how is land to be brought into the current of circulation ?

In the first place, of course, by abolishing all clauses which
restrict the power of alienating it ; clauses, for instance, such as
French law has decreed for the protection of the married woman,
the minor, or the legal person ; [1] or English law for the preservation of the entailed estate.

Secondly, by reducing to a minimum the formalities and costs
of alienation, which are at present proportionally heavier on lands

from a comparison of agricultural statistics from 1862 to 1892, as regards the
situation of landowners.

	1862	1892
Those who cultivate their own lands exclusively	1812	2199
Those who cultivate their own lands and are, at the same time, day labourers or tenant farmers	1987	1188
Those who do not cultivate their own lands themselves, but who do so by stewards or farmers	1441	1310
	5240	4697

The first category is obviously the normal type of peasant, i.e of small autonomous
producer. Now this class has increased over 21 per cent., while the other two
have decreased 30 per cent. Note that, as the figure for the third class is not
given for 1892, we have had to take it for 1882 ; it ought probably therefore
to be still further reduced.

[1] There are no end of articles in the French Code establishing the inalienability of landed property, or at least making its alienation subject to rigorous
formalities. For the Code Napoléon was inspired by the idea that immovable
property is the safest of all, the basis of the family, and that it should be *taboo*.
It was even worse in England until within recent years.

of smaller value, so that small property is more fettered than large. These costs vary, in France, from 7 per cent. on large sales, to 18 per cent. on small ones—an average of at least 10 per cent., not counting the solicitor's fees. The Torrens system (see p. 505), which was introduced into Australia in 1858, and has since spread to other countries, had this object in view. It consists, briefly, in applying to land the same system of registration as applies to persons. The history and the description of each piece of land are entered on a register and a copy is given to the owner. This certificate represents, as it were, the land in the owner's pocket. When he wants to sell it, he has only to take it to the registrar, who enters the transfer on the register and hands over a new title to the purchaser. There is therefore no necessity for the intervention of a solicitor or " man of law."

Lastly, the purchaser must be given complete security, so that he need fear neither eviction nor annoyance. The way in which property rights are authenticated in most countries, even in France, leaves much to be desired on this score. The purchaser is never perfectly certain that the seller was the true owner, and yet he can acquire no more rights than the seller had. In this respect the Torrens system is as superior in the security which it gives, as in its economy.

For the person inscribed on the register is always held to be the real owner; and even if, by mistake, he happens not to be, the true owner is none the less expropriated and has no other resort than to claim compensation from the State. It may seem hard that the right of property should be forfeited by a mere error of registration, but this sacrifice appeared indispensable in order to give an absolute value to the title, which represents property as the bank-note represents gold.[1]

---

[1] So harsh has this appeared to jurisconsults that, in old countries where the Torrens system has been introduced, the principle has been modified. The true owner takes possession of his land again, and the one who has been mistakenly inscribed on the State registers obtains compensation from the State. This is the case in England, where a system somewhat resembling the Torrens system was introduced, warily at first, and as a purely optional matter for landowners. Since 1897, it has been left to the discretion of the counties which might wish to adopt it.

In Germany, even before the appearance of the Torrens system, there were compulsory registers for the entering of property. Here, however, we are trenching on the domain of the jurisconsult.

IX: SYSTEMS FOR THE CONSERVATION
OF LANDED PROPERTY

WE now place ourselves at exactly the opposite point of view from that which we took in the last chapter. This does not, however, imply that the two points of view are irreconcilable.

Economists of the Social Catholic school, or at any rate those of a conservative spirit, readily allow, as a rule, the first of the three means indicated for acquiring land, namely, advances by the State; but the last two (division and mobilisation) are little to their taste.

In the first place, to cut up and coin the land, as it were, thus making it into merchandise is, in their view, contrary to the interests of cultivation and of the family. Land must not be robbed of its twofold characteristic of immobility and perpetuity, since it is these two qualities which associate it with the perpetuity of the family and the stability of lasting enterprises and long hopes.

The division of property into equal shares strikes them as a system inspired less by the love of small property than by the hatred of large; and, with its rough-and-ready mechanism, as going often contrary to the ends it has in view. It barely touches large estates, the owners of which are, as a rule, wealthy enough to settle the estate on one of the children while securing to the rest equivalent shares in money—and these, for the honour of the name, willingly lend themselves to such an arrangement; while the small landowner, on the contrary, whose sole fortune is his land, cannot avoid the knife. At each death, therefore, the small estate is subdivided anew, and this continues in geometrical progression until nothing is left but mere tatters of land, of absolutely no use unless perhaps for rounding off some great neighbour's estate. This system therefore compromises the interests of agriculture, and can plead no democratic compensation.

It is besides, in their opinion, too easy an optimism to say, as do some economists, that the subdivision of land will stop of its own accord so soon as it becomes harmful. There are innumerable instances where this pulverising process has ended in strips of land no wider than the scythe. If, they say, in the case of France, equal sharing has not been so destructive as it might have been, it is because it has been partly neutralised by two other causes, in their own way more deadly still: Malthusianism, which checks the division of the land among the children by checking the number of the children themselves; and emigration from the country, so that even where there are several children, only one—if that one—remains on the soil.

But what remedy would they propose ? To re-establish the liberty of bequest would not be tolerated by the spirit of equality of our race, which would see in it the resurrection of primogeniture. And even if, to avoid all suspicion of aristocracy, the liberty of bequest were limited to small estates, this would create the anomaly of two forms of succession, one for the rich and another for the poor, which would not be easily accepted. Le Play's school, without going so far as to claim for the father the right to dispose of his goods as he likes, asks that the proportion at his disposal should always be at least one-half, so as to enable him to transmit the estate to one of the children, and thus to maintain the *family stock*, an institution which, in his view, was as essential in the case of the rich as of the poor. If there were not enough money in the succession to give shares —even thus curtailed—to the other children, the latter were to be content with a mortgage on the estate. But this system would in all probability engender endless quarrels, and there is no guarantee that the heir would not be crushed under such a burden.[1]

A minimum limit, however, might be fixed below which all division would be forbidden, so that the heirs would have the alternative either of allowing the bit of land to be added to the lot of one of them, or of selling it. It would thus become the atom, as it were, of property.[2]

[1] In several of the German States there is a system very similar to that advocated by Le Play's school, known as the "right of the heir" (*Anerbenrecht*). The father may, by inscribing it on a public register, constitute a homestead which will not be divided at his death. It will pass to whichever of his children he has appointed, or to the eldest if he dies intestate. The one who keeps the land has a preferential right to one-third of the estate, and may even, if there is not enough money, pay the shares of his co-heirs, in the form of incomes. But he enjoys these privileges only for so long as he keeps the estate : if he sells it the whole is divided equally.

In France, also, a step has been taken in this direction by the law of April 10, 1908, which, while leaving untouched the principle that the shares should be equal in value, modifies it slightly where the estate does not exceed one hectare in area, and 1200 francs in value. It becomes possible to avoid compulsory sale if one of the heirs is able to purchase the estate, and the joint-possession, which must come to an end on the demand of any one of the heirs, may be prolonged for ten years where one of the heirs is a minor. This law is simply an extension of the law of April 12, 1906, which granted these same favours to cheap houses.

[2] The practical difficulty would be to fix this minimum. Obviously it could not be the same in the case of pasture land, vineyards, and market gardens. The *Congrès des syndicats agricoles*, which met at Orleans in 1897, asked that the minimum limit should be fixed at 50 ares (1¼ acres).

The excessive *subdivision* of property (*morcellement*), which consists in the land being divided among a great number of land-owners, is frequently accompanied by another evil, namely, *disper-sion* (*parcellement*), which consists in the same landowner possessing a large number of small pieces of land. Dispersion is not necessarily connected with small property. There may be, and, in certain districts, are large estates consisting of small scattered pieces of land, sometimes long distances apart. Here we find combined all the disadvantages of small and large property. There is, however, a clear remedy for this in what is called *consolidation*, or the exchang-ing by landowners among themselves of scattered patches of land for others beside their own estates. This operation has been prac-tised for a long time in Germanic countries, and even in certain parts of France.

In France, however, it can be done only by private arrange-ment ; and those who know the individualistic and distrustful nature of the French peasant will hardly expect it to spread. In Germany, particularly in Alsace, it is carried out in a more authoritative manner by compulsory syndicates, institutions which exist also in France, but only for the draining of marshes, irrigation works, or the making of roads (see p. 193, *Agricultural Associa-tions*). In communes where the majority of landowners are in favour of " consolidation," the recalcitrant minority are obliged to submit to it ; that is to say, to submit to expropriation. For re-memberment carries with it the suppression of all existing property rights and servitudes, replacing them by new rights, so that property, as it were, changes its skin. The measure is therefore a serious one. Certain Swiss cantons go a step further. The cantonal government may impose consolidation even when the majority have not voted it. It is superfluous to emphasise the benefits of this energetic operation from the point of view of cultivation.

If it is important that land should not be too much divided up, it is also important that it should not be rendered too mobile by facilities either for mortgaging, or for alienating, it. For what would be the good of creating a class of small landowners at great cost by advances from the State, if they are to be delivered over to improvi-dence and usury and brought down again into the ranks of the proletariat ? We must therefore counteract the facility of transfer by rendering so much land, at least, as is necessary for the existence and maintenance of the family inalienable, or at any rate not liable to distraint.

This institution of the *homestead*, as it is called in the United States, where it was established in 1839, is spreading in various countries. In France, after some fifteen years of hesitation and of bills laid before Parliament, the law of July 12, 1909, has finally consecrated the *homestead*, or, as it is called in French, the *bien de famille*.

To keep small property intact, this measure ought really to be compulsory and to make the *homestead* not only not liable to distraint, but inalienable. But no country has as yet gone this length. For, to put small property under such a civil disqualification would tend to set the small cultivators against it, and would thus defeat the very object in view. The American *homestead* is alienable,[1] subject, however, to the consent of the wife, as its preservation is in the interests of the family, not simply of the individual. This *bien de famille* must always include a house or home, as the name indicates. French law goes still further, requiring, if the wife be dead and the children under age, the authorisation of the court before alienation. In the United States the size of the homestead varies in the different States; in the French bill the limit was fixed not in size, but in value (8000 francs, including equipment and furniture). The law requires in every case that the land be cultivated by the proprietor in person.

This system, much advocated by economists of the Liberal, as well as of the Catholic, school, has, however, its adversaries.

It is certainly little consistent with the individualist doctrine, as it invites the small landowner to tie his hands together in order the better to defend himself. But the same may be said of the laws which, in France, exempt from distraint instruments of labour, indispensable furniture, and four-fifths of the working-man's wage. The objection, moreover, that it damages the credit of the small landowner is not admissible, since this is the very object aimed at. We have already said (p. 394) that the mortgage is, in our view, more harmful than otherwise, and, as to personal credit, the homestead in no way injures it.

X : URBAN PROPERTY

By urban property we must be understood to mean house property. Urban property is termed "immovable property" and, from the

[1] It may also in most States, though not all, be mortgaged, which seems absurd; for the homestead is thus protected only against ordinary creditors. The French bill rightly refuses to allow this.

juridical point of view, assimilated to property in land. The assimilation holds good from the economic point of view also, in this sense, that houses partake of the threefold character of land as shown above : they satisfy an essential want, they are limited in number, and they last, humanly speaking, for ever. The two first characteristics, indeed, are more accentuated in the case of houses than in that of land. This it is which has caused urban property to become the scandal of the present economic organisation. It is the most unjustifiable source of fortune and the cause, so far as can be seen, of the most terrible social miseries. If the present society is to perish, it will be by this rather than by capitalism that it will fall.

It is not the ownership of the house, as a building, which gives rise to social conflicts. The house, like anything else, is a product of human industry, and, although more lasting by nature than most things, is apt to depreciate rapidly in value by the competition of newer and more up-to-date buildings. What we are concerned with is the ownership of building grounds situated in towns. It is these latter which, through the growth of population in large centres, acquire fantastic surplus values and allow their owners to charge rents limited only by the capacity of tenants to pay.[1] There is no other value in the world in the original making of which the labour of man is so utterly lacking nor, on the other hand, where the action of social causes is so clearly at work. Schemes, then, for the abolition of private ownership, either by nationalising the land, or by taxing it, seem here to be more urgently necessary than even in the case of rural property.

Unfortunately, the remedy is not plain. To do away with the

[1] The newspapers reported that in 1908, in the centre of New York, at the angle of Broadway and Wall Street, a piece of building land was sold for 750 dollars per square foot. In 1808, just a century before, it had sold for a dollar and a half per square foot. The value, therefore, had increased more than a hundred-fold in 100 years. What would it be if we went back to the year 1624, when a Dutchman, Peter Minuit, bought the Island of Manhattan (on which the greater part of New York is built) from the Redskins for $25 paid in goods ?

In 1910, a shop situated in the centre of London, on lands belonging to the Duke of Westminster, paying a rent of £350, had, in order to obtain a renewal of its lease, to consent to a rise in rent of £5200, besides paying a sum of £50,000, and to undertake repairs for an equal amount.

Bastiat, in order to bring such cases under his *Economic Harmonies*, explained them by " the service " rendered to the tenant. And, without question, landowners render immense service to humanity. For it is no small boon to furnish mankind with his very means of work, or the lodging without which he cannot be born, live, or die. What is not so clear, however, is the principle of justice or social utility, by virtue of which some men have the pleasant privilege of being able to render such precious and highly paid services to their fellows.

private owning of city building grounds and of the houses on them, is not enough to bring down the value of the house and of its rent to cost price, as this value is due to an enormous and growing disproportion between supply and demand. It is obvious that, if houses became communal property and were offered for nothing, this disproportion would increase enormously. As land rent, it is said, does not determine the price of wheat, but the price of wheat on the contrary, determines land rent, so, we may say it is not building-land rent which determines city rents, but the price of city rents which determines building-land rent.

The only remedy consists in trying to balance supply and demand. The means to be employed we shall discuss in the chapter on Housing.

XI : THE OWNERSHIP OF FORESTS

IF there is some defence for private ownership in the case of cultivable land, this is not so as regards forests. Not only is the forest not the product of labour, but, save where it has been planted, it does not even involve, like the mine, the preliminary labour of search and discovery, and requires but little subsequent labour.

The forest was, in fact, the last category of property to come under private ownership, and even to-day it is only incompletely so. It is in forest land that the ancient communal ownership has survived longest, and, where the forest is privately owned, this is as a rule the result of usurpations which prescription alone has made legitimate.   .

Now, while the gradual invasion by private ownership had only good results in the case of cultivable lands, in that of forests it has had disastrous effects,[1] which all countries are doing their best to counteract.

Although wood is gradually giving way to iron for building purposes, and to coal for heating purposes, the forest has lost none of its social value ; and its utility is becoming more and more recognised to-day. It is the mother of rivers, and perhaps, though this is less certain, the dispenser of rains. It protects the valley against the mountain torrents, moderates floods, and, in a certain measure, purifies the atmosphere. Without going so far as to hold that the death of peoples follows on the death of their forests, we may say

---

[1] Proof being that forests are beginning to disappear in all countries (see p. 79). Even in young countries like Canada, where forest land seemed unlimited, the ravages of private appropriations are beginning to cause serious alarm.

that the preservation and, where possible, the restoration of forests are matters of social concern. Now, private ownership appears ill-qualified for this office of quasi-guardian of the forest. Not only is the individual as a rule indifferent to the interests of future generations, but personal interest urges him to draw an immediate profit from his property, either by clearing and realising the considerable capital it represents, or by cutting it down more than it can stand. In all treatises on Political Economy, the forest is taken as the classical example of the antagonism between individual ownership and the common good.[1]

Not that the State and the communes have shown themselves more faithful guardians of the forest. They too, in the course of centuries, have squandered this national patrimony with an improvidence hardly less reckless than that of private individuals. To-day, however, States are better advised. And the rural communes, although their only concern is the pasturing of the cattle and although they are not much to be relied on, are at any rate under the control of the State—a control unfortunately too often weakened by electoral interests.[2]

But there is another form of ownership which would be even better suited to forests than is individual, or communal ownership—that, namely, of " legal " persons, of corporations representing some great general interest—hospitals, institutions for charity and relief of all kinds, old-age funds, insurance societies, even savings banks, friendly societies, or, in general, all associations and institutions capable of possessing immovable property. These from their very perpetuity would find in forests exactly the kind of investment they require. All that is necessary is that the government, which subjects their investments to severe restrictions and often stupidly forces them to place their funds in government stock, should make this new investment possible for them.[3] For, if the forest gives too small or too long-deferred a return to be a suitable investment for individuals, the case is different with a " legal " person who has

---

[1] The greatest enemy of forests at this moment is the *newspaper*, most paper being made of wood. Each large daily paper in Europe and the United States absorbs annually some acres of forest.

[2] The large towns would offer better guarantees for the preservation of forests, but up till now this kind of property has been unknown to them. A few, however, are beginning to acquire it. The town of Orleans has had some idea of buying the forest of Amboise, which is threatened.

[3] The State refused this in the case of the Savings Banks' funds. To invest the billions of francs deposited by the public and payable on demand, in forests, would of course be absurd. But it should be quite admissible in the case of the personal fortune of these banks.

not to count with time. To this latter, such investment may bring in after fifty, or even twenty-one years, five or ten times as much as government stock, apart from the fact that the income from government stock is subject to conversion and the capital to many vicissitudes, while the surplus value of the forest is almost a certainty.[1]

The solving of the forest question therefore involves the following programme :

(1) *The preservation of what forest land still exists.*

(a) By making the forests belonging to the State and to the communes inalienable.

(b) By putting under State control not only the forests belonging to the communes and to public bodies, but those belonging to individuals and to private associations. This control would be more or less rigorous according to circumstances : in some cases the State would do no more than offer the help of its own agents in the better treatment of the wood ; in others it would limit the number and extent of the cuttings, as a bill before Parliament proposes ; or, as is done in India, Japan, and Würtemberg, take over the forest itself, allowing the owner only a regulated usufruct.

(c) By buying up private forests, either by arrangement or by expropriation. This last method, however, would require an expenditure which Parliament is not disposed to vote.

(2) The *extension of the forest domain by afforestation.* This afforestation might be undertaken :

(a) By the State. Sums have been voted for this purpose in all countries, including France. But how little ![2]

(b) By the communes. The laws of 1860 and 1906, in France, facilitate this work by allowing communes to let out the soil on leases of ninety-nine years, or to borrow from the *land banks* (*caisses régionales de crédit*) (see p. 400).

The planting of forests would be one of the best methods of capitalisation for creating pensions, since these last are compatible with long delay in the return. It has been calculated that a commune which planted every year half a hectare of pines per 100 inhabitants, would secure a pension of 360 francs at the age of sixty for all the children born after the date when the planting was begun.

---

[1] The planting of one hectare of forest costs 400 to 500 francs, and the return per hectare when it is producing varies from 70 to 190 francs.

It has been calculated (and verified by experiment, as in the forests of the Rhone) that a plantation of oak yields 4¾ per cent. after 21 years ; of wild pine, 15 per cent. after 50 years ; and of fir, 25 per cent. after 70 years.

[2] A credit of 3,377,000 francs in 1907. Prussia grants 8 million francs.

The *Conseil général* of Corsica expressed the desire (September 18, 1901) that the owners of chestnut forests should be forced to replant as many trees as they cut, or allowed to be cut, down. This drastic measure would be justified by the devastation that is taking place in the chestnut forests of Corsica, which are being sold by their owners for the manufacture of gallic acid.

(c) By individuals or private companies. A law of Frimaire, Year VII, grants a reduction in taxation of three-fourths during thirty years on land planted with trees, and Art. 226 of the *Code forestier* gives total exemption for the same length of time. But this is not enough to induce a landowner to do without income for thirty years. The government might perhaps find a better opening here, for its subsidies, than by bestowing them on the mercantile marine, linen, and cocoons. The most effective measure, no doubt, would be to restore the cult of the tree. In this direction the *associations post-scolaires* in France and the Touring Club Society are doing admirable work, which will perhaps show some results within the next generation.

XII : THE OWNERSHIP OF MINES

OF all forms of wealth, there is none, after the forest, in which private property is more difficult to defend than in mines. And for three reasons :

(1) Because minerals, whether gold, iron, or coal, are obviously a product of nature, not of labour. So is land, it may be said. But land, as a rule, is of no value when first discovered or occupied. So true is this that some have held—wrongly, as we have shown—that the value which it acquires later comes solely from the labour of clearing and cultivating it. The mine, on the contrary, has a value the moment it is discovered, proof being that, as a rule, it is formed into a company at once. No doubt much labour and expenditure are necessary to set it going, but it is not because of these that the mine is of value. It is, on the contrary, because the mine is held to be of great value that such works are undertaken.

The mine is treasure trove. It is a treasure slowly formed by subterranean forces, buried for centuries, often as well hidden and defended by nature as it could have been by any dragons of ancient legend ; and despite the use of scientific methods, it is discovered in most cases by chance.

Indeed, the very fact that chance plays so great a part in the discovery and surplus value of mines, is used as an argument to justify the enormous profits of certain mines, as these are balanced against the mines which have swallowed up capital. But this is as if in gambling we were to justify the gains of the winners by the losses of the losers—an argument which has neither moral nor economic force. For, if we take the total mining enterprises of a country, we find that profits far exceed losses, even after allowing the normal margin for the remuneration of capital.[1]

(2) Because mines are a really rare form of wealth, much more so than is cultivable land, rich mines in particular being much more scarce than fertile lands. Their contents too satisfy almost as pressing wants as do agricultural products. Iron and gold have done as much service to the human race as corn has, and their utility has increased at a much greater rate. To-day, it is the wealth of the subsoil, much more than that of the soil, which creates the great agglomerations of human beings called industrial cities. Mines are consequently able to yield enormous differential and monopoly rents, and the phenomenon of unearned increment is even more visible here than in the case of building land. For the mine is not a treasure once found and done with. It is a treasure whose value, as a rule, increases. True, building land lasts for ever, whereas the mine is gradually consumed by extraction, and its treasure exhansted ; but, as it may last for centuries, our argument is hardly affected.

(3) Because, within a very small space, mines may contain a thousand times more wealth than cultivated land.

The Potosi and the Comstock mines have yielded millions sterling in the form of silver, and the Anzin mines in the form of coal. The injustices of *unearned increment* are thus enormously magnified. This is why the nationalising of the mines takes the first place in Socialist, and even Radical-Socialist, programmes, far before even that of the land itself. Still, individual and co-operative ownership have also their champions. Four different theories of mineowning may in fact be distinguished : (a) the ownership of the mine may be claimed by the landowner ; (b) by the discoverer ; (c) by the State ; (d) by the miners. Each of these has been more or less put into practice.

(a) The *owner of the land* in which the mine is situated claims the mine on the ground that his right of absolute ownership carries with it the ownership of what is below, as well as above, the soil. Theoretically, this is absurd. It represents the landowner as possessing a pyramid whose vertex is the centre of the earth and whose

[1] See M. Simiand, *Le prix du charbon.*

s'

sides are prolonged into infinity. Practically, we should expect it to make the rational working of mines impossible, as the roads ought to stop at the exact limits of the estates on the surface. Yet this system has been admitted in England, one of the greatest of mining countries, without compromising the industry. The most absurd of theories may after all be made to fit facts. In England, estates are large and unbroken, and landowners, rather than exercise this right themselves, prefer to treat with the mining companies for royalties.[1]

(b) The *discoverer* has more weighty claims to ownership.[2] In the first place, if we admit, as we have done, that to produce is simply to discover a new utility, we may say of the discoverer that he has, in an immaterial but in the truly economic sense of the word, *produced* the mine (see p. 97). Yet, as such discovery is often the result of mere luck, it would be a very narrow basis for property of such consequence. It was not therefore this reasoning which determined certain countries—generally new countries and colonies —to attribute the ownership to the discoverer of the mine ; it was rather the practical consideration that the best way of encouraging the discovery of new mines was to declare them the property of the man who should find them. If every mine discovered belonged to the State, it is not at all likely that engineers would be as zealous in looking for them as are the hordes of prospectors stimulated by the prospect of a fortune.[3]

(c) The *State* may lay claim to the ownership of mines on the same ground as to the ownership of forests. Why, indeed, should not the State, instead of conceding the mine to capitalist companies, concede it to itself and exploit it directly, *en régie* as it is called (see p. 213) ? There can be no decisive objection to this, either on theoretical or on practical grounds, since the Prussian State works

---

[1] It has been calculated that the steamship *Lusitania* burns daily, at sea, 1680 tons of coal, bringing the owner of the mine £84 per day. The 333 stokers employed earn among them £79 per day, and for what labour !

[2] We have compared the mine to a treasure. Now, in the case of real treasure, French law attributes half to the person who finds it and half to the owner of the ground. Other legislatures, however, attribute part of it to the State.

[3] Thus in the French colonies there is a tendency to abandon the law of the mother country, and to adopt that of new countries, attributing the ownership of the mine to the *prospector*, to the person who first staked out the ground, or leased or bought it from the natives. The extent of the ground which may be occupied is, however, limited by law, and the final concession is made subject to the accomplishment of certain works and an inquiry. It is rare, moreover, that the person who discovers the mine asks the concession of it for himself. As a rule he has not enough capital, and prefers to resell his right with a profit.

the mines which form part of its vast and ancient royal domain no less profitably than do the great competing companies. In France, a bill to this effect has just been put before the Chamber. The crux of the whole matter lies in the question whether French administration is able to fulfil the conditions required, not for starting and working the mine—to this it is quite equal—but for obtaining good results commercially—a less certain matter.

(d) Lastly, we may conceive of the mine as collectively owned by the *workers* who exploit it.

Theoretically, there is no objection to this, but practically there is the immense difficulty that mining is, of all industries, the one which perhaps requires most capital ; and it is difficult to see where an association of working men could find it. This solution would be possible, therefore, only in the case of small concessions, like the few mines, already existing, in which miners' co-operative associations have been formed.[1] This system might be more easily carried out if combined with the preceding one, whereby the State, while retaining the actual ownership of the mine and providing the equipment, would concede the working of it to the workers themselves, grouped into societies. In this way the Associationist formula—not the Collectivist, as is sometimes mistakenly asserted—*the mine to the miners*—would be put into practice.

French legislation sanctions none of these four types of ownership, but hesitates between them. In theory, it admits that the mines belong to the State. It does not indeed distinctly say so ; it simply says that every mine must be conceded by the State. But how can the State concede the mines, and concede them to whomsoever it will, if it does not in the first instance consider them its own property ? Only, after rendering this theoretical homage to the eminent domain of the State, the law contradicts itself outright by giving the grantee an absolute and perpetual right of ownership [2] in the mine, save for the following privileges retained by the State :

(1) Right of control over the working of the mine, and the right to enforce certain measures of safety, in particular as regards flooding.

[1] There are only three in France, one of which, in the Pyrenees, dates back to the Middle Ages. They have not been very successful.

[2] The law of April 21, 1810, declares that " the grantees possess a perpetual right which they may dispose of and transmit like any other property, and which can be taken from them only in accordance with the forms prescribed for land-owners." Napoleon had insisted personally that this right should be clearly affirmed.

(2) A right to revoke the concession where the working is abandoned, or suspended long enough to affect national industry. In practice, this right has been exercised only once or twice at the beginning of the nineteenth century.[1]

Who, then, is this grantee, hardly to be distinguished from an out-and-out proprietor ? The State, we repeat, chooses whomsoever it thinks fit : probably the person whom, on inquiry, it thinks able, by his experience and his capital, to get most out of the mine.[2] The landowner and the discoverer are not debarred from obtaining the concession, but they are not given the preference. It is seldom, indeed, that the landowner obtains, or even demands, the concession : the law merely allows him a small due, called *droit de superficie*. As for the discoverer, when he is not the landowner, he is more often than not an engineer in the service of some company, which naturally obtains the concession. If it does not, he may claim compensation for his outlay from whoever obtains it.

This legislation is sharply criticised to-day. The general inclination at present is towards restoring the eminent domain of the State, and, in order to accomplish this, towards reducing this quasi-feudal ownership of the grantee to more modest proportions, such as we find in the case of other State concessions ; in particular : (1) by making the concession temporary or redeemable ; (2) by putting it up to tender, the State retaining a share in the profits ;[3] (3) by making it liable to certain charges for the benefit of the workers, such as profit-sharing, special pensions, etc.[4]

Reforms such as these appear only reasonable as regards all future concessions of mines, but in the case of mines already conceded they would amount to partial expropriation, as these concessions were made in perpetuity. The *Conseil d'État*, therefore, decided that

[1] " If the working is restricted or suspended in such a manner as to threaten public safety or the wants of the consumers." (Art. 49 of the law of April 21, 1810.) And yet, out of 1488 minin · concessions only 599 are being worked (1906).

[2] The mining companies already existing are, in general, the ones which best fulfil the conditions required in order to obtain new concessions. And as a rule they are preferred. There is a tendency, however, to-day against allowing the mining companies to become too large.

[3] At present, whoever obtains the concession pays a tax of 6½ per cent., calculated on the net proceeds, and an insignificant payment of 10 centimes per hectare.

[4] M. Millerand, at that time Minister of Public Works, declared in the Chamber (October 26, 1909) that it was the intention of the government to introduce into the law concerning mines a clause to which he attached great importance and value from the social point of view, obliging the concessionaire to admit his workers to a participation in the profits of the mine, either by means of labour shares or some other method to be determined.

the government could not modify the conditions of concession by way of decree, as it was contemplating doing, nor even, if it modified them by legislation, make the laws retroactive,[1] without abusing its power. Now, if legislation is to be reformed only in respect of new concessions, its field of application will be small. Still, there appear to be more mines than was once thought beneath the ancient soil of France.[2]

XIII : THE OWNERSHIP OF WATER

THE ownership of water is a much more difficult problem than that of land. Indeed, we may ask whether it is possible at all ; for water escapes through the fingers of whoever would try to take hold of it.

French law nevertheless declares that all water belongs to the owner of the land on which it rises. Theoretically, therefore, all water is privately appropriated. Happily, even if he wanted to, the landowner is not able, in the nature of things, to keep possession of running water. He is obliged by law to let it flow ; and, so soon as the stream becomes navigable, it ceases to be private and becomes public property.

Yet, when a commune or a town wants to obtain drinking water for its inhabitants, more often than not it is obliged to buy private sources at great cost.

Also, as regards irrigation, there are countries, *e.g.* certain regions of Spain and Algeria, where the ownership of water is of vital import-ance, since water is there the sole source of life, and he who is lord of the water, is lord of those who have none. In such countries, water for irrigation remains of necessity collective property, though in very different forms : sometimes under State control, as in Egypt ; sometimes under that of consumers' associations, as in the province of Valencia and in the oases of Algeria.[3]

In Europe, drinking water and water for irrigation are plentiful enough, but the question of water for motive power is very urgent.

[1] Belgian law, which was simply the French law of 1810, has just been modi-fied in the same direction, but only as regards future concessions.

[2] It is believed that important seams of coal, the continuation of the rich seams of German Lorraine, have been discovered in French Lorraine. Their concession is being deferred owing precisely to the desire of the government to apply a new legislation to them. New and large iron mines are also being worked in Normandy.

[3] For fuller information, see M. Brunhes' book, *L'Irrigation dans la Pénin-sule Ibérique et l'Afrique du Nord*, and the description given by Fromentin which we described p. 72, note.

In the case of navigable rivers, which are, as we have said, public property, it is the State which disposes of the motive force and concedes it to whomsoever it thinks fit.[1] But watercourses which are not navigable belong to the owners of the banks, and of the bed. These, it is true, do not exactly own the running water ; but, as it is impossible to capture or dam the water of a river without making use of the banks and the bed—consequently without the permission of their owners—it amounts to very much the same. And if, as often happens, the banks belong to different owners, these have to come to an understanding before the water can be used for motive force, or sold for such to a third person. The permission of the owner, moreover, is necessary not merely for damming and capturing the water, but for the laying of pipes and conduits, which must pass somewhere. And, as it is in these very streams, appropriated by private owners, that the best motive force for industry, namely, waterfalls, is to be found—navigable rivers having hardly any fall—what happens ?

More often than not the landowner has neither the inclination nor the means to carry out the works necessary for utilising the water, and confines himself either to hindering every one else from doing so—thus obstructing the employment of a natural wealth— or to demanding an excessive price for the permission, or for the cession of his strip of property—thereby heavily burdening industry. The situation is aggravated by the action of speculators, who buy up the best-situated waterfalls, and force manufacturers in search of motive force to pay a high price for it. Already the greater part of the *white coal* of France has been bought up in this way.

To solve this problem is one of the main concerns of the jurists of to-day. The simplest method perhaps would be to follow out the analogy between black and white coal, making the latter into a property conceded by the State in perpetuity. But the objections which we gave to the granting of an absolute right in the case of black coal, have much more force here. If concession, in the case of black coal, is limited by the lifetime of the mine, in the case of the waterfall it would be really everlasting. To concede the Niagara Falls to private enterprise for so long as the Niagara flows, would be truly absurd. The concession must therefore be made for a fixed term—a term long enough to give industry all the security it requires —the State reserving, if need be, the right of prior redemption.[2]

---

[1] Up till now, however, concession has always been on precarious tenure, so that this system is not very well adapted to the requirements of industry.

[2] This is the measure which passed its first reading in the Chamber and which

It is quite certain that the law of the future will attempt to make the concession of water power more lucrative for the State than has been the concession of the mines, either by putting it up to auction, or by giving the State or the commune the option of keeping it and exploiting it directly *en régie*, as is done in several of the Swiss cantons.

But such a law is as yet far off, and will probably come too late to save this natural wealth from private appropriation. The only course then open will be that of costly expropriation.

CHAPTER II : THE CAPITALIST *RENTIER*

I : THE SITUATION OF THE *RENTIER*

FROM the beginning of time, man, who has been well defined as a lazy animal, though he is no more lazy than other animals,[1] has shown a wonderful ingenuity in evading the law of labour ; slavery, parasitism, begging, theft, gambling, have no other origin.   But the best way of escaping labour, a way at once the most honourable and most secure, is to have an independent income.

Although the man of independent means does not work, he does not live the less well for that.   It is in his class that the largest incomes are found—larger and more regular than those from labour. Whether it snows or whether it blows, well or ill, young or old, at home or abroad, the income of the *rentier* never fails to find him. An " independent income," then, procures its owner two blessings, greater than all the enjoyments which other forms of fortune may bestow : security and independence. • This surely is a privileged situation, and we may well ask these happy mortals what god has vouchsafed them their leisure.   *Deus vobis haec otia fecit ?*

has since lain on a shelf :—concession by the State for a term of not more than fifty years ; limitation of the tariff in the case of public services (lighting, tramway, etc.) ; part of the force to be reserved for certain public services.

But over against this more or less socialistic measure, there is another, individualistic and conservative in nature, which would sanction and regularise the right of ownership of riverside proprietors, while at the same time preventing the ill-will of any one of them from obstructing the utilising of the force.

In Italy the system is that of concession for thirty years and payment to the State of 3 francs per h.-p. (about to be raised to 6 francs).

[1] The African negroes say that the monkey could speak quite well, but will not for fear of being made to work.

" Work," they answer, " nothing more nor less. We are living *on the product of past labour.*"

How much is this answer worth ? When this past labour is their *own*, when the man of means is a State official in receipt of his pension, or some one who has saved up for his old age, no objection can be raised. Men cannot be condemned to forced labour for life : when a man has worked during the productive period of his life, it is only just that he should be able to rest during the unproductive period. Even socialists like Bellamy [1] declare that, in the collectivist society of the future, man will be free at the age of forty-five from all services towards society, and from that age on will do what he likes, and live like an independent gentleman.

When, however, this past labour is the labour of *others*, of fathers, grandfathers, great-grandfathers, or even strangers who have created the fortune and left it to its subsequent possessor along with the right to consume it in idleness, the question is more embarrassing.

" Why ? " it may be asked. " We have already compared coins to consumption orders, giving the right to consume wealth up to the amount of their value (p. 239). Suppose, then, that a man by his labour has earned a large number of these orders, if, now or subsequently, he does not want to use them himself, surely he has the right to hand them over to some one to use in his stead ? "

From the economic point of view, perhaps so ; [2] but from the moral point of view we may be more exacting. Is the idle man of means quits with society by the simple fact that he has paid with a money which, on the most favourable hypothesis is no more than past labour, the labour of the dead ? Ought he not to pay in present and personal services the equivalent of the income which he is receiving ? For observe that the man of means is not living on past labour, as he thinks, but on *present labour*. What he is consuming daily are the products of living, not dead, labour—fresh bread, early fruit and vegetables, new clothes, the morning paper, etc. Now, justice demands that, in exchange for what his fellow men are doing for him, he should do something in return for them. A Classical economist has said that the man of means is a " wage-

---

[1] In his novel, *Looking Backward.*

[2] In reality, the man of independent means is much more favourably situated than if he were living on consumption " orders " destroyed by the very act of consumption ; for he lives on income obtained by lending these consumption orders, and this income is renewed indefinitely. (See *infra, Interest,* for explanation of this.)

earner who has been paid in advance." If he has been paid in advance, a certain amount of labour is due on his part. He ought, as the expression goes, "to make himself useful." If he is of no use, in vain will the economists demonstrate that he has paid in good money the full equivalent of what he has consumed. The fate of the parasite will be his, and he will be eliminated.

We must not, of course, confuse *idleness* with *leisure*. . The first is an evil which should be done away with; the second a blessing which all men should have.

Idleness is a state of revolt against the law of labour.

Leisure consists in respites from work in the course of an industrious and active life. It is not only useful, as recreation, making a man work better; it is indispensable for the development of his outer and inner life; for meditation, which ought not to be reserved for the wise alone; and for the accomplishing of many other duties besides that of earning a livelihood—family duties, social duties, good works, co-operation, public worship, political meetings, etc. etc.

It is not always easy to determine where idleness begins and leisure ends. The man who lives by begging, or by gambling, is easy to class; not so the man of independent means, the *rentier*,[1] of whom we spoke. Is he an idle man or simply a man of leisure?

We must admit that, from the historical point of view, the man of means has performed in the past a genuine social function of first importance—the creation, namely, of the arts, letters, sciences, politics, the higher culture—in a word, civilisation. All these blessings—in which the poor too have their share—we owe to the idle men of wealth of Greece, Rome, and Judea; of all the ancient societies, in fact, in which idleness appears in a particularly odious light, resting as it did solely on force, robbery, and slavery. But must it always be so? In order to direct rightly the great social interests, to unravel the subtle threads of politics and diplomacy, to wield the sceptre of good judgment with dignity in the kingdom of letters and the arts, will it always be necessary to have white hands unhardened by toil, minds free from the burden of tasks to fulfil or daily bread to earn? Perhaps not. These high functions would not be incompatible with even manual labour, were there only enough leisure for all workers.

---

[1] *Rentier* = holder of *rentes*—*i.e.* fundholder, stockholder, person of independent means. [TRANSLATOR.]

II : HISTORICAL SKETCH OF THE LOAN AT INTEREST—USURY

THROUGHOUT antiquity the loan at interest was practised, often under extremely hard conditions. But all the great men of ancient times, Moses, Aristotle, even the stern Cato himself, stigmatised it, and almost all religions have condemned it. After the advent of Christianity the attacks against it were redoubled in force in the writings of the Church Fathers ; and no sooner was the power of the Church solidly established than it was prohibited in civil as well as in canon law.[1] The law of Mahomet took the same attitude. " God has allowed sale, but forbidden usury," says the Koran. The true Mussulman will not touch interest on the money he has lent, not even at the Christian banker's, where he may have deposited it.[2]

Although this attitude has been treated subsequently with profound contempt, and considered as betraying an ignorance of all economic laws, it may, as a matter of history, be quite easily explained.

We have already pointed out (see p. 386, *Credit*) that, until a relatively recent date, credit, in the form of a loan of money, could not have a productive character. It could, and as a matter of fact did, serve only for consumption. When, therefore, the ancient economists declared the loan barren, they were not so far wrong as is sometimes imagined, and showed, on the contrary, that they had a very accurate notion of the economic state of their time.

In Rome, it was the poor plebeians who borrowed from the patri-

---

[1] " For money was intended to be used in exchange, but not to increase at interest. And this term (τόκος), which means the birth of money from money, is applied to the breeding of money, because the offspring resembles the parent. Wherefore of all modes of making money this is the most unnatural." Aristotle, *Politics*, i. 10.

" Quid foenerari ? quid hominem occidere ? " ("What is the loan at interest ? What is to assassinate ? ") Cato (quoted by Cicero).

" Thou shalt not lend upon usury to thy brother." Deut. xxiii, 19.

And the words of Christ, " and lend, hoping for nothing again," are well known. St. Luke vi, 35.

But it was not till the Council of Vienna, 1311, that the loan at interest among Christians was formally prohibited.

Jews, on the contrary, were allowed to lend to Christians, since it was felt that moneylenders could not be dispensed with, and that the Jews were rendering the Christians a very great service by taking this sin on their shoulders.

[2] See a curious book by M. Benali Fekar, *L'usure en droit musulman.*

The bankers at Cairo know well how to take advantage of this form of Mussulman piety.

cians in order to buy bread ; in the Middle Ages, it was impecunious knights who borrowed from the Jews and the Lombards to equip themselves for the Crusades—all for personal, and consequently unproductive, consumption. Naturally, when the term of the loan had expired, they could pay neither the interest nor the capital, and had to pay with their bodies, or with their labour, as slaves of their creditors.[1] Under such conditions, the loan at interest appeared in the lender as an abuse of the right of property, and, from the borrower's side, as an instrument of exploitation and ruin. This was quite enough to explain the ancient and stubborn reprobation of it.

At that time the very name of capital was hardly known ; land was practically the only wealth which brought in a return. The justice of farm rent was not disputed, since it was evident that the rent paid to the landowner did not come out of the farmer's pocket. It could be seen actually coming out of the land in the form of harvests. But such was not the case with money ; and Aristotle's observation that money does not breed[2] seemed perfectly true.

Nevertheless, then, just as in our own day, there were many persons in need of money, and no one was disposed to lend it for nothing. It was necessary therefore to compromise with principle, and the numerous and subtle expedients which the casuistry of the Middle Ages devised, form one of the most interesting chapters in the history of doctrines.[3] For instance :

(1) Whenever it was certain that the borrower could make a profit, e.g. by carrying on trade, and that the lender ran a certain risk, interest became legitimate, for it was no longer usurious.[4]

(2) Whenever the lender transferred absolutely to the borrower the capital of the sum lent, i.e. renounced repayment for ever, there

---

[1] The houses of the Roman patricians had cellars which were used as prisons (ergastula) for insolvent debtors. In the Middle Ages, in spite of Shakespeare's Shylock, manners and customs had become less rough. A powerful but insolvent debtor had only to send hostages to his creditors and pay for their food, which was still nevertheless a costly obligation. Does not this feature of history justify the canonists' saying, jus usurae, jus belli ?

[2] There is less excuse, however, for such an observation from Aristotle's pen, since the Greeks of his day knew well how to make a profit on capital employed in commerce.

[3] See a very good chapter on this in Ashley's Economic History of England.

[4] The Lateran Council of 1515 defined the situation quite clearly : " There is usury wherever there is gain which does not arise from a fruit-yielding thing and which implies neither labour nor expenditure nor risk on the part of the lender."

was no doubt about the legitimacy of interest, since the lender could not be expected to give up both the capital and the income. This was the loan in the form of perpetual annuity.

(3) If interest was stipulated for, as a penal clause, in the event of the capital not being repaid at the date fixed, it was considered just. And, as there was nothing to hinder the date fixed from being *the day after the loan was made*, we can see how easily the prohibition could be eluded.

The Reformation naturally caused a reaction against the canonist doctrine. Calvin was disposed to tolerate the loan at interest under certain conditions, and in the eighteenth century we find two great French Huguenot jurisconsults, Dumoulin and Saumaise, refuting the scholastic arguments against usury. Curiously enough, the Jesuits contributed quite as much as the Reformers to bring about the acceptance, in practice, of the loan at interest.[1] But it is not until we come to the economists, Turgot (*Mémoire sur les prêts d'argent*, 1769) and Bentham (*Defence of Usury*, 1787), that we find economic doctrine declaring itself positively in favour of the loan at interest. And from this time on economists have been unanimous in accepting it. And they are right. Why ? Because economic conditions have changed.

On the one hand, the rôles of lender and borrower are now reversed. It is no longer the needy who borrow from the rich ; the plebeians who borrow from the patricians. It is the rich and powerful —speculators, large companies, bankers, owners of gold mines, and particularly States—who borrow from the public, from men of small means, from the savings of the populace, from the peasant's stocking. The result is that it is not the weak and defenceless borrower whom public opinion and the law have to defend against the rapacity of the lender, but the ignorant lender who must be protected against the exploitation of the great borrowers of whom the financial history of to-day offers so many scandalous examples.[2]

On the other hand—and these two changes were concomitant—

---

[1] The *contractus trinus*, for instance, a three-sided contract by which the lender was supposed to share in the profits and risks of the enterprise, but at the same time insured himself against risk, and renounced profits in exchange for a fixed sum payable annually.

. [2] " Every one is aware of the brigandage that is carried on under cover of founding shareholding companies. Nothing is more brazen and more criminal. It is one of the saddest symptoms of public demoralisation. . . . . What the great bands of adventurers and brigands were, who fleeced merchants or pillaged the country in the remotest times of the Middle Ages, the shareholding companies are to-day ; only with greater security, impunity, leisure, and profit." This

the object itself of the loan contract has changed. Nowadays men borrow, not to obtain food, but to make fortunes. The loan, though still called by the jurists the *prêt de consommation* (loan for consumption), has assumed its true economic character of a mode of production. It is the *entrepreneur*, that is to say, the real agent of production (see p. 128), who borrows capital and pays interest, and this interest figures among the costs of production with as much right as do the wages of labour and the rent of the factory. To let the *entrepreneur* off paying interest, on humanitarian grounds, would therefore be absurd, since it would have no other result than to' increase his profits.

This change has not, of course, taken place everywhere. In the agricultural regions of the East—Russia, the Danube, Italy, and Algeria—credit has preserved its ancient forms, and it is often the borrower, the peasant, who is exploited and, finally, expropriated by the lender. This is at the root of the anti-Semitic movement, and it is for this reason that the old laws against usury may still be quite in keeping in some countries and under certain conditions.[1]

III : THE LEGITIMACY AND THE REGULATION OF INTEREST

THE question whether or not interest is legitimate is the oldest in Political Economy : we have just traced its principal phases. To-day this question has lost much of its former importance. To those, indeed, who see, in interest, simply a consequence of the right of ownership, the ground is cleared of all the old obsolete arguments. But to us it is of some concern to know what these scholastic arguments were.

(*1*) It was said that a distinction should be drawn according to

estimate appears somewhat exaggerated, especially from the pen of M. Leroy-Beaulieu (*Économiste français*, July 21, 1881). We quote it simply to show how entirely reversed to-day are the situations of lender and borrower.

[1] But even in those countries, associations of agricultural credit are beginning to bring about a change in the respective situations of creditor and debtor (see above, *Agricultural Credit*, p. 398).

In industrious countries, the loan for consumption, *i.e.* the borrowing of money in order to spend it, is only practised by rich prodigals, or by the customers of pawnshops. A great and deplorable exception must be made, however, in respect of the modern States which, within a century, have squandered in consumption, for the most part unproductive and even destructive, £6,000,000,000 of capital on which the unfortunate taxpayers will have to pay interest in perpetuity—or at least until the day of final bankruptcy. But this last class of borrower is too powerful to inspire pity, or to have need of protective laws.

whether or not the borrower had made a *productive use* of the capital borrowed.

But does this matter ? Even if the borrowed capital has not been, and cannot from the nature of the case be, put to a productive use—in other words, even where the money borrowed is not capital but a simple consumption-object—why should the owner of this wealth be obliged to lend it for nothing ? The precept *Lend, hoping for nothing again*, belongs to the evangelical, not to the economic, order. From the economic and juridical point of view, the simple principle that no one can be despoiled of his belongings, and that whoever consents to part with them to others has the right to do so on his own conditions, is clear enough to justify interest.

(2) It was said that a distinction should be drawn according to whether the lender had, or had not, *undergone a genuine privation*. But what difference can this make ? Since when has the remuneration I claim, whether in profit or wages, been according to the privations I undergo ? In virtue of what principle should I be constrained to put the goods which I cannot, or do not, care to use myself at the disposal of others for nothing ? Am I to let people settle in my flat because I am forced to be absent from it, or eat from my plate because I am not hungry ? This argument could be maintained only by starting from the premises that a man, in this world, has the *right only to the quantity of wealth strictly necessary for his consumption*, and that the surplus belongs by right to the mass—that is to say, by taking a frankly communist stand.

The logic on which the legitimacy of interest is based to-day is of the simplest, and may be put thus : '

Capital is very useful, whether for producing or not ; consequently every one wants it.

But all existing capital is in private hands, and up till now, at any rate, there has been none over. Those, therefore, who possess it and are willing to part with it for a time will only do so for a price—the highest price that the competition of other capitalist lenders will allow them to obtain.

Only, this reasoning takes for granted that the *private owning of capital is legitimate*. And our point is, do we admit this or not ? The ancient question then of the right to interest has changed its ground and has now become the question of the right to capital. Thus we find economists of the Classical school arguing that the ownership of capital is the result, first, of labour, like any other wealth ; secondly, of the saving or abstinence indispensable to transform products into capital, so that this ownership is, as it were, twice sacred.

On the other hand, the right to own capital has been severely attacked by socialists, and Karl Marx, in his *Capital*,[1] tries to show that the private ownership of capital is simply the result of spoliation in earlier times, and that it is the best way of continuing and aggravating this spoliation. Collectivists allow that the private ownership of capital may be legitimate when it appears in the modest form in which the Classical economists are pleased to consider it—Crusoe's hollowed canoe, the carpenter's plane, the crowns put away in an old stocking, or deposited in the savings bank by the peasant. But, they say, these are not true capital, not the capital which gives wealth and power. This last is never the product of the owner's personal labour. It consists, on the contrary, in the *savings made out of the product of the labour of others*, *i.e.* of hired wage-earners, and can only be increased by employing more workers in order to obtain more profits. No great fortune can be made in any other way.

Such reasoning would lead us to the conclusion that there are two classes of capital: small capital, the private ownership of which would be legitimate, since it is the fruit of individual and honest labour; large capital, vampire capital, the private ownership of which would be illegitimate, because it implies the appropriation of the result of the labour of others. Now, as large capital must obviously have begun by being small, it follows that the private ownership of capital is legitimate at the outset, and up to a certain point, while beyond that it becomes an abuse. It is with capital as with certain animals, which are good so long as they are little, and bad when they grow big. What determines this critical point ? It is the point at which capital, having become too large to serve as a mere instrument of labour to its master, is employed by him to make other men work—a sufficient number of men to enable him and his heirs to live independently for ever. Here we meet again the collectivist doctrine which we have already discussed (p. 483) and to which we refer the reader.

We would simply point out that we do not believe that capital, even when large, is necessarily and by nature an instrument of exploitation, nor that it can grow only by sucking the blood of

---

[1] And Rodbertus before him. The latter, neglected for a long time, has come into considerable favour within the last few years, as forerunner of the great collectivist doctrines. His book, also called *Capital*, dates from 1852, while that of Marx dates from 1867.

the working man. Vampire capital is not the normal form, but, on the contrary, a monstrous perversion of true capital, whose veritable rôle is to be the instrument and servant of labour. Of capital, as of money, it may be said, that it is a bad master, but a good servant. All that needs to be done is to put it back in its right place.

We would also call to mind what we have said before, that the private ownership of capital appears quite consistent with social utility. As a stock of accumulated wealth is absolutely indispensable to the development of production, we must consider the function of those who accumulate this wealth in order to offer it on the market—the manufacturers of capital—a very important one. And, certainly, the best method of encouraging these social economisers would appear to be to give them the ownership of the wealth which they have capitalised and the right to make a profit from it.[1] No doubt abuses will result—among others the possibility for the capitalist to be able to live without working. But it is a good thing for society that a certain number of its members should have leisure, not for idleness, but for *disinterested* occupations. This is one of the beneficent forms of the division of labour.

We have, however, the right to ask ourselves whether these " economisers " are not charging too high a price for the function they perform, and whether their services could not be obtained for less.

The Classical economists assure us that natural laws will see to it that the share of the capitalists is reduced to a minimum, through the inevitable fall in the rate of interest. But this is not altogether certain, as we shall see presently. Proudhon maintained that the organising of gratuitous credit would be enough of itself to rid us altogether of the necessity for paying capitalists.[2]

---

[1] We do not, however, go the length of saying, like many economists, that if interest were done away with, no more capital would be formed. We believe, on the contrary, that even more would be created ; only, the producers of capital would keep it in order to turn it to account themselves, or to hoard it up, and would not put it on the market. In the same way, if laws were passed prohibiting the leasing of houses, we should not, in all likelihood, build less, but most certainly there would be no more houses to let. Each person would build his own.

Fourier made the ingenious suggestion that the smaller the capital saved and invested, the higher the rate of interest on it should be, thus putting a premium on the most difficult saving—that of capital in its early stage. This idea was even carried out in some savings banks of a philanthropic character.

[2] Proudhon, in his famous discussion with Bastiat on credit, did not dispute the legitimacy of interest in the present economic organisation, and showed, not unreasonably, some impatience with Bastiat for insisting on proving to him a truth which he held self-evident. His aim was to organise a society in which, by a special institution called the *Banque d'Échange*, capital in the form of

The co-operative associations of credit, without going so far as this, aim, as we have seen (p. 398), at reducing the share of capital to a minimum, and capital itself to a subordinate rôle in production.

Lastly, the legislator in many countries intervenes to limit the share of capital. For it must not be thought that, during the century and a half that Political Economy has been proclaiming the right to interest as the natural attribute to the right to property, all the ancient laws prohibiting interest have been done away with. This is not the case.

(1) French law fixes a maximum rate of 5 per cent. for all loans which have not a commercial character, e.g. for mortgage loans, or loans for consumption. There is a trace here of the distinction drawn by the canonists. The law admits unlimited interest only when the loan is presumed to be really productive and at the same time risky, as when the money is sunk in industrial or commercial enterprises.[1]

(2) Not only has the creditor no right to claim more than 5 per cent., but the act of lending *habitually* above this rate, in civil loans, constitutes the offence of usury, and is punishable by imprisonment (law of December 19, 1850).

The Classical economists protest vigorously against the first of these laws. It is certain that the fixing of a maximum for the rent of money is quite an exceptional measure, since there is no limit for the rent either of houses, or of land. And, in our opinion, it might safely be dispensed with, provided that the second rule were left in force, *i.e.* the offence of usury. It is no more of a contradiction to allow liberty as regards the rate of interest, while punishing those who make a profession of lending at a high rate, than it is to allow consumers the liberty to drink, while punishing publicans who supply drunken men.

commercial paper could be put gratis at the disposal of all who needed it, which would of course bring down the rate of interest to zero.

[1] It is only since January 12, 1886, that this difference has been introduced between the commercial loan and the civil loan. During the whole of the nineteenth century, after the law of 1807, the legal limitation of interest and the offence of usury applied as much to commercial, as to civil, loans, with the sole difference that the limit was raised to 6 per cent. in the case of commercial loans. In Algeria the legal limit is 8 per cent. both for commercial and for civil loans.

There is also a *legal* rate, which must not be confused with the *conventional* rate, of which we have been speaking : it is that which concerns sums due, not for loans, but by virtue of decisions of the Law Courts. It was fixed by a law of April 7, 1900, at 4 per cent. for civil loans, and 5 per cent. for commercial loans.

IV : WHY CAPITAL PRODUCES INTEREST

THIS is not quite the same question as that of the last chapter. We are no longer asking whether the man who lends capital has the right to take interest for it—a matter which belongs entirely to the domain of law and ethics : we are asking *how* capital yields interest— a purely economic matter. The question to whom the apples of a tree should belong is one thing ; the question why an apple tree produces apples quite another. We can easily understand why the fortunate owner of capital does not lend it for nothing : what is not so easy to understand is how the borrower is able to pay indefinitely for it. Does this interest which he pays come out of his pocket, or does it correspond to some equivalent value received by him ? The first explanation must be rejected, although socialists declare it to be the only true one, since it would imply that all borrowers are of necessity ruined, which is not the case. The second must therefore be true. We must believe that, in general, the borrower receives something. What, then, is this value handed over to the borrower and represented by interest ? Whence does it come ? The question is by no means easy to answer, and various solutions have been proposed. We give the three principal ones :

(*1*) The first, called the *productivity theory*, explains the interest on capital by assimilating it to the rent of land. Interest is the *product of capital*. Why is land always able to be let for a rent ? Because it produces fruits, and the rent is the representation, as it were, of these fruits. So with interest. It is not, of course, claimed that capital has offspring, save in its original sense of cattle (*cheptel* = capital, meaning etymologically *lent cattle*). But capital is shown to produce by means of labour. As Bastiat said, in a famous apologue, a plane enables a worker to make twice, or even ten times, as many planks as he could make with his hand alone. These additional planks, then, due to the use of the plane, are what constitute the income from the plane. And if the owner of the plane, instead of using it himself, lends it to others, it is only natural that he should ask, as a kind of dividend. some of the additional planks thus produced. This is how the original income from capital becomes *contractual* interest.

But this explanation is not sufficient. In the first place, it holds good only for capital which has actually been put to a productive use. In the case of capital borrowed simply to be consumed, it is worthless, since in this case it obviously points to the non-existence, and therefore to the illegitimacy, of interest.

Even where capital is productively employed, as in our instance of the plane, it is not a very scientific explanation. For, although it is evident that the employment of capital enables labour to produce more in quantity and in utility, it is by no means certain that it allows it to produce more in *value*. To create abundance is not to create value (p. 47). Technical productiveness must not be confused with economic productiveness. Do machines, for instance, confer a higher value on the objects they have produced than does hand labour to the similar objects made by hand ? Under a monopoly, yes ; but not where there is competition. In this case the products, brought down to the cost of production, acquire no additional value through being made by machinery, or at least no additional value other than that represented by the value of the machine itself. We can understand that the price of the planks must cover the sinking fund necessary to replace the plane, but we cannot understand by virtue of what natural law it should cover an additional value called the *income* from the plane.

(2) The second theory explains the interest on capital by assimilating it to house rent. Interest is the *rent paid for capital.* Why does a house bring in a rent ? Obviously it does not yield fruit like land ; it provides, however, a number of utilities—shelter, home comforts, legal domicile, etc.—all of which are perpetual, or at any rate as long-lived as the house. Rent is the price paid for these enjoyments, the price of the services rendered by the house, and ought to last as long as they do. The rent, it is true, comes out of the tenant's pocket ; but it is given in exchange for equal value, like the price paid in return for food and drink. Capital is in exactly the same position. Capital renders more services than a house, since it allows a man to buy a house wherever he chooses ; and, as it may be used for an unlimited length of time, it should be paid for by a periodical rent, namely, interest. Interest is a phenomenon that springs not from production, but from exchange, as the etymology of the word indicates, *usura* meaning originally the *using* of capital without the unfavourable significance which it later acquired.

This explanation also is open to objection. As the capital the is the object of a loan is nearly always circulating capital—as a rule money—it is not a lasting possession like a house, but is destroyed in the very act of production. Coal thrown into the furnace disappears in smoke ; raw material is transformed ; money is spent in wages. How, then, can interest pay for the use of a thing the characteristic of which is that it is consumed at its first use ?

The jurisconsults bring out this opposition very strongly when they declare that, in a lease, the person who lets remains proprietor of the thing leased, while, in a loan—*prêt de consommation* as French law puts it, even when the object of the loan is production—the lender parts definitively with his money, and the borrower becomes absolute owner of it. Now, to admit that the borrower can be at the same time the owner and the lessee of a thing, is a contradiction.

These are all, however, objections of legal theory and of a purely scholastic order. From the economic standpoint it is easy to reply that the capital lent is neither the coal nor the money, but the *value*. Now, that is permanent, preserving its identity much better than a house, which sooner or later falls into ruins. Capital value, like the Proteus of mythology, remains eternal through all its metamorphoses. The borrower may become owner of the money and keep it as long as he likes ; but he has not become owner of its value, since he must give it back in the form of other money. The idea of a lease appears, therefore, to us the best simile for the loan of money, and the best explanation of interest.

There is, however, a third explanation which is more in fashion to-day, which refuses to assimilate interest with agricultural rent, or house rent. The lending of money is not a letting of it, they say ; it is, as we ourselves defined it (p. 384), the exchange of a present good (the value lent) for a future good (the value to be repaid). This exchange must, like every exchange, be made value for value. Now, if I give you 1000 francs cash in exchange for 1000 francs to be received a year hence, the exchange would not be equal, for the reason that *a future good is never worth so much as a present one*. Is not a dinner ready to be consumed at once of much more value than an invitation to dinner next year ? If any would deny this psychological truth, then we might as well say that a dinner a hundred or a thousand years hence is worth as much as a dinner to-night ! [1]

If we admit, then, this inequality in value which time creates between identical goods, it follows that, in order to restore equilibrium in exchanging a present for a future value, we must add to the latter a premium called interest. Interest is *the price of time*. Or, again, in exchanging a future for a present value (*e.g.* if we give a bill of exchange of three months' date for cash), we must deduct from

[1] This law appears to be simply a translation into scientific language of such popular sayings as, "A bird in the hand is worth two in the bush," etc. These, however, merely signify that all future satisfaction is uncertain, whereas the theory given above has a deeper meaning, namely, that future satisfaction even if certain, is *not worth* present satisfaction.

the sum to be received a fraction called *discount*. Here, perhaps, the price of time appears even more clearly than in the case of interest.

The explanation is the same when capital is not lent, but turned to account by its owner. If, as the owner of 1000 francs of capital, I prefer to put this into land as seed, or into a boiler as coal, or to give it out to workmen in the form of subsistence or wages, I am sacrificing in each case a present good for a future good in the form of harvests, or manufactured articles. It is always an exchange of the present for the future. Now, this would never occur if the future were not worth more than the present—if, at the end of the year, I did not expect to recover the 1000 francs *plus something*. This is what the capitalist unconsciously means when he says that his capital should bring him in interest. Every loan is an *advance*, as the expression goes ; and what does advance mean, if not a gaining of time ?

This is not an entirely new explanation ; the germ of it is to be found in Turgot.[1]   But it was the Austrian economist Böhm-Bawerk who gave it its fame.[2]

Like the others, this theory is not above criticism. If the superiority of a present good over a future good is self-evident whenever we are concerned with a *present* want, it is not so when we consider a *future* want.   In this case the situation may be reversed. A sack of wheat for sowing is worth much more to me when harvest-time comes, nine months hence, than now, in the month of January. And this is the situation of the lender of money.   For does not his very readiness to lend his money, show that he does not know what to do with it at the moment ; that he wants to save himself the trouble of keeping it and the fear of losing it ; that he thinks that it will be of much more use to him when the time comes for it to be repaid ?

Is not our general preference for cash simply due to the fact that we know we have always the power to invest it at interest, so that we are really reasoning in a circle ? [3]

---

[1] Even the canonists were acquainted with the argument that *interest is the price of time*.   But they refuted it nobly, saying that time could not be sold and had no price, since it belonged to God.   To-day, on the contrary, *Time is money*. Mr. Irving Fisher puts it picturesquely when he says, that the rate of interest is the *measure of impatience*.   (See his book, *The Rate of Interest*.)

[2] See M. Böhm-Bawerk's important works, *Capital and Interest* and the *Positive Theory of Capital*, translated into English by Smart ; also M. Landry, *L'intérêt du capital*.

[3] On the other hand, if it is evident that a present good is worth more than a future good, is it not also evident that *a present good is worth more than a past*

V : THE RATE OF INTEREST[1]

WE have seen that the rate of interest was for a long time limited by law, and that it still is, in France, for non-commercial loans. But the limit laid down by the legislator can sanction only what is practically the current rate ; otherwise it would be vain. What we want to know, then, are the economic and natural laws which determine the rate of interest, like the rate of wages and the prices of commodities.

If capital were lent in kind, in the form of mills, machinery, implements of production, etc. there would be a *different price for the hire of each kind* according to its quality, duration, and pro ductivity, just as the rent of houses varies with their comfort and situation, or that of lands with their fertility.

But capital is always lent in the form of money : first, because the borrower prefers to receive money, having thus more freedom to turn the loan to the uses for which he wants it ; and, secondly, because it is only in that form that capital is offered on the market by those who want to invest their savings. *Money capital*, indeed, is the only form of capital which can be created by saving.

Now, this substitution, which changes *letting* into a *loan of money*, produces some remarkable effects :

On the one hand, it tends to eliminate all causes of variation and to *equalise* the price of the hiring-out of all capital. For, as all capital is lent and borrowed in the same form, namely money, there is no difference in quality between the loans ; there is only a difference in quantity. And, as capital in this form is essentially mobile, flying instantaneously wherever a higher rate attracts it, the differences, if there are any, are rapidly levelled. Hence it is that on the national, and even the international, market there is only one single rate of interest at a given moment.

But, on the other hand, in fixing the price of the hiring-out of money, a cause of differentiation is called into play which is of

good ? If then, in giving you a dinner to-day instead of an invitation to dinner a year hence, I have the right to demand a premium, will not you, in giving me a dinner a year hence in return for a dinner already old and forgotten, have the right to think that you would be quits by giving me a poorer dinner ? This is certainly the feeling of all those who repay debts.

[1] The *rate* of interest is the relation between the figure for income and that for capital.

To express it more conveniently, capital is represented by the conventional figure of 100 and the rate of interest is then expressed in a percentage, 3, 4, 5 per cent.

enormous importance, namely, the *solvency* of the borrower.   For the borrower, as we have seen, is no longer a lessee : he acquires the absolute ownership of the money, and may use it as he thinks fit.   If, then, his solvency is doubtful, there will be a certain risk for the lender which will determine him to ask a higher rate of interest as *compensation in the event of the loss* of his capital.   It is an insurance premium, which the lender makes the borrower pay.

Interest must therefore be broken up into two parts :

(*1*) *Interest properly so-called*, which represents the price paid for the right to dispose of the capital, and which is the same for all loans on one and the same market and on the same date.

(*2*) An *insurance premium* against the risk of loss, which varies with each loan.[1]   This it is which almost solely determines the differences between the rates of interest in all Stock Exchange investments and securities.[2]

What, then, are the causes which determine the current rate of interest, in other words the price of the hire of money capital ?

We need no more hope to be able to find one single cause for the rate of interest than we were able to find one single cause for the value of commodities, or for the price of manual labour.   There are a great number of causes, all of which may, however, be grouped under the well-known formula, supply and demand.

The supply of capital in the form of money or securities depends, in the first instance, on the *saving power* of the nation, promoted by good institutions for saving, and by credit which opens outlets to it.   But it is not enough for capital to be plentiful in a nation ; it must be abundant on the market and offered for loan ; and this

---

[1] There is a third element, the sinking fund (*prime d'amortissement*) representing the annual payment which must be put aside to replace the worn-out capital if the capital be in kind, or to reconstitute the sum of money if the capital be in money.   But this is not interest.   It is a fraction of the new capital which is being built up to replace the capital consumed.

[2] The fact that capital is always offered in the form of money ought to have a third consequence, namely, that the rate of interest, the price of the hire of capital, should depend on the quantity of coin.   This is what the ordinary public believes when it says that when *money is plentiful, interest is low*.   And it is true in the case of short-term loans in the form of discount.   For we have seen that there is a necessary connection between the scarcity of money and the rise in the rate of discount (p. 446).   But it is not true in the case of long-term loans in the form of investments, the only ones which concern us here, since we are speaking of income.   For we have only to observe that income, just as much as capital, is in the form of money, and that the rate of interest, *i.e. the relation between the capital and the income*, cannot be affected by a cause which, like variations in the value of money, act equally and simultaneously on both terms of the relation.

implies the existence of a large class of persons *unable or unwilling to turn their capital to account by their own personal industry.* For it is clear that, in a country where each personally turns his own capital to account, there will be none to offer on the market, however abundant it may be. Lastly, the supply of capital depends on the *security* of the loan, without which capital, as in Persia, or Morocco, will be unproductively hoarded.

The demand for capital is determined by its *productiveness* ;[1] not so much the *average* productiveness of enterprises in a given country at a given moment, as the productiveness of the least productive enterprises among those for which capital is offered. For these, precisely because they cannot yield more, are the enterprises which determine the law of the market for capital. If they can give no more than 3 per cent. of interest, the other more remunerative enterprises will take good care not to.[2]

In a new country full of resources, with virgin soil to be cleared, mines to be opened up, means of communication to be established, the rate of interest will be very high : first, because capital there will be scarce, and those who have it will keep it to turn to account themselves and will not offer it on the market ; secondly, because enterprises which bring only small profits will be despised.

In an old country, on the contrary, the opposite causes will be at work. On the one hand, there will be no lack of capital, accumulated by centuries of saving ; on the other hand, the highly productive openings will be already occupied, and capital will be forced to look for less productive enterprises—all of which will weigh down the general rate of interest.

The loan at interest, like wages and farm rent, is a fixed contract ; that is to say, the lender gives up all right to a share in the profits, in return for a fixed annuity. Still, we have seen (p. 185) that,

---

[1] Not in the case of a consumption-loan, however. But it does not follow that the rate of interest is the less for that. On the contrary, in these loans the rate is limited only by the wants and the means of the borrower. It may therefore quite well become exorbitant. This is indeed the very category of loan that the usurer prefers.

[2] We may reach a more scientific explanation of the laws of interest, if we apply to the exchange value of capital the same reasoning that we applied to the exchange value of commodities (pp. 221-225). The rate of interest on one and the same market must satisfy the following conditions :

(1) It must be the same on all capital where there is equal risk ;

(2) It must be such as to make *the sums of capital offered and those demanded coincide ;*

(3) It must give satisfaction to the greatest possible numbers of lenders and borrowers.

for lenders who prefer the risk of profits and losses to the security of a fixed income, modern credit has created another combination. Instead of guaranteeing them a fixed income, the borrower promises them a share in the profits, if there are any, losses to fall in the first instance on the capital contributed by the shareholders. But this is no longer a loan contract legally speaking. It is a contract of *association.* The claim of these lenders, instead of being called an *obligation,* is called a *share,* and their income, instead of being called *interest,* is called a *dividend.* Naturally, the rate of the dividend is higher than that of interest, since it represents a more uncertain income, and must therefore include an insurance premium against the risk of loss. Generally it includes profit as well. But we shall return to this point when we come to the question of profits.

VI : DOES THE RATE OF INTEREST TEND TO FALL ?

IF from the social point of view it is desirable that wages should rise, it is equally desirable that interest should fall.

First, from the point of view of justice in distribution. For a fall in the rate of interest, by reducing the share appropriated by the *idle* capitalist out of the total product, increases, other things being equal, the share available for labour; the more so as the rate of interest determines not only the incomes of capitalists, but, indirectly, the rate of profits and the rent of buildings and of land, thus affecting all the incomes of the propertied classes.

Secondly, as a stimulus to production. For, by steadily lowering the price of capital and, in consequence, the costs of production, it enables enterprises to be undertaken which before were impossible. Here, let us say, is a piece of land waiting to be cleared ; here are workmen's houses waiting to be built ; but they will not bring in more than 3 per cent. If the current rate of interest is 5 per cent. it will be impossible to find capital for these enterprises, since they could only be undertaken at a loss. But suppose that the rate of interest falls to 2 per cent., no time will be lost in starting them. Turgot, in a celebrated passage, compares the fall in the rate of interest to a gradual withdrawing of the waters, allowing new lands to be brought under cultivation.

But, apart from being desirable, is such a fall probable ? Is it likely to be permanent ? Are we to consider it a veritable and natural economic law, like that of the increasing value of land or the decreasing value of metallic money ?

Political economists, particularly the French Optimist school,

T

from Turgot down to M. Paul Leroy-Beaulieu, have always answered in the affirmative. Bastiat included the gradual fall of interest among the most beautiful of his Harmonies.

Their answer is based on fact and on theory :

On fact, because the fall in the rate of interest, from 5 per cent. to 3 per cent., during the last thirty or forty years has been one of the most striking economic phenomena of the second half of the nineteenth century.

On theory, because most of the causes we have given as determining the rate of interest seem to act in a downward direction. It is only reasonable to think that, in a progressive society, capital, like all other forms of produced wealth, will become more and more *abundant*, and that consequently its final utility and value will continue to decrease. *Security* of investment ought also to increase, at least if civilisation be held to imply a greater faithfulness on the part of individuals and States in fulfilling their engagements, and more effective means of enforcing the payment of debts. Lastly, there is some reason for thinking that capital in the future will become *less productive* and that profits will diminish : in agriculture, owing to the law of diminishing returns ; in industry, and transport, because opportunities of employment are limited. It is undeniable, for instance, that all future railroads built in France will be much less productive than are the great lines already constructed.

There does not even appear to be an assignable limit to the fall in the rate of interest; there is no " cost of production " limit such as we find in the case of a commodity, nor " level of subsistence " limit such as we come upon in the case of wages. The only limit here is that below which the capitalist will cease to lend, and will prefer to hoard his capital or to consume it. But what this level is, whether 1 per cent. or 1 per 1000, who can say ? [1]

These, then, are the arguments of those who foresee an indefinite decline in the rate of interest. No one of them, however, is in our opinion conclusive.

[1] According to Bastiat, interest may fall below any assignable quantity without, however, reaching zero, like the well-known mathematical curves, which continually approach a straight line (asymptote) without ever meeting it. Foxwell, an English economist, has even gone so far as to assert that a day may come when capitalists, instead of receiving interest from those to whom they entrust their money, will pay them for keeping it. True, he is referring more particularly to loans made to banks in the form of deposits. And it is quite possible that in these cases banks, in consideration of the service they render the depositor, may not only give no interest on sums deposited, but may even, as formerly, make a charge for taking care of them.

As regards facts, the very suddenness of the fall which the rate of interest has undergone in less than a generation is sufficient indication that this is not one of the long, slow movements which characterise evolution, but a temporary and probably periodical oscillation. There is a rhythm in the movement of the rate of interest, as there is in so many other economic phenomena. Under the Roman Empire, the rate of interest was no higher than it was in the middle of last century ; and in Holland, in the eighteenth century, it was already as low as it is to-day. It is quite possible that the movement, from now on, may be in an upward direction, as, since 1900, there has been a marked rise in the rate of interest on government stock and on the principal securities.

As regards theory, forecasts as to the movements of the various factors which act on the rate of interest are, in our view, very uncertain. That capital will become increasingly abundant is indeed quite probable ; but this may very well be counteracted by the increasing demand for it. Do not all enterprises nowadays require increasing quantities of capital ? As for risks, does anyone imagine that there are fewer insolvent debtors, fewer failures, fewer colossal swindles, fewer quantities of capital thrown away in risky enterprises, or, in the bottomless gulf of armaments, to-day than in former times ? Assuredly not. What justifies us, then, in concluding that things will be otherwise in the future ? [1] As regards productiveness, it is true that no industry taken separately can be developed beyond a certain point ; but, if we look at production in general, we see that old industries are constantly being replaced by new ; and there is no ground for supposing that transport by automobile, for instance, will be less remunerative than transport by railway, or electric lighting less remunerative than gas.

To sum up, then, it appears to us more likely that the rate of interest, after having reached a minimum point, which is already behind us, will rise again and will pass in the future through the same long alternating periods of rise and fall as in the past.

This does not mean that we need give up all expectation of seeing the share taken by capital, whether in the form of interest or profit, reduced—the co-operatist programme—or even brought to so low a point that we should have the gratuitous credit of which Proudhon dreamed—the most practical form of collectivism. For what can it matter whether or not the capital remains in individual

---

[1] We have even a new risk to take into account, that of strikes, and also the charges which the law tends more and more to impose on employers and capitalists.

hands if every one can use it for nothing ?   What we would point out is simply that such a result would be due, not to the play of some natural law, but to the reasoned and persevering action of men, taking very probably the form of associations of mutual credit.[1]

CHAPTER III : WAGE-EARNERS

I : WHAT IS THE WAGE-EARNER ?

THE wage, as usually defined by the Classical economists, is the " income received by a man in exchange for his labour."

If we were to keep to this definition, wages would appear as the typical form of income, the form which has always existed and will exist for all time.   For it is impossible to conceive of a social state in which the individual lives otherwise than by exchanging his labour, or the product of his labour or his services, for a certain amount of wealth.   It was on this ground that the Classical economists included even the landowner and the *rentier* under the wage-earning class, and asserted with Mirabeau that all are wage-earners save thieves and beggars. [2]

But this definition is pure oratory, inspired by the perhaps half-conscious desire to represent wages as the most perfect form of remuneration that can be imagined, and the wage-earning system as a final state.   Now, the work of science is to distinguish between the different incomes that proceed from any one labour.   And the word wages, in economic language just as in that of every day, should be applied, not to every mode of the remuneration of labour, but only to a special mode known as *the price of labour hired and employed by an entrepreneur*, the *louage de services* as it is called in the French Code Civil (Art. 1780).

We have seen repeatedly that the *enterprise* is the characteristic feature of modern economic organisation.   Now the wage-earning system is as inseparable from the enterprise as is the act of sale from the act of purchase of one and the same commodity.   The commodity here is labour or handiwork : the wage-earner is the one who sells, the *entrepreneur* the one who buys.

Wages thus defined are therefore a relatively recent method of remuneration in economic history ; a method which only became

---

[1] See above, p. 403.

[2] " I know only three ways of existing in society : to be a beggar, a thief, or a wage-earner.   The landowner is himself but the first of wage-earners."

general with the modern capitalistic organisation of industry, and may quite possibly disappear along with it. This will be seen more clearly in the next chapter.

Our definition evidently includes all who work under an employer, in agriculture, industry, transport, or commerce ; whether they are manual labourers, employees, engineers, or even directors at a salary of 100,000 francs.[1] It does not include producers who work on their own account, that is to say, *autonomous producers*, such as peasants, retail dealers, artisans, although these are often poorer than wage-earners ; nor those who belong to the *professional classes*, *e.g.* doctors, barristers, artists, etc. These work for the public, for the *customer*, not for an *employer*.

Does it include (1) employees of the State and the communes, and (2) domestic servants ?

(1) As regards employees of the State we must distinguish between : (*a*) those who have charge of some public service or function, and are for that reason called *functionaries*. They are not wage-earners, for they are not in the service of an employer. The State, of course, pays them, but with the taxpayer's money and on behalf of the nation ; and they are refused the right to strike ; (*b*) workers and employees in the State shipbuilding yards, manufactories, etc. These differ in no way from ordinary wage-earners, save that they have certain advantages such as permanent employment, pensions, etc.[2]

[1] The figure which we gave (p. 500) for the total number of wage-earners in agriculture, industry and commerce, was roughly, 10 millions (including home wage-earners), of which 7 millions were men and 3 millions women.

This figure of 10 millions does not give the total of the wage-earning class ; for we must add, besides, all who depend on wage-earners and whose interests are consequently one with theirs—wives, children, old persons. Their number can be given only approximately. We may take it, however, that in the working class, as in the other classes, the number of the women is equal to that of the men. We thus get 14,000,000, including, of course, the 3,000,000 women wage-earners mentioned above. Children under thirteen years, the age below which they may not as a general rule work as wage-earners, may be estimated at one-fifth of the adult population, or about 2,800,000. Lastly, the number of super-annuated workers over sixty years of age is estimated at 300,000 or 400,000. This gives a sum total for the wage-earning class of a little over 17,000,000 persons, or 44 per cent., *i.e.* not one half of the population of France, which is 39 millions. This fact is of great importance from the social, and also the political, point of view.

[2] The number of State wage-earners, including the departments and the communes, is 550,000, and would amount to nearly 900,000 if we included all who are paid out of the budget (see above, p. 500, note). In any case, it is increasing day by day, having risen by about 15,000 or 20,000 per annum lately.

(2) Logically, domestic servants come under our definition of " wage-earners," as the master—the bourgeois—is certainly an employer. They are, however, usually classed apart. Indeed, from the economic point of view, they differ from the ordinary wage-earner in that they are not employed for production, and that their interests are necessarily bound up with those of the bourgeois in whose service they are. For this reason, and from the fact that " domesticity " renders them much more dependent, both as regards their persons and their time, than workers in industry, this profession is becoming less and less sought after. It is almost the only employment where the demand is greater than the supply. This is why it is one of the groups in which wages have risen most.[1]

II : HISTORICAL SKETCH OF THE WAGE-SYSTEM [2]

DURING the long period of " family industry " (see p. 158), when all that was necessary for the household was produced by the labour of serfs or of slaves, there was little room for the wage-earner. Of course, at all times, even in antiquity under the slave system, there have been men poor but free, who have hired out their labour to rich men in exchange for money or for goods, and who consequently come very nearly under the definition of the wage-earner. But the free workers of antiquity were more like the artisans of to-day, *i.e.* independent producers living by some trade or other, who were hired for extra help where there was not a sufficient number of domestic servants.[3]

There was hardly more room for the wage-earner under the second system, that of the guild, or corporative industry (see p. 158).

---

[1] The number of domestic servants (Census of 1906, t. i, part 2, p. 184) in 1906 was 946,000, of which 773,000 were women and 173,000 men. But this number is falling. There is already a " servant problem," which will become more and more important socially, since a great change will result in the habits of life of the bourgeois class when it can find no more servants ; the household will probably be replaced by something resembling the phalanstery.

There are a certain number of non-domestic wage-earners who are sometimes assimilated with domestic servants in statutes, because they, too, render personal services, and are not employed in production : waiters, hairdressers' assistants, etc. (about 66,000 in all).

[2] For the history of this system *see* M. Levasseur's masterly work on *L'histoire des classes ouvrières en France ;* for antiquity, M. Giraud's *Le travail en Grèce ;* and for the Middle Ages, M. Hauser's *Ouvriers du temps passé.*

[3] The master often let out his slaves to other persons for a price which might be called a wage, but which differed totally from the modern wage in that it was the master, not the slave, who received it.

The " journeymen " were, it is true, paid by the master, but they did not stand to him in the relation of wage-earner to employer. The etymology of the word *compagnon* (French for journeyman : *cum pane* = mess-mate) sufficiently indicates the nature of the relation between them, at the outset at any rate.   It was not merely one of common life and mutual help, but of reciprocal and fairly narrow obligations.   Journeymen could not be dismissed at the employer's pleasure, but they could not, on the other hand, leave him.   Their wages were regulated by the statutes of their guilds and sometimes by the local authorities, but they were unable to raise them.   All had in front of them, however, the hope of one day becoming masters, and in the case of many of them this hope was fulfilled.

On the whole, then, although the idyllic picture of the guild system is not quite true to facts, although coalitions of workers were not unknown at that time, we may say that this system of master and workers did not represent two opposing social classes, but two successive stages in a man's professional career.   And, according to M. d'Avenel, it was during the fifteenth century that the pay of the worker was highest.

Towards the end of the Middle Ages, the small town markets ceased to be the centre of economic life.   The great modern States began to be formed.   The opening of new roads gave rise to national, and even international, markets, and the small masters of former times were unable to produce on a large enough scale.   Their place was gradually taken by capitalists and wealthy merchants, who subsequently became the leaders of industry.   Thus the type of the modern employer gradually emerged.   At the same time the journeymen found the road to independence closed to them, and began to form a distinct class.   Shut out from the " maitrise " or mastership, and consequently from all share in fixing their wages, they formed associations of their own, composed solely of workers, the beginning, as it were, of the modern trade union.   Henceforth capital and labour went their separate ways.[1]

One step more was necessary to create the type of wage-earner as he exists to-day.   The restrictions and regulations which were at the root of the inferiority of the guild system, and bound the worker while protecting him, had to be done away with.   Labour had to be absolutely mobile before it could be freely organised.

---

[1] It was then that vehement recriminations first began to be heard, curious examples of which will be found in M. Mantoux's *La Révolution industrielle au XVIIIe siècle*.

This was accomplished in the first place by the creation of privileged
State manufactures, quite outside of the influence of the guilds, and
for that reason enfranchised from their regulations. Employers could
thus freely apply the principles of the division of labour and of
production on a large scale. The edicts of Turgot, and those of the
Revolution, put a finishing touch to this development by decreeing
the absolute liberty of labour.

From now on, the workers were free : free to sell their labour at
the price fixed by the Law of Demand and Supply on the open
market ; free to refuse it, or to leave their work when they chose.
But the employers were, of course, free also : free to pay the minimum
price for which they could obtain the labour of men, women, or
children ; free to turn them off at a moment's notice. The wage
contract was henceforth as free a contract as the contract of sale—in
one sense much more so, since the law took no notice of it—and
labour became a commodity the value of which was regulated by
the same laws as that of any other commodity. The modern wage-
system was now fully established.

No one, even among socialists, would dream of denying that this
system has given a great impetus to production and has powerfully
armed industry. But no open-minded person would deny, either,
that this reciprocal liberty at first benefited employers much more
than workers. The latter, isolated, disorganised, victims of a
legislation which did not allow them to associate, found themselves
in the worst possible situation for disposing of their labour, and were
obliged to sell it for next to nothing. And it is generally recognised
that, from the end of the eighteenth till nearly the end of the
nineteenth century, the condition of the hired wage-earner in Europe
was a very hard one—more degraded than that of the poorest
peasant—and that the *régime* of liberty was less advantageous to
him than the preceding systems had been.

But we must also admit that a change has taken place during the
last thirty years.

(*1*) Wage-earners have learned how to organise and group themselves for the better defence of their interests, and the legislative
prohibitions, which put obstacles in the way of their legitimate right
to do so, have been abolished.

(*2*) Quite a body of laws known as " factory legislation," which
we shall summarise further on, has been passed, practically re-
establishing in the modern factory the guarantees which had existed
under the guild system, but from which the latter had freed itself.
These laws regulate the hours of labour, insure workers against

accidents, and prescribe sanitary conditions, and, though they do not as yet fix a legal rate of wages, they at least provide some guarantees as to the method of payment and the discharge of workers.

III : THE WAGE CONTRACT

THE *entrepreneur*, the man whose function it is to gather together in his hands the implements and all that is necessary for production, naturally needs workers. He engages whatever number he requires ; that is to say, he hires them for a length of time which is as a rule undetermined, and for a price which is called a *wage*.

The wage contract, or labour contract, implies that the worker furnishes nothing but the labour. If he provides raw material as well, he is no more a wage-earner, but an *entrepreneur:* he no longer hires out his labour, he sells the products of it—a very different matter.

Juridically, then, the wage contract is a synallagmatic contract, creating reciprocal obligations ; the workman giving his labour, the employer giving a wage. But, under what legal category should it be classed ? We hesitate between three :

(a) By nature it belongs to the group of contracts *of hire :* like the hire of a house, *i.e.* lease ; the hire of land, *i.e.* farming ; the hire of capital, *i.e.* the loan at interest. Here the object let out is the labour, or, to use Karl Marx's celebrated expression, the " labour force " of the worker. What makes this contract unique and singularly difficult is that the object hired out is not distinct from the person to whom it belongs, as in the case of the house, land, or money. To hire out one's labour is to hire out oneself, and the identification between the object and the person is even more complete when the labour, instead of being specified, like that of the industrial worker or employee, is indeterminate, like that of domestic service. It follows that injustices, which are always possible and are more or less inherent in all contracts, fall here, as it were, on the living person, and are felt more keenly than in any other connection.

(b) But, as this assimilation of the hire of labour to the letting-out of other services is particularly odious to the workers, socialists prefer to assimilate it to a *sale*, since a sale implies no subordination of the one party, nor even a permanent relationship between the two contracting parties. We may, in fact, say that the worker sells his " labour force " at so much per hour, or for so much per task, just as water and electricity are sold at so much per hour, or cubic metre, or kilowatt. But this way of presenting the matter, if more

T'

flattering in form, changes nothing in the actual situation. A " contract of partnership " would perhaps be more in keeping with modern ideas as regards the hiring of labour ; unfortunately this would have serious practical drawbacks for the working man, as we shall see when we come to profit-sharing.

(c) What would be more in harmony with our present ideas would be a contract of association. Unfortunately the expression is rather one of possibility than of fact. Still we are approaching somewhere near it in profit-sharing and co-partnership.[1]

It is of more practical utility, however, to know the conditions and effects of this contract. The making of contracts is subject in law to certain essential conditions, the principal one being the free consent of the parties ; sometimes also to certain conditions of form, of which the most general is the drawing-up of a document signed by the parties as proof. The enumeration of these conditions in the case of sale, hire, marriage contract, mortgage, etc. fills many articles of the Code Napoléon. Respecting the contract of the hire of labour, however, the Code is much more brief, containing only two articles, one of which has been repealed while the other is but a simple declaration of principle.[2] And yet no contract holds a larger place in the life of mankind, governing as it does one half of the population—more, that is to say, than even the marriage contract. For marriage takes place perhaps once in a lifetime, whereas a worker may hire out his services twenty times a year. Jurisconsults are to-day trying to remedy this, and a law on the hiring of labour is at present in preparation in France.

The principal rules to which the contract of labour might in

---

[1] According to M. Chatelain (*De la nature du contrat entre ouvriers et entrepreneurs*) the wage contract is, already, juridically speaking, a contract of partnership, the worker contributing to the business his share in the future product of his labour.

This is a very attractive way of presenting it, but it expresses rather what ought to be than what is. For, to sell beforehand his share in the product of his labour, the worker must have a right of ownership over this product. Now the law admits this in no way. We have said (p. 461) that labour, of itself, is never enough to constitute a right of ownership.

[2] These two articles are : Art. 1780, which declares that a man cannot hire out his services in perpetuity—a quite superfluous precaution against serfdom ; and Art. 1781, which declares that, in a dispute as to the amount of the wage, the master's word is to be taken. This is the one which has been repealed. It created a humiliating inequality between the two parties ; but as a matter of fact, in the absence of any written proof, there is still nothing to do but accept the word of the debtor, *i.e.* the master, the judge having the power to take his oath according to the rules of procedure.

future be subjected, and which are already imposed by law in some countries, are :

I. That the fixing of the conditions of the contract should not be left to the discretion of the employer as is at present the case.

In large factories the conditions are stated in printed notices called workshop regulations, and the worker, by the very fact that he has taken on an engagement, is supposed to have accepted them. These regulations might be submitted to the control either of the State, as represented by labour inspectors, or to that of official representatives of the employers and of the workers, such as the *Conseils du Travail* or the *Conseils de Prud'hommes*. True, the employer will not readily accept such control, alleging his right to be master in his own place, and to engage labour on his own terms. Thus in countries where this control is organised (Germany, Belgium, Norway, etc.)[1] neither the State nor the workers have the right to demand alteration of the workshop regulations (save in the case of illegal clauses). The moral sanction, however, which results from publicity, or from a two-sided enquiry, has of itself a good effect.

Some clauses might with advantage be legally forbidden or, at least, regulated. The workers' grievance, for instance, against the workshop regulations is that, as a rule, they do away with the week's notice, etc., or compensation for dismissal, and in addition often impose *fines*. In Russia, and sometimes even in France, instances have been known where manufacturers looked on these fines as a normal supplement to their profits, or where foremen inflicted them in order to wreak their ill-will against the men, or to obtain satisfaction for their lusts from the women workers. And these abuses have not yet entirely disappeared. Still, the legislator hesitates to prohibit fines altogether,[2] seeing in them, from the legal point of view, not a confiscation of the worker's wage, but a penal clause for the non-execution of certain conditions of the contract—a clause which is also to be found in other contracts, *e.g.* those undertaken by *entrepreneurs* to complete certain works within a certain specified time.

---

[1] In Norway the law requires the workshop regulations to be submitted to the Labour Council, along with the observations of the workmen, who may elect a commission of five members and who have a fortnight within which to present their observations.

[2] The law on the payment of wages of which we shall speak presently, as voted first of all in the Chamber, prohibited fines. But the Senate would not ratify this prohibition, pointing out that the measure might be turned against the worker, since the employer would have no penalty left but dismissal. It simply limited fines to a maximum of one-fourth of the wage, and required that they should be put into a fund for the workers.

The workers also inflict fines on themselves through their trade unions or benefit societies. But at least the following guarantees should be exacted : (a) the fine should be inflicted only in the case of material injury caused to production ; (b) the amount of the fine should be proportional to the injury done, and therefore fairly moderate (in Belgium the maximum fixed by law is one-fifth of the daily wage); (c) the fines, with the reasons for them, should be recorded on a register and communicated to the labour inspectors, as is done in England ; (d) above all, the proceeds of the fines should be put into a special fund and applied to some collective work for the benefit of the workers.

II. That annulment of the contract should be allowed in cases of prejudice (*lésion*).

The Code Napoléon does not admit prejudice as a cause for annulment, save in two exceptional cases : the sale of immovable goods and the division of a succession. But the new German and Swiss Codes admit prejudice, in principle, in all contracts which have the character of an act of exploitation, one of the parties profiting by the ignorance or the embarrassment of the other. The question naturally arises whether the wage contract is not, of all contracts, the one in which this precaution is most needed. And the bill relating to this contract which has just been laid before the Chamber by the French Government declares that the contract may be rescinded whenever the conditions (for which read *wages*) are at variance with the normal conditions prevailing in that industry in the neighbourhood, or with the importance of the service rendered. The last clause of the sentence is somewhat dangerous, leaving as it does quasi-discretionary powers to the judge. Yet, if we were to stop short at the first clause only, a general fall in the rate of wages in the district, or in the industry, would be quite enough to render annulment on the ground of prejudice impossible.

We must be under no illusion as to the importance of this reform. For, if annulment can be effective in the case of a definite contract, such as a contract of sale or of division, it is not the same in a contract from day to day, like the hire of labour, which may be dissolved at any moment. If the worker considers that he is being taken advantage of, why does he not go ? Evidently because he does not think he will fare better elsewhere. But in that case he will not make a claim against the master. And if he nevertheless does, and obtains his case, what will be the consequence ? Damages equivalent to the loss of wage which he has suffered ? Good and well, but from what moment ? For it is impossible, after all, to admit that a worker who was free to leave when he chose, if he deemed himself prejudiced, should stay on in his employment for months and years in order to claim at the end of that time all that he has been deprived of. The bill fixes one month as the maximum period of time within which a demand for annulment must be made.

III. That the wages should be paid in legal money. .

To understand the usefulness of this rule we must know that for over a century the *truck-system* prevailed, so called because employers paid their workers, not in money, but in goods, sometimes with the very produce of their own factories.[1] Thus there were establishments whose workers had never had a gold piece in their hands during their whole lives.

In France, a law of February 19, 1910, requires that payment be made in money once a fortnight at least, and in the factory—this to avoid its being made in the public-house.

IV. That damages should be fixed for each of the two parties in certain cases of the wilful breaking of the contract.

In law every contract not made for a fixed term may be freely dissolved at the will of either of the two parties, (*e.g.* the hiring of a flat,) unless a term of years has been agreed on. Now, as the wage or labour-hire contract falls, as a rule, under this category, the employer may dismiss the worker, or the worker may leave his employer, the moment he chooses.

Custom has, however, taken away somewhat of the harshness of this legal provision. It has become usual, before the dissolution of a contract, to give at least a week's notice, or to pay an equivalent compensation; and the tribunals in France, *i.e.* the *Conseils de Prud'hommes*, give this custom the force of law. They cannot of course prohibit a clause to the opposite effect in the wage contract, and this is becoming more and more frequent. It is often stated in workshop regulations that the employer reserves the right to dismiss the worker at a moment's notice, the worker being free to leave in the same manner.

But, even supposing that the giving of a week's notice were the common practice, can we see in this brief grace of a few days, or in the small equivalent indemnity, a sufficient compensation for the enormous injury suffered by the dismissed worker? Let us take, *e.g.*—and it is a case unhappily only too frequent—a worker who has reached the age of fifty years and is dismissed as too old from a firm where he has perhaps worked all his life. At this age work

---

[1] This system was abolished in France by a law of 1910. See *infra*, *The Evolution of the Entrepreneur.*

elsewhere is closed to him, and dismissal is practically a death sentence. Yet all he can claim is a week's notice or eight days' wages. The legislature, moved by such a case of distress, added a clause, in 1890, to Art. 1780 of the Code Civil to the effect that the breaking of the contract by the will of one of the parties may give occasion to damages. But it does not specify in what cases there is abuse on the part of the employer. And jurisprudence has given up trying to find out, so that the law remains a dead letter. It was judged, however, that there was no abuse in the example which we have given above. Inhuman though such a decision may appear, we must admit that it is not easy to object to it, either from the juridical, or from the economic, point of view. For, to turn off a worker who is no longer any good for your work and with whom you have entered into no agreement, cannot be considered an abuse,[1] while, if the *entrepreneur* is to pay a life pension to every worker he dismisses, he will be at the mercy of his employees, if the enormous increase in his costs does not straightway ruin his industry. Or, again, if compensation is due after a certain number of years of service in the same firm, it is to be feared that many employers will dismiss their workers just before this limit is reached. This is certainly the most distressing and the most difficult of all the questions to which the wage-earning system gives rise, and is enough in itself to make us wish for the end of this *régime*.

V. A fifth reform in the wage contract, long and energetically demanded by the workers, is the abolition of the middlemen between the principal *entrepreneur* and the workers. It was the first of all their demands to which the law in France gave satisfaction. A decree of March 2, 1848, declared that " the exploitation of workers by sub-contractors or middlemen is abolished."

This decree remained, however, a dead letter, jurisprudence interpreting it as prohibiting the abuses to which the middleman gave rise, but not the middleman himself. The government, therefore, in order to satisfy the claims of the workers, has proposed a bill absolutely prohibiting, under penalty of imprisonment, any compact by which a sub-contractor undertakes to provide an *entrepreneur* with labour at his own expense. But in practice it is difficult to

---

[1] Note, moreover, that, even if the law decided that the act of dismissing a worker engaged for no fixed term constituted an abuse, nothing would be easier than for the employer to get round the law by specifying in the contract that the worker is only engaged by the week or by the day—with indefinite renewal of the engagement.

distinguish between this undesirable form of the labour contract and other more legitimate and even useful forms.

VI. That the individual contract of hire should give place to the *collective bargain.*

This reform is the great question of the day, and measures dealing with it have already been introduced in most countries, in France, Italy, etc. It had long been observed that the abuses in the wage contract were due for the most part to the extreme inequality of the contracting parties.[1] The worker offers a commodity, namely, himself, which cannot wait, since he must at the same time work in order to eat, and eat in order to work. The capitalist, by waiting, loses, at most, only the interest on his capital. But the situation is completely changed if, over against him, stands a body of workers forming one whole, and if, in addition, they are supported by a common fund which enables them also to wait and to bargain. In such a case the play of demand and supply is not perverted ; on the contrary, it is re-established on the same footing as in other contracts. This is what is called collective bargaining. Hitherto it has existed only in the form of agreements following on strikes. But why, instead of being resorted to exceptionally and to end a conflict, should not recourse be had to it as the normal form of labour contract ?

The difficulty is that every contract implies an exchange of wills, consequently real persons or persons legally represented Now it is not easy to see how to give a juridical personality and legal representatives to a group of workers. Who will sign the contracts ? And who will be bound by the signatures given ? To-morrow, perhaps, or in a little while, these workers will be replaced by others. Might they not be represented collectively by their trade unions ? This is the solution generally adopted as a last resort. But we shall see presently that the unions in France as yet include only a small fraction, about one-fifth, of the working population. It may be that none of the workers of the factory where this collective contract is to be drawn up belong to a union. In this case the employer will surely have the right to answer—it is the stereotyped phrase—" I am willing to make terms with my own workers, but not with strangers." And even supposing this difficulty were overcome, would the union itself offer a sufficient guarantee ? What responsibility would it take, in the case of non-fulfilment of the contract ? Would it pay damages, and with what, if its coffers were empty ?

[1] Thucydides said twenty-five centuries ago : " There can be no question of justice among men unless they treat with one another on an equal footing."

What puts employers against the collective bargain is the feeling that, in this new contract, it is they alone who will be morally and pecuniarily bound.[1] It must be admitted that, if the attempts at collective bargaining have given good results in England and even in Germany, this has not been the case in France. Contracts have very often been violated, each party throwing the responsibility for the rupture on the other. The collective bargain can only be effective where almost the whole of the working class is organised into trade unions and has awakened to its responsibility, or at least where the leaders have enough authority to sign in the name of all, and to force the workers to keep engagements undertaken in their name. On the other hand, it may be said that where such conditions are fulfilled there is little need of a written law to sanction the collective bargain. Thus in England and in Germany it works quite well of itself.[2]

Strictly speaking, the collective bargain is not a true wage contract. It does not oblige Peter to work for Paul, nor fix the price which Paul is to pay Peter. It is limited to laying down certain general rules to which employers and workers are to conform, e.g. a scale of wages, maximum hours of labour, the obligation to employ only trade-union men, etc. And, as such conditions cannot be laid down for an indefinite length of time, the term during which they are to hold good is generally fixed at two or three years. It is, as it were, a framework into which all individual contracts which concern the same firm, or even firms belonging to the same industry or district, must enter.[3] The collective bargain might thus be expanded into a kind of local legislation, save that the law, instead of being passed by Parliament, would be passed by working-men's and employers' unions. This would be a step in the direction of what is called the *compulsory trade union.* By this is meant, not that all workers would

[1] And we can understand that the declarations of certain militant socialists are not of a nature to reassure them. Thus M. Merrheim declared, at a public meeting, that they would accept the collective contract and even impose it by the force of their organisations, but *without any obligations on the part of the working class.*

[2] In England, at the present time, there are 1700 collective contracts involving 2½ million workers. In Germany certain industries, like typography, work altogether under the system of collective bargaining. In France, *l'Office du Travail* shows 202 collective contracts signed in 1911, 156 of which, however, were the result of strikes, which indicates but moderate progress.

[3] The French measure on this subject declares all employers and workers of the same industry and of the same district bound by the collective bargain, even if it has only been concluded by one single business firm, unless the contrary is expressly stated. But this forced solidarity has given rise to lively protests.

be compelled to join the union, but that all would be bound by its decisions.

After carrying out measures to make the contract of labour just from the workers' side, it would be not altogether unprofitable to do the same from the employers' side, and to look for some method of making sure that the worker carries out his part of the bargain. The increasing frequency of *sabotage*, not only active *sabotage*—which consists in damaging the employer's material—but passive *sabotage*, known in England as " ca' canny " and in France as *sabotage perlé*— which consists in doing the least possible amount of work—shows that such a precaution is not unnecessary. Unfortunately, it is hard to find any practical method of enforcing the obligations of the workers, unless it be the moral guarantee of a trade union ; for surety can hardly be demanded of one who has nothing.

Alongside of the laws which protect, so to speak, the wage of the worker against the employer, we must mention :

(*1*) Those which protect the wage of the worker against his creditors. The latter, generally tradesmen, can seize only one-tenth of his wage. If the employer has made advances to the worker or provided material for his labour, which frequently happens in home industry, he has the right to distrain another tenth. The worker may also give up one-tenth. This voluntary cession must not be confused with forced distraint. In any case there remain at least seven-tenths untouched for himself.

(*2*) Those which protect the wage of the wife against the husband, so that the husband may not live at the expense of the wife—as unfortunately happens only too often. For, in France, the legal system for all who marry without a marriage contract—and this is always the case in the working class—is that of community of goods administered by the husband alone.

IV : THE LAWS OF WAGES

To try to find the laws of wages is to try to discover the general causes which determine their rate and send them up or down ; it is to try to put their action into formulæ. This is one of the great problems of Political Economy, and has given rise to many famous theories.

We might, in the first instance, be tempted to ask ourselves whether there really are natural laws governing the rate of wages, since the rate of wages varies from trade to trade and from place to place ; and since, in each particular case, it is determined, as we have seen, by free, or presumably· free, discussion between the employer and the worker.

We should, however, be reasoning wrongly ; for the prices of goods also vary according to their nature, the place, and the time ; they, too, are the result of free bargaining between the seller and the buyer ; but this does not hinder us from looking for the laws which regulate them. There is nothing illogical in doing so. Prices and wages are, it is true, regulated by human conventions,[1] but these conventions are themselves determined by general causes which it is our business to discover. To believe in the existence of natural laws in Political Economy is simply to believe that men in their compacts are determined by certain psychological motives, or by certain outside circumstances of a general nature, which may be disentangled from the confused mass of particular cases.

Now, as labour in our present economic organization is but a commodity among others, bought and sold (or hired) on the market, it is evident that its price must be determined by the same laws as govern the price of any other commodity. These laws we have already studied in connection with value. They were summed up vividly and picturesquely by Cobden when he said that wages rose whenever there were two employers running after one worker, and fell whenever there were two workers running after one employer.

But this is a simple statement of fact, not an explanation. What we want to know is why, at one moment, it is the worker who is running after the employer ; why, at another, it is the employer who is running after the worker.

A satisfactory law of wages should be able to explain all the variations of wages ; in particular, why wages are higher (a) in one country than in another ; (b) at one time than another ; (c) in one trade than another.

Three theories of wages have been advanced, each of which was celebrated in its day and still has a certain number of adherents. We shall discuss them briefly :

(1) *The Wage-Fund Theory.* This was for a long time the classical theory in England and has held an important place among economic doctrines. It approaches most nearly to the theory of demand and supply, of which it is, in fact, simply a more precise statement.

---

[1] And it is no more accurate to say that wages are determined by individual agreements than that prices are ; every one knows that, just as there exists a general market price for each commodity, which can only be slightly influenced by the bargaining of the parties concerned, so there is a general rate of wages for each kind of labour.

Supply, on this theory, consists of the workers, the proletariat, who are in search of work in order to earn a living, and who offer their labour. Demand consists of capital seeking investment. We have already seen (p. 120), that the only way of employing capital productively is to apply it to making men work. *It is the relation between these two elements, the workers and the capital, which will determine the rate of wages.*

Take the circulating capital of a country, which English economists called the Wage-Fund, because in their idea its function was to support the workers in the course of their labours. Then take the number of workers. By dividing the first by the second, we obtain the average rate of wages. If, for example, the total circulating capital is 10 milliard francs, and the number of workers 10 millions, the annual average wage will be just 1000 francs.

Clearly, on this theory, wages can vary only as one or other of the factors varies. A rise in wages therefore is only possible in the two following cases :

(*a*) If the wage-fund, *i.e.* the total amount to be distributed in wages, is increased, and this can come about only through saving ;

(*b*) If the working population, *i.e.* the number of those who are to share it, diminishes—and this can happen only if the workers apply the principles of Malthus, and either refrain from marrying or limit the number of their children.[1]

Such a conclusion is certainly not reassuring for the future of the working class. It is to be feared that the divisor (the number of the working population) will increase much more rapidly than the dividend (the amount of available capital) ; from which it follows that the quotient (wages) will tend to decrease until it reaches the minimum below which it cannot go. And the reason is obvious. It is much easier to increase the number of children than to increase the supply of capital ; for the latter involves abstinence and the former precisely the contrary. Population increases spontaneously·; not so capital.

But this theory, though still defended by a few economists, is much discredited to-day.

---

[1] This was expressly stated by J. S. Mill, who developed most fully the doctrine of the wage-fund, which he later abandoned. " Wages depend on the proportion between the number of the labouring population and the capital or other funds devoted to the purchase of labour. . . . Wages not only depend upon the relative amount of capital and (labouring) population, but cannot under the rule of competition be affected by anything else." And naturally his conclusion is that there is no other safeguard for wage-earners than limiting the increase of population.

In the first place, the idea on which it is founded, namely, that a certain amount of circulating capital is necessary to enable the workers to work, is of interest only from the point of view of production, not of distribution. It is undeniable that wages are paid out of capital, or rather that the money which the *entrepreneur* uses for paying his workers is capital. But it by no means follows that the rate of these wages is determined by the total amount of this capital. It is one thing for an *entrepreneur* to ask himself whether he has means enough to employ workers, *i.e.* enough raw material and implements, and quite another to ask what is the share in the income from the business which he will be able to give them. The answer to the first question depends on what he possesses ; the answer to the second, on what he will produce. The demand for workers depends. certainly, on industrial activity, but this activity depends in turn on the expectations of *entrepreneurs* much more than on the sums which they have in hand or their credit at their banker's.

Further, the would-be precision of this theory is but a delusion. On closer examination, it amounts simply to saying that the rate of wages is obtained by dividing the total sum distributed in wages by the number of wage-earners—a mere truism ; or, if we take it in a wider sense, the wealthier a country the higher the wages—a proposition that needs no proof.

And this circulating capital, this wage-fund, whence does it come ? From labour itself. It is neither more nor less than the *income from labour* coming back to it in the form of wages. The explanation resolves itself, therefore, into a vicious circle. As Professor J. B. Clark has very well said, the wage-fund is a reservoir filled, as needs require, by a pump, and this pump is labour.

It must also be pointed out that, though this theory may explain the inequalities of wages from one period of time to another, or from one country to another—may explain, for example, why American wages are higher than our own by supposing that the wage-fund is larger in the United States—it does not succeed in explaining them from one trade to another. Can we say that the reason why the engraver earns ten francs a day, and the manual labourer one franc, is that the wage-fund is ten times greater for the first than for the second ? Such a statement would be quite unintelligible.

(2) *Theory of the Iron Law.* This theory also starts from the fact that manual labour or labour power is, under the present organisation of society, a commodity bought and sold on the market. Workers are the sellers ; employers are the buyers. Now, is it not

the case that wherever there is free competition the value of all commodities is determined by their cost of production ? This is what the Economists call their *natural price* or *normal value*. The same ought therefore to hold good of the commodity called manual labour. The price of labour, *i.e.* the wage, must also be determined by the cost of production.[1]

What we have to find out, therefore, is the meaning of the words " cost of production " when it is the worker that is the instrument of production.

Take for instance a machine. The costs of production are represented : (1) by the value of the coal which it consumes ; (2) by the sum which must be put aside annually in order to replace it when worn out. So, in the same way the cost of production of labour will be represented : (1) by the value of all that the worker must consume in order to maintain his productive force ; (2) by the sum necessary to replace him when he is no longer able to work, that is to say, the amount required to bring up a child to the adult age.

Wages are thus inevitably *reduced to the strict minimum necessary to support a worker and his family.*

This is the theory which Lassalle called by the name of the *Iron Law*—a name which sounded for thirty years as the refrain of a socialist war-song, and served as an admirable weapon for stirring up class hatred. For it proved to the workers that the economic organisation left them no chance of improving their lot. And yet, though it was the Collectivist school which gave this theory its name and fame, it was the Classical school which started it. Turgot was the first to declare that " in every sort of occupation . . . the wages of the artisan are limited to that which is necessary to procure him a subsistence." And Say and Ricardo expressed themselves in almost the same words.

To-day this theory is abandoned. Not only did the Liberal school hasten to disclaim it so soon as it saw the consequences which could be drawn from it, but the collectivists themselves formally disavowed it.[2]

They still maintain that wages tend to fall to their lowest limit ;

---

[1] " Like the price of all other merchandise, the price of labour is determined by the relations of supply and demand. But what determines the market price of any merchandise, or the average ratio of the supply and demand of a particular article ? The costs necessary for its production." Lassalle, *Bastiat, Schulze-Delitzsch*, chap. iv.

[2] If socialists believed in the Iron Law and the irreducible minimum, they would have no reason to object to the law coming down on wages for a contribution to old-age pensions or taxes, since clearly it could have no effect.

but the reason they give is a different, and a stronger one. It is, they say, the permanent existence of a body of unemployed, always ready to take the place of the worker who asks more. This brings us back to the law of supply and demand.

Indeed, if we were to take the theory literally, as meaning that the worker's wage can never rise above, or fall below, the *level of his material subsistence*, it is both too pessimistic and too optimistic, and manifestly contrary to facts. Under the sweating system wages go far below what is strictly necessary for the physical life ; while for many workers they are happily far above that level.

This theory, moreover, cannot explain the inequality of wages from one trade to another. Does an engraver or an engine-driver need to consume more nitrogen and carbon than a simple manual labourer or drudge? Why are the wages of country labourers lower in winter, when they are obliged to spend more in firing and clothing, than in summer, the " poor man's season," as Victor Hugo called it, because living is so easy then ? Why are wages higher in the United States than in Germany, or even in England ? What physiological reason is there why an American should eat more than a German or even an Englishman, his race-brother ? Why are wages higher to-day than a century ago ? Have we larger appetites than our forefathers had ?

And if we take the level of subsistence in the wider sense, as the minimum necessary to satisfy the complex desires of a man living in a civilised environment ; if we mean that the worker's wages are regulated by the habits and the way of living of the whole working class, by the sum total of physical and social, artificial and natural wants which characterise this level of existence ; if we admit that the *standard of life*, as it is called, is unequal, variable, progressive, and that it is naturally higher in the engraver's profession than in that of the manual labourer, in America than in France, in the twentieth century than in the thirteenth century, for the inhabitant of the town than for the country labourer ; then this is tantamount to saying that the law of wages, far from being " iron," is singularly elastic, varying according to race, climate, and epoch ; that it tends to rise continuously and inevitably as needs increase. And we must no longer call this singularly optimistic theory the " iron law," but, as has been cleverly said, the " golden law " of wages.[1]

---

[1] If we had asked Lassalle's disciples, for instance, why the wages of the day labourers in the country, which formerly only allowed them to eat black bread and to wear sabots, have risen nowadays so as to enable them to eat white bread and wear leather shoes, they would have answered : " It is *just because*

(3) Theory of the Productivity of Labour. A third theory, while, like the last, assimilating the law of wages to the law of value, nevertheless reaches quite opposite conclusions, as optimistic as the former are pessimistic.[1]

According to this theory, the value of wages cannot be assimilated to the value of an ordinary commodity, subject solely to the law of demand and supply under free competition. The worker is not a mere ordinary commodity : he is an instrument of production. Now, the value of an instrument of production depends above all on its productiveness. When an *entrepreneur* rents a piece of land, is not the rent he pays calculated according to the productiveness of the soil ? Why, then, when he hires labour, should not the rate of wages be calculated according to the productiveness of the labour ?

It is not of course maintained that wages are equal to the total value produced by an enterprise. That would be impossible, since it would mean that the employer was making no profit and would cease to employ labour. But it is claimed that the worker receives in the form of wages *all that remains* of the total product, when the shares of the other collaborators (interest, profit, rent) have been deducted. These shares are strictly determined, whereas his has the advantage of not being fixed. The wage-earner stands to the other sharers in the position, as it were, of residuary legatee.[2]

This theory, if sound, would be as encouraging as the other two are disheartening. For, if the level of wages depends solely on the productiveness of the worker's labour, his welfare is in his own hands. The more he produces, the more he will earn. Everything that can increase his productive activity—physical development, moral virtue, technical training, invention, and machinery—must inevitably increase his wages. On this theory, the wage contract would be even more profitable to the wage-earner than partnership,

their wants have increased and their habits have changed that their wages have gone up." Very good, but in this case we must also hold that, so soon as they take to eating meat with their bread and to wearing flannels under their waist-coats, their wages will rise to cover these new wants. Now what better can we desire ? It is no longer the wage which will determine the worker's standard of living, but his standard of living which will determine his wage. A radiant prospect !

[1] This more recent theory was first taught by the American economist Walker, in his book *The Wages Question* (1876), and later by most American economists. The eminent English economist, Jevons, also adopted it.

[2] He is called the *residual claimant*, the one who takes all that is left over. As Jevons said, " The wages of a working man are ultimately coincident with what he produces. after the deduction of rent, taxes, and the interest of capital."

or profit-sharing ; for the worker, and *the worker only*, would benefit
by every increase in the productiveness of labour. The other
collaborators would receive fixed, and on the whole decreasing,
shares.

We must admit that this theory is more successful than are the
other two in explaining the inequalities of wages. For, if the engraver receives more than the manual labourer, the American more
than the Frenchman, the worker of the nineteenth century more than
the worker of past centuries, is it not because the labour of the
former is more productive than the labour of the latter ? Do we not
consider apprenticeship useful to the worker simply because we
believe that a worker who knows his trade well produces more,
and, producing more, will be better paid ? [1]

It is evident also that the productiveness of labour exercises a
general influence on the rate of wages ; for, by increasing the wealth
of a country, it increases the total amount to be divided, and consequently the shares of all, including the workers.

This theory appears therefore not only more consoling than
the others, but nearer the truth. Still, it leaves in the background
one of the most essential elements of the problem, namely, the
abundance or scarcity of workmen, which often has a preponderant
effect on wages. Take, *e.g.* the United States. The productiveness of
labour has enormously increased there during the last twenty years ;
yet the rate of wages has not kept pace with it. Why ? Because
the proletariat has been so enormously swelled by the immigration of
foreign workers and by the private appropriation of the land. This is,

---

[1] To-day this theory of wages as determined by the productivity of labour
is presented in a more learned form. It has been taken up and perfected by the
economists who profess the theory of final utility. They simply apply to wages,
i.e. to the value of labour, the same arguments as to the value of things (see above,
p. 53). The wage, they say, is really equal to the product of the labour of the
worker, but of the *least productive* worker, the one who (in one and the same
industry) is employed under the worst conditions. The reason is, that it is
under these conditions only, and in the case of this worker alone, that the
product of his labour stands quite bare, so to speak. In the case of the other
workers, their productivity is due in part to outside circumstances independent
of them.

This theory of marginal productivity, expounded for the first time by a
German economist, von Thünen (*Der Isolirte Staat*). has been developed
and corrected by other economists (in particular Clark, *Distribution of Wealth*).
But it cannot be said to throw much light on the subject. For, if it is not
easy to obtain a clear idea of the utility of the " last fraction of a thing," it
is still more difficult to form a clear idea of the abstract personage " the
additional " or " marginal " worker who is supposed to determine the rate of
wages !

in fact, one of the main reasons for the legislative measures against
not only Chinese, but European immigration.[1]

To sum up then, just as we had to give up the attempt to find *one
single cause* of value (p. 56)—because there are any number of causes
so must we give up trying to find *one single cause* of wages.[2] The
price of labour is determined :

(*1*) By all the general causes which act on the value of all things,
and which we may, if we like, sum up roughly in the formula of
" final utility."

(*2*) By certain causes peculiar to the labour commodity, as this
commodity is not quite like any other since it is at the same time a
human being. Among these the most active are, the growing feeling
on the part of the worker of his social importance, and the organisations which he is creating in order to maintain his rights (see *infra,
Trade Unions*).

We have been trying to discover the economic laws which govern
wages. But the question may also be put a little differently. We
might try to find what, from the point of view of justice and reason,
wages *ought to be*. This is the celebrated question of the *just wage*,
which has occupied political economists from the Middle Ages
onward, but which is no nearer being solved now than it was then.
Pope Leo XIII himself gave his attention to it. In his famous
Encyclical on working men called *Rerum Novarum*, he declared : " It
is a natural law of justice that the wage should not be insufficient
to keep the worker sober and honest." According to this definition, it
is the needs, or rather the conditions of existence, of the social *milieu*
in which the worker lives that should determine the just wage. It
is practically the *living wage*. But why, in the case of the worker,

---

[1] Note, however, that the theory of productivity, taken in the sense of marginal
productivity, applies very well to this case of immigration ; for it is probable that
the immigrant workers are less productive than the older ones, at least until they
become acclimatised. They therefore play the part of marginal worker, and this
is why wages are determined by them.

[2] The multiplicity of causes that act on wages becomes more especially
apparent when we study the inequality of wages from one industry to another.
Adam Smith has a very interesting chapter on this subject. He shows how
wages vary from one trade to another according as the labour is more or less painful, or more or less honourable, or more or less intermittent, or requires a more or
less long apprenticeship. But if competition worked perfectly, which is far from
being the case, each person, in accordance with the hedonistic principle, would
try to find the maximum of satisfaction with the minimum of pain, and the
result would be that, as regards the balancing of pains and remunerations, all
trades would be equal.

should justice ask only enough for a modest existence, for a " sober " worker, when no such limit would be laid down for the other classes of society ? It is to the minimum wage, not to the just wage, that the above definition applies. What justice demands is that the wage should correspond exactly to the value created by the labour of the worker. Unfortunately, we have no criterion for determining this value.

The theoretical problem of the just wage is this. Given two factors co-operating in an undertaking, one of which is labour and the other capital, what is the share in the product which ought to come to each of them ? Here, say, is Crusoe, who provides a canoe and a net ; Friday, who furnishes his labour. At the end of the day Friday brings in ten baskets of fish. How much should go to Crusoe (capital), how much to Friday (labour)? A correspondent of *Le Temps* wrote, from Brazzaville, that, when the owner of his canoe, disputing with his paddlers as to the price of his passage, said, "What could the paddlers do without the canoe ? " the latter replied, "What could the canoe do without the paddlers ? "

The question is indeed on a level with that put by Marshall, when he asked whether it was the upper or the under blade of a pair of scissors that could be said to cut.

And it is precisely because it is theoretically insoluble that the wage problem is a source of continual conflict,[1] and that it is difficult to find a judge or an authority to determine what share should go to capital and what to labour.

V : THE RISE IN WAGES

WHATEVER be the laws which govern them, the fact remains that wages are always very low. According to the statistics of the *Bureau du Travail*, the average in 1911 was 7 francs 24 centimes per day in Paris, and 4 francs 22 centimes in the towns of the provinces ;

---

[1] Von Thünen, in a very remarkable book, tried to show by the aid of mathematics that the wage was the *square root* of two factors, the first being the value consumed for the upkeep of the labourer, the second the value produced by his labour. If a represents the first, and p the second, we have the formula $w = \sqrt{ap}$. Von Thünen calls the wage thus determined the *natural wage*. Why " natural " ? It is all one to Nature ! It would be better to have said " rational." But, even from the standpoint of reason and justice, this formula is not very satisfactory. It implies that the worker's share, in proportion to the product of his labour, diminishes as the product increases : if the product becomes nine times greater, the wage becomes only three times greater. Where are the reason and justice there ?

which, counting 300 working days per annum—a figure much above the average—gives an annual income of 2172 francs and 1266 francs respectively. But these are the wages of industrial workers. For country workers the average is not above 3 francs per day, or 900 francs per annum. And these are men's wages; in the case of women the average is 3 francs in Paris and 2 francs 10 centimes in the departments. Where the worker has a family, and can add to his own wage the wages of his wife and of his children over thirteen years who have not yet left home, his income during a short period of his life, is almost double that given above. But this accumulation can take place only over a short period, as he must wait until his children are thirteen years of age, and by the time they are eighteen or twenty they often leave home. We must add the fact that the worker is forced to retire much earlier than the ordinary middle-class man, or, at least, his wage falls rapidly.

Women's wages, in particular, are one of the most distressing questions of the present day. As they are at present, they are absolutely insufficient to keep a woman if she is alone, and are good only as an auxiliary wage to eke out the family income. But there are unfortunately many women living alone, spinsters or widows, or, as is often the case in the working class, women deserted by their husbands, or by the men with whom they lived without legal marriage. How are these to exist unless they find some one to keep them ? The causes of the low wage of women are not difficult to find. There is, in the first place, the competition of the women who simply wish to add a little to their incomes, with those who need to work for a living wage. There is also the lower level of subsistence and the fewer needs of the woman as compared with the man, due less to a natural law than to long acquaintance with poverty. Lastly, there is the absolute want of organisation among working women— inexperienced in the matter of trade unions and strikes—which leaves them without defence against the law of supply and demand and, above all, against the exploitation of the *entrepreneur*.

And yet, mean as all these wages are, they are large compared with what they once were. Half a century ago the average rate of wages in France was less than 2 francs a day.

The gradual rise in wages is an undeniable fact. Thousands of statistics drawn up in all countries enable us to conclude that wages (agricultural and industrial) have more than doubled in the course of the nineteenth century.[1]

[1] The following table, taken from the volume *Salaires et coût de l'existence aux diverses époques jusqu'en* 1910, published in 1911 by the *Office du Travail*, gives

Various circumstances must, however, be taken into account which render this rise less considerable and less beneficial than we might at first be inclined to think :

(1) In the first place, the "average wage" given by the statistics is presumed to be an *annual* and *regular* wage. Now, *unemployment* and *dead seasons*, which are becoming a chronic evil of industry, may enormously reduce the actual wage paid to labour —sometimes by one-sixth or one quarter. And this danger is all the graver that no effective method of insurance against it has been found.[1]

(2) In the second place, this rise in wages is in part nominal, since the value of money has depreciated. If money within half a century loses half of its purchasing power, what difference does it make to the worker that his wage rises from 1 franc to 2 francs ? He is no better off by the rise.

Now, it is a fact that money during the last century lost part of its value, and that this fall in the value of the monetary standard caused a general rise in prices. And, although the rise since 1900 has not yet reached the level of 1877, so that the buying power of money is still greater than it was forty years ago, and the worker's real wage may be said to be even greater than his nominal wage, we

the rise in wages, in France, during the nineteenth century in ten-yearly periods :

1806	.	.	.	.	40	1880	.	82
1830	.	.	.	.	45	1890	.	92
1850	.	.	.	.	51	1900	.	100
1870	.	.	.	.	71	1910	.	110

This gives, in the course of the whole century, a rise of 275 per cent. Wages have almost trebled.

The following index numbers, taken from the same source, give the cost of living (food, lodging, heating and lighting) over the century :

	Expenses	Index numbers
1810	990 francs	74
1830	1130 „	83
1850	1250 „	85
1870	1385 „	104
1880	1480 „	110
1890	1390 „	103
1900	1345 „	100
1910	1400 „	104

The calculation is based on the hypothesis that consumption has remained the same in quantity and quality. We see that the rise in 1910 is still a little below the maximum of 1880. But, as it has been continuing strongly since 1910, the figure for 1913 will probably be about 1450.

[1] See *infra*, *Working Men's Insurance*.

believe this to be too optimistic a conclusion since the rise in retail prices is greater than is indicated by the figures given.

There is no doubt about it in the case of housing, and the prices of foodstuffs (meat, vegetables, milk, butter, sugar, and even bread) have gone up considerably. The only articles which have gone down in price are groceries and manufactured goods such as clothing, furniture, etc. The prices of transport, posts and telegraphs, books and newspapers have also fallen greatly.

To sum up then, we find that, in France, from the beginning of the nineteenth century up till 1900, the rise in wages (40–110) was much greater than the rise in the cost of living (74–104), so that the margin of increase in *real* wages was considerable. If we take the last ten or twelve years, we find that the cost of living has risen as much as, if not more than, have wages, so that, although the rise in nominal wages continues, the real wage remains stationary or is falling. This is, no doubt, one of the causes of the restless and agitated state of the working class.

Is this rise in wages the result of natural or of artificial causes ? Has it, that is to say, come about spontaneously, or is it due to the efforts of the workers, of the State, or of the employers themselves ?

The uncompromising disciples of the Liberal school do not believe that wages, any more than prices, can be artificially raised. In their view, the rate of wages is determined by natural laws (see p. 586). such as govern the current prices of commodities, laws independent of the will of the parties concerned. To think that any bargaining, any coalition of workers, the text of a law, or even the generosity of an employer can send up wages would be as puerile as to think that we can bring fine weather by pushing round the pointer of the barometer.

There are, they admit, cases in which a strike has succeeded in raising wages ; but this is because the rise in wage was bound to come about in any case. The strike has here had the same effect as a slight blow would have on the dial of a barometer, causing the pointer to follow the mercury more quickly.

For wages to rise, at any rate in a country economically healthy, we have only, they say, to give free play to natural laws, and particularly, as regards the law of supply and demand, to make labour as mobile as possible—as mobile as capital or as gold.[1]

---

[1] This is why economists of the Liberal school would make labour an object of commerce : M. de Molinari, by means of *Bourses du Travail*, where labour would be quoted and transferred like movable values ; M. Yves Guyot, by *commercial labour companies* which would sell the labour of their members where it was most in demand, as industrial companies sell their coal or their cotton.

In answer to this optimistic language we may grant, it is true, that natural laws, that is to say, such causes as the scarcity or abundance of labour, the standard of living of the worker, above all the degree of general prosperity in a country, determine *in the long run* the rate of wages ; we may also grant that most of these causes act in an upward direction. But the working class that trusted solely to them would be very imprudent. For the rate of wages is apt to become crystallised, much more so than is the current price of goods. We see the same phenomenon, though in a lesser degree, in the retail prices of goods. This is what is meant when we say that the rate of wages, where workers are not organised, particularly where they are far from big centres, is governed by *custom*. The rate of wages is therefore, to return to our simile, a pointer which does not answer quickly to the movements of the atmosphere ; and if a blow, in the form of a strike, can quicken its pace by a few years, say the lifetime of a man, this will not be an altogether negligible result.

(3) Lastly, whatever the rise in wages may be, it has certainly been far outstripped by the increase in wants. And, as the feeling of ease or indigence is less a result of absolute income and of quantity consumed than of the relation between income and wants, the result is that, in spite of an increased wage, the working class may yet feel poorer. Such is the nature of man that ease may even appear misery when contrasted with the opulence of those around. And it must not be said that the increase of these wants is attributable to the working class itself. It is sufficiently obvious that most of them have been suggested in imitation of the wealthy classes.

It is not, moreover, a mere question of appetite unsatisfied. It is a question of justice. The workers hold that they have a right not only to an improvement in their condition, but to an increase of income proportionately equal to that of the other classes in society. Now are they getting this ? Has the rise in wages *been proportional to the general increase in wealth ?* All the economists of the Liberal school, Bastiat years ago, MM. Leroy-Beaulieu and Yves Guyot to-day, answer in the affirmative, and try to show that the share taken by labour has actually risen proportionally more than 'that taken by capital.

Unfortunately their proof is far from convincing, and the opposite contention seems much more likely to be the case. We saw in the last chapter that money wages had more than *doubled* within a century. Are we to believe that the share which would fall to each Frenchman, if the total income were to be divided among the total population, has only doubled during the same period ? The increase has been much greater than that. If we take, *e.g.* the annual total of inheritances transmitted, taking the years 1910–1912 as average, we find that it amounts to 7 billion francs.[1] Now, in 1826, the earliest figure available, it was only 1786 millions, and at the beginning of the nineteenth century it could not have been over 1 billion. As this sum is evidently proportional to the total of private fortunes, we may conclude that the total of private wealth has increased more than sixfold during the nineteenth century.

This is not enough, of course, to prove that the share of every capitalist has increased in like proportion, since obviously the number of capitalists, that is to say, sharers, has also increased considerably. The population of France during the nineteenth century rose from 28 to 39 millions. Still, this makes an increase of only 40 per cent. for the whole population, and, even admitting that the capitalist class has been swelled by a certain number of wage-earners on whom fortune has smiled, it seems fairly clear that the average share of the capitalist has increased more than that of the worker. In our opinion, we may say that it has at least quadrupled.[2]

VI : TRADE UNIONS

UNDER ordinary circumstances, when a worker bargains individually with his employer he is inevitably at a disadvantage ; he can neither defend nor dispute his wage ; all he can do is to take it or leave it. And if he is starving he gives in, for the following reasons :

(*1*) The capitalist can wait, while the worker cannot. The latter is in the position of a trader who must sell his goods or die, his goods here being his labour.

---

[1] Exactly 6179 millions in 1911, plus 1200 millions of donations and not deducting debts. But as debts were not deducted before the year 1901, they should not be taken into account in the comparison.

Owing to false declarations this figure is less than it should be. The difference between the official figure and the real figure is, indeed, increasing in direct proportion to the rise in the taxes on inheritances and to the more general use of bearer securities previously unknown. The total of inheritances ought to be over 8 billions.

It is true, on the other hand, as M. Leroy-Beaulieu has pointed out, that this increase is in part *apparent*, owing to the rise in the rate of capitalisation. A State *rente* of 3000 francs fifty years ago was worth only 60,000 francs in capital value. To-day it is worth 87,000 francs. And yet it is clear that the share which its owner obtains out of the national income is not greater than before.

[2] This is also the conclusion of M. Colson, who cannot be suspected of bias on this point. See *Cours d'Économie politique*, t. iii (*Finances*), p. 366.

(2) The employer can usually do without the particular workman in question. It is an easy matter to find another workman. If need be, he can be brought from abroad, or machinery may be substituted in his stead. The converse is not equally true. It is not so easy to find another employer. He cannot be imported by rail, or steamboat, and we have yet to discover the machine that can replace him.

(3) The employer is better acquainted with the condition of the market. He looks further ahead, and it is easier for him to come to an understanding with his colleagues, or at least to know what they are about.

But, so soon as the worker is able to form an association with his fellow workers, the positions are to a certain extent equalised.

(1) Association gives the worker the power to refuse work, since he is supported for the time being by the funds of the society. If the association has enough money, it creates an unemployment fund to prevent capitulation from starvation.

(2) Association unites in one common bond all the workers of one industry, so that the employer has to deal, not with one alone, but with all. The *collective bargain* thus takes the place of the individual bargain, which has really only the appearance of a bargain.

(3) Association enables the workers to start information offices with competent and experienced managers, who are as well acquainted with the current state of affairs as are the employers themselves.

To the Classical economists, then, who declare that trade unions cannot fix an arbitrary rate of wages, we must answer that this is not their object. They aim simply at securing such a wage as the general state of the market allows, so that the worker is not at the mercy of such accidental and disturbing circumstances as the fact of having had no dinner, or being without work, or having a large family to feed.

And yet the right to unite and to form associations has only recently been conquered by the working classes.

Associations of workers of the same trade go back, indeed, through the journeymen's corporations [1] of the Middle Ages, to the workers' associations of Rome and of antiquity. But these venerable institutions were abolished in France by the laws of the Revolution, and, as a survival of the *ancien régime*, underwent the same fate as the guilds.[2] It was not till a century later, on the initiative of Waldeck

---

[1] Not through the mediæval guilds strictly speaking, which were generally composed of masters and resembled rather the employers' unions of to-day.

[2] The fears of the men of the Revolution concerning any reawakening of the corporative spirit and the peril which it might cause to individual liberty, were

Rousseau, that the celebrated law of March 21, 1884, restored to the workers (and to the employers also) the right to form the unions called, in France, *syndicats professionnels*.[1] This right to associate to defend trade interests was a real privilege, since it was refused to all other persons in France for any object whatever.

In 1912, the number of trade unions in France was 5217, with nominally 1,064,000 members. Nearly all of these belonged to industry and commerce, and nearly all were men, only 8 per cent. of the members being women.

If we compare the number of trade unionists (950,000, excluding women and country labourers) with the total number of workers employed in industry and commerce, which amounts roughly to 4 millions (excluding women), we see that the proportion of members of unions is less than one-fifth. And many of these figure only nominally on the lists. The proportion of members of unions varies, moreover, greatly from one trade to another. It is much above the average among miners, engineers, and printers, although even among

not unfounded from the individualistic point of view at which they placed themselves. No sooner, indeed, are these trade unions created than we find them, in the name of solidarity, governing their members despotically, and trying even to enforce their decisions on non-union men. Hence the incessant conflicts which have given rise to so many lawsuits. The legislature itself has vainly tried, by various abortive measures, to reconcile the rights of union men with the liberties of non-union men.

[1] In Great Britain trade unions number 2,400,000 members. With considerable resources at their disposal (over £6,000,000 of income), grouped into vast confederations directed by prudent and distinguished men, some of whom have been elected to the House of Commons, they hold large annual congresses, and constitute a veritable social power.

Up till recently they devoted themselves to practical objects, to raising wages and to reducing the length of the working day, without asking for government intervention. They have been moderate in the use of the formidable weapon—the strike—preferring to devote the greater part of their resources to funds for unemployment, old age, or sickness. They have been reproached, indeed, with an over-conservative spirit, and with trying to form a kind of aristocracy of working men. Since the famous London dock labourers' strike, however, the movement has spread to the ranks of the unskilled workers, who have also formed a number of trade unions, poor but much more socialist in spirit. These are more disposed to claim the aid of the State, owing to their slender resources, and seem to be leading trade unionism in the direction of collectivism, or at least towards the temperate form of English socialism called Fabianism, which would be content with socialising the land and mines. (See *History of Trade Unionism*, by Mr. and Mrs. Webb.)

Germany has outstripped England to-day and left the other countries far behind, the number of workers belonging to trade unions being over 2½ millions. But if we compare the proportion of members to the total population, it is Denmark and Sweden which stand in the first rank, and England next.

U

the miners, who hold the record, it is not over 40 per cent., while in many other trades it falls far below this.

In order to be *legally constituted* these unions must include only members *exercising a trade* and *the same trade*.[1] The legislature, indeed, had in mind only workers in industry, commerce, and agriculture. Those following the liberal professions, and State employees, were thus debarred from forming unions.

In regard to the liberal professions, however, a special law gave medical men the right to form unions, and to-day this right is practically admitted for all professions.

The case of employees of the State, the communes, and the departments has given rise in the last few years to vehement controversies. The right to form unions was given, in the first instance, to State workmen, and to employees who worked for the State under the same conditions as ordinary employees, *e.g.* the workers in State factories and railways. But when postmen, teachers, clerks, etc., in public administrations demanded the same right, the government refused it, on the ground that it could not allow agents in the State service, *i.e. functionaries,* "to defend their professional interests" against the State. Their professional interests must be subordinate to the public interest. In actual fact, however, a number of these functionaries have formed unions, which have been tolerated, pending legislation on the subject.

For the rest, since the right of association has become a right common to all French citizens without distinction as to whether or not they are functionaries, whether or not they exercise a trade ; and since association under common law confers practically the same rights as does trade-union association, it is a little difficult to understand the passion with which the right to form unions is demanded.[2] But just because it has been refused it has become a sort of rallying cry for discontented functionaries, and the symbol of an ostensible community of interests with the proletariat.

[1] Workers who have changed their trade, or have retired, have thus to leave their union. And this is a great drawback, since they are the very ones who have most experience and most leisure to administer the union. In actual fact, however, the law is not very strictly enforced.

[2] The legal position of trade-union associations constituted by the law of 1884 differs, however, in some features from that of associations constituted under common law by the law of 1901. The former may constitute themselves more simply, and have the right to receive legacies, which is refused to the latter. On the other hand, the latter are freed from the obligation to recruit from one single occupation, and may freely possess immovable property, while the former may possess only the amount of immovable property necessary for working purposes.

These trade unions are, in turn, grouped either into federations. *i.e.* groups of unions, of the same industry, *e.g. la Fédération des travailleurs du Livre*, which is the best-organised union in France ; or into *Bourses du Travail, i.e.* groups of unions of the same district.[1] These *Bourses du Travail*, which exist also in Germany, play a particularly interesting part. They date no further back than 1886 ; but the original idea belongs to the Liberal economist M. de Molinari, who suggested them over fifty years ago, in order to regulate the price of labour on the labour market by finding out where labour was scarce and where it was abundant. This is, in fact, what they do. And, to enable workers to move from place to place more easily they have resuscitated the travelling money, the *viaticum*. They also take charge of the technical training of workers. There are over 150 of these *Bourses du Travail* in France.[2]

In order to be legal these unions must concern themselves solely with trade interests, otherwise they lay themselves open to dissolution by the courts. They have no right to go in for commercial or industrial transactions, nor for politics. The first of these rules is generally respected by the unions of working men and employees. The militant working men, indeed, have no desire to go in for business undertakings, which might shackle them in their class conflict, and make them conservative through the possession of capital and the pursuit of gain.[3] As for the second, many of the working-men's unions ignore it altogether. Not only do they go in for politics, but "syndicalism," as it has been called, has a complete social programme of its own (see *supra*, p. 492), namely, to organise the conflict of the classes and to obtain directly, without applying to the government or the legislative power, all the rights necessary for the working class by means of single strikes or, if need be, the general

---

[1] These unions of trade unions do not enjoy the same legal position as the trade unions ; in particular they may not possess immovables.

[2] See Pelloutier, *Histoire des Bourses du Travail*. In England the government has just created about 100 Labour Exchanges wholly on the lines of M. de Molinari's plan. They are simply labour bureaus, intended to ward off crises of unemployment, and are looked on with little favour by trade unionists, who see in them a means for the employer to recruit "blacklegs."

[3] A measure has, however, been proposed to confer on unions the right to carry on industry and commerce, *e.g.* to constitute within themselves co-operative societies of production (see *infra*). It is thus hoped to lead the activity of the unions into a practical channel, and at the same time to provide them with capital and resources.

Many trade-union members, even among the non-revolutionaries, object to this, as turning the unions aside from what should be their true aim, the struggle against capitalism. For what would become of this struggle if the unions themselves were to become capitalist employers ?

strike. In the *Confédération Générale du Travail* this programme has of late found an organ which is causing a real uneasiness to the government and to the bourgeoisie.[1]

All trade unions are not, however, revolutionary. Many are *reformist*,[2] or trade union in the English sense of the word ; that is to say, they aim rather at practical improvements, their methods being :

(*1*) To make employers accept the union as the normal inter-mediary in all negotiations between them and their workers, and to make them, if possible, agree to the principle of collective bargaining.

(*2*) To fix a minimum wage, called the Standard Rate, below which employers cannot go without the risk of a strike, and below which workers are forbidden to accept work.

(*3*) To start insurance funds against unemployment, and labour bureaux—the latter intended not only to attract workers to the unions, but to save them from having to accept whatever employ-ment turns up at a starvation wage.

(*4*) To inspire members with a feeling of loyalty to the union, a loyalty enforced, if need be, by the boycotting of refractory members or renegades.[3]

---

[1] *La Confédération Générale du Travail*, or the C.G.T., dates back no further than the year 1902, and the number of its members seems by no means propor-tional to the authoritative rôle it takes upon itself. In 1912 it comprised sixty federations, and all the *Bourses du Travail* (600,000 enrolled and 400,000 paying members), or about one-half of the total trade-union members, and only one-tenth of the working population. True, it attaches more importance to a militant minority than to large battalions.

[2] Besides the revolutionaries and the reformists, there is a third not very numerous party, which seeks rather to ally itself with the employers ; it is even said to be supported by the employers. Its members are known as the *jaunes* (yellows), a name which the *rouges* (reds) have given them, but which they accept to-day and display with some ostentation. We shall return to their programme when we come to profit-sharing.

[3] This generally takes the form of a demand sent to the employer to dismiss the refractory workman on penalty of declaring a strike. It has given occasion to numerous lawsuits, the victims of it claiming damages against the unions. Although the injury thus done to the worker may be terrible, since he may find himself shut out from all other workshops and reduced to exile and starvation, jurisprudence has decided that, so long as the union aims only at defending its own interests and those of the working class, and provided that it does not act from personal enmity, it is making a legitimate use of the right con-ferred on it by law.

The question of the civil responsibility of unions for the prejudice caused, not only to their comrades by the act of boycotting them, but to employers or third persons by reason of strikes, is one of the most difficult.

(5) To develop the technical and social training of the workers (by lectures for apprentices, libraries, newspapers, etc.), and to limit the number of apprentices.

(6) To issue labels[1] to be attached to products made by union labourers, and to recommend houses which pay the standard wage.

On the whole, in spite of their too often tyrannical way of understanding working-class solidarity ; in spite of their arrogance towards all that is not working class ; in spite of their too frequent abuse of the strike and even of *sabotage*, trade unions have rendered the workers undoubted services. It is to be hoped that they will be accepted by all employers without reservation, and that they will gradually number among their members the whole of the working population. Only so will they cease to be an instrument of social disturbance and become a preponderant factor in economic evolution.

VII : STRIKES

THE *strike*, that is to say, the refusal to work, is generally considered the sole end and essential function of the trade union ; but this is a grave mistake. A well-organised union wins the day without strikes, as a general gains victories without battles. It is indeed the best-organised and most powerful unions which declare the fewest strikes. Still, the strike constitutes the *ultima ratio* of the trade union when all other means have failed.

What is the strike ? It is not a mere refusal to work, for such an act has never been punishable by law ; nor is it the abandonment of work begun, for the right to repudiate exists in the case of the labour contract, just as in that of any other contract that is not for

---

[1] The label is of American origin. It has spread extraordinarily in the United States. In France, up till now, it has hardly been used except by the printers of the *Fédération du Livre*. It can give good results only where it is supported by the public—the consumers ; for it is only in so far as the manufacturer knows that the *label* will be an effective advertisement and will bring him faithful customers that he will be inclined to accept the conditions of the union in order to obtain the right to use it. Consumers, therefore, must first of all be educated up to it. This work might perhaps be undertaken by the *Ligues sociales d'acheteurs* (see *infra*, Book IV).

The *label* has for counterpart the *boycott*, most often practised in Germany. While the label recommends the purchase of articles manufactured in conformity with trade-union rates, the boycott prevents the sale of articles manufactured in contravention of them. Union members not only refrain from buying these articles themselves, but try to persuade the public, by all means in their power, to do the same. This process may, however, occasion lawsuits, in France at any rate, as an attack on the liberty of trade.

a fixed term. The strike is a means of constraint exercised by one contracting party over the other, in order to obtain certain modifications of the contract, *e.g.* a rise in the wages previously agreed on. It is not the sole means of constraint : there may be others, such as *sabotage ;* [1] but in the case of the strike the coercion consists in the sudden interruption of labour and the injury which results for the employer. This means of constraint is effective only if exercised collectively by a large number of workers, by all who belong to the factory, or, if possible, by all who belong to the same industry, so that employers cannot help one another ; or—and in this case it reaches its maximum of effectiveness—by all workers in all industries, that is to say, by the general strike. The characteristic of the strike, then, is that it is an *a priori* understanding, a *coalition ;* this is, indeed, the only name by which it is known in French law.

The strike ought therefore to be considered as a method of war, since its object is to obtain by force what cannot be obtained otherwise. The tactics of the strike, too, are beginning to follow more and more closely those of real warfare. Hostilities are begun without previous declaration, in order to strike unexpectedly ; [2] a staff is organised by the union, or by the *Confédération Générale du*

---

[1] We know that the workers call *sabotage* the act of inflicting injury on an employer, either by damaging the raw material or implements, *e.g.* putting sand into the machinery ; or by wasting the goods for sale, *e.g.* giving double the quantity to the consumer for the same price ; or by not working efficiently ; or even (an original kind of *sabotage* invented by the railway employees in Italy) by fastidiously applying all the rules in such a way that the service cannot proceed. The first only of these modes of *sabotage*, material damage, is liable to be punished by law (*Code Pénal*, Art. 443), although the punishment is never applied. The others escape the law altogether.

This method of attack on the employer is at once less costly than the strike for the workers, as they continue to draw their wages, and quite as effective against the employer, as it does away with his profit.

[2] Jurisprudence has tried to put an end to this by forcing strikers to give warning, or in default of it to pay an indemnity (see above, p. 581). But apart from the fact that this penalty is inapplicable so soon as the strikers are numerous, many economists and jurisconsults contest the legitimacy of it. The notice they say, is necessary only in the case of a repudiation of the labour contract ; now, in the strike, there is no breach of contract, but only interruption of work. The workers do not want to leave the workshop, or they would go and get work elsewhere, in which case there would be no strike ; nor has the employer expressed any intention of dismissing his workers.

For our part, we hold that the strike does not constitute in itself a dissolution of contract, and consequently gives the employer no right to claim an indemnity from the workers ; but it gives him nevertheless a legitimate ground for dissolving the contract without being bound to pay an indemnity. And yet, if the strike is of a purely defensive character, it is open to question whether the courts should

Travail; headquarters are taken up ; a commissariat service and communist soup kitchens are started to feed the strikers and their families ; children are quartered on other villages in order to reduce expenses ; sentinels and pickets are set to guard the works to hinder non-strikers, blacklegs, from entering, and even at the approaches to railway stations to prevent them from arriving ; finally, armed force is used either against the renegades, who are looked on as traitors, or against the troops sent to protect them, and, sometimes even, factories are burnt down. Do we not recognise here all the signs of war ? And it is as such that the working-class trade-union party understands the strike, seeing in it the typical expression of class conflict.[1] The strike, moreover, is employed to-day not only in conflicts between employers and workers, but also in political conflicts. Thus, in Belgium, more than once a general strike has been declared for the purpose of obtaining universal suffrage.

It is not surprising, then, to find that the strike, or, in general, the coalition, was till quite recently in every country an offence specially foreseen and punishable by law. In France, however, the right to strike was recognised before the right of association, as the law abolishing penalties for strikes dates from May 25, 1864,[2] while that recognising the right of trade association dates only from March 21, 1884. To-day no one contests the legitimacy of the strike. To give the economists of the Liberal school their due, they were, indeed, the first to announce it, long before it was legally recognised, on the ground that, even if the strike be considered a violation of the principle of social liberty—an act of war—yet the working class must

not allow the strikers whose places have been filled a right to compensation. For fuller discussion of this difficult point, as of all the questions in this chapter, see a lecture by M. Perreau in a volume of lectures by various authors on *Le Droit de Grève.*

[1] See in particular M. Georges Sorel's book, *Réflexions sur la violence.*
At a congress, in 1910, the federation of stokers and engine-drivers declared that " in such cases the honest methods are the most violent."

[2] The law of 1864, which modified Arts 415, 416 of the *Code Pénal,* did not, however, abolish all penalties special to strikes It retained those of Art. 414 regarding " violence, menace, or fraudulent dealings." But why special penalties for these acts, since they are already considered misdemeanours under common law and punished by other articles of the *Code Pénal* ? Because, said the author of the law, M. Émile Olivier, it was held necessary that the law which restored the *liberty to strike* should protect in a special manner the *liberty to work,* and because it was to be expected that the penalties of common law would here be insufficient. The actual facts, the acts of violence against workers who wish to continue working, which to-day accompany nearly all strikes, seem fully to justify this precaution. Still, there is a strong trend in favour of repealing this article as the last vestige of the repressive penalties against strikes.

be allowed the right to defend its interests as best it may, in the absence of courts competent to solve the conflicts between labour and capital.

It would be all the more unjust to refuse the right of coalition to the workers, since it is impossible to refuse it to employers. In reality, all law punishing coalition falls only on the workers. For, if the law can effectively prevent the workers from taking the measures necessary to organise strikes, such as the calling of meetings, and various manifestations, it is quite powerless to prevent a few employers from meeting at one of their houses and coming to an agreement to cut down wages.[1] Adam Smith had already pointed out, in his day, that there is always a tacit state of coalition among employers, which is the more easy as they are fewer in number. If there were not some counterbalancing weight on the side of the workers, these last would necessarily go under. The condition under which men exist is, unfortunately, a state of war, and this implies, for so long as it lasts, and pending the advent of a new *régime*, the *morale* of warfare.[2]

There are, however, cases in which the strike appears so dangerous for public security that we may very naturally ask whether, in these exceptional instances, its penal character should not be maintained. First of all, there is the case of functionaries and employees of the State, or of public services. In the last few years, in different countries, we have seen strikes of postal employees, State railway employees, workers in the State shipbuilding yards, and even, at Lyons, in 1905, a strike of policemen ! All the governments concerned have energetically refused to their functionaries, even those to whom they allowed the right to form trade unions, the right to stop their service on pretext of a strike, and have considered the interruption of service as an act of rebellion, involving dismissal at the very least. They point out to their functionaries, who claim the right to strike, that their situation is not quite the same as that of worker to employer. On the one hand, their *nomination* has nothing in common

---

[1] The lock-out, much in use in England, has been introduced into France only quite recently and somewhat timidly. It is an answer on the part of the employer to a manœuvre of the strikers called the *grève par échelons*, or *grève tampon*, which consists in declaring a strike first in one factory, and then, when it has capitulated, in another, and so on, the strikers being supported successively by the comrades who continue working. The *lock-out* checkmates these tactics by shutting out all the workers of the same industry and region.

[2] This condition and *morale* of warfare need not hinder us from foreseeing a future state in which, in the words of M. Jaurès, "the memory of strikes will horrify mankind reconciled."

with a contract ; and, on the other, their salary is fixed by law, and consequently can be altered only by the legislative power. All compulsion with a view to obtaining a modification of their salary by any other than the regular legislative channel constitutes, therefore, a veritable act of rebellion. In France, however, there exists no law which formally forbids them to strike.[1]

There are also many other enterprises which, though not carried out by State employees, are none the less essentially " public services," the interruption of which may be exceedingly harmful to public security, e.g. the water-supply, the lighting of the streets, the railway service, even when the railways are in the hands of private companies. The stoppage of the railways is no less serious than that of the posts, since the posts cannot work without the railways.[2]

The problem is a difficult one, for it is not easy to know just where to stop. If electrical and railway workers are to be refused the right to strike, why not also bakers' assistants ? A town may more easily dispense with light than with bread. On the other hand, it is difficult to see what penalty would be effective in enforcing such a law. Prison ? But how prosecute, judge, and imprison thousands of men ? Fines ? But how force workers to pay if they have nothing ? Dismissal ? This is indeed the only effective penalty. But to apply it there is no need of a special law. The employer and the State have always the right to dismiss a worker who neglects his

[1] It is, however, frequently said that they are forbidden by law, on the strength of Art. 126 of the Code Pénal, which decrees severe penalties against functionaries who concert to resign their posts in such a way as to hinder the performance of a public service But it is not at all certain that this applies to strikes, since the strike does not imply resignation. Far from it !

[2] In many countries there are laws punishing strikes in public services, e.g. in Holland, Italy, Russia, in the case of the railway services ; in England, in that of water and lighting. or any strike which attacks life and property. But there has never been occasion to apply this law. In most countries, railway strikes have been crushed out by the expedient of mobilising the strikers. This method was found effective, but its legality is open to criticism, and it is dangerous as a training in anti-militarism. In France it was applied, for want of a better method. in the recent railway strike (1910).

The Canadian system appears to be the best. The right to strike is not withdrawn from railway employees, but it is subject : (1) to a sufficiently long delay to enable an official inquiry to be made ; (2) to appearance before a Conciliation Board. If these slower methods fail, the field is then left open for a strike as ultima ratio. But, as a rule, the parties come to an understanding.

In any case, if it is held indispensable to deny the right to strike to certain categories of workers or employees, they must be given, in compensation, a court of arbitrage before which they may carry their grievances. This project, however, is not being very well received either by the workers or the employers.

U′

work or refuses to do it. Only, in practice, this penalty would seldom be inflicted by the employer, and still more seldom by the State.[1]

All that we have said concerning strikes, then, amounts simply to this, that the strike, precisely because it is an act of war, is by its nature beyond the action of law. And it is our view that, though the legislator ought to try to punish such acts as take the form of attacks on the liberty of persons, or on property, yet, in dealing with the large strikes which attack the very existence of society, he should count mainly on the force of public opinion. This is no illusory guarantee. Far from it. For, if the public is indifferent or even sympathetic to strikers so long as it sees in the strike no more than a conflict between worker and employer, it is quickly roused so soon as it sees in it a blow aimed at its own interests, or finds the satisfaction of its daily wants endangered. The reason why the strikes of postal, tramway, or railway employees have hardly ever succeeded is, simply, that they have touched the consumer. And the force of public opinion will be still more effective when it is organised, when, for instance, Consumers' Leagues and Co-operative Societies for Consumption have educated the consumer. It is on him, after all, that we have to fall back as third party in any attempt to solve the conflicts between Capital and Labour. It is quite possible that the consumer may one day reach the point of organising bands of volunteers to prevent the interruption of public services, as he has already, on more than one occasion, organised the boycotting of manufacturers (in the case of gas and beer) when he thought they were in the wrong.[2]

Strikes are increasing to a disquieting extent. Statistics show a very rapid increase in their number in all countries, even in England.[3] Apparently this increase must not be put, as is often

---

[1] A written undertaking not to strike might perhaps be required of each candidate for public services; but we should not need to rely too much on the moral value of any such pledge.

[2] See Book IV, *The Rôle of the Consumer.*

[3] If, for France, we compare the two five-yearly periods 1899–1903 and 1906–1910, we see that, in the first, the average number of strikes was 649 with 169,000 strikers, while in the second it was 1237 with 237,000 strikers—a perceptible increase! We must not, however, exaggerate the meaning of these figures, as do the newspapers in order to alarm the bourgeois. The number of strikers, 237,000, is certainly much below that of workers involuntarily unemployed from want of work. Whereas the average period of voluntary unemployment for each striker is sixteen days, the average period of involuntary unemployment for each worker is much more. Of the total number of work-days furnished by the working class, the number lost by unemployment is estimated at 8 per cent., while that

done, solely to the account of trade unions, since strikes are as frequent in industries where there are no unions as in those where there are many ; and since the country in which the organisation of trade unions is most advanced, namely, England, is also the country where strikes were, for a long time, on the decrease.[1] Strikes, it would seem, are determined rather by economic causes, particularly by the desire to obtain a rise in wages when the rate of profits goes up. It is only natural, indeed, that the worker, also, should try to benefit by favourable conditions of industry, the more so as it is at such times that strikes have the best chances of success.[2]

It is, however, a much disputed point as to whether strikes are able effectively to raise wages. Economists of the Liberal school are not inclined to admit that they can, believing, as they do, that the rate of wages, like the current price of commodities, is determined by natural laws, which govern from above all the bargains and disputes of the parties concerned. Still, in our view, this violent method has unquestionably contributed to raise the rate of wages, and, in particular, to reduce the working day. The action of natural law here would be really incomprehensible. The efficacy of strikes must not be gauged from the actual numbers of those which have failed or succeeded.[3] One successful strike may send wages up in a host of industries. Besides, what acts more strongly in this direction than even the strike itself is the ever-present fear of one.

resulting from strikes is not more than 1 per *thousand*. (See M. Picquenard's lecture in the volume referred to above.)

[1] The number of strikes in England was over 1200 in 1889 and fell to 400 between 1902 and 1905. Since then strikes have been increasing, the year 1911 giving 903 with nearly 1 million strikers.

[2] Mr. Rist, in the *Revue d'Économie politique* (March 1907), shows that the number of strikes varies in direct ratio with the increase in exports and in inverse ratio with the increase in unemployment.

[3] According to the numerous strike statistics published in all countries, we may count an average of 20 per cent. of complete successes, to 45 per cent. of complete defeats, and the remaining 35 per cent. of reciprocal concessions. So that in more than half, and sometimes in two-thirds, of the number of cases, the workers obtain more or less important advantages.

The following are the percentages of total failures for five countries during the period 1901–1910 :

Austria	34·1 per cent.
France	40·2 ,, ,,
England	43·9 ,, ,,
Germany	44·9 ,, ,,
Belgium	65·5 ,, ,,

Thus Austria has two-thirds of partial or complete successes against one-third of total failures, while Belgium has only one-third of complete or partial successes.

Those who deny the efficacy of strikes as a means of raising wages point out that the rise in wages has been at least equal, if not higher, in industries in which strikes never occur, or in those in which there are no organised unions, *e.g.* among agricultural labourers and domestic servants. But why is this ? It is simply because these classes of workers have benefited indirectly from the rise in wages in the organised industries. If wages have risen in the country, it is because country labourers have migrated to the towns in search of better pay. The wages of domestic servants, also, follow the rise of industrial wages. The organised trades are thus becoming the regulators of the labour market, which was formerly weighed down by the great poverty-stricken crowd. Economically and morally this is an immense advantage.

The workers, it is sometimes said, lose more than they gain even by a victorious strike. The wages which they lose during the time they are idle, their small savings which they are forced to use up in order to live, the debts they contract to their tradesmen, more than outweigh any increase in wage which they may win. But the calculations made by the *Offices du Travail* in France and Italy show that this argument is worthless. If the increase in the wage were to last but one year, even deducting the wages lost, it would leave a considerable balance over.[1] And this hypothesis is much too unfavourable, since once a rise has been won it generally continues for ever.

It is also a difficult matter to know the exact influence of strikes on the prices of products and, as a result, on consumers. There is a prevalent opinion that they have a real action in sending up prices, and that the recent rise in prices is in great part due to them. We could wish, indeed, that such an opinion might become widely accredited, as it would shake the consumer out of his lethargy and show him that it is not merely railway and postal strikes which affect him. But it must be admitted that there is not much scientific foundation for it.[2] No doubt it is sometimes possible to point to a paral-

---

[1] There would be a gain even if we were to deduct the wages lost without compensation by the strikers who fail altogether. These, of course, have done a bad stroke of business so far as they themselves are concerned ; but, they are only a minority. The working class, taken as a whole, gains each year an increase of income by strikes. True, it may be said that there is no proof that as much, if not more, might not have been gained, without loss, by friendly negotiation ; and the example of England is quoted as a case in point. But the miserable wage of working women is certainly due, in part at least, to the fact that they do not strike.

[2] In refutation of it, the *Confédération Générale du Travail* has just published (September 1910) some curious figures showing, on the one hand, the rise in the price of bread, meat, wine, and sugar, and, on the other hand, wages in the baking,

lelism between the movement of strikes and the movement of prices ; but, even so, it is quite possible that it is the second that acts on the first. A rise in profits is bound to exercise a pressure on strikes in two ways at once. By raising the cost of living it impels workers to demand a higher wage ; by increasing profits it gives them a better chance of obtaining it.[1]

VIII : CONCILIATION AND ARBITRATION

POLITICAL conflicts, which used to be the source of constant warfare, arc now frequently settled by arbitration. Why should not the conflicts between labour and capital be solved in the same peaceful manner ? There is indeed in most countries a strong incl nation to do so, and already numerous boards of conciliation and arbitration, elected by employers and employed, are successfully at work.

Some, like the *Conseils d'usine* (workshop boards), operate, as their name indicates, within the limits of the factory. Their rôle is to receive the complaints of the workers, discuss the workshop regulations, and share in the internal government of the works. Their decisions, however, are not binding on the employer.[2]

Others, such as the conciliation board of the iron trade in the North of England, embrace nearly a whole industry.[3] There are even a number in the United States which have an official character and apply to a whole State.

We must distinguish carefully between *conciliation* and *arbitration*. Though they often work through the same organs, they differ essentially in character.

butchering, wine-growing, and sugar-making trades. The rise in price of these four products, between 1900 and 1910, has varied from 40 per cent. to 100 per cent., while wages have remained absolutely stationary.

[1] Still, it is said, the rise in wage gained by a strike must come from somewhere. True, but it may quite well come from a curtailing of profits, or from a reduction in the cost of production. There is no more fruitful stimulus to progress in machinery than strikes. We do not deny that in some industries a rise of wages, as the result of a strike, may involve a rise in prices. We have only to point to the house-building trade during the last few years. But we do not believe that strikes can determine a *general rise* in prices. Only a variation in the value of money can have such an effect as that (see p. 231).

[2] There are a fair number of them in Austria. In Belgium they are known by the name of *Chambres d'explication*. In France there are only two or three.

[3] These conciliation boards exist to-day in nearly every industry in England. There are 262 permanent boards in existence which concern nearly 2 million workers, and their pacific effect may be measured by the fact that, out of the 7508 conflicts settled by them between 1900 and 1909, in only 104 cases was there a stoppage of work.

(*a*) They deal with different stages of the problem. Conciliation takes place before the conflict breaks out. Its object is to prevent conflict. Arbitration does not come in as a rule until after the conflict has lasted some time. Its object is to settle the conflict.

(*b*) They follow a different procedure. In conciliation the two parties come together to discuss the matter in hand, and to try to convince each other. In arbitration there is always a third party as well, and the two concerned plead before the arbitrator like litigants before a judge.

(*c*) Above all, they differ in their results. In conciliation the two parties are pledged to nothing ; if they do not succeed in convincing one another, they retire and nothing is done. In arbitration a solution is bound to be reached, and is accepted in advance by both parties concerned. This is so well understood that, as soon as arbitration is accepted, the strikers resume work.[1]

Arbitration, then, is a much more serious matter than conciliation, and not so lightly resorted to, since it implies entire abdication of both parties in favour of a third person. But for this very reason it is much more effective. It is only natural, then, to ask whether it could not be made compulsory on employers and workers.

Compulsory courts of arbitration exist in a few countries, but only for serious conflicts, *e.g.* such as concern the State and its employees, or services of public utility (railways, etc.). Danish law establishes compulsory arbitration in every case of collective bargaining, giving the party which complains that the agreement has been broken the right to summon the other.

There is one essential difference between the rôle of judge in a civil suit and the rôle of judge in conflicts between capital and labour. The first judges according to the written law, or at least according to generally admitted principles of law ; the last has no criterion.[2] Here, say, is a worker who demands a wage of

---

[1] This, at any rate, is the custom in England, and the law in Australia. In France it is far otherwise ; not only do the strikers never dream of resuming work the moment arbitration is accepted, but they often make difficulties about resuming it when the verdict is not to their liking.

[2] Conciliation and arbitration boards must not be confused with industrial courts, such as the *Conseils de Prud'hommes* in France. . The latter are veritable tribunals. They decide, not economic questions, such as the demand for a rise in wages, but juridical questions, such as the claim for a wage which has not been paid, *i.e.* not general, but individual cases. The reform of these courts is also being studied at the present moment.

Nor must they be confused with the *Conseils consultatifs du Travail*, an official institution which is intended to " give advice to the government " on working-men's problems, but has not yet been put in operation.

5 francs, and an employer who declares he is able to give him only
4 francs. What is—I do not say the written law—but the economic
law, the moral law, according to which the judge will pass sentence ?
Is his criterion the just wage ? But what is the just wage ? Is it
the wage as measured by the legitimate wants of the worker ? Is
it the wage as measured by the utility of the labour he performs,
or by the value of the products of that labour ? Economists have
wrestled with these problems for centuries. What can we expect
the judge to do ? [1] This is the reason why we can hardly imagine
compulsory arbitration.

And yet, in New Zealand, there has been in existence for some
twenty years a compulsory court of arbitration—a veritable tribunal—
from whose jurisdiction none can escape. This institution, created
by law, in December, 1894, and adopted later by the other Australasian
States, gave good results for some time, and was supposed to be
ushering in an era of social peace. To-day, it is beginning to provoke
lively hostility, not only on the part of employers who have an
official wage forced on them by the court of arbitration, but on the
part of the employees, who will not be deprived of the right to strike,
and who, on several occasions have refused to comply with the
decision of the Court. These States are, of course, small countries,
in which trade unions are already powerfully organised, including, as
they do, the whole working population, and where industry has
nothing to fear from foreign competition. It would be no easy
matter, for instance, in France, supposing the trade unions refused
to submit to the decision of an arbitration court, to apply to them
the heavy fines inflicted in New Zealand (£10 per head, or £500 for
the union).

A French law of December 27, 1893, introduced optional arbitration and conciliation in a somewhat timid form. The magistrate (*juge
de paix*) is called upon to invite the parties to come to terms. He
cannot intervene officially, unless a strike has been declared, or
unless at the demand of one of the parties. If the two parties
consent, they nominate delegates, who· discuss the matter before
the magistrate. If the discussion leads to nothing, the magistrate
proposes to nominate an arbitrator—never himself, as he has no
technical competence. The parties are free to accept or refuse.

The results given by this law are unsatisfactory, and mark a backward, rather than a forward, step. The law has been applied in about
one-fourth of the conflicts, but it has been able to settle no more than
8 per cent. by conciliation and less than 3 per 1000 by arbitration.

[1] See what we have said on the just wage (p. 593).

In the absence of compulsory arbitration, the question has arisen whether the attempt at conciliation, that is to say, the summoning of the two parties before an elected council, could not be made compulsory, as it is in civil suits, and an inquiry imposed. The parties would remain free not to come to an agreement, but the mere fact of their coming together, and the publicity of the inquiry, might give good results. In spite of some practical difficulties, this measure has more to commend it than any hitherto tried for the prevention of strikes.[1]

IX : THE REGULATION OF LABOUR

THE regulation of labour belongs strictly to the domain of what is called *working-class legislation*. From the beginning of the nineteenth century, but particularly towards the close of it, the State intervened :

(1) To limit the working day.

(2) To secure for the worker safe and sanitary conditions of work.

(3) In some cases to secure for him a minimum wage.

(4) Lastly, by international treaties, to spread the reforms carried out in each country.

This is not to say, however, that the State is the sole factor in the regulation of labour : the employer also has his share. Indeed, by means of the workshop regulations (p. 579), it was he who, until quite recently, regulated the conditions of labour. Since, however, the workers have begun to organise themselves, their unions, through the collective bargains which they impose on employers, are taking a more and more active part in regulating labour. Economists of the Liberal school, indeed, insist that these last two factors are sufficient of themselves for regulating labour, and that it is unnecessary and harmful to call in the heavy hand of the State. The most progressive trade unionists are of the same opinion, being in favour of *direct action*, and holding that the working class should carry out itself what it thinks best for its own interests. They show the profoundest contempt for reforms granted by the State, and for all socialists—whether State socialists or Marxian socialists— who expect any result from them.

And yet economic history shows how effective is the action of law in this matter. Those who point to the example of England, where the hours of adult labour have only lately been limited by law, and

<hr>

[1] It is imposed by Canadian law (see p. 609, n. 2).

where nevertheless workers have been able to win a nine-hours day, forget that England was the first country to limit by law the hours of labour for children and young persons, and that this reduction has reacted on the length of the adult working day. In France, State intervention long anticipated private action, on the part both of employers and workers. It must not be forgotten that, under the system of free competition, the most philanthropic employer cannot curtail the working day nor give the weekly day of rest, unless his competitors follow suit. Before such reforms are possible there must be one single law for all. Now, the State alone can compass this. It alone can enforce measures concerning the sanitary condition of workshops, which are special police measures ; it alone can sanction such reforms by means of international treaties.

Not only are laws indispensable, but *inspectors* are necessary to see that they are carried out effectively ; otherwise, experience has shown that the law will remain a dead letter. We may groan, indeed, at seeing the number of functionaries increase with each new regulation ; but the public conscience is not yet so well developed— particularly in regard to labour legislation—that it can be counted on, of itself, to apply the law. And the control of inspectors themselves is insufficient unless backed by strong working-class organisations.[1] No doubt labour legislation is vexatious ; it is a mechanism lacking in elasticity. But, in the matter of social reform, we must often be content with the lesser of two evils.

1. THE LIMITATION OF THE WORKING DAY

Of the four instances we have just given of the regulation of labour, the most important is the limitation of the hours of labour. The wage received is only one side of the wage-earning question : the other is the amount of labour furnished. The improving of the worker's condition may lie quite as much in the reduction of his labour as in the increase of his income.

The shortening of the working day is one of the reforms to which the greatest importance is nowadays attached. Socialists look upon it as a means of emancipating the worker, of freeing him, in part, from the exploitation of the employer, and of enabling him to prepare himself for the social and political struggle. Workers see in it a way of doing less work without a reduction of wage, perhaps even with the chance of a rise, thanks to the shortage of labour that will be

---

[1] There are 134 labour inspectors in France, whose duty it is to inspect 550,000 establishments employing over 4 million workers. We may calculate, therefore, the average for each !

caused by the reduction of working hours. But the real significance of the movement lies in the fact that it is a means of raising the intellectual, moral, and even physical level of the worker, giving him the leisure necessary for *recreation*, in the deep and real sense of the word, so that for a certain number of hours each day he may cease to be a producing machine and may become a man. A man's business is not his whole life : family life, civic life, intellectual life claim also their share.[1]

The problem presents itself in a different light according as we are dealing with the child, the woman, or the man.

(*1*) *Child labour.* As regards the child, every civilised country, with a few rare and shameful exceptions, are to-day of one accord in forbidding the employment of children in factories. The age limit alone differs. In England it is fourteen years ; in France thirteen, this being the age when compulsory education ceases and the child is supposed to receive his certificate. The limit ought to be raised to fourteen years, as in England, Switzerland and Austria, since the age of thirteen is still too early not only to begin industrial work, but to stop primary education.[2] In any case, if the age limit be kept at thirteen years, in order that the burden of the children may not be too heavy on the parents, it is important that a certain number of hours per week should be reserved for technical training (see *Apprenticeship*).

It must not be thought, however, that this protection of children was carried without opposition. The campaign, inaugurated in England, in 1802, by the Health and Morals of Apprentices Act, ended only in 1833, and its success was due to the heroic perseverance of Lord Shaftesbury ; while, in France, it was not until 1841 that an age limit was fixed at eight years. The reform met with the same objection as was urged later against compulsory education, namely, that the responsibility for the children must be left to the parents. In both cases, however, the answer is, that parents, when pressed by want, are too ready to sacrifice the health, education, and future of their children for an addition to their income. The law, the guardian of the future, must prevent this.

In the case of adolescents of thirteen to eighteen years of age, the law in France is content to fix the length of the working day at ten hours. In England, from the age of twelve to fourteen,

---

[1] One reason for the failure of popular universities was certainly the over-long working day, which left the workers too tired to listen.

[2] Particularly in France, where the number of illiterates, after decreasing steadily, seems to have begun to increase. On a yearly average, 8800 conscripts, or nearly 3 per cent. of the total number per annum, can neither read nor write.

the working day is only half that of an adult, or else one day in two.

(2) *Women's labour.* The problem is more difficult in regard to women. Some uncompromising spirits urge the entire exclusion of women and children from factory work. And they have no lack of arguments in their favour. They point to the breaking-up of the home, the frightful mortality among children left alone, the dangers of factory life for the morality and health of the young girl and the woman, the risk of abortion and still-birth in the case of wives.

On the other hand, it must be urged that, at a time when so much is being said in favour of the emancipation of woman and the equality of the two sexes, it would be an unheard-of thing to disqualify all women from working for their living. It is difficult enough for them, as it is, to earn it honestly, without closing the doors of the factories against them. And, if we were imprudent enough to limit the disqualification to married women and mothers, we should strike a deadly blow at marriage and maternity, more dangerous in France than in any other country.

The result, then, has been a compromise. The law does not forbid married women to work in factories, but is content with regulating their labour in the interests of health and morality. These regulations may be brought under four headings :

(*a*) Limitation of the hours of labour : in France ten hours.

(*b*) Prohibition of night labour, with certain exceptions which, in practice, give rise to abuses.[1]

(*c*) Prohibition of underground work in mines.

(*d*) Cessation of work for several weeks before and after child-birth. Factory work, when a woman is pregnant, is apt to cause miscarriage ; and even when confinement takes place at the right time, the child is liable to be born rickety. It also necessitates the feeding of young children artificially. Hence the enormous infant mortality among the working classes in certain poor quarters of

---

[1] These exceptions are :

Permanent, in three or four categories of labour only, the principal one being newspaper folding ;

Temporary, in certain seasonal industries, like the manufacture of jams (and sardine packing), which can be carried on only at certain times of the year ;

Partial, *i.e.* where the worker does not work during the whole night, but only for a part of it, as in the millinery and dressmaking industries. This last exception, which was the most important and gave rise to the most serious abuses, has just been abolished (Decree of February 17, 1910), except in the case of ready-made mourning. There was no reason for it, indeed, except the caprices of rich customers, and it was bound to disappear so soon as the moral education of the consumer was a little more advanced.

towns (30 per cent. in the case of infants under a year, instead of the average 11 per cent.). This is therefore a vital question for the nation.[1] The mother herself is apt to suffer seriously in health by returning to work immediately after confinement. A law forbidding a woman to work during the critical periods which precede and follow confinement would be only too well warranted.

Such a measure of protection does not yet exist in France, where the law confines itself to forbidding an employer to dismiss a woman for suspension of work during eight weeks before and after confinement. French legislation did not forbid work altogether, fearing to injure the health of the mother still more by depriving her of her wage at the very moment when she most needed nourishment.[2]

(3) *Adult male labour.* The limitation of the hours of labour is still more difficult in the case of the adult male. We know the argument of the Classical school, that individuals who have attained majority ought to be left free to regulate the employment of their time and their labour ; that they are the best judges of their own interests. To this we would reply that, under the present system of large-scale industry, such liberty does not exist. The worker has to enter and leave the factory when the bell rings ; no matter what his wishes may be, he must work the number of hours imposed not merely by the employer, but by custom and competition. There is no question therefore of liberty. We have merely to consider whether a reduction of the hours of labour contributes to the well-being of the working class, or whether it is necessary for the progress of the nation. Now, the experience of countries where it has already been tried would appear decisive on this point.

The reduction of the hours of labour does not, it would seem, necessarily involve a curtailment of production or a fall in wages [3]—

---

[1] Institutions intended to remedy in a certain measure this social sore are : the *crèche*, a private establishment where children are kept and looked after during the absence of the mother in accordance with the health regulations ; and the *Salles d'allaitements* started in certain factories.

[2] A Bill before Parliament proposes a State pension during the critical period. Meanwhile societies called *Mutualités Maternelles* undertake to provide the working-class mother with what she requires during this time. And their efficacy is admirably shown in the notable decrease in infantile mortality.

[3] We must not, of course, push this theory to the verge of absurdity and declare, as socialists continually do, that the less a man works the more he will produce. We must beware of arguing in two opposite directions at once, and of asserting that the shorter working day will make labour more productive and at the same time give more work to all, thereby doing away with unemployment. It is evident, that if the workers while working less produce more, there will be no need of more workers. We must choose between the two arguments.

one of the objections most often urged against it. The workers, less over-driven, less exhausted, with more time for their intellectual, moral, and physical development, are able to produce more ; and if they produce more, there is no reason why their wage should fall. As a matter of fact, the countries which have the shortest working day— Australia, the United States, and England—are the countries in which wages are highest and the output per worker greatest. Only, before the shortening of the working day can give such good results, certain previous conditions are necessary which do not exist in all countries.[1]

(1) Workers must be willing to *intensify* their labour, so as to make up for the shorter hours. Now, in France, the workers refuse to do this, declaring that they would exhaust themselves as much as before, for the profit of the employer. What they want is, that the reduction of the hours of labour should force the employer to engage a greater number of men. This, they believe, would do away with unemployment and would send up wages.

(2) Even if the workers have the will to work harder in less time they must be physically capable of doing so ; for this intensification of labour presupposes an endurance and an energy with which all races are not endowed. The French worker is unable to work as many looms at a time as the American worker does.

(3) The equipment must be so improved as to admit of this intensification of labour, and even to require it : the machinery must not be more backward than the worker. Now, this is the business of the employer ; the worker can do nothing towards it. So complex are these conditions, that the reduction in the hours of labour, when introduced suddenly, has more than once had deplorable results and has had to be abandoned.[2]

In the case of men, the legal limitation of the hours of labour is the exception. France gave the initiative more than half a century ago by the law of 1848, when she fixed the limit at twelve hours. But, in actual fact, this law, which was much in advance of the economic development of the time, remained a dead letter till nearly the end of the century.[3] A few other countries followed later—

---

[1] See a remarkable article entitled *Les rapports entre le salaire, la durée du travail et sa productivité*, still true, though written some time ago by M. Louis Brentano in the *Revue d'Économie politique* (April 1893).

[2] *E.g.* the experiment of the eight-hours day in the State shipbuilding yards in France sent up the cost of production enormously. This was because the three stimulating conditions which increase output were almost entirely lacking.

[3] In France the legal limit for over a million adult workers is not more than ten hours, since all workers, even adults, who work *on the same premises* as women

Switzerland, Austria, Norway, Russia, Spain—fixing the maximum
length of the working day at eleven hours.

It is well known that workers are making a further demand.
They claim the eight-hours day of the English song :

> *"Eight hours to work, eight hours to play,*
> *Eight hours to sleep, and eight shillings a day "* ;

and great demonstrations are organised every First of May in all
countries to demand this reform. As yet, however, this minimum
exists in no written law. It is actually in force in Australia, but
there it was conquered fifty years ago by the trade unions. In
England, labour hours are generally fifty-four per week, making
about nine and a half per day and six on Saturday. In the United
States, they are somewhat more than this. In France, they vary in
large industry from ten to eleven hours per day.

It is in home work that the length of the working day is excessive ; and this is curious, since it is here that the worker is free to
regulate his hours as he wishes. But he is pushed along, as it were,
at the point of the bayonet by the lowness of his wage. The long
hours, the low wage, the unhealthy conditions of work in a room
which is often the living-room of the whole family, and the existence
of the middleman between employer and worker, are what mark
the sweating system (see Book I, *Home Work*). It is here that the
intervention of the law would do most good, but it is here also that
it is most difficult. For not only must the home be respected, but
home workshops, even where subject to inspection, are difficult to
find and to inspect satisfactorily.[1]

The question of the *weekly day of rest* is connected with that of
the working day. In most countries it is imposed by custom, if not

and lads of under eighteen, cannot be kept at work longer than these (law
of March 30, 1900). A factory, indeed, must shut at the same hour for all
its workers. The measure has, however, this objection that, in order to avoid
it, employers sometimes turn off all their young apprentices (see above, *Apprenticeship*). It is probable, however, that the ten-hours limit will soon apply to all
workers : a bill is already before Parliament to that effect.

The miners' working day has been limited by law to eight hours (June 29,
1905) ; for railway stokers and engine-drivers there are also special regulations.

[1] French law does not allow government inspectors to enter home workshops, except where a mechanical motor is used, and then only with a view to
security, not to controlling the hours of labour. In England, the employer who
employs home labour must register the names and addresses of the workers
whom he employs and the wages he pays. The question of sweated industry
is one of the questions of the day. Exhibitions of sweated articles organised
in London, Berlin, and Paris have greatly stirred public feeling.

by law. It is one of the instances of how powerless individual goodwill is to carry out a reform, unless supported by law. True, the
law here is not easy to apply. The difficulties experienced in France
in enforcing the recent law of 1907 regarding the weekly day of
rest, were so great that, in practice, it had to be given up in a great
number of cases. Without entering into details, it is easy to understand that, if the weekly day of rest is to be the *same day*, *i.e.*
Sunday, as it is in all Christian countries, it cannot be strictly
observed in all kinds of work without completely suspending social
life. Some must therefore continue to work while others play.
In order that a million Parisians may go and enjoy themselves in
the country, there must be thousands of tramway and railway
employees to transport them, and waiters in cafés and restaurants to
supply them with food and drink. The law cannot work without
numerous exceptions. Either employees must take their days off
in rotation, or the Sunday rest must be made up to them by one
whole day, or two half-days, during the week. Hence innumerable
complications.

On the other hand, as the law aims at protecting only employees,
it does not apply to small shopkeepers who have none. These, therefore, may open their shops on Sunday and profit by the closing of
those of their competitors—a profit all the greater as Sunday is the
chief purchasing day of the working classes. It is now demanded,
therefore, that all shops be closed without distinction. This is the
rule in most German towns. But it is rather sacrificing the liberty
of the small shopkeeper.

The loss caused to shopkeepers would be less if workers had the
Saturday afternoon free for their purchases, as in England.[1] The
" week-end " habit is indeed tending to spread to the Continent.
It already exists, to all intents and purposes, in the Paris banks and
a few administrations, but it has not yet been sanctioned by law.
There is also an inclination to grant a certain number of days
holiday to the workers, during which wages would, of course, be
paid, as otherwise these holidays would be mere unemployment,
of which the working class has had more than enough. But this
has not as yet become law.

[1] In England there are holiday agencies to enable workers and employees to
take advantage of week-ends, and to pass forty hours out of town, for the moderate
price of £1.

2. MEASURES OF HYGIENE AND SECURITY

These measures are too technical to enumerate here. We shall confine ourselves to pointing out that they bear mostly on the size and ventilation of workshops ; fencing of machinery ; the manipulation of poisonous materials—much more common than is thought,[1] certain substances being so pernicious that the use of them has had to be absolutely prohibited by law, *e.g.* white phosphorus and white lead ; the providing of cloakrooms and lavatories ; the forbidding of meals to be taken in the workshop.

Manufacturers consider these measures as in many cases vexatious and useless ; and more often than not the workers themselves share this feeling. Certainly it would be better if private initiative rendered them unnecessary ; and there is no doubt that the magnificent installations in some of the large English and American factories go far beyond what is required by law.[2] Unfortunately it is hardly to be hoped that the mass of employers will follow suit ; and here, as elsewhere, if we trust to the principle of *laisser-faire*, the most progressive will be the ones to suffer for their generosity.

8. THE LEGAL MINIMUM WAGE

The fixing by law of a minimum wage is a measure urgently demanded by socialists, and even by a good number of the "Social Catholic" school.

It may be said that it is no more arbitrary to fix a minimum rate of wages than a maximum rate of interest. But the danger of fixing a legal minimum wage is that if it be fixed too low it may bring down the average wage to its level ; while, if it be fixed too high, it may determine employers never to engage labour worth less than this minimum, so that all inferior workers—beginners, the old, the infirm, and the unskilled—who might still make a low wage by poor work, will henceforth find no employment and will fall on the rates. So true is this that, in Australia, legislation was obliged to authorise wages below the legal rate for "half-workers." Still, it may be said that a social *régime* in which the capable receive good wages and the incapable are assisted by the rates is perhaps better than such a system as our own, where the competition of the bad worker too often drags down the wage of the good worker.

---

[1] See the volume published by the *Office du Travail*, under the eloquent title *Les poisons industriels*.

[2] In particular Port Sunlight and Bournville, celebrated as garden cities. See our *Économie Sociale*.

It is to be feared, however, that women—unless a different tariff were fixed for them, thus sanctioning an inequality between the two sexes against which they justly protest—would find themselves driven out of trades in which they might still gain a miserable livelihood. We have therefore to proceed with caution.

Notwithstanding these difficulties, many countries have taken a step in this direction, viz., Australia, since 1896, and England, where, since 1909, Trade Boards have been constituted, composed of representatives of employers and workers, whose business it is to fix a minimum rate of wages in certain industries,[1] to be ratified by the Board of Trade. There is no question of fixing a general legal minimum wage, but simply of drawing up a scale of pay in certain industries—particularly those in which the sweating system is prevalent—a scale fixed by the parties concerned and to which the legislator simply gives legal force. This is more of the nature of a compulsory collective bargain.

The miserable conditions of home labour are so obvious, and have stirred the public so deeply, that it is probable that these protective measures will spread to all countries. Employers themselves raise no objection to them in principle ; they simply point out the practical difficulties of applying such tariffs.[2]

4. INTERNATIONAL LABOUR TREATIES

It is often said that economic solidarity, or rather the competition between nations, is so intense at the present day that it would be impossible for one country to shorten its working day without finding itself at a dangerous disadvantage compared with the rest. Attempts are now being made, therefore, to create a general under-

---

[1] In England only five industries come under the minimum wage :

(1) Ready-made and wholesale bespoke tailoring ; (2) the finishing pro-cesses of machine-made lace ; (3) paper-box making ; (4) certain kinds of chain-making, and (5) since the great miners' strike of 1911–1912, coal-mining. But the list may be lengthened at discretion by the Board of Trade.

[2] In France the *Conseil supérieur du Travail* has just adopted an analogous system, but only for women in the clothing industries. Wages in these industries must not be lower than the ordinary woman's wage for non-specialised work in the district, and the *Conseils de Prud'hommes* are entrusted with passing judgment on any breach of the rule.

The minimum wage, which would be fixed by law for all workers, must not be confused with the minimum wage which the State undertakes to pay *in its capacity of employer* (e.g. the 5 francs a day promised in France to the employees on State railways) ; nor with the wage imposed by the State in all works undertaken by *entrepreneurs* on behalf of the State. The wage here specified is not, strictly speaking, a minimum wage, but simply the current wage of the district, which must be ascertained by inquiry.

standing among all civilised countries, and the problem is thus becoming international, a fact not tending to speedy solution.[1] International regulation would, no doubt, be useful ; but it must not be taken as a pretext by the different countries to justify their tardiness in taking the first step. Experience has shown, that the nations advanced enough *morally* to limit the length of the working day, are also advanced enough industrially not to need to fear the competition of countries where hours are long. Still, it is obviously preferable for countries which are practically at the same level of civilisation to adopt the same regulations. An attempt has been made during the last few years to bring this about ;—either by general diplomatic conventions, such as those concluded at Berne in 1906 between seven States (France, Germany, Italy, and the neighbouring States) for suppressing the use of white phosphorus, and between thirteen States for prohibiting the night work of women in industry ;— or by treaties between two States, such as the Franco-Italian Treaty of 1904 relative to accidents, savings bank deposits, etc.

X : GUARANTEES AGAINST RISKS

To receive a fair wage and not be subjected to too crushing labour is not everything for the worker. There is a third condition, namely, *security*, without which his life will be full of anxiety. The man who lives from hand to mouth must have some guarantee against the risks which threaten at any moment to take away his work, and, with it, his livelihood. There are six risks to which he is exposed. Four of these are common to all mankind, viz., *sickness, old age, death*, and *invalidity ;* two are peculiar to his economic condition, viz., *accidents* and *unemployment*. And all have the same effect, namely, of depriving him of his wage, and consequently of reducing him and his to poverty. What can he do against so many enemies ? Not much indeed !

As regards *prevention*, the worker may, by temperance and a

---

[1] In April, 1890, an International Conference, at which all the great nations of Europe were represented, was convoked at Berlin by the Emperor William II. A body of resolutions was drawn up which remained unaccomplished. But, in 1900, on the initiative of some French and Belgian professors of Political Economy, an *International Association for the Legal Protection of Workers* was constituted in Paris, to which fourteen countries adhere, the headquarters of which are at Basle. It publishes an international bulletin of working-class legislation—besides the publications of the separate countries—and holds annual congresses. The French section issues very instructive memoirs on all questions relating to working-class legislation.

strict observance of the laws of health avoid illness and delay old age and death to the extent that his small means allow; but the other two risks are hardly within his control. His own prudence will do something towards avoiding accidents, but that of his employer and of the State can do much more. And it must be admitted that in all industries, including mining, the proportion of accidents to workers is steadily decreasing. Against unemployment, however, the worker is powerless.

As regards positive *provision against risks*, the worker may, by saving, manage to scrape together enough to carry him over the bad days, or to last him through his old age. But who can really imagine that saving—such saving as is that of the poor man— even eked out by the ingenious combinations of Friendly Societies, etc., is enough to secure him and his the equivalent of a wage of which he has been deprived by some fatality, some prolonged illness, or invalidity resulting from an accident or old age?

True, there are insurance companies which give a high insurance in case of death, accident, or even old age. But their premiums are quite beyond the working-man's means, and they do not cater to the small working-class *clientèle*. Moreover, as few even among the bourgeois insure against these two risks, we can hardly expect the worker to have more forethought. In any case there are no insurance companies against unemployment.

If the worker, then, is powerless of himself to make provision against the risks to which he is exposed, must he not turn to others to help him? And to whom if not to the employer and to the State?

(*1*) To the employer, as regards at any rate the risks of accident and unemployment. For if, under the present wage system, the worker is no more than an instrument in the service of the employer, the latter ought surely to bear the cost of breakage or wear, as he does in the case of his other machines. The employer, again, is able in a certain measure to prevent unemployment by regulating his output, as he knows very well how to do, through trusts and cartels, when there is any danger of selling his products at a loss.

Even in the case of risks common to all mankind—sickness, old age, death—the employer is not entirely without responsibility, since sickness may be aggravated, and death and old age hastened, by the unhealthiness of the trade. It is only too certain that illnesses due to unhealthy occupations are much more frequent, and old age and death much more premature, in the working class than in any other class of society. There would be no injustice, therefore, in making employers participate to some extent in the insurance against these last risks.

(2) To the State, as representing the nation; and because of the law of social solidarity, which declares that, as all members of society share in the fruits of production, all must share also in the burdens— particularly that of unemployment, which is always due to social causes (pp. 88–89).

Only, if the State undertakes to guarantee the worker against the risks of life, surely it has the right in return to force him to co-operate, so far as he is able, in this insurance, and the employer likewise. The intervention of the State leads thus quite naturally to *compulsory insurance.*

The legal obligation to insure, and the co-operation, in varying proportions according to the nature of the risk, of the three factors— the wage-earner, the employer, and the State—are the characteristic features of what is called the German system of insurance introduced into that country by three celebrated laws (1883 for sickness, 1886 for accident, 1889 for old age),[1] and partially adopted since in France. The following is a short summary of it :

In the case of sickness and small accidents which do not cause disablement for more than thirteen weeks, the employer pays one-third and the employee two-thirds of the premium.

For old age and invalidity, half of the insurance premium is paid by the employer and half by the employee. As the costs are much heavier in this case, the State comes to the aid of both employer and employee by undertaking to pay an annual sum of fifty marks for each retired worker. This sum is invariable, whatever the amount of the pension, so that the participation of the State is relatively much larger in the smaller pensions. It is an ingenious device for giving the poor an advantage.

Accidents the German law lays wholly to the charge of the employer, thus sanctioning the theory, to which we shall return, called by jurisconsults the theory of " industrial risk," that accident should enter under the provisions and general costs of every industry.

This mechanism, which embraces not only the whole working-class population, but clerks, small officials, etc., and practically what is called the middle class, which distributes £84,000,000 in compensation and pensions per annum, and which has already £100,000,000 of capital, is the most imposing experiment of State Socialism ever attempted. There are, however, two great risks against which the German system makes no provision—unem-

---

[1] Codified under a general law June 1911.

ployment and death; insurance against the first appearing too difficult and against the second too costly.

Having indicated thus summarily the guarantees against risks in the working-man's life, we give a few words on each of these risks separately.

(1) *Sickness.* This is the only one of the five with which private initiative has been able to cope with any measure of success, its method being association. For if sickness, even of the shortest, makes a terrible breach in the budget of the individual worker, and is one of the most frequent causes of pauperism, it is not less true that, for the aggregate of men collectively, this risk is fairly small. Statistics show that, for the average man, the number of days of sickness is not over seven or eight per annum.[1] To lose his wage for one week each year, even if we add doctor's fees and medicine, is not a crushing burden for the normal working man. Hence the success of the associations against the risk of sickness, called in France *sociétés de secours mutuels*, and in England Friendly Societies. For a small subscription, varying from 1 fr. 50 to 3 francs a month according to the locality, the French societies guarantee their members in case of sickness : (a) the costs of medical treatment, doctor, and chemist ;[2] (b) an indemnity equal to half the wage ; (c) as a rule a few other services, such as funeral expenses, moderate help for widows and orphans, and about one-third of them give a modest old-age pension.

However numerous these *sociétés de secours mutuels* may be, they are far from including the whole of the working-class population.[3]

---

[1] This figure varies, of course, with the age, from six days at twenty years of age, to thirty-five days at seventy years of age. It is for this reason that the younger workers often prefer to create a new society for themselves alongside of the old, and we see egoism penetrating even into mutual benefit schemes. This is one of the causes of the ridiculous multiplication of small societies in the same town.

[2] The society makes the bargain with the doctor fixing either a very small price per *visit*, or paying him an annual fixed sum for the whole society, or an annual fixed sum for each member who has chosen him for doctor. This last system of composition has the fewest objections.

[3] The *sociétés de secours mutuels* numbered at the beginning of 1910 (the last official statistic published) 19,500 with 5,648,000 members. But this figure must be considerably reduced if we would have the real number of insurers against sickness, since, in the first place, it includes 500,000 honorary members, and 800,000 members of children's societies (*mutualités scolaires*); secondly, many of its members, honorary or not, belong to more than one society ; lastly, some of the largest of these societies do not concern themselves with sickness, but only with old-age pensions. We find, then, the number of insurers against sickness reduced to about 3,000,000, only one-third of which, at most, belong

They are, besides, recruited rather from among small shopkeepers, artisans, clerks, cultivators, and even modest *rentiers*, than from the working class strictly speaking. There are therefore a number of workers who do not belong to any association, and who have no other resource, when sick, than to go to hospital. It was to avoid this extremity that the German law made insurance against sickness compulsory for all workers whose income is under 2000 marks, tempering the obligation by making the employer, as we said above, pay one-third of the subscription.[1]

These societies are very popular in France. They are also very ambitious, and would like to cover not only sickness, but its causes, tuberculosis, alcoholism, insanitary dwellings, and risks such as invalidity and unemployment. They would also, if possible, become the organs for carrying out the law of old-age pensions. Unfortunately, the sacrifices which they impose on themselves are far below the measure of their programme. The subscription of members is not, on an average, more than 13 francs per head.[2]

(2) Accidents. An accident sustained in the course of work differs from sickness in its causes, but not in its effect, which is more or less prolonged unemployment, occasionally permanent if the accident has involved mutilation. Accident differs from sickness mainly in that the employer's responsibility is much greater. For, if responsibility for the illness of the worker can be laid at his door only in exceptional cases where it is due to the nature of the work, on the contrary it is difficult for the employer to avoid responsibility for accident, even when not in the ordinary course of work. The very fact that the accident has taken place on his premises, or while

to the working class. Insurance against sickness does not therefore by any means include all who have need of it.

The corresponding English Friendly Societies are concentrated into colossal unions containing hundreds of thousands of members, and are much richer than the French ones. It is only recently that the French *sociétés de secours mutuels*, which were isolated, grouped themselves into departmental unions and into a national federation.

[1] Why should the employer be made to pay one-third of the cost of sickness for the workers ? There are two reasons : the first, a general one, viz., that a good number of the illnesses which attack the workers are caused by the work itself ; the second, peculiar to German legislation, viz., that accidents the consequences of which do not last longer than three months are assimilated to sickness and fall on the same funds.

[2] Barely enough to cover the costs for sickness (excluding women, children, and illnesses of more than six months duration). The receipts are swelled by the subscriptions of honorary members, by State and communal subsidies (over 10 millions per annum), by gifts, legacies, lotteries, *i.e.* by charity disguised as solidarity.

working for him, is enough to involve the responsibility of the employer. Even when the accident is the worker's own fault ? Yes, because the negligence, imprudence, or even disobedience of the worker to the workshop regulations are themselves industrial risks which ought to enter under the normal previsions and general costs of the *entrepreneur*.[1]

As compensation for the responsibility laid on employers, the law fixes the amount of the damages so as to remove all cause of dispute : (1) For temporary disablement, half of the wage ; (2) for permanent, but only partial, disablement, half of the reduction suffered by the wage ; (3) for permanent and total disablement, two-thirds of the wage ; (4) for death, 60 per cent. of the wage at most, for the whole family.

But, since it is the employer who is liable to pay the compensation, it is he, and not the worker, who henceforth insures against this risk. Ought he to be forced to insure or not ? In Germany he is obliged to by law. In France, however, the employer insures only if he wants to, and where he wants to— in an ordinary company, a friendly society of employers, by forming a guaranteeing syndicate with other employers in the same industry, or at the *Caisse Nationale des retraites*.[2] A number of the very

---

[1] French law, however, in the case of *culpable* negligence on the part of the worker, allows the judge to reduce the indemnity, as also to raise it in the case of culpable negligence on the part of the employer. But the courts rarely find for cases of culpable negligence, even when due to drunkenness ! It goes without saying that, if the accident is *intentional*, the employer is not responsible.

This theory of industrial risk did not pass into law till April 19, 1898. Up till then the worker could not obtain damages except under common law, *i.e.* by proving that the accident was due directly or indirectly to the employer. He had therefore no redress in cases, which are by far the most frequent, when the accident was due to ill-luck or to his own imprudence. Even when the accident was due to the employer, the proof was difficult to establish. In the long legal discussions raised by this question, it was asked whether the burden of proof ought not to be put on the employer, and the responsibility for the accident laid at his door. But, even so, each accident would have given rise to a lawsuit in which the worker would always have been at a disadvantage. This was what the legislator wanted to avoid, by adopting the theory of industrial risk and drawing up a fixed tariff of damages. Common law is still the only means of redress for a good many wage-earners—agricultural labourers (except where steam or other motive forces are used), domestic servants, etc. For the law of 1898, although completed by the law of 1906, applies only to workers in industry, transport, and commerce ; and only to those whose wages are below 2400 francs.

[2] The *Caisse Nationale* insures only for serious accidents entailing permanent incapacity. Its agents would not be able to exercise sufficient vigilance in cases of ordinary accident, and the State would always come off worst. But its field of action is thereby very much restricted.

large manufacturers prefer to do their insurance themselves, while many of the very small ones find the cost of insurance too heavy and prefer to run risks. In these cases the State stands as security for the solvency of the employer, as otherwise the worker might be left without compensation.[1]

(3) *Old Age.* It may seem strange to class old age among risks, since it is, on the contrary, expected and hoped for by every one : the risk, indeed, is rather of dying before old age. Nevertheless—and it is here perhaps that the inequality of social conditions is most cruelly felt—old age, unprovided for, with only the bitter prospect of the workhouse, or of dragging on as a burden to the children, is the nightmare of all wage-earners. The man who lets himself be over-taken by it unawares may perhaps be reproached with improvidence, seeing that old age may be foreseen a long while beforehand, and that a man has all his life in which to provide against it ; but even if he is willing, he must be *able* to save for his old age. Now, for a working man to save sufficient capital to bring in an income equal to half of his wage—say for a man who earns 2000 francs a year, to save 25,000 francs—he must, even at compound interest, put aside about 500 francs a year for thirty years. This is an impossibility for him. To try to provide an annuity for the years between superannua-tion and death would be less chimerical, but still very costly, as an income of half the wage, with reversion to the widow, would absorb about 15 per cent. of the wage. While even if a man were to insure for no more than a franc a day for himself alone, this would mean forty francs a year, which, if he died prematurely, would be sacrificed without any profit to him or his.[2]

[1] To cover this risk the State levies an additional tax of 2 per cent. on manu-facturers' licences (*patente des industriels*) and ½ per cent. on shopkeepers' licences (*patente des commerçants*). Experience has shown that this is much more than is necessary.

[2] The amount of the premium varies with four factors : (a) the amount of the pension ; (b) the age at which it is to be paid ; naturally the more remote this is, the smaller is the premium, not only because it gives the interest a longer time in which to capitalise, but because there will be less chance of the insured man living till that date ; (c) the age at which the premiums begin to be paid ; if at birth, a very small premium will be enough to give a large income for the two reasons given above ; (d) lastly, the rate of interest, since the capitalisation of the premiums will give larger or smaller results, according as the rate of interest is higher or lower. Taking the lowest tariffs, those of the *Caisse Nationale*, twenty-five years as the starting-point, and sixty years as the age of retirement, 365 francs as the amount of the annuity, and 3½ per cent. as the rate of interest, the amount of the premium would be 42 francs. If a man were to insure at the age of three years, the premium would be 14 francs ; if at the age of forty, however, it would be 95 francs.

As a matter of fact, individual foresight has shown itself powerless to provide for old age, even in France, where the pension is such an attraction that it has been enough, of itself, to attract numbers of candidates to State employment, and to induce them to accept very low pay.

The schemes proposed are numerous, but may be reduced to three types :

(a) The German system. On this system, insurance for old age is compulsory on every wage-earner, and a minimum number of premiums must be paid towards it (1200 weeks in Germany). On the other hand, the employer is bound to make an equal contribution, and the State also bears a share; this allows the worker's compulsory subscription to be reduced to a moderate figure in proportion to his wage. The employer is responsible for the payment of the workers' premiums, and deducts them from their wages.

This system has the advantage of securing a pension to nearly every one (all but the few who will not subscribe the minimum). But it has some serious objections. It lays a burdensome tax on all employers and wage-earners ; it necessitates a bureaucratic organisation and a costly and complicated system of book-keeping ; it accumulates in the hands of the State an enormous sum of capital which the latter may be tempted to misapply ; and lastly—this is the great objection of the Liberal school—it discourages and competes with private saving, sometimes even rendering such saving impossible. For it substitutes compulsorily, for all the various ways of individual saving, the most egoistic way of all, that by life annuity.[1]

(b) The Belgian system. Insurance against old age is optional for every one. Only, in order to encourage it, the State grants a subsidy equal to, or even larger than, the amount contributed by the worker. This is the system called " *subsidised liberty*." The State says to the person concerned, " Help yourself and I will help you." The State, in fact, subsidises only those who belong to a Friendly Society. This system obviously does not give rise to the same

---

[1] Obviously the worker's savings go to provide a life annuity. They die with him and are of no benefit to his family, whereas if they are employed in buying movable values, or land, or houses, though the interest on them would be much less than a life annuity, the capital at least would remain. Now, it is a serious thing for the legislator to force a poor man to put his savings into the first of these investments, and thereby to close the second to him.

By French law, the insured person may put part of his contribution into other forms of saving as well as the life annuity, such as the buying of a piece of land or a house.

objections as the last ; in particular, it does not discourage private saving. It has, however, the objection of leaving unaided all the improvident, many of whom perhaps are more sinned against than sinning, and consequently the most deserving of pity. There is, of course, always poor relief for these to fall back on.[1]

(c) The English system. Since the law of 1908 the State, without asking any contribution from the workers or from the employers, grants a pension to all citizens who have reached the age of seventy without means, or whose income is below a certain figure. The amount of the pension is calculated so as to provide a minimum income for those who have nothing, and to supplement the income of those who have something up to the point beyond which the pension stops. The right to the pension is subject to certain conditions, and was at first denied to paupers or to those who habitually refused to work—a check that was not easy to exercise. English law has simply adopted a system which has been in force for some years in New Zealand. Such a system is naturally much preferred by workers and socialists to the two preceding ones, but it is a great burden on the finances of the State.[2]

In France, as we shall see (p. 635), assistance has lately been instituted for indigent old age, though in more modest proportions than in England. If, after thus providing for the improvident, we had introduced the Belgian system of State-aided saving to encourage the provident, we should, by combining these two systems, have done all that could be desired. Why did we prefer the German system ? Because the English is, in reality, only a system of poor relief; and nowadays it is taught that foresight ought to take the place of relief, solidarity that of charity. The German system seemed, therefore, more in keeping with modern ideas. But, to tell the truth, this is but a difference of words. On the German system, too, the old man, to the extent to which he is assisted by the employer and by the State, is receiving relief : whoever receives much more than he gives is receiving relief. Still, the compulsory old age pension follows logically enough from compulsory relief ;

---

[1] Under the Belgian system, the local bodies, as well as the State, contribute, so that in some cases the amount contributed by the worker is multiplied five times over. This is, of course, only for small contributions of less than 15 francs, the State naturally reserving its generosity for small savers. As the latter are relatively scarce, its sacrifices on this score are not very large.

[2] The expenditure for old age pensions in the United Kingdom has greatly exceeded what was anticipated, amounting in 1912 to over £12½ millions for 942,000 persons. In Australia, in 1910, it was £1,520,000 for 65,000 persons or about £24 per head.

for if the State undertakes to come to the aid of every citizen who approaches the end of his life without means, it has the right, in return, to oblige every citizen to make the necessary effort to lighten the burden.

The French law voted on April 5, 1910, after interminable discussions, reproduces the essential features of the German law, viz., (1) *compulsory* insurance for every wage-earner, the employer deducting the premium from his wage ; (2) *equal contribution* by employer and worker ; (3) *State subsidy* in the form of a supplement to the pension ; (4) right to a retiring pension, the amount of which will vary *according to the number of contributions paid* (at least thirty payments a year must be made) ; (5) *capitalisation of contributions* in order to guarantee the right of each insurer, and through the action of compound interest to lessen the burden of contribution on the worker.

But the French law is much more favourable to the worker in three respects : (1) The age limit is sixty, whereas in Germany it is seventy ; (2) it fixes a uniform rate of subscription, 9 francs per annum for men, 6 for women, and 4 fr. 50 for lads of under eighteen and for employers, whereas in Germany there is a scale of contributions according to wage varying from 10 fr. 40 to 31 fr. 20 ; [1] (3) the State supplement to each pension is 100 fr. instead of 50 marks. It must not be thought that these are slight differences. They mean a heavy increase of burden for the State, particularly the lowering of the age limit. For it is between the years of 60 and 70 that there are the greatest number of deaths.

What will be the pension received by the worker at the age of sixty years ? On the most favourable hypothesis, and supposing that contributions have been uninterrupted from the age of fifteen to sixty, it may amount to 387 francs.[2] But in reality it is not very easy to say. And it is still less easy to determine the cost that

[1] In the original measure the contribution was fixed at 2 per cent. of the wage for the worker and the same for the employer. The actual rate represents barely ½ per cent. of the average wage.

[2] If the worker is able to continue his payments and do without his pension till he is sixty-five, the amount of the pension is increased much more than we might suppose from the slight difference of five years. It then amounts to 478 francs. This is because the capitalisation of interest is much greater towards the end of the time. The pension is slightly raised for those who have brought up three children.

In Germany, the old-age pension varies with the wage from 135 to 285 fr. per annum. But in most cases, as we have already pointed out, the German workman is able to obtain as an alternative the disablement pension, which is much more advantageous as it may amount to 435 fr.

will fall on the State. This is estimated at 300 million francs per annum.[1]

The difficulties of applying this law are so great that it has not yet been possible to set it in action. The law has, moreover, aroused strong opposition not only among employers but among the Friendly Societies, who fear the competition of this compulsory insurance.[2] The workers too are not anxious to make a sacrifice by which many of them will not benefit—none at any rate who die before the age of sixty-five—and they fear that the employers' contribution will eventually fall on them in the form of a reduction of wage.[3] This fear is but little founded, as it is much more likely that their own share will be thrown on to the employers—by strikes if need be.

(4) Invalidity. Invalidity implies absolute incapacity to work. It may result either from an incurable disease, accident involving serious mutilation, old age, or from some congenital infirmity, as in the case of those who are born deaf and dumb, cripples, idiots or lunatics. It is in this last form only that invalidity should be classed separately, as in the others it is but the further consequence of the risks we have already discussed. Still, by reason of its extreme gravity, invalidity is generally put under a separate heading. In its economic consequences, indeed, it is much more to be dreaded than old age, as it may strike a man at any age, even at birth, without shortening his life, thus constituting a longer and more crushing burden for a family. And yet no risk is more deserving of pity, since it escapes all foresight, and consequently implies no responsibility in the victim.

Happily, if the risk of invalidity is heavy, it is also relatively very rare—unless at the end of life we count old age as invalidity—so that,

---

[1] What makes all forecast uncertain is the fact that the law will not be in full action for 50 years. As we may imagine, the workers will not be asked to wait till then! The law has provided for this delay by a temporary measure which consists in allocating pensions to all workers as they reach the age of sixty-five; and, as the workers have contributed nothing, the State has to pay the difference. The pension of course is a smaller one, but the cost will nevertheless be great.

Another cause of uncertainty is the power which has been given to certain classes of society who are not wage-earners, but independent producers—or even small employers who have not more than *one* employee—artisans, peasants, tenant farmers, *métayers* to avail themselves of the law.

[2] In order to relieve the vehement expressions of apprehension of these Societies that they will be deserted so soon as the wage-earner is obliged to contribute to compulsory insurance, the law allows them to collect the compulsory subscriptions themselves and to benefit by a small percentage.

[3] A socialist paper even wrote the day after the passing of the law: "It is done! The crime is committed!"

when the State takes over this risk, the cost of insurance, owing to
numbers, is not very great. The German law, generally referred to
as the Law of Insurance against Old Age, in reality bears the title
" Law on Invalidity," and it is this last that it has particularly in
view. Insurance against invalidity may indeed be taken as exempting
a man from insurance against old age. For there are only two alter-
natives ; either the old man is disabled, in which case he can benefit
by the insurance against invalidity, or he is able-bodied and can work,
in which case it does not seem very necessary to compensate him.
Still, even in Germany, insurance against invalidity does not absolutely debar a man from insuring against old age, for the reason that
it is held only just that the old man should have the right to rest, even
though he can still work. After the age of seventy years, therefore,
German law grants the pension for old age without requiring proof
of invalidity. But, it gives, as we have seen, a very small pension,
that for invalidity being twice as large. The aged have therefore
every interest in proving that they are disabled, and this is, in
fact, what four-fifths of the aged in Germany do.

The French measure, on the contrary, has only old age in view,
answering in this to public feeling on the matter. For every one
wants to insure against old age, as every one hopes to live till then,
whereas insurance against invalidity interests only a few, since no
one counts on being disabled. A pension after a certain age, moreover, appeals singularly to the French temperament, as every Frenchman hopes one day to become a small *rentier*. Lastly, insurance
against old age is much less liable to abuse than insurance against
invalidity ; for old age is determined by the indisputable proof of
birth certificates, whereas invalidity is determined by medical reports,
often uncertain and arbitrary, into which favouritism may easily
creep.[1]

(5) *Premature Death.* This is one of the most dreaded of all
risks ; for the premature death of the head of the house is one of the
most frequent causes determining the fall of working-class families

---

[1] For what is to be the criterion of invalidity ? That the invalid is absolutely incapable of all labour ?   On this score, no one, not even the man who has
had both arms amputated, would be an invalid.   German legislation admits that
there is invalidity when the capacity for labour has been reduced by two-thirds.
But how can we verify that the man who has hitherto earned three francs can
henceforth earn only one ?   To do so, obviously we should have to resort, in the
last instance, to official doctors, as in Germany, or to jurisprudence, as in France,
where a tariff is fixed for the consequences of accidents.   According to this tariff,
the loss of the right hand represents a diminution of labour power of 80 per cent. ;
that of a finger, 5 per cent.

into pauperism. Insurance against it, however, would be so costly that Friendly Societies, and the State itself own themselves, powerless to cope with it. The premium necessary to ensure the widow and family an income equivalent to the lost wage would be almost equal to one-sixth of the wage (over 15 per cent.). Even in the bourgeois class, insurance against death is found too costly, in France at any rate, and is rarely resorted to. We must not forget that death resulting from an accident in the course of work comes on the employers' liability, and gives an income varying from 20 to 60 per cent. of the wage, according to relationship and to the number of those who are to benefit by it.

Insurance against death and unemployment were omitted in the vast German system of insurance. But a law of 1912 grants a small pension of 200 francs to widows whose husbands were insured, and who are not themselves already insured as working women, as also small sums to orphans, the total of which must not exceed the pension which the father would have had in case of invalidity.[1]

In England, and in the United States, insurance societies against death are very numerous, although the sums insured for are small —not sufficient to replace the labour of the breadwinner, but simply enough to tide the family over the crisis caused by the death. Even in this modest form they render a real service.[2]

(6) *Unemployment.* This is the most frequent, and therefore the most serious, of all risks for the wage-earner. It consists in a stoppage of work owing to dismissal, combined with the difficulty of finding employment elsewhere. Dismissal may be due either to the dead season, to an economic crisis involving the suspension or slowing down of production, or to the shutting of the workshop from such causes as fire, bankruptcy, the death of the employer, etc.

The number of unemployed may vary, according to the industry and the season, from 2 per cent. to 12 per cent. in skilled industries, up to 50 per cent. or more in casual labours, such as stevedoring. It is not of course the same man who is unemployed the whole year round—it is now one, now another; but every wage-earner has in fact to count on one to six weeks of unemployment per annum, according to his trade. Against this terrible evil there are two remedies, both inadequate.

---

[1] In France, the law on old age pensions gives widows and orphans only a small temporary help during three to six months.

[2] In France, there are a certain number of societies called *franc au décès*, in which, whenever a member dies, each of the other members has to pay one franc, and the total goes to the family of the deceased. This is, however, simply as a help towards funeral expenses, and cannot be called insurance against death.

(a) *The Finding of a Situation.* Special institutions undertake this. In France, the register offices which charged a fee for doing so gave rise to such abuses that a law (March 14, 1904) gave the municipalities the right to expropriate them with compensation. Those which still exist may charge a fee only to employers. All towns of over 10,000 inhabitants must create a free register office. As a matter of fact, however, only a very few have done so, and their offices do but little business.[1]

There are also a number of philanthropic societies for finding situations for the unemployed. The trade unions would like to have the monopoly of this business, since, by finding situations only for union men, they would have a sure means of recruiting all workers and of exercising a sovereign control over them. But it goes without saying that employers try to keep the disposal of vacant situations in their own hands—and this is the more easy, as it is they who have the places to offer. In Germany, where employers are very powerfully organised, many employers' unions oblige their members to engage workers only through an employers' registry. This is what is called the " Hamburg system."

Between these two extremes, however, there is a mixed system, which is preferable, consisting in employment bureaux, chosen partly by employers, partly by workers. These are the most numerous and render the best services. Most of them have been created by the municipalities, but there are also a few private ones.[2]

But employment offices are after all an insufficient remedy for unemployment. Statistics show that, with the exception of a few industries, the demand for situations is always much greater than the supply. To what is this due ? When we think of the number of men who have not even the necessaries of life, it seems extraordinary that there should be this surplus, this " army-reserve of labour "[3] as Karl Marx called it, which might, it would seem, so

---

[1] Barely 100,000 situations were found in 1908, half of which were in Paris. The German municipal bureaux do ten times as much.

In England, the number of situations found, in 1912, was 516,841, in addition to 116,731 casual jobs.

[2] To find employment for a man is not enough. He must be able to go where the work is waiting for him. Some trade-union federations therefore. in particular those of the *Travailleurs du Livre* and the *Bourses du Travail*, give the *viaticum* to enable the worker to go to the town where he may find work. In Germany, those who have a certificate from a register office pay only half-fare.

[3] An official inquiry in Germany, in connection with the law of 1904 on register offices, gave the following figures : for 100 offers of employment, 146 demands. Even supposing each situation were filled, which is never the case—85 per cent. being the average—46 per cent. would still be out of work.

easily be employed in providing what is lacking.   It is due no doubt
to the fact which we indicated above (p. 88), that machinery and, in
general, all that is known as industrial progress tends to reduce the
quantity of labour necessary for a given result.

In any case it is a strange feature of our economic organisation,
and one which does indeed point to the fact that " something is
rotten in the state of Denmark," since the man who is willing to
earn his living by his labour is often unable to do so.   Thus the
socialism which preceded the Revolution of 1848 demanded that the
Right to Work should be secured by the State to every man.   It even
went the length of seeing, in the legal consecration of this right, the
whole solution of the social problem.   We know that the deplorable
experiment of national workshops was based on this idea.   To-day
we speak no more of the right to work.[1]   It has been seen how impossible it is for the State to provide useful work for all and sundry
—work, that is to say, really productive.   What is important
to the worker, moreover, is not the right to work, but the right to a
wage ; so that modern socialism turns rather to the minimum wage,
pending the socialising of the instruments of production which is to
transform unemployment into leisure, and turn an evil into a
good.

(b) *Insurance*, whereby the worker is compensated to the extent
of whole or part of the wage lost, as is the case with any other risk.
But we must point out that insurance here would be much more
difficult, not only because of the extent and frequency of the risk,
but because it is almost impossible to distinguish true unemployment,
due to lack of employment, from false, due to laziness.   No association
therefore has tried to insure against this risk, and the few attempts
made by municipalities have given wretched results.[2]   Only think

---

[1] The right to work has to-day been modestly converted into the right to
relief given in work.   This is the most commendable form of relief, particularly
when it takes the form of agricultural work, since the money given is not altogether
lost.

Many philanthropic societies organise this form of relief by means of special
workshops, as do also the municipalities, which open yards for public works.
Yet even within these modest limits, it is almost impossible to provide work
that has not the two objections : (1) if unproductive, of degrading the unemployed
by giving him a useless task ; (2) if productive, of creating injurious competition
with workers.

[2] The experiment of *compulsory* insurance was made by the town of St. Gall
in Switzerland.   It had to be given up after two years with a large deficit.   As
might be foreseen, it was those who could never be made to pay their subscriptions who claimed most compensation, and the good workers, who were
hardly ever out of work, soon tired of paying for the bad who were always un-

of the number of unemployed there would be if the State undertook to provide incomes for all who were without work !

England, however, has not been afraid to enter on this path— not, of course, as yet for the whole working population, but for that part of it which is employed in industries particularly liable to unemployment. Employers and workers are obliged each to pay 4*d.* per week, the State making up another third. In return for this, the worker has a right to 1*s.* per day of unemployment benefit during fifteen weeks at the outside (the first week not being counted). It must be said that the dangers of such an experiment are, to some extent, neutralised by the parallel organisation of a very complete system of Labour Exchanges, established in all industrial towns— there are some 400 of them—whose duty it is both to find situations and to pay the unemployment money. Needless to say this last is paid only to those who are unable to find work.

It is too early to estimate the results of this imposing mechanism. So far the workers do not appear to look on it with too favourable an eye.[1] It would seem true, indeed, that they have not a sufficient share in the working of it. There is only one institution fitted by its nature to attempt this adventure, viz., the trade union. It alone is in a position to distinguish the true unemployed from the false ; and, if it had charge at the same time of finding situations, it could easily circumvent those who were not genuinely unemployed by obliging them to accept the work offered them. Insurance against unemployment, moreover, would be a powerful weapon in the hands of trade unions for keeping up the level of wages, since it would enable the unemployed to wait, instead of having to capitulate from hunger. The English trade unions devote a large part of their resources to out-of-work benefit. In other countries, unfortunately, the unions are not nearly so wealthy and can grant only very inadequate allowances for unemployment. Hence the idea has arisen of making the trade unions and the municipalities collaborate, the latter furnishing the necessary funds, the former organising the insurance and paying the sums necessary.

There are objections, however, to making the trade union the official dispenser of help for unemployment, and to conferring on it, in this way, a kind of monopoly. It is, in a manner, to make member-

---

employed. In towns (Basle, Bern, Cologne, etc.) where it was made optional the results were better. Compulsory insurance against unemployment has still, however, some partisans, and was defended at the Congress on unemployment held in Paris, September 1910.

[1] They object that it serves mainly for finding situations for " blacklegs."

ship of it compulsory. Many municipalities will probably refuse to adopt this line, or, if they do follow it, the trade unions may be sure that the municipal subsidy will not be granted without a certain amount of official, and perhaps vexatious, superintendence.

We find therefore two systems at work which differ somewhat from one another, in principle at any rate. Under the system of Liège, which dates from 1897, the subsidy is granted by the municipality directly to the trade unions and is proportional to the contributions paid by the workers. In the much more celebrated system of Ghent, which dates from 1901, the subsidy is granted through an autonomous organ called the " unemployment funds of the city of Ghent," and is proportional to the benefits paid to the unemployed. The Ghent system does, as a matter of fact, work as a rule through the trade union,[1] but it gives those who do not belong to a trade union, nor even to an association against unemployment, but who simply insure by means of deposits at the savings banks, an equal right to a subsidy. In this last case the subsidies are proportional to the amount of money withdrawn from the savings bank, just as, in the case of the man who has insured, they are proportional to the amount of insurance he has received. It is thanks to this neutral attitude that the system of Ghent has been spread so much more widely than that of Liège. It has been adopted by a large number of towns in all countries.

France is very backward as regards this form of insurance. About forty towns give grants for unemployment either in the form of work, or in that of subsidies to insurance companies, or to trade unions, but not on any definite plan. The State itself has taken up this line, and, since 1905, has allocated to unemployment an annual sum of 100,000 francs in its budget. But the results have been poor in this sense that the subsidy has not succeeded in creating a large number of insurance societies, either within or without the trade unions. It has even been found impossible to utilise the total amount granted by the State, a very rare phenomenon in the history of subsidies.[2]

---

[1] On condition, of course, that the trade union has itself organised an insurance against unemployment, and levies subscriptions for it from its members. This condition also applies to Liège. The subsidy granted by the municipality does not exceed the modest sum of 4 fr. 50 per week.

Another difference is that, on the Liège system, unemployment resulting from a *lock-out* is assimilated to unemployment due to accidental causes, and is compensated, whereas on the Ghent system it is treated as a case of strike, and the municipality remains neutral.

[2] In 1909 the State was called on to pay only 42,000 francs ; the total amount of insurance paid from the insurance funds did not exceed 200,000 francs ; and

If the proposal of the *Conseil du Travail* passes into insurance association against unemployment (whether a trade-u association or not) will have the right to a contribution from the employer, the commune and the State, provided that it fulfils certain conditions.

XI : PROFIT-SHARING AND CO-PARTNERSHIP

WE have shown the disadvantages of the wage-system ; the conflict of interests which it creates between employer and employed ; the uneconomic way in which labour is utilised, and the consequent poor return which it gives.

To remedy this state of affairs two different methods have been tried :

1. The one consists in simply increasing the return from labour by varying the wage according to the return :

(a) By substituting for the fixed daily wage a *piece-work* wage, that is to say, a wage based not on time, but on the quantity of work actually done. This mode of remuneration greatly stimulates the activity of the worker, and for that reason is becoming more and more common in industry. It has, however, the serious objection, from the employer's and the consumer's point of view, that it sacrifices quality to quantity, particularly where the work cannot be directly controlled. For this reason piece-work can rarely be resorted to in agriculture.

(b) By substituting for the individual piece-work wage a collective piece-work wage—not to be confused with the collective bargaining of which we have spoken. The employer negotiates with a group of workers *en bloc*, who undertake to perform a certain piece of work for a certain price, which they divide among them as they think fit. As regards productiveness, this system gives about the same results as individual piece-work, but it is as a rule better received by the workers on account of the independence which it leaves them. It is like a kind of small co-operative association formed within the bosom of the employer's factory, which sells the product of its labour to the employer.

(c) By adding to the fixed wage a *premium* calculated either according to the output above a certain minimum, or to the economies made in raw material and coal. These premiums lend themselves to an infinite variety of combinations ; they may be simple, progressive, etc.

the numbers of workers insured was only 33,000. The *Fédération des Travailleurs du Livre* in itself alone makes up the greater number of these.

The workers, as a rule, are hostile to all these modes of payment. In their opinion, they enable the employer to gauge exactly the worker's capacity for work and to regulate the normal wage on the basis of maximum output, to the great disadvantage of those who are not able to do so much; they increase unemployment by pushing one man to do the work of two, and they establish between the capable and vigorous worker and his less gifted comrades an inequality repugnant to their idea of justice. The attraction of greater gain moreover pushes the worker on to overwork, ruins his health, and thus causes him to sacrifice the future to the present.

2. The other method consists in modifying the wage-contract itself, giving it more or less the character of a contract of association, either by *profit-sharing*, or by *co-partnership*.

(a) *Profit-sharing* has been practised from time immemorial among fishermen. But the first experiment to have striking success was that tried in Paris, in 1842, by a house-painter, Leclaire.[1]

Profit-sharing may assume the most varied forms, but it must always be *contractual*; that is to say, it must form an integral part of the contract of labour, it must be inscribed in the rules of the firm, and it must be recognised as a right—without distinction of persons, and under general conditions fixed *in advance*. The profits distributed are generally shared among the workers in proportion to their respective wages, taking into account the length of their services. Profit-sharing, it must be observed, is quite distinct from the giving of simple gratuities.

The shares given to the workers may be paid either in money, or put to their account in some savings bank or pension fund. This last method, sometimes called " deferred sharing," is the one most prevalent in France. It has the advantage of ensuring that the supplementary remuneration is put to a good use; but, by postponing the enjoyment of it to some distant date, it weakens the stimulating effect to be expected from profit-sharing.

Profit-sharing has enthusiastic partisans who see a number of advantages in it from the moral, as well as from the economic, point of view.

(*1*) It is to reconcile labour and capital, and to raise the dignity of the working man by transforming him from an instrument of production into a partner.

---

[1] In France there is a society for the practical study of profit-sharing, founded in 1879 by Charles Robert, which carries on active propaganda for the development of this institution. Among the numerous publications on this subject, see *La Participation aux bénéfices* by Waxweiler, and, rather against it than otherwise, *La Participation aux bénéfices* by M. Bureau.

(2) It is to increase the productiveness of labour by stimulating the worker's activity, and by interesting him in the success of the enterprise.

(3) It is to increase his income by adding to his ordinary weekly wage, which he will continue to devote to current expenses, an annual dividend which he may save up or use for extra-ordinary expenses.

(4) It is to ward off unemployment by creating permanent ties between employer and employed.

But profit-sharing has also many adversaries : among Classical economists and employers on the one hand, among socialists and workers on the other.

On the part of socialists this is easy to understand. If profit is a theft committed by employers at the expense of workers, a so-called reform which would render this theft legitimate by making the robbed participate in it is the height of impertinence.

Workers fear that profit-sharing will be used as an inducement to the sole end of making them produce more value, by harder work, than they will receive back in the form of additional income.

As for employers, they consider unjust a participation in profits which does not also imply a participation in losses. And they object strongly to letting their workers, and through them the public, know the amount of their profits, or, worse still, the lack of them.[1]

Lastly, the Classical economists, without formally condemning profit-sharing, see in it simply a " condiment," as M. Leroy-Beaulieu puts it, to make the wage-system more palatable, analogous to the bonuses given by certain firms. They urge against it the serious objection that workers have, strictly speaking, no right in the profits, since these are in no way their work, but exclusively that of the employer. Profits, they say, are the result, not of the material and technical manufacture of the article, but of its sale at the right moment and in the right place—an entirely commercial art with which the workers are altogether unacquainted. Proof of this is to be found in the fact that everywhere, in mines, railways, etc. some enterprises may be seen making large profits, while others, employing an absolutely identical staff of workers, suffer losses.

If, by this, the economists mean that the manufacturer makes profits in his capacity of merchant only, not of manufacturer, their statement is distinctly paradoxical. If they mean that his profits are due more to fortunate circumstances than to anything else, we

---

[1] This objection does not hold, however, against enterprises in the form of joint-stock companies, since these have to publish their accounts.

agree (see below, *Profits*); but why should not the workers also have the right to share in these favourable opportunities which could not be turned to account without their help ? Observe that this right is considered only natural in the case of capitalist shareholders, although the profits are assuredly still less *their doing* than that of the workers.

The fact remains, anyhow, that profit-sharing is far from fulfilling the great expectations to which it gave rise, and the number of firms which practise it has decreased perceptibly in all countries during the last ten years.[1]

This is in part due to the disfavour which attaches to all forms of patronage—to anything which tends to tighten the bonds between employer and employed. What both of these are trying for, on the contrary, is to be as independent of one another as possible. " Profit-sharing," says M. Trombert, secretary of the Society for the Development of Profit-Sharing, " requires the existence of good feeling in the workshop," but this " good feeling," in the sense of family feeling, is rare indeed.

Still, this institution has not said its last word.[2]

In the first place, there are two large branches of production where it has not yet been seriously tried, although they would seem to be the most promising, and, curiously enough, are the very ones in which it was first practised, viz., agriculture and sea-fishery.

Further, it might be made compulsory in a certain number of enterprises. The French Government has a clause on its programme to make profit-sharing compulsory in enterprises conceded by the State, or by municipalities.[3] This would be no small domain into which profit-sharing would thus be thrust by sheer force, since these concessions include mines, railways, tramways, town lighting, etc.[4]

---

[1] For statistics on this point, as on all the working-class institutions which we have been studying, see our *Économie sociale*.

[2] Several Cabinet ministers of late years, in particular M. Briand, have declared that the participation of workers in the profits of industry is a matter to be seriously studied (M. Briand, Speech at St. Étienne, 1910).

[3] Why not also in enterprises managed directly *en régie*, by the State ? Because these enterprises are not intended to give profits, but to provide resources for the State in the place of taxes. It would be absurd to admit workers to share in the proceeds of taxes. By what right should the workers in tobacco manufactories have a share in the proceeds of the sale of tobacco which, sold at a price raised artificially by 500 per cent., brings in over one million francs per day to the Treasury ?

[4] It has even been proposed to make profit-sharing compulsory in all enterprises in the form of joint-stock companies, on the pretext that, as these companies hold their juridical personality from the law, they ought to accept the conditions of existence which the law imposes. This theory is not very sound from the juridical point of view, and would certainly not be without danger from

It would be larger still if the law were made retroactive, and were applied to all existing mining and railway exploitations.

Let us say, in conclusion, that there is a great tendency to over‑value the rate of profits. The fact that the profits of an enterprise go to one man, while wages are distributed among hundreds or thousands, gives rise to false ideas as to their relative importance. If all employers were abolished and their profits were divided up among the workers, the latter would be unpleasantly surprised to find how small the increase in each man's share would be.[1]

(b) A still more radical modification of the wage-contract would be to transform it into a veritable partnership, involving for the worker a share, not in profits only, but in administration and respon‑sibility, including losses. At first sight this seems impossible ; for how is the worker who has no capital, to bear the losses, and how can we expect the employer to submit to the control of the worker in the administration of the business ? This twofold difficulty could easily be overcome, however, if the worker possessed shares in the business.   In this case he would share in the administration and in the losses in the same measure as any other shareholder.   This method is called *co-partnership (l'actionnariat ouvrier)*.[2]

the economic, since it would divert a large mass of capital existing in the form of shareholding companies, only to drive it abroad or throw it back into the archaic form of individual enterprise.

   [1] Statistics of the mining industry for a period of twenty-seven years (1881-1908) allow us to compare the total profits with the total wages.   The average yearly profit actually obtained per worker employed was 302 francs which. on an average wage of 1242 francs, comes to a little over 25 per cent.   This, then, is the maximum amount by which the wage might have been increased if all the dividends had been divided up among the workers.   That is to say, each worker would have had 5 francs per day instead of 4 francs.   This is something, of course, but much less than we should have expected from the passionate denun‑ciations of profit by the socialists.   Before the elimination of profit can do much to alter the situation of the present-day worker, there must be much more than a mere transfer of income from the hands of the employer to those of the worker—which is a small thing.   We must suppose that the abolition of the wage-system, of which the abolition of profit is only a secondary consequence, will transform the mentality and activity of the worker, so that the wealth created by each will increase.

   [2] In connection with this question, see M. Granier, *Les Actions de Travail*, 1910, and a book with the same title by M. Antonelli, 1912, as also an article of our own in the *Revue d'Économie politique*, January 1910, under the name of *L'actionnariat ouvrier*.   Co-partnership stands as the fundamental article in the programme of the *syndicats jaunes*.   These, in order, no doubt, to obtain the credit of having invented it, have baptized it with the curious name of *pro‑priétisme*, meaning thereby that the object is to make the worker proprietor of his instruments of production—not in the form of individual property, but in

The practical difficulty, as we may very well conceive, is to provide the worker with the means of acquiring shares. Profit-sharing is the simplest way, as the profits have only to be converted into shares in the business ; but it may also be done in another way, by splitting up the shares until they are within reach of the worker's savings.

It has even been proposed to allow the workers a certain number of free shares in every enterprise started in the form of a joint stock company ; either when the company is formed (why not, indeed, since free shares, called founders' shares, are given to capitalists ?) or at any rate as soon as the capital shares have been paid back. In either case the shares would be allotted, not individually, but collectively to all the workers, perhaps to their trade unions.

For it is more difficult than is generally thought to persuade the worker to become a shareholder in the business.[1] So little anxious is he to avail himself of this opportunity where it has been given him, that it has sometimes been necessary to turn it into an obligation and to make him a shareholder, whether he will or no, by converting *ex officio* his profits into shares.[2] Only, there may be some doubt as to the moral and social efficacy of a system which makes the wage-earner a partner in spite of himself. If co-partnership were grafted on to profit-sharing, and so organised as to work automatically and indefinitely, with no limit to the capital which could come into the hands of the workers, it is clear that, sooner or later, the employer would be eliminated and the business transformed into a sort of co-operative association for production. It was in this very way that the most prosperous co-operative associations for production in France, those of the *Familistère* at Guise and the firm of *Leclaire* to which we referred, were founded.

This leads us naturally to the question of co-operative association for production.

the form of collective property. This is no other than the Co-operatist programme which we have already discussed.

[1] The extreme reluctance of the workers to become shareholders in the business in which they work is easily explained not only by their hostility to any association with the employer, but also from a more *bourgeois* point of view, by the fear of seeing their savings swallowed up if the business fails.

[2] Thus the London gas companies, which are the most successful instances of co-partnership, found it necessary to compel the worker to allow at least half of his profits to be converted into shares in the business.

XII: CO-OPERATIVE ASSOCIATION FOR PRODUCTION

Co-operative association for production is an advance on the pre-ceding forms of the wage-system. Association is no longer that of workers *with* the employer, but of workers *without* the employer.[1]

France is considered, and rightly, as the birthplace of institutions of this kind. It was there that the first working-men's association for production was founded, in 1834, by Buchez, a French publicist. It was not till the close of the Revolution of 1848, however, that the movement took on a real impetus, and over 200 working-men's societies for production were started. All failed with the exception of three or four which have survived to the present day ; but in 1866–1867, there was a renewed activity in this direction, and during the last few years the number of societies has increased so rapidly that to-day (1912) they number a little over 500, and some of them are very prosperous.[2]

The obstacles encountered by the co-operative associations for production are many,.and explain only too well their want of success

(1) The first is *lack of capital.* We know very well that, in produc-tive enterprises, although it is possible to do without the capitalist, it is impossible to do without capital. Large-scale industry is daily demanding greater and greater quantities. How can simple workers procure these ? By putting aside a few sous a day from their savings ? This, to be sure, is possible, and has been done in a few enterprises on a small scale, but only at the cost of heroic sacrifices ; and it

---

[1] J. S. Mill saw the solution of the social problem in free co-operative associa-tion for production. This was also the system advocated by Lassalle. The latter, however, wanted the State to become a sleeping partner in the co-operative societies for production to the extent of some hundreds of millions of marks, in order to enable them to compete victoriously with the enterprises of private employers.

To-day collectivism is frankly hostile to co-operation for production. For co-operation for production, though it aims at abolishing the wage-system, retains the private ownership of capital as the basis of its organisation, its true object being to make the workers co-proprietors of their instruments of production. Collectivism, on the contrary, proposes to " socialise " the instruments of produc-tion, *i.e.* to withdraw them from individual ownership, *even from that of the workers themselves.* This opposition of ideas became clear during the strike at Car-maux, in 1900, when the question of creating a co-operative glass manufactory arose. The socialists protested, declaring that what was wanted was not a glass manufactory belonging to glass-workers, but one belonging to the whole working class.

[2] They number 20,000 members, and their production amounts to 70 million francs. But the figure for their profits, which would be of most interest to us, is not known.

cannot be counted on in a general way. By getting it on loan from the State ? The experiment was made in 1848, but the 2 million francs thus distributed brought little success to the companies which received them. Nothing is so easily wasted as money given for nothing, especially if it be given by the State.

Still, we do not consider this difficulty insurmountable. Experienced and well-organised working-men's associations would easily be able to borrow all the money they required, either by forming a common bank (one such already exists in France, see p. 405), or by applying to the co-operative societies of credit, or for consumption, both of which have large sums at their disposal (see p. 393).

(2) The second consists in *want of custom.* Working-men's associations for production are not, as a rule, powerfully enough equipped to produce cheaply, and for the large consumption of the masses. On the other hand, their trade-mark is not sufficiently well known to attract wealthy customers. In France, fortunately for them, they have found customers in the State and the municipalities, and it is due to these that many of the societies are still in existence. But under such conditions their life is somewhat artificial.

(3) The third is the *lack of economic education* in the working class, which makes it impossible for it to find within its own ranks men capable of directing an industrial enterprise. Even supposing the right men are to be found, the workers do not know enough to choose them and keep them as managers, their very superiority frequently causing their exclusion ; or, if their guidance be accepted, the rank and file, unable to appreciate sufficiently the superiority of intellectual over manual labour, are unwilling to give them a share in the proceeds equivalent to the services which they render.

(4) The fourth and last obstacle is that these associations tend—so difficult is it to change a social system—to *reconstitute the very institutions which they are seeking to eliminate,* viz., the employer class and the wage-system. Only too often co-operative associations, so soon as they are successful, close their ranks, and, refusing all new members, engage hired workmen, becoming themselves neither more nor less than partnerships of small employers.[1] This is the

---

[1] Most of them indeed employ auxiliaries ; thus 336 out of 510 societies, *i.e.* two-thirds, employ auxiliary workers in the proportion of one-third auxiliaries to two-thirds members. A case has been known in which there were 13,600 members and 7521 auxiliaries.

The co-operative society for production of the spectacle-makers in Paris has 225 members *plus* 1200 paid workers, and the value of its shares has risen from 300 francs to 50,000 francs. It is clearly co-operative only in name. To

principal objection which socialists urge against them, and it must be admitted that it is not without ground. On the other hand, to ask the workers of the first hour of the day, who, by privation and perseverance, have succeeded in founding a prosperous enterprise, to admit on equal terms the workers of the eleventh hour, is really to expect a rare act of disinterestedness. Still, here, too, education is doing its work, and, thanks to the control of the *Chambre Consultative*, such deviations from the co-operative principle are becoming more and more rare.

The creation of co-operative associations for production may be facilitated :

(*1*) By profit-sharing, when the employer prepares his own abdication by so organising participation that the workers become partners during his lifetime, and successors after his death. The best-known examples of this method were given by Godin in the Familistère at Guise, and by Mme. Boucicaut in the case of the Bon Marché.[1]

(*2*) By trade unions. Several co-operative associations for production in France owe their origin to trade unions. In this case the associations do not set all the members of the union to work at once, since they have neither sufficient capital nor sufficient markets, but only those who ask to become members, and in their turn.

(*3*) By co-operative societies for consumption. These, when sufficiently developed and united into federations, are able to support co-operative societies for production, and to provide them with precisely the elements they lack for success—*capital*, in the form of loans ; *customers*, consisting of the consumers' societies themselves ; and *management*. This third element is the more easily supplied owing to the double control which the co-operatives exercise in their twofold capacity of sleeping partner and customer. The English co-operative societies for consumption are beginning to follow this policy.

It is in this direction that the future of association for production lies. But it is important to distinguish here two systems, which we may call the Federalist and the Autonomist systems.

prevent this kind of abuse the French Government has brought in a measure obliging the co-operative societies to let their workers participate in the profits.

[1] The Bon Marché is not a true co-operative association for production, although there are no shareholders but the employees : for the profits are distributed not according to labour—the co-operative principle—but according to shares—the capitalist principle.

Under the autonomist system, that which we have indicated above, the initiative is taken by the workers themselves, who form societies producing on their own account ; the rôle of the consumers' societies is here restricted to lending them capital and ensuring them markets. On the federalist system, the consumers' societies, either in groups, or singly if they are powerful enough, start manufactories for the direct production of some article or other of their consumption. In this case the workers whom they employ remain simple wage-earners and are in no sense co-proprietors of the manufactory. As a rule, they have not even a share in the profits, these being kept exclusively for the consumers.[1] But this system has given rise to lively opposition, the workers and employees of the associations for consumption demanding co-partnership in the enterprise, or a share, at least, in the profits. This demand, rejected by the English associations, has been granted by the Scottish Co-operative Wholesale Society.[2]

XIII : THE FUTURE OF THE WAGE-SYSTEM

THE question as to whether the wage-system will last for ever, or whether we are to see in it merely a temporary phase of economic evolution, brings out very clearly the characteristic features of the divergent schools of economists.

The Liberal school looks on the wage-system as a final state, since it considers the wage contract the sole and universal mode of the remuneration of labour. No better can be found, since it is the type of the " free contract."[3] The reason why it has developed so greatly in our modern societies is because of its decided superiority : (1) in giving the worker a secure and immediate income, independent of the risks of the enterprise ; (2) in leaving to the employer, along with the ownership of the products, the management and responsibility of the industry.

This school does not, it is true, deny that wages are often insufficient, and that it would be desirable to see them raised. Only, it says, the sole means of raising them is to make the wage contract as free as possible. It rejects therefore the " family " and " patriarchal " conception of the wage-system, as antiquated, and is no

---

[1] It goes without saying that if the workers are members of the society for consumption, they receive, *qua* consumers, their share of the profits like every other member. But that is not the point.

[2] See our book *Les Sociétés coopératives de Consommation.*

[3] M. Paul Leroy-Beaulieu in his great *Traité d'Économie politique,* t. ii. See also M. Levasseur's *Le Salariat.*

more favourable to a wage regulated by custom or by law, making as it were a kind of *statute* of the wage-system. It tries to put the worker and the employer on the same footing as the seller and the buyer of a commodity, and to this end it proposes to create—either, like M. de Molinari, *Bourses du Travail* where labour would be quoted as are securities on the Stock Exchange—or, like M. Yves Guyot, *commercial societies of labour* which would sell the labour of their members under better conditions than isolated workers are able to do.[1] As for the just wage, there can be none other than that which results from the law of supply and demand, or from the natural laws which we have explained above. It is the most just because it is the one most in conformity with social utility. There is no more reason for fixing a just wage on an *a priori* principle, than for fixing a just price for corn or coal, or a just rent for the capitalist landowner. The worker has a right to all that he can earn, no more, no less.

The Catholic Social school accepts the wage-system as a normal, even a providential, state ; for, through it, the rich are able to make the poor live and the poor, the rich. The wage ought not. however, in their view, to be delivered over to the play of supply and demand, nor to the often oppressive liberty of bargaining between employer and worker. The best way to obtain the just wage would be to reconstitute the guilds composed of both workers and employers, and leave it to them. Failing these, the law should intervene.

The Socialist school, on the contrary, sees in the wage-system simply a historical category, the third phase in an evolution of which the first two stages were slavery and serfdom ; a phase which, in its turn, will give place to a social system under which the workers, now become masters of the instruments of production, will enjoy the whole product of their labour. What, in their view, at present characterises the wage-system is the inevitable dependence in which the worker stands towards his employer, as also the deduction made by the employer from the product of the worker's labour. Now, this deduction made by the capitalist, whether it be in the form of profit, interest, or rent, is inseparable from the institution of private property : the only way therefore of doing away with the wage-system is to do away with private property.[2]

---

[1] De Molinari, *Les Bourses du Travail ;* Yves Guyot, *Les conflits du Travail et leur solution.*

[2] The statutes of the *Confédération Générale du Travail* declare (Art. 1) that it (the C.G.T.) groups together, quite outside of any political school, all workers

Lastly, the Co-operative or Solidarity school, like the Socialist School, sees in the wage-system no more than a temporary mode of remunerating labour, a mode which is bound up with the capitalist *régime*, and will pass away with it.[1] This school does not deny that the wage-system was a great advance on previous systems, but it reproaches it :

(a) With creating an unavoidable *conflict of interests* between the employer and the employed, identically the same as that which exists between the seller and buyer of a commodity—the one trying to give the minimum wage in exchange for the maximum labour ;[2] the other trying to give the minimum labour in exchange for the wage received—and thus intensifying the class conflict.

For, in reality, *other things being equal*, the higher the wage the smaller the profit, and *vice versa*. This is what Ricardo meant when he said that " every diminution in the wages of labour raises profits," whereas " a rise of wages invariably lowers profits." We emphasise the words *other things being equal*. For it is evident that, if the conditions of productiveness change, if, *e.g.* the total output of the enterprise doubles, wages and profits might double simultaneously ; and in new countries, where productivity is great, high wages and large profits are not infrequently found together.[3] But the antagonism of interests is present nevertheless, and the incessant strikes are witness to it. In the actual economic order, then, employer

alive to the struggle which must be carried on to bring about the disappearance of the wage-system and the employer system. The " reformist " trade unions, however, do not consider the wage-earners ready as yet to do without the employer (see p. 604).

[1] In France the Radical-Socialist party has adopted exactly the same programme as the Co-operative or Solidarity school. This party, at the Congress of Nancy, in 1907, declared in its programme that it encouraged all institutions by which the proletariat could enforce its rights, *bring about the abolition of the wage-system, and arrive at individual ownership, the very condition of its freedom and dignity.*

[2] In the inquiry of 1889, in Belgium, we find the following bare-faced declaration of an employer : " The science of industry consists in obtaining the greatest possible sum of labour out of a human being for the lowest possible remuneration." Quoted by Vandervelde, *Enquête sur les Associations professionnelles*, t. iii, p. 98.

[3] An employer may even find it to his interest to employ more highly paid workers, or to raise the wages of those whom he already employs, if he thinks that he will thereby obtain such an increase of output as will bring him in a higher return. Obviously what matters to the *entrepreneur* is not the expenses, but the results. The labour of an English worker paid 5s. a day will be cheaper in the end than that of an Indian coolie paid 5d. a day, if the former turns out twenty yards of cotton stuff for the latter's one. But, all the same, if the employer can pay the English worker 4s., his profits will be still higher.

and employed stand over against one another in an attitude of mutual defiance, yet bound together, as it were, by an iron chain.

(b) *With taking away the worker's interest in turning out good work*, thereby seriously affecting production. For, as the worker has no claim on the profits of the enterprise, having sold his share of the product of his labour for a fixed sum, he has no other stimulus to work than the *fear of being dismissed*. Now if such a motive is enough to determine him to do a minimum amount of work, it is not enough to determine him to use his productive capacities [1] to their utmost, for it makes labour a veritable task. The fixed contract reduces the worker to a purely passive rôle, robbing him of all interest in the success, as in the failure, of the business. It is difficult to convince the workers that they have no rights on all this wealth which comes forth from their hands : it is impossible to prevent them from viewing with bitterness one generation of employers and shareholders after another becoming rich from some mine or factory in which they too have worked from father to son, and yet remained poor. True, they are but *hands*. The English expression is as accurate as it is cruel ; but it is just the evil of our social organisation that one man may be nothing more than an instrument for another. The first principle of morals, as formulated by Kant—what he called the supreme practical principle— was, that we should always remember to look on the person of our fellow man as an end, not as a means. The present organisation of labour, according to which workers in an employer's service are but a means whereby he makes a fortune, is far from carrying out this noble maxim.

The Co-operative school, however, breaks away from the Socialist school as regards the means to be employed for doing away with the wage-system. To attempt to do this by abolishing property appears to it a contradiction ; it is this very lack of property which, by creating a state of dependence, has created the wage-system.

---

[1] In industry the inferiority of paid labour is not so noticeable, as this labour may be closely overseen, and its results immediately controlled, and as the system of piece-work is used wherever possible. It is in agricultural production that it is most felt :

(a) Because surveillance is much more difficult there than in the factory, particularly if the estate be large ;

(b) Because the results of the agricultural labourer's work cannot as a rule be appreciated till long after the work is done, and then only in a very uncertain way ;

(c) Because the method of piece-work cannot be applied to agriculture, the good execution of the work being much more important than the speed at which it is done.

Only by making property general, therefore, can the workers be emancipated.

For, after all, when we speak of doing away with the wage-system, what exactly do we mean ?

The only way to do away with it would be to make each wage-earner independent, producing with his own means and on his own account, like the artisan, or the peasant. But such a system appears to be incompatible with large industry and with the whole trend of economic evolution, and is advocated by none, not even by socialists. The term " abolition of the wage-system " then must be taken to mean simply that workers will henceforth be co-proprietors of the enterprises in which they work : that they will manage them themselves and keep all the profits.

Now, how does Collective Socialism think of carrying out this programme ? By " socialising the means of production," the workers henceforth working, not for capitalist employers, but for society, which will give them back the exact equivalent of what they have produced, retaining merely enough to cover general costs and expenditure for the common good. But it may be doubted whether this scheme, even if it worked, would do away with the wage-system. It is not very clear in what way those who are to work henceforth for " society "—whether this society be the nation, the commune, or the trade-union federation—will differ from the wage-earners who work to-day for the State, or for the big companies.

On the other hand, it is very evident that, under this system, all the autonomous producers of to-day, just because they are not wage-earners, will be doomed to disappear.

The Co-operative school, therefore, flatters itself that it comes nearer the desired end by transforming wage-earners into partners. These, working henceforth for associations of which they are themselves the members, will have only themselves to obey, and will receive the whole product of their labour. In a word, they will become their own employers. Theoretically the solution is perfect ; in practice there is some difficulty. For, if the association be confined to one particular enterprise (say a co-operative association for production), its action must surely be somewhat limited, and it cannot hope to change the condition of the working masses. While, if it be general, as in the case of the large co-operative societies for consumption, the worker, being only a unit among many, has no longer the feeling that he is working for himself, and his situation approaches very nearly that of the worker under the Collectivist *régime*. A combination, however, of these two modes of co-operation might perhaps enable us to steer clear of this dilemma (*see* p. 651).[1]

CHAPTER IV: THE *ENTREPRENEUR*[2]

I : HISTORICAL EVOLUTION OF THE *ENTREPRENEUR*

WE have already had occasion to speak of the personage called in economic language the master, or *entrepreneur*. We have seen (in the Book on *Production*) that it is he who takes the initiative in all production. But he occupies no less important a place in distribution, since it is he also who is the great distributor, giving to each of his collaborators their pay, that is to say, their incomes : to the worker his *wage*, to the capitalist his *interest*, to the landed proprietor his *land rent*, or his *house rent*. Whatever is left over after these constitutes his own income, viz., *profit*.[3]

The old idea of the employer as, in a sense, a patron (*cf.* French *patron* = employer) demanding rights from, and owing duties to, his workers, standing to them somewhat as a chief to his subordinates, has undergone curious transformations within the last century. We many distinguish three periods :

(*1*) At the opening of the industrial period, and till the middle of the nineteenth century, the *entrepreneur* was concerned solely with his economic functions, *i.e.* with producing the most possible output at least cost, and with utilising to the best of his interests the labour force available, not of men only, but the more lucrative, because

---

[1] See, however, in the report for October 1905 of the *Société d'Économie politique* the discussion on co-operation for production : " *La coopération peut-elle abolir le salariat ?* " which was answered in the negative.

[2] Adam Smith and the English school did not distinguish the *entrepreneur* from the capitalist. It was J. B. Say who first brought out the distinction, although the name *entrepreneur* is to be found in Quesnay. M. Yves Guyot proposes to use the word *employeur* after the English, as symmetrical with *employé* or wage-earner, but it has the disadvantage of somewhat contracting our conception of the *entrepreneur* ; the latter does much more than merely give employment to labour.

[3] The *entrepreneur*, instead of distributing the shares *after* the value of the products has been realised, may do so in advance. This is generally done in the case of wages, but it makes no difference in the function of the *entrepreneur*.

The *entrepreneur* very frequently himself provides some of the elements of production : generally the ground, all or part of the capital, and a certain amount of labour. This also makes little difference, since, in this case, he assigns himself incomes, theoretically distinct, as capitalist, landowner, and wage-earner, as we shall see under each of these headings.

less costly, labour of women and of children.   It was the *régime* of *laisser-faire*, as characteristically revealed in the famous answer of an English employer, who, when asked what would become of his dismissed workers, replied, "I leave that to natural laws."

No doubt, from the economic point of view, the capitalist employers of this heroic age were the creators of large modern industry ; but from the moral point of view their history is hardly edifying.[1] We must, of course, except a few individuals, and foremost among them Owen, the great Scottish manufacturer, to be remembered rather as the first creator of a model factory than for his communist theories.

(2) Towards 1850 a new conception, that of the *good employer*, arose, in a group of Protestant manufacturers in the town of Muhlhausen, at that time French.   Its formula is to be found in the no less famous words of another employer, Dollfus : "The employer owes the worker *more than his wage*." This was equivalent to saying that the payment of labour, as fixed at the current rate by the law of supply and demand, did not exhaust justice, and that there still remained something due to the worker ; that the latter must be looked on, not as a mere instrument of labour, but as a collaborator with the employer, who in his turn should try to find out the worker's wants and provide for them.   In this way was inaugurated the great *employers' movement* which found expression in workmen's dwellings, employers' stores, funds and pensions, sometimes even in profit-sharing and children's schools.

Unfortunately, this generous impulse frequently degenerated into a control over the private life of the worker which became intolerable to him.[2] It was only natural that the good employer, who recognised that he had duties towards his worker, should also attribute to himself the rights of a father, and should be willing only to make sacrifices with his eyes open, and for workers whom he had found worthy.   But it was also to be expected that the worker should show himself ungrateful, and this did not fail to happen. Taking into account the mentality of the working man of to-day, trained to the idea of class conflict, it is evident that the idea of

---

[1] The miseries of the working class at this epoch were the object of numerous inquiries in England—and in France of a famous work by M. Villermé, published in 1840, *Tableau de l'état physique et moral des ouvriers dans les filatures de coton, de laine et de soie.*

[2] It must be added that these institutions often degenerated into such scandalous exploitations that the legislator had to interfere.   In France, the law of March 21, 1910, did away with the truck system save, under certain conditions, in the railway companies.

the employer as a father must appear to him grotesque and hateful. He does not believe in the so-called sacrifices of the employer ; and even if he did, he would refuse them as charity. He claims his due in the form of an increase of wage, neither more nor less.

The economists of the Liberal school, again, show very little sympathy with the system of the " good employer." They are at one with the worker in declaring that the contract of labour should be a contract of *do ut des* ; that it should involve no obligations on either side other than those inherent in the contract itself—that is to say, the good execution of the work promised, on the part of the worker, and the payment of a wage fixed according to the market rate of labour, on the part of the employer. They hold that it is useless, and even dangerous, to graft moral obligations on to Political Economy.[1]

To-day the Catholic Social school and the school of Le Play alone defend the " patron " system, and even they disown the patriarchal, or paternal conception of it, and limit themselves to declaring that the function of employer is moral as well as economic, and cannot lose its moral character without detriment to society as well as to itself.[2] Only, the rôle of the employer should nowadays be not so much to provide for the wants of his workers, as to stimulate them to organise themselves ; that is to say, the employer, instead of starting " truck-shops " or workmen's dwellings, should give the workers facilities for forming co-operative societies for consumption, or for building. These schools recommend the large employer to gather round him *social engineers*, who, as distinct from the technical engineers, would deal solely with problems of the social order.

In our opinion, the modern employer should keep to his industrial function and abstain from all intervention in the life of the worker outside of the works, even by way of " doing him good " ; but he should do his utmost to give him *within the works* the best conditions of labour as regards security, hygiene, and comfort. These, indeed, contribute towards maximum productivity. This example has already been given by some of the large employers in England and the United States.

(*3*) A third period has begun recently when employers, confronted with organised workers who declare that they will have no dealings

[1] For this criticism of the patriarchal employer, see in particular the books of M. Yves Guyot, where it is continually emphasised.

[2] On the rôle of the modern employer, see numerous articles by M. Cheysson. The factory of M. Harmel at Val-des-Bois, near Rheims, is renowned in France as the model of the " patron " system as conceived by the Catholic Social school.

with their employers save on the basis of class conflict, have been forced to think, not of the protection of their workers, but of their own defence.[1] Thus the " patron " institutions have given way in turn to what might be called militant institutions, the object of which is to set up, over against the working-men's organisations, powerfully armed employers' organisations, ready to give blow for blow, to answer strikes by lock-outs, to enrol strike-breakers, to answer boycotting on the part of workers by the black-listing of their leaders, to create, over against the trade union funds for strikes, employers' funds for insuring against strikes, etc.   The *métier* of employer is going to become a very difficult one.   It will no longer be a simple case of handing down a patrimony from father to son.   Many employers will retire from the struggle, and a natural selection will increase the power of the employing class.

It must be pointed out that the socialists themselves—those, at any rate, who are logical—in no way dispute the right of employers to organise in defence of their class interests ;[2] they even in a sense desire such action as bringing the class conflict into prominent relief and, in all probability, hastening its end.   Philanthropic concessions on the part of the employing class merely cause delay by minimising the struggle, and by weakening the class-consciousness of the workers.   But it goes without saying, of course, that the Catholic Social school sees, with apprehension, the employer starting along a road which leads towards the opposite pole to that of social peace.   Still, after all, perhaps this meeting of powerful and antagonistic organisations may, by bringing the forces into equilibrium, be the best means of securing an armistice, and ultimately of imposing arbitrage.

II : WHAT IS PROFIT ?

PROFIT is *the excess of sale price over cost price*. How is profit calculated ? Nothing, it would seem, is easier. The smallest *entrepreneu*r

---

[1] It is in the United States and Germany that militant employers' organisations have developed on the largest scale.

Insurances against strikes have been in existence for some years in Germany and Austria, and two similar organisations have just been created in France. We can understand that an insurance of such a very special nature is not easy to organise, not only because of the difficulty of making good, or even of estimating, the injury done, but because the strike may very often be provoked by voluntary action on the part of the employer. Compensation, therefore, is granted only *if the strike is judged legitimate by the committee*. This is a guarantee against ill-timed strikes, which may have a conciliatory effect, rather than otherwise.

[2] This is what M. Georges Sorel, for example, declares in his book *Réflexions sur la violence.*

knows how to do it for himself. He simply subtracts his cost of production from the value of the manufactured article, that is to say, from its current market price, and the result he gets is his profit.

Yet this sum involves one of the most difficult points of economic theory, the difficulty, namely, of knowing exactly what is to be included under " costs of production."

In the first place—and there is no difficulty about this point— it must include the wages paid by the *entrepreneur* to the workers whom he has employed ; also, if he has borrowed all or part of the capital, the interest which he owes to the capitalist; lastly, the rent for the ground, if it has been leased. These are the three essential elements in the cost of production. If we represent the value of the article manufactured by V, the wage by W, interest by I, and rent by R, then profit, P, will be given by the simple formula :

$$P = V — (W + I + R)$$

As regards land rent, the English economists, basing their argument on Ricardo's theory, have always declared that land rent did not enter into cost of production, seeing that it itself is determined by that cost. This doctrine is true of differential rent (see above, pp. 510, 511 note); but, in all the cases in which rent is the result of a veritable monopoly, *e.g.* in the case of ground situated in towns, or near waterfalls, it certainly figures among the costs, and, if the *entrepreneur* is obliged to pay rent, this rent has as good a right to figure among his costs as have wages and interest.

In short, then, the *entrepreneur* must deduct from the value of the product the shares due to all his collaborators. Nothing could be simpler than this first operation (see above, p. 128).

But, as a rule, the *entrepreneur* also contributes something himself : perhaps the land and the buildings, the whole or part of the capital, or, at any rate, a certain quantity of labour in the form of organisation and management. Why should not these elements be written down among the costs of production on a line with the contributions of his collaborators ? What difference does it make that they happen to be personal to himself, that he does not need to borrow them ? If he had not employed them in this particular enterprise, he would have been able to obtain something from them in some other way : from his ground if he had let it, from his capital if he had invested it, from his labour and intelligence if he had applied them elsewhere. His own enterprise, then, must yield him at least the equivalent of what he would have been able to have made, in some other way, from these values which he possesses, otherwise he will

not undertake it.[1] Here, then, is a second layer of costs of production.

Now, how are we to calculate the value of these different elements
of production which are brought into the business by the *entrepreneur?*

In the case of rent it is simple enough : all we have to do is to
find out the price which the *entrepreneur* would have had to pay for
similar ground and buildings.

In the case of capital it is equally simple : interest is calculated
at the current rate, that which the *entrepreneur* would have had to
pay if he had borrowed the capital. And, as a matter of fact, in all
good systems of book-keeping, the *entrepreneur* writes down under a
separate heading the interest on the capital which he has himself
contributed.

This interest, however, should be calculated at a higher rate than
the current rate of interest. For the *entrepreneur* has to take into
account : (*a*) the wearing out of his capital (buildings, machinery,
etc.) ; [2] (*b*) the risk of losing it if the business is not a success ; (*c*) the
uncertainty of return in all industrial enterprises, as it may sometimes happen that the income from a business is less than the current
rate of interest. Suppose, *e.g.* the return from an enterprise is so
variable that it gives profits only every second year. Obviously,
if the *entrepreneur* is to draw from his business an income equal,
on an average, to the current rate of interest, his rate of profit must
be at least double that of the current rate of interest. This difference
in rates is simply compensation for losses, not a real profit at all.[3]
It is the same difference as exists between the rate of interest on
bonds, and the rate of dividends on shares.

It is not until we come to calculate the personal labour of the
entrepreneur that the difficulty begins. What is the salary which

---

[1] And yet, if we look closely, we shall find a number of enterprises in all
countries which do not produce enough to *remunerate the capital invested in them
at the current rate.* How, under such conditions, do they keep going ? This
apparent contradiction is easily explained when we consider the nature of the
capital sunk. If it is in the form of fixed capital, it is impossible to turn it to
any other account than that for which it was intended. The only choice therefore is either to abandon it altogether, or be content with the income, however
small, which can be drawn from it. This frequently happens in the case of
railways, tramways, mines, etc. ,

[2] We do not mention the sinking-fund for replacing money capital borrowed,
we are speaking here of capital belonging to the *entrepreneur.*

[3] This insurance premium must not be confused with the premium which we
referred to under the same name when showing how the rate of interest was
calculated (p. 567). That premium was calculated to cover possible loss of the
capital ; this is calculated only to cover the variability of income.

he ought to receive ? The answer is : As much as he would give
a good manager capable of replacing him ; or, the salary which
he could himself obtain if he let out his services. The remuneration
thus calculated is, no doubt, somewhat arbitra:y. Still, many
entrepreneurs enter the salary wh:ch they take as an item in their
costs. The salary will be larger as a rule than that which the
entrepreneur would give an employee of equal merit, or would
claim himself if he were seeking the post of manager. And this
we can quite understand. For we must take into account the
responsibilities, the anxieties, and the risks of the occupation of
entrepreneur—not the risk of losing his capital, which we have
already counted, but that of losing his position and his commercial
honour. If a man cannot earn more as *entrepreneur* than as
salaried manager, it would be better for him to enter some one else's
service : he would at least have peace of mind. There are indeed
only too many Frenchmen who reason in this way.

Here, then, the calculation ends. We have only to subtract this
total from the value produced, and what remains will be *profit*—
profit pure and simple. Only, after we have taken into account
and deducted all the elements enumerated above, we may ask our ·
selves, *will there be anything left over ?*

There can be a remainder only if the value of the finished product
is greater than the total sum of the costs of production. Now, this
is possible only in so far as the *entrepreneur* is invested, legally or
de facto, with a monopoly of some sort, a privileged situation. If
he has not a monopoly, if the industry is open to free competition,
if, that is to say, the *entrepreneur* brings nothing more to the market
for services than what all the rest of the world may bring, then there
will be no remainder. And there is nothing surprising in this. For,
if the competition of *entrepreneurs* is free, since it will be most active
wherever there is a profit to be gained, it cannot fail to bring down ·
the value of the product to the level of cost of production.[1]

¹ Professor Walras employs a striking, and at first sight surprising, formula
when he declares that the *normal rate of profits is zero.* By this he means that,
under the hypothetical system of free competition on which he bases his system
of mathematical equations, the price at which the *entrepreneur* buys productive
services (including his own), and the price at which he sells the articles manufactured, must necessarily be equal. Profits are therefore obviously reduced to
zero.

This amounts to saying that the only *normal* income of the *entrepreneur* is
that which he receives in his capacity of *worker* or *capitalist*, and that the surplus
(what is generally called profit) is only an accidental stroke of luck.

This theory, although apparently paradoxical, is perhaps more in accordance
with facts than we might at first sight think. Take, for instance, two capitalists

III : THE LEGITIMACY OF PROFIT,

FOR the very reason that the *entrepreneur* has played the leading part on the economic scene, the part of hero, he and his income have been the centre of attack and defence in the matter of profits. For the opinion which we may have as to the legitimacy of profits evidently depends on the manner in which we understand the rôle of *entrepreneur*.

(*1*) French economists, beginning with Say, drew a dividing-line between the function of *entrepreneur* and that of capitalist, making a distinct personage of the former. It was they who baptized him by the name of *entrepreneur*. The character which, in their view, was predominant in the *entrepreneur* was that of worker.[1] Profit therefore appeared to them a *remuneration of labour*—a labour very different in its nature from that of the manual labourer, superior in productiveness, and consequently calling for a higher remuneration than the simple wage. For it involves :

(*a*) *Invention*, the capital act of all production, as we saw (p. 97). The great industrial fortunes (Bessemer steel, Singer's sewing machines) are all the result of invention. We saw that the really productive act is the idea. Now, the function of the *entrepreneur*, they say, is just to have ideas—not ideas of genius, but commercial ideas. Above all, the *entrepreneur* must discover what will please the public. It is not enough for him to invent new models : he must, if I may so put it, invent new wants.

(*b*) *Management*. It is one of the fundamental laws of Political Economy that collective labour is more productive than isolated labour, but only when organised, disciplined, regimented. There must therefore be some one to distribute tasks and assign to each his place. This is the rôle of the *entrepreneur*, and it is for this reason that he has been called the " captain of industry." For industry is like warfare ; it is the general who wins the battle. Good soldiers,

who have invested equal sums in the same enterprise, the one in shares, the other in bonds. The above theory means simply this, that in the long run—say fifty years—these two capitalists, the one getting interest, the other dividends, will have received exactly the same income. This conclusion is, we believe, generally confirmed by business men. It is not impossible, taking everything into account, that the *income in dividends may be smaller than that in interest*, owing to the psychological law which makes men always over-estimate chances of success and under-estimate those of failure.

[1] Still, the employer is sometimes considered as a capitalist and profit is justified as an insurance premium against risk—an explanation without ground in our view, as we have explained above that insurance against risk can only involve *compensation*, not *profits*.

like good weapons, contribute to it, but they are only the conditions of success, not the efficient cause of it; proof being that the same troops with the same equipment, badly led, will be routed. So we continually find one enterprise succeed where another fails, though the workers employed may be equally intelligent.

(c) *Commercial speculation.* To produce is nothing : the important thing is to sell, to find markets. Thus enterprises to-day are becoming more and more commercial in character. This is another feature of the *entrepreneur's* labour, and one of the highest social importance, since, by his commercial speculation, the *entrepreneur* works unconsciously towards keeping production and consumption in equilibrium.

Such, then, is the explanation which makes profit the remuneration of a higher order of labour. In spite of a certain amount of truth which it contains, this theory does not bring out the essential nature of profit, and seems inspired rather by the desire to justify it against socialist attacks. For it must be pointed out that, of all the labours mentioned as characteristic of the *entrepreneur*—invention, management, and even the search for markets—there is not one which may not be, and in most of the large joint-stock enterprises is not, entrusted to paid managers, engineers, chemists, commercial travellers, etc. And we have seen that, when *entrepreneurs* themselves undertake this labour, they give themselves a salary for it, obviously considering this remuneration as coming under the heading of cost of production, not of profits.

(2) Socialists, on the other hand, look on profit as a spoliation of the worker.

Robert Owen, at the beginning of last century, saw in profit the epitome of all economic ill, and did his best to abolish it by starting a labour exchange where workers could exchange their products for labour coupons and *vice versa*, without having to pass under the yoke of the *entrepreneur*, or having to pay him tribute in the form of profit.

But it was not till Karl Marx's book on *Capital* appeared that profit was definitely attacked. The following are, shortly, the arguments by which this doughty champion demolishes the income of the *entrepreneur*, or employer.

The assimilation of the rôle of *entrepreneur* to that of worker is, he says, absurd, or at any rate out of date. In former times, the employer worked side by side with his workers, *primus inter pares*, and could be considered as a worker and a producer. The case may still be found, exceptionally, in small industry. But in large industry—which, for Marx, is the only form of industry in the

Y

future—the employer is exclusively a capitalist, and is employer only because he is rich, just as, under the *ancien régime*, a man was an officer because he was noble. The employer gets profit from his capital like any other ordinary merchant, simply by selling : he buys in order to sell. What does he buy ? The force of the worker in the form of labour. What does he sell ? This same force in the form of concrete goods. And the surplus between the two constitutes his profit.

But where does this surplus come from ? For we must not forget that, on the Marxist theory, labour alone can confer value, and that value is measured by the quantity of the labour (pp. 49–53). Can the employer, then, resell the products of the worker's labour for a higher value than he has paid for that labour ? This is the knot of the problem, the " mystery of iniquity," the discovery of which is Marx's claim to glory. Let us listen to his argument.

The article put by the *entrepreneur* on the market has a value determined by the labour which it has cost. Suppose that it has taken the worker ten hours to make, its value will be measured by ten hours of work : *the article will be worth ten hours.*

But what is this work or labour-force of the worker worth ? It is determined, like that of the product itself, or of any commodity, say a machine, by its cost of production. Now, in the case of this human machine, the cost of production is nothing less than the cost indispensable to raise a worker, that is to say, to bring him up and support him. Suppose that the expenditure required to support this worker and keep him in good condition is equal to five hours' work a day : his labour, then, *is worth five hours' work*, neither more nor less. In giving him, therefore, in the form of wages a value equivalent to five hours' work, the employer is paying labour exactly what it is worth according to the laws of value and exchange. But, as the product of the labour of this same worker is worth ten hours, there is a difference between the buying price and the cost price—a surplus value of five hours. This is what Marx calls *Mehrwert* : it is the keystone of his doctrine.

For there are five hours of work by which the employer profits without paying for them, five hours during which the worker works for nothing. *Profit is thus a certain quantity of labour unpaid* : this is the whole secret of capitalist exploitation.[1] And it goes without saying

---

[1] Marx's demonstration is too complicated to be given in full. To obtain an accurate idea of it one must distinguish between *profit* and *surplus value.*

Surplus value can come only from capital employed in making men work— capital, that is to say, expended in wages—and it is proportional to the quantity

that these unpaid hours are multiplied by the number of workers employed, so that the more workers are employed the greater will be the profit.

This demonstration may be put in a simpler, if less precise, form, by taking as starting-point the fact that the *value produced by a man's labour is generally greater than the value required to support him*. This is true even of the isolated and primitive worker. Were it not so, civilisation could never have arisen, nor population have increased. How much more true, then, is it of the civilised worker, whose power is multiplied by the division of labour and by collective organisation ! Now, the employer who has become possessed of this labour-force by purchase invents a thousand ingenious ways of increasing its surplus value—lengthening the working day as much as he can, stimulating the worker by the deceptive device of piece wages, introducing machinery which enables him to utilise the feeble arms of women and children. On the other hand, technical progress, by enabling all that is necessary for the material life and the support of the worker to be produced at less cost, reduces, by the same amount, the value of his labour, since this value cannot exceed that of the cost of maintenance. If, *e.g.* the productiveness of labour increased to such an extent that five minutes were sufficient to produce the subsist- ence of a man working ten hours a day, the value of a working-man's day of ten hours would henceforth be equivalent to no more than five minutes' work. This would be the wage which the employer would henceforth pay, and the surplus, *i.e.* the value produced during the remaining nine hours fifty-five minutes, he would keep.

This elaborate scaffolding of dialectic, raised in order to prove

of this capital, which Marx calls *variable capital*. But capital in the form of machinery or even of raw material, which Marx calls *constant capital*, does not give any surplus value, as the labour of the worker who manipulates them merely reproduces their value, no more, no less.

Profit, on the contrary, results from the employment of capital in general, without distinction : its rate is determined by competition and has no relation to the proportions of variable or constant capital employed in any particular industry.

But then, here is an industry, say, which employs only manual labour, and spends under this head £80,000 in wages : there is another more advanced industry which spends only £40,000 in wages, since it has replaced the half of its workers by machines. On Marx's reasoning, the surplus value of the first industry would be double that of the second. And yet very probably it will be the second which will make the most profits. This is one of the great stumbling-blocks in the Marxist theory. There is a contradiction between the Marxist doctrine and facts which it is not easy to explain, although the Marxists have done their best. See *History of Doctrines*, by Gide and Rist (English translation).

that profit, by its very nature, is a spoliation [1] consisting in a certain quantity of unpaid labour, rests on a single pin-point,[2] viz., the idea that the value of labour, like that of any other commodity, is determined solely by the quantity of work necessary to produce it. If, however, we do not admit the theory of value as based on labour —and few do so to-day—(see p. 52), the whole structure falls to the ground.

Marx's reasoning possesses, however, a real value, less as a criticism of profit than as a criticism of the wage-system. For, we are bound to admit that, under this system, labour has certainly been treated as a commodity to be bought and sold ; that the employer has always tried to pay as little as possible for it ; and that for many centuries he succeeded admirably in doing so. But this is not to say that the employer is a simple merchant, buying " labour force " in order to sell its products. His function is more complex. Labour, moreover, does not allow itself to be thrown about like a bale of merchandise. Trade unions, working-class legislation, co-operation, etc., all tend to regulate the rate of wages by other laws than those which govern the market price of commodities, to recognise in the wage-earner the rights of a joint-sharer.

(3) Both of these attitudes, the one justifying, the other attacking profits, are somewhat too sweeping. Profit is a bundle of heterogeneous elements which cannot be appreciated *en bloc*. At least two kinds of profit must be distinguished :

(a) Profit as understood by the Economists, which takes the form of remuneration for the labours of co-ordination, management, and the finding of markets, and compensation for risks. To speak accurately, this is not profit but one of the necessary factors in the cost of production. Even if the capitalist *régime* were to be replaced by a collective, or co-operative *régime*, a sum would still have to be taken for the above ; only, instead of being paid to the employer, it would be paid to the manager, or put into a reserve fund.

(b) Profit which would be better named *surplus profit*, due to certain favourable circumstances which enable the *entrepreneur* either to *produce below the normal cost of production*, and thus to benefit by a veritable differential rent analogous to that of the

---

[1] Marx to be accurate, does not set out to show the illegitimacy of profit— he puts aside all moral, or what he calls *normative* considerations—but simply to give the scientific explanation of it, the employer, he says, not being able to do other than he does. Still, his " explanation," whether intentionally or not, tends obviously to present profit in the light of spoliation.

[2] Still, it is going a little too far to call it " altogether infantile," as does M. Paul Leroy-Beaulieu, *Cours d'Économie politique*, vol. ii, p. 211.

landed proprietor,[1] or to sell above *the normal cost of production,* thus benefiting by a veritable monopoly.

This last situation is much more frequent than we might think. It may, in the first place, be legal, resulting from a patent for invention, or from a customs tariff. But it may also result from such circumstances as the possession of a more or less considerable amount of capital, which, in a new or poor country, would constitute a sort of monopoly ; the fact of bearing a name already well known in industry ; or of occupying a good site—for instance, a public-house situated close to a factory, or even to a cemetery. Who is there who has not his small monopoly ? It is this surplus profit which, when exceptionally favourable circumstances arise, creates great fortunes. Shakespeare must have been thinking of it when he said :

> "*There is a tide in the affairs of men*
> *Which, taken at the flood, leads on to fortune.*
> *Omitted, all the voyage of their life*
> *Is bound in shallows and in miseries.*"

Surplus profit does not, of course, appear either as necessary, or as legitimate as ordinary profit, since by the nature of the case it implies a privilege, or at least an inequality of luck. Still, the distinction we have drawn must be borne in mind. If the surplus profit is the result of some happy invention, answering to a desire on the part of the public, or of a saving realised in the cost of production, it is simply a premium on invention and industrial progress, and, far from involving any tribute from the consumers, like monopoly or rent, it implies a greater profit to them than even to the *entrepreneur*.[2] For the *entrepreneur* keeps, as a rule, in the form of

---

[1] Land rent makes its appearance, as we have seen, whenever, on a market, the price is regulated by the *maximum* cost of production—which is the case whenever supply is less than, or simply equal to, demand. This often happens with agricultural products. With industrial products, however, although a maximum cost may regulate prices *at a given moment*, the moment does not last long, since industrial competition quickly increases the supply beyond demand. Thereafter it is, on the contrary, the minimum cost of production which regulates prices.

[2] Numerous and amusing instances may be quoted of enormous profits and fortunes made by inventions which have nothing of the nature of genius about them ; the shoe-lace, the safety-pin, steel pen-nibs, roller skates. What a fortune the inventor of the picture post-card would have made if he could have patented it !

M. Paul Leroy-Beaulieu, who takes this view (see *Essai sur la répartition des richesses*), quotes, as an example, the Bessemer process of manufacturing steel, which brought a million or so sterling to the inventor, but much more to industry in general.

profits, only a small part of the saving economised, and even this just remuneration is not long in being torn from him by competition ; so that what was at first a minimum cost of production for him alone soon becomes the normal cost of production for every one. But, if it is due to a monopoly enabling the *entrepreneur* to sell above the current price, it is a tax which must be abolished.   Observe, however, it is a tax on the purse of the consumer, not on the wage of the worker.

For the rest, this somewhat scholastic question of the right to profit resolves itself really into another question, viz., whether the function of employer is indispensable or not. If it is possible to do without the *entrepreneur*, clearly there is no reason to remunerate him. This is what we must now inquire into.

IV: THE ABOLITION OF THE *ENTREPRENEUR*

THE abolition of the *entrepreneur*, or employer, is a formula which appears as frequently in socialist manifestos as the abolition of the wage-system itself.   They are not, however, as we might think, the same thing.   The *entrepreneur* may quite well disappear while the wage-system remains.   The abolition of the wage-system, the abolition of the employer, the abolition of profit—these are kindred propositions but yet distinct.

By the abolition of the employer we must be taken to mean simply the substitution of enterprise in a collective form for enterprise in an individual form.   That such substitution is possible admits of no doubt, since we see it realised to-day on the largest scale. And economists of the Liberal, as well as of the Socialist, school predict that this evolution will not stop until it includes all production. This, however, has yet to be verified.[1]   Certainly, in the joint-stock companies, neither the wage-system nor profit is abolished !

The spread of the limited liability company, or the *société anonyme*, as it is called in France, is pointed to by collectivists as a proof that the employer is henceforth of no more use and has become a simple parasite.   The very term *anonymous*, they say, is a clear indication that there is no longer an employer in the sense in which the Economists use the word—that is to say, an individual at the same time proprietor and manager of an enterprise, receiving profits, but giving daily labour in return. The employer has been eliminated, or, rather, has been broken up into managers and salaried officers

---

[1] From an inquiry made by M. Camille Sabatier for the *Ligue de la Propriété*, at Toulouse, it would seem that the number of small employers is on the increase.

on the one hand, and a host of idle shareholders on the other, who sometimes know no more of the enterprise in which they are so-called partners than the name of the company written on their share certificates. Abolish them, and the enterprise would go on just the same as before. Now, as a result of the present evolution, which is substituting large production for small, and the joint-stock company for individual enterprise, all employers, they say, will soon be reduced to mere shareholders, their activity limited to tearing off their coupons. Their uselessness will then be openly demonstrated, and the rôle which they play in society will be at an end.

But the example of the capitalist joint-stock companies is not quite to the point. For employers still exist there. It is not, of course, the shareholders, simple moneylenders—*sleeping partners* as they are so well named in England—who are the employers. It is the Board of Directors—sometimes only a few of its members, say the chairman, or secretary—who keep the whole business going. The government is no longer that of an hereditary monarchy, but of an oligarchy chosen by a small number of capitalists, and invested with full powers, after the fashion of the republic of Venice.

The case of the co-operative society is different. Although here, also, the business is kept going by one or two individuals, the manager is chosen by universal suffrage and is always liable to be dismissed, so that this is really a democratic republic. And the example of the co-operative societies proves, in fact, that the employer is not altogether indispensable. It must be observed, however, that the co-operative, like the municipal or State form of enterprise, is best adapted to businesses which have already reached a certain stage of maturity, and which can work in a quasi-automatic fashion. It does not follow that in the starting of new businesses the *entrepreneur* can be altogether dispensed with. It is doubtful, for instance, whether such an enterprise as aviation would ever have developed so extraordinarily, or even perhaps arisen, had not a few wealthy and bold individuals made it their business. So soon, however, as travelling by aeroplane becomes as commonplace as travelling by tramway or by railway, it will be possible for aviation, like the tramways, and the railways, and the grocery business, to become a co-operative, or a municipal, or social undertaking.

The elimination of the employer, even if it could be carried out, would not necessarily involve the abolition of profit—witness the joint-stock companies, where profit under the name of dividends is greater than ever. Our next question, then, is whether profit itself is not destined to disappear.

This seems not improbable : its end is already predicted on different sides, not only by socialists, but by economists of the Classical school. The latter teach that the rate of profits, at any rate, is doomed, like the rate of interest, to an inevitable fall, save where such accidental circumstances as a sweeping destruction of capital, or some great new invention might temporarily raise it. Some have even laid it down as a mathematical axiom that, under a hypothetical system of free competition, the rate of profits *would go down to zero*.

We must, however, draw a distinction. Normal profit, that which represents remuneration for the labour of co-ordination and recompense for risks incurred, and which is entitled on this twofold ground to be entered under costs of production, can never be done away with, since, as we have said, it is one of the conditions necessary for all production. The only profit, therefore, which there can be any question of suppressing is that which we have called surplus profit : profit, that is to say, due to inequalities of economic situation, or to monopolies. And it is quite possible to admit, in theory at least, that this profit may disappear, either by the suppression of the monopoly, or by some mechanism which, like collectivism or co-operation, would hand back the surplus to the community.

This is being actually done by the co-operative societies for consumption, and it is precisely their ushering in of a new economic order which makes them so interesting. Profit, as salary of management, and as interest on capital, is not suppressed, because it cannot be, and it figures under the costs of production. But surplus profit, arising from lucky contingencies such as result in reduction of cost price, or raising of sale price, is abolished. Even if we have the semblance of it, in practice, in the distribution of bonuses, it is restored to those from whom it was taken—the buyers. It is not really profit ; it is, as the French co-operatives rightly call it, a *ristourne*, that is to say an *overcharge* returned.

There still remains the question what would be the effect on production of the abolition of profit ? The Classical economists who, like John Stuart Mill, proclaim the law of the decline of profits, foresee as a consequence of it the " stationary state " (see p. 89). In their view, so soon as the possibility of profiting by lucky chances is withdrawn from men, one of the most powerful springs of industry will be slackened.

This is quite probable, but doubtless by that time other motives will have arisen for human activity; and even should we reach a stationary state in industry, the prospect need not alarm us over-much. Mill himself looked forward to it with equanimity.

CHAPTER V: THE DESTITUTE

I: THE DIFFERENT CATEGORIES OF DESTITUTE

At all times, and in all countries, there has existed at the opposite end of the scale from the idle-rich, a more or less large class of idle-destitute; that is to say, persons who, having no property and being unable or unwilling to live by their labour, can live only by what they take out of the incomes of others.[1]

Their idleness may be due to three causes:[2]

(1) They may not have the *strength* to work. This is the case with children, the aged, and all who suffer from chronic disease or permanent infirmity.

[1] The number of paupers in France is estimated at 1,400,000, or 3·6 per cent., *i.e.* 1 person in 28. But many out of this number do a little work, and are only partially assisted by the State.

[2] A number of investigations have been made into the causes of poverty. We give two which, although they differ somewhat in classification, confirm one another fairly well as regards results.   The table on the left was drawn up by M. Morel Fatio, at Geneva; that on the right by Mr. Warner, at New York:

MISFORTUNE.

	Per cent.				Per cent.
Illness	. 26		Illness		. 27
Old age	. 9		Old age		. 10
Unemployment	. 15		Unemployment		. 29
Insufficient wage	. 17		Premature death		. 12

VICE.

Vice	. 16		Alcoholism		. 11
Idleness and incapacity	. 8		Idleness		. 10
Mendicity	. 9		Unclassified		. 1
	100				100

It will be seen that involuntary causes—what we call misfortune—represent 67 per cent. of the cases in Geneva, and 78 per cent. in New York.   That is to say, destitution is much more largely due to misfortune than to the fault of the destitute.

But some causes of first importance seem to have been omitted in both investigations, *e.g.* the desertion of wives and children, unfortunately a frequent cause of poverty in the working population; also the large size of working-class families.

v′

(2) They may not have the *means* to work. For it is not enough to have the will to work ; a man must also be able to find work, *i.e.* he must have materials or implements at his disposal. Now, in unemployment both of these are lacking.

(3) They may not have the *will* to work. All work, as we know, involves more or less painful effort ; so much so that many men, rather than make this effort—above all, rather than submit to the discipline which all work demands—prefer to run the risk of starving.

What is society to do, faced with these three categories of destitute ? For it cannot refuse to grapple with the problem which they present.

It has to make provision for the first from reasons of social solidarity. It is, above all, to its interest to maintain and educate the children, since they represent the future. In the natural order of things it is of course the family which should undertake this charge. But the family in our days is frequently scattered ; sometimes, as in the case of illegitimate children, it does not even exist. There are cases, again, where children have to be taken from parents who are exploiting, or perverting them. As for the aged and infirm poor, society has no interest in keeping them alive, since, economically speaking, they are worthless, and all that is given them is so much the less for the active portion of the population. But the moral evolution of a people is no less important than its economic evolution ; and a society which would leave its aged and infirm to die of hunger would be singularly backward in this respect, less humane, for all its civilisation, than the savage hordes which strangle their aged, but piously, that they may not suffer long.

Society has to make provision for the second, for it is in a measure *responsible* for their misfortune.[1] It is the present economic constitution of society which has separated the worker from the implements of his labour and has forced him to ask for work in order to live.[2] It is the law of progress itself, as we see it in large production, mechanical inventions, international trade, competition, which brings about unemployment and crises (see pp. 88, 144). It is therefore only just

---

[1] This reasoning also applies to the next category. Society has its share of responsibility in vice as well as in poverty.

[2] It must not be forgotten that people still die of hunger. In London, according to the official statistics (1907), the number of deaths from hunger, properly speaking, *i.e.* from actual exhaustion owing to lack of food, amounted to forty-eight, or about one a week; but according to the Salvation Army it amounts to about 200 per annum !

that society, which benefits as a whole by every forward step, and which, in the great battle of life, reaps all the fruits of victory, should bear the burden of the fray and come to the relief of the wounded and vanquished. This is what is meant by social solidarity (see p. 32).

Lastly, society cannot neglect the third category, since it constitutes a *public danger*. It is from this population of drunkards and vagabonds that the army of crime is recruited; and as, once they have committed an offence, society is obliged to maintain them, and the maintenance of a prisoner is a costly matter, it is both more prudent and more economical to take preventive measures.[1]

Society, we say, then, is under the obligation to help; but do we mean a *legal*, or only a *moral*, obligation? Ought the obligation to exist in the form of law, thus recognising in the pauper a veritable *right* which he can enforce if need be in the courts of justice? If our standpoint is simply that of charity or brotherly love, we shall discard all idea of official or compulsory assistance; for official or compulsory love is a contradiction in terms. But we believe, for the reasons which we have just given, that assistance—so much, at any rate, as is indispensable to life—is a real obligation on society, an obligation which should be written not only in the law, but in the State and communal budgets, and that some procedure should be organised to enable the poor to enforce their claims.

This legal relief, moreover, would by no means render private relief superfluous. It could only undertake the strictly necessary, leaving the rest to private charity. The margin of misery and suffering will still be wide enough to absorb all the activities of the latter.

II: THE DANGERS OF POOR RELIEF

RELIEF, when legal and administrative, is not without dangers, particularly when it constitutes a " right " on the part of the destitute. These dangers have been denounced by all the Classical economists, but by none more forcibly than by Malthus. They may be summed up in the following formula : " *The number of paupers tends to increase in direct ratio to the help they may count upon.*" And this danger, say the Economists, is particularly to be feared when the aid is given by the State. The reasons they give are the following :

(1) Official relief as a " right " tends to *develop improvidence.*

[1] In the new model prisons of to-day a prisoner's cell costs 6000 francs !— the price of a good working-man's house.

A number of persons, who might perhaps make both ends meet if they had only themselves to depend upon, neglect to provide for their future, or for that of their children, so soon as they know that they can count on the help of the State. As the song of the English country labourers says :

> " *Hang sorrow and cast away care,*
> *The parish is sure to find us !* "

(2) Legal relief, once secure and to be counted on,.leads to an *increase of population in the pauper classes.* Paupers have no anxiety regarding the maintenance of their children, since they do not have to support them. They gain, in fact, by having families, since relief is distributed according to the size of the family. A premium is thus, as it were, involuntarily put on the increase of the destitute, and a large substratum of paupers is formed in the lowest depths of society, inscribed on the registers of public relief, just as are the *rentiers* on the *Grand Livre,* transmitting their rights as well as their vices—a race despised, but too degraded to be unhappy at their lot, or to strive to rise above it.

(3) Relief is apt to *impoverish the productive classes of society,* and thus militates directly against the law of natural selection, which tends, on the contrary, to perfect the organism by making the higher elements predominate over the lower ones. For, obviously the desti-tute classes constitute neither the most sane, nor the most healthy, portion of the social organism. And as the State is able to main-tain them only by taxation, that is to say by the resources which it takes from the product of the labour of those capable of producing, and as the class of destitutes is continually increasing, the tribute which it levies on the industrious class is becoming more and more heavy, and may finally force this class in turn into the gulf of pauperism.

But if these reasons are ample proof that we cannot be too careful in organising the right to poor relief, they are far from sufficient to induce us to do away with it altogether.

It is quite possible that the prospect of relief may tend to reduce productive activity and saving, but it is also possible that, when intelligently administered, it may have a stimulating effect. And why, after all, do we fear ill-effects from it only in the case of the poor and not of the rich ? The certainty of a pension, the hope of an inheritance, or the possession of funds, should produce a much lazier frame of mind.

The fear that assisted persons will have too large families is somewhat fanciful, while the so-called law according to which all systems of public relief increase the number of paupers is belied by experience. At no time has public relief been more highly organised than at the present day; never have its resources been greater, its scope wider; and yet the proportion of paupers is decreasing in all nations, even in England, the country which may be taken as the standing example of legal relief and which served as a case in point for the sinister predictions of Malthus.[1]

It is possible that to maintain and preserve in society all the sick, the infirm, the incapable, and the lazy, may entail a certain waste of wealth and force; but this waste would exist in any case—unless we go the length of exterminating all the good-for-nothings, including the idle rich, an alternative which no one has yet dared to propose. On the other hand, relief may save some one worth saving, and may spare society the still greater hurt that results from crime, prostitution, and drunkenness. Indeed, the object of assistance, as understood to-day, is less to care passively for the sad fruits of destitution than to fight the causes of it as revealed in the two tables given above.

The simplest, oldest, and most venerable of all forms of private relief is *almsgiving*. It has a noble history, but to-day it is generally recognised as the most ineffective, and as the most liable to develop professional begging and lying. It is therefore only resorted to exceptionally, and is everywhere giving place to foundations, that is to say, to associations, or private institutions, which act as inter-mediaries between the reliever and the relieved, receiving the money from the former in subscriptions, and handing it over to the latter in the form of aid, as far as possible *in kind*. But, as these foundations develop, they assume almost of necessity the same administrative and bureaucratic characteristics as are laid to the charge of public relief. They no more develop feelings of charity in the subscriber than do taxes in the taxpayer. And if they spend relatively less in general expenses and staff than does individual charity, if those who direct them have the advantage of greater experience, still we cannot forget the scandals to which they have sometimes given rise, nor the way in which they have often wasted the money confided to them.

The best way of avoiding pitfalls, while retaining the advantages of both methods, lies, it would seem, in uniting private and public

---

[1] The number of persons in receipt of relief in the United Kingdom, after rising to the alarming number of 63 per 1000 in 1849, or 1 pauper in every 16 inhabitants, has fallen to-day (1913) to 19 per 1000, or 1 in 52 inhabitants.

relief, as is done under the famous Elberfeld [1] system.   On this
system inquiries are made, and home-visiting is undertaken by
voluntary *visitors*, to each of whom a district is allotted. The duty
is in no way legally binding, but it is one which custom and the
habits of the people have rendered morally so.   The funds are
provided by the municipality, which naturally reserves control over
them ; but it exercises this right in a very liberal spirit.

It is the fashion at present, among social and political speakers,
to say that *assistance* has had its day and must give way to *insurance*;
in other words, charity is to retire before solidarity.   Since destitution
is the result of misfortune or improvidence, we have only to make
providence compulsory and to organise insurances against all the
risks of life, in order to end them.   But, even supposing insurance
could avert all the primary causes of poverty—which it cannot—
how are we to insure against alcoholism, gambling, idleness, the
wandering instinct ? [2]   We must not forget that social insurances
and Friendly Societies are profoundly penetrated by assistance,
since it is only by means of subsidies from the State—that is to say
the taxpayer—and contributions levied on employers and voluntary
gifts, that they are able to work.

For the rest, it is a mistake to present insurance as a means of
abolishing poverty. It is only a reparation. Insurances against
fire and hail do not keep off fire and hail. They simply indemnify
the victims.   To abolish poverty we must go much further back,
and change the economic and moral conditions which develop social
plagues, or weaken the resisting force of man.

III : THE ORGANISATION OF POOR RELIEF

THE ill-effects of legal assistance would be reduced to a minimum
if poor relief were organised on the following lines :

(*1*) If it were *communal*. The commune,[3] just because it is as a
rule a small association, is in a much better position to discriminate
between those who really need relief and those who do not, and it
is as a rule more careful of the pence of the ratepayers. Still, as the
incomes of communes vary almost as much as do those of individuals,
and as the poorest communes are often, though not always, those

[1] A town of Rhenish Prussia. This system was introduced there in 1853.

[2] There are quite a number of men who, by inclination or reversionary
instinct, prefer vagrancy to a regular life of daily work. Every civilised society
still has its savages.

[3] A small territorial division in France, the *département* being the largest
territorial division. [TRANSLATOR.]

where there are the greatest number of poor, it is indispensable for the State, or some administrative group such as the department or the province, to come to their aid. The threefold solidarity of commune, department, and State is the French system.

(2) If it were administered in *special institutions*, divided where possible into three categories corresponding to the three classes of paupers mentioned above—invalids, professional beggars, and unemployed ; and if it exacted a certain amount of work in return for help given. Also, as regards outdoor relief, if it simply subsidised and controlled private help.

(3) If *legal begging were strictly prohibited*. For clearly there can be no rational organisation of assistance so long as the destitute can find help without working, by means of begging.

Only, we must take care not to put the cart before the horse and prohibit begging before we have organised public assistance. The law may forbid a man to hold out his hand, but not if it leaves him to die. Yet this is how the matter stands in France. Begging and vagrancy, that is to say, "the having no home nor means of subsistence," constitutes an offence. This does not, however, prevent beggars from swarming. There is need of entirely new legislation on the point, and attention is being given to it at the present moment.

In England, legal and compulsory relief has been organised by a series of laws, going back to the time of Elizabeth, which constitute a veritable monument of legislation. Each parish is bound to maintain its poor in *workhouses*, or by outdoor relief, and must raise the money required for this purpose by a special Poor Rate, the sum total of which amounts to nearly £15,000,000.

This organisation has been the subject of innumerable studies and official inquiries.[1] Now it is detention in the workhouse which is advocated, in order to avoid the abuses of outdoor relief. Now public opinion, disgusted by the degrading effects of detention on the paupers, returns to outdoor relief, whereupon the number of the relieved increases beyond all bounds. A law of 1908 granted to all persons over seventy years of age, whose income does not exceed £31 10s. per annum, a pension varying from 1s. to 5s. per week, without requiring any previous contribution. Denmark and New Zealand had already passed similar laws.

As regards legislation on public assistance, the countries of Europe may be divided into two distinct classes. Protestant countries admit the principle of compulsory public assistance—assistance, that is to say, inscribed in the letter of the law. Catholic countries have

[1] See *Majority and Minority Reports of the Royal Commission*, 1905.

hitherto admitted only the principle of optional public assistance. There is a historical reason for this curious opposition. During the whole of the Middle Ages, Catholic religious orders had undertaken the charge of the destitute, and in the countries into which the Reformation penetrated, the State, when confiscating the property of these communities, took over as a rule their duties also, and first among them that of relieving the poor.

Thus, in France, when the Revolution handed over the possessions of the Church to the State, the Declaration of Rights confirmed the idea that society owes a living to its unfortunate citizens by giving them either work, or food if they are unable to work ; and similar declarations figure in nearly all subsequent constitutions. They have, however, so far remained a mere empty statement of principle, as no law has ever organised this assistance in a practical manner. Public assistance has, of course, existed in France for centuries in the form of *hospitals* and *charitable boards*. But these establishments have existed as a rule on their private fortunes, with optional grants from the government.[1]

To-day matters are changed. This optional relief is being transformed into legal relief in the strict sense ; that is to say, it is becoming a form of expenditure compulsory on the State, the departments, and the communes. The main stages of this evolution have gradually included :.

(1) *Deserted children*, whether foundlings, orphans, or children taken from their parents by a decree of the courts owing to illtreatment.[2] For this class of unfortunates relief has always existed, though not perhaps very well organised. The most elementary humanity prevents a civilised State from neglecting such a duty. But the education of these children is one of the most difficult problems, and is as yet far from solved. The boarding of them out with agriculturists' families in the country is the best expedient so far tried ; but the results as yet have not been very satisfactory.

(2) *Lunatics*, for whom also relief has always existed, not so much from philanthropic reasons as for the sake of public security. In France, this relief was organised by the law of June 30, 1838, a law which occasioned famous abuses in the matter of arbitrary sequestration, but which it is not easy to evade.

---

[1] Their funds are derived from donations and legacies, the interest on which has accumulated for centuries, and from certain special taxes, such as the 10 per cent. on all public performances.

[2] By the law of July 24, 1889, one of the most useful ever promulgated, which declares the parental authority of unworthy parents forfeit, and puts the children under the care of the State or of private societies.

(3) The *sick poor.* Until the law of July 15, 1893, the indigent sick were cared for in the local hospital, if there was one, and if there happened to be room in it. Public relief therefore was very uncertain. Since this law, which may be considered as really marking the introduction of compulsory relief in France, every sick pauper may claim free treatment from his commune in case of illness, either at the hospital or, if there is not a hospital, at his home. The application of this law cost a little over 20 million francs for 1,000,000 persons treated.

(4) *Aged and infirm.* In the first edition of the Principles we said that the distress of the aged poor in France was a disgrace to the country. The law of July 14, 1905, has redressed this. Henceforth every French citizen without resources,[1] of over seventy years of age, or of any age whatever if he be infirm, may claim from his commune a pension varying from a minimum of 60 francs to 240 francs a year (360 francs in Paris). The law leaves to each commune the charge of drawing up the list of those whom it deems paupers, while giving those who think their claims have been neglected the right to appeal to a cantonal commission. This law has relieved much unjust suffering, but, like all laws of social reform, it has given rise to numerous abuses, some communes having no names on their list, from a spirit of economy ; others having the names of all, from a spirit of equality ; others, again, writing down only the names of friends of the municipality. And the idea is gradually gaining ground, particularly since the passing of the Old-Age Pension Act (see below), that all aged persons, indigent or not, have a right to a pension. This assistance constitutes an expenditure that is increasing as it is becoming more widely known. It amounted in 1912 to nearly 100 million francs, for 640,000 persons assisted, one half of which falls on the State and the other half on the communes and the departments.

---

[1] What are we to understand by the expression " without resources " ? Is the man who has something to fall back on from *his labour,* or from *private charity,* or who has laid by a certain provision for himself by his savings, to be refused a pension ? No ; the first case the law does not consider incompatible with the right to a pension ; for this would be to punish the man for his willingness to work. As for the other two cases, the law takes account of them up to a certain point, being unwilling to discourage saving and private charity.

One of the most difficult cases is where an aged person. without resources, has children who are well off and legally bound to give him or her an allowance. The law has not in this instance thought itself justified in refusing the pension, but it gives the commune the right to proceed against the children—a right more often than not illusory.

CHAPTER VI: THE STATE

I: THE RÔLE OF THE STATE IN DISTRIBUTION

IN treatises on Political Economy the State never appears among the joint-sharers. We ourselves did not formerly class it among them. And yet the State has really a twofold claim to a place under distribution.

(*1*) As *joint-sharer*,[1] and its share is no small one, since it amounts to 5 billion francs for the State strictly speaking, and over 6 billions if we include, as we ought, under the word State, the various local governments, *i.e.* the departments and the communes. The State thus takes about one-fifth of the whole income of France (see above, p. 476).[2] Its share is greater than that of the landowners, and probably than that of the capitalists, the former being valued at 3½ billions only, and the latter at 4 or 5 billions.

But, it will be said, is not this share taken by the State merely a second-hand income, like the incomes of paupers?

It is quite true that, through taxation, it comes out of incomes already received by the citizens of the State. But this way of presenting the State as a mere parasite is not quite accurate. The State also produces wealth; and, though it is difficult to distinguish exactly what is productive and what is unproductive expenditure, we certainly cannot say that these 6 milliards are all unproductive.

We no longer, it is true, explain and justify taxation, on the individualist theory, as a contract of exchange or insurance between the State and the citizen, a *do ut des*, an exchange of services. On such a hypothesis we should have to lay down, as a principle of social justice, that taxation must be proportional to the *benefit received* from society. Now, on the contrary, it is taught that taxation should be proportional to the ability to pay—a very different conception.[3] But, by the very fact that men live in society and

---

[1] The tax has its origin in the right which the State has to claim its share in the distribution of the social income (Rossi, *Principes d'Économie politique*, chap. viii).

[2] From an inquiry made by M. Beaurin Gressier for the *Société de Statistique*, in 1895, we see that, in the case of the family which had been the object of inquiry—the middle-class family with an income of 20,000 francs—taxation, under its various forms, took 23 per cent. of the total income, which confirms the above general estimate.

[3] The two conceptions approach one another, however, if we consider that the ability to pay (*i.e.* the resources of each member) is due precisely to social causes, and is, as it were, a share in the profits of the national enterprise.

. form a nation, they tacitly admit that they must accept the collective burdens in return for the advantage which they obtain. It is the State, as representing society, which assumes these burdens; and it must have the wherewithal to meet them by means of compulsory contributions levied on all the members of society. Here again, as in so many other instances, we find the idea of solidarity.[1]

(2) As *distributor*—quite a different rôle from the preceding one. The State, standing in the name of social justice and solidarity, as it is called to-day, takes from those who have too much in order to give to those who have not enough.[2] It goes without saying that the Liberal school energetically refuses to acknowledge the right of the State to play such a part, and to arrogate to itself in this way the dispensation of wealth and the redressing of wrongs. But, whether we approve, or whether we disapprove, the fact remains that the modern State is marching in this direction. What is the object of the recent social laws passed in Germany, France, and England, if not to distribute to certain categories of destitute the resources taken by proportional or progressive taxation from the propertied minority—such laws, for instance, as those lately passed in France concerning gratuitous medical aid and the relief of the aged and disabled; or the recent law passed as to old-age pensions, which will lay a burden of some hundred million francs on the budget? The increasing number of subsidies given to agricultural associations, Friendly Societies, etc., has no other object in view than this. It is here that the idea of taxation as based on service rendered to the taxpayer, falls to the ground; for the service is rendered, on the contrary, by the taxpayer to others, whether he be willing or not.

[1] For example, I have to contribute to-day, perhaps in perpetuity, a fairly large share of my income to pay the interest on the war loans of 1870. No one can say that I am paying therein a service rendered to me, or to my father, still less that I am paying the insurance premium of that disastrous adventure. But it would be right to tell me that, since I am a French citizen, I ought to bear the consequences, good or ill, of the acts of those who have preceded me on this land of France; and that I ought even to accept the responsibility for their foolishness and misfortunes, just as I benefit by the friendly soil and the relatively happy life which they have prepared for me.

The " service " theory is accurate, however, in some cases, as in that of the examination fee paid by students.

[2] See an article in the *Revue d'Économie politique*, of 1909, by M. Chatelain, *L'impôt comme instrument de répartition*. Professor A. Wagner considers the tax as the main instrument of social reform : he counts on it to prevent the " Marxist binome," or the concentration of wealth at one pole and of poverty at the other.

Although this distributive function of the State has been, in the .
main, a development of late years, it must not be thought that it was
unknown in the past. It has always existed, and under much worse
conditions than to-day, since, in former times, taxation took from
the poor in order to give to the rich.[1]

How, and by whom, is the share of the State, in other words, the
amount of taxation, fixed ? Originally the sovereign determined
his own share, as still happens in countries which have not a
constitution. The tax was for a long time a survival of the tribute
levied by the conqueror on the conquered. The first victory of the
commons—that which inaugurated the parliamentary era—was the
enforcing of the principle of no taxation without representation.
Thereafter it was the citizens themselves who fixed the share of
their incomes which they would give up to the State. To-day this
great principle of individualist justice is beginning to waver, and
we are advancing fairly rapidly towards a system inspired by the
principle of social solidarity, in which, as formerly, the taxes will be
paid by those who have not voted them, and voted by those who
will not pay them. For the fiscal policy of democracies, which is
to grant large exemptions and reductions of taxation to the wage-
earning masses while levying at the same time a progressive tax
on incomes and successions, tends to concentrate the burden on a
smaller and smaller number of the wealthy. And as, under the
system of universal suffrage, it is the majority who ultimately make
the laws, including those relating to taxes, the share of the State
must inevitably increase ; for it will be fixed by the majority
who are to benefit by it, and taken from the propertied minority.[2]
This is one of the principal causes of the increase in public
expenditure.

II : THE SHARE OF THE STATE
IN DISTRIBUTION—TAXATION

THE State, differing in this from ordinary individuals, who have
to regulate their expenses according to their income, regulates its
income as a rule according to its expenses. In France, where it

[1] Even to-day protective duties have often this result.

[2] Thus, in connection with M. Caillaux's scheme for an income tax, an inquiry
was made by the government which showed that, out of 11 million taxpayers,
6 millions (or over half) would be exempt from the proportional tax as having
an income of less than 1250 francs in the country, and 2500 in the towns ; and
only 481,000 (1 in 23) would pay the progressive tax on income from all sources,
as having an income over 5000 francs. .

requires about 5 billion francs, it asks 5 billion francs of the taxpayers.[1]

But it is not an easy matter to squeeze from a nation a sum amounting, along with the taxes of the communes and of the departments, to over 6½ billion francs, or an average of over 600 francs per family.   And the whole art of the statesman and the financier, until recently, consisted in trying to discover sources of public revenue which would weigh as lightly as possible upon the taxpayer and might even escape attention altogether. To-day, as we shall see, the principle acted on is quite different. The following are the sources from which the State obtains its revenue :

1. MANUFACTURES AND STATE LANDS

This category of revenue is not taxation. Nothing is demanded from the taxpayer.   The revenues under this heading are drawn from properties owned by, or from industries worked by, the State or municipalities. The revenue here consists of rents, or profits, which the State receives in its capacity of landowner, or *entrepreneur*, and which by rights ought not to appear in this chapter, since they come under the heading of profits and are not a special category of revenue. The State here is " earning its living " like any other person.

As regards industrial enterprises, we have seen already (see pp. 204–208) that the State is becoming increasingly active along this line, and that such operations figure largely in the budgets of several nations.   But, we have to take into account the pressure, constantly brought to bear on the State and on municipalities by consumers, who are at the same time electors, to lower the prices of public services to cost price or even below.

As regards State domains, they were, during feudal times, the main source of the income of the State, as they still are in semi-barbarian societies, where the fortune of the sovereign is not yet distinct from that of the nation. The sovereign princes of India, like the ancient kings of France, live, in great part, and keep up their armies, from the revenues of their domains.   But in most civilised countries the domain of the State has been reduced to next to nothing. In Prussia, however, and in some of the German States, the State still draws from its domains, which include not only forests but vineyards, mines, factories, etc. a revenue of a good many millions sterling. In France, the only State domain left consists in forests and in a large number of unproductive monuments. It is therefore but a drop in the budget.

[1] See *infra, Public Expenditure.*

If the theory of land nationalisation were ever to be carried out (see pp. 525–528), if, *e.g.* new countries were, from now on, to reserve to themselves the ownership of their public lands, granting them to individuals only by way of temporary concession, we might see, in the future, large revenues accruing to the State, which would allow it to do away with all, or part, of the taxes. This is one of the arguments urged in favour of land nationalisation. The programme of the single-tax system proposed by Henry George and M. Walras, for instance, is the abolition of all taxes weighing on the individual, on his labour, or on the products of his industry : the State living henceforth solely on the rent from its lands, which when bought back would constitute its own domain.[1]

2. TAXATION

As its domain is now so reduced, the State has to ask almost the whole of its resources from the contributions of its citizens, by laying taxes either on acts, on commodities, or on persons.

(1) Taxes on acts.

It is a very ancient fiscal idea to lay taxes on certain acts of life—donations, alienations, payments, lawsuits, etc.—by means of stamp and registration duties. These taxes have the twofold advantage from the fiscal point of view :

(*a*) Of corresponding to a service rendered by the State—a service which consists, namely, in authenticating a deed and giving it legal force. To tell the truth, we could very well do without this service ; but the State may, after all, say that it is due to it, to its officers and to its law courts, that these deeds of civil life are respected. As regards successions—the largest item under this category of receipts—the State may say that the transmission of goods at death is a concession accorded by the legislator to the successor, particularly in the case of succession *ab intestat*, or between distant relations or strangers (see above, p. 469).

(*b*) Of falling only indirectly on the taxpayer, or at least of touching him at the moment when he least feels it. The person who enters into an inheritance, particularly if it be unexpected,

---

[1] It is true that, in France, the total net income from land, which is valued at only 3½ billions, would be insufficient for the needs of the State. But Walras replies that the State ought to regulate its expenditure according to its resources, and that to limit its resources to income from land would have the advantage of putting a limit to public expenditure which does not at present exist. Nature, so to speak, would fix it herself. For the results which Walras expected from this system, from the point of view of the distribution of wealth, see his *Économie sociale*.

can afford to give up a share to the State without too much grumbling. The person who buys land, knowing in advance the amount of transfer duty he will have to pay, calculates his price accordingly. The 10-centime stamp on every receipt above 10 francs worries neither the buyer, since he thinks that it is the tradesman who pays, nor the tradesman, who puts it into his price.

This is not to say, however, that certain of these duties have not serious disadvantages from the economic point of view, particularly the transfer duties, since they make the transfer of land more difficult, and thereby run counter to modern ideas, which are all in the direction of making land more mobile (see p. 534).

(2) *Duties on commodities.*

These too are of very ancient origin. The duties still levied by municipalities under the name of *octrois* bring to mind the times when the strange, or foreign, merchant was taxed for the protection of the local merchant; and, even at the present day, the greater part of these contributions in France come from duties on imported goods, *i.e. customs duties.* Gradually, however, the duties on foreign goods were extended to such home products as are, or originally were, of the nature of luxuries: tobacco, sugar, alcohol, wines, candles, etc.

This mode of contribution was formerly much in favour, both with the Treasury and the taxpayer, for it had the great practical advantage of not being felt. Few Frenchmen realise, when buying a pound of sugar or a railway ticket, that they are paying a third or a tenth of the price to the Treasury. These taxes are therefore called in France *indirect contributions.* We may even say that these contributions are, in some sort, *optional,* since we pay the tax only if we buy the article, and we have after all the option of refraining.

Customs duties appear at first sight to have the advantage of making the foreigner, not the citizen, pay. This would surely be the ideal tax. Unfortunately, we have already seen that this idea is for the most part an illusion (p. 360).

Indirect contributions, including customs duties and monopolies, represent considerable sums in the budgets of all countries. In France, they amount to over 2100 million francs, or over two-fifths of the budget. Yet the number of articles which may be thus taxed is not very great. For they must combine two conditions in some respects contradictory: (1) they must be objects of large consumption, in order to offer a sufficient basis for taxation;

(2) they must not be articles indispensable to life, or the tax would be too unjust.[1]

These taxes are much discredited to-day as not being proportional to income, and as falling often more heavily on the poor man [2] than on the rich. This is obvious as regards the duties on salt, petroleum, and even on alcohol : the enormous tribute of 330 million francs collected under this last heading is paid almost wholly by the working class. It is true that they could escape it by giving up drink ; but this is a moral, not a fiscal, consideration.

(3) *Taxes on persons.*

Here there is no disguise. The State demands a fixed sum from each taxpayer, and, if he refuses to pay, pursues him with a succession of summonses, and finally distrains and sells his goods. The personal tax bears the imprint of its ancient origin, when it was the *tribute* or ransom imposed by the conqueror on the conquered. Thus, of all categories of taxes, it is the one which appears most burdensome and vexatious to the taxpayer ; and governments, for fear of unpopularity, used to avoid this method of obtaining revenue. When, for instance, after the War of 1870, France had to find 700 millions per annum of new resources, almost the whole of this was raised from indirect taxation.

Everything, however, points now to a radical change in men's minds ; and, curiously enough, it is the same fear of unpopularity which is at present pushing modern governments to reduce indirect taxation, and to demand the greater part, if necessary the whole, of their public revenue from direct taxation. We gave above (p. 684) the explanation of this singular change of opinion. Men are concerned nowadays rather to find the most just, than the least vexatious, tax. And their anxiety regarding the irksome nature of a tax will be still less when the burden has been shifted on to the minority. There is a tendency at present to regard taxation as a means of correcting an unfair distribution of wealth. In a word, the point of view adopted is social and political, rather than economic and

---

[1] There is, however, one article of prime necessity which has long been taxed in France, and whose fiscal history is really atrocious : it is salt. The salt tax has been retained to-day on the ground that it represents only a small burden for the taxpayer (a little less than one franc per head) ; for salt, although indispensable to life is consumed only in small quantities.

[2] Duties on commodities might be made more equitable if they were levied according to the value of the article, as in this case they would constitute a tax on expenditure. But in practice it is impossible to do this, as it would necessitate a valuation of each product. We have seen that even the *ad valorem* customs duty is difficult to apply.

fiscal; and, from this standpoint, the personal tax has two incontestable advantages over all others :[1]

(*1*) From the fiscal point of view, it is the only tax which, by reason of its personal character, allows the burden to be distributed according to the fortune of the taxpayer, which admits, that is to say, of the rich being made to pay more than the poor.

(*2*) From the moral point of view, its personàl and unpleasant nature is held to be considered an advantage. For it is not good that a tax should be unfelt. It is indispensable that each citizen of a free country should feel directly, and in a manner which he cannot ignore, the consequences of all expenditure incurred by the State, *i.e.* by his chosen representatives. It is the best way of giving him his political education.

The personal tax may take three forms :

(*a*) It may be assessed according to presumptive or external signs, without inquiry and without declaration on the part of the taxpayer. In this case it falls on the property (capital or income) most easy to value, no pretence being made of aiming at strict proportionality. This is the French system. Thus there is a tax on *doors and windows (portes et fenêtres)*, an external sign conveniently easy to verify, but obviously without much relation to the real value of the house. There is a tax on trade and manufacturing licences (*patentes*), based on an arbitrary professional classification, on the rent paid, the population of the locality, the number of employees—without inquiry, however, as to the figure for profits. As for the *land tax (impôt foncier)*, it falls on lands classified according to a survey three-quarters of a century old, which has no longer any relation to real income. The *contribution mobilière*, which is a tax calculated according to the amount of the rent, is the only one which at all nearly approaches the proportional income tax, of which we shall speak.[2]

Although crude and out-of-date from the scientific point of view, although it allows many categories of income to escape its meshes—incomes from professions, mortgages, government stock, and

---

[1] There is, indeed, a general tendency just now to substitute the *personal* for the *real*. We have already pointed this out in the case of credit.

Remark, that in primitive societies the personal tax is the only one known (apart from the revenue from the State domain, which is not a tax). This is another instance of the regressive evolution which we have already had occasion to point out.

[2] These four taxes, *les quatre vieilles* as they are called, are the oldest and most important of the direct taxes ; but there are others, one in particular strictly proportional to income, viz., the tax of 4 per cent. on incomes from movable values.

functionaries' salaries[1]—this tax has the advantage of being the least vexatious of all for the taxpayer, and of being consecrated by long usage.

(b) It may be established in a more scientific way so as to fall on all categories of income without exception, and be so discriminated that the burden falls differently on each kind of income, more heavily, for instance, on income from capital than on income from labour. This may be called the tax by schedules, or, more simply, the tax on incomes, to distinguish it from the global income tax which we shall discuss presently. This system of income tax by schedules has, however, two serious objections :

In the first place, taxation according to the kind of income gives rise to the shifting of incidence, and is thus less apt to fall on the capitalist and the proprietor, at whom it is aimed, than on the consumer, whom it is intended to spare. A tax on land rent sends up the price of foodstuffs ; a tax on house rent sends up rents ; a tax on trade licences sends up the price of commodities.[2]

In the second place, it is equivalent to a *partial confiscation of capital*, the more unjust that it falls only on the person who has the bad luck to possess it at the time when the tax is established. A tax of 10 per cent. on land rent brings down the value of the land 10 per cent. ; a tax of 4 per cent. on incomes from movable values diminishes the value of each share or bond by 4 per cent., etc. As those who buy the land or the security after this will deduct from the price they pay the amount of the tax capitalised, they will in reality pay no tax. It is as if the State were to appropriate as perpetual co-owner the tenth or twentieth part of the value of the capital, and the rest only were to remain private property.

(c) Lastly, the tax may be laid upon total income without distinction of categories : this is called *l'impôt global*. As a rule it is also made progressive.

---

[1] Exemption in the case of government stock and functionaries' salaries is indeed quite justifiable. As regards the first it was considered that, as the State pays interest on its stock, as debtor so to speak, to keep a part of it back as taxation would be a sort of partial bankruptcy—particularly since the State has, more than once, when issuing loans, promised that the *rentes* should not be taxed. As regards the second, it was held that, as the State is bound in the long run to pay a sufficient salary to its functionaries, it would be somewhat absurd to take with one hand what it is obliged to give back with the other.

[2] The problem on whom a tax finally falls is famous under the name of *Incidence*. The tax does not always fall on the person who ought legally to pay it. More often than not he throws it on to others—the house-owner, for instance, on his tenants ; the tradesman on his customers ; the lender on the borrower, etc. For all these different operations, which can be dealt with properly only in a financial treatise, see Seligman, *Incidence of Taxation*.

This last system is strongly advocated to-day in democratic countries, and figures in the French Government bill as a supplement to the tax by schedules. This is not only because it is theoretically simple, but because it is the only one which allows us to pass from the proportional to the progressive tax. It is evident that, if we would regulate according to the fortune of the taxpayer not merely the *amount* of the tax, but the *rate* at which it is assessed—which is the characteristic of progressive taxation—it is absolutely necessary to know the total figure of his income.[1]

It is much in favour among the socialist and radical-socialist parties, and is supported by the new theories of value and of final utility (pp. 38 n., 53). The fact too that, as a rule, social and collective causes contribute more in the formation of large fortunes than in that of small ones, makes it seem only just that the large should contribute more to society than the small. It is a sort of debt which they are paying off. We see therefore no essential objection to the progressive tax, so long as it aims merely at establishing a *more exact proportionality than simple arithmetical proportionality.* But, if its object be to throw on the wealthy classes the whole burden of public expenditure and to relieve the wage-earning class completely, it would have disquieting political consequences. For, under the system of universal suffrage, it is the wage-earners who make the laws. Now, the first principle of all government is that those who govern should be responsible for their acts, otherwise we should be reviving, only upside down, the privilege of the *ancien régime*, which exempted from taxation the governing classes, the nobles and the clergy.

While approving therefore of progressive taxation, we hold that, as a counterpoise, there should also be a universal income tax, *i.e.* a tax, however small, on every citizen, even the humblest wage-earner.

---

[1] It is impossible to deal here with the weighty question of progressive taxation. We refer the reader to the treatises on financial science of Leroy-Beaulieu, Jèze, Allix, and in particular Seligman, *Progressive Taxation.* Also, as the most favourable to progressive taxation, the book of the Belgian professor, Hector Denis, entitled *l'Impôt.*

The ordinary argument is, that the progressive tax is the only really proportional tax. Can we talk of equal sacrifice, for instance, when a worker who has only 1000 francs of income pays 100 francs, while a rich man who has 100,000 francs pays 10,000 ? Certainly not. The first has to take the 100 francs out of his necessaries, while the second takes them only from his superfluities. Real proportionality, from an economic point of view, would make not merely the *amount* of the tax vary with the income, but the *rate* at which it is levied : would ask, for instance, 1 per cent. from the man who has an income of only 1000 francs, and 10 per cent. from the man who has 100,000 francs.

What is to be feared is not so much progressive taxation as the abuse which is at present being made of degressive taxation, and the exemptions on which it is based. It is said, in answer, that the proletariat already pays sufficiently in the form of indirect and consumption taxes. But we have already remarked that taxes which are paid unconsciously do not involve sufficient responsibility on the part of the taxpayer.

This global and progressive tax, however, if the best in theory, gives rise to the gravest difficulties when it comes to be applied. Checks which are sufficient for the tax by schedules are powerless here. We can no longer trust to outside signs, to the amount of the rent, to the more or less arbitrary estimates of the Treasury officials. On the other hand, the resistance of the taxpayer— especially the French taxpayer—to disclosing the amount of his fortune is invincible. It is therefore to be feared : (1) either that, if we rely on the declarations of taxpayers, the honest will pay for the dishonest, and this tax, which appears the most just, will in reality be the most unjust ; (2) or that, if income is estimated officially by the Treasury, it will be necessary, in order to penetrate into the secrets of private life, to employ singularly vexatious and probably ineffective measures, since in all probability they will fall only on the small capitalists, the large ones being always able to escape through the thousand and one combinations of credit, or by investing their money abroad.

In our opinion, then, it would be better to keep simply to the declaration of income, and, without wasting too many threats on the refractory taxpayer, to impose, as sanction, the *publicity* of the declaration. However unpleasant this method may be deemed, it is necessary for the education of public morals. Each man's fortune is well enough known in his own immediate circle to prevent him from willingly exposing himself to the conviction of lying ; and many, no doubt from sheer pride, would be unwilling to declare their income below its real value.[1]

[1] In France the progressive tax exists for successions, the rate varying, in the case of children, from 1 per cent. on successions below 2000 francs to 6½ per cent. on successions above 50 million francs ; and for strangers in blood from 18 per cent. to 29 per cent.

For the last twenty years the income tax has been the object of innumerable measures in France. The last, already passed in principle by the Chamber, establishes a system of two stages : (a) the proportional tax on each category, with exemption if the total income is under 1250 francs, or 2500 francs, according to the locality ; (b) a progressive tax on the total income starting from 5000 francs.

BOOK IV: CONSUMPTION

CHAPTER I: CONSUMPTION IN ITS RELATIONS TO PRODUCTION

I: WHAT IS THE MEANING OF THE WORD "CONSUMPTION"?

To consume wealth is to utilise it for the satisfaction of our wants; it is to apply it to the uses and ends for which it was made. Consumption is therefore the final cause, and, as the word so well expresses it, the " consummation " of the whole economic process—production, circulation, and distribution. Its importance is far greater than the small space devoted to it in treatises on Political Economy would lead us to suppose. The domain of consumption is infinitely rich, and as yet half explored; it is from here probably that economic science will one day start anew. Logically, indeed, economic science should start with the study of consumption. In the earlier part of this book, when we were speaking of wants and final utility, we were already in the domain of consumption. The chapters dealing with them must therefore be read again in connection with the following.

We must beware of several misapprehensions to which the word " consumption " gives rise.

In the first place we must not think that consumption is synonymous with *destruction*. It is true—and this is what leads to the confusion—that certain wants, say the want of food or of warmth, can be satisfied only by the transformation of the objects which serve to feed and to warm us. To utilise bread or wine, *i.e.* to turn them into flesh and blood, we are obliged to consume them ; to warm ourselves with wood, we are obliged to burn it, that is to say, to reduce it to cinders and smoke ; it is a troublesome necessity.[1]

But there are, fortunately, many other forms of wealth which may be utilised without being destroyed : houses, gardens, money, furniture, curios. These, it is true, are not everlasting either, and they

---

[1] Moreover, by the word " destruction " we must be taken to mean destruction of the utility and value only, not the annihilation of the matter ; for it is evident that, just as a man can create nothing by production (p. 96), so he can destroy nothing by consumption. The chemist with his scales will always be able to find the object consumed, to the last atom.

generally perish sooner or later by accident, or by wear and tear; but this destruction must not be imputed to consumption. The proof is that we try to make things last as long as possible, and if we could make them so that they would never wear out (clothing, linen, furniture, houses, etc.) they would fulfil their economic purpose even better. On this hypothesis they could be utilised in perpetuity, and this would be the ideal of consumption.

Even where consumption destroys utility, a wise economy finds a way of obtaining something out of the dead utilities, making them rise from their ashes in some new form : paper from rags ; manure from the *débris* of food, or the cinders of iron furnaces ; a whole gamut of perfumes and colours from coal residual products ; soap and light from household refuse. The power of utilising residues, *e.g.* in the oil refineries, is one of the causes of the superiority of large-scale industry. Thus, in a perfect economy, no utility would perish : all would be transformed. And the history of consumption would be simply a history of the metamorphoses of wealth.

On the other hand, if we must not take consumption as synonymous with *destruction*, neither must we take it as synonymous with *production*.

No doubt, all production of wealth involves a constant consumption of raw material, coal, etc.—in a word, of circulating capital. And in this sense we may say that consumption is the indispensable condition, even the cause of production, and that production is proportional to consumption. The economic process is a closed circuit : man produces in order to eat, and eats in order to produce. So true is this that, just as some economists have considered the sowing of seed an act of consumption, others, like Jevons, have looked on eating as an act of production, seeing in the food consumed by the workers the one true type of capital in the form of *advances* made to labour. But if we are to make any headway at all we must mark at some point or other the end and beginning of the circuit. Now, the end of the whole economic process is the satisfaction of man's wants ; it is at this moment only that wealth is definitely consumed ; up till then, and throughout all its transformation, it has simply been in process of being produced. The " lordly sweep of the sower's arm " must remain for ever the typical symbol of the act of production ; to call it an act of consumption, thereby assimilating two such opposites as the sowing of corn and the eating of it, can be justified only by the poverty and inaccuracy of economic terminology.[1]

---

[1] Economists, as a rule, refer to consumption such as this as *reproductive*

There is often, moreover, confusion as to the action of consumption on production. As consumption is the end of all production, it is obvious that if men cease to consume, they will cease to produce ; if they stop eating corn, they will stop sowing. But we must beware of thinking that, though consumption is the *final cause* of production, it is the *efficient cause*, and of concluding that in order to push on production we must push on consumption. This idea, as we shall see, is what makes public opinion so indulgent towards prodigality.

No doubt intense consumption like that of the United States is a powerful stimulus to production. But the only real causes of production are the factors we already know—labour, land, and capital ; and it is clear that it is not consumption that can create or increase any one of these. On the contrary, consumption does its best to undo their work, and to empty the reservoir they are labouring to fill. If this reservoir were fed by a continuous stream, so that the water flowed in as fast as it flowed out, we could excuse the mistake of thinking that the more wealth is consumed, the more will be produced. But this is not the case. No one will pretend that the more fruit we gather, the more the orchard will produce ; the more fish we take out, the more there will be in the sea ; the more wood we burn, the higher and denser will the forest grow.

II : WHETHER PRODUCTION WILL ALWAYS KEEP PACE WITH CONSUMPTION.—THE LAWS OF MALTHUS

ALTHOUGH consumption, as we have just said, does not necessarily imply destruction, still most forms of it, particularly the consumption of food, involve the daily absorption of an increasing quantity of products. Hence the question at the head of this chapter.

This is a subject which used greatly to agitate economists. Every man who comes into the world brings with him a mouth and two arms ; but the mouth begins to work at once, while the arms do not begin for some fifteen or twenty years. Thus, in the natural order of things, consumption has a long start. Nor is this all. Economists, as we have seen, are oppressed by the fear that

consumption, to distinguish it from the other consumption which serves for the immediate satisfaction of our wants, which they call *unproductive* consumption. But this last is the only true consumption, and it is for this alone that we should reserve the name.

production—that of food, at any rate—may be limited in the future by the law of diminishing returns (pp. 77–82), whereas the number of mouths to feed seems destined to increase indefinitely. And there is no reason to think that the appetite of the man of the future will be less than that of the man of to-day. We may well ask then whether production will always be able to keep pace with consumption.

These fears were expressed with singular force a little over a century ago by an English economist, Malthus. In a formula, which has since become world-famous, he asserted that population *tended to increase in geometrical progression, while the food-supply only increased in arithmetical progression.* He expressed this law by the following figures, which were, of course, intended merely to illustrate his meaning, not to be taken literally :

> Progression of population .. 1 2 4 8 16 32 64 128 256
> Progression of production .. 1 2 3 4 5 6 7   8   9

The average period within which population doubled he calculated at twenty-five years, and concluded that, at the end of two centuries, population would be to the means of subsistence as 256 to 9 ; at the end of three centuries as 4096 to 13 ; and that, after some thousands of years, the difference would be beyond calculation. Production, therefore, far from keeping pace with consumption, would remain further and further behind.

It was not for a more or less remote future that Malthus expressed his fears. In his view, this pressure of population was going on at the moment, as it had always done in the past. The balance between production and consumption had been maintained only by a frequent cutting down of the human species, by wars, epidemics, famines, destitution, prostitution, and other abominable scourges, which, however, from this new point of view, appeared truly providential.[1]

He hoped, however, for the future, that men would have the wisdom to substitute *preventive* for *repressive* checks, and voluntarily limit the increase of population. To this end he advised abstention from marriage until sufficient means had been accumulated to support children,[2] that is to say *moral*, not *legal* restraint ; for

---

[1] Providential, not only as serving to maintain the balance between production and consumption, but because, by exterminating the weak and incapable, they contributed to the general perfectioning of the human race. It is well known that Malthus inspired Darwin, as Darwin himself acknowledged.

[2] Contrary, however, to the general opinion and to what the Neo-Malthusians teach to-day, Malthus never advocated limiting the number of children

it was never his idea that marriage should be prohibited by law, as it was till recently in some of the German States, in the case of persons who could not show that they had more than a given income.

A century has passed since the publication of this celebrated doctrine, and experience has not yet justified the pessimistic forebodings of its author. It would seem indeed as if both of his famous progressions have been entirely contradicted by events.

Everywhere we see wealth increasing at a greater rate than population—in new countries like the United States as well as in old countries like France. So that to-day our first concern is rather in the opposite direction. At the present moment, when our markets are so encumbered with industrial and agricultural products that States are raising customs barriers to protect themselves against what they call the inundation of foreign products, the question is rather: Will production find sufficient markets?

The prophecy as to the over-rapid increase of population, again, is being strikingly belied. Even supposing that a slowing-down of production is possible at some more or less remote date, the slowing-down of the birth-rate has already begun in all countries, especially France. The main consideration at the present moment is exactly the opposite of that of Malthus, namely: What is to be done to keep the birth-rate up? [1]

in marriage (see Gide and Rist, *History of Economic Doctrines*, English translation). It was *before*, not *after*, marriage that moral restraint was to be exercised. He considered six children as the normal number, and added that husbands and wives could not know that they would not have more.

While recommending celibacy to those who could not afford to bring up children, Malthus still more sternly proscribed illegitimate unions, as their results, from the point of view of the birth-rate, would be the same or worse. Moral restraint, he categorically declares, implies abstention from all sexual relationship.

[1] It is not only in France that the birth-rate is rapidly decreasing. This phenomenon is found almost everywhere. Although in France, between 1850 and 1912, it fell from 27 to 19 per 1000 inhabitants, in England it fell in the same time from 33 to 25 per 1000, and in Germany from 38 to 30. In Germany, however, the fall is quite recent. In the States of Australasia the birth-rate, which was 40 per 1000 in 1870, has fallen to 27. And in the older States of the United States the rate would be almost the same as in France, were it not that the high birth-rate among immigrants keeps up the average.

This does not alter the fact that the situation of France is very critical from the political, military, and economic point of view. For the decrease in the birth-rate began half a century earlier in France than in the other nations Moreover, as the death-rate of the other nations is decreasing still more rapidly than their birth-rate, their annual increase of population, up till the present time at any rate, has remained the same, or is even growing.

This change of attitude, surprising at first sight, may easily be explained. It is due to the fact that the causes which formerly impelled towards procreation have weakened simultaneously: (a) *Economic* causes. Whereas formerly children were set to work from the tenderest age, to add to the family income, and remained for a long time in the home, to-day education and Factory Acts forbid the lucrative employment of children. They, again, so soon as they are in a position to earn something leave the paternal roof. It is a bad business, then, to have children, particularly for the poor. (b) *Social* and *moral* causes. Whereas formerly there was a strong desire to perpetuate the family, to increase the strength of the city or fatherland, to ensure ancestor worship, to create immortal souls, or at least to hand on the torch of life, to-day the family is being broken up, not only by the abandoning of tradition, but by factory life. Patriotism is being diluted into internationalism; the commandments of the Churches forbidding Neo-Malthusian practices are no more obeyed; and, as for the sexual instinct, to which above everything else Nature has entrusted the care of preserving the race, mankind has found more and more easy and sure ways of giving it free play without running the risks of paternity or maternity.

Malthus' mistake lay, therefore, in not having perceived the number and force of all these new motives which conspire to prevent the increase of population; or in not having realised their efficacy, since he naïvely and honestly thought that this increase could be prevented only by moral restraint—a means which appeared to him, not without reason, as unlikely to be widely practised.[1]

Many laws of population have been discussed since Malthus' day. The true law, according to M. Paul Leroy-Beaulieu, is that the birth-rate varies inversely with the degree of civilisation— meaning by that " the development of well-being, of education, and of new and democratic ideas."[2]   Put thus, the law would be some- what too flattering to France. There are countries more advanced than France in education and even in well-being—Scandinavia, Germany, Holland, etc.—the birth-rates of which are nevertheless high. Statistics show, however:

(1) That the birth-rate is lower among the wealthy than among

[1] He was not ignorant of the other preventive measures, and even classed them under the heading of " vice." But he did not foresee how general they would become in practice thanks to the teaching of those who have usurped his name.

[2] *Traité d'Économie politique,* t. iv, p. 672; and in various articles in the *Ec nomiste français.*

the poorer classes. We can understand, indeed, that, among the rich, a host of wants compete with and weaken the genetic want which, among the poor, is almost the only one along with that of food. We may therefore conclude that the birth-rate will fall in proportion as all classes rise towards ease and the nation itself progresses in well-being. This conclusion is amply confirmed by facts.

(2) That, other things being equal, the birth-rate seems to fall more rapidly in the more democratic countries. In the United States and Australia, it has fallen almost as low as in France. One explanation given for this is, that, under a democracy, the individual, by what Dumont called the law of *capillarity*,[1] has a better chance of rising in life when unburdened by a family. The explanation is not very convincing. Still, we may say that the democratic system tends to weaken the family and to develop " feminism," and thus to limit the natural functions of wife and mother in proportion to the social functions which it opens to them.

It is also true that, in every country, the " proletariat " class becomes less prolific as it becomes more well-to-do ; although, if we were to accept the doctrine of Malthus, we should expect to find, on the contrary, that the more it had to eat the more children it would have. The reason is that with ease comes thought for the future, and wants grow even more quickly than means.

For all these reasons, the human race to-day is more than reassured as to the possibility of an exaggerated increase in population. France, indeed—and the other countries will probably soon follow her lead—is trying, on the contrary, to find ways of stimulating population, or at least of clearing away the obstacles which keep it from increasing. But the remedies proposed—viz., large premiums on every child after the third, supplementary pay for officials who have large families, the abolition of protective duties in order to bring down the cost of living, a reform of the laws of succession,[2] a simplifying of the formalities of marriage, exemptions

---

[1] Arsène Dumont, *Dépopulation et Civilisation*.

[2] This is the principal remedy proposed. The Romans, as is well known, had recourse to it, their *caducary laws* being passed with the object of fighting the same evil ; and although they are said to have been ineffective, we do not really know one way or the other. Various ingenious systems have been proposed in France. Le Play's school lays most of the blame for the decrease in population on the law of equal sharing, holding that it is to avoid this division that the father of the family will not have children. It would therefore re-establish freedom of bequest, or, at least, increase the proportion at the disposal of the father. But the same law of equal sharing exists in other countries which nevertheless have a very high birth-rate.

from military service, even a tax on bachelors—seem powerless against the general causes which we have indicated above. The first is the only one which might prove effective, but it is doubtful if it would tend towards the perfecting of the race on " eugenic " lines.

III: THE RÔLE OF THE CONSUMER
—SOCIAL LEAGUES OF BUYERS

One of Bastiat's last remarks on his death-bed was : " We must learn to look at everything from the point of view of the consumer." In that he was only expressing the general opinion of the Liberal school of Political Economy. But, faithful to the spirit of their school, the Liberal economists consider it unnecessary to take any steps to bring about this reign of the consumer, holding that free competition will do all that is required. For, they say, under the system of free competition, every producer is bound to do his best for his customer, the consumer, giving him the greatest value at the lowest price. M. Yves Guyot has even written a bright and paradoxical little book, under the name of *La Morale de la concurrence*, showing how producers, passing their lives in doing their utmost to serve others, realise perfect altruism. The consumer, like a king, has only to let himself be served.

Facts do not confirm this optimistic picture. No doubt the producer finds it to his interest to satisfy the customer, since this is as a rule the surest means of getting more custom and higher profits. But it is after all only a secondary object ; the immediate one is not the service of others, but gain. And if he can increase his gain by raising his prices, or by adulterating his produce, experience shows that he will not hesitate to do so. It is a well-known fact that, of late, the rise in prices and the adulteration of foodstuffs in all countries have taken on alarming proportions.[1] No doubt professional honour and good business repute are a certain guarantee to the consumer ; but here we are trenching on moral ground and leaving that of Political Economy.

The consumer would do well, then, not to leave his interests to the tender mercies of the *laissez-faire* principle, nor to fall asleep in his rôle of *roi fainéant*. He needs must defend his interests

---

[1] Is it necessary to recall the history of the meat-preserving industry in Chicago and Mr. Sinclair's *Jungle*, which caused such a sensation ? In September 1908, a congress was held in Germany on the best means of preventing the adulteration of foodstuffs. See *infra, The Rôle of the State in Consumption.*

energetically, for they are also the interests of society ; therein lies their superiority.

To accomplish this he must resort to the producers' methods, viz., association. Consumers' associations are of two different types : the one aims at showing the consumer his *rights* and his interests, and the means by which he may satisfy them ; the other aims at teaching him his *duties* and the means by which he may perform them. For, if the consumer is king in the economic order, his kingship is not without responsibility. It is within the power of the consumer, by changing the nature of his expenditure, to turn capital and labour from the channels where they are being employed into whatever others suit him. Even when he lives as a simple *rentier*, he exercises a decisive influence over the three factors of production—land, labour, and capital—saying to the one, " Go, and he goeth," and to the other, " Come, and he cometh." It is this power of command which lays on the rich special obligations which up till now they have but little understood.

Among the consumers' associations which aim at defending the rights of the consumer, the most important are the societies *for consumption* (see p. 201). But these are not, as is sometimes thought, the only ones. There have been many others : leagues against Protection, such as the famous Anti-Corn Law League, which played so great a part in the economic history of England in 1840 ; leagues against the adulteration of food, as the *Société de l'Aliment pur* in France ; and, more recently, the *Ligue française des consommateurs*, which aims at grouping all these separate interests together.[1]

It is not by means of organisation and association only, that consumers defend their rights : like producers, they, too, of late have occasionally resorted to strikes, which have proved no less successful in their hands than in those of the working men, *e.g.* the strike of consumers against the *Beef Trust* in the United States, the strike against the brewers in Germany, the strike against the gas companies in various towns in France.

Consumers' associations of the second type, which aim at teaching the consumer his duties and how to practise them, must be subdivided into two classes :

(*a*) Those which combat noxious, immoral, and ruinous consumption, foremost among which stand temperance associations,

---

[1] The associations which aim at defending the interests of consumers of certain public services, *e.g.* the *Society of telephone subscribers* in France, are of the same family. There ought to be an *association against tips*.

vegetarian societies,[1] and associations against the use of tobacco or opium, or against the using of the spoil of animals for apparel, particularly the wearing of birds' feathers on ladies' hats.[2]

(b) Those which aim at putting a stop to selfish consumption such as lays extra labour on the working classes, e.g. the ordering of dresses at the last moment, involving night work, or extra hours ; Sunday deliveries ; the use of trunks too heavy for porters ; the taking of flats where the kitchens and servants' accommodation are inadequate. They are called the Social Leagues of Buyers. The earliest were founded in New York, but there is also one in Paris, which was founded in 1900 by Mme. Brunhes.[3] These societies have either *white lists* on which they write the names of the shops which undertake to conform to certain conditions as regards wages, rest for their workers, etc. ; or else distribute labels to be attached to the goods as certificates. It is obvious that, if these leagues included a large number of wealthy consumers, tradesmen would find it greatly to their interest to appear on the white list, or to obtain labels, and would thus be stimulated to treat their workers well.

These leagues of buyers, the object of which cannot be too highly praised, and which form a new era in economic organisation, have, however, latterly called forth some lively criticism, the more unexpected that it comes from the economists of the Liberal school.[4] They hold that the consumer is totally incompetent to occupy himself with the technical organisation of labour. Perhaps so ; but

[1] Vegetarian societies consist of those who consider the slaughter, or, worse still, the breeding, of animals for food an inhuman act ; and those who think this animal food anti-hygienic and anti-economic, or as giving, at the same price, a much smaller quantity of nutritive elements than do vegetables. Some vegetarian societies forbid not only all animal food, but all animal products— milk, butter, eggs, honey.

[2] The societies against the slaughter of birds are inspired not only by a generous sentimentalism, but also by the fact that the disappearance of birds in the country is one of the main causes of the increase of the vermin which devour the crops.

[3] In England, nearly a century ago, a league of consumers undertook not to consume " slave " sugar, *i.e.* sugar produced in the States where slavery existed. This was the first league of consumers.

In 1908, these buyers' leagues held their first congress at Geneva. Four countries have already organised leagues (United States, France, Switzerland, and Germany).

[4] See a pamphlet by M. Wuarin, professor at Geneva, on this subject, and an article by M. Yves Guyot in the *Journal des Économistes*, of 1907.

It was in connection with an inquiry into the manufacture of chocolate, by the Swiss League of Buyers, that discussion arose on this point. The manufacturers whose chocolate was not considered worthy to figure on the white lists were naturally irritated.

he is not too ignorant to judge of his own wants, and to distribute good or bad marks to producers. We can only say that, as regards the workers or employees, these leagues would do well to come to an understanding with the trade unions and employers' unions, better qualified than they to find what improvements are possible.

It is interesting to note that, on this question of the function of the consumer, socialists are no less critical than the Individualist economists. They hold that it is to the side of the producer that we must look, and that he alone must rule. It is on the association of producers, not of consumers, that society in the future must be built; it is through this form of association that the ethics of the future will evolve. The idea of the sovereignty of the consumer, they say, is a notion worthy only of a bourgeois.[1] And we can easily understand that the supremacy of the consumer is irreconcilable with the essential theories of Marxist Socialism, namely, class conflict and the victory of the working class. For the function of consumer ignores all division into classes. Production, of necessity, divides men by creating an antagonism of interests, of groups, and of classes. Consumption makes no exception of persons or of classes: it is in this that it seems to us superior.

CHAPTER II: EXPENDITURE

I: THE DISTRIBUTION OF EXPENDITURE

EXPENDITURE is the price paid to procure objects of consumption; it is consumption expressed in money.[2]

Every one is obliged to regulate his expenditure according to his income. Nothing is more important than this distribution of expenditure, since it is that which determines the maximum of

---

[1] See in particular M. Georges Sorel: "There are philanthropists who preach co-operation, and constantly repeat that the order established by capital must be overthrown, that we must give back to consumption its directing power; such sentiments are natural in persons who, living on their incomes, salaries, or emoluments, are outside of the producing power; their ideal is the life of the idle man of letters. Quite other is the socialist ideal." (*Introduction à l'Économie moderne*, p. 125.)

For the opposite point of view, see our book, *La coöpération*, and in particular the lecture entitled *Le règne du consommateur*.

[2] We must not think that the money spent is consumed. It is only transferred from the buyer to the seller. This is why, in the eyes of the public, every expenditure, even the most foolish, appears inoffensive, since it only takes from Peter to give to Paul. Nay more, they hold it praiseworthy as " benefiting

satisfaction which may be got out of a given income. It is not so easy as it appears; for, as most men's wants are greater than their resources—particularly in the case of the poor—they have to set their wits to work to "make the most" of their incomes. Now, the consumer can satisfy one want only by sacrificing another. The plaything which the workman brings home to his child means the renunciation of a packet of tobacco of equal value. The consumer is in the situation of a barterer, who can obtain one thing only by giving up another, and who balances in his mind the utility of that which he is giving up and that which he wants to consume, deciding in favour of whichever seems best. (We must not forget that the word utility is to be taken here in its economic sense of desirability—a very different thing from rational utility. Few, indeed, are the budgets in which expenditure is regulated in accordance with veritable needs. In most cases they are regulated according to the intensity of different desires.[1])

The Austrian school has tried to put this law of the distribution of expenditure into more precise words, as follows : *To obtain the maximum of satisfaction, the final utilities of the last objects consumed in each category of expenditure must be equal.* Here, for instance, is a consumer who has 6 sous a day on which to satisfy two wants : that of smoking and that of reading the newspaper. He distributes his expenditure thus : four cigars at 1 sou each, two newspapers at 1 sou. The above law states that the satisfaction obtained from the last cigar smoked (No. 4) and the last newspaper read (No. 2) are

trade." To judge expenditure rightly we must look, not at the money, but at the wealth paid for in money, and see whether it has been usefully consumed or not (see below, *Luxury*).

It is a delicate question to know what is precisely the action which spending has on production. J. S. Mill devotes a difficult chapter to it in his treatise. He tries to show that it is *investment*, not *spending*, that promotes industry and gives work. And this is our own view (see *infra*, *Investment*). Still, if spending cannot *create* production, nor *keep production going*, it none the less exercises a capital influence in that it *commands* it (this is the current expression) ; that is to say, it directs production into whatever channel it wants.

[1] It is evident that the utility of one and the same thing is far from being the same for all consumers. A thirsty traveller, dying of fatigue, pays the same price for a glass of beer, or a seat in a tramway, as any other consumer, although he would willingly give twice, or three times as much. The gratification which he obtains from it may therefore be measured by the excess of the price which he would be willing to pay over the price he actually pays. This is what Marshall calls *Consumers' Rent*. As each commodity has only one price on the market, in spite of very different costs of production on the side of the producers, and very different subjective utilities on the side of consumers, the result is differential advantages on both sides, which are called, not without some subtlety, by the same name of *rent*.

equal. For if they were not—if, for example, the satisfaction obtained from the last newspaper read were less than that obtained from the last cigar smoked—the consumer would obviously have preferred to smoke an additional cigar and read a newspaper less.

More practically useful than this psychological analysis is the study of the budgets of individuals and families, especially those of the working classes. This study was started by Le Play half a century ago, as the best instrument of social investigation ; [1] to-day it constitutes an important branch of statistics. Among other interesting facts it is seen that the smaller the means, the larger is the place taken by food in the working-man's budget. [2]

There is another more difficult distribution of expenditure, viz., that between present and future we nts, or, in other words, between spending strictly speaking and saving. But we shall consider this in the chapter on Saving.

II : SOCIETIES FOR CONSUMPTION

As men do not like to deprive themselves of anything, they have sought a way of reducing their expenditure which would not involve the necessity of saving, *i.e.* of reducing the quantity or the quality of the things they consume ; this they have discovered in various kinds of association.

(1) *The common household.* If several persons join together to share one house, one fire, one table, they will certainly obtain the same sum of satisfaction at much less expense. The maintenance of monks in convents, soldiers in barracks, boys in a boarding school, is a daily proof of this.

The economy is due to the same causes which make large production cheaper than isolated production (see p. 1C2), causes which we know already, and which we have only to transpose with slight changes to the domain of consumption.

Thus the Communists conclude that our present way of living, grouped into separate families, is very expensive, involving a real waste of wealth, as regards housing, cooking, etc., and that it would be a great step in advance, and a boon to the whole human race, if

---

[1] *Les Ouvriers Européens*, 1854. These budgets serve as framework for the different monographs on working-class families. The investigation of them has been continued by Le Play's school, and to-day over a hundred of them have been published.

[2] Two-thirds in a budget of £40, coming down to a quarter in a budget of £200 and over. This law, known as " Engel's law," after the German statistician who formulated it, has been verified by numerous observations.

it could be replaced by life in common. No one has developed this idea with more spirit and amplitude than Fourier in his " phalanstery."[1]

Observe that most of the advantages of the common household may be realised without the common mess, or *table d'hôte*. All that is necessary is common service for all the inhabitants of one house, each family living in its separate flat. This is already carried out in a number of large hotels in summer resorts. And the system is certainly tending to spread, particularly in countries like the United States, where the desire for comfort is very great, and domestic service very costly.

(2) *Common purchase.* Even while retaining the present mode of life in separate households, it is possible to realise many of the advantages of common living by means of associations for consumption. A certain number of persons, for instance, associate to buy in common—consequently wholesale—all or some of the objects which they need. They are thus able to obtain them more cheaply.[2]

For this new form of commercial association we refer the reader to the details which we have given (pp. 200–204). Its aim goes far beyond the mere reduction of the cost of living. Still, this advantage is certainly the *raison d'être* of a great number of the societies in existence, and it is not a negligible one, as the reduction varies from 5 to 15 per cent. The English societies save their members £12,000,000 annually.

III : HOUSING—BUILDING SOCIETIES

OF all forms of expenditure, that on house rent deserves special study, not only because it tends to absorb an ever-increasing share of the family income, but because, of all private wants, it is the òne the social importance of which is greatest—greater even than that of food.

In antiquity, the house was not only the home, but the altar of the household gods ; and every person, rich or poor, had his own. Now that the exigencies of modern life have brought man back, as it were, to the nomadic stage, and he is no longer rooted to the place in which he was born, most men live in hired apartments. And all the social, economic, and political causes which force human

[1] See the small edition of *Œuvres choisies*, by Fourier, which we have published with an introduction.

[2] Some associations go no further than this, viz., the Civil Service, and the Army and Navy Stores in London, which rival in importance the *Bon Marché* and the *Louvre*. These, however, are considered by true co-operatists as an inferior form of co-operation.

beings to congregate in great cities—centralisation, large production, the development of railways, fêtes, spectacles, café-concerts —tend continually to raise rents, to the great profit of the city proprietor, but to the great detriment of the public.[1] Seventy years ago (in 1846) urban population represented a little less than one-quarter of the population of France (24·40 per cent.). In 1896, it represented over one-third (39·10 per cent.) ; soon it will be equal to one-half. In other words, urban population has increased over 60 per cent. in half a century. And France is one of the countries with the fewest large towns.

The evil is great even for the well-to-do classes, which have often to economise in their food in order to pay their lodging ; but in the case of the poor it is much worse. The rise in house rent, by forcing working men to crowd together in wretched hovels, produces the most deplorable effects both from the hygienic, and from the moral, point of view.[2] As we may imagine, the larger the family, the less money it will have to spend on its rent, the smaller therefore will be the space into which it will have to crowd, particularly as many landlords refuse to take in large families.

Most of the vices which afflict the working-class population— the loosening of family ties, the frequenting of the public-house, precocious debauchery, the transmission of contagious diseases— are due to this cause. The dignity of life, both for the man and for the woman, is intimately bound up with the comfort of the home.

The only remedy which would be of any avail would be an evolution in the opposite direction to that which is at present taking place, viz., a cessation in the growth of cities, and a return to country life on the part of the population which has abandoned it. But there

---

[1] From an inquiry published by the *Ministère du Travail*, it appears that, for the same dwelling in Paris, rent increased as follows :

	Francs			Francs
1810	80	1870	220
1830	100	1900	320
1850	120	1903	350

Rent therefore has more than quadrupled in a century, a much higher progression than that of wages (see above, p. 596 n). And a rise of at least 10 per cent. must be counted between 1903 and 1913.

[2] A dwelling is said to be *overcrowded* when there are more than two persons per room. Now, M. Bertillon estimates that there are 321,000 persons in Paris —one-eighth of the population—living three persons *or more* in a room.

And Paris is not the worst town in this respect ; the proportion of persons ill-housed is greater still not only in big capitals like Vienna, but in middle-sized provincial towns, such as Brest, St. Etienne, Lille, etc., where we should not expect to find a lack of space.

is no sure prospect of any such return, although a certain centri-
fugal movement may be remarked in our large cities, in some of
which rents in the centre of the town have gone down to one-half.
This movement is encouraged by the low price of transport (omni-
buses, tramways, and railways) which allows workers and employees
to find healthier and cheaper dwellings far from the centre of the
city. Working men, however, do not care to go far from their
centre of occupation and recreation.

The rise in house rent is not due solely to the surplus value of
building ground. It is due also to the cost of construction, which
is daily increasing, owing to the fact that house building has not had
the advantage of the mechanical progress which other industries have
had. We must add the fact that builders prefer to build houses
for the wealthy. Not that houses for the poor do not bring in a
large interest; but they entail much expense and trouble.

What is to be done against the evil of overcrowding ? .

We might resort to measures of public health and impose by
law a certain cubic space, and hygienic conditions with regard to
dwellings; or we might even go the length of expropriation and
demolish the houses and insanitary quarters. In most countries,
laws to this effect exist and are applied with varying rigour.[1]

But these measures, it must be admitted, in certain respects
only aggravate the evil. They are bound to raise the cost of building
small dwellings, and thus to put them beyond the reach of the
poor. We have therefore no other resource than to call for the
collaboration of all the factors of social progress—Friendly Societies,
employers, philanthropists, municipalities, the State, the workers
themselves associated in co-operatives—and ask them for the
capital necessary to build the largest possible number of houses under
the most economic conditions, with no expectation of profit, so as
to bring rents down to cost price.

Numerous schemes have, indeed, been tried :

(1) *Garden Cities,* which consist in houses built by employers or

---

[1] The laws are very strictly applied in England, and much less so in France,
although a law of April 15, 1902, confers somewhat extensive powers on municipalities. Application for permission to build has to be made to them ; they
control all building plans and have the right to impose certain repairs, to
forbid letting, and even to expropriate. But the municipalities are by no
means anxious to undertake these troublesome responsibilities, particularly as
expropriation in France is very costly. English law makes their work easier
for them by giving them the power to deduct from the value of the house:
(1) the fictitious increase in rent due to overcrowding ; (2) the amount for
repairs necessary to put the house in good condition ; where this is impossible,
they need pay no more than the price of the ground.

by companies for their workers.[1] These " cities " are not built solely from philanthropy. They are indispensable in the case of factories and mines situated far from the centre of towns, for which workers could not be recruited unless some lodging were provided for them. This is one of the most important forms of what we have called the " good employers " movement (see above, p. 658). It has undergone the same fate as the institutions which were the outcome of this movement. The workers, believing themselves exploited, even when their rent does not represent the cost price of their dwelling, are anything but grateful to their employers, and look on this form of lodging as a kind of serfdom.

In England and the United States, some of these workmen's villages are marvels of comfort, hygiene, and even of artistic accommodation—in particular the celebrated garden cities of Port Sunlight, near Liverpool, and Bournville, near Birmingham.[2]

The garden city, however, touches but distantly the question of rent. It is in the town, not in the country, that the question of rent is acute.

(2) *Co-operative building societies*, formed by the workers themselves. There are several thousands of these societies in England and in the United States. In the city of Philadelphia, called for this reason the *City of Homes*, over 60,000 houses have been built by them, each inhabited by a workman's family.

The organisation of these building societies is very complex. Some buy the land, build the houses, and sell or let them to such of their members as want them, the profits on the sales or leases coming back in the end to the working-class landlord, or tenant, in his capacity of member. Most of them, however, particularly in England, do not undertake the building of the houses, but simply lend the money for it, on a system of very ingenious and economic combinations. And as these loans are perfectly guaranteed, they serve as investments for the savings of those members who are obliged to wait a long while for their turn, or of those who do not want to become owners of their houses. So that these societies act even more as savings banks than as building societies.

In France, they are spreading but slowly and have great difficulty in obtaining the necessary capital. They cannot ask the workers

---

[1] In France, the collieries alone, between 1850 and 1907, had built 38,312 houses, representing a capital of 125 million francs. See the annual reports of M. Cheysson to the *Conseil supérieur des habitations à bon marché*.

[2] See M. Georges Benoit-Lévy, *Les Cités-Jardins en Angleterre, et aux Etats-Unis* and our *Économie Sociale*.

for it, nor can they apply to the ordinary lender of capital, as the interest they offer must be very small if rents are to be low. They have, therefore, to turn to disinterested lenders, such as the *Caisse des dépôts et consignations,* or Public Assistance.[1]

(3) Societies of a *semi-philanthropic, semi-capitalistic* nature, which undertake to build and endow comfortable and sanitary houses for working men, and which limit in advance the profits they will take to the moderate figure of 3 per cent.[2]

(4) The building of houses by *municipalities.* A number of towns in England, Germany, and Switzerland have begun to do this. They have, in fact, been forced into it for the reason indicated a moment ago. If they cause insanitary dwellings to be closed they must of necessity try to replace them. The municipalities may either give subsidies to the societies for the building of working-men's houses, or they may buy the ground in order to avoid its being bought up by private individuals, and so benefit by the increment. In Germany, there are many different ways in which the municipalities may intervene. In England, so soon as the mortality in a quarter exceeds a certain rate, the municipality has it demolished and replaced by new houses, which it lets at cost price. In London alone no less than £2,000,000 has been thus spent, and 30,000 persons have been housed anew.[3]

It is to be feared, however, that if this system becomes general, municipalities will find themselves on the horns of a dilemma. If they lower their rents too far their finances will suffer ruinously, and they will aggravate the hypertrophy of the large cities. So soon as lodging is free in Paris, few Frenchmen will forgo the pleasure of living there. If, on the other hand, they force their tenants to pay

[1] In France, in 1912, there were only 210 co-operative building societies, all very small, and 122 philanthropic building societies. In Germany, there were over 2000. *Co-operative societies for consumption* also build houses for their members. As these societies aim at providing their members with all that is necessary, why should they not also provide lodging ? The English consumers' societies have already built 46,000 dwellings, either directly or, more often, by granting loans to their members. Very often they recoup themselves by keeping back the bonuses due to members, so that the latter find themselves in possession of a house without having paid a penny more than the price of their daily purchases.

[2] The typical example of this kind of society is the celebrated Peabody Trust in London, founded by the philanthropist Peabody, who gave £500,000 for the purpose thirty years ago. To-day over 20,000 tenants are lodged in 6000 flats built by this fund. An endowment of almost equal importance (10 million francs), but which does not capitalise its rents, has been created in Paris by Messrs. de Rothschild.

[3] In England the municipalities have to build, within a radius of two miles at most, enough houses to lodge one half of the ejected population.

their " quarter " punctually, and evict them in case of non-payment, they will promptly become as unpopular as the landlord of to-day, and will have much more difficulty than he has in obtaining their rents.

In all of these schemes there have been two aims : to give the worker healthy and cheap housing ; to make him the owner of his house. It was thought that this last, in particular, would give him a taste for saving, for ownership, for home. To-day, however, this patriarchal theory is much shaken. The ownership of a house, in spite of the advantages which it has from the moral and economic point of view, has also serious objections for the worker. By tying him down to one particular spot, it deprives him of the mobility which is so precious to him, if he is to move whither his work is most in demand. It makes him more dependent on the employer. It must be added, that French law, which imposes actual division of the estate at death, and which thus constrains houses to be sold (or even, if there are children under age, compels judicial sale, with costs which may exceed the value of the house), is well calculated to discourage it.[1] On the other hand, if the problem of working-men's dwellings rises out of the private ownership of land and houses, it would seem that, by transferring this ownership to the worker, we are only displacing the evil, not curing it. Thus, in England, *Copartnership Tenant Societies* are being started, which aim at providing their members with comfortable dwellings at the lowest possible price, but which retain the ownership of the dwellings. This enables them to control the houses from the hygienic point of view, and to give the whole community the benefit of the surplus value of the land. This is the path of the future, and many employers and philanthropic societies, particularly municipalities, are adopting this system. The tenant finds in it almost all the advantages without the drawbacks of ownership ; for, provided he observes the conditions laid down by his society, that is to say conditions made by himself, he need fear neither the raising of the rent nor eviction.[2]

[1] True, this legislation has been improved on by the law of November 30, 1894, and by that of April 12, 1906. Apart from incidentally encouraging the building of cheap dwellings by exemptions from taxation, by the creation of departmental committees to spread building societies of all kinds, and by giving certain public institutions the power to lend them money, these laws also modified the code, making it easier to transmit these houses by succession. The house may now be put into the share of one of the heirs only, or may remain undivided for a longer period of time than common law allows, which, in principle, is only five years.

[2] This admirable institution dates from 1903 and numbers as yet only 24 societies, which have built about 6600 houses.

We must mention one other unpretending, but most beneficent system, which consists in *the hiring and fitting-up by philanthropic societies of dwellings already built*, with the object of sub-letting them to working men on better conditions, and of providing to some extent for the moral and economic education of those who are to live in them. This system, closely associated with the name of Miss Octavia Hill, is more modest than the preceding, and is designed primarily for the poorest classes. Miss Hill found, from practical experience, that it is useless to install poor people in good dwellings unless we first change their habits and inculcate in them some sense of cleanliness, comfort and *home;* and she has created an organisation admirably adapted to this end.

IV : CREDIT FOR CONSUMPTION—PAWNSHOPS

WE have seen (pp. 394–405) that there are a number of credit institutions for facilitating production; why should not there also be some for facilitating consumption? If credit may be indispensable to provide a man with the implements of his labour, it may be equally so to provide him with bread while he is waiting to earn it.

Credit for consumption is, in fact, practised on the largest scale, by the wealthy as well as by the working classes. *Sale on credit* is the rule with certain tradesmen, such as bakers and tailors; and it is well known that large shops have been created and organised almost solely with the idea of selling furniture and novelties on credit. This is, however, generally condemned as a cause of the ruin, and often the moral degradation, of those who resort to it. And co-operative societies for consumption have made it a rule—often violated, however—to refuse all credit and to sell for cash only.

There are indeed serious objections to credit for consumption:

(1) It incites the consumer to spend, by allowing him to satisfy his desires without any immediate sacrifice. An improvident buyer, particularly a woman, not very expert at balancing accounts—and it is generally women who go in for these purchases—will find it difficult to resist the temptation of taking away whatever pleases her without having to undo her purse-strings.[1]

(2) It places the consumer in a position of veritable servitude towards the tradesman, particularly when the consumer is poor and unable to pay. For he is no longer able to change his tradesman,

---

[1] The large stores, though they have abolished sale on credit, have substituted a no less dangerous attraction, viz., the power to return goods if they do not please.

and is obliged to submit to inflated prices or to the most inferior goods without daring to utter a complaint. Even rich consumers—particularly women of the world who have not paid their bills—are not safe from blackmail on the part of their tradesmen.

(3) It inflicts a double loss on the shopkeeper—the loss of interest and the loss resulting from not being paid.[1] This has to be made good by raising the prices of articles, so that all consumers suffer, beginning with those who pay punctually, and who are thus made to bear the share of the bad customers.

These evils, however, real though they are, are not serious enough, to induce us to condemn credit for consumption without exception.

It is true that, for articles of daily consumption and small value, such as bread, sale on credit can be justified only by exceptional circumstances, such as unemployment—circumstances which, alas, occur only too frequently in the existence of the working man !

But for articles of slow consumption and high price, such as furniture or even clothing, sale on credit may be the sole means of obtaining them, and may therefore render great service. Young people who have not enough money to buy their own furniture will perhaps remain unmarried, or, if they marry, will be obliged to take furnished lodgings, which will be extremely dear. A bed and a table are a species of capital which may be as indispensable to " setting up," as a sewing-machine or a loom ; credit therefore may be quite as justifiable in the one case as in the other.

On the other hand, furniture and clothing sold on credit are generally sold on the *hire system ;* that is to say, the price is paid in small monthly or weekly instalments, spread over a long period. Under such conditions, buying on credit takes on the aspect rather of saving—a " saving of consumption," as M. Boucher paradoxically puts it.[2] Instead of being incited to spend, the working-men's families convert this money—money which they would probably have spent in some unproductive way, which, as they put it, " burns their fingers "—into lasting goods ; and these will perhaps become something to fall back on in the bad days, when they are reduced to carrying them to the pawnshop.

Pawnshops should be considered as coming under the heading of credit for consumption. They are banks the object of which is

---

[1] Such losses have caused the failure of numbers of tradesmen, and what is scandalous, they occur most frequently among the tradesmen who supply the upper classes. Dressmakers, for instance, have been ruined by rich customer. who never troubled to pay their bills.

[2] *De la vente à tempérament.* Thèse du doctorat, 1906.

to make advances—not to persons needing them in order to produce, but to persons needing them in order to provide the necessaries of life. The borrower renounces the satisfaction of some superfluous or less urgent want, in order to satisfy some other more urgent want. He pledges his marriage-ring or his watch, or even his sheets, in order to have the wherewithal to buy bread. It is well known that these institutions—originally of a religious character—established, in Italy, in the twelfth century (*monte* in Italian meaning bank; *cf.* the French name *Mont-de-piété*), have become to-day institutions, so to speak, of secular relief controlled by the State. They lend on pledge—the borrower, by his very situation, being unable to offer personal guarantee—and charge a rate of interest which, though fixed to cover costs only, is bound to be fairly high, since the expenses of valuation, protection, and registration are considerable. If the loan is not repaid on the due date, which may be renewed indefinitely, the pledge is sold, and anything over is put at the disposal of the borrower.

The enormous *clientèle* of these institutions, and the importance of their operations (73 million francs, 45 million being for Paris alone), show that they answer to a social want. The incomes of the poor, and even of many of the rich, are intermittent : they pledge in bad days and redeem in good ones. The pawnshop thus plays the part of flywheel, as it were, regulating consumption in budgets which are not easy to balance.

V : LUXURY

THE word " luxury," in its ordinary acceptation, means the *satisfaction of a superfluous want*. This definition does not of itself imply an unfavourable judgment, for, as Voltaire cleverly put it, " The superfluous is very necessary." We ought to wish for a little of the superfluous, that is to say, a little luxury, for every one, even for the poorest. Nature herself offers us examples of the most splendid and sometimes extravagant luxury, in the petals of her flowers, the wings of her butterflies, and the coats of her most microscopic insects. History, on the other hand, shows us that every want, when it first appears, is considered superfluous. It is, indeed, bound to be so : first, because no one has ever felt it before ; secondly, because it probably requires a great deal of labour for its satisfaction, and industry, being inexperienced, will have to feel its way. If there is an object considered indispensable to-day, it is surely our under-linen ; " to be reduced to one's last shirt " is a proverbial expression for the lowest degree of destitution. Yet, at one time, a shirt was considered an object of great luxury, and was a royal present. A thousand other things have had the same history.[1] If, then, we had followed out the doctrine of the ascetics and suppressed all desire for luxury, we should have stifled straight away all the wants which make civilised man; and our condition would be no better to-day than was that of our ancestors of the Stone Age.

Luxury, then, must not be confused with wastefulness. A pot of flowers on a working-woman's window-sill is luxury, not wastefulness : to break the glasses after a convivial dinner is wastefulness, not luxury. Luxury, it is true, may easily degenerate into wastefulness : it is in this case only that it is blameworthy. It remains for us, then, to find out where to draw the line between the two.

Public opinion, in estimating luxury, considers only the amount of money spent. But this criterion is of no value. Whether a man spends his fortune in collecting postage-stamps, or in giving his cook the wages of an ambassador, or in horse-racing, these acts, blameworthy perhaps from a private point of view, are of no concern to society ; for the money which comes from the prodigal's pocket is simply transferred to that of his tradesman, his butler, his jockey, or the parasites who live at his expense.[2]

From the point of view of society, the true criterion is not the amount of money·spent, but the quantity of wealth or labour consumed in satisfying a given want. Now, we must bear in mind always that the sum total of existing wealth is insufficient at present to satisfy the elementary wants of the great majority of mankind (see p. 478), and that the productive forces—land, labour, and capital—which feed and renew the reservoir of wealth are all limited in quantity. It is evidently, then, an imperative duty not to turn aside for the satisfaction of a superfluous want, too great a share of the forces and wealth available for the necessaries of existence.[3] The question is one of proportion. Unjustifiable luxury, or waste, consists in a *disproportion between the quantity of social labour consumed*

---

[1] *E.g.* forks, watches, bicycles, and to-day motor-cars and aeroplanes.

[2] We must not forget, however, that if expenditure ultimately involves a destruction of wealth, this is a loss for society, as Bastiat's famous fable of *La Vitre cassée* shows ; but there is not always destruction, as the above examples prove.

[3] Does it follow from our definition that so soon as societies are wealthy enough to secure all superfluities for their members, no luxury will be culpable ? We believe so. If Nature, as we were saying, is able to allow herself an almost insolent luxury in her works, it is because time, force, and matter cost her nothing.

and the degree of individual satisfaction obtained. We give a few examples.

The taste for flowers—altogether unknown to our ancestors—which has only spread within the last thirty years in France,[1] is certainly a luxury in the first sense of the word, since it answers to a superfluous want, and is pleasing, elevating, and within reach even of the poor. But, if we adorn our drawing-rooms with orchids brought from Madagascar or Borneo by expeditions which have cost thousands of pounds, and perhaps the lives of men; or with blue dahlias which have been raised in hothouses requiring more coal than would keep ten families warm during a whole winter, luxury here comes under the second definition which we have given.

There is no objection, so far as we can see, to a lady wearing a dress the cut of which alone has cost £80; for, to repeat, our concern is not with the amount of money spent, which merely passes from one person to another, but with the material and labour expended. Now, it is not likely that this dress has taken much more stuff or workmanship than an ordinary one. But if this same lady has several yards of lace put on to it which have cost years of labour by a lacemaker, this is what we call abuse.[2]

It is quite justifiable for an English lord to spend a million sterling on a picture gallery, although it would have been better still had he used it to endow a public museum; but if, like his rougher baronial ancestors, he were to bolt enough meat and wine at his meal to feed twenty persons, or if, to have the pleasure of giving his guests a few grouse to shoot, he were to convert into moors land which would have produced enough food for several hundreds of his fellow citizens, thereby condemning them to exile, this is abuse. For observe, that in all these cases there is no question of industrial or artistic progress.[3]

---

[1] In Paris, in 1870, there were only thirty florists' shops; to-day there are over 500.

[2] But, it may be said. the lacemaker will be much distressed at having no more lace to make, since this is her means of livelihood. No doubt, but would it not be better for things to be so arranged that she could earn her living by making dresses for those who have none?

M. Leroy-Beaulieu points out that the desire for luxury has a stimulating effect on production in general: it is perhaps with the sole object of "enabling his wife to wear laces that the husband has earned millions." (*Précis d'Économie politique.*) It is certain that the vainest luxury may exercise a stimulating influence, if only by the envy which it excites. But, if the labour to which it gives rise is in turn employed in producing articles of luxury, then it is as the labour of the Danaïdes.

[3] The two positions, for and against luxury, have been the object of con-

It must not, however, be thought that unjustifiable luxury, in the form of waste of labour and of wealth, is to be imputed only to the rich. There is a wastefulness among the poor which is no less costly to society. What is the value of the pearl which Cleopatra threw into her cup compared with the hundreds of thousands of pounds which poor consumers throw daily into their glasses in the form of opal-tinted absinthe ? At least the Queen of Egypt was not poisoned by her draught.

What are we to say of art ? Is it to be considered a luxury ? This is indeed the general opinion, and economists are somewhat at a loss to justify art. Still, if we recall the definition which we gave of luxury, we shall see that it implies no condemnation of art, even from the purely economic point of view, since true art does not require an amount of labour disproportionate to the result. On the contrary, a block of marble and a chisel, or a square yard of canvas and some tubes of colour, with a few days' labour, are enough to provide exquisite enjoyment for generations of mankind. An American once paid £100,000 for a picture by Raphael ; [1] but what does it matter whether this enormous sum belongs to him or to the picture dealer ? It is the picture alone that we must consider. Did the painting cost the artist a sum of labour or of capital out of proportion to the beauty created ? No ; for it is the characteristic of art to produce great enjoyment by very simple means. Now, this is precisely the opposite of our definition of unjustifiable luxury.

VI : NOXIOUS CONSUMPTION—ALCOHOLISM

Section V leads us to the consumption which passes beyond luxury, in that it injures both the health and morality of the consumer. The dividing-line is obviously not easy to draw, and may always be a matter of dispute, particularly as the evil results rather from the abuse of consumption, than from the act of consumption itself. It might be questioned, for instance, whether there is not abuse in the 500 million francs' worth of tobacco annually consumed in France.

There is, however, one form of consumption which has assumed the proportions of a national peril, and which cannot be omitted in this chapter : it is that of alcohol. In France, the consumption of

troversy since antiquity. Against luxury, see M. de Laveleye, *Le Luxe ;* and for it, M. Leroy-Beaulieu, *Traité d'Économie politique*, iv. For documents, consult the four volumes of M. Baudrillart on *l'Histoire du Luxe*.

[1] The same sum was offered to Lord Lansdowne in February 1911, for a landscape by Rembrandt.

alcohol increased four times over during the nineteenth century, and by 1900 reached almost 5 litres of pure alcohol per head per annum. From that date on it fell to a little over 3 litres per head, in 1907, so that it was thought that this terrible scourge had been overcome.[1] Since 1907, however, the figure has risen again to 4 litres. To realise what this means, we must remember : (1) that these 4 litres are pure alcohol and represent about 10 litres of ordinary brandy ; (2) that the figure given is obtained by dividing total consumption by total population, three quarters of which are women and children, so that, if we count only the adult male population, we must multiply the figure by 4, giving 40 litres per head ; (3) that we must add the contraband alcohol consumed, which should raise the last figure by one quarter. Ultimately, then, we get an average consumption of 50 litres per head.[2]

This fact is the more disturbing in that France, formerly, was far from being one of the most alcoholic countries. True, the evils of alcohol are not necessarily in relation to the consumption of it. Denmark, for instance, where the consumption of alcohol reaches its highest point, is nevertheless the first country in Europe, perhaps in the world, for longevity, birth-rate, education, and all the virtues of association and co-operation.[3]   But, alcoholism acts as a cultural solution for all that is bad in a nation, multiplying tendencies to crime, suicide, lunacy, violence, and, above all, laziness.

The remedies that have been tried against alcoholism are very numerous, but few have shown any great results. They may be classed as follows :

I. Action by legal constraint : (a) *Prohibition of the sale, or*

[1] This fall was probably due not to the anti alcohol campaign, but to the increase in the duties on alcohol in 1900.

[2] The following table shows the movement of the consumption of alcohol in France during the last few years in absolute figures and per head.

	Hectolitres.	Litres.
1907	1,289,000	3·31
1908	1,339,000	3·44
1909	1,342,000	3·46
1910	1,399,000	3·59
1911	1,574,000	4·06

The figures for England and Germany are :

	England	Germany.
1907	2·37	6·10
1911	1·77	5·20

[3] There is, however, one shadow in this glowing picture : it is that Denmark is one of the countries which number the most suicides, 232 per million inhabitants, or almost the same figure as France ; whereas, in England, the proportion is only 89, and in Norway 45.

even of the production, of alcohol. The sale of alcohol is prohibited in several of the United States. In others *local option* is practised, that is to say, each district is allowed the faculty of decreeing prohibition.[1] Legal prohibition has had hardly any result save that of provoking fraudulent sales ; but local prohibition has been more successful, implying as it does an effective support on the part of public opinion. As for the prohibition of production, this is becoming more and more difficult with the progress that is being made in the art of distilling : to-day it is possible to distil alcohol from all organic matter, even from logs of wood, and to manufacture it directly by chemical synthesis.

(b) *Penal repression of drunkenness.* This remedy, which exists in French law but which is never applied, may give good results from the point of view of order and public decency, particularly when it is the publican who is punished for supplying drink to a drunken man. But, even if it were stringently applied as it is in other countries, it is of no use against alcoholism ; for alcoholism is a chronic state, very different from intermittent fits of drunkenness, and much more grave.

II. Action by example and propaganda. It is possible to carry on the fight by *education, i.e.* by the simple appeal to hygiene, economy, and the dignity of the human being. This teaching, particularly when it is given in such a propitious environment as the school and the army, is certainly not without result. Effective also, in a different way, are the associations of disinterested men who, in order the better to fight alcoholism, make their members undertake to abstain from alcoholic drinks. These are very numerous and of the most varied types. The oldest, called the Good Templars, which was started in the United States in 1851 and has spread into all countries, imposes on its members complete abstinence not only from every distilled but from every fermented drink.[2] The Blue Cross Society, of Swiss origin (1877), is somewhat less rigid in that it does not exact a lifelong pledge, and the *Ligue nationale française*

---

[1] Recent laws in Belgium and in Switzerland have prohibited the sale of absinthe, and a measure to this effect has been proposed in France ; but it is little likely to be carried, in spite of the fact that " absinthism " has reached a critical point in that country.

[2] It is a much disputed question whether these societies ought to impose abstinence from all alcoholic beverages, even those which are simply *fermented*, such as wine and beer ; or only from *distilled* drinks. In reality, the aims of the various societies are different. Societies of total abstinence try mainly to convert those who are already alcoholic or dipsomaniacs, and for these certainly the only remedy is total abstinence. Temperance societies aim mainly at preventing the evil, and for that moderation in consumption is quite enough.

anti-alcoolique is still less severe, since it asks no pledge at all and works mainly by propaganda.

These societies, though often the object of ridicule, have had a powerful influence. We may even say that they have been the most effective of all the weapons hitherto tried. In England, Scandinavia, and the United States, they have really saved a large proportion of the population from alcoholism. But their action is effective only where it finds a solid support on moral and religious ground.

III. Action against the abettors of alcoholism, namely the producers and sellers. These two social categories are necessarily interested in the development of alcoholism since they live by it. And, as their electoral power is very great by reason of their number,[1] they form an insurmountable obstacle to all efforts of the legislature or of private initiative.

The fight against these powers of alcoholism may be carried on by the following means :

(*a*) *By limiting the number of public-houses.* This remedy has been tried in different countries, particularly in Holland, and has been the object of several bills in France. But the vested interests of the wine merchants have always frustrated it, although, in order to disarm them, the method proposed was that of extinction, which would have favoured survivors with practically a monopoly.

(*b*) *By active competition against public-houses, carried on by philanthropic anti-alcohol societies.* These may take the form either of *temperance cafés* which sell non-alcoholic drinks only : their success has been mediocre ; or of public-houses which sell alcoholic drinks, but do not try to attract customers.

This is what is called the Gothenburg system, after the Swedish town in which it was first tried in 1865. The municipalities do away with the publicans—either by expropriation or, where the law enables them to do so, by simply refusing the licence—and substitute private companies in their place. These companies, in managing the public-house, must aim, if not at disgusting the consumer, at any rate at not attracting him. For this purpose, they must make the premises as bare and uncomfortable as possible, not even offering customers chairs.

It certainly seems as if this system ought to give good results, since it reverses the magnet, as it were ; and for a long time it was spoken of as something marvellous, and as having completely

---

[1] In France, there are 500,000 publicans and over a million distillers. In England, the number of public-houses is decreasing, being 91,000 in 1911. This gives 1 per 400 of the population as against 1 per 83 in France.

eliminated alcoholism from the two Scandinavian countries. To-day, however, its fame has somewhat abated. These humanitarian public-houses, it is said, have come in many respects to resemble their predecessors ; the companies which direct them do not disdain profits, or, at any rate, the towns which reserve a certain share of the profits try to push on sales.

This does not mean that the consumption of alcohol has not considerably declined in Norway and Sweden ; but the action of other factors, particularly of temperance societies, has perhaps more to do with it than the Gothenburg system.

(c) *By the suppression of distillers' privileges.* In France, growers harvesting their wine and cider may transform it into alcohol for their own consumption without paying duties.[1] Although by law the quantity so allowed is limited, in actual fact it is unlimited. Not only does the State lose millions sterling every year under this head, but the whole country population is steeped as it were in this clandestine fount. The *bouilleurs de cru*, as they are called, play in the country the same rôle as do the publicans in the towns.

(d) *By State monopoly of the manufacture or sale of alcohol.* In Russia, as is well known, the State has monopolised sale, and sells brandy in its shops as the French State sells tobacco.[1] In France, it has been proposed more than once that the State should monopolise the distilling and sale of alcohol, and Professor Alglave headed an active campaign in favour of the proposal. It is not likely that it will succeed, however, as the distillers and the retailers have combined against any such reform.

For the rest, if the question of monopoly is of great interest from the fiscal point of view, bringing in, as it does in Russia, nearly £100,000,000 gross (nearly £72,000,000 net), and in France £40,000,000, it is of interest as a means of fighting alcoholism only in so far as it results in suppressing or controlling *bouilleurs de cru* and retailers. It is true that, both in Russia and in Switzerland, the State promises part of the proceeds of the monopoly to the fight against alcoholism ; but we should be very simple to imagine

---

[1] In Russia the State sells brandy in closed flasks only, so that the customer cannot consume it on the spot. But, as he simply goes across the road to drink it at the eating-shop opposite, there is not much gain in the way of temperance. The State used to employ some £400,000 per annum of its enormous profits in subsidising "temperance committees" ; but it has already reduced this sum to one half.

In Switzerland, the State sells only wholesale and to retail dealers, and thus makes but modest profits (some £250,000). Part of this it hands over to the Cantons to fight alcoholism, but they as a rule apply it to poor relief.

that the State, as philanthropist, will apply itself to drying up its resources as treasurer.

VII : ABSENTEEISM

Absenteeism is the name given to the habit among landowners, or men of wealth, of living abroad, or at least away from their estates. This custom is very common in some of the countries of Western Europe, particularly Ireland ; and the question arises as to whether it involves undesirable consequences for the home country and *vice versa*, desirable consequences for the country in which these absentees reside.

From the moral point of view, absenteeism is severely condemned. But it is necessary to draw a distinction. Condemnation is well founded in the case of landed proprietors, since the owning of land is, as we have seen, a social function, and ought, like all public functions, to be performed personally and not by proxy. Private ownership of land, which is justified only by public utility, has no longer any foundation if the owner does no more than collect his rents, and shows, by his very absence, that he is living as a parasite. Besides, apart from theory, experience has many a time shown, in Ireland for example, that the absenteeism of landowners who delegate their powers to agents or to middlemen, is the ruin both of cultivators and of agriculture.[1]

But the case of the man of independent means is somewhat different. His social function—for he too has one, viz., the creation and administration of capital—does not bind him down to one particular spot. On the contrary, a certain degree of cosmopolitanism is very useful if he would invest intelligently, and keep trace of his investments afterwards.

From the economic point of view, absenteeism is criticised on the ground that the man who spends his money abroad allows strangers to benefit by it, instead of his fellow citizens. Is not the sojourn of rich foreigners in Switzerland, Italy, Paris, and the Riviera looked on, with good reason, as a source of wealth to the populations there ? Surely, then, if the absentee, by the mere fact of his presence, confers a benefit on the country in which he resides, he must by the mere fact of his absence be inflicting an equal loss

---

[1] From the social and political point of view—which must also be considered —it was the absenteeism of the great French landowners which contributed to the decadence of the French aristocracy.

In Roumania landed proprietors residing abroad are very heavily taxed.

on the country he has left. The money that a man spends abroad he can neither spend nor invest at home.

It will be said, perhaps, that the absentee does not give his money for nothing, but expects to receive an equal value in the form of food, lodging, and various services. If the English, *e.g.* spend 50 million francs in Switzerland, is it not just the same as if there were an export of 50 million francs of Swiss products into England, the only difference being that the buyers have come to consume them on the spot?[1] No. It may be pointed out that the sum paid by the English residents gives a much higher profit than would be obtained by exporting these goods or services to England, for two reasons: (1) Foreigners as a rule pay *more for things than they are worth*, since the law of competition is not at work here. Leaving aside the morality of such a proceeding, we are bound to admit that there are few towns frequented by foreigners where there are not two prices for goods, one for the foreigner and one for the natives of the country. (2) Very often the foreigner pays for the use of wealth that is not *by nature consumable or destructible.* When he takes a villa for the season, or hires a guide for the day, and pays for the right to enjoy a clear sky, to breathe fresh air, to look at a blue sea or snow-white mountains, he takes nothing away from the wealth of the country; he pays it a veritable rent similar to that by which every landowner profits who has the monopoly of some natural advantage. Why, indeed, should not the Swiss panorama, the blue gulfs of the Riviera, the waterfalls of Norway, the great memories which cling to the Italian cities, be sources of wealth for these countries, just as much as coal-mines or petroleum wells? It is exactly what happens in the case of the individual. If I have some natural curiosity, a grotto or a ruin, on my estate, and make visitors pay a franc each to see it, it is clear that my income is increased by the amount which these travellers are spending.

The absenteeism of *persons* is very different from that of capital. We shall return to the last when discussing investment.

VIII: STATE CONTROL OF CONSUMPTION

FROM earliest times governments have held it incumbent on them to see that their peoples did not suffer from famine, or excessive dearness, or the bad quality of manufactured products; just as

---

[1] Moreover this English money will probably come back to England in payment for English goods in accordance with the economic law of barter (see *supra*, pp. 335–337).

they held it their duty to limit, or prohibit, consumption which they deemed contrary to the public welfare. Without encroaching on history, which is beyond the scope of this chapter, we have only to recall the action of Joseph in Egypt when he filled the granaries against the seven years famine ; the distributions of corn to the Roman citizens, inaugurated at the time of the Gracchi, and lasting until the Empire ; the measures taken under the *ancien régime* up till the eve of the French Revolution for ensuring the provisioning of the corn market ; the edicts which established maximum prices ; the sumptuary laws regarding dress and the wearing of furs, cloth of gold, etc. ; or the *Code Michaud* under Louis XIII, which prohibited the wearing of laces and fixed the number of dishes to be served at table ; the innumerable and meticulous regulations regarding goods for sale—not food only, but all articles, even clothstuffs, the very threads of which were counted.

The Classical economists, in inaugurating the liberty of labour, established at the same time liberty of consumption ; and, during the whole of the reign of the Liberal school, the control of the State in this domain almost entirely ceased. The consumer was admitted to be the best judge of his own interests, and consumption was considered a purely private matter with which the State had nothing to do. But the reaction in favour of intervention which has since manifested itself, first in commerce and in production, has not been slow to make itself felt in consumption also. It is but natural that protection should spread from producers to consumers. The State is, moreover, only obeying a new power, one which is becoming day by day more imperious—Social Hygiene. It is almost wholly in the name of this last that State control in the matter of consumption is exercised to-day.

The so-called *sumptuary* laws were abandoned, not merely because they were as a rule ineffectual and vexatious, but because, as we have seen (p. 714), it is difficult and dangerous to draw the line above which luxury begins. Still, taxes on certain objects and services of luxury (on motor-cars and carriages in France, and on domestic servants in some countries) may act partially as sumptuary laws.

The different ways in which the State intervenes in consumption may be put under five headings. It endeavours :

(*1*) To ensure consumers a *sufficient quantity*. This solicitude extends only to foodstuffs, and almost solely to bread. We have just called to mind the measures formerly taken by governments in this matter, which would fill volumes. To-day, haunted as we are

less by the fear of famine than by that of over-production, this
first mode of intervention may be considered abandoned. Still,
the customs duties on corn and cattle have no other excuse than
to ensure the production of food in the protected country. We may
also mention, in this connection, the plans for providing *free bread*
for all, which were proposed by M. Barrucand in France and
Dr. Alfred Russel Wallace in England, but which were no more
than a nine days' wonder.

(2) To protect consumers against an *inflation of prices* in products
of prime necessity, which might put them beyond the reach of the
poorer classes. The solicitude of the State here is of the same order
as in the preceding case, and concerns, like it, only bread, and
occasionally meat. Thus, in France, a law passed at the time of the
Revolution, July 22, 1791, gives municipalities the right to price bread
and meat. And it is a curious fact that, in spite of lively criticism
on the part of the economists of the Liberal school, this law is still
in vigour after 122 years! It is the most venerable of all the
weapons in the legislative arsenal.

True, in the case of meat it has fallen into disuse, since,
owing to its very different qualities, it is impossible to fix a maximum
price for meat without falling back on a very complicated tariff,
or to prevent butchers from passing a piece of meat from one category
to another. Sometimes, however, mayors have taken advantage
of this law to threaten butchers' combines. Bread, as a homogeneous product, is more easily priced, and the law is still frequently
applied in regard to it. But bakers have, nevertheless, many
devices 'for eluding the tariff—by putting in flour of an inferior
quality, or by adding water, or salt, to their dough. Probably the
creation of municipal butcheries and bakeries as at Verona and
Catania, or, failing these, some official support to co-operative
bakeries and butcheries, would be a better and more scientific
guarantee for consumers than this survival of old edicts as to
maximum prices.

(3) To protect consumers against the *adulteration of foodstuffs*.
Whereas the last two modes of State intervention are falling into
desuetude, this, on the contrary, is rapidly spreading. It is due,
on the one hand, to the really marvellous progress which has taken
place in the art of adulteration (see p. 136 n. 1); and, on the
other, to the parallel progress in our knowledge of the laws of hygiene,
that is to say, of the properties of food substances and of the best
way of ultilising them for maintaining our force and energy. Laws
have been passed in all countries against adulteration in wine, butter,

milk, sugar, meat, etc. Finally, in France, a law of August 5, 1905, has extended legal control to all products " which serve for the food of man or of animals." *Bureaux d'hygiène* are to be created in all towns of over 20,000 inhabitants ; samples are to be taken from all shops by these bureaux and analysed in the municipal laboratories, and, if a case of adulteration is found, it is to be taken before the court.

Of all modes of State intervention, this is the one which economists of the Liberal school find most irksome and irrelevant.[1] They put up with intervention perforce when it is a question of production or circulation, since public interest is there at stake ; but when it comes to consumption, this intermeddling of the legislator in the domain of private life appears to them simply grotesque.

Yet how can we doubt that the adulteration of food is a matter of public interest, after seeing, in 1907, the four departments of the south of France rise in a body to the cry of " Down with fraud " ; or after the preserved meat scandals of Chicago, which disgusted the whole world ; or after the International Congress of Geneva, of 1908, to inquire into the adulteration of food ? As for thinking that the consumer is sufficiently able to know what he is consuming and to look after his own interests, this is simply to ignore the fact that were he possessed of all knowledge of hygiene, he is often unable to choose his food, especially if he is one of the poorer customers. Are the infants poisoned by milk the " best judges of their own interests " ? Moreover, if the consumers are the best judges, what better can we do than listen to them when they demand, as they are doing in all countries, the intervention of the legislator ?[2]

We do not deny that these measures of protection are very difficult to apply. Hygiene is still far from infallible, and nothing is more difficult than to determine where adulteration begins and what is to be understood by a " true " or " pure " product. It is

[1] See, in particular, M. Yves Guyot's continual protests, in his books, against the repressive laws on adulteration, and even against those which try to stamp out alcoholism.

[2] In France in 1901, they had even created a society with the eloquent title " *League for the Defence of Human Life* "—which was not, however, strong enough to live.

We may also cite Switzerland, where the Federal Council has submitted to the referendum a plan for modifying the constitution which would give the Confederation " the right to legislate on the commerce in foodstuffs, articles of household consumption and utensils, in so far as these may be a danger to health or life." And although the cantons are very jealous of their autonomy, this bill was voted (July 11, 1897) by 162,250 votes to 86,955, and resulted, in 1907, in a law on the repression of fraud by means of inspection at the frontier.

evident that, if we were to take adulteration to mean every modification of a natural product, it would be necessary to prohibit everything, since most foodstuffs undergo at least the artificial modification of cooking. The watering and sugaring of wine are rightly
considered adulteration, and yet Nature herself, in the making of
wine, uses hardly any other elements than these. But if practical
difficulties call for great prudence in applying the law, they do not
make the law any the less necessary.[1]

It is true that consumers may protect themselves by private
associations—leagues of consumers or buyers, societies against
adulteration (see above, p. 701), agricultural syndicates, the co-operative consumers' societies of which we have spoken—particularly if
these are invested, as are English private societies, with the right
to prosecute.[2] But they need the law behind them, just as the
law, in turn, needs them, since without their aid it will probably
prove ineffective.

(4) To prevent the consumption of *noxious products*, either by
prohibiting the consumption itself—a measure which is difficult
to carry out and is, moreover, an attack on the liberty of the individual—or by prohibiting the sale and manufacture of them,
which is, in practice, quite as effective. Thus, in Belgium and Switzerland, the sale of absinthe has recently been prohibited. China, by
a decree of November 21, 1906, has forbidden the consumption of
opium under severe penalties, and this campaign is being strongly
supported by " Young China." It is devoutly to be wished that
French Indo-China would follow her example ; but opium, there, is
a very lucrative government monopoly.[3] Even in France, the consumption of this narcotic is taking on alarming proportions, although
the importation of it is forbidden. In some countries, as we know,
the sale of alcohol itself and of distilled drinks is prohibited (see
p. 719).

The legislative measures taken in many countries to protect
the inhabitants of towns, particularly the poor, against unsanitary
dwellings must also be included under this heading ; for lodging

---

[1] As a curious example of intervention in the name of hygiene, we may quote
the municipal decrees of a few German towns which prohibit ladies from wearing
long dresses, on the ground that they raise the dust of the roads.

[2] French law refuses this right to private societies, but jurisprudence admits
it in the case of trade unions when they can prove that they are pursuing trade
interests, and the agricultural unions have made use of this right more than
once. They are, however, often non-suited, on the ground that the union
has suffered no pecuniary loss, and consequently has no ground on which to
claim damages.

[3] On the fight against opium, see Paul Gide, *L'opium*, 1910.

also falls under consumption. We know what minute conditions—though rarely observed outside of the large centres of population—are prescribed as to the number of cubic feet which rooms must contain, the height of ceilings, doors and windows, etc. (see above, *Housing*).

The State also concerns itself with *gambling, betting,* and *lotteries,* either prohibiting them, regulating them, or profiting by them. We ought perhaps to have spoken of these under *Distribution*; and if we had devoted a whole chapter to spoliation in all its forms, we should not have failed to reserve a place for them. Still, they are, strictly speaking, acts of consumption, or at least of expenditure—and an expenditure which is not a mere transfer of money, since the sums lost by gambling or by betting are nearly always unproductively consumed, being either wasted by the winners, or used to keep up a host of parasites. The alarming increase of these habits in the middle and lower classes, not only in France but in all countries, has attracted the attention of many governments; but these have hitherto been more intent on making money by them than on repressing them.[1]

Lotteries, we know, were carried on in former times, and still are to-day in Italy, Spain, the town of Hamburg, and various German States, by the governments themselves, as a more or less lucrative form of State enterprise.[2] In France, the government has renounced them, and they are allowed only if previously authorised by the administration, or by parliament, according to the importance of the sums at stake. But this permission is very freely granted on the most futile philanthropic pretexts.[3] It may be urged in excuse that the lottery is less dangerous than gambling and betting: first, because the losses suffered by the players are limited and are too

---

[1] Legislation on race-course betting and on gambling-houses is plentiful. Public gaming-houses in France were, till lately, prohibited by the State. But it was easy to evade this prohibition by means of clubs and casinos, so-called private associations, which are, however, in reality open to all. The Government has therefore temporised, and has authorised games in watering-places, in return for a tax of 15 per cent. on the gross proceeds.

As for betting on race-courses, all agencies are forbidden save the one known as the *pari mutuel*, which the State obliges to pay 7 per cent. of the amount of the bets in return for its privilege.

[2] Thus in Italy the *lotto* yielded 74 million francs gross between 1903 and 1904, and, deducting the payments to the winners and costs, 33 millions net.

[3] M. Clemenceau, when Prime Minister, declared in the Chamber, in 1908, that he had had requests for lottery permits to the amount of 537 million francs, but that he had authorised them only to the amount of 100 millions. Since then, however, the administration seems to have become more strict as regards permits.

small to cause their ruin; secondly, because the money of the losers, or even of the winners, may be usefully employed. Even as a mode of distributing wealth, the lottery, though it has the bad effect of intensifying the action of chance and of accustoming public opinion to the idea of wealth acquired without labour, offers every one at least more equal chances than do gambling and betting, where the inequality of luck and of information borders on swindling. It even satisfies a certain not very far-sighted sentiment of justice.

(5) Lastly, the law may intervene, not this time to protect the interests of the consumer, but to lay certain duties on him incumbent on his social function, in particular forbidding the waste of certain forms of natural wealth, *e.g.* prohibiting fishing during several months of the year, etc. There are many articles the sale of which will doubtless one day be forbidden, since the consumption of them implies stupid or pernicious destruction—for example, the wearing of birds' feathers in hats. Up till now, only a few private leagues have tried, without much success, to fight this " Redskin " fashion.

IX: PUBLIC EXPENDITURE [1]

THE continuous increase in public expenditure is one of the most characteristic facts of our time. At the beginning of the century, and until about 1830, the budget of expenditure in France was hardly more than a billion francs; to-day it is nominally 4665 millions, but really a good deal over 5 billions. In less than the lifetime of a man, then, it has increased fivefold.[2] If we add to this the expenditure of the communes and of the departments, the

[1] If this chapter be read in connection with that on Public Credit (p. 405) and that on Taxation (p. 684), the reader will obtain a summary of what is called Public Finance (*Économie Financière*), which is a distinct branch of study in the Law Faculties in France.

[2] The following figures give the successive increases in the French budget during the last few centuries:

	Million francs.
Louis XVI (1785)	610
Napoleon I (1815)	931
Charles X (1830)	1095
Louis-Philippe (1848)	1771
Napoleon III (1869)	1·04
„ (1872)	2723
Republic (1913)	4665

We take the end of each reign as marking the stages. For the Second Empire, however, we take the year 1872 instead of 1870, in order to bring in the liquidation of the Franco-German War.

2 A

figure reaches 6 billions. The causes of this phenomenon, which is general, as it shows itself equally, or even more markedly, in other countries,[1] are not difficult to find.

(1) The first is connected with the *depreciation of money* (see also pp. 63, 235), owing to which expenditure appears greater than it really is. A certain amount must, therefore, be deducted in order to obtain the real increase.

(2) The second is the *development of the military spirit* with all its consequences—war, and the armed peace which alone costs more than the wars of former times. Over a quarter of the 4½ milliards of State expenditure mentioned for France is set aside to pay the cost of past wars, in the form of interest on the loans which were contracted to carry them on. The army and navy budgets in France, including the defence of the colonies and military possessions, amount to over 1500 million francs ; and this is less than those of England, Germany, Russia, and the United States.[2] Expenditure on fleets, in particular, has assumed extravagant proportions during the last few years, each Super-dreadnought costing from 65 to 70 million francs.

(3) The third is the *gradual extension of the attributes of the State*. Every public expenditure corresponds, in fact, to some State

[1] The following is the increase in the budgets of the 4 principal European States during the last 20 years in millions of francs. The figures in brackets give the increase per head.

	1882		1913
Russia	3,114 (40)	..	7,948 (50)
England	2,192 (70)	..	4,895 (108)
Germany	2,695 (55)	..	10,700 (165)
France	3,573 (90)	..	4,665 (120)

From the figures for Germany, we must deduct about 3400 million marks for various State undertakings, which leaves about 5200 million marks (6500 million francs) yielded by taxation, or about 100 francs per head.

[2] The following figures give the increase in military expenditure in millions of francs (army and fleet, exclusive of colonies, military pensions, etc.).

	1883	1912	Increase
Russia	894	1,920	115 per cent.
England	702	1,779	153 ,,
Germany	504	1,648	227
France	789	1,343	70
Austria-Hungary	318	674	112
Italy	311	649	109

And the figures for the ensuing years will be higher still.

The most curious example of the increase of military expenses is Switzerland. Although a small country and protected by its neutrality, its war budget has increased from 7 million francs in 1874 to 45 millions in 1911, *i.e.* a much higher rate of increase than that of any other country.

function Now, in all countries, even England, the country of self-help, there is a more and more marked tendency to widen the attributes of the State (see above, p. 204), not only by developing the older public services, such as education, public works, etc., but by creating new departments, or at least large ministerial services, such as agriculture, commerce, labour, poor relief, public health (dealing with insanitary dwellings, epidemics, adulteration of foodstuffs), social insurances, etc.

It goes without saying that this gradual extension of the attributes of the State means a proportional increase in public expenditure. Still, it would be unjust to lay the heaviest share of responsibility for this enormous increase of public expenditure at the door of State Socialism, as it is called. If, from the total of State expenditure in France, which is 5000 millions, we subtract 1500 millions for the army and navy, and 1200 for the national debt —which is for the most part due to war; if, besides, we subtract the 400 or 500 million francs which the collection of taxes costs, we find only 1800 million francs of public expenditure left to put to the account of the various departments. Now, if we call to mind that the total income of France is estimated at over 30 billions, we shall not really find it exorbitant that less than 6 per cent. of this should be devoted to expenditure for the public good.[1]

It appears that, for a long while during the course of the nineteenth century, the upward march of public expenditure did not surpass, if it even equalled, the rise in the general wealth of the country. Although, as we said, the budget increased fivefold within a century, the total wealth of the French nation increased sixfold within the same time (see above, p. 599). The proportion of public expenditure to national income therefore diminished. But, during the last few years there has apparently been a change. The increase of wealth seems to be slowing down, while the budget appears to be increasing at an enormous rate.

And those who fondly imagine that the rising tide of expenditure is about to stop are under a singular delusion. In view of the laws for the relief of the aged and infirm, which are not as yet in full play; the law, just applied, regarding old-age pensions; the

[1] True, 1250 millions must be added for expenditure by the communes and departments, which is also for the common good, raising the proportion to 9 per cent.

It is clear that the military spirit counts for nothing, or for very little (say the building of a few barracks), in the increase of municipal expenditure. The latter, therefore, can be attributed only to the extension of the functions of municipalities.

insurance schemes lately started for unemployment and invalidity;
the requirements of city hygiene in the matter of the demolishing of
unhealthy quarters and the reconstruction of houses ; the urgency, if
a general strike is to be avoided, of raising the miserable pittances of
nearly a million functionaries (among whom are 120,000 discontented
teachers, who are embittering the rising generation); the necessity,
if we are to keep up a sufficient army in face of the falling birth-rate,
of lengthening the period of military service, of paying those
who are willing to re-enlist ; of creating flotillas of aeroplanes and
dirigibles ; the no less imperious necessity to maintain a war
fleet of at least secondary power; lastly, the rise in prices, which, of
course, enhances public just as much as private expenditure—in
view of all these, we may expect within a short time an increase
in expenditure of over a milliard francs. And the rise will not stop
there. It will not be long before we shall have exceeded the sixth,
and find ourselves well on our way towards the seventh milliard.

It is the opinion of many that, with such a prospect in view, the
ruin of France and of other countries is inevitable. This may be,
but it does not necessarily follow as a consequence of this evolution.
For what is expenditure on the part of the State ? It is money taken
from Peter to give to Paul. Who is Peter ? The taxpayer. Who
is Paul ? The functionary, the *rentier*, the old-age pensioner, every
one who receives from the State. The 6 milliards of expenditure
to-day,[1] the 7 or 8 milliards of expenditure to-morrow, represent
nothing more than a transfer of money. The whole question
from the economic point of view [2] is whether these milliards taken
from the capital and labour of the nation are being wasted or whether
they are being used for the real needs of the country. It cannot
be said that the money employed in constructing roads and ports, in
organising technical teaching, insurances, etc., or even in avoiding
a disastrous war [3] is money lost. If governments were infinitely
wise and knew how to spend money better than do individuals, the
increase in public expenditure would be a cause of wealth, not of

---

[1] Including the expenditure of the communes.

[2] We say " from the economic point of view," as the transfer of money, even
by law, from one person's pocket to another raises a question of justice, with
which, however, we have not to concern ourselves here.

[3] It is often said, that expenditure upon armament may be looked on as
an insurance premium. Suppose the cost of a war between France and Germany
were 30 milliard francs for the conquered nation, a premium of 2 milliards per
annum, or 6 per cent., does not seem too much. But, as war expenditure may
also provoke a war, and as it refunds nothing if the war takes place, the operation, from the economic point of view, has nothing to commend it.

poverty. Such a state of affairs is, of course, unlikely ; hence in·crease in expenditure causes anxiety. Still, if ruin is to come, it will come not from the increase in public expenditure, but from the uses to which this increase has been put.

CHAPTER III: SAVING

I: THE TWO ASPECTS OF SAVING

THE word *saving* is applied to two very different categories of acts which have no relation with one another, although in everyday language, and even in treatises on Political Economy, they are often mistaken for one another.

(*1*) By saving we mean the art of satisfying our wants while consuming as little as possible, that is to say, the art of obtaining the most possible out of our material or our money—in short. of *economising* them. It is simply an application of the hedonistic principle of obtaining the greatest satisfaction at least sacrifice. A clever housewife will be able to cook her dinner with half the amount of coal and butter that a more wasteful one would use. Better still, she will be able to provide a more nourishing meal for her husband and children on a smaller sum of money. It is not simply in food, but in necessaries of all kinds, that economy finds its place. A careful man will keep his coat as good as new three times as long as some more careless neighbour, and may, out of a more modest income, manage to obtain as much satisfaction as another man who lets his money run through his fingers.

Now, this is not a negligible form of saving in the national economy. Taken separately, it is true, each of these economies is of small account ; but, repeated in every act of consumption, they mount up to an enormous total, and may represent a notable portion of the national income. The waste which goes on in consumption in America, even among the working classes, is a well-known fact. It is claimed that to this rapid consumption is due, in part, their great productive activity. Perhaps so ; but to this is also due the fact that they get a much smaller amount of well-being out of their activity than we should expect, from their large wages and large incomes. It is, on the other hand, owing to their wise economy, that French families are able to live with comfort on incomes which would mean misery for Americans.

It is not in family consumption only, but in national consumption, that economy finds a sphere of action. This is a domain which up till now has been too much neglected—at least from the theoretical point of view; for, in practice, great progress in economy has been made of late, particularly as regards the utilising of *industrial refuse*, and the preserving of perishable goods by refrigerating processes. By means of these inventions, an enormous quantity of wealth is saved which was formerly lost.

Nations, further, make a bad use of their resources; and perhaps the greatest advantage of the Protectionist system, if it were rationally applied, would be the education which it would give countries in this respect. Professor Patten points out, for example, that cotton and maize, native products of the United States, might be substituted with advantage for other textiles and cereals imported from abroad. The curious project of the Daylight Saving Bill, in England, comes under the same order of ideas, being a bill to economise daylight by adapting the civil—that is to say the working—day to the solar day, and so saving artificial light.

Economy is a veritable art, which, like all other arts, needs to be learned. It would be a great blessing and a great source of wealth if it were taught, particularly to those whose business it is more especially to practise it—to women. The teaching of domestic economy is spreading. In England and Germany, there are schools for teaching both the theory and practice of it, in which kitchens take the place of laboratories. There are also travelling kitchens, with teachers who travel from village to village.

(2) But we use the word " saving " in a second sense, meaning not consumption *economised* but consumption *postponed*. Man, instead of satisfying his present wants, thinks of his future wants, feeling them as strongly as if they were present, and " puts something aside " for the morrow, or for his old age, or for his children. This is not simply economy; it is *foresight*.[1]

In ordinary speech, saving is as a rule associated with *investment*, that is to say, the productive employment of savings. But the two acts are really quite independent. Saving finds its own end within itself and can stand alone. For to provide for future wants

[1] In an interesting book, entitled *Introduction à l'étude de la prévoyance*, M. Anatole Weber reproaches teachers of Political Economy with having no theory or general view and definition of foresight. And this is the definition he gives: " Every act of an individual which is done with the object of arming him against the uncertainty of the morrow." It does not seem to us to differ essentially from our own definition, which he also quotes, save that it is too general. On this definition to sow, plant, build—all acts of production indeed—would be acts of foresight.

is, of itself, an important economic act. We shall speak of investment in another section.

Saving was long advocated by the economists of the Liberal school as the sole source of fortune, or, at least, as the only means of salvation for the working class.

Public opinion, on the contrary, has never looked on it with much favour; and a lofty spirit like Montesquieu even went so far as to write, " If the rich do not spend much, the poor die of hunger."

We might be tempted, perhaps, to reconcile these two opinions by saying that it is for the poor to save and the rich to spend. And this, in fact, is what we often hear said. But what are we to think of these contrary counsels ?

As regards the poor, to whom saving is more especially recommended, the injunctions of economists and moralists have perhaps exceeded the limit. We do not say that saving is often impossible for them, for it is always possible, even for the poorest : man's wants are wonderfully elastic and may be stretched out indefinitely or compressed almost to nothing. A man with no more than a pound of bread a day may accustom himself to eating only every alternate day, and so save half of it. Besides, do not the working classes spend millions sterling on brandy and tobacco ? Now, it is certain that they could save on these if they wanted to, and that it would be much better for them if they did.

If, in spite of this, we hold that the advice to save, given with so much unction to the poor, is not always justified, it is because saving is more harmful than useful whenever it curtails necessaries or legitimate wants. It is absurd to sacrifice the present for the future if the sacrifice of the present be *such as to jeopardise the future*. Every private or public expenditure which results in developing a man physically, or mentally, should be sanctioned without hesitation, not only as good in itself, but as *preferable even to saving*. What better use can a man make of his wealth than to build up his health and develop his intelligence ? The consumption of brandy and stimulants should, no doubt, be discouraged ; but the money so badly spent in this way may perhaps find more useful employment at the butcher's, grocer's, or hosier's than at the savings bank. For this expenditure on alcohol is taken less from the superfluities, than from the necessaries of life. Nourishing food, good clothing, a healthy dwelling, comfortable furniture, more attention to health, instructive books, walks or even voyages, certain sports, concerts, the education of children, are all not only desirable forms of expenditure, but more to be recommended than saving. They are, in fact, not so much an expense as an investment, and the best investment of all, since they raise the value of the man and his productiveness.

And, if the worker has something over, he would do better to put it into some union, co-operative, friendly society, or unemployment fund, than save it up himself. This form of saving, *collective in aim* as well as in organisation, gives better results at less sacrifice than individual saving can possibly do. It tends to create an impersonal fund at the service of all, and appeals to the spirit of solidarity as much as to individual interest. It is not without good reason, then, that collective saving is held more in esteem among the working classes than is the individual saving of the bourgeois class.

Let us pass now to the rich. Is the advice to spend which Montesquieu gave them justified ? But if the rich do not save who will, since we have seen that it is often impossible, and not even desirable, for the working class to save ?

In the first place, if the saving of the rich man takes the form of investment, as it generally does, he is only transferring his faculty of consumption to others, among whom are precisely the workers. His saving therefore will not cause these to die of hunger, but will, on the contrary, give them a living.

Even when the rich man does not turn his money to a productive use, but *hoards* it up in the narrowest sense of the word—which very rarely happens—he really harms no one but himself. For what are these coins that he buries in the earth or in his strong-box ? Each one, as we know, is a sort of " order " giving its possessor the right to take a certain share of wealth out of the total in existence (see p. 289). Now, the man who saves does nothing worse than abandon for the moment his right to take his share. Very good. He is free to do so, and harms no one. The share which he might have consumed and does not will be consumed by others, that is all.[1]

---

[1] What makes avarice so justly contemptible from the moral point of view, is that, by taking his money out of circulation, the miser is depriving himself of all social duties, thus necessarily living as an egoist. But, from the economic point of view, he is quite an inoffensive personage.

Hoarding could be harmful to society only if the objects hoarded did not keep, in which case it would result in a veritable destruction of wealth, as for example the hoarding of the miser in Florian's tale, who kept apples until they were rotten, and

> *Lorsque quelqu'une se gâtait*
> *En soupirant il la mangeait !*

The social utility of saving consists in forming, by the accumulation of private savings, a mass of capital available for new enterprises. Saving possesses, therefore, the same utility for society as for individuals, viz., that of providing for future wants. If France has been able to hold her rank honourably as an industrial power with countries which are her superior in population, activity and equipment, it is mainly to her power of saving that she owes it.[1]

Since saving, then, is useful to a country, it is a duty incumbent on all who are able to save—that is to say, on the rich; for they alone are able to do so without leaving some legitimate want unsatisfied.

But, even in the case of the rich, we do not hold that saving should be their sole or even their principal duty. For them, too, there are ways of spending—philanthropic, æsthetic, scientific, etc.—which constitute a much more urgent social duty than saving. If they do not take on themselves these forms of public expenditure, the State and the towns will have to do it at the cost of taxes which will fall upon every one. There is one form of expenditure, in particular, which they have much less right to refuse than have the working classes, namely the renewing of the human capital of the country—population. It is certainly the saving of the middle classes in this respect, imitated gradually by the workers, which is responsible for the advance of Neo-Malthusianism. If we do not take thought, we shall come to a state of society in which the poor will be subsidised to keep up the population.

We may say therefore, by way of conclusion, that, however far-fetched the association of the words may seem, saving is a luxury

Still, it is said, if the rich were to begin to save all their incomes, and from a spirit of penitence were to live simply on bread and water, what would become of industry and commerce ?

In this case, the production of wealth intended for the consumption of the rich would doubtless cease from lack of demand ; but the production of products necessary for the consumption of the people would still continue. And as this production would be the only outlet for all the investments of the rich, it would receive a powerful stimulus. It is probable, therefore, that these products would become more abundant and cheaper.

[1] Herr von Bülow said in the Reichstag, November 1908, not without a little flattering exaggeration: " France owes her wealth to her grateful soil, the activity and the ingeniousness of her inhabitants, but more still to her admirable spirit of economy, to the force of saving which distinguishes each Frenchman and Frenchwoman. France has become the world's banker. For her backwardness in production, as compared with us, she makes up in saving."

But during the last few years, the annual saving in Germany has been estimated officially at 5 billions. It should therefore be greater than our own.

possible only to rich societies, and among these, is confined to the small number of persons .who have a superfluity of wealth.

Statistics, indeed, show us, that the countries which really save are few in number, while their figure for saving rarely represents more than one-tenth of the national income.[1]

II : THE CONDITIONS OF SAVING

SAVING, labour, and the division of labour, are perhaps the only economic acts which are common to animals and to man ; to which, therefore, we may give the name of " natural " *par excellence*. Certain animals—of which the ant is the type—know and practise saving in the form of hoarding.[2]

Still, we must not think that saving is spontaneous. Before it can take place, a number of somewhat difficult conditions must be fulfilled:

(*1*) As a subjective condition, there must be a certain degree of *foresight* in the saver, *i.e.* of the peculiar faculty which consists in feeling a future want as if it were a present one. The man who intends to save weighs two wants—a *present* want which he refuses to satisfy, say a desire for bread to satisfy his actual hunger ; and a *future* want which he wishes to provide for, say a desire to have bread for his old age. On the one hand, he is held back by the thought of the sacrifice which he will have to make ; on the other, he is attracted by the advantage which he expects from saving. His will swings to and fro between these two opposing forces, and is determined by the stronger.[3] Note that the present want is a reality ; it is an actual physical feeling ; the future want is an abstraction and is felt only in imagination. Before we can save, then, we must have certain habits of mind, certain moral propensities, which have familiarised us with abstraction. And these can only be the result of an already advanced state of civilisation.

Our education and occupations at the present day force us to think constantly of the future. Scientists, trying to penetrate the secrets of future ages, politicians anxious for the morrow, business men launching into speculations, simple tradesmen concerned with their monthly accounts and their annual stocktakings—all unconsciously and in varying degree have become familiar with this

---

[1] The proportion of the annual saving of France is estimated at 2 to 3 billion francs out of a total income of 25 to 30 billions.

[2] Saving, in the form of the accumulation of reserves for future needs, is a phenomenon frequently found, even in the vegetable world.

[3] We pointed out a similar conflict in the case of labour (p. 105).

unknown future and bring it into their calculations. But this is an intellectual effort beyond the savage, who feels only the want of the moment, and who, in Montesquieu's famous expression, " cuts the tree at the bottom to have the fruit " ; difficult, too, for those of our fellow citizens who, in social condition and mental habits, are not far removed from primitive man, and who live from hand to mouth. Savages, children, paupers, vagabonds, all are equally, and for the same reasons, improvident.[1]

(2) Labour must be productive enough to yield something over and above the necessaries of life. For, if it is imprudent to sacrifice future to present wants, it would be madness to sacrifice present to future wants. To reduce ourselves to dying of hunger now for fear of dying of hunger next year, would be worse than miserly. We have just seen (p. 735) that it is contrary to the interest of society, as well as of the individual, to make too great a sacrifice in present consumption for the sake of postponed consumption. For the man who has just enough to live on and no more, saving is a painful and even dangerous operation and may involve the fore-going of some essential satisfaction. But for the man who has more than enough wealth, saving can hardly be looked on as a meritorious sacrifice.[2] It may, indeed, become a necessity; for, when all is said and done, the consuming power of each man is limited, be it as great as that of Gargantua. Our needs, and even our desires, have a limit which Nature herself has set us, in satiety (see above, p. 37).

(3) As an objective condition, there must be a certain quality in the thing saved : it must be *capable of being preserved*. Now, this quality is rare in the state of nature. There are few objects the con-sumption of which may be postponed without danger of deterioration or total loss of the object. Some things are destroyed as quickly when they are laid aside as when they are in use. Furniture and

---

[1] See *The Growth of Capital*, in Bagehot's *Economic Studies*. As a curious example of improvidence, we may quote the savages of the Orinoco, who, it is said, will readily sell their hammocks in the morning but not in the evening. And the negroes of Senegal, who sell their millet at 15 centimes the kilogramme before the harvest, and 3 centimes after. (Deberme, *L'Afrique Occidentale*.)

[2] The Liberal economists have tried to emphasise the sacrifice involved in saving. Senior, who called it abstinence, looked on it as the creative cause of capital. They therefore exaggerated its merits and virtues. Socialists, on the other hand, made light of this so-called abstinence, and the privations of the capitalists, and it was against them that Lassalle let fly his sharpest arrows. These two opposite points of view are in reality inspired by the desire either to justify or to discredit the private ownership of capital. As a matter of fact, both are right ; for the sacrifice involved in saving may run through the whole gamut from infinity to zero.

clothes fade ; linen cuts or turns yellow in the chest ; iron rusts ; foodstuffs go bad or are devoured by insects ; even wine after a certain time loses its flavour ; and the very grain stored by the ant—though grain is one of the most easily preserved forms of wealth—cannot be kept for more than a year without great care.[1]

Saving, in fact, was little practised for want of suitable objects to save, until money, or at any rate the precious metals, were used as accumulators of value. Gold and silver are, as we have seen, almost the only immutable substances. They are not, to be sure, objects of consumption themselves ; but what does that matter, since, at any moment, they may be exchanged for such objects ? Instead, then, of saving up perishable goods, the man who wants to save exchanges these for money, which he puts away in a safe place ; and at any subsequent time he, or his great-grandchildren, have only to exchange this money for whatever wealth they want. When a treasure which has been buried for centuries is found, it is a *postponed* consumption that is being finally consummated, to the advantage of the fortunate discoverer.

Furthermore, since the invention of credit, saving has found a more wonderful instrument than even money. Here, say, is an individual with 1000 francs at his disposal : he might consume it, but prefers to postpone his consumption and write his name, as it were, for a value of 1000 francs on the *Grand Livre*[2] of society. At any future time, either he or his descendants will have the right to draw from the then existing mass of wealth, not the actual wealth which he had put into it and which has long since been consumed by others, but the equivalent of it.

(4) Lastly, there must be *instruments*, or institutions, for facilitating saving—if it be but barns or cellars in which to store corn and wine, or safes in which to keep money. These institutions will be the subject of our next section.[3]

---

[1] This is why we said on page 734 that the new processes for preserving products are an important aid to saving.

[2] In France, all holders of government stock are inscribed on what is called the " Grand Livre."

[3] Is there not another essential condition for saving ? Must not *capital bring in a certain rate of interest* before people will save ?

This is what most treatises on political economy teach—mistakenly in our opinion. A certain rate of interest is, as we shall presently explain, indispensable for *investment*, but not for *saving* in the strict sense : for saving has its end in itself, *i.e.* in the providing against future and unforeseen wants. We may even say, without paradox, that, if investment at interest were to become for some reason impossible, saving or hoarding, instead of being checked, would be strongly *stimulated*. For the man who, to-day, is content to save 100,000 francs, deeming

III: INSTITUTIONS FOR FACILITATING SAVING

IN all civilised countries there are ingenious institutions for facilitating saving.

(1) The best-known are the *Savings Banks*, properly so called. These institutions are intended to facilitate saving by taking charge of the sums saved.[1] They render the depositor the service of keeping his savings safe against thieves, still more perhaps against himself.

For the best way to aid the growth of small savings is to put it out of the owner's power to yield to the desire of spending them. The penny bank, so familiar to children, is simply an application of this idea. The money cannot be withdrawn without breaking the money-box, and, although this may easily be done, it is thought that this slight obstacle will give the child time for reflection, and enable him to resist temptation.[2]

The savings bank is only a more perfect money-box. The small sums deposited remain, of course, at the disposal of the depositor, but they are not at hand in his pocket ; and, in order to recover them, a few formalities and a little more time and trouble are necessary than merely breaking the money-box. It is, besides, a money-box in which the money bears fruit ; for, in order to encourage saving, these banks give the depositor a small interest. This interest must be looked on only as a sort of premium or stimulus to saving, and must not be too high. For the savings bank is not an institution for investment.[3] It exists to enable persons to put aside small sums and to accumulate a little capital. If, once this capital is formed, depositors want to invest it or turn it to account, they have only to withdraw it. The rôle of the savings bank is finished, and there

that he can live sufficiently well on 3000 or 4000 francs of income, would, so soon as he found that he had to live on the capital itself, be eager to save up as much as possible.

[1] In 1908, the centenary of the first Savings Bank, created by Duncan at Ruthwell, in Scotland, was celebrated.

[2] This device is still employed in some countries. Since 1906, the Paris Savings Bank, to stimulate a spirit of economy, gives a savings bank book up to the sum of 10 francs, and a money-box which it lends for nothing, and which it only can open. Within four years, over 2300 money-boxes have been brought to be opened, and the sums thus saved amount to nearly 1,500,000 francs. A similar scheme has just been started in England.

[3] This is why in France, by the law of 1895, the maximum of each deposit, which was formerly 2000 francs, has now been reduced to 1500.

The rate of interest, which used to be 4 per cent.—thus causing a loss to the State, as these funds deposited in the *Caisse des dépôts et consignations* and invested in State stock brought in barely 3 per cent.—is now regulated according to the current rate of capitalisation.

are other appropriate institutions (banks, *crédit foncier*, etc.) which will take charge of it.

Savings banks were formerly private, or municipal, institutions. To-day, however, in most countries there is a *State savings bank* with branches in all the post offices. That of Vienna is celebrated for its perfect mechanism, which almost realises the *comptabilisme social*, or social accountancy of which we spoke (p. 327, n. 2).

In France, the savings banks receive nearly six milliard francs of deposits, and this sum would be much larger were it not that each deposit is limited by law to 1500 francs. The law is, however, often evaded. Savings banks, even when private, have not the right to use the deposits as they think fit. They are obliged by law to invest them in government stock. The State does not, however, hold itself responsible for the deposits of the banks. These, therefore, if their cash in hand will not meet the withdrawals, are forced to sell their stock in order to obtain the ready money needed.

This requirement of the law, although intended to give depositors absolute security, has been roundly criticised, and with reason.

On the one hand, the funds swallowed up by the Treasury, are doing absolutely nothing, and might easily be turned to better account. In Italy, where savings banks are remarkably well organised, the greater part of their funds is put into land, or agricultural, loans. As the interest paid to depositors is very low, the banks are able to ask a very low rate of interest from agriculturists, and this is an inestimable advantage to agriculture. And, as their investments are much more varied, they offer much better security to depositors than do the French savings banks, which, bound as they are to put their money into government stock only, are at the mercy of a revolution or an unfortunate war.[1]

The continuous buying of government stock by the savings banks [2] certainly helps to keep up the credit of the State; but it

[1] A campaign, due to the initiative of M. Eugène Rostand, has been started in France to obtain for French savings banks the same freedom as have the banks of other countries. A law of July 20, 1895, made a somewhat timid start along this line, by allowing, not the savings banks themselves, but the *Caisse des dépôts et consignations*, in which their deposits are kept, to invest not only in government stock but in securities guaranteed by the State, as also in land, and communal, bonds. It has given a little more freedom still as regards the investment of funds which are the property of the savings banks themselves—for these have as a rule some property of their own. Thus they may invest in local securities up to the amount of one-fifth of their capital, and of the whole of their income. In particular they may lend to societies for the building of working-men's houses.

[2] It is owing to these daily purchases that French stock is quoted at a higher rate than that of other countries whose credit is at least equal to that of France.

might compromise it seriously in the case of a panic. For the savings banks, in order to face a run, would be obliged to sell all their government stock, and this would bring down the public funds with a crash. So real is this danger, that the law has provided a safeguard against it by a clause allowing the banks to repay depositors in instalments of not more than 50 francs once a fortnight.

It is a great exaggeration to say, as is constantly done, that the savings banks represent working-class saving : in reality, only about one quarter of the workers, in the strict sense, whether of the country or of the towns, make use of the savings banks.[1]

(2) *Mutual Prudential Societies*, formed by persons who pay monthly subscriptions and at the end of a certain time, say, twenty years, divide the capital thus accumulated, or more generally the income from it. These societies differ from insurance companies in that they do not fix beforehand the amount of the annuity which they will pay.

How is it that men are able to save more when thus organised than when isolated ? It is, in the first place, because the rule of monthly subscription makes saving an obligation and a habit; in the second, because a society is better able than an individual to turn to account the marvellous power of compound interest ; lastly, because in most of these societies the survivors benefit by the subscriptions paid by those whom they outlive. The *Prévoyants de l'Avenir* is the best-known society of this type ;[2] it is practically

---

[1] The following is the distribution of deposits, January 1, 1910.

	Per cent.
Industrial and agricultural workers	23
Clerks, etc.	5
Domestic servants	8
Landowners and *rentiers*	16
Small employers	9
Liberal professions	1
Military men and sailors	1
Children	37
	100

It must be remarked that the greater number, if not all, of the 37 per cent. of children's savings bank books belong to the bourgeois class.

And if, instead of counting the number of depositors, which does not mean much, we could count the amount of the *total sums deposited* belonging to the working class, we should see that it is very small : no doubt it is this class that owns the 2,571,000 books of less then 20 francs of savings, representing a mere 22 million francs in all.

[2] These societies for saving are very numerous (over 500 in Paris) but give rise to many abuses. In the first place, their meetings are held too frequently

a *tontine*, a mode of speculating on the death of members. The accumulated effect of these three causes together gives surprising results.[1]

(*3*) *Co-operative societies for consumption.* These, although their name indicates consumption rather than saving, act also as saving institutions by removing the obstacle which renders saving so painful and which yet seems inseparable from it, viz., abstinence or privation. They create, as has been aptly said, " automatic saving " by the simple and ingenious mechanism which we explained above (p. 202). The produce bought wholesale by the society is sold retail to its members, and the profits thus realised on purchases are put to their accounts, and handed over to them at the end of the year, or kept on deposit in their names.

If a working-man's family buys 1000 francs' worth of goods in a co-operative store, and the store is making a profit of 10 per cent., at the end of the year he will have made a saving of 100 francs, *which will have cost him nothing*—that is to say, no restriction of consumption. He will have consumed just as much as before ; he will have been supplied with goods of a better quality ; he will have paid no more for them than he would elsewhere ; and, in spite of all this, he will actually have saved money. And the more he purchases, the more he saves ; so that a means seems to have been found, as some one has paradoxically put it, of saving by spending.[2]

(*4*) *Co-operative societies of credit,* which, although mainly banks of deposit and discount for lending to the public, to artisans, and to shopkeepers, act equally as savings banks. They have even been called " improved savings banks." The *people's banks* of the Schulze-Delitzsch type are of this character.

at the public-house. In the second, the older members often benefit exorbitantly from the contributions of new members, particularly if the latter come in numbers. So great was this abuse that a special law had to be passed limiting the pensions to be paid to these older members.

[1] Thus we find, in many post offices in France, an advertisement of the *Caisse Nationale des Retraites,* announcing that a subscription of 1 franc a week from the age of twenty years will give 586 francs of income at the age of sixty ; or that, if a subscription of 100 francs be paid in once and for all for a child of three years old, he will have an annuity of 115 francs when he reaches the age of sixty.

[2] The facilitating of individual saving is, like cheapness, only a subsidiary aim of co-operation (see above, p. 203). Still, the capital of the English co-operative societies and their deposits, which are almost solely the result of savings made by their members, amount to over £68,000,000.

IV: INSURANCE

THE object of saving is, as a rule, to provide against future, but certain, wants ; a man saves for his old age or for his children. But saving is no less necessary to provide against the *unexpected*, to make good future losses which may result from the numerous risks that menace either persons (illness, accidents, invalidity, death, etc.) or things (fire, hailstorms, theft, etc.), and which involve the destruction of wealth,[1] or at any rate the unproductive consumption of it.

Individual saving, however, is not well fitted for this task. It is difficult for a single individual to accumulate a reserve fund large enough to provide against such risks as fire—a fund which would often be useless, as the risk might never be incurred. On the other hand, it is just here that association works wonders. For, as chance misfortunes like theft, or fire, will probably fall on only a few members ; and as even common risks such as illness, and certain risks such as death, will not fall on all members at once, it will be enough for each to put aside a very small sum, for the total to cover every risk wherever it may befall.

Experience, for example, has proved that a sum equal to the thousandth part of the value of a house is more than enough to cover its value in case of fire, if the association comprises enough members. And so with all other risks. This is what is called *insurance*.

Insurance is a very wonderful invention, and one of the most remarkable instances of solidarity. It consists in rendering harmless (from the pecuniary point of view only, of course) the most enormous risks, which would crush a single individual, by spreading them over a multitude of persons at a very slight sacrifice to each. Still, we must not exaggerate its virtues : as distinct from saving, which implies an increase of wealth, insurance simply prevents impoverishment, and an individual one at that. For it is evident that insurance cannot prevent the destruction of the wealth. The house is burnt ; the ship is sunk. For society, therefore, there is a dead loss ;[2] but for the individual, insurance renders this loss innocuous by reducing

---

[1] There are, in France, year in, year out, 2500 *fires*, causing a loss of hundreds of millions of francs—the eighteen principal companies alone pay 75 million francs of insurance claims—and 80,000 to 100,000 *thefts* amounting, in the parcel post alone (which is under the administration of the railways in France) to some dozens of millions.

[2] Indeed, the loss from the social point of view, as M. Leroy-Beaulieu points out very rightly in his *Traité d'Économie politique*, far from being diminished by insurance, is increased by it ; since, in addition to the destruction of values resulting from, say, the fire, we must add the costs necessary to organise the insurance.

it to an insignificant sacrifice.[1] Even from the social point of view the consequences of the destruction of the wealth are lessened by the fact that it is immediately repaired. Without insurance the city of San Francisco, which was destroyed by fire, would have taken much longer to rise from its ashes.

Needless to say, insurance is possible only in the case of misfortunes which are independent of the human will. If the misfortunes be due, even in part, to a man's own fault, he must take the consequences. Insurance would here be quite immoral, as it would tend to deaden responsibility. It would, besides, be ruinous for any insurance company, since it would put the company at the mercy of the insured. It is easy to see that insurance against failure in examinations, against bankruptcy, against celibacy, would be absurd. But there are also many risks against which insurance, without being impossible, would be very difficult. We have seen instances of them in connection with insurance against unemployment and strikes (pp. 640, 641, note).

There are, on the other hand, certain forms of insurance which may be considered dangerous. Thus, no longer than a century ago, when the *Code Civil* was promulgated, life insurances were forbidden,[2] on the ground that the prospect of receiving a sum of money on the death of another person would create the desire for his death, or at least the temptation to hasten it. And this fear is not altogether fanciful ; for it is stated as a fact that the insuring of the lives of children among the working-class population in the department of the Nord, where it is practised on a fairly large scale for small sums, gave rise to criminal·speculation, and raised the rate of infant mortality.

But on that score it would surely be better to begin at the beginning and do away with succession altogether l These exceptional instances cannot be weighed in the balance against the infinitely greater number of cases in which the insuring of life is a provident act.

[1] Insurance is a purely *reparative* measure. Preventive measures for avoiding the destruction of wealth are beyond all insurance schemes. It is even to be feared that insurance in some measure paralyses them, since the certainty that a loss will be made good, weakens, to this extent, the eagerness to prevent it.

We may mention as *preservative* measures, the organisation of the fire brigade, lifeboats, lighthouses, etc., even safes against theft. These have indeed an important economic function and really deserve a chapter of their own in the vast and little explored domain of consumption.

[2] Insurance is said to be *en cas de décès* when the sum is payable at death ; *en cas de vie* when it is payable at a fixed age, say on reaching one's majority ; and *mixed* when the capital is to be paid whether the insured person lives or dies. This is the most advantageous, but also the most costly form of insurance.

Can anything be more moral than for the head of a family to provide for his premature death, and to insure for an amount of capital which will save his family from poverty ? Moreover, if he is forced to borrow and has no guarantee but his labour, he will perhaps have some difficulty in finding money, whereas his life insurance will always be accepted as sufficient pledge. This form of insurance has spread very widely in England and in the United States. It is much less practised in France.

Insurance may take four different forms :

(1) The simplest is that of the *guarantee association*, all members undertaking to pay their share of the compensation due to those who have suffered loss. It is the form most frequently practised by manufacturers to cover their responsibility for accidents ; and by landowners in insuring against the mortality of their cattle. It requires neither capital nor fixed subscriptions ; but it involves great risks, and is suitable only for small groups of rich persons who know one another.

(2) The *mutual insurance*, which takes the form of subscriptions calculated to cover, so far as possible, all risks that can be foreseen, and the constitution of a guarantee fund. But there is still a fair amount of risk about this form of insurance, since, if there are more mishaps than were provided against, it becomes necessary either to demand additional subscriptions, or to reduce the compensation.

(3) It is for these reasons that the best-known form of insurance, that of *fixed premiums*—which may also be called the *capitalist* form of insurance—was created. These are enterprises in the form of joint-stock companies, which accumulate enormous reserves, and guarantee integral repayment of loss in return for an annual fixed premium.[1]

---

[1] Is *co-operative insurance* a special form of insurance, or does it come under one or other of those indicated above ?

It is easy to distinguish it from capitalist insurance : (1) because insurers and insured are one : it has for clients only its own shareholders, as in the co-operative associations for consumption or for credit ; (2) because it pays over to its clients any profits made out of them.

This last characteristic is not, however, of itself a sufficient distinction, since some, even among the capitalist insurance companies, pay back a part of their premiums to their clients, so that the latter sometimes find that they have no subscriptions to pay. This is frequently the case in the United States, where many large companies call themselves, though without justification, mutual insurance companies.

It is not so easy to distinguish co-operative from mutual insurance, since the latter also insures only its own members. Still co-operative differs from mutual insurance in that it has a constituted capital in the form of shares, that it charges fixed premiums, and makes good the whole of the loss incurred. As,

These companies were the most brilliant financial enterprises of the first half of the nineteenth century. Certain among them distributed annual dividends, which amounted to much more than the actual capital paid up ; and the price of their shares rose sometimes to twenty or even fifty times their orig'nal value. The monstrous profits which they reaped, and the enormous capital which they amassed, had the advantage besides of providing every guarantee to the insured.

But it became apparent in the end that these insurance companies distributed almost as much in dividends and in commissions to their agents, as they did in indemnities ;. that is to say, they were making their clients pay twice as much as there was any need for. The tendency to-day, therefore, is to return to mutual insurance, on a large enough scale, however, to obviate the risk mentioned above.

(4) There is a fourth possible mode of insurance, viz., *State insurance*. This may be either optional or compulsory. It exists in Switzerland for fire, and in Germany, as we have seen, for accidents, invalidity, and old age. There is more and more talk of it in France, as the growing charges on the budget are obliging the State to look for new resources. The monopoly of insurance is, along with the monopoly of alcohol, the last hope of the Treasury. Socialists strongly recommend this mode of insurance, not only as a fiscal expedient, but as a step towards the socialising of all capitalist enterprises. State Socialists and " Solidarists " also advocate it, as realising in the best sense the ideal of social solidarity—" All for each."

It has, however, no lack of adversaries. These declare that State insurance will by no means bring in the profits expected. In the first place, the State, they say, will not be able to avoid compensating the expropriated companies, and will thereby burden itself with a large debt. Further, insurance lends itself to endless frauds, since those who insure either hide the bad risks, or send in exaggerated claims, or provoke disasters at a favourable moment. As it is, capitalist companies and mutual insurance associations

however, it demands only a very small contribution of capital from each member (25 francs) it is not easy for it to collect the large amount of capital required, nor to offer the same guarantees as companies which call in outside capital. This is why co-operative insurance is not very often found as an independent enterprise, although it is beginning to spread as a graft on co-operative associations for consumption. It is only natural that a society of consumers, which would provide for all the economic wants of its members, should also take thought for their security and insure them against risks.

have great difficulty in defeating these frauds ; and it is to be feared
that the State will simply be plundered, as it has neither dividends
to defend like the big companies, nor the easy reciprocal check of
the small mutual insurances, and as it cannot even count on the
public conscience, which, in France at any rate, frankly avows that
to steal from the State is not to steal at all.[1]

State partisans answer that State insurance ought to be more
economical for the insured than is the insurance of capitalist companies, for the very reason that it has no dividends to pay—more
economical than even that of mutual insurances, since, owing to its
legal and compulsory character, it has the power to make all the
inhabitants of a district subscribe, and thus, by force of numbers, to
reduce premiums to a minimum.[2] The State, they say, may also
save the enormous commission spent by the companies on agents
and touts. This, however, is doubtful as the State also will need
agents and inspectors.

For the rest, even supposing the State does not itself undertake
the business of insuring, it may intervene in various ways.

(1) By encouraging, or even subsidising, the mutual insurance
societies in cases where public interest is directly concerned such
as fires, illness, invalidity, mortality of cattle, and perhaps hailstorms and floods. This it already does in the case of the agricultural associations and working-men's associations against unemployment

(2) By exercising, as it does at present, a control over the management of the capitalist companies. French law requires reserve funds
to be put aside, calculated mathematically, and, in the case of foreign
companies, an adequate guarantee fund in French securities.

V : INVESTMENT

IF we consider investment under the same chapter as saving, it is
because the two acts are always associated in our minds ; they are,
however, in their nature essentially different.

Investment, it is true, presupposes saving, for we can invest
only what we have put aside. Hence the connection we are apt to
establish between the two facts. But whereas *saving* is an act of

---

[1] It is for this reason that, as we saw (p. 631, note 2), the *Caisse Nationale*
refuses to insure accidents in the course of labour other than those which involve
permanent incapacity, since simulation in the latter case is more difficult. This
mistrust is eloquent.

[2] We spoke of the agricultural mutual insurance associations (p. 195).

consumption, investment is always an act of *production.* To save is
to abstain at the present moment in view of a future want; it is
postponed consumption. To invest, on the other hand, is *to turn to
account.* It is to transform the power of consuming into the power
of producing; that is, it is to renounce the power of consuming in
order to transfer it to others (as a rule in the form of wages).

In former times land was almost the sole form of investment.
Any other opportunity was difficult and almost impossible for two
reasons :

(*1*) The lack of *openings.* At a time when lending at interest
was prohibited, or could be effected only in an indirect way, when
the principal borrowers, viz., the large joint-stock companies and
the modern States, did not as yet exist, and when even the letting
of houses was unusual, there could be but little opportunity for
investing money. All that could be done was to hoard, and this is
still the case in Eastern countries.[1]

(*2*) *Lack of security.* Unless the lender can be guaranteed against
the risks of robbery, invasion, governmental confiscation, or the
dishonesty of a powerful debtor, he will not part with his savings,
nor hand them over to productive consumption. He must first have
the certainty of getting them back again.

To-day these two obstacles have disappeared. On the one hand,
political security is sufficiently well guaranteed in every civilised
country—although perhaps the moral security which comes from
faithfulness to one's engagements, still leaves much to be desired.
On the other hand, our epoch offers a thousand openings for investment unknown to our forefathers. In 1815, only five securities were
quoted on the Paris Bourse; by 1869, there were 402. To-day
there are over a thousand, not to speak of the hundreds of others
quoted in the departments or on Stock Exchanges abroad. Industrial and financial enterprises, shareholding companies, agricultural
and land operations, above all the continual loans issued by States
in the form of government stock, offer endless facilities to those on
the look-out for investment.[2] All hold out the prospect of a more or

---

[1] In 1907, Lord Cromer, then Governor of Egypt, quoted in his report the case
of a village sheik who, after purchasing a property for £25,000, reappeared half
an hour after the signature of the contract with a string of mules carrying on
their backs the sum which he had just dug up out of his garden.

[2] At the Congress of movable values (*valeurs mobilières*), during the Paris
Exhibition of 1900, the total amount of securities quoted on the stock exchanges
of all countries was estimated at £20,000,000,000—out of which £6,000,000,000
represented Government stock, and the rest shares and bonds in industrial
concerns. Prodigious as this figure may appear, it must be much higher to-day.

less high rate of interest ; many what amounts to a veritable bonus in the form of repayments larger than the original sums lent; and, in certain cases allowed by law, lottery prizes to a value of from 100,000 to 500,000 francs—an inducement of very questionable morality. We may even be inclined to think that there are too many openings for investment. For they make it too easy to live the life of the idle *rentier*, a life which, though it has its good points, should not be carried to excess (see p. 553). If men were unable to find so many opportunities of investing their money they would be stimulated to turn it to account for themselves.

In any case, it is to this facility that the swarm of small capitalists is due. For land, even when it is most broken up, does not lend itself to such an extreme subdivision as does the investment of capital. To take French Government stock alone, the number of persons holding it is estimated at over 2 millions.

The utility of investment, from the point of view of production, is nevertheless beyond dispute. It is investment which provides for all great enterprises the capital without which they would be impossible.

From the point of view of society, again, investment must be considered as a more altruistic employment of wealth than even hoarding or spending. For hoarding is always, and spending very often, egoistic ; whereas the investor, instead of employing his wealth in satisfying his present or future wants, transfers it to others to consume in reproduction. He does not do so, of course, from a philanthropic motive ; he is pursuing his own gain. But although his altruism is unconscious, the results are the same as if it were intentional. As J. S. Mill rightly said : " We help the workers, not by what we consume, but only by what we ourselves *do not consume*." [1] Suppose a man employs his savings in buying stock issued by a mining or railway company.[2] He pays the company the value of this stock in money. Does the company shut this money away in

The total quantity of securities issued, that is to say, of loans issued by States or companies, has risen during the last fifteen years to an annual average of £640,000,000.

[1] Account must be taken, however, of our remarks on the social function of the consumer, p. 700.

[2] We say advisedly stock at the moment of its issue by the company ; for if it is bought on the stock exchange, it is merely *transferred* : our capitalist is simply substituting himself for its previous owner. Even in such a case as this, however, Investment generally means a productive use of capital ; for the capitalist who has sold his stock is obliged to find employment for the money he has received in exchange. It is probable, indeed, that he sold it only because he had in view some more productive use for the money

its safes ? Certainly not ; if such had been its intention, it would
never have borrowed it. It will use it in sinking new shafts, constructing new lines, buying coal, rails, sleepers, above all, in paying
its employees and in engaging new hands. And it is the same with
every investment.

Yet the popular prejudice against hoarding extends even to the
man who invests his money. It is assumed that the man who locks
up securities in his safe is veritably hoarding, and withdrawing
money from circulation ; and it is not seen that, on the contrary,
his money is scouring the world, stimulating commerce, and setting
men to work in all parts of the globe—Chinamen perhaps on the
railways of Asia, or Kaffirs in the Transvaal mines. It is possibly
just such cases as these which give some foundation to the popular
prejudice ; for the capital which is giving work to foreign labour
cannot give it to the home workers. Investment may very often
be a kind of absenteeism in capital. But we must consider this
question somewhat more fully.

VI : THE EMIGRATION OF CAPITAL

THE emigration of capital has been a much-debated question of
late years. It has been denounced as a national peril, an anti-
patriotic, almost treasonable, act.[1] The total amount of investments
abroad have been calculated, for France, at over 40 milliard francs.

It is not merely in loans that the emigration of capital takes
place ; it may come about through the buying of foreign securities,
or through industrial enterprises. The complaint is often heard,
in France, of the number of enterprises of all sorts—mines, banks,
etc.—which are in the hands of foreigners.[2]

What is meant by this financial anti-patriotism ? That the
capital thus exported will serve for the manufacture of arms or
cruisers to be turned against the home country ?

But on this ground we should tax with treason the French firms
which sell arms, or the raw material for them, to the foreigner. And

---

[1] In his report on the budget of 1910, before the French Chamber, M. Dumont
spoke of the " Hervéisme of capital." And a newspaper, Le Rappel, said in all
seriousness, " Let us show no mercy towards those who, having all the social
advantages of the home country, betray it still more criminally under the sway
of a contemptible and ferocious cupidity."

In Germany, however, it was the Conservative and agrarian party which
protested against the emigration of capital.

[2] Many of the best marks of champagne, and the iron mines recently discovered
in Normandy, belong to Germans.

yet, by a curious contradiction. we are doing our best to make foreign nations buy their guns from Le Creusot and build their warships in our shipbuilding yards.

A more moderate meaning is, that the capital thus exported will be so much less for our national industry. But might we not say, in reply, that it is the national enterprises that are lacking ? Why make it a crime against capital that it turns elsewhere for the investment which it cannot find at home ?

Notwithstanding, the French Government, influenced by vehement protests, has begun to concern itself with the emigration of capital.

This phenomenon has appeared to it alarming from the *fiscal* point of view, as an evasion ; from the *economic* point of view, as a danger to French saving ; and from the *political* point of view, as sometimes contrary to French interests.

(*1*) From the fiscal point of view, the government has tried to prevent evasion by entering into negotiations with foreign governments, and has obtained agreements with England and Belgium regarding the declaration of successions. But not much need be expected from agreements of this nature. They are never likely to become general ; there will always be countries only too happy to act as asylums for capital.[1] For capital, even when only on deposit, brings many advantages to the towns where it is allowed to accumulate, turning them into great financial centres. To prevent the flight of capital, it has been suggested that the law should require all movable values to be nominative. But, if a country were to adopt such a measure as this, it would strike a fatal blow at its national industry while bringing no corresponding gain to its treasury. An international understanding would be necessary, and we have just explained why there is little hope of it. In our view, the Treasury would do better to renounce this chase after movable values, from which it stands to return empty-handed. and which simply develops in the taxpayer the ingenuity of the hunted hare ; more especially as it is not the large capitalists who would walk into its traps, but the small ones, ignorant of financial combinations (see what we said above concerning the income tax, p. 692).

It must not be supposed, moreover, that the capitalists who deposit their securities in foreign banks do so with the sole object

---

[1] In 1880, the deposits in the Swiss banks rose to 472 million francs ; in 1909, to 1655 millions. The greater part of this increase was certainly due to foreign deposits. And these hundreds of millions of deposits in money are a drop in the bucket compared with the deposits in *securities*.

of defrauding the Treasury. Many do so in the belief that they are safer there in the event of revolution or war, or stand a better chance of finding profitable investment.

(2) From the point of view of the commercial interest of the country, the government has inaugurated a new policy, which consists in authorising foreign loans only if the borrowing country will give certain advantages in return, *e.g.* if it will set aside part of the money lent for orders to French industry, or grant concessions in its customs tariff.[1]

How can the French government prevent the loan of capital to foreign countries? By refusing to authorise quotation on the Paris Bourse. This, no doubt, will not prevent shrewd French capitalists, particularly those who have bankers abroad, from subscribing to these loans. But it makes subscription impossible, or at least very difficult, to the mass of small capitalists, especially if the large credit establishments, whose indications they, as clients, follow blindly, associate themselves with this boycotting on the part of the government.

Although this policy has been generally approved by public opinion, it is, in our view, to be regretted. It offends the pride of the countries on whom these conditions are imposed; while, by obliging them to look for other lenders, it shows them that France has not, as she is only too ready to believe, the monopoly of the lending of capital. It also injures French capitalists; for, by turning away borrowers, it naturally reduces the demand for their capital and consequently the rate of interest.

It is unpleasant, no doubt, to think that the money lent to this country or to that may help to carry on industries which are competing with our own; or, in the case of a new country, may be used to give orders to rival, if not hostile, nations. But we cannot prevent this by refusing the loan. The only result of our action is that the rejected countries go elsewhere to find their capital and France loses the benefit of their orders as well as of their borrowings—not to speak of the enormous commissions and charges which bankers and the State levy on the issue of foreign loans.

[1] It was owing to such conditions that requests for loans on the part of the Argentine Republic in 1909, Hungary and Turkey in 1910, and Bulgaria in 1912, fell through. In the case of the Argentine Republic, the government ultimately went back on its decision; but in that of the others its refusal was final and they borrowed elsewhere.

The government refused also to admit the shares of the German Bagdad Railway on the Paris Bourse. This did not, however, hinder the undertaking from being carried out.

The State, indeed, in the matter of national saving is not competent to play the part of financial adviser, and ought to leave it to the bankers whose trade it is. For to forbid the public to subscribe to certain loans and to invite it to subscribe to others is to undertake heavy responsibilities.

(3) From the political point of view, the government lays stress on the danger of furnishing resources to enemies and of raising diplomatic complications in cases where the insolvency of the borrowing State necessitates strong measures and the intervention of the " mailed fist."

Such a consideration might have some value in the case of loans issued by States themselves, but not of those issued by private companies. As for the intervention of the mailed fist to protect the interests of lenders and to enforce the payment of claims which are sometimes usurious, it ought to be absolutely forbidden by the law of nations. A loan is a purely private act and it is for the lender to obtain information and assume risks.[1]

To sum up, the foreign loan is an operation which, like everything else, has its bad sides ; but its advantages far outweigh its disadvantages. By the payment of interest it creates a regular current of cash which renders the balance of trade and of exchange favourable—both conditions of a sound financial situation. Indirectly, also, it creates commercial currents ; for the currents of cash are ultimately transformed into currents of merchandise, which are thus paid for without the passing of a penny ; and the public credit, and even the political influence, of the lending country are thereby greatly strengthened. Like commerce, the foreign loan exercises a pacific influence by the business relations which it establishes between countries, as obviously the creditor country is concerned in the prosperity of the debtor country, though the converse is not equally true. We must learn to be content with these advantages, and not risk losing them by imposing conditions foreign to the loan itself. We must realise that to lend at interest is not an act of liberality, and that when a lender receives the maximum interest that the state of the market allows him, nothing more is owing to him ; that if he demands additional advantages he is coming very near usury.

If the country which exports capital has no reason to regret its foreign investments, the country which imports the capital has still

[1] This was indeed the position defended by the Argentine Minister, M. Drago, at the International Arbitration Congresses.

less. It gains in an increased demand for labour, and part, at any rate. of the goods produced remain in it. No doubt it would be better for it to utilise itself its natural resources than to have these colonised, as it were. But it is better that they should be turned to account by foreign immigrants than not at all.

It is the rôle—we might almost say the mission—of old and rich countries to become exporters of capital. England began, France followed, and now it is Germany's turn. In like manner, it is a necessity for new countries to become importers of capital. And this distribution of rôles is for the good of all.

INDEX

2 B

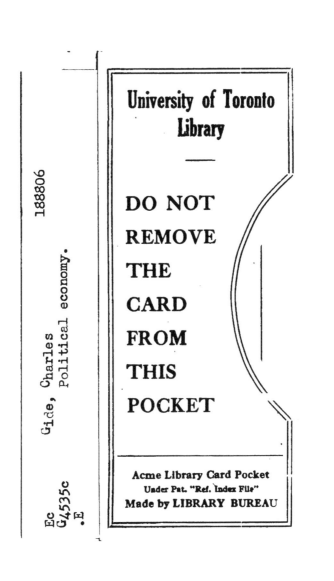

Lightning Source UK Ltd.
Milton Keynes UK
UKHW020205080119
335173UK00013B/1928/P